Problems of International Politics

Editors:
Keith Darden, *Yale University*
Ian Shapiro, *Yale University*

The series seeks books central to the understanding of international politics that are empirically rich and conceptually innovative. The editors are interested in works that illuminate the evolving character of nation-states within the international system. The series sets out three broad areas for investigation: identity, security, and conflict; democracy; and justice and distribution.

Competitive Authoritarianism
Hybrid Regimes After the Cold War

Competitive authoritarianism – regimes that combine competitive elections with serious violation of democratic procedure – proliferated in the post–Cold War era. This book explains the rise and diverging fate of competitive authoritarian regimes since 1990. Based on a comparative study of 35 cases in Africa, Asia, the Americas, and post-communist Eurasia, the book finds that extensive ties to the West led to democratization. By raising the external cost of abuse, linkage to the West brought democracy even where domestic conditions were unfavorable. Where such ties were limited, external democratizing pressure was weaker. Regime outcomes in these cases hinged on the character of state and ruling-party organizations. Where incumbents possessed robust coercive and party structures, competitive authoritarian regimes were durable; where incumbents lacked such organizational tools, regimes were unstable but rarely democratized.

STEVEN LEVITSKY is Professor of Government at Harvard University. His research interests include political parties, political regimes, and informal institutions, with a focus on Latin America. Professor Levitsky is author of *Transforming Labor-Based Parties in Latin America: Argentine Peronism in Comparative Perspective* (2003); is coeditor of *Argentine Democracy: The Politics of Institutional Weakness* (2005) and *Informal Institutions and Democracy: Lessons from Latin America* (2006); and is currently coediting a volume on the rise of the Left in Latin America in the 2000s. He has published articles in the *Annual Review of Political Science, Comparative Political Studies, Comparative Politics, Journal of Democracy, Journal of Latin American Studies, Latin American Politics and Society, Latin American Research Review, Party Politics, Perspectives on Politics, Studies in Comparative International Development*, and *World Politics*. He is on the editorial board of the *Journal of Democracy*.

LUCAN A. WAY is Assistant Professor of Political Science at the University of Toronto. His research interests include political regimes and weak states, with a focus on post-communist Eurasia. Professor Way is currently completing a book, *Pluralism by Default: Sources of Political Competition in the Former Soviet Union*, and has published articles in *Communist and Post-Communist Studies, Comparative Politics, East European Politics and Societies, Journal of Democracy, Journal of Communist Studies and Transition Politics, Politics & Society, Post-Soviet Affairs, Studies in Comparative and International Development*, and *World Politics*, as well as numerous book chapters. He is on the editorial board of the *Journal of Democracy*.

More praise for *Competitive Authoritarianism*

"This landmark contribution to the comparative study of political regimes will be widely read and cited. In an epic act of theoretical synthesis, Levitsky and Way weave careful empirical research on three-dozen countries across five world regions into a convincing account of patterns of regime change. In distinguishing democratic transitions from a range of authoritarian outcomes, they reach nuanced conclusions about the relative explanatory influence of international factors (linkage and leverage) and domestic power politics (rulers versus oppositions). Above all, they help us understand how autocrats learn to live with elections. Strongly recommended."

— Michael Bratton, University Distinguished Professor of Political Science and African Studies, Michigan State University

"This is the most anticipated book in comparative politics in more than a decade. Written in a single authorial voice, Levitsky and Way's arguments about the distinct trajectories of competitive authoritarian regimes are theoretically grounded, conceptually nuanced, geographically wide ranging, and empirically well supported. I expect this book to have a major impact on the field for many years to come."

— Marc Morjé Howard, Georgetown University

"Regimes that blend meaningful elections and illicit incumbent advantage are not merely resting points on the road to democracy; Levitsky and Way guide us along the multiple paths these regimes can take and provide powerful reasoning to explain why nations follow these distinct paths. This deeply insightful analysis of an important subset of post–Cold War regimes is conceptually innovative and precise, empirically ambitious, and theoretical agile, moving fluidly between international and domestic causes of regime dynamics. Read it to understand the dynamics of contemporary hybrid regimes; then read it again to appreciate its many lessons for our general understanding of regime change."

— David Waldner, University of Virginia

Competitive Authoritarianism

Hybrid Regimes After the Cold War

STEVEN LEVITSKY
Harvard University

LUCAN A. WAY
University of Toronto

CAMBRIDGE
UNIVERSITY PRESS

CAMBRIDGE
UNIVERSITY PRESS

32 Avenue of the Americas, New York NY 10013-2473, USA

Cambridge University Press is part of the University of Cambridge.

It furthers the University's mission by disseminating knowledge in the pursuit of education, learning, and research at the highest international levels of excellence.

www.cambridge.org
Information on this title: www.cambridge.org/9780521709156

© Steven Levitsky and Lucan A. Way 2010

First published 2010
7th printing 2013

A catalog record for this publication is available from the British Library.

Library of Congress Cataloging in Publication data
Levitsky, Steven.
Competitive authoritarianism : hybrid regimes after the Cold War / Steven Levitsky, Lucan A. Way.
    p. cm. – (Problems of international politics)
Includes bibliographical references and index.
ISBN 978-0-521-88252-1 (hardback) – ISBN 978-0-521-70915-6 (pbk.)
1. Authoritarianism – Case studies. 2. Democratization – Case studies. 3. Political development – Case studies. 4. Political stability – Case studies. I. Way, Lucan, 1968–
II. Title. III. Series.
JC480.L45 2010
321.9–dc22   2010005438

ISBN 978-0-521-88252-1 Hardback
ISBN 978-0-521-70915-6 Paperback

For Zareen

For Liz and Alejandra

Contents

Acknowledgments

This book grew out of a conversation over lunch in the old Coolidge Hall cafeteria at Harvard University's Weatherhead Center for International Affairs (WCFIA). What began as a discussion of political scandals involving leaked tapes and autocrats in Peru and Ukraine led to a realization that the two countries' regimes were surprisingly similar – and that we had no term for these regimes. We wrote a conference paper on the two cases, never imagining that the project would grow to encompass 35 countries across five continents (or that both of our initial cases would turn out to be outliers!). Nor did we have quite the right label – until Tim Colton inadvertently invented the term "competitive authoritarianism" when he misremembered our inferior moniker in a conversation in the hallway.

This book took a long time to write, and during that time, we accumulated many debts. Our initial ideas about competitive authoritarianism were shaped by conversations with Keith Darden and Richard Snyder, two fellow members of the Berkeley mafia, and with Jason Brownlee and Dan Slater, two then-graduate students who were already at the forefront of a new wave of research on authoritarianism.

Two figures exerted an enormous intellectual influence on this project. Andrew Janos, who taught us comparative politics at Berkeley, first helped us understand the centrality of the international environment in the evolution of political regimes. Samuel Huntington, who was Director of the Harvard Academy for International and Area Studies when this project began, was a major influence for both of us. His ideas about political organization and regime stability pervade this book.

We owe an important debt of gratitude to several institutions. First, the WCFIA provided an intellectual home – and generous funding – to both of us. The WCFIA and the Harvard Academy for International and Area Studies, where Lucan was a Scholar, provided us with a critical opportunity to work together under the same roof during the project's early stages. Steve thanks the WCFIA and its extraordinary staff for providing a friendly and supportive environment in which to work, as well as a wide variety of forums for scholarly feedback and exchange, beginning with the hallways and extending to a range of seminars, conferences, and an invaluable authors' conference. Lucan is grateful to the Kellogg Institute at the University of Notre Dame for stimulating discussions about political regimes during his time there, as well as to the Connaught Fund, Social Science and Humanities Research Council of Canada, and Temple University, whose support made possible research trips to Belarus, Moldova, Tanzania, and Ukraine. Lucan is also grateful for the camaraderie and intellectual exchange provided by faculty and students at the Centre for European, Russian, and Eurasian Studies (CERES) at the University of Toronto.

A large number of graduate and undergraduate students have contributed their research assistance and/or editing skills to this project. We are particularly thankful to Mark Adomanis, Francisco Flores, Catherine Kelly, Maria Koinova, Alicia Llosa, Gabriel Loperena, Elena Maltseva, Jonathan Luke Melchiorre, Mason Pesek, Peter Schwartzstein, Jonathan Taylor, and Lisa Turkewitsch for their able research assistance. We thank James Loxton, John Sheffield, and George Soroka for their extraordinarily careful editing and fact-checking.

We also owe a special debt of gratitude to the editors of the *Journal of Democracy*, Larry Diamond and Marc Plattner, who encouraged this project from the beginning, backed it throughout, and provided an important forum for our ideas. Larry's encouragement convinced us to write this book, his feedback improved it, and his prodding helped to ensure that we actually finished it. Larry, our debt to you is enormous.

While researching and writing this book, we received valuable (and sometimes painful) feedback from numerous colleagues. We owe a particular debt of gratitude to Timothy Colton, Jorge Domínguez, Gerald Easter, Marc Howard, Dan Slater, Hillel Soifer, Nicolas van de Walle, and David Waldner, who read large portions of the manuscript and provided critical advice. We also thank Mark Beissinger, Eva Bellin, Valerie Bunce, Michael Coppedge, Richard Deeg, M. Steven Fish, Robert Fishman, Francisco Flores, Gustavo Flores, Barbara Geddes, Kenneth Greene, Anna Grzymala-Busse, Axel Hadenius, Frances Hagopian, Henry Hale, Antoinette Handley, Stephen Hanson, Jeffrey Herbst, Susan Hyde, Pauline Jones-Luong, Charles Kenney, Jeffrey Kopstein, Beatriz Magaloni, Scott Mainwaring, Michael McFaul, María Victoria Murillo, Thomas Pepinsky, Kenneth Roberts, James Robinson, Ed Schatz, Andreas Schedler, Joe Schwartz, Oxana Shevel, Susan Solomon, Alfred Stepan, Susan Stokes, Ronald Suny, Jay Ulfelder, J. Samuel Valenzuela, Brenda Way, Laurence Whitehead, Sean Yom, and Daniel Ziblatt. Their comments and suggestions contributed much to this book.

Robert Austin, John Gledhill, and Milada Vachudova provided much-needed help on Chapter 3. Serhiy Kudelia, Taras Kuzio, Ora John Reuter, Richard Sakwa, Vitali Silitski, Christoph Stefes, Cory Welt, and Jonathan Wheatley offered useful comments and assistance on Chapter 5. Kate Baldwin, Joel Barkan, Robert Bates, Michael Bratton, John Harbeson, Goran Hyden, Nahomi Ichino, Nelson Kasfir, Catherine Kelly, Michael Lambek, Staffan Lindberg, Carrie Manning, Susanne Mueller, Jacqueline Solway, and Richard Whitehead generously offered their time and feedback on Chapter 6.

We are also grateful to Lew Bateman, Eric Crahan, and Jason Przybylski at Cambridge University Press and to Keith Darden and Ian Shapiro, the editors of the Problems of International Politics series. Their patience, support, and suggestions (as well as their willingness to take on such a large manuscript!) are much appreciated.

Portions of the book draw on materials previously published as "The Rise of Competitive Authoritarianism," *Journal of Democracy*, 13 (2): 51–64 (April 2002); "Linkage versus Leverage: Rethinking the International Dimension of Regime Change," *Comparative Politics*, 38 (4): 379–400 (July 2006); "The dynamics of autocratic coercion after the Cold War," *Communist and Post-Communist Studies*, 39 (3): 387–410 (September 2006); and "Why Democracy Needs a Level Playing Field," *Journal of Democracy*, 21 (1) 57–68 (January 2010).

Finally, we owe enormous gratitude to our families. Steve thanks Liz Mineo and Alejandra Sol Mineo-Levitsky, who do not care very much about competitive authoritarianism (and make life much better as a result). Lucan thanks Zareen Ahmad for her seemingly limitless capacity to share in both the joys and the frustrations that this project has brought. We dedicate this book to them.

Acronyms and Abbreviations

ABIM	Malaysian Islamic Youth Movement
ADEMA	Alliance for Democracy (Mali)
ADP	Agrarian Democratic Party (Moldova)
AFORD	Alliance for Democracy (Malawi)
ANM	Armenian National Movement
APEC	Asia–Pacific Economic Cooperation
APSA	American Political Science Association
AREMA	Vanguard of the Malagasy Revolution (Madagascar)
ASEAN	Association of Southeast Asian Nations
BA	Alternative Front (Malaysia)
BDP	Botswana Democratic Party
BN	*Barisan Nasional* (Malaysia)
BNF	Botswana National Front
CAFTA	Central America Free Trade Agreement
CARICOM	Caribbean Community
CCM	Party of the Revolution (Tanzania)
CDN	Nicaraguan Democratic Coordinator
CDR	Democratic Convention (Romania)
CEP	Provisional Electoral Council (Haiti)
CIO	Central Intelligence Organization (Zimbabwe)
CIS	Commonwealth of Independent States
COSEP	Superior Council of Private Enterprise (Nicaragua)
CPDM	Cameroon People's Democratic Movement
CPP	Cambodian People's Party
CRN	National Reconciliation Committee (Madagascar)
CSCE	Commission on Security and Cooperation in Europe
CUG	Citizen's Union of Georgia
DAP	Democratic Action Party (Malaysia)
DN	National Directorate (Nicaragua)

DOS	Democratic Opposition of Serbia
DPA	Democratic Party of Albanians (Macedonia)
DPP	Democratic Progressive Party (Malawi, Taiwan)
DSS	Democratic Party of Serbia
DUI	Democratic Union for Integration (Macedonia)
EC	European Community; Electoral Commission
EPP	European People's Party
EPS	Sandinista Popular Army (Nicaragua)
EU	European Union
EZLN	Zapatista National Liberation Army (Mexico)
FAPSI	Federal Agency for Government Communications and Information (Russia)
FDPM	For a Democratic and Prosperous Moldova
FDSN	Democratic National Salvation Front (Romania)
FJKM	Church of Jesus Christ in Madagascar
FL	Lavalas Family (Haiti)
FORD	Forum for the Restoration of Democracy (Kenya)
Frelimo	Front for the Liberation of Mozambique
FSB	Federal Security Service (Russia)
FSK	Federal Counter-Intelligence Service (Russia)
FSLN	Sandinista National Liberation Front (Nicaragua)
FSN	National Salvation Front (Romania)
FUNCINPEC	National United Front for an Independent, Neutral, Peaceful, and Cooperative Cambodia
GDF	Guyana Defense Forces
GDP	gross domestic product
GPRTU	Ghana Private Rural Transport Union
HDZ	Croatian Democratic Union
HNP	Haitian National Police
HSP	Croatian Party of Rights
HZDS	Movement for Democratic Slovakia
ICFY	International Commission on Former Yugoslavia
ICTY	International Criminal Tribunal for the Former Yugoslavia
IFE	Federal Electoral Institute (Mexico)
IFES	International Foundation for Electoral Systems
IMF	International Monetary Fund
INGO	international nongovernmental organization
IO	international organization
IPPG	Inter-Party Parliamentary Group (Kenya)
IRI	International Republican Institute
ISA	Internal Security Act (Malaysia)
JCE	Central Elections Board (Dominican Republic)
JOC	Joint Operation Command (Zimbabwe)
KANU	Kenya African National Union
KGB	Committee for State Security (Belarus, USSR)
KMT	Kuomintang (Taiwan)

KNP	Khmer National Party (Cambodia)
KPRF	Communist Party of the Russian Federation
LDP	Liberal Democratic Party (Kenya)
MB	Ministry of Security (Russia)
MCA	Malaysian Chinese Association
MCP	Malawi Congress Party
MDC	Movement for Democratic Change (Zimbabwe)
MFN	Most Favored Nation
MIC	Malaysian Indian Congress
MMD	Movement for Multiparty Democracy (Zambia)
MP	Member of Parliament
MYP	Malawi Young Pioneers
NAC	National Affairs Conference (Taiwan)
NAFTA	North American Free Trade Agreement
NARC	National Alliance Rainbow Coalition (Kenya)
NATO	North Atlantic Treaty Organization
NCA	National Constitutional Assembly (Zimbabwe)
NCEC	National Convention Executive Council (Kenya)
NDA	National Democratic Alliance (Malawi)
NDC	National Democratic Congress (Ghana)
NDI	National Democratic Institute for International Affairs
NDP	National Development Party (Kenya)
NDU	National Democratic Union (Armenia)
NED	National Endowment for Democracy
NGO	nongovernmental organization
NPP	New Patriotic Party (Ghana)
NRIIA	National Republican Institute for International Affairs
NUF	National United Front (Cambodia)
OAS	Organization of American States
ODM	Orange Democratic Movement (Kenya)
OPL	Lavalas Political Organization (Haiti)
OSCE	Organization for Security and Cooperation in Europe
OVR	Fatherland-All Russia
PA	Provincial Administration (Kenya)
PAN	National Action Party (Mexico)
PAS	Islamic Party of Malaysia
PCRM	Communist Party of Moldova
PD	Democratic Party (Albania)
PDG	Gabonese Democratic Party
PDS	Senegalese Democratic Party
PDSR	Party of Democratic Socialists (Romania)
PHARE	Poland and Hungary: Assistance for Restructuring their Economies
PLC	Constitutional Liberal Party (Nicaragua)
PLD	Dominican Liberation Party
PNC	People's National Congress (Guyana)

PNDC	Provisional National Defense Council (Ghana)
PNU	Party of National Unity (Kenya)
PPP	Progressive People's Party (Guyana)
PRD	Dominican Revolutionary Party; Party of the Democratic Revolution (Mexico)
PRES	Party of Russian Unity and Concord
PRI	Institutional Revolutionary Party (Mexico)
PRM	Greater Romania Party
PRPB	Popular Party of the Revolution (Benin)
PRSC	Social Christian Reformist Party (the Dominican Republic)
PS	Socialist Party (Albania, Senegal)
PSD	Social Democratic Party (Romania)
RB	Benin Renaissance
Renamo	Mozambican National Resistance
SAP	Stabilization and Association Process
SBU	Committee on Security in Ukraine
SDF	Social Democratic Front (Cameroon)
SDP	Social Democratic Party (Croatia)
SDSM	Social Democratic Union of Macedonia
SIN	National Intelligence Service (Peru)
SPS	Socialist Party of Serbia
SRI	Romanian Intelligence Service
SRP	Sam Rainsy Party (Cambodia)
SRS	Serbian Radical Party
SVR	Foreign Intelligence Service (Russia)
TACIS	Technical Aid to the Commonwealth of Independent States
TANU	Tanganyika African National Union (Tanzania)
TC	Constitutional Tribunal (Peru)
TTS	Youth Aware of Responsibilities (Madagascar)
UDF	United Democratic Front (Malawi)
UMNO	United Malays National Organization
UNDP	National Union for Development and Progress (Cameroon)
UNIP	United National Independence Party (Zambia)
UNO	National Opposition Union (Nicaragua)
UNTAC	United Nations Transition Authority in Cambodia
UPC	Cameroon People's Union
USIA	United States Information Agency
VMRO-DPMNE	Internal Macedonian Revolutionary Organization
ZANU-PF	Zimbabwe African National Union-Patriotic Front
ZAPU	Zimbabwe African People's Union
ZCTU	Zimbabwe Congress of Trade Unions; Zambian Central Trade Union
ZNA	Zimbabwe National Army
ZUM	Zimbabwe Unity Movement

I

Introduction and Theory

1

Introduction

The end of the Cold War posed a fundamental challenge to authoritarian regimes. Single-party and military dictatorships collapsed throughout Africa, post-communist Eurasia, and much of Asia and Latin America in the late 1980s and early 1990s. At the same time, the formal architecture of democracy – particularly multiparty elections – diffused across the globe.

Transitions did not always lead to democracy, however. In much of Africa and the former Soviet Union, and in parts of Eastern Europe, Asia, and the Americas, new regimes combined electoral competition with varying degrees of authoritarianism. Unlike single-party or military dictatorships, post–Cold War regimes in Cambodia, Kenya, Malaysia, Mexico, Nigeria, Peru, Russia, Serbia, Taiwan, Ukraine, Zimbabwe, and elsewhere were competitive in that opposition forces used democratic institutions to contest vigorously – and, on occasion, successfully – for power. Nevertheless, they were not democratic. Electoral manipulation, unfair media access, abuse of state resources, and varying degrees of harassment and violence skewed the playing field in favor of incumbents. In other words, competition was real but unfair.[1] We characterize such regimes as *competitive authoritarian*. Competitive authoritarian regimes proliferated after the Cold War. By our count, 33 regimes were competitive authoritarian in 1995 – a figure that exceeded the number of full democracies in the developing and post-communist world.[2]

The study of post–Cold War hybrid regimes was initially marked by a pronounced democratizing bias.[3] Viewed through the lens of democratization, hybrid regimes were frequently categorized as flawed, incomplete, or "transitional" democracies.[4] For example, Russia was treated as a case of "protracted"

---

[1] On post–Cold War hybrid regimes, see Carothers (2002), Ottaway (2003), Schedler (2006a), and the cluster of articles in the April 2002 *Journal of Democracy*.

[2] See, for example, the scoring of Diamond (2002: 30–1) and Schedler (2002b: 47).

[3] For a critique, see Carothers (2002).

[4] See Collier and Levitsky (1997).

democratic transition during the 1990s,[5] and its subsequent autocratic turn was characterized as a "failure to consolidate" democracy.[6] Likewise, Cambodia was described as a "nascent democracy" that was "on the road to democratic consolidation"[7]; Cameroon, Georgia, and Kazakhstan were labeled "democratizers"[8]; and the Central African Republic and Congo-Brazzaville were called "would-be democracies."[9] Transitions that did not lead to democracy were characterized as "stalled" or "flawed." Thus, Zambia was said to be "stuck in transition"[10]; Albania was labeled a case of "permanent transition"[11]; and Haiti was said to be undergoing a "long,"[12] "ongoing,"[13] and even "unending"[14] transition.

Such characterizations are misleading. The assumption that hybrid regimes are (or should be) moving in a democratic direction lacks empirical foundation. Hybrid regimes followed diverse trajectories during the post–Cold War period. Although some of them democratized (e.g., Ghana, Mexico, and Slovakia), most did not. Many regimes either remained stable (e.g., Malaysia and Tanzania) or became increasingly authoritarian (e.g., Belarus and Russia). In other cases, autocratic governments fell but were succeeded by new authoritarians (e.g., Georgia, Madagascar, and Zambia). Indeed, some regimes experienced two or more transitions without democratizing.[15] As of 2010, more than a dozen competitive authoritarian regimes had persisted for 15 years or more.[16] Rather than "partial," "incomplete," or "unconsolidated" democracies, these cases should be conceptualized for what they are: a distinct, nondemocratic regime type. Instead of assuming that such regimes are in transition to democracy, it is more useful to ask why some democratized and others did not. This is the goal of our study.

This book examines the trajectories of all 35 regimes that were or became competitive authoritarian between 1990 and 1995.[17] The study spans five regions, including six countries in the Americas (the Dominican Republic, Guyana, Haiti, Mexico, Peru, and Nicaragua); six in Eastern Europe (Albania, Croatia, Macedonia, Romania, Serbia, and Slovakia); three in Asia (Cambodia, Malaysia, and Taiwan); six in the former Soviet Union (Armenia, Belarus, Georgia, Moldova, Russia, and Ukraine); and 14 in Africa (Benin, Botswana, Cameroon, Gabon, Ghana, Kenya, Madagascar, Malawi, Mali, Mozambique, Senegal, Tanzania, Zambia, and Zimbabwe).

---

[5] This view of Russia was widely shared in the 1990s. This quote comes from McFaul (1999); see also Colton and Hough (1998); Aron (2000); Nichols (2001).

[6] Smyth (2004).

[7] Brown and Timberman (1998: 14) and Albritton (2004).

[8] Siegle (2004: 21).

[9] Chege (2005: 287).

[10] Rakner and Svasand (2005).

[11] Kramer (2005).

[12] Gibbons (1999: 2).

[13] Erikson (2004: 294).

[14] Fatton (2004).

[15] Examples include Georgia, Haiti, Madagascar, and Moldova.

[16] These include Armenia, Botswana, Cambodia, Cameroon, Gabon, Kenya, Malawi, Malaysia, Mozambique, Senegal, Tanzania, Zambia, and Zimbabwe.

[17] Thus, cases of competitive authoritarianism that emerged after 1995, such as Nigeria and Venezuela, are not included in the study.

The book asks why some competitive authoritarian regimes democratized during the post–Cold War period, while others remained stable and authoritarian and still others experienced turnover without democratization. Our central argument, which is elaborated in Chapter 2, focuses on two main factors: ties to the West and the strength of governing-party and state organizations. Where linkage to the West was high, competitive authoritarian regimes democratized. Where linkage was low, regime outcomes hinged on incumbents' organizational power. Where state and governing party structures were well organized and cohesive, regimes remained stable and authoritarian; where they were underdeveloped or lacked cohesion, regimes were unstable, although they rarely democratized.

This introductory chapter is organized as follows. The first section defines competitive authoritarianism and presents the case for a new regime type. The second section examines the rise of competitive authoritarianism. It attributes the proliferation of competitive authoritarian regimes to the incentives and constraints created by the post–Cold War international environment. The third section shows how competitive authoritarian regime trajectories diverged after 1990 and provides an overview of the book's central argument and main theoretical contributions.

WHAT IS COMPETITIVE AUTHORITARIANISM?

"Politics . . . is not like football, deserving a level playing field. Here, you try that and you will be roasted."

– Daniel arap Moi, President of Kenya[18]

Competitive authoritarian regimes are civilian regimes in which formal democratic institutions exist and are widely viewed as the primary means of gaining power, but in which incumbents' abuse of the state places them at a significant advantage vis-à-vis their opponents. Such regimes are competitive in that opposition parties use democratic institutions to contest seriously for power, but they are not democratic because the playing field is heavily skewed in favor of incumbents. Competition is thus real but unfair.

Situating the Concept

Competitive authoritarianism is a hybrid regime type, with important characteristics of both democracy and authoritarianism.[19] We employ a "midrange" definition of democracy: one that is procedural but demanding.[20] Following Dahl, scholars have converged around a "procedural minimum" definition of democracy that includes four key attributes: (1) free, fair, and competitive elections;

---

[18] Quoted in Munene (2001: 24).
[19] For discussions of hybrid regimes, see Karl (1995), Collier and Levitsky (1997), Carothers (2002), Diamond (2002); Levitsky and Way (2002), Schedler (2002a, 2002b, 2006a, 2006b); Ottaway (2003), and Howard and Roessler (2006).
[20] See Diamond (1999: 13–15).

(2) full adult suffrage; (3) broad protection of civil liberties, including freedom of speech, press, and association; and (4) the absence of nonelected "tutelary" authorities (e.g., militaries, monarchies, or religious bodies) that limit elected officials' power to govern.[21] These definitions are essentially "Schumpeterian" in that they center on competitive elections.[22] However, scholars have subsequently "precised" the concept of democracy by making explicit criteria – such as civil liberties and effective power to govern – that are implicitly understood to be part of the overall meaning and which are viewed as necessary for competitive elections to take place.[23]

Although we remain committed to a procedural-minimum conception of democracy, we precise it by adding a fifth attribute: the existence of a reasonably level playing field between incumbents and opposition.[24] Obviously, a degree of incumbent advantage – in the form of patronage jobs, pork-barrel spending, clientelist social policies, and privileged access to media and finance – exists in all democracies. In democracies, however, these advantages do not seriously undermine the opposition's capacity to compete.[25] When incumbent manipulation of state institutions and resources is so excessive and one-sided that it seriously limits political competition, it is incompatible with democracy.[26]

A level playing field is implicit in most conceptualizations of democracy. Indeed, many characteristics of an uneven playing field could be subsumed into the dimensions of "free and fair elections" and "civil liberties." However, there are at least two reasons to treat this attribute as a separate dimension. First, some aspects of an uneven playing field – such as skewed access to media and finance – have a major impact between elections and are thus often missed in evaluations of whether elections are free and fair. Second, some government actions that skew the playing field may not be viewed as civil-liberties violations. For example, whereas closing down a newspaper is a clear violation of civil liberties, de facto governing-party control of the private media – achieved through informal proxy or patronage arrangements – is not. Likewise, illicit government–business ties that create vast resource disparities vis-à-vis the opposition are not civil-liberties violations per se. Attention to the slope of the playing field thus highlights how regimes may be undemocratic even in the absence of overt fraud or civil-liberties violations.

It is important to distinguish between competitive and noncompetitive authoritarianism. We define *full authoritarianism* as a regime in which no viable

---

[21] See Dahl (1971), Huntington (1991: 5–13), Schmitter and Karl (1991), Collier and Levitsky (1997), Diamond (1999: 7–15), and Mainwaring, Brinks, and Pérez-Liñan (2001). Other scholars, including Przeworski and his collaborators (Alvarez et al. 1996; Przeworski et al. 2000), employ a more minimalist definition that centers on contested elections and turnover.

[22] See Schumpter (1947) and Huntington (1989).

[23] On conceptual precising, see Collier and Levitsky (1997).

[24] See Levitsky and Way (2010).

[25] Thus, although district-level competition in U.S. congressional elections is marked by an uneven playing field, incumbents of both major parties enjoy these advantages.

[26] Greene (2007) describes this as "hyper-incumbency advantage."

channels exist for opposition to contest legally for executive power.[27] This category includes closed regimes in which national-level democratic institutions do not exist (e.g., China, Cuba, and Saudi Arabia) and hegemonic regimes in which formal democratic institutions exist on paper but are reduced to façade status in practice.[28] In hegemonic regimes, elections are so marred by repression, candidate restrictions, and/or fraud that there is no uncertainty about their outcome. Much of the opposition is forced underground and leading critics are often imprisoned or exiled. Thus, in post–Cold War Egypt, Kazakhstan, and Uzbekistan, elections served functions (e.g., a means of enhancing regime legitimacy, generating information, or distributing patronage) other than determining who governed[29]; opponents did not view them as viable means to achieve power.

Competitive authoritarian regimes are distinguished from full authoritarianism in that constitutional channels exist through which opposition groups compete in a meaningful way for executive power. Elections are held regularly and opposition parties are not legally barred from contesting them. Opposition activity is above ground: Opposition parties can open offices, recruit candidates, and organize campaigns, and politicians are rarely exiled or imprisoned. In short, democratic procedures are sufficiently meaningful for opposition groups to take them seriously as arenas through which to contest for power.

What distinguishes competitive authoritarianism from democracy, however, is the fact that incumbent abuse of the state violates at least one of three defining attributes of democracy: (1) free elections, (2) broad protection of civil liberties, and (3) a reasonably level playing field.[30]

Elections

In democracies, elections are *free*, in the sense that there is virtually no fraud or intimidation of voters, and *fair*, in the sense that opposition parties campaign on relatively even footing: They are not subject to repression or harassment, and they are not systematically denied access to the media or other critical resources.[31] In fully authoritarian regimes, multiparty elections are either nonexistent or noncompetitive. Elections may be considered noncompetitive when (1) major candidates are formally barred or effectively excluded on a regular basis[32]; (2) repression or legal controls effectively prevent opposition parties from running public campaigns; or (3) fraud is so massive that there is virtually no observable relationship between voter preferences and official electoral results.

---

[27] Our category of full authoritarianism thus includes a wide range of authoritarian regimes, including monarchies, sultanistic regimes, bureaucratic authoritarianism, and single-party regimes. The differences among these regimes are vast and of considerable theoretical importance (Snyder 2006). For the purposes of this study, however, all of them lack significant legal contestation for power.

[28] We borrow the distinction between closed and hegemonic regimes from Schedler (2002a). See also Howard and Roessler (2006).

[29] See Lust-Okur (2007) and Blaydes (forthcoming).

[30] For a full operationalization of competitive authoritarianism, see Appendix I.

[31] See Elklit and Svensson (1997).

[32] Effective exclusion occurs when physical repression is so severe or the legal, administrative, and financial obstacles are so onerous that most viable candidates are deterred from running.

Competitive authoritarian regimes fall in between these extremes. On the one hand, elections are competitive in that major opposition candidates are rarely excluded, opposition parties are able to campaign publicly, and there is no massive fraud. On the other hand, elections are often unfree and almost always unfair. In some cases, elections are marred by the manipulation of voter lists, ballot-box stuffing, and/or falsification of results (e.g., the Dominican Republic in 1994 and Ukraine in 2004). Although such fraud may alter the outcome of elections, it is not so severe as to make the act of voting meaningless.[33] Elections also may be marred by intimidation of opposition activists, voters, and poll watchers, and even the establishment of opposition "no-go" areas (e.g., Cambodia and Zimbabwe). However, such abuse is not sufficiently severe or systematic to prevent the opposition from running a national campaign. In other cases (e.g., Botswana), voting and vote-counting processes are reasonably clean but an uneven playing field renders the overall electoral process manifestly unfair. In these cases, unequal access to finance and the media as well as incumbent abuse of state institutions make elections unfair even in the absence of violence or fraud.[34] Thus, even though Mexico's 1994 election was technically clean, skewed access to resources and media led one scholar to compare it to a "soccer match where the goalposts were of different heights and breadths and where one team included 11 players plus the umpire and the other a mere six or seven players."[35]

Civil Liberties

In democracies, civil liberties – including the rights of free speech, press, and association – are protected. Although these rights may be violated periodically, such violations are infrequent and do not seriously hinder the opposition's capacity to challenge incumbents. In fully authoritarian regimes, basic civil liberties are often violated so systematically that opposition parties, civic groups, and the media are not even minimally protected (e.g., Egypt and Uzbekistan). As a result, much opposition activity takes place underground or in exile.

In competitive authoritarian regimes, civil liberties are nominally guaranteed and at least partially respected. Independent media exist and civic and opposition groups operate above ground: Most of the time, they can meet freely and even protest against the government. Yet, civil liberties are frequently violated. Opposition politicians, independent judges, journalists, human-rights activists, and other government critics are subject to harassment, arrest, and – in some cases – violent attack. Independent media are frequently threatened, attacked, and – in some cases – suspended or closed. In some regimes, overt repression – including the arrest of opposition leaders, the killing of opposition activists, and the violent repression of protest – is widespread, pushing regimes to the brink of full authoritarianism.[36]

---

33 For example, vote fraud in Serbia in 2000 and Ukraine in 2004 accounted for about 10% of the vote, which was large enough to alter the results but small enough to make voting meaningful.

34 See Greene (2007) and Levitsky and Way (2010).

35 Castañeda (1995: 131).

36 Examples include Cambodia, Zimbabwe, and Russia under Putin.

More frequently, assaults on civil liberties take more subtle forms, including "legal repression," or the discretionary use of legal instruments – such as tax, libel, or defamation laws – to punish opponents. Although such repression may involve the technically correct application of the law, its use is selective and partisan rather than universal. An example is Putin's Russia. After Mikhail Khodorkovsky, the owner of Russia's largest oil company, began to finance opposition groups in 2003, the government jailed him on tax charges and seized his company's property and stock.[37] On a more modest scale, the Fujimori government in Peru "perfected the technique of 'using the law to trample the law,'"[38] transforming judicial and tax agencies into "a shield for friends of the regime and a weapon against its enemies."[39] Rivals – often internal ones – also may be prosecuted for corruption. In Malaysia, Mahathir Mohammad used corruption and sodomy charges to imprison his chief rival, Anwar Ibrahim; in Malawi, President Bingu wa Mutharika had his chief rival, ex-President Bakili Muluzi, arrested on corruption charges; and in Ukraine, Leonid Kuchma used corruption charges to derail Prime Minister Pavlo Lazarenko's presidential candidacy.[40]

Perhaps the most widespread form of "legal" repression is the use of libel or defamation laws against journalists, editors, and media outlets. Thus, in Malaysia, the Mahathir government entered into a "suing craze" in the wake of the 1998–1999 political crisis, making widespread use of defamation suits to silence critical reporting[41]; in Cameroon, more than 50 journalists were prosecuted for libel in the late 1990s and several newspapers were forced to close due to heavy fines[42]; and in Croatia, independent newspapers were hit by more than 230 government-sponsored libel suits as of 1997.[43] In some cases (e.g., Belarus, Cambodia, and Russia), the repeated use of costly lawsuits led to the disappearance of many independent media outlets. In other cases (e.g., Malaysia and Ukraine), the threat of legal action led to widespread self-censorship.

Although "legal" and other repression under competitive authoritarianism is not severe enough to force the opposition underground or into exile, it clearly exceeds what is permissible in a democracy. By raising the cost of opposition activity (thereby convincing all but the boldest activists to remain on the sidelines) and critical media coverage (thereby encouraging self-censorship), even intermittent civil-liberties violations can seriously hinder the opposition's capacity to organize and challenge the government.

An Uneven Playing Field

Finally, nearly all competitive authoritarian regimes are characterized by an uneven playing field.[44] Obviously, a degree of incumbent advantage exists in all democracies. Indeed, many new democracies in Eastern Europe and

---

[37] Goldman (2004, 2008).
[38] Youngers (2000a: 68).
[39] Durand (2003: 459, 463).
[40] Darden (2001).
[41] Felker (2000: 51).
[42] Fombad (2003: 324).

[43] Pusic (1998).
[44] For discussions of uneven playing fields in hybrid regimes, see Schedler (2002a, 2002b), Mozaffar and Schedler (2002), Ottaway (2003: 138–56), Greene (2007), and Levitsky and Way (2010).

Latin America are characterized by extensive clientelism and politicization of state bureaucracies. To distinguish such cases from those of unfair competition, we set a high threshold for unfairness. We consider the playing field uneven when (1) state institutions are widely abused for partisan ends, (2) incumbents are systematically favored at the expense of the opposition, *and* (3) the opposition's ability to organize and compete in elections is seriously handicapped. Three aspects of an uneven playing field are of particular importance: access to resources, media, and the law.

ACCESS TO RESOURCES. Access to resources is uneven when incumbents use the state to create or maintain resource disparities that seriously hinder the opposition's ability to compete.[45] This may occur in several ways. First, incumbents may make direct partisan use of state resources. In a few cases, this funding is legal. In Guyana and Zimbabwe in the 1980s, governing parties were financed by special public ministries and/or official state subventions to the exclusion of other parties. More frequently, state finance is illicit. In Mexico, for example, the Institutional Revolutionary Party (PRI) reportedly drew $1 billion in illicit state finance during the early 1990s[46]; in Russia, tens of millions of dollars in government bonds were diverted to Yeltsin's 1996 reelection campaign.[47] Incumbents also may systematically deploy the machinery of the state – for example, state buildings, vehicles, and communications infrastructure – for electoral campaigns, and public employees and security forces may be mobilized en masse on behalf of the governing party. In former Soviet states such as Belarus, Russia, and Ukraine, this mobilization included not only low-level bureaucrats but also teachers, doctors, and other professionals.[48] In underdeveloped countries with weak private sectors, such abuse can create vast resource advantages.

Incumbents also may use the state to monopolize access to private-sector finance. Governing parties may use discretionary control over credit, licenses, state contracts, and other resources to enrich themselves via party-owned enterprises (e.g., Taiwan), benefit crony- or proxy-owned firms that then contribute money back into party coffers (e.g., Malaysia), or corner the market in private-sector donations (e.g., Mexico and Russia). In Malaysia and Taiwan, for example, governing parties used control of the state to build multibillion-dollar business empires.[49] The state also may be used to deny opposition parties access to resources. In Ukraine, for example, businesses that financed the opposition were routinely targeted by tax authorities.[50] In Ghana, entrepreneurs who financed

45 For a sophisticated discussion of how incumbent abuse of state resources shapes party competition, see Greene (2007).

46 Oppenheimer (1996: 88).

47 Hoffman (2003: 348–51).

48 See Allina-Pisano (2005) and Way (2005b). In Guyana and Peru, soldiers were mobilized for electoral campaigns; in Serbia, the security apparatus provided logistical support for the "anti-bureaucratic revolution" movement that helped Milošević consolidate power (LeBor 2002: 200–201).

49 On Malaysia, see Gomez (1990, 1991) and Searle (1999); on Taiwan, see Guo, Huang, and Chiang (1998) and Fields (2002). Similarly, in Mexico, the PRI raised hundreds of millions of dollars in donations from business magnates who had benefited from government contracts, licenses, or favorable treatment in the privatization process (Oppenheimer 1996; Philip 1999).

50 As a former head of Ukraine's security services stated, "If [your business is] loyal to the authorities, they will ignore or overlook

opposition parties "were blacklisted, denied government contracts, and [had] their businesses openly sabotaged"[51]; in Cambodia, the opposition Sam Rainsy Party (SRP) was "starved for funds by a business community told by [the government] that financing SRP was committing economic suicide."[52]

In these cases, resource disparities far exceeded anything seen in established democracies. In Taiwan, the $200 million to $500 million in annual profits generated by the $4.5 billion business empire of the Kuomintang (KMT) gave the party a financial base that was "unheard of...in any representative democracy,"[53] which allowed it to outspend opponents by more than 50-to-1 during elections.[54] In Mexico, the PRI admitted to spending 13 times more than the two major opposition parties *combined* during the 1994 election, and some observers claim that the ratio may have been 20-to-1.[55] In Russia, the Yeltsin campaign spent between 30 and 150 times the amount permitted the opposition in 1996.[56]

ACCESS TO MEDIA. When opposition parties lack access to media that reaches most of the population, there is no possibility of fair competition. Media access may be denied in several ways. Frequently, the most important disparities exist in access to broadcast media, combined with biased and partisan coverage. In many competitive authoritarian regimes, the state controls all television and most – if not all – radio broadcasting. Although independent newspapers and magazines may circulate freely, they generally reach only a small urban elite. In such cases, if radio and television are state-run and state-run channels are biased in favor of the governing party, opposition forces are effectively denied access to the media. Thus, even after the Banda dictatorship in Malawi gave way to elected President Bakili Muluzi, incumbent control of the media was such that one journalist complained, "Before it was Banda, Banda, Banda – every day. Now it is Muluzi, Muluzi, Muluzi."[57]

In other cases, private media is widespread but major media outlets are linked to the governing party – via proxy ownership, patronage, and other illicit means. In Ukraine, for example, President Kuchma controlled television coverage through an informal network of private media entities. The head of the Presidential Administration, who also owned the popular 1+1 television station, issued orders ("temnyki") to all major stations dictating how events should be covered.[58] In Malaysia, all major private newspapers and private television stations were controlled by individuals or firms linked to the governing *Barisan Nasional* (BN).[59] In Alberto Fujimori's Peru, private television stations signed "contracts" with the state intelligence service in which they received up to $1.5 million a month in exchange for limiting coverage of opposition parties.[60]

anything. If you are disloyal, you or your business will be quashed immediately" (Way 2005b: 134).
[51] Oquaye (1998: 109).
[52] Heder (2005: 118).
[53] Chu (1992: 150); see also Fields (2002: 127).
[54] Wu (1995: 79).
[55] Oppenheimer (1996: 110); Bruhn (1997: 283–4).
[56] McFaul (1997: 13).
[57] *Africa Report*, November–December 1994, 57.
[58] Human Rights Watch (2003c); Kipiani (2005).
[59] Nain (2002); Rodan (2004: 25–6).
[60] Bowen and Holligan (2003: 360–1).

BIASED REFEREES: UNEVEN ACCESS TO THE LAW. In many competitive authoritarian regimes, incumbents pack judiciaries, electoral commissions, and other
nominally independent arbiters and manipulate them via blackmail, bribery,
and/or intimidation. As a result, legal and other state agencies that are designed to
act as referees rule systematically in favor of incumbents. This allows incumbents
to engage in illicit acts – including violations of democratic procedure – with
impunity. It also ensures that critical electoral, legal, or other disputes will be
resolved in the incumbent's favor. Thus, in Malaysia, a packed judiciary ensured
that a schism in the ruling United Malays National Organization (UMNO) was
resolved in Prime Minister Mahathir's favor in 1988; a decade later, it allowed
Mahathir to imprison his main rival, Anwar Ibrahim, on dubious charges. In
Peru, Fujimori's control over judicial and electoral authorities ensured the legal-
ization of a constitutionally dubious third term in 2000. In Belarus in 1996,
the constitutional court terminated an impeachment process launched by parliamentary opponents of President Lukashenka, which facilitated Lukashenka's
consolidation of autocratic rule. In Venezuela, the electoral authorities' 2003
ruling invalidating signatures collected for a recall referendum against President
Hugo Chavez delayed the referendum long enough for Chavez to rebuild public
support and survive the referendum.

Competition without Democracy: Contestation and Uncertainty in Nondemocracies

Table 1.1 summarizes the major differences among democratic, full authoritarian,
and competitive authoritarian regimes (for a full operationalization, see Appendix I). As suggested in the table, a distinguishing feature of competitive authoritarianism is *unfair competition*. Whereas full authoritarian regimes are characterized
by the absence of competition (and, hence, of uncertainty) and democracy is characterized by fair competition, competitive authoritarianism is marked by competition that is real but unfair. Opposition parties are legal, operate aboveground,
and compete seriously in elections. However, they are subject to surveillance,
harassment, and occasional violence; their access to media and finance is limited; electoral and judicial institutions are politicized and deployed against them;
and elections are often marred by fraud, intimidation, and other abuse. Yet such
unfairness does not preclude serious contestation – or even occasional opposition victories.[61] Stated another way, whereas officials in full authoritarian regimes
can rest easy on the eve of elections because neither they nor opposition leaders
expect anything but an incumbent victory, incumbents in competitive authoritarian regimes cannot. Government officials fear a possible opposition victory
(and must work hard to thwart it), and opposition leaders believe they have at
least some chance of victory. In competitive authoritarian regimes, incumbents
are forced to sweat.

---

[61] Examples include opposition electoral victories in Nicaragua in 1990; Zambia in
1991; Guyana in 1992; Belarus, Malawi, and
Ukraine in 1994; Albania in 1997; Croatia in
2000; and Kenya in 2002. Indeed, even violent regimes, such as Cambodia, Serbia, and
Zimbabwe, may be quite competitive.

TABLE 1.1. *Comparing Democratic, Competitive Authoritarian, and Closed Regimes*

	Democracy	Competitive Authoritarianism	Full Authoritarianism
Status of Core Democratic Institutions (Elections, Civil Liberties)	Systematically respected. Widely viewed as only route to power.	Exist and are meaningful, but systematically violated in favor of incumbent. Widely viewed as primary route to power.	Nonexistent or reduced to façade status. Not viewed as a viable route to power.
Status of Opposition	Competes on more or less equal footing with incumbent.	Major opposition is legal and can compete openly, but is significantly disadvantaged by incumbent abuse.	Major opposition banned, or largely underground or in exile.
Level of Uncertainty	High	Lower than democracy but higher than full authoritarianism.	Low

What this suggests is that uncertainty and even incumbent turnover are not defining features of democracy. Influential scholars, particularly Adam Przeworski and his collaborators, have argued that uncertainty of outcomes and the possibility of electoral turnover are what distinguish democratic from nondemocratic regimes.[62] Such a conceptualization ignores the real possibility that serious violation of democratic procedure may occur in competitive elections. At times during the 1990–2008 period, elections in Albania, Armenia, Belarus, Cameroon, Cambodia, Gabon, Kenya, Madagascar, Malawi, Mozambique, Russia, Ukraine, Zambia, and Zimbabwe were characterized by considerable uncertainty and, in some cases, incumbent defeat. However, none of them was democratic and some were not even remotely so. We therefore must be able to conceptualize regimes that are sufficiently competitive to generate real uncertainty (and even turnover) but which fall short of democracy. As this book demonstrates, such regimes were widespread during the post–Cold War period.

Alternative Conceptualizations of Hybrid Regimes: Do We Need a New Subtype?

Scholars should create new regime subtypes with caution. Studies of democratization in the 1980s and 1990s generated hundreds of new subtypes of democracy.[63] As Collier and Levitsky warned, such an "excessive proliferation of new terms and

[62] See Przeworski (1986, 1991) and Alvarez et al. (1996); see also McFaul and Petrov (2004: 5–6). Przeworski famously characterized democracy as a "system in which parties lose elections" (1991: 10).

[63] Collier and Levitsky (1997).

concepts" is likely to result in "conceptual confusion."[64] Similarly, Richard Snyder has called for a "conservative bias with regard to concept formation." Rather than fall prey to the "naturalists' temptation to proclaim the discovery, naming, and classification of new political animals," Snyder argues, scholars should "carefully evaluate the null hypothesis that the political phenomena of interest . . . are actually *not* sufficiently novel to warrant new categories and labels."[65]

We contend that competitive authoritarianism *is* a new phenomenon and that no existing term adequately captures it.[66] First, these regimes routinely proved difficult for scholars to categorize during the post–Cold War period. For example, the Sandinista regime in Nicaragua was described as "a hybrid perhaps unique in the annals of political science"[67]; Fujimori's Peru was said to be a "new kind of hybrid authoritarian regime"[68]; and the PRI regime in Mexico was labeled a "hybrid, part-free, part authoritarian system" that does "not conform to classical typologies."[69]

Which existing regime categories might be appropriate for these cases? One scholarly response has been simply to label them as democracies. Regimes in Ghana, Madagascar, Malawi, Mozambique, Peru, Russia, Ukraine, and Zambia were routinely labeled democracies during the 1990s. Even extreme cases such as Belarus, Cambodia, Haiti, and Russia under Putin occasionally earned a democratic label.[70] The problem with such a strategy is straightforward: Regimes with serious electoral irregularities and/or civil-liberties violations do not meet procedural minimum standards for democracy. To label such regimes democracies is to stretch the concept virtually beyond recognition.

Another conceptual strategy has been to use generic intermediate categories, such as hybrid regime,[71] semi-democracy,[72] or Freedom House's "partly free,"[73] for cases that fall between democracy and full authoritarianism. The problem with such categories is that because democracy is multidimensional, there are multiple ways to be partially democratic. Competitive authoritarianism is only one of several hybrid regime types. Others include (1) *constitutional oligarchies* or *exclusive republics*, which possess the basic features of democracy but deny suffrage to a major segment of the adult population (e.g., Estonia and Latvia in the early 1990s)[74]; (2) *tutelary regimes*, in which elections are competitive but the power of elected governments is constrained by nonelected religious (e.g., Iran), military (e.g., Guatemala and Pakistan), or monarchic (e.g., Nepal in the 1990s) authorities; and (3) *restricted* or *semi-competitive* democracies, in which elections are free but a major party is banned (e.g., Argentina in 1957–1966 and Turkey in

---

[64] Collier and Levitsky (1997: 451). For a similar critique, see Armony and Schamis (2005).

[65] Snyder (2006: 227).

[66] See Diamond (1999: 25; 2002), Carothers (2000a, 2002), Linz (2000: 33–4), and Schedler (2002b, 2006b).

[67] Leiken (2003: 183).

[68] Burt (1998: 38).

[69] Cornelius (1996: 25).

[70] On Belarus, see Korosteleva (2006); on Cambodia, see Brown and Timberman (1998: 14) and Langran (2001: 156); on Haiti, see Gibbons (1999: 2) and Shamsie (2004: 1097); on Russia, see Nichols (2001: v–vii).

[71] Karl (1995).

[72] Mainwaring, Brinks, and Pérez-Liñán (2001).

[73] See Freedom House (http://www.freedom house.org).

[74] See Roeder (1994).

the 1990s). The differences among these regimes – and between them and competitive authoritarianism – are obscured by categories such as semi-democratic or partly free. For example, El Salvador, Latvia, and Ukraine were classified by Freedom House as partly free – with a combined political and civil-liberties score of 6 – in 1992–1993.[75] Yet, whereas in Latvia the main nondemocratic feature was the denial of citizenship rights to people of Russian descent, in El Salvador it was the military's tutelary power and human-rights violations. Ukraine possessed full citizenship and civilian control over the military, but it was competitive authoritarian. "Semi-democratic" and "partly free" are thus residual categories that reveal little about regimes other than what they are not.

Another strategy is to classify hybrid regimes as subtypes of democracy.[76] For example, Larry Diamond used the term *electoral democracy* to refer to cases in which reasonably fair elections coexist with a weak rule of law and uneven protection of human and civil rights, such as in Colombia, Brazil, India, and the Philippines.[77] Similarly, Fareed Zakaria applied the term *illiberal democracy* to "democratically elected regimes" that "routinely ignore constitutional limits on their power and [deprive] their citizens of basic rights and freedoms."[78] Subtypes such as "defective democracy," "managed democracy," and "quasi-democracy" are employed in a similar manner.[79] However, the value of such labels is questionable. As Andreas Schedler argued, many hybrid regimes:

… violate minimal democratic norms so severely that it makes no sense to classify them as democracies, however qualified. These electoral regimes … are instances of authoritarian rule. The time has come to abandon misleading labels and to take their nondemocratic nature seriously.[80]

Similarly, Juan Linz argued that although scholars "might positively value some aspects" of hybrid regimes, they "should be clear that they are not democracies (even using minimum standards)." To avoid confusion, Linz proposed "the addition of adjectives to 'authoritarianism' rather than to 'democracy.'"[81]

Competitive authoritarianism does not easily fit existing subtypes of authoritarianism (e.g., "post-totalitarianism" and "bureaucratic authoritarianism") in large part because these regimes are noncompetitive. As Diamond noted, none of Linz's seven principal types of authoritarianism even remotely resembles competitive authoritarianism – and "for good reason. This type of hybrid regime, which is now so common, is very much a product of the contemporary world."[82]

---

75 See Freedom House (http://www.freedom-house.org).

76 See Collier and Levitsky (1997).

77 Diamond (1999: 9–10; 2002: 27–31). Although Diamond (2002: 27–9) considers such regimes less democratic than "liberal democracies," he treats them as fully competitive – and therefore distinct from competitive and other authoritarian regimes.

78 Zakaria (1997: 22–3). Zakaria applies this term loosely, including everything from democracies (Argentina) to closed regimes

(Kazakhstan) to collapsed states (Sierra Leone).

79 On managed democracy, see Colton and McFaul (2003); Balzer (2003) uses the term managed pluralism; on quasi-democracy, see Villalón (1994). On defective democracy, see Croissant and Merkel (2004).

80 Schedler (2002b: 36).

81 Linz (2000: 34). See also Brown (2005: 2).

82 Diamond (2002: 24). See also Linz (2000: 33–4).

Newer subtypes of authoritarianism, such as electoral authoritarianism and semi-authoritarianism, are closer to ours in that they refer to nondemocracies with multiparty elections.[83] However, they have generally been defined broadly to refer to *all* authoritarian regimes with multiparty elections – both competitive and hegemonic.[84] Thus, the concept of electoral authoritarianism encompasses both competitive authoritarian regimes and noncompetitive regimes such as those in Egypt, Kazakhstan, and Uzbekistan.

Our conceptualization is more restrictive. We limit the category to regimes in which opposition forces use democratic institutions to contest seriously for executive power. Such a narrow definition is not a mere exercise in conceptual hair-splitting. Competitiveness is a substantively important regime characteristic that affects the behavior and expectations of political actors. As we argue later in this chapter, governments and opposition parties in competitive authoritarian regimes face a set of opportunities and constraints that do not exist in either democracies or other forms of authoritarian rule. Furthermore, competitive authoritarianism is widespread. More than 40 countries – including Malaysia, Mexico, Nigeria, Russia, Serbia, Taiwan, and Venezuela – were competitive authoritarian at some point after 1989. Indeed, competitive authoritarian regimes easily outnumbered democracies in Africa and the former Soviet Union. Thus, the conceptual space we are carving out – that of competitive nondemocracies – may be narrow, but it is both densely populated and substantively important.

THE RISE OF COMPETITIVE AUTHORITARIANISM

"[Why liberalize?] When you see your neighbor being shaved, you should wet your beard. Otherwise you could get a rough shave."

– Julius Nyerere, President of Tanzania[85]

"Don't you know how these Westerners are? They will make a fuss [about electoral fraud] for a few days, and then they will calm down and life will go on as usual."

– Eduard Shevardnadze, President of Georgia[86]

---

[83] Schedler (2006b: 3) defines electoral authoritarianism as a regime that is "minimally pluralistic," "minimally competitive," and "minimally open" but which "violate[s] the liberal-democratic principles of freedom and fairness so profoundly and systematically as to render elections instruments of authoritarian rule." Thus, elections are "minimally competitive" but opposition parties are "denied victory" (2006b: 3). On semi-authoritarianism, see Carothers (2000a) and Ottaway (2003).

[84] For example, Schedler (2002b: 47) distinguishes between "competitive" electoral

authoritarian regimes, in which the electoral arena is a "genuine battleground in the struggle for power," and "hegemonic" electoral authoritarian regimes, in which elections are "little more than a theatrical setting," but he finds it useful to "collapse both into one broad category." See also Ottaway (2003) on semi-authoritarianism. Hyde and Marinov (2009) similarly conceptualize competitive authoritarianism to include both competitive and noncompetitive regimes.

[85] Quoted in Morna (1990: 24).

[86] Quoted in Karumidze and Wertsch (2005: 24).

Competitive authoritarianism is a post–Cold War phenomenon. Although a few competitive authoritarian regimes existed during the interwar and Cold War periods,[87] they proliferated after the fall of the Berlin Wall. This was not a coincidence. Beginning in the late 1980s, major changes in the international environment undermined the stability of many closed regimes and encouraged the rise of electoral ones. First, the end of the Cold War led to a withdrawal of external support for many superpower-sponsored dictatorships. Soviet-backed Leninist regimes and U.S.-backed anti-communist regimes faced a precipitous decline in external military and economic assistance. In many cases, the elimination of Cold War subsidies coincided with mounting economic crises, which undermined the stability of many autocracies. States became bankrupt, patronage resources disappeared, and – in many cases – coercive apparatuses began to disintegrate, leaving autocrats with little choice but to liberalize or abandon power.[88]

The collapse of the Soviet Union also led to a marked shift in the global balance of power, in which the West – particularly the United States – emerged as the dominant center of economic and military power. In the post–Cold War era, as in interwar Eastern Europe,[89] the disappearance of a military, economic, and ideological alternative to the liberal West had a major impact on peripheral states. For example, it created an "almost universal wish to imitate a way of life associated with the liberal capitalist democracies of the core regimes,"[90] which encouraged the diffusion of Western democratic models.[91] Yet diffusion was also rooted in an instrumental logic: The primary sources of external assistance were now located almost exclusively in the West. Effectively "[r]eading the handwriting on the (Berlin) wall," many autocrats adopted formal democratic institutions in an effort to "position their countries favorably in the international contest for scarce development resources."[92]

The end of the Cold War was also accompanied by a major shift in Western foreign policy.[93] With the disappearance of the Soviet threat, the United States and other Western powers stepped up efforts to encourage and defend democracy through a combination of external assistance, military and diplomatic pressure, and unprecedented political conditionality.[94] In 1990, the United States, United

---

[87] In interwar Eastern Europe, competitive authoritarian regimes emerged in Bulgaria, Estonia, Hungary, Latvia, Lithuania, Poland, and Romania. During the Cold War period, cases of competitive authoritarianism included Argentina under Perón (1946–1955); Zambia in the late 1960s; the Dominican Republic during the 1970s; Senegal after 1976; and postcolonial Guyana, Malaysia, and Zimbabwe.

[88] See Herbst (1994) and Joseph (1997). Outside of Eastern Europe and the former Soviet Union, regimes that were particularly hard hit by the end of the Cold War include those in Benin, Cambodia, Guyana, Haiti, Liberia, Madagascar, Mozambique, and Nicaragua.

[89] See Janos (2000).

[90] Whitehead (1996b: 21).

[91] See Sharman and Kanet (2000), Schmitz and Sell (1999), and Kopstein and Reilly (2000).

[92] Bratton and van de Walle (1997: 182–3). See also Joseph (1999a).

[93] See Carothers (1991, 1999), Diamond (1992), Burnell (2000a), von Hippel (2000), and Schraeder (2002a).

[94] U.S. funding for democracy-assistance programs "took off" (Burnell 2000b: 39–44), increasing from near zero in the early 1980s to $700 million at the turn of the century (Carothers 1999: 6; Burnell 2000b: 49).

Kingdom, and France announced that they would link future economic assistance to democratization and human rights. Western governments and multilateral institutions began to condition loans and assistance on the holding of elections and respect for human rights.[95] Although it was never applied consistently, the "new political conditionality" induced many autocrats to hold multiparty elections.[96]

Political conditionality was accompanied by efforts to create permanent international legal frameworks for the collective defense of democracy.[97] Thus, the 1990s saw the emergence of an "international architecture of collective institutions and formal agreements enshrining both the principles of democracy and human rights."[98] These efforts went farthest in Eastern Europe, where full democracy was a requirement for European Union (EU) membership.[99] However, they also were seen in the Americas, where the Organization of American States (OAS) adopted new mechanisms for the collective defense of democracy.[100]

Finally, the post–Cold War period saw the emergence of a transnational infrastructure of organizations – including international party foundations, election-monitoring agencies, and a plethora of international organizations (IOs) and nongovernmental organizations (INGOs) – that were committed to the promotion of human rights and democracy.[101] Strengthened by new information technologies such as the Internet, transnational human-rights and democracy networks drew international attention to human-rights abuses, lobbied Western governments to take action against abusive governments, and helped protect and empower domestic opposition groups.[102] Due to the presence of these networks, rights abuses frequently triggered a "boomerang effect:" they were widely reported by international media and human rights groups, which often led Western powers to take punitive action against violating states.[103] At the same time, the growing number and sophistication of international election-observer missions helped call international attention to fraudulent elections, which deterred an increasing number of governments from attempting fraud.[104]

These changes in the international environment raised the external cost of authoritarianism and created incentives for elites in developing and post-communist countries to adopt the formal architecture of Western-style democracy, which – at a minimum – entailed multiparty elections. The change

---

95 See Nelson and Eglinton (1992) and Stokke (1995a).

96 The term *new political conditionality* is taken from Callaghy (1993: 477). See also Clinkenbeard (2004).

97 Farer (1996a), Schraeder (2002b), and Pevehouse (2005).

98 Diamond (1995: 38).

99 Pridham (2005) and Schimmelfennig and Sedelmeier (2005).

100 See Farer (1993, 1996b) and Halperin (1993).

101 See Sikkink (1993), Keck and Sikkink (1998), Middlebrook (1998), Carothers (1997b, 1999, 2000b), Risse, Ropp, and Sikkink (1999), Burnell (2000b), Florini (2000), and Ottaway and Carothers (2000).

102 Keck and Sikkink (1998) and Risse and Sikkink (1999).

103 Keck and Sikkink (1998: 12–13).

104 See McCoy, Garber, and Pastor (1991), Rosenau and Fagen (1994), Carothers (1997b), Chand (1997), and Middlebrook (1998).

was particularly striking in sub-Saharan Africa, where the number of *de jure* single-party regimes fell from 29 in 1989 to zero in 1994,[105] and in post-communist Eurasia, where only one *de jure* one-party regime (Turkmenistan) endured through the 1990s.

Yet if the post–Cold War international environment undermined autocracies and encouraged the diffusion of multiparty elections, it did not necessarily bring democracy. External democratizing pressure was limited in several ways. First, it was applied selectively and inconsistently, with important countries and regions (e.g., China and the Middle East) largely escaping pressure.[106] Second, external pressure was often superficial. In much of the world, Western democracy promotion was "electoralist" in that it focused almost exclusively on multiparty elections while often ignoring dimensions such as civil liberties and a level playing field.[107] As Zakaria observed:

In the end ... elections trump everything. If a country holds elections, Washington and the world will tolerate a great deal from the resulting government. ... In an age of images and symbols, elections are easy to capture on film. (How do you televise the rule of law?).[108]

The international community's focus on elections left many autocrats – both old and new – with considerable room to maneuver.[109] Governments "learned that they did not have to democratize" to maintain their international standing.[110] Partial liberalization – usually in the form of holding passable elections – was often "sufficient to deflect international system pressures for more complete political opening."[111] In short, the post–Cold War international environment raised the minimum standard for regime acceptability, but the new standard was multiparty elections, not democracy.

Even in the post–Cold War international environment, therefore, full democratization often required a strong domestic "push." Where favorable domestic conditions such as a strong civil society and effective state institutions were absent (e.g., much of the former Soviet Union and sub-Saharan Africa), transitions were more likely to result in regimes that combined multiparty elections with some form of authoritarian rule.[112] In other words, they were likely to result in competitive authoritarianism.

The proliferation of competitive authoritarian regimes in the early 1990s was striking. In 1985, when Mikhail Gorbachev became the Soviet leader, only a

---

[105] See Bratton and van de Walle (1997: 8) and Joseph (1997).

[106] See Nelson and Eglinton (1992), Carothers (1999), Lawson (1999), and Crawford (2001).

[107] On electoralism, see Karl (1986). See also Carothers (1999), Diamond (1999: 55–6), Lawson (1999), and Ottaway (2003).

[108] Zakaria (1997: 40).

[109] See Stokke (1995b), Joseph (1997, 1999a), Carothers (2000b), and Ottaway (2003).

[110] Joseph (1999a: 61).

[111] Young (1999a: 35). As Carothers (1997a: 90–1) wrote, governments learned how to "impose enough repression to keep their opponents weak and maintain their own power while adhering to enough democratic formalities that they might just pass themselves off as democrats."

[112] See Carothers (1997a, 2000a, 2002), Joseph (1999a), and Ottaway (2003).

handful of competitive authoritarian regimes existed in the world.[113] By 1995, nearly three dozen countries were competitive authoritarian. Thus, although the end of the Cold War triggered a wave of democratization, it also triggered a wave of hybridization. The "fourth wave" was at least as competitive authoritarian as it was democratic.[114]

DIVERGING OUTCOMES: COMPETITIVE AUTHORITARIAN REGIME TRAJECTORIES, 1990–2008

Competitive authoritarian regimes are marked by an inherent tension. The existence of meaningful democratic institutions creates arenas of contestation through which oppositions may legally – and legitimately – challenge incumbents. At times, authoritarian governments manage these arenas of contestation without difficulty. When incumbents enjoy broad public support (e.g., Botswana and Peru in the mid-1990s) and/or face very weak opposition (e.g., Tanzania), they may retain power without egregiously violating democratic institutions. However, the existence of multiparty elections, nominally independent legislatures, judiciaries, and media creates opportunities for periodic challenges, and when incumbents lack public support, these challenges may be regime-threatening. Most frequently, opposition challenges take place at the ballot box, as in Serbia (2000), Kenya (2002), Ukraine (2004), and Zimbabwe (2008). However, they also may emerge from parliament (e.g., Russia in 1993 and Belarus in 1996) or the judiciary.[115]

Such contestation poses a serious dilemma for incumbents. On the one hand, thwarting the challenge often requires a blatant assault on democratic institutions (i.e., stealing elections or closing parliament). Because such challenges are legal and generally perceived as legitimate (both at home and abroad), openly repressing them may be quite costly. On the other hand, if incumbents allow democratic procedures to run their course, they risk losing power. In effect, such challenges force incumbents to choose between egregiously violating democratic rules, at the cost of international isolation and domestic conflict, and allowing the challenge to proceed, at the cost of possible defeat. The result is often a regime crisis, as occurred in Cambodia and Russia in 1993, the Dominican Republic in 1994, Armenia in 1996, Malaysia in 1998–1999, Peru and Serbia in 2000, Madagascar in 2001, Ukraine in 2004, Kenya in 2007, and Zimbabwe in 2008. It is perhaps for this reason that Huntington wrote that "liberalized authoritarianism" is "not a stable equilibrium. The halfway house does not stand."[116]

Yet competitive authoritarian regimes were not bound to collapse; in fact, many of them proved strikingly robust. In several cases, incumbents either

---

[113] Cases included Botswana, Gambia, Guyana, Malaysia, Mexico, Nicaragua, Senegal, and Zimbabwe.

[114] The term "fourth wave" is taken from McFaul (2002).

[115] Examples include the Constitutional Tribunal's 1997 ruling against Fujimori's bid for a third term in Peru and the Zimbabwean Supreme Court's 2000 ruling against the Mugabe government's land-reform program.

[116] Huntington (1991: 137). See also Howard and Roessler (2009).

TABLE 1.2. *Competitive Authoritarian Regime Trajectories, 1990–2008*

Democratization	Unstable Authoritarianism	Stable Authoritarianism
Benin	Albania	Armenia
Croatia	Belarus	Botswana
Dominican Republic	Georgia	Cambodia
Ghana	Haiti	Cameroon
Guyana	Kenya	Gabon
Macedonia	Madagascar	Malaysia
Mali	Malawi	Mozambique
Mexico	Moldova	Russia
Nicaragua	Senegal	Tanzania
Peru	Zambia	Zimbabwe
Romania		
Serbia		
Slovakia		
Taiwan		
Ukraine		

repeatedly thwarted opposition challenges or maintained such effective control that no serious challenge emerged. In other cases, incumbents were defeated by opposition challenges but successors ruled in a competitive authoritarian manner – in other words, the government changed but the regime did not. Indeed, 19 of our 35 cases remained competitive authoritarian for 15 years or more,[117] a lifespan that is comparable to even the most durable bureaucratic authoritarian regimes in South America.[118] Hence, it appears that many halfway houses *do* stand.

Competitive authoritarian regimes followed three distinct paths between 1990 and 2008 (Table 1.2). The first is *democratization*, or the establishment of free and fair elections, broad protection of civil liberties, and a level playing field.[119] Democratization may be overseen by authoritarian governments, as in Ghana, Mexico, and Taiwan, or they may occur after those governments fall from power,

---

[117] The lifespan of all 35 competitive authoritarian regimes in our sample are Albania (1991–), Armenia (1992–), Belarus (1992–1999), Benin (1990–2006), Botswana (1966–), Cambodia (1992–), Cameroon (1991–), Croatia (1992–2000), Dominican Republic (1986–1996), Gabon (1990–), Georgia (1992, 1995–), Ghana (1991–2000), Guyana (1985–1992), Haiti (1994–2004, 2006–), Kenya (1991–), Macedonia (1991–2007), Madagascar (1989–1993, 1997–), Malawi (1993–), Malaysia (1957–), Mali (1992–2002), Mexico (1982–2000), Moldova

(1992–), Mozambique (1992–), Nicaragua (1983–1990), Peru (1992–2000), Russia (1992–2007), Romania (1990–1996, 2000–2004), Senegal (1976–), Serbia (1990–2003), Slovakia (1993–1998), Taiwan (1991–2000), Tanzania (1992–), Ukraine (1992–2004), Zambia (1990–), and Zimbabwe (1980–).

[118] Military regimes in Brazil and Chile survived for 21 and 16 years, respectively.

[119] We score outcomes as democratic if regimes remain democratic for at least three presidential/parliamentary terms and/or were democratic at the end of 2008.

as in Croatia, Nicaragua, Peru, Serbia, and Slovakia. Although the removal of authoritarian incumbents is not necessary for democratization,[120] all of our democratizing cases experienced turnover. Between 1990 and 2008, 15 of our 35 cases democratized: Benin, Croatia, the Dominican Republic, Ghana, Guyana, Macedonia, Mali, Mexico, Nicaragua, Peru, Romania, Serbia, Slovakia, Taiwan, and Ukraine.

The second outcome is *unstable authoritarianism*, or cases that undergo one or more transition but do not democratize. In these cases, authoritarian incumbents were removed at least once but new governments were not democratic. Successors inherited a skewed playing field and politicized state institutions, which they used to weaken and/or disadvantage their opponents.[121] Ten cases fell into the unstable authoritarian category: Albania, Belarus, Georgia, Haiti, Kenya, Madagascar, Malawi, Moldova, Senegal, and Zambia.

The third outcome is *stable authoritarianism*. In these cases, authoritarian incumbents or their chosen successors remained in power for at least three presidential/parliamentary terms following the establishment of competitive authoritarian rule.[122] This category includes cases that became more closed over time (e.g., Russia). During the 1990–2008 period, 10 of our 35 cases remained stable and nondemocratic: Armenia, Botswana, Cambodia, Cameroon, Gabon, Malaysia, Mozambique, Tanzania, Russia, and Zimbabwe.

This diversity of outcomes challenges the democratizing assumptions that underlie much of the post–Cold War literature on regime change. Neither the breakdown of authoritarian regimes nor the holding of multiparty elections necessarily led to democratization during the post–Cold War period.[123] Indeed, most (20 of 35) of our cases failed to democratize between 1990 and 2008. These regime patterns suggest that – *contra* Lindberg and others – multiparty elections are not by themselves an independent cause of democratization.[124] They also make it clear that electoral turnover – even where longtime autocrats are removed – should not be equated with democratic transition. In many cases – from Albania, Belarus, Malawi, Moldova, Ukraine, and Zambia in the 1990s to Georgia, Kenya, Senegal, and Madagascar in the 2000s – the removal of

---

[120] Arguably, democratization occurred in Mexico and Taiwan before incumbents lost elections.

[121] Cases of brief democratization followed by a reversion to competitive authoritarianism (e.g., Madagascar 1993–1997) are scored as unstable authoritarian.

[122] Cases in which incumbents remained in power but three full terms had not yet been completed as of December 2008 (e.g., Cameroon and Tanzania) are scored as stable.

[123] Carothers (2002) and Brownlee (2007a) make similar points.

[124] See Lindberg (2006a, 2006b, 2009a, 2009b). See also Rigger (1999, 2000). All of our

regimes held regular multiparty elections, and some did so for three (Zimbabwe), four (Senegal), and even five (Malaysia and Mexico) decades without democratizing. The holding of elections thus cannot explain why some competitive authoritarian regimes democratized whereas others did not. Neither can they explain why Guyana, Mexico, and Taiwan democratized via elections during the 1990s but not during previous decades. More generally, Brownlee (2007a) has shown that holding of multicandidate elections has no independent causal impact on authoritarian stability.

autocratic incumbents brought little institutional change, and successor parties did not govern democratically. Such cases are too numerous to be ignored or treated as exceptions.

EXPLAINING DIVERGENT OUTCOMES: THE ARGUMENT IN BRIEF

This book explains the diverging trajectories of competitive authoritarian regimes since 1990. As a starting point, we assume that incumbents seek to retain power and that they are willing to use extralegal means to do so. We argue that incumbents' capacity to hold onto power – and the fate of competitive authoritarian regimes more generally – hinges primarily on two factors: (1) *linkage to the West*, or the density of ties (economic, political, diplomatic, social, and organizational) and cross-border flows (of capital, goods and services, people, and information) between particular countries and the United States and the EU; and (2) incumbents' *organizational power*, or the scope and cohesion of state and governing-party structures.

We make a three-step argument. First, where linkage to the West was extensive, as in Eastern Europe and the Americas, competitive authoritarian regimes democratized during the post–Cold War period. By heightening the international salience of autocratic abuse, increasing the likelihood of Western response, expanding the number of domestic actors with a stake in avoiding international isolation, and shifting the balance of resources and prestige in favor of oppositions, linkage raised the cost of building and sustaining authoritarian rule. High linkage created powerful incentives for authoritarian rulers to abandon power, rather than crack down, in the face of opposition challenges. It also created incentives for successor governments to rule democratically. Among high-linkage cases, not a single authoritarian government remained in power through 2008 and nearly every transition resulted in democracy. This outcome occurred even where domestic conditions for democracy were unfavorable (e.g., Guyana, Macedonia, and Romania).

Where linkage was low, as in most of Africa and the former Soviet Union, external democratizing pressure was weaker. Consequently, regime outcomes were driven primarily by domestic factors, particularly the organizational power of incumbents. Where state and/or governing parties were well organized and cohesive, as in Malaysia and Zimbabwe, incumbents were able to manage elite conflict and thwart even serious opposition challenges (both in the streets and at the ballot box), and competitive authoritarian regimes survived. Indeed, in nearly all low-linkage cases in which incumbents had developed coercive and/or party organizations, autocrats or their chosen successors remained in power through 2008.

Where state and governing-party structures were underdeveloped and lacked cohesion, regimes were less stable. Because incumbents lacked the organizational and coercive tools to prevent elite defection, steal elections, or crack down on protest, they were vulnerable to even relatively weak opposition challenges. Consequently, regimes were more open to contingency than in other cases.

In this context, a third factor – states' vulnerability to Western democratizing pressure (which we call *Western leverage*) – was often decisive. Where countries' strategic or economic importance inhibited external pressure (e.g., Russia), or where assistance from counter-hegemonic powers blunted the impact of that pressure (e.g., Cameroon, Gabon, and post-1994 Belarus), even relatively weak regimes survived. Where Western leverage was high, such governments were more likely to fall. In these cases, turnover created an opportunity for democratization. Indeed, fragile democracies emerged in Benin, Mali, and Ukraine. However, in the absence of close ties to the West or a strong domestic push for democracy, transitions frequently brought to power new authoritarian governments (e.g., Georgia, Malawi, and Zambia). In low-linkage cases, therefore, low organizational power was associated with unstable competitive authoritarianism.

Like all theories of regime change, ours cannot explain all cases. Regime outcomes are influenced by a variety of factors – including economic performance, the strength and strategies of opposition movements, leadership, and historical contingency – that lie outside of our theoretical framework. It is not surprising, therefore, that some of the regimes analyzed in this study follow trajectories not predicted by our theory (e.g., democratization in Benin, Ghana, and Ukraine). Nevertheless, linkage, leverage, and organizational power explain a striking number of cases.

THEORETICAL IMPLICATIONS

Our research has a range of implications for the study of contemporary political regimes and regime change. For example, it contributes to the emerging literature on the international dimension of regime change. The massive wave of democratization that swept across the developing world in the 1980s and 1990s defied nearly all established theories of democratization. Framed in terms of Dahl's cost of toleration versus cost of suppression,[125] many leading theories expect stable democracy to emerge when either (1) increased societal wealth or equality reduces the cost of toleration[126]; or (2) a strengthening of civil society or opposition forces – often a product of socioeconomic modernization – increases the cost of repression.[127] Neither of these phenomena occurred on a large scale prior to the transitions in Latin America, Africa, or communist Eurasia. What *did* change was the international environment. Changes in the post–Cold War international environment heightened the cost of suppression in much of the developing world. Thus, it was an externally driven shift in the cost of suppression, not changes in domestic conditions, that contributed most centrally to the demise of authoritarianism in the 1980s and 1990s.[128]

This book presents a new framework for analyzing the international influences on regime change. The recent literature highlights a dizzying array of international influences including diffusion, demonstration effects, conditionality,

---

[125] Dahl (1971: 15).

[126] Lipset (1959/1981); Dahl (1971); Przeworski and Limongi (1997); Boix (2003); Acemoglu and Robinson (2005).

[127] See Dahl (1971) and Rueschemeyer, Stephens, and Stephens (1992).

[128] We thank David Waldner for drawing our attention to this point.

transnational civil society, and new information technologies. We organize these various mechanisms into two dimensions: Western *leverage* and *linkage* to the West. This framework enables us to capture cross-national variation in the nature and degree of external democratizing pressure. We find that the impact of the international environment varied considerably across cases and regions, and that this variation was rooted, to a large degree, in the extent of countries' ties to the West. Where linkage was high (e.g., Eastern Europe and the Americas), regimes often democratized – even in the absence of favorable domestic conditions; where it was low (e.g., Africa and the former Soviet Union), domestic factors predominated. Moreover, we find that although political conditionality and other forms of direct (or leverage-based) pressure may be effective, the democratizing impact of conditionality is far greater in countries with extensive linkage to the West.

Second, this book highlights the role of incumbent organizational power in shaping regime outcomes. Recent studies of democratization have given considerable attention to the role of societal or opposition-centered factors, including civil society,[129] organized labor,[130] mass protest,[131] and opposition cohesion,[132] in undermining authoritarianism and/or installing democracy. However, in much of post-Cold War Africa, Asia, and post-communist Eurasia, civil societies and opposition parties were weak and fragmented; as a result, the societal push for democratization was meager.[133] In many of these cases, regime outcomes were rooted less in the character or behavior of opposition movements than in incumbents' capacity to thwart them. Where incumbents possessed a powerful coercive apparatus and/or party organization, even well-organized and cohesive opposition challenges often failed. By contrast, where incumbents lacked the organizational tools needed to steal elections, co-opt opponents, or crack down on protest, transitions occurred even when oppositions were weak. Indeed, this book shows that successful opposition movements were often rooted in state and party weakness. Much of the financial and organizational muscle behind successful opposition challenges in Zambia (1990–1991), Kenya (2002), Georgia (2003), and Ukraine (2004) was provided by ex-government officials who had defected only weeks or months before the transition.

Two implications are worth noting. First, although strong parties and states are widely – and correctly – viewed as critical to democratic stability, they also are critical to stable authoritarianism.[134] Where incumbents lacked strong state and party organizations, they rarely survived during the post–Cold War period. In a competitive authoritarian context, therefore, successful state- or party-building (e.g., Zimbabwe in the 1980s, Armenia and Cambodia in the 1990s, and Russia in the 2000s) may contribute not to democratization but rather to authoritarian

---

[129] See Fish (1995), Diamond (1999), and Howard (2003).

[130] See Rueschemeyer, Stephens, and Stephens (1992), Collier (1999a), and Bellin (2000).

[131] See Bratton and van de Walle (1997), Beissinger (2002, 2007), Thompson and Kuntz (2004, 2005), Bunce and Wolchik (2006a, b), and Tucker (2007).

[132] Howard and Roessler (2006).

[133] On the weakness of civil society in post-communist countries, see Howard (2003). On opposition weakness in Africa, see Rakner and van de Walle (2009).

[134] See Huntington (1968, 1970) and, more recently, Way (2005a), Brownlee (2007a), and Slater (forthcoming).

consolidation. Second, many post–Cold War transitions were rooted more in the weakness of incumbent governments than in the strength, strategies, or mobilization of opposition forces. Such transitions were marked by a paradox: The weakness of state and governing-party organizations made it more likely that an autocrat would be forced from power but *less* likely that the transition would result in democracy. Transitions by collapse generally occurred in a context of weak states, parties, and civil societies – conditions that were hardly propitious for democratization. Because both institutional and societal checks on successor governments tended to be weak, transitions often gave rise to new authoritarian incumbents.

This book also speaks to the emerging literature on political parties and author- itarian stability. Scholars such as Barbara Geddes, Jason Brownlee, and Beatriz Magaloni have highlighted the role that parties play in maintaining elite cohesion, which is widely viewed as central to authoritarian stability.[135] For these scholars, parties manage elite conflict mainly through the organization and distribution of patronage. By providing institutional mechanisms for rulers to reward loy- alists and by lengthening actors' time horizons through the provision of future opportunities for career advancement, parties encourage elite cooperation over defection.[136]

Not all ruling parties are alike, however. As our study demonstrates, author- itarian parties vary considerably in their organizational strength and cohesion. This variation has important implications for regime stability. Indeed, our case analyses show that strictly patronage-based parties – even institutionalized ones – are often vulnerable to collapse during periods of crisis. During the post–Cold War period, established ruling parties in Kenya, Malawi, Senegal, and Zambia were decimated by defection in the face of economic and/or succession crises. By contrast, cohesion is greater in parties that are bound by salient ethnic or ideological ties or a shared history of violent struggle, such as revolutionary or liberation movements (e.g., Frelimo in Mozambique, the FSLN in Nicaragua, and ZANU-PF in Zimbabwe). Such nonmaterial bonds often help hold parties together even in the face of declining patronage resources. Frelimo, the FSLN, and ZANU remained intact despite severe economic crises and serious threats to their hold on power. Thus, parties that combined patronage with nonmaterial ties – such as those rooted in violent conflict or struggle – provided the most robust bases for authoritarian rule during the post–Cold War era.

THE DISTINCTIVE LOGIC OF COMPETITIVE AUTHORITARIAN POLITICS

This book also highlights the importance of taking seriously the dynamics of con- temporary authoritarian regimes.[137] Until recently, the assumption that hybrid regimes were "in transition" to democracy biased analyses in important ways.

---

[135] Geddes (1999); Brownlee (2007a); Magaloni (2008). See also Smith (2005).

[136] Geddes (1999) and Brownlee (2007a).

[137] Here, we echo the calls of Linz (2000: 32–8), Brown (2005), Schedler (2006b), and Snyder (2006).

Scholars gave disproportionate attention to factors that shaped the performance and stability of democracy, such as constitutional design, executive–legislative relations, electoral and party systems, and voting behavior. As a result, the factors that contribute to building and sustaining contemporary nondemocracies, as well as the internal dynamics of these regimes, were left underexplored.[138] In treating competitive authoritarian regimes as "transitional" democracies, scholars often assumed that political processes (e.g., candidate selection, electoral campaigns, and legislative politics) worked more or less as they do under democracies. Yet such assumptions are often misguided. The coexistence of meaningful democratic institutions and authoritarian incumbents creates distinctive opportunities and constraints for actors, which – in important areas of political life – generate distinct patterns of political behavior. We examine some of these areas in the following sections.

Informal Institutions

One characteristic of competitive authoritarianism is the centrality of informal institutions.[139] Informal institutions exist in all regimes but, given the disjuncture between formal (i.e., democratic) rules and actual behavior that is inherent to competitive authoritarianism, their role in such regimes may be particularly important. Recent work suggests that actors frequently employ informal institutions as a "second-best" strategy when they cannot achieve their goals through formal institutions but find the cost of changing those institutions to be prohibitive.[140] By raising the cost of formal (e.g., single-party) authoritarian rule, the post–Cold War international environment created incentives for incumbents to employ informal mechanisms of coercion and control while maintaining the formal architecture of democracy. Because informal means of coercion are more difficult for international observers to identify than formal mechanisms of repression (e.g., press censorship or bans on opposition), they were often critical to the survival of post–Cold War autocracies.

This book highlights a range of informal rules, practices, and organizations used by incumbents in competitive authoritarian regimes. In the electoral arena, for example, incumbents who cannot cancel elections or ban opposition candidates frequently turn to illicit strategies such as vote buying, ballot-box stuffing, and manipulation of the vote count.[141] Although they are frequently ad hoc,

---

[138] This lacuna began to be filled in the 2000s. See Brownlee (2002, 2007a, 2007b), Slater (2003, 2010), Way (2003, 2004, 2005a), Bellin (2004), Smith (2005, 2007), Waldner (2005), Schedler (2006a), Magaloni (2006), Greene (2007), Lust-Okar (2007), Darden (2008), Pepinsky (2009b), and Blaydes (forthcoming);

[139] Informal institutions may be defined as socially shared rules, usually unwritten, that are created, communicated, and enforced outside of officially sanctioned channels (Helmke and Levitsky 2004). On informal institutions and political regimes, see O'Donnell (1996), Lauth (2000), Collins (2002, 2003), and Helmke and Levitsky (2004, 2006).

[140] Mershon (1994: 50–1); Helmke and Levitsky (2004).

[141] See Mozaffar and Schedler (2002), Schedler (2002b), and Hartlyn and McCoy (2006).

practices such as ballot-box stuffing (e.g., Mexico) and vote-buying (e.g., Taiwan) may be institutionalized.

Another informal institution found in many competitive authoritarian regimes is organized corruption. Bribery, blackmail, proxy ownership, and other illicit exchanges are often critical to sustaining authoritarian governing coalitions.[142] For example, in Cambodia, Peru, Russia, Ukraine, and elsewhere, corruption networks played a central role in ensuring the compliance of state actors during the 1990s.[143] In Malaysia, Mexico, Peru, Senegal, Russia, and Taiwan, institutionalized corruption and patronage and proxy-ownership networks bound key economic, media, and civil-society actors to governing parties.

Competitive authoritarian governments also employ informal mechanisms of repression. For example, many of them use "legal" repression, or the discretionary use of legal instruments – such as tax authorities and libel laws – to target opposition and the media. Although such repression is formal in the sense that it entails the (often technically correct) application of the law, it is an informal institution in that enforcement is widely known to be selective. The value of this form of repression is its legal veneer: Prosecution for tax fraud or corruption can be presented to the world as enforcement of the rule of law rather than repression.

Finally, authoritarian incumbents employ informal or "privatized" violence to suppress opposition.[144] When the cost of imposing martial law or banning opposition activity is prohibitively high, incumbents may opt for violence that is "orchestrated by the state … but carried out by nonstate actors, such as vigilantes, paramilitaries, and militias."[145] Examples include organized war veterans in Armenia and Zimbabwe, "ethnic warriors" in Kenya, miners in Romania, party "youth wings" in Kenya and Malawi, "kick-down-the-door gangs" in Guyana, *chiméres* in Haiti, and "divine mobs" in Nicaragua. Because such thug groups are not formally linked to state security forces, they provide a "certain invisibility as far as international opinion is concerned."[146] They therefore help incumbents achieve the goal of "containing the broad popular challenge to their government, while attempting to distance themselves from human-rights abuses."[147]

Succession Politics

Competitive authoritarianism also generates distinct challenges in the realm of executive succession. Succession poses a serious challenge to most autocracies.[148] Unlike most democracies, authoritarian succession is often a high-stakes game. Outgoing incumbents often face serious risks, including possible seizure of wealth and prosecution for corruption or human-rights violations.[149] Indeed, many former rulers in competitive authoritarian regimes have been exiled or

---

[142] See Darden (2008).
[143] On Cambodia, see Gottesman (2003). On Ukraine, see Darden (2008). On Peru, see Rospigliosi (2000), Durand (2003), and Cameron (2006).
[144] See Kirschke (2000) and Roessler (2005).
[145] Roessler (2005: 209).

[146] Holmquist and Ford (1994: 13).
[147] Roessler (2005: 211).
[148] See Brownlee (2007b).
[149] For this reason, immunity is often a central issue for departing autocrats. This was the case, for example, in Georgia, Russia, Serbia, Ukraine, Zimbabwe, and elsewhere.

imprisoned after leaving office.[150] For this reason, incumbents often seek a successor who they can trust to protect them.[151] At the same time, however, they face a challenge that does not exist in other authoritarian regimes: the need to win competitive elections. A loyal successor is of no value if he or she loses elections. Trustworthiness and electability are often in tension with one another. On the one hand, the most electorally viable candidates are often figures with independent resources and/or support bases, which make them more difficult to control. On the other hand, regime insiders – particularly those who lack independent stature or resources – are more likely to remain loyal, particularly if their close connection to the regime makes them vulnerable to blackmail. However, such politicians often lack the voter appeal to win elections.[152]

Finding a successor who is both electable and trustworthy is often difficult. In Malawi (1994), Kenya (2002), and Ukraine (2004), outgoing rulers erred on the side of safety, choosing loyal but weak candidates who lost elections. In Ukraine, for example, President Kuchma chose Viktor Yanukovych – a corrupt official with a criminal past – apparently because he could be controlled via blackmail, but the unpopular Yanukovych lost the 2004 election. By contrast, in Malawi (2004) and Zambia (2001), successors won elections but subsequently turned on their patrons. In Peru, the inability to find a viable successor contributed to Fujimori's decision to seek an illegal (and, ultimately, ill-fated) third term in 2000.

Party Behavior

Finally, party behavior is distinct under competitive authoritarian regimes. As Scott Mainwaring has noted, standard assumptions about party behavior – for example, that parties are vote-maximizing – hold only where elections are the "only game in town."[153] In such a context, parties take the political regime as given and work within it: They participate in elections, seeking to maximize votes; if they lose, they turn to parliamentary opposition. In unconsolidated democracies and hybrid regimes, however, parties often play a "dual game" that encompasses both electoral and regime objectives.[154] In other words, conventional vote-maximizing strategies are complemented – and sometimes trumped – by strategies aimed at shoring up or undermining the existing regime.

Parties clearly play a dual game in competitive authoritarian regimes.[155] On the one hand, unlike most authoritarian regimes, parties must take seriously elections and other democratic institutions; their ability to gain or maintain power

---

[150] Former presidents who were prosecuted after leaving office include Fatos Nano in Albania, Levon Ter-Petrosian in Armenia, Kamuzu Banda and Bakili Muluzi in Malawi, Alberto Fujimori in Peru, Slobodan Milošević in Serbia, and Frederick Chiluba in Zambia. Nano, Fujimori, and Milošević were imprisoned.

[151] It is often for this reason that many autocrats opt for a dynastic solution, tapping a son or other close relative (Brownlee 2007b).

[152] It is perhaps for this reason that unlike hegemonic regimes in Azerbaijan, Jordan, North Korea, and Syria, no competitive authoritarian regime except Gabon underwent a dynastic succession between 1990 and 2010.

[153] Mainwaring (2003).

[154] Mainwaring (2003: 8–17). See also Schedler (2009a).

[155] For an insightful discussion of this dual game, see Schedler (2009a, 2009b).

hinges – at least, in part – on their ability to win votes and control legislatures. On the other hand, however, competing on a skewed playing field often requires strategies that have little to do with vote-maximization. Thus, in all but a few of our cases,[156] opposition parties combined conventional (i.e., electoral or parliamentary) strategies with extra-institutional ones. For example, oppositions may boycott elections in an effort to undermine their domestic or international legitimacy.[157] Major opposition parties boycotted at least one round of presidential or parliamentary elections in Ghana (1992), Cameroon (1992 and 1997), Haiti (1995 and 2000), Zambia (1996), Zimbabwe (1996 and 2008), Mali (1997), Serbia (1997), Peru (2000), Benin (2001), and Senegal (2007).

When opposition parties participate in elections, conditions may induce them to adopt strategies that differ markedly from those seen in democratic regimes. One is thug mobilization.[158] In a context of widespread violence or lawlessness, candidates' ability to win votes may be just as important as their ability to physically protect or deliver them. Thus, although recruiting and deploying armed thugs rarely enhances parties' electoral appeal, it can be critical to their ability to campaign and protect the vote. As Zoran Đinđić, the main architect of Serbia's "bulldozer revolution" in 2000, stated, oppositions must "clearly show they are ready to use violence to fight back in case of repression.... Security forces must realize they cannot resort to violence without risks."[159] Indeed, successful oppositions mobilized both votes and thugs in Benin (1991), Malawi (1994), Serbia (2000), and Kenya (2002).

Opposition strategies also differ between elections. Rather than confine its activities to parliament, oppositions in competitive authoritarian regimes may engage in mass protest aimed at toppling the government (or forcing it to undertake democratizing reform) before the end of its mandate. Such tactics were adopted in Cameroon (1991), Madagascar (1991 and 2009), Albania (1991 and 1997), Ukraine (1993), Venezuela (2002), Haiti (2003), and Georgia (2003 and 2007).

Alternatively, opposition parties may adopt a coalitional strategy, joining the government in pursuit of state resources, media access, protection, and other benefits.[160] Although often characterized as "naked opportunism,"[161] coalitional

---

[156] In Botswana, the Dominican Republic, Romania, Slovakia, and post-1992 Ghana, opposition contestation was limited to constitutional (i.e., electoral and parliamentary) channels. Conventional opposition strategies generally predominate where competitive authoritarian regimes are relatively soft and opposition parties possess the resources needed to survive (usually due to the existence of a robust private sector and civil society).

[157] See especially Lindberg (2006c). In Africa, opposition parties boycotted more than a third of presidential elections between 1989 and 2003 (Lindberg 2006c: 150–1).

[158] See Ichino (2007).

[159] Tomic (2001).

[160] Such coalitions are distinct from those in democratic regimes in at least two ways. First, they are usually not necessary for and are often unrelated to the formation of parliamentary majorities. In most cases, incumbents already enjoy such majorities. Second, they generally have no programmatic or ideological bases.

[161] Ihonvbere (2003a: 47–8). Also Chege (1996: 354).

strategies may be critical to party survival. In countries characterized by extreme underdevelopment (e.g., Cambodia and Malawi) or extensive state control of the economy (e.g., Belarus and Gabon), civil society and the private sector are generally small and impoverished, leaving the opposition with limited access to resources. Unless parties have a generous external patron (e.g., Nicaragua and Slovakia) or established organizations, identities, and core constituencies (e.g., Albania, Guyana, and Malaysia), joining the government may be the only viable means of securing the resources and media access necessary to remain a viable political force.

From a vote-maximizing standpoint, coalitional strategies are often suboptimal. Joining an unpopular (and, in many cases, corrupt and repressive) government may erode opposition parties' electoral and activist bases.[162] However, where access to resources is so limited that four or five years in opposition can be tantamount to political suicide (e.g., much of Africa and the former Soviet Union), politicians may conclude that joining the governments is the best means of preserving their organizations in order to "play another day."

Coalitional strategies at times have been successful. In Ukraine, after oligarch Yulia Tymoshenko's bank accounts were frozen in the late 1990s, she abandoned the opposition and created the progovernment Fatherland Party. An alliance with the government allowed Tymoshenko to regain her assets and build a powerful organization before moving back into opposition, where she would become a major player in the Orange Revolution.[163] Similarly, the entry of Abdoulaye Wade's Senegalese Democratic Party (PDS) entry into government coalitions in 1991 and 1995 brought the party access to patronage resources that it used for organization building, while other opposition parties languished.[164] Wade won the presidency in 2000. In Kenya, opposition leader Raila Odinga led his National Development Party (NDP) into a "partnership" with the Moi government during the late 1990s in exchange for police protection and access to patronage resources.[165] In 2001, the NDP joined the cabinet, which "permitted Odinga to organize dissent from within."[166] A year later, Odinga led a massive defection that helped ensure the 2002 electoral defeat of the Kenya African National Union (KANU).

---

[162] For example, after Cambodia's largest opposition party, FUNCINPEC, joined the Hun Sen government in 1998, it came to be viewed as a government "lap dog" (Marston 2002: 98) and suffered electoral decline. In Cameroon, the opposition UNDP joined the government after the 1997 elections and was "all but wiped out" in the 2002 legislative election (*Africa Confidential*, August 30, 2002, pp. 1–2). In Serbia, several opposition parties aligned with the Milošević government during the 1990s to gain access to patronage, but Milošević used these alliances to discredit these parties (and thus splinter the opposition) at key moments. Indeed, Vojislav Koštunica emerged as the strongest opposition challenger in 2000 in part because he had never cooperated with Milošević.

[163] By contrast, politicians – such as Oleksandr Moroz – who remained in opposition throughout the Kuchma period remained marginal and enjoyed less electoral success.

[164] Beck 1999: (205–208).

[165] Kanyinga (2003: 112–13); Ndegwa (2003: 150).

[166] S. Brown (2004: 336); see also Odiambo-Mbai (2003: 78–80).

Under competitive authoritarianism, therefore, opposition parties play a dual game, trying to win by the existing rules while simultaneously seeking to change them. This means that although opposition parties must take seriously electoral competition and vote-maximization, they may also pursue strategies (e.g., electoral boycotts, mass protest) aimed at undermining the regime. Moreover, they may adopt strategies (e.g., thug mobilization, alliances with unpopular governments) that – although suboptimal from a vote-seeking standpoint – allow them to compete and survive on a skewed playing field.

CASE SELECTION AND METHODS

Our study examines all 35 regimes in the world that were or became competitive authoritarian between 1990 and 1995. We exclude from the analysis other types of hybrid (or "partly free") regimes, including a variety of regimes in which political competition exists but nonelected officials retain considerable power, such as (1) those in which the most important executive office is not elected (e.g., Iran, Jordan, Kuwait, and Morocco)[167]; (2) regimes in which top executive positions are filled via elections but the authority of elected governments is seriously constrained by the military or other nonelected bodies (e.g., Guatemala, Pakistan, Thailand, and Turkey in the early 1990s)[168]; and (3) competitive regimes under foreign occupation (e.g., Lebanon in the early 1990s). In all of these regimes, the power of actors outside the electoral process generates a distinct set of dynamics and challenges not found under competitive authoritarianism. We also exclude "illiberal" electoral regimes, in which mainstream parties compete on a reasonably level playing field but widespread human- or civil-rights abuse – often targeting nonmainstream political parties or ethnic groups – persist (e.g., Colombia and Sri Lanka in the early 1990s). Because violations do not directly affect mainstream political competition, such hybrid regimes are not competitive authoritarian.

We also exclude cases in which competitive authoritarianism collapses before the completion of a single presidential or parliamentary term,[169] as well as cases in which state collapse makes it difficult to identify *any* kind of organized political regime.[170] Finally, we limit our study to regimes that were competitive authoritarian prior to 1995 in order to evaluate the impact of our variables over a significant period (at least 13 years). Thus, cases that became competitive authoritarian after 1995 (e.g., Nigeria and Venezuela) are excluded from the sample.[171]

Our criteria for scoring cases (and the actual coding) are elaborated in Appendix I. Our criteria for democracy are strict. Regimes "cross the line" from

---

[167] Likewise, Uganda is excluded from the sample because there were no elections for the executive and political parties were banned between 1990 and 1995.

[168] Other tutelary regimes during the early 1990s include Bangladesh, El Salvador, Honduras, and Nepal.

[169] Cases include Niger, where a competitive authoritarian government was toppled in a coup in 1996, and Bulgaria, where a competitive authoritarian government fell prey to mass protest in 1997.

[170] Cases include Angola, Bosnia-Herzegovina, Liberia, Sierra Leone, and Zaire/Congo in the 1990s.

[171] Other regimes that might be characterized as competitive authoritarian after 1995 include Congo-Brazzaville, Gambia, Kyrgyzstan, Niger, and Uganda.

democratic to competitive authoritarian if we find evidence of centrally coordinated or tolerated electoral manipulation, systematic civil-liberties violations (i.e., abuse is a repeated rather than an exceptional event and is orchestrated or approved by the national government), or an uneven playing field (i.e., opposition parties are denied significant access to finance or mass media or state institutions are systematically deployed against the opposition).

Our method of scoring may be illustrated with reference to a few cases that fall near the border between competitive authoritarianism and democracy. During the initial period (1990–1995), we scored Botswana as competitive authoritarian due to extreme inequalities in access to media and finance; the Dominican Republic as competitive authoritarian due to the Balaguer government's packing of the electoral commission and large-scale manipulation of voter rolls; and Slovakia as competitive authoritarian due to Mečiar's abuse of media and harassment of parliamentary opposition. On the other side of the line, Brazil and the Philippines suffered serious problems of democratic governance – including extensive clientelism, corruption, and/or a weak rule of law – in the early 1990s, but we found no evidence of systematic electoral abuse, civil-liberties violations against political opposition, or skewed access to media or finance. Hence, these cases were scored as democratic and excluded from the analysis.

Turning to regime outcomes in 2008, we scored Senegal as competitive authoritarian due to harassment and arrest of opposition politicians and journalists, and we scored Georgia as competitive authoritarian due to harassment of major media in the 2004 elections and closure of television stations during the 2007 state of emergency. On the other side of the line, we scored Benin as democratic because the 2006 election was widely characterized as clean and we found no evidence of serious abuse under President Yayi Boni. Likewise, Guyana, Macedonia, Romania, Serbia, and Ukraine were scored as democratic because – notwithstanding repeated institutional crises and serious problems of corruption – elections were clean, critics suffered no systematic harassment, and opposition parties enjoyed access to media and finance.

With respect to the line between competitive and full authoritarianism, our main criterion is whether opposition parties can use democratic institutions to compete seriously for power. If parties or candidates are routinely excluded, either formally or effectively, from competing in elections for the national executive,[172] or if electoral fraud is so extensive that voting is essentially meaningless, then regimes were scored as noncompetitive and excluded from analysis.[173] Based on these criteria, Cambodia, Serbia, and Zimbabwe in the 1990s were scored as competitive because – notwithstanding widespread state violence – opposition parties were able to seriously contest national elections. Likewise, Malaysia was scored as competitive because, despite highly institutionalized authoritarian controls, opposition parties operated legally and seriously contested nearly all

---

[172] Viable candidates may be effectively deterred from running via severe physical repression or the imposition of extreme legal, administrative, and financial obstacles to electoral participation.

[173] Examples include Burkina Faso, Ethiopia, Kazakhstan, Uzbekistan in the early 1990s.

parliamentary seats. By contrast, Singapore was scored as fully authoritarian because restrictions on speech and association made it nearly impossible for opposition groups to operate publicly and because legal controls and other institutional obstacles prevented opposition parties from contesting most seats in parliament. Egypt was scored as noncompetitive because the Muslim Brotherhood was banned and thousands of its activists were imprisoned. Azerbaijan was scored as fully authoritarian because all major opposition candidates were excluded from the 1993 election, allowing Heydar Aliyev to win with 99 percent of the vote.[174]

Two points are worth noting here. First, as in any study of this type, there exist borderline cases that arguably could be included in the sample but that we judged to be either insufficiently authoritarian (e.g., Namibia and Philippines) or insufficiently competitive (e.g., Azerbaijan, Singapore, and Uganda) for inclusion. Nevertheless, few of these borderline cases appear to run counter to our theory (see Chapter 8). Second, competitive authoritarianism is a broad category that ranges from "soft," near-democratic cases (e.g., the Dominican Republic and Slovakia in the early 1990s) to "hard," or near-full authoritarian cases (e.g., Russia and Zimbabwe in the mid-2000s). Indeed, despite considerable political reform in Kenya and Senegal between 1991 and 2008, both cases were scored as competitive authoritarian throughout the given period. Although this may be unsatisfying, the problem is hardly unique to competitive authoritarianism: Germany, Sweden, El Salvador, and Mongolia were all widely considered democracies in 2008.

The medium-n analysis employed in this study has both limitations and advantages. Our analysis is bounded in two ways. First, it is bounded by regime type. The fact that our sample includes only competitive authoritarian regimes – and thus is not representative of the broader universe of regimes – limits our ability to make general claims about the effects of linkage and organizational power. We do not, therefore, offer a general theory of regime change. Second, our study is bounded historically. Our theory of linkage's democratizing effects is relevant only for periods of Western liberal hegemony. We do not expect ties to the West to have had similar effects during the Cold War period. As this book suggests, the causes of democratization changed considerably after 1989, with the international dimension having a far more important role than in earlier periods. Hence, it appears that the factors that explain regime outcomes during the 19th century or the Cold War era differ from those that explain regime outcomes during the post–Cold War era. If that is the case, then the generalizability of theories based on analyses of other historical periods *also* may be limited.[175]

---

[174] For similar reasons, we exclude Côte d'Ivoire and Kazakhstan in the early 1990s. In this sense, our operationalization differs from that of Hyde and Marinov (2009), who classify as competitive authoritarian all regimes in which multiparty competition exists, including those in which opposition candidates stand no chance to win.

[175] For example, Przeworski and Limongi's (1997) finding that poor democracies are unlikely to endure may need to be refined in light of evidence from the post–Cold War period. Where linkage was high, as in much of Central America and the Caribbean, low-income democracies proved surprisingly robust during the 1990s and 2000. See Mainwaring and Pérez Liñan (2005).

Our research design also has important advantages. First, intensive case analysis yields greater measurement validity than is possible in most large-n cross-national studies.[176] Rather than relying on preexisting datasets that were not designed to measure competitive authoritarianism (e.g., Freedom House, Polity IV), or proxy variables whose measurement validity is often questionable (e.g., per capita military spending as a proxy for coercive capacity), we developed measures that closely approximate our concepts. The indicators used for each variable, as well as the actual coding of cases, are provided in the appendices. Thus, although our coding process is "subjective," in the sense that we make the scoring decisions in each case, it is transparent, consistent across cases and regions, and easily falsifiable – characteristics that are not shared, for example, by Freedom House.[177] This method allows us to maximize measurement validity while retaining a level of rigor and standardization that is sometimes lacking in more qualitative studies.

Second, detailed case studies allow us to examine and test for causal relationships in a way that large-n cross-national studies generally fail to do.[178] Our research design sets a high bar for testing our hypotheses. Rather than simply show a correlation between theory and outcome among the universe of competitive authoritarian regimes, we must demonstrate that the predicted causal processes are at work in each case. Thus, our case analyses show – over multiple observations – how linkage shapes actors' behavior in ways that make democratic outcomes more likely. Likewise, the case studies demonstrate the causal processes by which low state or party cohesion undermines regime stability (e.g., by preventing governments from cracking down or facilitating elite defection) during crises. Intensive case analysis also allows us to test alternative explanations by examining whether the causal mechanisms posited by rival approaches (e.g., inequality, economic crisis, institutional design) are at work.

At the same time, our medium-n analysis yields considerable variation in terms of both the dependent variable (i.e., regime outcomes) and various potential explanatory factors. Whereas most small- and medium-n analyses are limited to one or two regions, this study compares cases across five regions,[179] which

---

[176] See Adcock and Collier (2001) and Collier, Brady, and Seawright (2004a).

[177] As our research makes clear, Freedom House scores suffer from serious comparability problems over time and across region. For example, in 1997, Brazil – which was widely considered a full democracy – received a worse Freedom House score than either Malawi (where there were frequent attacks on the opposition and media) or Russia (where the government had bombed parliament and elections had been marred by fraud and manipulation). In the early 2000s, Botswana (where the playing field is so skewed that the opposition has never won a national election) received a better Freedom House score than Argentina and Mexico, both of which were widely considered full democracies. Inconsistencies over time are even more egregious. For example, Mexico's Freedom House score in 1979, when it was clearly authoritarian, is identical to its score in 1999, when, after a series of far-reaching electoral reforms, it was arguably a democracy.

[178] See Collier, Brady, and Seawright (2004a, 2004b).

[179] Among recent studies, Waldner's (2005) work on postcolonial regimes in Latin America, the Middle East, Asia, and Africa comes closest to ours in geographic breadth.

provides variation along dimensions that are essentially controlled for in single-region studies. For example, because linkage generally does not vary much within regions but varies considerably *across* regions, regional analyses often understate its impact.[180] Similarly, the relative weakness of states and governing parties across much of Africa and the former Soviet Union – and, thus, the relative lack of variation across these cases – may lead scholars to understate the role of incumbents' organizational capacity in sustaining or undermining political regimes.[181] In summary, a comparative study of 35 cases enables us to capture considerable variation (on both the independent and dependent variables) while retaining both measurement validity and close attention to causal processes.

PLAN OF THE BOOK

The remainder of the book is organized as follows. Chapter 2 describes our theory of competitive authoritarian regime change, focusing on the role of linkage to the West and incumbent state and party strength. In the chapters that follow, we examine competitive authoritarian regime trajectories in five regions. Chapters 3 and 4 focus on the high-linkage regions of Eastern Europe and the Americas. In both regions, high linkage and leverage resulted in widespread democratization, even in cases with unfavorable domestic conditions for democracy. Chapter 5 (the former Soviet Union), Chapter 6 (Africa), and Chapter 7 (Asia) examine competitive authoritarian regime trajectories in regions with lower levels of linkage. In these regions, domestic factors predominated. Where states and governing parties were strong, competitive authoritarian regimes remained stable; where they were weak, regimes were more likely to break down. Finally, the conclusion evaluates the findings of the five empirical chapters, highlights the book's central theoretical argument via paired cross-regional comparisons, examines general implications of our theory, and explores additional theoretical issues raised by the case analyses.

---

[180] For example, recent studies of the impact of the EU have emphasized the importance of conditionality in shaping democratization (cf. Vachudova 2005b and Schimmelfennig and Sedelmeier 2005) while largely ignoring the impact of linkage. This relative inattention to how linkage enhances the effectiveness of conditionality can be traced, in part, to the fact that these studies focus almost entirely on high-linkage cases.

[181] For example, because of the ban and destruction of the Communist Party during the collapse of the Soviet Union, virtually all post-Soviet regimes had weak ruling parties. As a result, the weakness of ruling parties has largely been ignored in discussions of elite defection and instability in the region (cf. Hale 2006).

2

Explaining Competitive Authoritarian Regime Trajectories

International Linkage and the Organizational Power of Incumbents

This book explains the diverging competitive authoritarian regime paths during the post–Cold War period. As noted in Chapter 1, we divide post–Cold War (1990–2008) regime trajectories into three categories: (1) *democratization*, in which autocrats fell and their successors governed democratically; (2) *stable authoritarianism*, in which autocratic governments or chosen successors remained in power through at least three terms[1]; and (3) *unstable authoritarianism*, in which autocrats fell from power but their successors did not govern democratically. Our central question, therefore, is why some competitive authoritarian regimes democratized after 1990, while others remained stable and authoritarian and still others experienced one or more transitions without democratization.

Our explanation combines a domestic structuralist approach to regime change with insights from recent work on the international dimension of democratization. Whereas earlier studies of regime change – ranging from the structuralist theories of the 1960s and 1970s to the agency-centered literature of the 1980s – focused overwhelmingly on domestic variables,[2] widespread democratization after the Cold War compelled scholars to take seriously the international environment.[3] The spatial and temporal clustering of third- and fourth-wave

---

[1] We also code as stable cases in which incumbents remain in power for at least two terms but three full terms had not yet been completed as of December 31, 2008.

[2] Classical regime analyses that focused on domestic variables include Lipset (1959/1981), Almond and Verba (1963), Moore (1966), and O'Donnell (1973). In the most influential agency-centered analysis of the 1980s, O'Donnell and Schmitter (1986: 18) concluded that it "seems fruitless to search for some international factor or context which can reliably compel authoritarian rulers to experiment with liberalization, much less which can predictably cause their regimes to collapse."

[3] On the international dimension of democratization, see Huntington (1991), Pridham (1991a), Starr (1991), Diamond (1992, 1995), Whitehead (1996a), Pridham et al. (1997), Grugel (1999a), Kopstein and Reilly (2000), Gleditsch (2002), Schraeder (2002a), Kelley (2004), Levitsky and Way (2005, 2006), Mainwaring and Perez Liñan (2005), Pevehouse (2005), Vachudova (2005b), and Brinks and Coppedge (2006).

transitions convinced even leading proponents of domestic-centered approaches that it was "time to reconsider the impact of the international context upon regime change."[4] The debate thus turned from *whether* international factors matter to *how much* they matter. Some scholars posited the primacy of external factors, arguing that international effects outweigh those of domestic variables.[5] In this view, international pressure may so decisively change actor calculations that "the influence of many traditionally important domestic variables may be mitigated."[6] Other scholars argued that the international environment plays a secondary role,[7] or that its effects are largely superficial, yielding "virtual" or "artificial" democracies.[8]

We offer a somewhat different perspective on this debate. Rather than assert the primacy of either international or domestic factors, we argue that their relative causal weight varies, in predictable ways, across countries and regions.[9] In states with extensive ties to the West, post–Cold War international influences were so intense that they contributed to democratization even where domestic conditions were unfavorable. In these cases, we concur with those who posit the primacy of international variables. However, where ties to the West were less extensive, post–Cold War international pressure was weaker, and consequently, domestic factors weighed more heavily. In these cases, regime outcomes are explained primarily by domestic structural variables, particularly the strength of state and governing-party organizations.

THE INTERNATIONAL DIMENSION: LINKAGE AND LEVERAGE

Analyses of the international dimension of democratization proliferated in the post–Cold War era. These studies point to at least five distinct mechanisms of international influence.[10] The first is *diffusion*, or the "relatively neutral transmission of information" across borders, via either demonstration effects in neighboring countries or modeling on successful democracies.[11] Facilitated by the spread of new information and communication technologies,[12] diffusion is said to account for the "wave-like" temporal and regional clustering of democratic transitions.[13]

4 Schmitter (1996: 27).
5 See Kopstein and Reilly (2000), Gleditsch (2002), Kelley (2004), Pevehouse (2005), and Vachudova (2005b).
6 Pevehouse (2005: 209). See also Vachudova (2005b).
7 See Linz and Stepan (1996) and Bratton and van de Walle (1997).
8 On "virtual democracies," see Joseph (1999b); on "artificial" democracies, see Pinkney (1997: 216).
9 Kopstein and Reilly (2000), Gleditsch (2002), and Brinks and Coppedge (2006) make similar arguments.
10 For summaries of the various mechanisms of international influence, see Diamond (1993, 1995), Schmitter (1996), Whitehead (1996a), Grugel (1999b), Burnell (2000b), and Schraeder (2003).
11 Whitehead (1996b: 5–8). On diffusion, see Huntington (1991), Starr (1991), Drake (1998), O'Loughlin et al. (1998), Schmitz and Sell (1999), Kopstein and Reilly (2000), Gleditsch (2002), Starr and Lindberg (2003), Brinks and Coppedge (2006).
12 On the role of the Internet, see Ferdinand (2000), Simon (2002a, 2002b), and Kalathil and Boas (2003).
13 See Huntington (1991), Starr (1991), O'Loughlin et al. (1998), Gleditsch (2002), Bunce and Wolchik (2006a, b), Brinks and Coppedge (2006), and Beissinger (2007).

A second mechanism of international influence is *direct democracy promotion* by Western states, particularly the United States.[14] Here, the primary force for regime change is "efforts by the world's most powerful liberal state to promote democracy abroad,"[15] via diplomatic persuasion, threats, and – in a few cases (e.g., Haiti, Panama, and Serbia) – military force.

A third mechanism of international influence is *multilateral conditionality*, in which external assistance or membership in international organizations is linked to countries' democratic or human-rights performance.[16] Forms of conditionality range from negative conditionality – or the withdrawal of external assistance to recalcitrant autocrats – to positive or membership conditionality employed by regional organizations such as the EU. The EU offered aid and extensive integration into Western Europe in exchange for far-reaching political, administrative, and economic reform.[17]

A fourth mechanism is external *democracy assistance*.[18] Western governments, party foundations, and international organizations dramatically increased funding in the 1990s for civic-education programs, electoral assistance, legal and legislative reform, and independent media and civic organizations.

Finally, *transnational advocacy networks* constitute a fifth mechanism of external influence.[19] Human-rights, democracy, and election-monitoring NGOs grew rapidly in size, number, and influence during the 1980s and 1990s. These organizations drew international attention to human-rights violations, electoral fraud, and other violations of international norms, and they lobbied Western governments to take punitive action in response to them.[20]

Despite this heightened scholarly attention, however, the relationship between the international environment and regime change remains poorly understood. Two problems are worth noting. First, there has been little effort to either adjudicate among the various mechanisms of international influence cited previously or integrate them into a coherent theoretical framework.[21] Most studies either simply present a laundry list of the various mechanisms of international influence or limit the focus to a single mechanism.

---

[14] Whitehead (1996b: 8–15) calls this democratization "by control." See Carothers (1991), Lowenthal (1991), Smith (1994), Robinson (1996), Whitehead (1996c), Peceny (1999), Cox, Ikenberry, and Inoguchi (2000), Rose (2000), von Hippel (2000), and Schraeder (2002a).

[15] Peceny (1999: 185). See also von Hippel (2000).

[16] See Nelson and Englinton (1992), Stokke (1995a), Crawford (2001), Zielonka and Pravda (2001), Linden (2002), Clinkenbeard (2004), Schimmelfennig and Sedelmeier (2005), and Vachudova (2005b).

[17] On EU conditionality, see Pridham (1991a; 2005), Pridham, Herring, and Sanford (1997), Jacoby (2004), Kelley (2004), Pevehouse (2005), Schimmelfennig and Sedelmeier (2005), Vachudova (2005b).

[18] See Diamond (1995), Carothers (1999, 2000b), Ottaway and Chung (1999), Elklit (1999), Burnell (2000a, 2000b), Ottaway and Carothers (2000), and Ethier (2003). U.S. funding for democracy-assistance programs "took off" in the 1990s (Burnell 2000b: 39–44), increasing from near zero in the early 1980s to $700 million at the turn of the century (Carothers 1999: 6; Burnell 2000b: 49).

[19] On transnational human-rights networks, see Sikkink (1993), Keck and Sikkink (1998), Risse, Ropp, and Sikkink (1999), Florini (2000), and Orenstein and Schmitz (2006).

[20] Keck and Sikkink (1998); Risse and Sikkink (1999).

[21] For a similar critique, see Pevehouse (2005: 204).

Second, many analyses of international democratizing pressure give insuffi-cient attention to how it varies – in both character and intensity – across cases and regions.[22] For example, democratic diffusion has been shown to be "spa-tially dependent."[23] Thus, diffusion effects were far more pronounced in the Americas and Eastern Europe than in Asia and the former Soviet Union.[24] Regional variation was also manifested in Western efforts to promote democ-racy: Whereas Western powers invested heavily in democracy promotion in Eastern Europe and Latin America during the 1990s, democracy promotion was trumped by "power politics" in much of Asia[25]; in Africa, democracy promotion was largely "rhetorical."[26] The effectiveness of political conditionality also var-ied by region: Whereas EU membership conditionality was relatively effective,[27] conditionality had only a limited democratizing impact in Africa.[28] Finally, the impact of transnational advocacy networks varied by region: Human-rights net-works exerted greater influence in Eastern Europe and Latin America during the 1990s,[29] whereas Middle Eastern and sub-Saharan African states were "severely underrepresented" in these networks.[30]

In summary, the international dimension was decidedly thicker in some regions (Eastern Europe and Latin America) than others (Africa and the for-mer Soviet Union) in the post–Cold War period.[31] To capture and explain this variation and to integrate the large number of seemingly disparate mechanisms of international influence into a concise theoretical framework, we organize the post–Cold War international environment into two dimensions: *Western leverage* and *linkage to the West*.[32]

Western Leverage

Western leverage may be defined as governments' vulnerability to external democratizing pressure. Our conceptualization of leverage encompasses both (1) regimes' bargaining power vis-à-vis the West,[33] or their ability to avoid

---

[22] An exception is the literature on diffusion. On regional variation in international influences, see Whitehead (1996e: 395–6), Kopstein and Reilly (2000), Gleditsch (2002), Mainwaring and Pérez Liñan (2003, 2005), Brinks and Coppedge (2006), and Orenstein and Schmitz (2006).

[23] Kopstein and Reilly (2000: 1–2); see also Starr (1991), O'Loughlin et al. (1998), Gled-itsch (2002: 4–5), and Brinks and Coppedge (2006).

[24] Starr (1991); Chu, Hu, and Moon (1997); Prizel (1999); Whitehead (1999); Kopstein and Reilly (2000).

[25] See Inoguchi (2000).

[26] Bratton and van de Walle (1997: 241); Dia-mond (1999: 55–6).

[27] Linden (2002); Kelley (2004); Pevehouse (2005); Schimmelfennig and Sedelmeier (2005); Pridham (2005); Vachudova (2005b).

[28] Bratton and van de Walle (1997: 182, 219); Roessler (2005: 210–11).

[29] Sikkink (1993: 435–6); Risse and Ropp (1999: 240); Kumar (2000: 137); Smith and Wiest (2005).

[30] Florini and Simmons (2000: 7).

[31] See Kopstein and Reilly (2000), Gleditsch (2002), Mainwaring and Pérez Liñan (2003, 2005), and Pevehouse (2005).

[32] Stallings (1992) used the terms *linkage* and *leverage* in her analysis of international influ-ences on economic policy.

[33] Our treatment of "the West" is highly aggre-gated. It is obvious that Western powers do not always act in a monolithic way. EU and

Western action aimed at punishing abuse or encouraging political liberalization; and (2) the potential impact (in terms of economic health or security) of
Western punitive action toward target states. Leverage thus refers not to the
exercise of external pressure, per se, but rather to a country's vulnerability to
such pressure.[34] Where countries lack bargaining power and are heavily affected
by Western punitive action, leverage is high; where countries possess substantial
bargaining power and/or can weather Western punitive action without significant
harm, leverage is low.

Leverage is rooted in three factors.[35] The first and most important factor is the
size and strength of countries' states and economies. Governments in weak states
with small, aid-dependent economies (e.g., much of sub-Saharan Africa) are more
vulnerable to external pressure than those of larger countries with substantial
military and/or economic power (e.g., China and Russia). These latter states
have the bargaining power to prevent pressure from being applied; therefore, the
various types of pressure employed by Western powers – such as aid withdrawal,
trade sanctions, and the threat of military force – are less likely to inflict significant
damage.

Second, leverage may be limited by competing Western foreign-policy objectives. Where Western powers have countervailing economic or strategic interests at stake, autocratic governments often possess the bargaining power to ward
off external demands for democracy by casting themselves – and regime stability – as the best means of protecting those interests.[36] Thus, Western powers
have exerted little democratizing pressure on major energy producers (e.g., Saudi
Arabia and Kuwait) or states that are deemed strategically important (e.g., Egypt
and Pakistan). In such cases, efforts to take punitive action often divide Western
governments, thereby diluting the effectiveness of those efforts.[37]

Third, leverage may be reduced by the existence of what Hufbauer et al.
call "black knights," or counter-hegemonic powers whose economic, military,
and/or diplomatic support helps blunt the impact of U.S. or EU democratizing
pressure.[38] Russia, China, Japan, and France played this role at various times
during the post–Cold War period, using economic, diplomatic, and other assistance to shore up authoritarian governments in neighboring (or, in the case of
France, former colonial) states. Examples include Russia's support for autocrats in
Belarus and France's support for autocrats in former colonies such as Cameroon
and Gabon. In Eastern Europe and the Americas, by contrast, no significant countervailing power existed during the post–Cold War period. For countries in those

---

U.S. policies differed during the post–Cold
War period, and their own policies were
often inconsistent across cases and over time.
As Kopstein (2006) notes, the EU and the
United States have often employed distinct
democracy-promotion strategies. However,
EU and U.S. policies toward competitive
authoritarian regimes were sufficiently coher-
ent after 1989 to merit theorizing about the
West as a unitary actor.

[34] This definition thus differs from that used by
Vachudova (2005b), who treats leverage as
the actual exercise of political and economic
pressure.

[35] For operationalization of leverage, see Appendix II.

[36] Nelson and Eglinton (1992: 20) and Crawford
(1997: 87).

[37] Crawford (2001: 211–27).

[38] See Hufbauer, Schott, and Elliott (1990: 12).

regions, the EU and the United States were effectively the "only game in town," which heightened the vulnerability of those countries to Western democratizing pressure.

Leverage raised the cost of building and sustaining authoritarianism during the post–Cold War period. Where leverage was high, autocratic holdouts were frequent targets of Western democratizing pressure.[39] External punitive action often triggered fiscal crises, which – by eroding incumbents' capacity to distribute patronage and to pay salaries of civil servants and security personnel – seriously threatened regime survival. Indeed, even the threat of punitive action or – in the case of Eastern Europe – the promise of external reward may powerfully shape autocratic behavior. Thus, Western pressure at times has played a major role in toppling authoritarian regimes (e.g., Haiti and Serbia) or forcing them to liberalize (e.g., Kenya, Mozambique, Malawi, and Nicaragua); in blocking or rolling back coups (e.g., Guatemala, Haiti, and Paraguay) or stolen elections (e.g., the Dominican Republic, Serbia, and Ukraine); and in dissuading governments from stealing elections in the first place (e.g., Romania and Slovakia).

Yet leverage alone rarely translated into effective democratizing pressure, for several reasons. First, Western democracy-promotion strategies (with the exception of EU membership conditionality) were markedly "electoralist," in that they focused on holding multiparty elections while often ignoring dimensions such as civil liberties.[40] Thus, whereas coups and other blatant acts of authoritarianism often triggered strong Western responses, "violations that are less spectacular yet systematic tend[ed] to be left aside."[41] Even in internationally monitored elections, incumbents often got away with harassment of opponents, abuse of state resources, near-total control over the media, and substantial manipulation of the vote.[42] Moreover, Western pressure tended to ease up after the holding of multiparty elections, even if the elections did not result in democratization.[43]

Electoralism was exacerbated by difficulties in monitoring and enforcing conditionality. Although external pressure may be effective for easily monitored "one-shot" measures, such as the holding of elections, it is less effective at guaranteeing other aspects of democracy, such as civil liberties and a level electoral field.[44] Outside of the EU, the mechanisms of monitoring and enforcement required to impose the full package of democracy were largely absent. Hence, it is not surprising that cross-national studies have found that political conditionality had little impact on regime outcomes during the post-Cold War period.[45] Even in

[39] Nelson and Eglinton (1992: 20); Crawford (2001: 210–27).

[40] On "electoralism," see Karl (1986). See also Diamond (1999: 55–6).

[41] Stokke (1995b: 63).

[42] See Geisler (1993), Carothers (1997b), and Lawson (1999).

[43] During the mid-1990s, for example, autocratic governments in Armenia, Georgia, Kenya, Mozambique, Peru, Tanzania, and Zambia faced little external pressure after elections were held.

[44] Nelson and Eglinton (1992: 35); Stokke (1995b: 63–7); Ottaway (2003).

[45] According to one study, conditionality made a "significant contribution" to democratization in only 2 of 29 cases in the 1990s (Crawford 2001: 187). See also Nelson and Eglinton (1992), Stokke (1995b), and Burnell (2000b: 26–7).

sub-Saharan Africa, where Western leverage is perhaps greatest, scholars have found no positive relationship between conditionality and democratization.[46]

Leverage alone thus generated blunt and often ineffective forms of external pressure during the post-Cold War period. Even where political conditionality was applied, autocrats frequently enjoyed considerable room to maneuver. Although compelled to hold elections, they often got away with minimal reforms that fell short of democracy – for example, adopting multipartyism without guaranteeing civil liberties or a level playing field.[47] In other words, leverage was sometimes sufficient to force transitions from closed to competitive authoritarianism but it was rarely sufficient to induce democratization.

Linkage to the West

The second dimension, *linkage*, is central to understanding variation in the effectiveness of international democratizing pressure during the post–Cold War period. We define linkage to the West as the density of ties (economic, political, diplomatic, social, and organizational) and cross-border flows (of capital, goods and services, people, and information) among particular countries and the United States, the EU (and pre-2004 EU members), and Western-dominated multilateral institutions.[48] Linkage is a multidimensional concept that encompasses the myriad networks of interdependence that connect individual polities, economies, and societies to Western democratic communities.[49] Six dimensions are of particular importance:[50]

- *economic linkage*, or flows of trade, investment, and credit
- *intergovernmental linkage*, including bilateral diplomatic and military ties as well as participation in Western-led alliances, treaties, and international organizations
- *technocratic linkage*, or the share of a country's elite that is educated in the West and/or has professional ties to Western universities or Western-led multilateral institutions
- *social linkage*, or flows of people across borders, including tourism, immigration and refugee flows, and diaspora networks

---

[46] Bratton and van de Walle (1997).

[47] Carothers (1997a, 1999, 2000a); Joseph (1999a, 1999b); Ottaway (2003: 193–4).

[48] This discussion draws on the work of Whitehead (1991, 1996b, 1996d, 1996e), Pridham (1991b), and Kopstein and Reilly (2000).

[49] This conceptualization draws on Keohane and Nye's (1989: 33–4) work on "complex interdependence," a central characteristic of which is "multiple channels of contact among societies." However, whereas Keohane and Nye focus on linkage *among* Western powers, we examine countries' ties *to* Western powers. Our conceptualization of linkage is broadly

similar to those of Rosenau (1969b), Pridham (1991b, 1991c), and Stallings (1992). It also is comparable to Scott's (1982) use of "informal penetration," Li's (1993) use of "penetration," and Kopstein and Reilly's (2000) use of "flows." Our conceptualization differs from international-relations work on "linkage diplomacy," which has been defined as government attempts to project power "from an area of strength to secure objectives in areas of weakness" (Oye et al. 1979: 13; Haas 1980; Stein 1980; Li 1993).

[50] For operationalization of linkage, see Appendix III.

- *information linkage*, or flows of information across borders via telecommunications, Internet connections, and Western media penetration
- *civil-society linkage*, or local ties to Western-based NGOs, international religious and party organizations, and other transnational networks

Linkage is rooted in a variety of historical factors, including colonialism, military occupation, and geopolitical alliances. It is enhanced by capitalist development – which increases cross-border economic activity, communication, and travel – as well as by sustained periods of political and economic openness. However, the most important source of linkage is geographic proximity.[51] Proximity "induces interdependence among states" and creates "opportunity for interaction."[52] Countries that are geographically proximate to the United States and the EU, such as those in the Caribbean Basin and Eastern Europe, generally have closer economic ties; more extensive diplomatic contacts; and larger cross-border flows of people, organizations, and information than countries in less proximate areas, such as sub-Saharan Africa or the former Soviet Union.[53]

Linkage serves as a transmitter of international influence. Many international effects that are commonly described as "global" are, in fact, rooted in concrete ties – networks; organizations; and flows of people, information, and resources – among states.[54] Thus, research on diffusion suggests that it is facilitated by "intensive and long-term contacts,"[55] which are rooted in networks of communication and flows of people and resources.[56] Similarly, transnational pressure has a greater impact where NGO networks are "strong and dense" and interstate relations are characterized by extensive interaction.[57] In short, many "globalizing" forces are not felt evenly across the globe. Post–Cold War demonstration effects, "CNN effects," and "boomerang" effects were most pronounced in countries with extensive ties to the West. Where ties to the West were minimal, these external influences were "weaker and more diffuse."[58]

Linkage contributed to democratization in three ways during the post–Cold War period: (1) it heightened the international reverberation caused by autocratic abuse; (2) it created domestic constituencies for democratic norm-abiding behavior; and (3) it reshaped the domestic distribution of power and resources, strengthening democratic and opposition forces and weakening and isolating autocrats. These mechanisms are *material* rather than normative or ideational.

---

[51] See Kopstein and Reilly (2000), Gleditsch (2002), and Brinks and Coppedge (2006).

[52] Gleditsch (2002: 4–5).

[53] Although linkage varies with region, the two are far from perfectly correlated. Some cases – Taiwan is a clear example – exhibit far greater linkage than their regional position would lead us to expect. Moreover, one finds considerable variation within each region. In East Asia, for example, cases range from high (Taiwan) to medium (Malaysia) to low linkage (Cambodia). Although the Americas is generally a high-linkage region, several cases within it score as medium linkage (e.g., Haiti and Peru).

[54] Gleditsch (2002: 13).

[55] Bostrom (1994: 192).

[56] Kopstein and Reilly (2000); Brinks and Coppedge (2006); Pérez-Armendáriz and Crow (2010).

[57] Risse-Kappan 1995a: 30–1; 1995b: 286–7); Keck and Sikkink (1998: 206).

[58] Whitehead (1996e: 395–6). See also Kopstein and Reilly (2000).

Although linkage may facilitate the diffusion of ideas and norms,[59] it also has a powerful impact on actors' interests, incentives, and capabilities. We focus on these latter effects.

Shaping Incentives: International Reverberation and the Cost of Government Abuse

Linkage heightens the international reverberation triggered by government abuse, thereby raising the cost of such abuse. Extensive media, intergovernmental, and NGO penetration, as well as flows of people and information, increases the level of external monitoring so that acts of fraud or repression are more likely to become news in Western capitals. The activities of transnational NGO networks, exile communities, and multilateral organizations have an amplifying effect, turning what otherwise would be a minor news item into an international scandal.[60] In such a context, even relatively minor abuse may gain substantial attention in the West. Thus, whereas stolen elections in Armenia, Cameroon, and Gabon went virtually unnoticed in the U.S. media during the 1990s, fraud in Mexico's *gubernatorial* elections gained widespread U.S. media coverage in 1991.[61] Likewise, the 1994 Zapatista uprising attracted a massive influx of international media and human-rights organizations to Southern Mexico, and the army's initial attempt to repress the Zapatistas "inspired an overwhelming reaction from civic groups throughout the United States."[62] In Eastern Europe, a dense array of multilateral organizations resulted in a level of detailed monitoring not seen in other parts of the world.[63] For example, the Slovak government was once cited for violating *informal* parliamentary norms of committee assignment.[64] By contrast, where Western media and international nongovernmental organization (INGO) penetration is weak, even egregious abuse often fails to make international headlines. Thus, in parts of Africa, even regimes that "rely overwhelmingly on violence and exclusionary tactics...manage to slip almost completely beneath the radar of the international media."[65] Likewise, months after the 2005 massacre of more than 100 protesters by Uzbek security forces, even Western regional experts knew "very little" about what had happened.[66]

Linkage also increases the probability that – all else being equal – Western governments will take action in response to reported abuse. Extensive media coverage and lobbying by INGOs, exile and diaspora communities, and religious and party networks often generates a "do-something" effect that puts

[59] See Risse, Ropp, and Sikkink (1999), Beissinger (2002, 2007), Bunce and Wolchik (2006a, 2006b), Orenstein and Schmitz (2006), and Pérez-Armendáriz and Crow (2010).

[60] Risse and Sikkink (1999: 18).

[61] Dresser (1996b: 332).

[62] Kumar (2000: 117); see also Dresser (1996b: 334).

[63] Pridham (2002, 2005); Schimmelfennig (2002).

[64] Vachudova (2005b: 158).

[65] Joseph (2003: 160).

[66] Oral presentation by Victoria Clement, "Yellow Revolution? Recent Referendums and Elections in Central Asia," at the conference "Shades of Revolution: Democratization in the Former Soviet Union," University of Illinois, 12 September 2005. See also *The Economist*, October 1, 2005: 39–40.

pressure on Western governments to act.[67] In Haiti, for example, lobbying by refugee organizations, human-rights groups, and the Congressional Black Caucus helped convince the Clinton Administration to take action against the military regime.[68]

Western governments are also more likely to take action in high-linkage cases because they perceive direct interests to be at stake. For the United States and EU members, the potential social, political, and economic effects of instability in the Caribbean Basin and Eastern Europe are greater than those of instability in sub-Saharan Africa or most of the former Soviet Union. For example, threats of regional instability and refugee flows caused by Serbia's proximity to Western Europe explains why the North Atlantic Treaty Organization (NATO) opted for a military response in Kosovo but took little action in response to similar or worse crises (in terms of refugees and internal displacement) in Afghanistan, Angola, and Sudan.[69] Similarly, the domestic impact of refugee flows encouraged Western intervention in Haiti (1994) and Albania (1997). In the former case, "the impact of seeing so many small boats on the television screens of average homes in the United States became too stark for Washington to ignore"[70]; in the latter case, "[t]he Albanian problem became an Italian problem" as the Italian press "kept Albanian events on the front page for months."[71]

Where linkage is less extensive, the probability of a Western response is lower. For example, due to limited media coverage, weak political ties, and the relative weakness of Africa-oriented lobbies and human-rights networks, Western governments have felt little pressure to take action against autocratic abuse in sub-Saharan Africa.[72] Because U.S. politicians view it as "politically unwise to incur the possibility of alienating their constituencies by focusing on Africa," even severe problems – such as the civil war in Congo – have often "failed to rise to the level of a policy-making crisis" in Washington.[73] A similar pattern can be seen in the former Soviet Union; for example, there existed relatively little pressure on Western governments to respond to Russian human-rights abuses in Chechnya or the 2005 massacre of unarmed protestors in Uzbekistan.[74]

In summary, linkage increases the probability that government abuse will gain the attention of – and trigger responses by – Western powers, thereby narrowing autocrats' room to maneuver. In such a context, even leaders who engage in relatively minor abuse, such as Mečiar in Slovakia, are likely to be tagged as rogue autocrats, even though they are often less repressive than governments in low-linkage countries that are accepted – and even embraced – by the West (e.g., Ethiopia and Uganda in the 1990s).

---

[67] von Hippel (2000: 102–103).

[68] Malone (1998: 166); I. Martin (1999: 725–6).

[69] Daalder and O'Hanlon (2000: 194).

[70] Ballard (1998: 77–8). See also von Hippel (2000: 102).

[71] Belloni and Morozzo della Rocca (2008: 182). See also Johnson (2001).

[72] Moss (1995: 198–9); Shraeder (2001: 391–4).

[73] Schraeder (2001: 392).

[74] On the Western response to Russian abuse in Chechnya, see Cornell (1999); Goldgeier and McFaul (2003: 138–44).

Shaping Interests: Creating Domestic Constituencies for Democratic Behavior

Linkage also shapes the distribution of domestic preferences, increasing the number of domestic actors with a stake in adhering to regional or international democratic norms. Where linkage is extensive, a plethora of individuals, firms, and organizations maintain personal, financial, or professional ties to the West. Because international isolation triggered by flawed elections, human-rights abuses, or other violations of democratic norms would put these ties – and, consequently, valued markets, investment flows, grants, job prospects, and reputations – at risk, internationally linked actors have a stake in avoiding such behavior. For example, regional economic integration increases the number of businesses for whom a sudden shift in trade or foreign-investment flows would be costly. These economic actors have a stake in their governments' adherence to regional democratic norms.[75] As a European official describing the effect of integration stated:

> You can never prevent an adventurer trying to overthrow the government if he is backed by the real economic powers, the banks and the businesses. But once in the [European] Community, you create a network of interests for those banks and businesses...; as a result, those powers would refuse to back the adventurer for fear of losing all those links.[76]

This dynamic was apparent in the Dominican Republic, where – despite a severe political–economic crisis in the early 1990s – business leaders opposed a coup out of fear that it would "hurt the country's economic prospects, affect tourism, and impact relations with the United States."[77]

A similar logic applies to technocrats with ties to Western universities, INGOs, and international organizations such as the World Bank and International Monetary Fund (IMF). Not only are technocrats sensitive to developments abroad, but they also often aspire to funding from or positions in Western universities or IOs in the future.[78] Fearing the professional or reputational costs of association with a norm-violating government, they are more likely to advocate reforms that improve the country's international standing and oppose government actions that risk international rebuke. Likewise, ties to the West may induce ruling-party politicians to seek to reform those parties from within, as occurred in Croatia, Macedonia, Mexico, and Taiwan, or to defect to the opposition, as occurred in Slovakia in the mid-1990s.[79] Linkage may even shape voter preferences. Citizens who expect integration with Europe or the United States to bring prosperity are likely to vote against parties whose behavior appears to threaten the process

---

[75] Pridham (1991c: 220–5); Pevehouse (2005).
[76] Quoted in Pridham (1991c: 235).
[77] Hartlyn (1993: 166).
[78] For example, Mexican President Carlos Salinas aspired to be President of the World Trade Organization after his term ended (Kaufman 1999: 185). His successor, Ernesto Zedillo, became head of Yale University's Center for the Study of Globalization after leaving the presidency. Similarly, Ganev (2006: 79) argues that adherence to European norms in Bulgaria was motivated in part by "the prospect of moving up the trans-European bureaucratic ladder and eventually landing well-paid jobs in Brussels."
[79] Vachudova (2005b: 161, 163, 172).

of integration. Thus, oppositions in Croatia and Slovakia focused their election campaigns on a promise to end their countries' relative estrangement from the EU.[80]

Linkage thus creates domestic constituencies for adherence to regional and international norms. By heightening domestic actors' sensitivity to shifts in a regime's image abroad, linkage blurs international and domestic politics, transforming international norms into domestic demands. When much of the elite perceives that it has something to lose from international isolation, it is more difficult to sustain a coalition behind authoritarian rule. For example, Serbia's increasing isolation from the West in the late 1990s led key military and security officials to defect, which undermined Milošević's ability to crack down on opposition protest.[81] Likewise, when President Fujimori's 1992 coup threatened Peru's reintegration into the international financial system, technocrats and business allies convinced him to abandon plans for dictatorship and call early elections.[82] By contrast, in Armenia, Belarus, Cambodia, Malaysia, and Zimbabwe – where Western-linked elites were less numerous and influential – authoritarian coalitions remained cohesive in the face of criticism and even isolation from the West.

Shaping the Distribution of Power and Resources
Linkage also reshapes domestic-power balances in ways that favor democratization. First, ties to the West help to protect opposition leaders and groups who otherwise would be vulnerable to repression. Because individuals who gain Western media attention and have influential allies in the West are more difficult to kill or imprison, governments in high-linkage contexts are often forced to tolerate voices of criticism and opposition that they otherwise might have silenced. For example, although the Mexican army possessed the coercive capacity to destroy the Zapatista rebels, international media attention and the presence of thousands of international human-rights observers "made it literally impossible for the Mexican government to use repression" against them.[83] Likewise, in Romania, international criticism brought about by intense European engagement in the early 1990s helped convince the Iliescu government to cease government-sponsored violence by coal miners.[84]

Second, ties to Western governments, transnational party networks, international agencies, and INGOs may provide critical resources to opposition and prodemocracy movements, helping to level the playing field against autocratic governments. Where autocrats monopolize access to the media and sources of finance, opposition parties are often so starved of resources that they cannot mount effective national electoral campaigns. External ties may help compensate for these resource asymmetries by providing assistance to opposition parties, independent media, and human rights and election monitoring groups. Intense Western engagement may also help encourage fragmented oppositions to unite.[85] Thus, in Slovakia, support from the EU and European party networks helped a

[80] Vachudova (2005b: 177); Fisher (2006).

[81] Cohen (2001a: 214); Bujosevic and Rado-vanovic (2003: 24–6).

[82] Mauceri (1996: 89).

[83] Castells (1997: 80).

[84] Vachudova (2005b: 102).

[85] Vachudova (2005b); Fisher (2006).

weak and fragmented opposition defeat Mečiar in 1998;[86] in Serbia, U.S. and European assistance helped level the playing field by financing independent media, opposition activists' salaries, and a massive get-out-the-vote campaign;[87] and in Nicaragua, where a weak and fragmented opposition stood little chance of wresting power from the Sandinistas on its own, U.S. officials helped unify anti-Sandinista forces, select a presidential candidate, and run a national election campaign.[88] In East Asia, by contrast, opposition party ties to the West are weaker,[89] and power and resource asymmetries have often been more difficult to overcome.[90]

Third, ties to the West may enhance domestic support for democratic opposition groups. Western media penetration heightens citizen awareness of their country's international standing – and its consequences. In such a context, opposition politicians who enjoy close ties to the West may gain prestige and support, either because they are identified with valued Western ideals or because they can credibly claim an ability to improve their country's international standing (e.g., by securing EU entry or improving relations with the United States). Thus, in Nicaragua, where the Sandinista government suffered a costly U.S.-sponsored war and trade embargo, the National Opposition Union's ties to the United States allowed it to "claim with confidence that if it won the election, the United States would end its economic embargo... and open the floodgates of U.S. economic assistance," which proved to be a critical source of electoral support.[91] At the same time, linkage may erode domestic support for autocratic incumbents. Leaders whose pariah status is perceived to threaten their countries' regional or international standing may pay a significant cost in terms of domestic support. In Slovakia, for example, most voters and politicians viewed Vladimir Mečiar as an obstacle to European integration – a goal that enjoyed broad public support.[92] Not only was Mečiar's pariah status a major issue in the 1998 election, but it also undermined his party's ability to find coalition partners with which to form a government.[93]

Finally, linkage may alter the balance of power *within* autocratic parties, helping to strengthen reformist tendencies. In Croatia, for example, widespread frustration with international isolation and strong ties to the European People's Party helped reformists wrest control of the Croatian Democratic Union from radical nationalists after the death of Franjo Tuđman.[94] Linkage also strengthened the hand of reformist factions in the Mexican PRI and Taiwanese KMT.

Linkage effects are often indirect and diffuse. Linkage influences a variety of state and nonstate actors, generating multiple and often decentralized forms of pressure that may operate below the radar screens of outside observers. Thus,

---

[86] Pridham (1999a: 1229–30).

[87] Carothers (2001).

[88] López Pintor (1998: 41–4).

[89] See Sachsenroder (1998: 13).

[90] See Gomez (2002a) and Rodan (2004).

[91] Moreno (1995: 240); see also Anderson and Dodd (2004: 152–4).

[92] Vachudova (2005b: 174–5); Schimmelfennig, Engert, and Knobel (2005: 40); Fisher (2006).

[93] Schimmelfennig, Engert, and Knobel (2003: 515). Pariah politics also played a role in Croatia and Romania, where the EU discouraged alliances with parties that were viewed as nondemocratic, and governments pushed those parties out of ruling coalitions.

[94] Houghton and Fisher (2008: 450).

although scholars have rightly attributed democratic successes in Eastern Europe and the Americas to external pressure by the EU and the United States, the intensity and efficacy of such measures was rooted, to a considerable degree, in linkage.[95]

Three final points about linkage are worth noting. First, linkage has a "cluster" effect; that is, it is the cumulative impact of a diversity of ties that is critical to shaping political outcomes. Thus, it is only where ties to the West are extensive on all (or nearly all) dimensions – as opposed to being concentrated in one or two dimensions (e.g., economic ties to Persian Gulf states or Western ties to opposition groups in ex-Soviet states) – that we should observe the linkage effects described above.[96]

Second, linkage and leverage may overlap, and when both are high, they can be difficult to disentangle. In Eastern Europe, for example, many of the institutions created by the EU accession process simultaneously enhanced linkage and served as mechanisms of external pressure. Moreover, because linkage raises the cost of international norm-violating behavior for individual actors (e.g., lost business, professional, or funding opportunities), it also may be viewed as a form of leverage. Nevertheless, the analytic distinction between linkage and leverage is important: Not only do cases vary considerably along both dimensions (compare the Dominican Republic and Slovakia, where linkage and leverage are high, to Cambodia and Malawi, where leverage is high but linkage is low), but – as we demonstrate – this variation also matters for regime outcomes.

Third, not all linkage is Western. A few of our cases are characterized by substantial social, economic, or political ties to important non-Western states (e.g., China and Russia) or communities (e.g., the international Islamic community). Where these ties are strong, they can be expected to shape how governments respond to Western pressure. The existence of a significant non-Western audience may blunt the impact of ties to the West. Indeed, in a few of our cases, extensive *non-Western linkage* appears to have had such an effect. In Malaysia, for example, social, political, and civil-society ties to the international Muslim community increased the UMNO government's sensitivity to developments in the Muslim world and countered the political influence of Western actors.[97] In Belarus and Ukraine, ties to Russia – rooted in the Soviet era – similarly blunted the impact of Western pressure.

Linkage, Leverage, and Democratization

Although linkage and leverage both raised the cost of authoritarianism in the post–Cold War era, they did so in distinct ways and to different degrees. As noted previously, leverage alone generates inconsistent and superficial democratizing

---

[95] Pridham (1991b) and Whitehead (1991, 1996d, 1996e, 1996f) make similar arguments.

[96] The clustered nature of linkage makes it difficult to isolate the effect of a particular dimension relative to others. Thus, membership in regional or international organizations may facilitate democratization (Pevehouse 2005), but only because it is embedded within dense social and information ties.

[97] Nair (1997).

pressure. Where linkage is low, external monitoring and sanctioning is usually limited to elections and large-scale human-rights violations, which leaves autocrats with greater room to maneuver. Even where external pressure succeeds in removing autocrats from power, transitions may not result in democracy. Without extensive ties to the West – and usually facing little domestic pressure – new governments have weaker incentives to play by democratic rules. Indeed, low-linkage transitions frequently have ushered in new autocratic governments.[98]

Where linkage is high, leverage is more likely to generate pressure for full democratization. Linkage enhances the democratizing impact of leverage in at least three ways. First, it improves external monitoring by increasing information flows concerning even minor democratic abuses. In a context of extensive penetration by international media, INGOs, and multilateral organizations, authoritarian governments face intense scrutiny. Crucially, this scrutiny extends beyond elections to include civil liberties, media freedom, and other democratic procedures – in other words, the full package of democracy. Moreover, monitoring tends to be permanent rather than limited to crises or election cycles. Consequently, Western attention is less likely to wane after elections are held and/or autocrats are removed.

Second, linkage increases the probability that Western states actually will use leverage for democratizing ends. Because authoritarian abuse is more likely to reverberate in Western capitals and trigger demands for a response, norm-violating governments are more likely to suffer punitive action. In other words, the "boomerang effect" discussed by scholars of transnational advocacy networks is more likely to be triggered in a context of extensive linkage.

Third, linkage magnifies the *domestic* impact of external pressure by increasing the likelihood that it will trigger broad domestic opposition. Because economic elites, politicians, technocrats, and voters are more aware of how their country is perceived abroad and more likely to believe that they have something to lose from international isolation, norm-violating governments confront a *double boomerang effect*: Abuse triggers hostile reactions on both the international and domestic fronts (Figure 2.1). For example, after Guatemalan President Jorge Serrano's 1993 "self-coup" was condemned by the U.S. government, the "threat of international . . . isolation loomed in the minds of both economic and military elites, both of which valued their international contacts." Indeed, "fear of the international consequences of allowing the coup to stand" led them to mobilize against Serrano and ultimately oust him.[99]

Linkage also increases the likelihood that authoritarian collapse will lead to stable democratization. In a high-linkage context, successor governments have stronger and more permanent incentives to play by democratic rules. First, in nearly all cases, officials in successor governments maintained close ties to Western actors that were forged during periods of opposition. In Croatia, the Dominican Republic, Nicaragua, Peru, Romania, Serbia, Slovakia, and elsewhere, opposition leaders relied heavily on Western allies for resources, protection, and legitimacy. In some cases, their domestic public support was rooted in a promise to

---

[98] Examples include Belarus, Georgia, Kenya, Madagascar, Malawi, Moldova, and Zambia.   [99] Pevehouse (2005: 190–2).

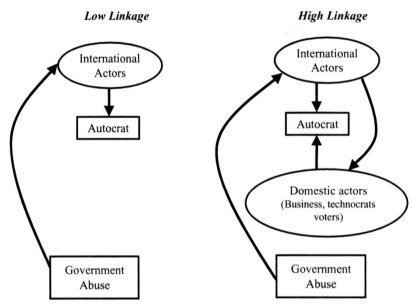

FIGURE 2.1. Linkage and the "double boomerang" effect.

deliver better relations with the West. Once these opposition leaders came to power, they were unlikely to "bite the hand" that helped get them there.[100] Second, because the infrastructure of international monitoring remains in place, new governments generally face the same level of scrutiny as their autocratic predecessors. Hence, even former opposition leaders who are not committed to democracy face strong pressure to behave democratically.

Where linkage is low, by contrast, opposition groups have weaker ties to the West and – in the absence of an infrastructure of media, NGOs, and other transnational actors – new governments enjoy greater room to maneuver. As long as domestic prodemocracy forces are weak, then, they have few incentives to play by fully democratic rules. Consequently, transitions are more likely to bring new nondemocratic governments to power (e.g., Georgia and Zambia); where regimes democratize (e.g., Benin and Mali), they are more vulnerable to authoritarian reversal.

In summary, the democratizing impact of Western leverage varies with linkage. In the absence of linkage, external pressure is often too limited and inconsistent to bring stable democratization. Where linkage is high, external pressure is more effective in both bringing down autocrats and ensuring stable democratization.

The dimensions of leverage and linkage thus help us understand cross-national variation in international pressure for democratization.[101] As shown in Table 2.1,

---

[100] Examples include Violeta Chamorro in Nicaragua, Emil Constantinescu in Romania, Mikulas Dzurinda in Slovakia, Leonel

Fernández in the Dominican Republic, and Alejandro Toledo in Peru.

[101] See Levitsky and Way (2005, 2006).

TABLE 2.1. *How Variation in Linkage and Leverage Shapes External Pressure for Democratization*

	High Linkage	Low Linkage
High Leverage	Consistent and intense democratizing pressure	Often strong, but intermittent and "electoralist," pressure
Low Leverage	Consistent but diffuse and indirect democratizing pressure	Weak external pressure

different combinations of leverage and linkage create distinct external environments. Across these environments, the relative influence of domestic and international factors varies considerably.

Where linkage and leverage are both high, as in much of Eastern Europe and the Americas, external democratizing pressure is consistent and intense. Violations of democratic norms routinely gain international attention and trigger costly punitive action, which is often magnified by opposition among domestic constituencies. In such a context, autocracies are least likely to survive and turnover is most likely to bring democratization. It is in these cases, therefore, that international influences are most pronounced. Democratization is likely even where domestic conditions are unfavorable.

Where linkage is high but leverage is low (e.g., Mexico and Taiwan), external democratizing pressure will be diffuse and indirect but nevertheless considerable. Even in the absence of direct external pressure, governments face intense scrutiny from international media, transnational human-rights networks, and internationally oriented domestic constituencies. Consequently, governments will be sensitive to shifts in international opinion. Even if governments are not directly pushed to democratize, the pursuit of international legitimacy creates incentives to avoid egregious abuse and may induce them to build credible democratic institutions.

In low-linkage countries, international democratizing pressure is weaker. Where both linkage and leverage are low, as in Russia, external pressure is likely to be minimal. In such a context, even serious abuses may fail to trigger a strong international reaction; when punitive action is undertaken, it is unlikely to have a significant impact. Consequently, governments will have considerable room to maneuver in building or maintaining authoritarian regimes. In this context of relative international permissiveness, regime outcomes hinge primarily on domestic factors. Democratization in such cases thus requires a strong domestic "push."

Where linkage is low but leverage is high, as in much of sub-Saharan Africa, international pressure may be significant but it tends to be limited and sporadic. Governments that fail to meet international electoral or human-rights standards may confront debilitating cuts in external assistance. However, such pressure is often limited to the holding of minimally acceptable elections, thereby leaving autocrats substantial room to maneuver. Even when autocrats fall, regimes may not democratize. In the absence of extensive linkage, international pressure often ceases after an electoral turnover, which may allow successor governments to violate democratic norms at low external cost. Hence, although a high-leverage/low-linkage environment may raise the cost of authoritarianism, it is less propitious for democratization.

THE DOMESTIC DIMENSION: ORGANIZATIONAL POWER AND AUTHORITARIAN STABILITY

Our domestic-level analysis centers on the balance of power between autocrats and their opponents.[102] Much of the literature on democratization has focused on the opposition – or societal – side of this story. A large body of scholarship highlights the centrality of organized labor and other class actors, civil society, mass protest, and insurgency in undermining authoritarianism and/or installing democracy.[103] Other recent studies point to the importance of opposition strategy. For example, Marc Howard and Philip Roessler link the formation of broad opposition coalitions to the liberalization of competitive authoritarian regimes, whereas Valerie Bunce and Sharon Wolchik attribute the success of "electoral revolutions" in Georgia, Ukraine, and Kyrgyzstan in the 2000s to the diffusion of particular opposition techniques and tactics that were initially developed in Eastern Europe.[104]

Yet regime outcomes also hinge on incumbents' capacity to resist opposition challenges.[105] Authoritarian governments vary considerably in their ability to control civil society, co-opt or divide oppositions, repress protest, and/or steal elections. Consider the story of the three little pigs. Setting normative preferences aside, imagine that the pigs are autocratic incumbents, their houses are their regimes, and the wolf represents prodemocracy movements. The wolf huffs and puffs at all three houses, but the impact of his huffing and puffing varies across cases: Whereas the houses of straw and sticks quickly collapse, the house of bricks remains intact. The key to explaining these outcomes lies not in the wolf's abilities or strategies but in differences in the strength of the houses.

Many recent analyses of regime change – for example, the literature on the "color revolutions" of the 2000s – focus on democratic "huffing and puffing"

---

[102] Here, we draw on Theda Skocpol's work (1973, 1979) on the causes of social revolution, as well as more recent regime analyses that highlight the role of state and party organization and the balance of power between state and societal actors, including Rueschemeyer, Stephens, and Stephens (1992), Slater (2003, 2010), Bellin (2004), Smith (2005), Waldner (2005), Way (2005a), and Brownlee (2007a).

[103] On organized labor and class actors, see Rueschemeyer, Stephens, and Stephens (1992), Collier (1999a), and Bellin (2000);

on civil society, see Fish (1995), Diamond (1999), and Howard (2003); on protest, see Bratton and van de Walle (1997), Beissinger (2002), Thompson and Kuntz (2004, 2005), and Tucker (2007); and on insurgent democratization, see Wood (2000).

[104] Howard and Roessler (2006); Bunce and Wolchik (2006a, b).

[105] On this issue, see Skocpol (1973, 1979), Snyder (1998), Brownlee (2002), Slater (2003, 2010), Bellin (2004), and Way (2005a, 2005b).

but pay insufficient attention to the strength of authoritarian houses.[106] In some countries, bankrupt states; weak, underpaid, and disorganized security services; and fragmented elites left regimes vulnerable to collapse in the face of minimal protest. Thus, as Jeffrey Herbst observed, it was "the weakness of African states rather than the strength of democratic opposition" that drove many regime transitions in that region. African democracy movements frequently confronted states that "were rotting from within. With a mere push many would collapse."[107] Way finds a similar dynamic in the former Soviet Union.[108] For example, in Georgia, where police had not been paid in three months, Eduard Shevardnadze abandoned power in the face of "undersized" crowds, largely because he "no longer controlled the military and security forces" and was "too politically weak" to order repression.[109] Likewise, in Kyrgyzstan in 2005, the police stepped aside as a few hundred protestors seized regional governments and demonstrations of no more than 10,000 people led President Askar Akayev to abandon power.[110] Finally, in Haiti, the Aristide government was "toppled by a rag-tag army of as few as 200 rebels."[111] The rebels "did not fight a single battle. The police simply changed out of their uniforms, grabbed bottles of rum, and headed for the hills."[112]

In other cases, the story played out differently. Where state and/or governing party structures were well organized and cohesive, autocrats often thwarted serious opposition challenges. For example, the Armenian government, backed by army veterans who had recently returned from a successful war with Azerbaijan, faced down crowds of up to 200 thousand protesters following the rigged 1996 presidential election.[113] In Zimbabwe, opposition plans for "mass action" to protest the flawed 2000 elections were "deferred indefinitely" in the face of brutal police repression[114]; after the 2002 election, opposition leaders were "unwilling to consider" mass action "given the vast repressive machinery that would confront them."[115] In Malaysia, although the 1998 arrest of Anwar Ibrahim gave rise to an unprecedented *Reformasi* movement, regime opponents confronted a "highly effective and repressive police force."[116] Protest was met forcefully by riot police and ultimately "posed no threat to the government's stability."[117] Finally, in Serbia, opposition forces were mobilized throughout the 1990s, but autocratic breakdown occurred only after military defeat and a severe economic crisis had weakened the state. Opposition movements in Armenia, Zimbabwe, and Malaysia were stronger than those in Haiti, Georgia, and Kyrgyzstan. The fact that regime change occurred in the *latter* cases (or, in Serbia, only *after* the state was battered

[106] The recent literature on authoritarian stability has paid far greater attention to issues of incumbent strength. See Geddes (1999), Slater (2003, 2010), Bellin (2004), Smith (2005), Magaloni (2006), Brownlee (2007a), Greene (2007), Pepinsky (2009b), and Blaydes (forthcoming).

[107] Herbst (2001: 364, 361).

[108] See Way (2002a, 2005a, 2005b).

[109] Mitchell (2004: 345, 348).

[110] Radnitz (2006).

[111] *The Economist*, March 6, 2004, p. 39. See also Wucker (2004).

[112] Dudley (2004: 27).

[113] See Fuller (1996a: 45) and Stefes (2005).

[114] *Africa Today*, January 2001, p. 25; see also Raftopoulos (2001: 23).

[115] Raftopoulos (2002: 418).

[116] Slater (2003: 89).

[117] Felker (1999: 46); see also Hilley (2001: 151).

by successive military defeats) suggests that the fate of authoritarian regimes rests not only on the opposition forces but also on the robustness of the regime that they are up against.

Variation in incumbent power is particularly important in the analysis of competitive authoritarianism. The regimes analyzed in this study had not democratized by 1990 (or, in a few cases, suffered authoritarian reversals in the early 1990s) despite a highly favorable international environment. In nearly all of these cases, the domestic impetus for democratization was weak.[118] With a few exceptions (most notably Mexico and Taiwan), civil societies lacked the organization, resources, and rural presence to sustain the kind of robust democracy movements seen in countries such as Poland, South Korea, and South Africa. Given this lack of variation, opposition-centered variables are of limited utility in explaining diverging outcomes.

Our approach to incumbent power is *organizational*. As Samuel Huntington observed, organization is "the foundation of political stability."[119] Sustaining modern authoritarianism is a complex and costly endeavor. It entails dissuading diverse social and political actors from challenging the regime (through co-optation, intimidation, or repression), as well as maintaining the loyalty and cooperation of powerful actors within the regime. These challenges are especially great in competitive authoritarian regimes because incumbents must deal with myriad actors (parties, media, judges, NGOs) and arenas of contestation (elections, legislatures, and courts) that do not exist – or are merely a façade – in fully closed regimes. In all but the most traditional societies, these tasks require organized mechanisms of coordination, monitoring, and enforcement.[120]

Building in part on Lucan Way's work on failed authoritarianism and pluralism by default in the former Soviet Union,[121] we focus on two organizations: states and parties. Effective state and party organizations enhance incumbents' capacity to prevent elite defection, co-opt or repress opponents, defuse or crack down on protest, and win (or steal) elections. Where states and governing parties are strong, autocrats are often able to survive despite vigorous opposition challenges. Where they are weak, incumbents may fall in the face of relatively weak opposition movements.

State Coercive Capacity

The role of state coercive capacity has received relatively little attention in recent regime studies.[122] Recent analyses highlight the importance of state strength to democracy. Scholars such as Guillermo O'Donnell and Stephen Holmes argue that an effective state, grounded in the rule of law, is essential to protecting basic

---

[118] Howard (2003).

[119] Huntington (1968: 461).

[120] See Selznick (1960), Slater (2003, 2010), Smith (2005), and Brownlee (2007a).

[121] Way (2005a).

[122] Exceptions include Thompson (2001), Way (2002a, 2005a, 2005b), Slater (2003, forthcoming), Bellin (2004), and Darden (2008).

liberal-democratic rights.[123] As an earlier generation of scholarship made clear, however, strong states also enhance autocratic stability.[124] Whereas some state institutions check executive power and uphold a democratic rule of law, others provide mechanisms to suppress opposition and maintain political hegemony. *Authoritarian* state institutions – from security forces to local prefects to intelligence agencies – furnish governments with tools to monitor, co-opt, intimidate, and repress potential opponents, both within and outside the regime.[125] Although these state institutions often perform illiberal and even illegal functions, they nevertheless may be effective.[126] And the more effective they are, the more stable authoritarian regimes will be. State-building is thus as important to authoritarianism as it is to democracy.[127] Where post–Cold War autocrats inherited weak states and failed to rebuild them (e.g., Albania, Georgia, Haiti, and Madagascar), they rarely endured in power. Where authoritarians invested seriously in state-building – as in Zimbabwe during the 1980s, Cambodia and Armenia during the 1990s, and Russia under Putin – the result was not democracy but rather more robust authoritarianism.

State coercive capacity is critical to regime outcomes. The centrality of state coercive structures was highlighted in Theda Skocpol's seminal study of social revolution.[128] Only where states' coercive apparatus was weakened (often by war), Skocpol found, did autocracies fall prey to revolution. More recently, Eva Bellin has highlighted the role of strong security apparatuses in sustaining authoritarianism in the Middle East. As Bellin argued, "democratic transition can be carried out successfully only when the state's coercive apparatus lacks the will or capacity to crush it."[129] Likewise, Way has shown how limited coercive capacity undermined autocratic consolidation in the former Soviet Union.[130]

Coercive capacity is central to competitive authoritarian stability. The greater a government's capacity to either prevent or crack down on opposition protest, the greater are its prospects for survival. Incumbents may employ distinct forms of coercion. Some, which we label *high-intensity coercion*, are high-visibility acts that target large numbers of people, well-known individuals, or major institutions. An example is the violent repression – often involving security forces firing on crowds – of mass demonstrations, as occurred in Mexico City in 1968 and Tiananmen Square in China in 1989. Although such massacres are uncommon in competitive authoritarian regimes, violent repression of protest – in each case, with dozens of reported deaths – occurred in Cambodia, Kenya, and Madagascar. Other forms of high-intensity coercion include campaigns of violence against

---

[123] See O'Donnell (1993, 1999) and Holmes (1997, 2002). See also Linz and Stepan (1996), Mengisteab and Daddieh (1999), Sperling (2000), Carothers (2002: 16), Bunce (2003: 180–1), Joseph (2003), Bratton (2005), and Bratton and Chang (2005).

[124] See especially Huntington (1968) and Skocpol (1973, 1979).

[125] Slater (2003, 2010).

[126] See Darden (2008).

[127] See Way (2002a, 2005a).

[128] Skocpol (1979).

[129] Bellin (2004: 143).

[130] Way (2002a, 2005a). See also Slater (2010).

opposition parties (e.g., Cambodia and Zimbabwe), imprisonment (e.g., Malaysia and Russia), attempted assassination of major opposition leaders (e.g., Belarus and Ukraine), and high-profile assaults on democratic institutions such as parliament (e.g., Russia in 1993).

Competitive authoritarian regimes also rely on other, less visible, forms of coercion, which we label *low-intensity coercion*. Because these coercive acts do not involve high-profile targets and thus rarely make headlines or trigger international condemnation, they are often critical to sustaining competitive authoritarian rule. Low-intensity coercion takes myriad forms. One of them is surveillance. Governments in Belarus, Nicaragua, Russia, Taiwan, and Zimbabwe used vast surveillance apparatuses and informant networks to monitor opposition activity throughout the country.[131] Another type of low-intensity coercion is low-profile physical harassment, or localized attacks on opposition activists and supporters. This includes the use of security forces or paramilitary thugs to break up opposition meetings; vandalize opposition or independent media offices; and harass, detain, and occasionally murder journalists and opposition activists. Low-intensity coercion also may take nonphysical forms, including denial of employment, scholarships, or university entrance to opposition activists; denial of public services – such as heat and electricity – to individuals and communities with ties to the opposition; and use of tax, regulatory, or other state agencies to investigate and prosecute opposition politicians, entrepreneurs, and media owners.[132]

Whereas high-intensity coercion is often a response to an imminent – and highly threatening – opposition challenge, low-intensity coercion is often aimed at preventing such challenges from emerging in the first place. Where it is effective (e.g., Singapore and Belarus in the 2000s), many opposition supporters conclude that antigovernment activity is simply not worth the risk, leaving only the most die-hard activists to oppose the regime.[133] By deterring opposition protest (or nipping it in the bud), successful low-intensity coercion thus reduces the need for high-intensity coercion. Where opposition movements are so thoroughly beaten down that they pose no serious challenge, incumbents have little need to steal elections or order police to fire on crowds.

Coercive capacity may be measured along two dimensions: *scope* and *cohesion*.[134] Scope refers to the effective reach of the state's coercive apparatus, or what Michael Mann calls infrastructural power.[135] Specifically, we focus on the size and quality of the "internal security sector," or the "cluster of organizations with direct responsibility for internal security and domestic order."[136] This includes

---

[131] In some cases (e.g., Peru and Ukraine), surveillance targeted agents within the regime itself, allowing executives to use blackmail as a means of maintaining discipline within the government and security forces (Cameron 2006; Darden 2008).

[132] Such measures have been employed in Belarus and Ukraine. On Ukraine, see Allina-Pisano (2005).

[133] For an excellent analysis of these dynamics in Mexico, see Greene (2007).

[134] These dimensions are operationalized in Appendix IV.

[135] Mann (1984).

[136] Weitzer (1990: 3). See also Williams (2001a).

army and police forces, presidential guards, gendarmes and riot police, secret police and other specialized internal security units, and the domestic intelligence apparatus,[137] as well as paramilitary organizations such as death squads, militias, and armed "youth wings."[138] It also may include a variety of other state agents – local prefects, tax officials, and state enterprise directors – who are mobilized to harass the opposition. Where scope is high, as in Belarus, Malaysia, Nicaragua, Russia, Taiwan, and Zimbabwe, the state possesses a large and effective internal security sector – usually equipped with extensive intelligence networks and specialized police and paramilitary units – which is capable of engaging society across the national territory. Security forces are well funded and well equipped, and they have a demonstrated capacity to penetrate society, monitor opposition activity, and put down protest in all parts of the country.

Where scope is low, as in Albania, Georgia, Haiti, and Macedonia, armed forces are small, poorly equipped, and often lacking in specialized internal security agencies. Security forces do not effectively penetrate the national territory; law-enforcement agents are nonexistent – or maintain only a token presence – in much of the country; or, alternatively, are underpaid to the extent that they are largely ineffective and refuse to obey orders. Such cases frequently are characterized by extensive "brown areas,"[139] or territories that lack even a minimal state presence. For example, in Georgia in the early 1990s, the military consisted mainly of "weekend fighters and volunteers" who had to feed and arm themselves.[140] Similarly, Haiti possessed no standing army after 1994, and its police force was one of the smallest, per capita, in the world.[141] The Haitian police "often lack[ed] the means to conduct basic operations" and were not present in many rural areas.[142]

Scope is particularly important for low-intensity coercion. Systematic surveillance, harassment, and intimidation require an infrastructure capable of directing, coordinating, and supplying agents across the national territory. Where such an infrastructure is absent or ineffective, incumbents' ability to monitor and check grassroots opposition activity is limited.[143] This (often de facto) space for mobilization makes it easier for opposition groups to organize electoral campaigns or protest movements. Indeed, the (attempted) use of high-intensity coercion is often evidence that mechanisms of low-intensity coercion are weak or have broken down.

Cohesion refers to the level of compliance *within* the state apparatus. For coercion to be effective, subordinates within the state must reliably follow their superiors' commands. Where cohesion is high, incumbents can be confident that even highly controversial or illegal orders (such as firing on crowds of protesters, killing

[137] Weitzer (1990: 3).
[138] See Roessler (2005).
[139] O'Donnell (1993).
[140] Zürcher (2007: 137–9).
[141] Erikson and Minson (2005a: 4).
[142] Schulz (1997–1998: 85).

[143] An extreme example is Haiti, where security forces failed to prevent the emergence and spread of armed gangs – in urban slums, rural towns, and – crucially – along the Dominican border – that eventually overthrew the Aristide government (Fatton 2002: 151–2; Erikson 2004).

opposition leaders, and stealing elections) will be carried out by both high-level security officials and rank-and-file soldiers and bureaucrats. Where cohesion is low, leaders cannot be confident that such orders will be complied with, by either high-level security officials or the rank and file. Noncompliance takes a variety of forms; in extreme cases, security officials may openly disobey presidential orders and even cooperate with (or defect to) the opposition (e.g., Georgia in 2003, Madagascar in 2002, and Ukraine in 2004) and rank-and-file soldiers may desert en masse (e.g., Haiti in 2004).[144]

Cohesion is critical to the success of high-intensity coercion. Acts of high-intensity coercion are risky ventures. Because they are likely to trigger strong negative reactions both at home and abroad, such acts often exacerbate regime crises and may even contribute to regime collapse.[145] State officials responsible for ordering or carrying out the repression thus run considerable risks because if it fails and the regime collapses, they will be vulnerable to retribution. Hence, acts of high-intensity coercion pose a particular threat to the chain of command, increasing the likelihood of internal disobedience. A breakdown in coercive command structures undermined incumbents' capacity to engage in high-intensity coercion in Benin (1990), Georgia (1991 and 2003), Russia (1993), Ukraine (1994 and 2004), and Madagascar (2002). Only where the state apparatus is cohesive (e.g., Armenia, Malaysia, and Zimbabwe) can incumbents confidently order acts of large-scale repression or abuse.

State cohesion is rooted in several factors. One factor is fiscal health.[146] Unpaid state officials are less likely to follow orders – especially high-risk orders such as repression and vote-stealing. Thus, in much of Africa and the former Soviet Union, deep fiscal crises eroded discipline within states during the immediate post–Cold War period. In extreme cases, such as Benin, Georgia, and Malawi, the noncompliance of unpaid security forces left incumbents' without means to crack down on opposition protest. However, material resources are neither necessary nor sufficient to ensure cohesion. In Armenia, Mozambique, Nicaragua, and Zimbabwe, state apparatuses remained intact despite severe fiscal constraints. Indeed, incumbents who rely strictly on material payoffs are often vulnerable to insubordination during such crises.

The highest levels of cohesion are usually found where there exists one of three alternative sources of cohesion. The first is shared ethnic identity in a context of a highly salient ethnic cleavage. In a deeply divided society (e.g., Guyana and Malaysia), autocrats may enhance loyalty within security agencies by packing them with ethnic allies.[147] Second, cohesion may be enhanced where state

---

[144] Subtler forms of noncompliance include calling in sick when coercive action is expected, promising compliance but failing to carry it out, and carrying out orders in ritualistic – and thus ineffective – ways. See, for example, Bujosevic and Radovanovic's (2003: 19–20) description of police response to protests in Serbia in 2000.

[145] Examples include the assassinations of Pedro Joaquin Chamorro in Nicaragua (1972) and Benigno Aquino in the Philippines (1983).

[146] See Decalo (1998) and Gros (1998a: 9–10).

[147] See Enloe (1976, 1980) and Decalo (1998: 19–21). Thus, cohesion is enhanced when governing parties and militaries are "bound together in a joint communal mission" (Enloe 1980: 179).

elites are bound by a salient (often nationalist or revolutionary) ideology, as in Croatia, Nicaragua, and Serbia.[148] Third, cohesion may be rooted in solidarity ties forged in a context of violent struggle, such as war, revolution, or liberation movements.[149] Where top state positions are controlled by a generation of elites that won a war (Armenia) or led a successful insurgency (Mozambique, Nicaragua, and Zimbabwe), state actors are more likely to possess the cohesion, self-confidence, and "stomach" to use force.[150]

Measuring cohesion is problematic. It is often unclear how cohesive an organization is until it is seriously tested. However, using state responses to regime crises during the period under study as an indicator of cohesion would be tautological. To avoid this problem, we rely on two types of indicator.[151] First, wherever possible, we examine levels of cohesion in periods *prior to* the period under study. For example, coercive apparatuses in Mozambique and Nicaragua remained cohesive despite serious external challenges during the 1980s, whereas those in Benin and Haiti showed evidence of repeated indiscipline during the 1980s.[152] Second, we look for evidence of non-material sources of cohesion: ethnic or ideological ties (in a context of deep ethnic or ideological polarization) or a history of shared struggle. Where we find evidence of either prior discipline under stress or nonmaterial bases of cohesion, we score cohesion as high. Where we find evidence of prior indiscipline, we score cohesion as low. All other cases are scored as medium.

Party Strength

Like states, strong parties are important pillars of authoritarian rule.[153] As scholars such as Barbara Geddes, Jason Brownlee, and Beatriz Magaloni argue, governing parties help manage elite conflict, often through the organization and distribution of patronage.[154] By providing institutional mechanisms for rulers to reward loyalists and by lengthening actors' time horizons through the provision of future opportunities for career advancement, parties encourage elite cooperation over defection.[155] As long as the party is expected to remain in power, losers

---

[148] Both Selznick (1960) and Skocpol (1979: 169) and argue that ideology plays an important role in sustaining the cohesion of revolutionary leaderships.

[149] Studies of the origins of states and parties have long emphasized the role of conflict in generating strong and cohesive organizations (Huntington 1970; Tilly 1975, 1992; Shefter 1994; Hale 2005a, 2006).

[150] Along similar lines, Mark Thompson (2001) and Andrew Nathan (2001) argue that the survival of the revolutionary generation in the Chinese Communist Party was critical to its decision to crack down on protestors in 1989.

[151] For full operationalization, see Appendix IV.

[152] Such an assessment is more difficult in post-communist (and particularly post-Soviet) cases, where the extent of state transformation in 1989–1991 makes it meaningless to use capacity in the 1980s as a measure for capacity in the 1990s. In these cases, we look for evidence of patterns of discipline or indiscipline in areas of state activity unrelated to regime outcomes (i.e., tax collection, the draft) in the post-communist period.

[153] See Zolberg (1966), Huntington (1968), Huntington and Moore (1970), Geddes (1999), Smith (2005), Way (2005a), and Brownlee (2007a).

[154] Geddes (1999); Brownlee (2007a); Magaloni (2008).

[155] Geddes (1999); Brownlee (2007a).

in short-term power or policy struggles are likely to remain loyal in the expectation of access to spoils in future rounds.[156] Where governing parties are weak or absent, regime elites see fewer opportunities for political advancement from within and are thus more likely to seek power from outside the regime.[157] Such elite defection is often a major cause of authoritarian breakdown.[158]

Yet parties do more than manage intra-elite conflict. For example, they often help to maintain authoritarian stability "on the ground." Grassroots party structures often play a major role in mobilizing support for autocrats. Thus, the KMT's mass organization "transformed millions of Taiwanese into members and supporters,"[159] which provided the regime with "overpowering" mobilizational capacity.[160] The Serbian League of Communists helped mobilize as many as five million supporters in the "anti-bureaucratic revolution" that allowed Milošević to overcome local opposition and consolidate power.[161] Party organization also may enhance coercive capacity. Autocratic governments may use local party cells, youth wings, and other grassroots structures to monitor and suppress opposition, transforming them into an "extension of the state's police power."[162] In Kenya, for example, KANU served as an "adjunct to the security forces in monitoring and controlling opposition," deploying its youth wing to "patrol the country, instill support for the party, and monitor dissent."[163] In Taiwan, the KMT's extensive network of informers was deployed to "keep watch over neighborhoods, factories, military units, businesses, and government offices."[164]

Mass organization also helps deter defection by ensuring that defectors will fail.[165] Where parties are well organized at the grassroots level, defectors often have difficulty mobilizing support. Lacking cadres on the ground, even high-profile defectors (such as Tengku Razaleigh in Malaysia, Edger Tekere and Simba Makoni in Zimbabwe, and Augustine Mrema in Tanzania) could not compete in the trenches and performed poorly in elections. Thus, strong parties not only make elite defection less likely, as Geddes and others argue, but they also ensure that defectors are less likely to succeed.[166]

---

[156] Geddes (1999: 129, 131).

[157] Way (2002a); Brownlee (2007a).

[158] This argument is made by Easter (1997), Geddes (1999), and Brownlee (2007a) and is line with earlier work by O'Donnell and Schmitter (1986).

[159] Rigger (2000: 137).

[160] Cheng (1989: 482).

[161] Thomas (1999: 44–51). Similarly, the Mexican PRI's "gigantic human network of clientelist relations" (Pacheco Mendez 1991: 255) was critical in "organizing, supporting, and controlling popular demands" (Centeno 1994: 53).

[162] Widner (1992a: 8).

[163] Widner (1992a: 7, 132).

[164] Hood (1997: 59). See also Gold (1997: 170). Grassroots party structures were also used for surveillance and intimidation in Cambodia, Guyana, Mozambique, Nicaragua, Serbia, Tanzania, and Zimbabwe.

[165] Even the strongest governing parties occasionally suffer high-level defections. Examples include Mexico in 1940, 1946, 1952, and 1987; Malaysia in 1986 and 1998; Zimbabwe in 1988 and 2008; Taiwan in 1993; and Tanzania in 1995.

[166] The current literature on parties and authoritarian durability (Geddes 1999; Brownlee 2007a; Magaloni 2008) focuses on party mechanisms to prevent elite defection but says little about why defectors succeed or fail after moving into opposition.

Strong parties are particularly important in competitive authoritarian regimes because unlike other authoritarian regimes, incumbents must retain and exercise power through democratic institutions. Most important, strong parties help win elections. Elections in competitive authoritarian regimes are often hard-fought contests. Winning them usually entails some mix of voter mobilization and fraud, both of which require organization. Mass parties provide an infrastructure for electoral mobilization. In Tanzania, for example, the massive Chama Cha Mapinduzi (CCM) network of 10 House Party Cells made it "very easy for the party to reach everyone in the country."[167] Likewise, the Mexican PRI's vast organization allowed it to become "one of the world's most accomplished vote-getting machines."[168] Parties also help *steal* votes. Ballot-box stuffing and other forms of fraud require coordination, discretion, and discipline among numerous lower-level authorities – which party organizations provide.[169] For example, the PRI organization facilitated various ballot-box–stuffing strategies, including "flying brigades," in which voters were trucked from precinct to precinct so they could cast multiple ballots.[170]

Parties also help control legislatures. Legislative control is critical in competitive authoritarian regimes.[171] For one, it enhances the executive's capacity to manipulate and control other areas of politics. Because top judicial and electoral authorities often are chosen directly by legislatures or require legislative approval, executive control over constitutional courts, electoral commissions, and other agents of horizontal accountability often requires a reliable legislative majority. Control over the legislature also may allow the governing party to modify the constitution (for example, eliminating presidential term limits) to extend or deepen authoritarian rule.[172] Finally, legislative control has a defensive purpose: to eliminate the legislature as a potential arena for contestation. When not controlled by the executive, legislatures may thwart presidential appointments, create new mechanisms of oversight, conduct high-profile investigations into government abuse, and even threaten the incumbent's political survival by voting to remove him or her (as in Madagascar in 1996 and as nearly occurred in Russia in 1993 and 1999).

Strong parties facilitate legislative control in two ways. First, they are more likely to win legislative elections. Presidents without such parties (e.g., Soglo in Benin, Fujimori in Peru, and Yeltsin in Russia) have weaker coattails: They often fail to translate their own electoral success into legislative majorities. Second, well-organized, cohesive parties help maintain legislative control between elections, for they offer incumbents a variety of means to keep legislative allies in line (mechanisms of patronage distribution, a well-known party label, ideological

---

[167] Lucan Way, interview with Joseph Warioba, Prime Minister of Tanzania 1985–1990, Dar es Salaam, November 22, 2007.

[168] Cornelius (1996: 57).

[169] For example, the Mexican PRI carried out fraud in a highly disciplined manner. Instructions issued by the Interior Ministry were passed on to governors and then carried out by local party officials (Carbonell 2002: 85).

[170] Cornelius (1996: 60).

[171] On the role of legislatures in nondemocratic regimes, see Gandhi and Przeworski (2007).

[172] See Magaloni (2006).

or other sources of cohesion). Where governments lack such a party, legislative factions are more prone to internal rebellion and schism.[173] Such crises create opportunities for opposition forces to gain control of the legislature, which can result in parliamentary efforts to remove the president from power.[174]

Finally, strong parties facilitate executive succession. As discussed in Chapter 1, succession poses a difficult challenge for most autocracies. Because they must worry about prosecution after leaving office,[175] incumbents generally place a high value on finding a successor who will ensure their protection. This requires not only winning the election but also doing so with a candidate who can be trusted or controlled. Strong parties facilitate succession in several ways: They have a larger pool from which to draw strong candidates, they offer mechanisms to prevent the defection of losing aspirants, and they possess electoral capacity that is independent of the outgoing executive. Thus, it is not surprising that smooth successions almost always occur in competitive authoritarian regimes with strong governing parties (e.g., Malaysia, Mozambique, and Tanzania). Where party structures are undeveloped, succession is more traumatic: Candidate pools are smaller, the likelihood of internal conflict and defection is greater, and the party's electoral viability is less certain.

Like state strength, party strength may be measured in terms of scope and cohesion.[176] *Scope* refers to the size of a party's infrastructure, or the degree to which it penetrates the national territory and society. Where scope is high, as in Taiwan, Malaysia, Nicaragua, and Tanzania, parties possess mass organizations, usually with large memberships and activist bases. These organizations maintain a permanent and active presence across the national territory – down to the village and/or neighborhood level – and, in some cases, they penetrate the workplace and much of civil society as well. For example, UMNO's 16,500 branch organizations allowed it to penetrate "every village in the country" and assign a party agent to monitor every 10 households.[177] Similarly, the CCM's 2-million–member mass organization enabled it to operate a "10-house" cell structure in villages throughout the country.[178] Where scope is low, governing parties either do not exist at all, as in Ukraine under Kravchuk, or lack even minimal organization, memberships, or activist bases, as in Benin and Peru. Thus, party operations are confined to major urban centers, the president's home region, and – in some cases – the presidential palace.[179]

---

[173] See Way (2005a: 200–204).

[174] Examples include Russia in 1993 and Belarus and Madagascar in 1996.

[175] See Shlapentokh (2006).

[176] For operationalization, see Appendix IV.

[177] *Far Eastern Economic Review*, June 24, 1999, p. 1; Case (2001a: 52, 2001b: 37).

[178] Berg-Schlosser and Siegler (1990: 81); Barkan (1994: 16). Where scope is medium (e.g., KANU in Kenya and UNIP in Zambia), parties possess national structures, with

offices in most of the country, but they are not mass organizations that penetrate or mobilize society in any significant way.

[179] In Peru, for example, Alberto Fujimori's New Majority "had scarcely any organizational presence outside the national congress" (Roberts 2002: 18). After Fujimori's 1995 reelection, "there wasn't even ... a party headquarters where the president could celebrate his victory" (Degregori 2000: 62).

Cohesion refers to incumbents' ability to secure the cooperation of partisan allies within the government, in the legislature, and at the local or regional level. Cohesion is crucial to preventing elite defection, particularly during periods of crisis, when the incumbent's grip on power is threatened. Where cohesion is high (e.g., Malaysia, Mozambique, Nicaragua, Serbia, and Zimbabwe), allied ministers, legislators, and governors routinely support the government, implement presidential directives, and vote the party line. Internal rebellion or defection is rare, even in the face of major crises or opposition challenges; when defections occur, they tend not to attract many followers. For example, the Sandinistas did not experience a single public schism during the 1980s in the midst of civil war and severe economic crisis.[180] Where cohesion is low, as in Benin, Georgia, Ukraine, Zambia, and Russia under Yeltsin, parties are little more than loose coalitions of relatively autonomous actors, many of which derive their power and status from outside the party. Incumbents routinely confront insubordination, rebellion, or defection within the cabinet, in the legislative bloc, and among regional bosses. Consequently, regimes are vulnerable to internal crises triggered by splits within the governing coalition, which result in opposition takeovers of the legislature or strong electoral challenges from erstwhile regime insiders. Indeed, in several cases (Georgia in 2001–2003 and Mali in 2000–2002), internal crises emerged even in the absence of economic problems or a major opposition challenge.

Sources of party cohesion vary. Although much of the literature on parties and authoritarian stability focuses on mechanisms of patronage distribution,[181] patronage is a relatively weak source of cohesion. Patronage may help hold elites together during normal times, but parties that are based exclusively on patronage ties often become vulnerable during periods of crisis. When economic crisis threatens incumbents' capacity to distribute patronage, or when incumbents appear vulnerable to defeat, patronage-based parties often suffer large-scale defection (e.g., Zambia in 1990–1991, Senegal in 2000, Kenya in 2002, and Georgia in 2001–2003). In such cases, elite access to patronage often has been much better secured by going over to the opposition than by remaining loyal to the ruling party. As one defecting member of the ruling UNIP in Zambia explained in 1991, "only a stupid fly... follows a dead body to the grave."[182]

Cohesion tends to be greater when it is rooted in nonmaterial ties such as shared ethnicity (e.g., Guyana and Malaysia) or ideology (e.g., Nicaragua) in a context of deep ethnic or ideological cleavage. Bonds of solidarity forged out of periods of violent struggle are perhaps the most robust source of cohesion. Parties that emerge from successful revolutionary or liberation movements (e.g., Mozambique, Nicaragua, and Zimbabwe) tend to be highly cohesive – at least while the founding generation survives.

Again, efforts to measure cohesion must be careful to avoid tautology. Therefore, we do not use levels of internal discipline during the period of study as

---

[180] Similarly, ZANU in Zimbabwe experienced strikingly few defections during the 2000–2008 crisis.

[181] Geddes (1999); Brownlee (2007a).

[182] Quoted in Ihonvbere (1996: 70).

evidence of cohesion. Instead, we operationalize party cohesion in the following way[183]: Cases in which presidents rule without a party (e.g., Belarus), are backed by multiple and competing parties (e.g., Russia under Yeltsin), or govern with newly formed parties that are organized around patronage (e.g., Benin, Georgia, Mali, and Peru) are scored as low cohesion. Established parties in which patronage systems are institutionalized but are the only real source of cohesion (e.g., Kenya and Zambia) are scored as medium. Two types of party are scored as high cohesion: (1) parties that exhibit strong ideological (e.g., Serbia) or ethnic (e.g., Guyana and Malaysia) ties where that cleavage is highly salient; and (2) parties whose origins lie in revolutionary or liberation movements and which are still led by the founding generation (e.g., Mozambique, Nicaragua, and Zimbabwe).

State Economic Control as a Substitute for Coercive and Party Organization

Discretionary state control over the economy also may enhance incumbents' capacity to preempt or thwart opposition challenges.[184] Where such control is extensive, it may substitute effectively for powerful coercive and party organizations. Incumbents' economic power may be considered high where resources are concentrated in state hands and governments enjoy substantial discretionary power in allocating those resources. Economic resources are concentrated where the state maintains control over key means of production and finance, as in many partially reformed command economies,[185] or where a large percentage of national income takes the form of rents controlled by the state, as in many mineral-based rentier states.[186] Rulers exert discretionary control where they can routinely use the tax system, credit, licensing, concessions and government contracts, and other economic policy levers to punish opponents and reward allies.[187]

Discretionary economic power furnishes incumbents with powerful tools to compel compliance and punish opposition. Where the livelihoods, careers, and business prospects of much of the population can be affected easily and decisively by government decisions, opposition activity becomes a high-risk venture. Businesses linked to the opposition may be denied access to government credit, licenses, contracts, or even property rights; independent media may be deprived of access to newsprint or advertising; public employees may be forced to work for the governing party; and critics may be fired, blacklisted, or denied access

---

[183] For a full operationalization, see Appendix IV.

[184] Dahl (1971: 48–61); Fish (2005); McMann (2006); Greene (2007).

[185] Fish (2005).

[186] Our view of the causal link between oil and autocracy differs somewhat from many standard approaches (cf. Ross 2001). In our view, reliance on oil promotes autocracy not only because it limits the need for taxation or provides resources for patronage and security, but also because it allows autocrats to monopolize control over a large share of societal wealth. In this sense, oil facilitates autocratic rule in the same way that extensive state control of the economy does.

[187] In the absence of substantial discretionary power, even extensive state intervention may be compatible with democracy (e.g., Sweden).

to essential goods and services. Discretionary state economic power also may be used to starve oppositions of resources.[188] For political oppositions to be viable, they must have access to resources. Unless those resources are distributed equitably by the state, they must come from the private sector and civil society. Where states control most means of production or monopolize the main sources of wealth, private sectors will be small and civil societies will be poor, leaving "no conceivable financial base for opposition."[189] Where vast discretionary power allows governments to punish businesses for their political behavior, opposition parties, independent media, and other civic groups will have few reliable channels of finance.[190]

In some cases, then, discretionary economic power may partly substitute for strong party and state organizations in limiting elite defection and thwarting opposition challenges. Where state economic power is extensive, as in Belarus, Botswana, and Gabon, it may be so costly for elites to defect and so difficult for opposition forces to mobilize resources that incumbents go largely unchallenged, even in the absence of strong state or party organizations.

Combining State and Party Strength

Strong states and parties contribute to authoritarian stability in different ways. State coercive and economic power enhances incumbents' capacity to suppress opponents and critics and to defuse or preempt potential opposition movements through intimidation, co-optation, and deprivation of resources. Strong parties help incumbents manage intra-elite conflict, mobilize support, and win or steal elections.

State and party functions often overlap and, to an extent, they are substitutable. For example, strong parties may be so successful at mobilizing support and maintaining elite cohesion that incumbents can survive even in the absence of strong states (e.g., Mozambique and Tanzania). In addition, strong parties facilitate incumbent control over a wide range of state institutions through the provision of loyal cadres bound by a partisan identity. Finally, well-organized parties may perform state-like coercive functions, including surveillance and other forms of low-intensity coercion.

Strong states also may partially substitute for weak parties. State agencies may be deployed as what Henry Hale calls "party substitutes."[191] In Peru and Ukraine, state intelligence agencies played a central role in maintaining elite cohesion through surveillance, blackmail, and bribery.[192] In other cases, incumbents used state agencies as party-like mobilizational tools. In Ukraine, governments mobilized public teachers and doctors for electoral campaigns; in Peru

---

[188] Greene (2007) and Levitsky and Way (2010).

[189] Riker (1982: 7). See also Dahl (1971: 48–61) and Fish (2005: 156–7).

[190] By contrast, where economic liberalization shifts resources into the private sphere and strips governments of tools of econo-

mic coercion, as in much of Eastern Europe and the Americas during the 1990s, entrepreneurs often play a major role in financing opposition.

[191] Hale (2006).

[192] Cameron (2006); Darden (2008).

and Serbia, army, police, and other security branches were used for campaign activities.[193]

There are limits to substitutability, however. In Peru and Ukraine, succession crises and legislative weakness – both exacerbated by party weakness – contributed to crises that ultimately toppled regimes.[194] Moreover, elite conflict rooted in party weakness may undermine incumbent control over coercive and other state agencies. When the governing elite is divided, security forces may be paralyzed by conflicting orders, and state officials may resist carrying out risky coercive action on behalf of any side. Incumbents may lose control over entire security agencies – or be sufficiently uncertain about their loyalty that they cannot order repression.[195]

Organizational power is thus highest where both states and parties are strong. These are clear cases of "brick houses": Strong state and party organizations give incumbent governments the capacity to hold together, even under serious crisis, and to thwart even relatively strong opposition movements – both at the ballot box and in the streets. Malaysia, Nicaragua, Taiwan, and Zimbabwe fall into this category. Organizational power is lowest where both state and party organizations are weak. These are unambiguous cases of "straw houses": Incumbents lack substantial capacity to win (or steal) elections or to crack down on protest. Moreover, they routinely suffer intra-elite conflict and defection. As a result, governments are vulnerable to collapse in the face of even modest opposition challenges; examples include Benin, Georgia, Haiti, Madagascar, Malawi, and Ukraine under Kravchuk.

Other cases exhibit mixes of state and party strength. A few cases, including Mozambique and Tanzania, are characterized by strong governing parties but relatively weak states. In these cases, incumbents' capacity to win elections and limit intra-elite conflict may be sufficient to ensure regime stability. However, regimes remain vulnerable to opposition mobilization. In other cases, including Armenia, Belarus, and Putin's Russia, incumbents possessed relatively high state capacity but lacked cohesive parties. Although such regimes may be less vulnerable to mass protest, they are more vulnerable to internal conflict than those with strong governing parties.

The Impact of Opposition Strength

Incumbent organizational power, of course, is only one side of the story. Opposition strength is also important in explaining regime trajectories. The strength, cohesion, and strategies of opposition forces are widely viewed as critical to

---

[193] On Ukraine, see Allina-Pisano (2005) and Way (2005b); on Peru, see Planas (2000: 357–8); on Serbia, see LeBor (2004: 200–201).

[194] Although such crises did not occur in Belarus and Russia through 2009, the absence of a cohesive party – and the potential for elite

defection – remained a point of vulnerability.

[195] See Way (2005a: 238). This was particularly evident in Ukraine in 2004, when important elements of a well-paid and well-trained security force defected to the opposition amid a regime crisis (Way 2005b).

democratization.[196] Strong civic and opposition movements shift the balance of power and resources away from state elites, which raises the cost of sustaining authoritarianism. Where opposition forces mobilize large numbers of people for elections or protest movements, incumbents must employ more nakedly autocratic means to retain power (e.g., steal elections or crack down violently on street protest), which then erode public support, generate tension within the regime elite, and risk international punitive action. Thus, the greater the opposition's mobilizational and electoral capacity, the higher is the probability that incumbents will opt for toleration over repression.[197]

Opposition strength is clearly important in explaining regime outcomes. During the Third Wave, opposition mobilization played a central role in democratization in Argentina, the Philippines, Poland, Spain, South Africa, South Korea, and elsewhere. Among our cases, opposition strength was critical to democratization in Mexico, Taiwan, and – to some extent – Ghana and Serbia. In these countries, political and civic organizations developed a capacity to mobilize citizens across territory and over time. This gave opposition forces the ability to launch sustained protest, compete effectively in elections, and monitor electoral processes, which increased the cost of repression and fraud. In other cases (e.g., Benin in 1988–1990, Zambia in 1990–1991, Madagascar in 2001–2002, and Ukraine in 2004), large-scale protest – even in the absence of a highly developed civil society – was critical to the removal of autocratic governments (even if its longer-term democratizing impact was open to question).

In general, however, the weakness of opposition forces limited their impact on competitive authoritarian regime outcomes. Because they were poor and predominantly rural societies with small middle classes (e.g., Cambodia, Haiti, and much of sub-Saharan Africa), or because they had recently emerged from decades of Leninism and state socialism (e.g., Eastern Europe and the former Soviet Union), most of the cases examined in this study lacked the raw materials for a strong opposition movement. Private sectors were weak, civil society was small and narrowly based, and political parties lacked organization and any significant presence in the countryside.[198] In none of these cases did opposition forces possess the infrastructure or resources to challenge incumbent power over the long term.

Even where mass protest played an important role in dislodging autocrats from power, transitions were often facilitated by incumbent weakness. In many seemingly protest-driven transitions, incumbents' inability to prevent large-scale elite defection (Ukraine, and Zambia) or use coercion to crack down on opposition protest (Benin, Georgia, Madagascar, and Malawi) contributed directly to their fall from power. In effect, protesters knocked down a rotten door. By contrast, where coercive and/or governing party structures were strong (e.g., Armenia,

---

[196] See Rueschemeyer, Stephens, and Stephens (1992), Bratton and van de Walle (1997), Collier (1999a), Diamond (1999), Wood (2000), Thompson (2001), Howard (2003), and Howard and Roessler (2006).

[197] Dahl (1971).

[198] On the weakness of civic and opposition forces in post-communist countries, see Howard (2003).

Malaysia, and Zimbabwe), incumbents often withstood even strong and sustained opposition challenges.

Indeed, in some cases, opposition strength is endogenous to incumbent capacity. For example, where incumbents possess powerful instruments of physical and/or economic coercion, they may use them to systematically undermine opposition organization. Thus, systematic coercion may weaken opposition movements by making civic political participation so risky that all but the most diehard activists exit the public sphere. Repression weakened opposition forces in Armenia, Cambodia, and Zimbabwe; in Belarus and in Putin's Russia, effective low-intensity coercion deterred strong opposition movements from emerging in the first place. Discretionary economic power also may be used to weaken or deter opposition movements. In Belarus, Gabon, and Russia in the 2000s, economic coercion and co-optation helped starve opposition movements nearly out of existence.

At the same time, incumbents' organizational weakness may enhance opposition strength. In Georgia, Kenya, Malawi, Senegal, Ukraine, and Zambia, much of the financial and organizational muscle behind successful oppositions came from political, economic, and military actors who had recently defected from the governing coalition. In Ukraine, key financial and organizational resources behind the Orange Revolution were provided by business oligarchs who had only recently abandoned the government.[199] Likewise, in Kenya, the defection of Raila Odinga and other KANU barons just prior to the 2002 election was critical to the ruling party's defeat.[200] In these cases, it was ultimately incumbent weakness rather than opposition strength per se that drove transitions.

SYNTHESIS OF THE ARGUMENT

Our theory synthesizes the international and domestic arguments presented above. We make a three-step argument. First, where linkage is high, as in Eastern Europe and the Americas, democratization is likely. Due to extensive penetration by international media, transnational human-rights networks, and multilateral organizations, even minor abuses reverberate in the West and are likely to trigger responses from Western powers. Because many domestic actors maintain ties to the West, the threat of isolation (or even a tarnished international image) is likely to trigger strong opposition at home. The cost of abuse increases the likelihood that incumbents will tolerate rather than repress opposition challenges, and that they will cede power when they are defeated. Because opposition forces maintain close ties to the West (and often view Western support as critical to their success) and because they face the same external constraints that had toppled their predecessors, new governments should rule democratically. Linkage should have a democratizing effect *even where organizational power is high*. High linkage creates incentives for incumbents to underutilize coercive capacity and tolerate opposition challenges that they could otherwise suppress – effectively wiping out the effect of domestic power balances.

---

[199] Way (2005b).   [200] Ndegwa (2003: 150).

High linkage also should lead to democratization where leverage is low (e.g., Mexico and Taiwan), although the process may require a stronger domestic push. In such cases, governments face less direct external pressure to democratize. Nevertheless, linkage increases the elite's sensitivity to their country's international standing, which creates incentives for incumbents to avoid egregious abuse and maintain their power via credible political institutions. Such a strategy may succeed when oppositions are weak; however, under-utilization of coercive capacity creates space for opposition activity, and when strong opposition challenges emerge, governments may be trapped by their efforts to maintain international credibility. Unwilling to pay the external and domestic costs of repression, they may be forced to accept defeat and abandon power.

Where linkage is lower, regime outcomes are driven largely by domestic factors. In the absence of extensive linkage, government abuse is less likely to gain international attention or trigger an external punitive response. Even where punitive action is taken, it is rarely sustained and is less likely to trigger substantial opposition at home. As long as incumbents avoid massive repression or fraud, they enjoy considerable room to maneuver.

The second step of the argument thus centers on the *organizational power of incumbents*. In low-linkage cases, high organizational power should bring authoritarian stability. Where incumbents possess strong state and/or party organizations, they are well equipped to contain elite conflict and thwart opposition challenges, both in the streets and at the ballot box. Governments are often able to pre-empt serious opposition challenges; when such challenges arise, they possess the cohesion and the coercive power to withstand or repress them. Where organizational power is high, then, competitive authoritarian regimes should survive even in a context of high leverage.

Where organizational power is low, competitive authoritarian regimes are less stable. Incumbents are vulnerable to elite defection and frequently ill-equipped to thwart even modest opposition protest or electoral challenges. In such cases, due to the weakness of both progovernment and antigovernment forces, regime outcomes are often fluid and contingent.

In this context, *Western leverage* – the third step in the argument – may be decisive. Where leverage is low, even relatively weak incumbents are likely to survive, for they will encounter limited external democratizing pressure. Where leverage is high, governments that lack organizational power will be vulnerable even to weak opposition challenges. In such a context, the probability of turnover is high, which creates an opportunity for democratization.[201] Where successor governments under-utilize power or undertake reforms to level the playing field, democracies may emerge. However, in the absence of linkage, transitions characterized by weak states, parties, and civil societies create numerous opportunities for incumbent abuse. Hence, turnover is more likely to result in a new competitive authoritarian government. More generally, given the difficulty of consolidating

---

[201] Along these lines, van de Walle (2003: 307–308) argues that in sub-Saharan Africa, democratic outcomes are more likely when party systems are fragmented and governing parties are weak, as in Benin and Mali.

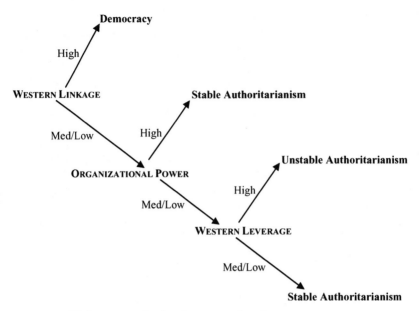

FIGURE 2.2. Linkage, organizational power, and regime outcomes.

any form of rule – democratic or authoritarian – in a context of party and state weakness, the most likely outcome is a pattern of *unstable authoritarianism.*

The predictions generated by our theory are summarized in Figure 2.2. As shown in the figure, we expect all high-linkage cases to democratize, regardless of organizational power and leverage. Where linkage is not high, we expect high organizational power to bring authoritarian stability. Finally, we expect cases of low and medium organizational power to hinge on Western leverage: Where leverage is high, we predict turnover (but not democratization); where leverage is medium or low, we predict regime survival. Cases of medium organizational power and high leverage generate the most difficult prediction. Such cases, which typically are established civilian regimes governed by patronage-based machines, should be more stable than those of low organizational power. However, we predict regime instability because although such regimes are often stable during normal times, they are vulnerable to crisis – and some type of crisis (e.g., economic or succession) was likely during the 18-year period covered by this study.

Two potential methodological concerns are worth addressing. First, it may be argued that linkage is endogenous to political regimes. For example, Western powers may establish closer ties to democratizing regimes. Likewise, non-democracies may reduce linkage by placing restrictions on travel, international media, and INGOs. Although states' behavior undoubtedly affects linkage, our treatment of linkage as exogenous and fixed is defensible on several grounds. Most important, linkage is a slow-moving variable. Levels of migration, education abroad, cross-border communication, and even trade and investment most often are rooted in historical factors such as geography, economic development, and long-term geopolitical alliances, and thereby tend not to change dramatically over the short term. Furthermore, linkage consists of a wide array of ties. Countries rarely experience significant shifts along multiple dimensions simultaneously, and short-term fluctuations in any single area (e.g., trade) are unlikely to alter substantially a country's overall linkage score. Finally, although closed regimes (e.g., Burma and North Korea) may reduce linkage, competitive authoritarian regimes usually do not. Even the most repressive competitive authoritarian regimes generally avoided behavior (e.g., expelling Western media and NGOs, restricting foreign investment, or limiting travel and communication to the West) that would have a significant effect on linkage.[202] Indeed, few of the regimes examined in this study were subject to long-term or encompassing Western isolation. Even where Western sanctions were applied, however (e.g., Nicaragua and Serbia), levels of overall linkage remained high.

A second methodological issue concerns our organizational power variable. Incumbent organizational power may be viewed as an overly proximate cause of regime outcomes and perhaps even a source of tautology. If an incumbent's fall from power were taken as evidence of weakness, or if an incumbent's survival were taken as evidence of strength, then the argument indeed would be tautological. To avoid tautology, we use clear *ex ante* indicators of organizational power that are analytically distinct from – and chronologically prior to – the performance of state and party organizations during the period under study. These indicators are easily distinguishable from regime outcomes. Indeed, the fact that several of our high-organizational-power cases experienced turnover (e.g., high linkage cases such as Guyana, Mexico, Nicaragua, Serbia, Slovakia, and Taiwan) makes it clear that outcomes are not being used to measure organizational power.

From a theoretical standpoint, organizational power is a structural and slow-moving variable. Powerful coercive and party structures rarely emerge or disappear overnight, and they are almost never the product of short-term crafting or institutional design. As the extensive literature shows, strong states and parties are often rooted in previous periods of conflict and mobilization.[203] Indeed, in nearly all of our cases of high organizational power, incumbents inherited structures that were forged during earlier conflicts or regimes.[204] In Malaysia and Zimbabwe, governments inherited a powerful security apparatus built up by colonial or settler regimes[205]; in Belarus and Russia, governments inherited the Soviet intelligence and security apparatus; and in Armenia and Taiwan, a powerful coercive apparatus emerged from large-scale military conflict or threat. Where incumbents inherited weak state apparatuses (e.g., Albania, Benin, Georgia, Haiti, and Malawi), they had to build coercive capacity from scratch – an exceedingly difficult task. Similarly, the strongest parties examined in this study emerged

---

[202] Where such behavior occurred in our cases (e.g., Belarus, Russia, and Zimbabwe), it did so only at the tail end of the period under study – as regimes were closing.

[203] See Huntington (1968, 1970), Shefter (1977, 1994), Skocpol (1979), Cohen, Brown, and

Organski (1981), Tilly (1985, 1992), Smith (2005), and Slater (2010).

[204] Slater (2010) offers an excellent analysis of how early periods of conflict shaped state-building processes in Southeast Asia.

[205] Weitzer (1990); Stubbs (1997).

from intense mobilization and conflict, including revolution (e.g., Nicaragua), liberation movements (e.g., Mozambique and Zimbabwe), and civil war (e.g., Mozambique and Taiwan).[206] These conditions are not easily replicated. Party-building is costly and time-consuming; sitting executives, who can make use of state resources (and who are often averse to independent power centers) have little incentive to invest in it.[207] This is particularly true in the contemporary period, in which mass media often substitute for party organization.[208] Thus, where incumbents did not inherit strong party structures – as in much of Africa and the former Soviet Union – governing parties were almost invariably weak. Far from a proximate cause of regime outcomes, then, organizational power is a historically rooted phenomenon that is rarely subject to dramatic short-term change.

ALTERNATIVE APPROACHES

Before proceeding to the case analyses, it is worth examining alternative approaches that explain competitive authoritarian regime trajectories; specifically, we examine economic, institutionalist, and leadership-centered approaches.

Economic Explanations: Modernization, Inequality, and Economic Performance

One set of alternative explanations focuses on socioeconomic variables; prominent among these is economic modernization.[209] It may be hypothesized, for example, that the democratization of competitive authoritarian regimes will be more likely in wealthier societies with higher levels of education, larger middle and/or working classes, and more developed civil societies. Indeed, socioeconomic development contributed to democratization in two of our cases: Mexico and Taiwan. Yet the overall utility of modernization theory in this study is limited, which is due in part to the nature of our sample. Scholars generally agree that the relationship between development and democracy is clearest at high levels of development: Wealthy industrialized countries are likely to become (or remain) democratic. However, as shown in Table 2.2, all of our cases except Taiwan were classified by the World Bank as either low- or middle-income countries in 1991. In none of these cases would level of development lead scholars to confidently predict the installation and/or survival of democracy.[210] It is not surprising that regime outcomes among low- and middle-income cases varied considerably.[211]

---

[206] On the relationship between party strength and previous periods of conflict, see Smith (2005).

[207] Zolberg (1966: 125); Shefter (1977, 1994).

[208] Levitsky and Cameron (2003).

[209] For various interpretations of the relationship between economic development and democracy, see Lipset (1959/1981),

Rueschemeyer, Stephens, and Stephens (1992), Przeworski and Limongi (1997), Boix (2003), and Boix and Stokes (2003).

[210] Przeworski and Limongi (1997); Geddes (1999: 118–19).

[211] Economic development may *indirectly* shape competitive authoritarian regime outcomes in two ways. First, it enhances

TABLE 2.2. *Economic Development and Competitive Authoritarian Regime Outcomes (World Bank Classifications Based on Per Capita GNP in 1992)*

	Stable Authoritarianism	Unstable Authoritarianism	Democracy
Low Income	Cambodia Mozambique Tanzania Zimbabwe	Haiti Kenya Madagascar Malawi Zambia	Benin Ghana Guyana Mali Nicaragua
Middle Income	Armenia Botswana Cameroon Gabon Malaysia Russia	Albania Belarus Georgia Moldova Senegal	Croatia Dominican Republic Macedonia Mexico Peru Romania Serbia Slovakia Ukraine
Upper Income			Taiwan

Source: 1994 World Bank World Development Report, pp. 251–2.

A second socioeconomic explanation centers on the role of income inequality.[212] For example, Carles Boix argues that because the redistributive demands of the poor are greater in highly unequal societies, elite resistance to democracy (which presumably allows poor majorities to tax the rich) will be greatest when inequality is high. Thus, competitive authoritarian regimes should be more likely to democratize in countries with lower levels of inequality. However, there are reasons to expect the impact of inequality to be limited. First, in much of the developing and post-communist world, nondemocratic regimes often did not represent the interests of the wealthy, as assumed in the models employed by Boix and others.[213] Many competitive authoritarian regimes were leftist or populist in origin, represented lower-class constituencies, and

---

opposition capacity. Capitalist development strengthens civil society (Lipset 1959/1981; Rueschemeyer, Stephens, and Stephens 1992). It is therefore not surprising that strong opposition movements emerged in Mexico and Taiwan during the 1990s or that opposition forces remained weak in poor, rural countries such as Cambodia, Haiti, Madagascar, Malawi, and Tanzania. Second, development often enhances linkage. Capitalist development increases economic integration, cross-border communication, travel, education, and more extensive ties to transnational civil society, all

of which raise the cost of authoritarianism. Thus, relatively industrialized countries such as Malaysia and Taiwan are more closely linked to the West than is Cambodia. Hence, although level of development is less helpful than linkage or organizational powers in explaining post–Cold War competitive authoritarian regime outcomes, modernization's long-term effects are important. We thank Susan Stokes for highlighting this point.

[212] Boix (2003); Acemoglu and Robinson (2005).
[213] See Pepinsky (2009b).

TABLE 2.3. *Heritage Foundation Index of Economic Freedom Scores: Stable Competitive Authoritarian Regimes versus Democratizers (Average Annual Scores 1995–2008)*

	Fiscal Freedom (Tax burden)	Overall Score
Stable Competitive Authoritarian Regimes (*)	74.5	56.1
Democratizers: Before Transition (**)	71.1	55.7
Democratizers: After Transition	75.6	59.2

Notes:

Index is 0–100 (100 = most freedom)

* Armenia, Botswana, Cambodia, Cameroon, Gabon, Malaysia, Mozambique, Russia, Tanzania, and Zimbabwe.

** Benin, Croatia, Dominican Republic, Ghana, Macedonia, Mali, Mexico, Peru, Romania, Slovakia, Taiwan, and Ukraine. Guyana and Nicaragua are excluded because they democratized prior to 1995, the first year for which Heritage Foundation data are available. Serbia is excluded due to lack of data.

Source: Heritage Foundation Index Of Economics Freedom (online: www.heritage.org/index/explore.aspx).

embraced redistribution.[214] Second, global financial integration limited states' policy-making autonomy in the post–Cold War period, particularly in developing countries.[215] In a context of high capital mobility, the cost of redistribution was such that even democratically elected governments had strong incentives to avoid it.[216] Hence, even in highly unequal societies, the wealthy had little to fear from democratization.

A brief examination of our cases suggests that democratization did not impose a greater burden on the wealthy. Table 2.3 compares the average annual Heritage Foundation Index of Economic Freedom scores among our cases of stable competitive authoritarianism and cases of democratization, both before and after the transition. As shown in the table, there is no evidence of a relationship between democratization and either "fiscal freedom" (which measures tax burden) or overall economic freedom. Hence, democratization in these cases does not appear to have posed a threat to the economic interests of the wealthy. This is true even in cases of extreme inequality. Six of our democratizers consistently had a GINI score of greater than 0.40 during the 1990s: the Dominican Republic, Guyana, Mali, Mexico, Nicaragua, and Peru. In all six cases, overall Economic Freedom scores were higher in 2008 than they had been in 1995. The absence of a relationship between democratization and redistribution – even in highly unequal countries – suggests that income inequality is not an important causal factor in shaping competitive authoritarian regime outcomes.

---

[214] Examples include Cambodia, Guyana, Haiti, Malaysia, Mozambique, Nicaragua, Serbia, Tanzania, and Zimbabwe.

[215] Mosley (2003); Wibbels (2006).

[216] Boix (2003) himself highlights the role of capital mobility in reducing elite fears of democracy.

A third socioeconomic approach focuses on economic performance. Economic growth is widely cited as an important factor in shaping regime stability.[217] Economic crises tend to undermine authoritarian regimes by eroding public support, triggering mass protest, or sapping governments of resources needed to distribute patronage and/or finance the coercive apparatus.[218] Economic growth is likely to bolster public support and expand the resources available for patronage and public-sector salaries. Following this logic, competitive authoritarian regimes with healthy economies should be most stable, whereas those that fail to deliver economic growth should be vulnerable to collapse.

Although these arguments have much validity, economic booms and crises do not affect all regimes equally[219]; rather, their impact is mediated by organizational power and linkage. For example, the political effects of economic crises may be blunted in regimes with extensive organizational power. Where state and party cohesion are high, incumbents often possess the wherewithal to prevent elite defection, crack down on protest, and win (or steal) elections even in the face of widespread voter dissatisfaction. Thus, in Nicaragua, the Sandinista regime survived a 33 percent decline in gross domestic product (GDP) during the mid-1980s; in Armenia, the Ter-Petrosian government survived a 60 percent economic contraction in 1992–1993; and, as of mid-2010 the Mugabe government had survived Zimbabwe's spectacular post-2000 economic collapse. Each of these governments could rely on cohesive state and (in Nicaragua and Zimbabwe) party structures forged during periods of intense military conflict. In general, it is only where state and party cohesion are low that fiscal crisis undermines discipline within the security forces, the withdrawal of patronage resources triggers elite defection, and autocratic governments succumb easily to protest (e.g., Albania in 1997 and Madagascar in 2002), armed rebellion (e.g., Georgia in 1992 and Haiti in 2004), or electoral defeat (e.g., Zambia in 1991 and Belarus, Malawi, and Ukraine in 1994).

The benefits of economic growth also are mediated by organizational power. A growing economy clearly makes life easier for autocrats, but where organizational power is low, it is often not sufficient to sustain them. Thus, in Madagascar (2002, 2009), Mali (2002), Georgia (2003), and Ukraine (2004), intra-elite conflict – in the absence of a strong governing party – and/or the disintegration of a weak coercive apparatus brought down incumbents despite high growth rates.

Finally, linkage also mediates the impact of economic growth. Where linkage is extensive, the external cost of fraud and repression remains high no matter what the growth rate. Thus, in several high-linkage cases, incumbents undertook

---

[217] See Bermeo (1990: 366–7), Huntington (1991: 50–8), Haggard and Kaufman (1995), Przeworski and Limongi (1997), Geddes (1999), and Przeworski et al. (2000). In their analyses of postwar regime outcomes, Przeworski et al. (2000) found that growth rates were positively associated with the stability of both democratic and authoritarian regimes.

[218] There is little question, for example, that economic crises contributed to the liberalization or collapse of many Africa autocracies in the early 1990s (Herbst 1994).

[219] See Smith (2006) and Pepinsky (2009b).

democratizing reforms (Mexico, and Taiwan) or lost power (Slovakia, Taiwan, and Romania) despite growing economies.

In summary, economic performance clearly affects regime stability, but its impact is mediated by organizational power and linkage. Where linkage is high or organizational power is low, autocratic incumbents are often vulnerable even when growth rates are high. Where organizational power is high and linkage is low, autocrats often survive even in the face of severe economic crisis.

Institutional Design

Another alternative approach focuses on institutional design. During the past two decades, a vast literature examined how constitutional and other formal institutional arrangements shape post–Cold War regime outcomes. For example, drawing on earlier work by Juan Linz and others,[220] scholars of post–Cold War hybrid regimes link presidentialism – and in particular, powerful presidencies – to nondemocratic outcomes.[221] Thus, according to Steven Fish, *super-presidentialism* – defined as a "constitutional arrangement that invests greater power in the presidency and much less power in the legislature" – has "inhibited democratization" in Russia and other post-Communist countries by undermining accountability and inhibiting the emergence of strong institutions, parties, and experienced political elites.[222] Along somewhat different lines, Timothy Colton and Cindy Skach point to *semi-presidentialism* as a cause of Russia's slide into authoritarianism. In their view, semi-presidential systems are prone to interbranch conflict and immobilism, which create incentives for presidents to "dominate the political process and rule by decree," which places regimes on a "slippery slope to dictatorship."[223] Finally, several studies have highlighted the role of constitutional courts, electoral commissions, and other institutions in deterring or blocking autocratic abuse.[224]

We find institutional design to be of limited utility in explaining post–Cold War regime outcomes. From an empirical standpoint, there is no clear relationship between constitutional design and competitive authoritarian regime outcomes. Among our cases, 13 of 29 presidential or semi-presidential regimes democratized between 1990 and 2008, compared to only 1 of 6 parliamentary regimes.[225] Among high-linkage cases, all presidential regimes democratized.

More generally, there is reason to be skeptical about the impact of the institutional design in competitive authoritarian regimes. Institutionalist analyses hinge

---

[220] See Linz (1990), Stepan and Skach (1993), and Linz and Valenzuela (1994).

[221] Reynolds (1999); Fish (2001a, 2005, 2006).

[222] Fish (2005: 248–50).

[223] Colton and Skach (2005: 116–17).

[224] See, for example, Ganev (2001: 194–6), Elklit and Reynolds (2002), and Horowitz (2006).

[225] Cases of presidentialism and semi-presidentialism that democratized are Benin, Croatia, the Dominican Republic, Ghana, Guyana, Mali, Mexico, Nicaragua, Peru, Romania, Serbia, Taiwan, and Ukraine. Among parliamentary systems, Slovakia democratized, but Albania, Belarus (1992–1994), Botswana, Cambodia, and Malaysia did not.

on the assumption that formal institutions are (1) regularly enforced, and (2) minimally stable.[226] In other words, they take for granted that parchment rules actually constrain actors in practice. Indeed, it is only under these conditions that institutional design can be expected to have a significant independent effect on regime outcomes. Although these assumptions hold up relatively well in the advanced industrialized democracies, they travel less well to other parts of the world.[227] Indeed, a striking characteristic of many competitive authoritarian regimes is the extent of sheer institutional weakness.

In most competitive authoritarian regimes, for example, formal institutions are highly unstable. The Russian constitution was changed nearly four hundred times between 1992 and 1993.[228] In Madagascar, constitutional arrangements have been "tampered with so much . . . as to be unrecognizable"[229]; consequently, constitutional rules "functioned less as a constraint on the behavior of elites than as the object of elite manipulation."[230] In Malaysia, the governing UMNO could "change the constitution at will,"[231] and even ex–Prime Minister Mahathir complained that the "frequency and trivial reasons for altering the constitution" had reduced it to a "useless scrap of paper."[232]

Competitive authoritarian regimes also are characterized by weak enforcement of formal rules. For example, although Mexico's 1917 constitution formally prescribed a weak executive, a strong legislature, and an independent Supreme Court, in practice, PRI presidents enjoyed vast "metaconstitutional" powers that reduced Congress to a "rubber stamp."[233] Democratic provisions in Peru's 1993 constitution "were transformed into facades"[234]; in Cambodia, many constitutional provisions remained "dead letters"[235]; and in Romania, politics was characterized by the "nonobservance of the Constitution, its letter, its spirit, and its guarantees."[236] Such constitutions routinely fail to constrain powerful executives. Thus, in Croatia, "the problem [was] not that the president ha[d] strong constitutional powers but that [President] Tuđman [was] going beyond them."[237] In Haiti, "no head of state has felt constrained by constitutions, even his own."[238]

In most competitive authoritarian regimes, formal rules and agencies designed to constrain governments were frequently circumvented, manipulated, or dismantled by those governments. In Belarus, President Lukashenka paid no attention as the Constitutional Court cited him for violating the Constitution 16 times in his first 2 years in office. In Gabon, the nominally independent electoral commission created during the 1990s "proved neither autonomous nor competent"[239]; in 1998, many of its functions were unconstitutionally transferred back to the

---

[226] Levitsky and Murillo (2009).
[227] See Huntington (1968) and Levitsky and Murillo (2009).
[228] Filatov (2001: 180).
[229] Marcus (2004: 2).
[230] Marcus (2005: 156).
[231] Crouch (1996b: 115).
[232] Quoted in Lee (1995: 109).
[233] Eisenstadt (2004: 40). See also Weldon (1997).
[234] Degregori (2000: 377).
[235] Jennar (1995: 2).
[236] Weber (2001: 213).
[237] *Uncaptive Minds* (1994: 41).
[238] Weinstein and Segal (1992: 62).
[239] Freedom House, "Freedom in the World 2004: Gabon." (online: www.freedomhouse.org)

Interior Ministry.[240] In Malawi, when Electoral Commission Chair, Anastazia Msosa, asserted her independence in 1998, the Muluzi government "promptly removed her" and then packed the commission with allies.[241] In Peru, after the newly created Constitutional Tribunal (TC) ruled against President Fujimori's bid for a third term in 1997, the pro-Fujimori Congress sacked three TC members, leaving the country's highest constitutional authority dormant for three years.

The failure of formal institutions to constrain executives also is seen in the case of presidential term limits. Although term limits were imposed throughout much of Africa during the first half of the 1990s, Bruce Baker observes that "in political circles across the continent the talk is of altering constitutions to allow [Presidents] to stay on for a longer term, another term or for an unlimited number of terms."[242] In Burkina Faso, Cameroon, Chad, Gabon, Namibia, Niger, Togo, Uganda, and Zimbabwe, presidents modified or eliminated constitutional term limits to extend their stay in office.[243] Term limits were similarly sidestepped or overturned in Azerbaijan, Belarus, Peru, Tajikistan, Ukraine, and Venezuela.

Where formal rules do not effectively constrain powerful actors, they are unlikely to have a significant independent effect on regime outcomes. Indeed, the causal story is often reversed: Rather than shaping regime outcomes, formal institutional arrangements are frequently endogenous to those outcomes.[244] For example, although presidentialism may contribute to democratic breakdown in some cases, it has frequently been imposed by regimes that were *already authoritarian*. In postcolonial Cameroon, Gabon, Ghana, Guyana, Kenya, Madagascar, Malawi, Senegal, Tanzania, Zambia, and Zimbabwe, the consolidation of autocratic power preceded – and surely facilitated – shifts from parliamentary to presidential constitutions. In Zimbabwe, for example, Westminster parliamentarism was replaced by presidentialism *after* violent repression of opposition had created a "de facto one party state."[245] Guyana underwent a similar change only *after* the Burnham government had "ruthlessly suppressed" opposition.[246]

Similarly, many contemporary super-presidentialist constitutions were products – rather than causes – of authoritarianism. Thus, throughout much of post-communist Eurasia, autocratic governments imposed highly presidentialist systems *after* they had concentrated power.[247] Russia's super-presidentialist 1993 constitution was drawn up only after Yeltsin had closed the legislature in a presidential coup; Belarus' highly presidentialist constitution was imposed after Lukashenka had emasculated the legislature and constitutional court; and Romania's strong presidency was created after the ruling National Salvation Front had consolidated power and violently put down opposition protest.[248] Likewise, Peru's 1993 constitution, which expanded presidential power, was drawn up

[240] Gardinier (2000: 236).

[241] Patel (2002: 157).

[242] Baker (2002: 286).

[243] See Baker (2002) and S. Brown (2003: 329).

[244] Easter (1997).

[245] Nordlund (1996: 153–4).

[246] Premdas (1994: 48).

[247] In Kazakhstan, Turkmenistan, and Uzbekistan, super-presidentialist constitutions were imposed by leaders who had already monopolized political control by the time Mikhail Gorbachev introduced semi-competitive elections in 1990.

[248] Sellin (2004: 122–4).

after Alberto Fujimori's 1992 coup had closed Congress and dissolved the old constitution.[249] At the same time, stronger parliaments may be a product – rather than a cause – of democratization. Thus, in Croatia, parliament and the judiciary were strengthened after opposition forces had removed the autocratic Croatian Democratic Union (HDZ) from power.[250]

We are not making a general claim that formal institutions do not matter. Rather, the impact of institutions – that is, the degree to which formal rules actually shape expectations and constrain behavior – varies across cases. Where formal institutions are regularly enforced and minimally stable, the causal power of institutional design may be considerable. In much of the developing world, however, formal institutions are weak: Rather than constraining political elites, they are routinely circumvented and manipulated by them; rather than structuring the political game and determining winners and losers, they are repeatedly restructured by the winners at the expense of the losers. In such cases, the independent causal power of formal institutions is limited.

The Role of Leadership

A third alternative approach to explaining competitive authoritarian regime outcomes centers on contingency and leadership. During the 1980s and 1990s, democratization in countries with seemingly formidable structural obstacles triggered a paradigm shift in regime studies. Following the influential work of Guillermo O'Donnell and Philippe Schmitter, scholars began to treat transitions as periods of extraordinary uncertainty, in which contingent events and the choices of political elites could be decisive in shaping regime outcomes.[251] Many of these scholars highlighted the role of leadership in "crafting" successful transitions.[252] For example, Fish pointed to Mongolia's democratization as a "triumph of choice, will, leadership, agency, and contingency over structure, history, culture, and geography."[253] Along similar lines, scholars attributed nondemocratic outcomes to either "poor elite decisions" or contingent events.[254] Other scholars stressed the importance of political leaders' commitment to democracy and compromise.[255]

---

[249] Conaghan (2005: 57–8).

[250] *RFE/RL Newsline* November 10, 2000 (online: http://www.rferl.org/archive/en-newsline/latest/683/683.html). Observers have often noted that all eight of the Eastern European countries admitted to the EU in 2004 (i.e., Czech Republic, Hungary, Estonia, Latvia, Slovakia, Slovenia, Poland, and Lithuania) had either parliamentary systems or presidential systems with weak presidencies (Stepan 2005; Colton and Skach 2005: 123). Yet, in seven of the eight countries, institutional design and full democratization were implemented simultaneously immediately following the collapse of Soviet rule – suggesting that constitutional design and democratization may have been the product of a common prior factor.

[251] See O'Donnell and Schmitter (1986), Przeworski (1986), Di Palma (1990), Karl (1990), and Higley and Gunther (1992).

[252] O'Donnell and Schmitter (1986); Di Palma (1990); Fish (1998).

[253] Fish (1998: 140).

[254] Moser (2001a: 10); see also McFaul (2001) and Tanaka (2005).

[255] Fish (1998); Gros (1998a: 4–7); McFaul (2002).

Leadership obviously affects regime outcomes, particularly in the short run. It is difficult to understand the emergence of competitive authoritarianism in Serbia, Slovakia, and Venezuela, for example, without reference to the committed, risk-taking leadership of Milošević, Mečiar, and Chavez. At the same time, surprising levels of pluralism in Russia in the 1990s and Ukraine after 2004 were rooted in part in the unusual tolerance of incumbents. Leaders also vary considerably in their will to face down – violently, if necessary – mass protest. In this sense, Hun Sen in Cambodia and Mugabe in Zimbabwe differed markedly from Zedillo in Mexico and Kaunda in Zambia.

However, evidence suggests that over time, leadership is less important than international and domestic structural variables in shaping competitive authoritarian regime trajectories. The distribution of regime outcomes during the post–Cold War period, in fact, was much more structured than the early transitions literature would lead us to expect. Widespread democratization in the Americas and Eastern Europe, and considerably less democratization in sub-Saharan Africa and the former Soviet Union, suggest that – unless we are prepared to believe that leaders in the former regions were exceptionally skilled democrats – regime outcomes were not particularly open to contingency and leadership choice.

Indeed, our case analyses suggest that leaders' choices often are heavily structured by the domestic and international context in which they operate. In numerous cases, erstwhile authoritarian leaders (e.g., Iliescu, Kaunda, Kérékou, and Rawlings) and parties (e.g., the Nicaraguan FSLN, Mexican PRI, Taiwanese KMT, and Croatian HDZ) behaved democratically, allowing free elections and leaving power peacefully. At the same time, a striking number of "democratic" opposition leaders – including Sali Berisha in Albania, Levon Ter-Petrosian in Armenia, Alyaksandr Lukashenka in Belarus, Zviad Gamsakhurdia and Mikheil Saakashvili in Georgia, Vladimir Mečiar in Slovakia, Bakili Muluzi in Malawi, and Frederick Chiluba in Zambia – governed in a nondemocratic manner after coming to power.

Even when leaders' behavior had important short-term effects, the effects frequently did not endure much beyond that leader's tenure in office. Thus, Yeltsin's tolerance of opposition and media pluralism during the 1990s did little to prevent Putin's subsequent authoritarian crackdown. Similarly, the relatively benign rule of Viacheslau Kebich in Belarus (1992–1994) quickly gave way to Lukashenka's autocratic regime. Likewise, abuse of democratic procedure by Tuđman in Croatia, Balaguer in the Dominican Republic, and Mečiar in Slovakia in the mid-1990s did little to prevent their successors from consolidating democratic rule immediately after coming to power. Hence, with a few exceptions, leadership generally has had only a marginal impact on longer-term competitive authoritarian regime outcomes.

It is more useful, therefore, to assume that incumbents in competitive authoritarian regimes seek to maintain their power, using both democratic and – when available – nondemocratic means. What determines whether these leaders behave democratically, therefore, is not so much their beliefs as the opportunities and constraints that confront them. Where leaders possess effective coercive apparatuses and few international constraints, as in Belarus, Malaysia, Russia, and

Zimbabwe, they generally use those instruments to govern autocratically – especially when their power is at stake. By contrast, where leaders lack a strong coercive apparatus (Benin, Georgia, Moldova in the 1990s, and Ukraine under Kravchuk) and/or face heavy international constraints (Mexico, Nicaragua, Romania, and Taiwan), their behavior is more likely to be consistent with democratic norms.

CONCLUSION: A STRUCTURALIST ARGUMENT

Our study is more structuralist than most analyses of contemporary regimes. Whereas research on 19th-century, interwar, and postwar regime patterns routinely focuses on structural variables,[256] most explanations of third- and fourth-wave regime outcomes center on contingency, elite choice, and institutional design.[257] Although our study focuses on post–Cold War regimes, it assigns less causal weight to contingency and leadership. Instead, our argument centers on factors that are rooted in long-term historical processes – and that are not easily changed by individual leaders. At the international level, linkage to the West (with the partial exception of EU-led integration) is less the product of elite decisions than of geography, economic development, colonialism, and long-standing geostrategic alliances. Similarly, at the domestic level, strong coercive and party organizations are rarely the product of short-term crafting or institutional design.

Post–Cold War regime outcomes are far more patterned than contingency, choice-centered, and institutional design approaches would suggest. Two structural factors – that is, linkage to the West and incumbent organizational power – go a long way toward explaining variation in the trajectory of post–Cold War competitive authoritarian regimes. We examine these cases in the chapters that follow.

---

[256] See Lipset (1959/1981), Moore (1966), O'Donnell (1973), Skocpol (1979), Collier and Collier (1991), Luebbert (1991), Przeworski et al. (2000), Boix (2003), and Acemoglu and Robinson (2005).

[257] See O'Donnell and Schmitter (1986), Di Palma (1990), Fish (1998, 2005), McFaul (2001, 2002), Bunce and Wolchik (2006a, 2006b), Howard and Roessler (2006), and Beissinger (2007). An exception is the literature on oil-based regimes (cf. Ross 2001).

II

High Linkage and Democratization

Eastern Europe and the Americas

Chapters 3 and 4 examine the fate of hybrid regimes in Eastern Europe and the Americas, where proximity to Europe and the United States resulted in high linkage in 10 of 12 cases (and nearly high linkage in the other two).[1] Extensive ties to the United States or Western Europe generated strong and persistent external democratizing pressure, which resulted in democratization in 9 of 10 high-linkage cases. In many of these cases, linkage-based pressure was so intense that democratization occurred in the face of significant domestic obstacles, including underdevelopment (e.g., Guyana, Macedonia, Nicaragua, and Romania); severe ethnic tension (Guyana and Macedonia) and/or civil war (Croatia and Serbia); powerful incumbents (Croatia, Guyana, Mexico, Nicaragua, Serbia, and Slovakia); and extreme civic and opposition weakness (everywhere except Mexico and Serbia). Among high-linkage cases, only Albania – which was characterized by underdevelopment, extreme state weakness, and a recent history of Stalinist rule – failed to democratize, and it came very close to democratization by 2008.

The mechanisms of external interference differed between the two regions. For example, EU democratization efforts in Eastern Europe were more institutionalized and top-down than anything seen in the Americas. The leverage of EU membership had no equivalent in the Americas. Yet, in both regions, linkage motivated extensive Western engagement – including strong diplomatic pressure, a high level of attention to even minor abuse, and even military intervention (Nicaragua and Serbia) that powerfully constrained autocrats and created openings for democratic opposition that were not seen in low-linkage cases. Domestic actors (politicians, technocrats, economic elites, and even voters) were highly sensitive to external pressure, which made it far more difficult for incumbents to maintain authoritarian coalitions. In some cases (e.g., Nicaragua and Slovakia),

---

[1] All six cases in Eastern Europe were scored as high linkage. In the Americas, the Dominican Republic, Guyana, and Mexico were high linkage; Haiti and Peru were medium linkage.

the incumbent government's pariah status became an issue that benefited the opposition at election time. Finally, Western engagement and ties to a variety of Western actors critically strengthened otherwise weak and divided opposition forces in both regions.

These external influences distinguished the Eastern European and Latin American/Caribbean regime paths from most of the other cases examined in this book. Although a few low-linkage countries experienced important periods of Western engagement (e.g., Cambodia and Mozambique in the early 1990s; Ukraine in 2004), such engagement did not reshape actors' capacities and incentives to the same degree as in Eastern Europe and the Americas – and it was rarely, if ever, sustained. Indeed, linkage effects were remarkably persistent in these latter regions, which resulted not only in regime transitions but also in relatively stable democratization.

3

Linkage, Leverage, and Democratization in Eastern Europe

This chapter examines the trajectory of the six competitive authoritarian regimes that emerged in post-communist Eastern Europe: Albania, Croatia, Macedonia, Romania, Serbia, and Slovakia.[2] Conditions for democratization in Eastern Europe were relatively unfavorable. Not only were some countries (e.g., Albania, Macedonia, and Romania) underdeveloped, but even in the more advanced countries (e.g., Croatia and Slovakia), decades of Leninist rule created obstacles to democratization that arguably exceeded those in most Latin American/Caribbean cases. Communist regimes were far more repressive and closed, banning virtually all forms of independent political expression, which resulted in weak civil societies in the 1990s.[3] Moreover, legacies of central planning made it easier for post-communist autocrats and their allies to secure (formal or informal) control over key economic assets, thereby limiting opposition access to resources.[4] Finally, every country except Albania experienced severe ethnic tension, and Croatia and Serbia suffered ethnic civil war.[5]

Despite these obstacles, five of six Eastern European cases (Croatia, Macedonia, Romania, Serbia, and Slovakia) democratized during the post–Cold War period; the sixth case, Albania, very nearly democratized. This outcome, we argue, was rooted in a combination of linkage and leverage. Although the imposition of Soviet control after 1945 closed off ties to Western Europe throughout most of the region,[6] the collapse of communism brought a dramatic expansion of linkage – in the form of rapidly expanding trade with the West; large-scale migration;

---

[2] By "Eastern Europe," we are referring to post-communist countries outside the former Soviet Union in Central and Southeast Europe.

[3] See Wehrle (1999: 157) and especially Howard (2003). Among the cases discussed in this chapter, only Serbia emerged from communism with a highly mobilized civic opposition.

[4] Miklos (1997).

[5] See Silber and Little (1996) and Vachudova and Snyder (1997).

[6] See Radio Free Europe (1978), Collins and Rodrick (1991: 37–40), Tismaneanu (2003), and Linden (2008: 130–1).

and an invasion of Western media, NGOs, international organizations (IOs), and party organizations.[7] Moreover, linkage, geographic proximity, and security concerns motivated an unprecedented degree of Western intervention in the domestic politics and policies of Eastern European states.

Sources of Western engagement and influence in Eastern Europe were myriad, including a variety of U.S. agencies and U.S.-based NGOs and IOs.[8] However, the most important source of linkage and leverage was the EU. Initially slow to embrace Eastern European membership,[9] the EU formally committed to expansion in 1993 and began membership negotiations in 1998. By the early 2000s, the EU was arguably "the most successful democracy promotion program ever implemented by an international actor."[10]

The EU's role was distinctive in several ways. First, it is unique among regional organizations in its long-term commitment to democratic membership conditionality. Democracy was introduced as a criterion for membership in the early years of the European Community (EC) and was used to exclude Greece, Portugal, Spain, and Turkey from membership in the 1960s.[11] By the 1990s, the EU commitment to democracy had expanded considerably.[12] The 1993 Copenhagen criteria stipulated that candidate states must have stable institutions that guarantee "democracy, the rule of law, human rights and respect for and protection of minorities."[13] Democratic conditionality was deepened by the 1997 Treaty of Amsterdam, which provided for suspension of existing membership for those states that violate "the EU's principles of liberty, democracy, respect for human rights and fundamental freedoms and the rule of law."[14]

The EU's fusion of linkage and leverage allowed it to apply democratic conditionality consistently, thoroughly, and effectively. EU conditionality was accompanied by unprecedented integration (codified in some 80 thousand pages of the *acquis communautaire*) that engaged "virtually all identifiable sectors of public activity and interest."[15] It fostered a multiplicity of political and institutional ties via the European Parliament, European party organizations, numerous regional organizations and commissions, and programs such as "twinning," which matched candidate-country bureaucracies with their counterparts in Western European governments.[16]

Integration also brought a striking level of external intervention into the domestic politics of candidate countries. The Europe Agreements of the early 1990s created an extensive system of consultation and monitoring that

[7] On trade, see R. Martin (1999: 184); on migration, see Mansoor and Quilin (2006: 34); and on media, NGOs, and IOs, see Pridham (1999b), Reichardt (2002), Vachudova (2005b), and Fisher (2006).

[8] See Bunce and Wolchik (2006a, 2006b).

[9] See Schimmelfennig (2001: 55–7) and Grabbe (2003).

[10] Vachudova (2005a: 67). See also Kelley (2004); Knaus and Cox (2005); Schimmelfennig and Sedelmeier (2005); Pridham (2005);

Schimmelfennig, Engert, and Knobel (2006); and Cameron (2007).

[11] Pridham (2002: 206); Thomas (2006).

[12] Malova and Rybar (2003: 100); Pridham (2005: 25–34).

[13] See Baun (2000: 44) and Malova and Rybar (2003: 101).

[14] Pridham (2002: 206); see also Henderson (1999: 223).

[15] Pridham (2005: 5).

[16] Grabbe (2002: 261); Pridham (2005: 125–6).

encompassed virtually every level of government.[17] Beginning in 1997, the EU conducted intensive annual reviews of compliance on all membership requirements. Thus:

> ... political monitoring of applicant countries is really perpetual. While officially satisfaction of the Copenhagen political criteria is necessary for the opening of membership negotiations, these are not regarded as being fulfilled once and for all.[18]

EU institutions were reinforced by a dense network of regional and international organizations – including the Organization for Security and Cooperation in Europe (OSCE), the Council of Europe, NATO, transnational party organizations, and a variety of NGOs – that monitored democratic developments across the region.[19] The result was a set of democratic benchmarks that were both highly detailed and systematically monitored and enforced. These organizations provided multiple and overlapping sources of monitoring, as well as potential sources of elite socialization.[20]

Finally, the benefits (real and perceived) of ties to Europe powerfully shaped the incentives of domestic actors. Permanent and extensive ties to the wealthy European core constituted a "big prize" that resonated broadly among both the Eastern European elite and the general public.[21] As a result, enlargement became "one of the most important variables of political life" for countries in Eastern Europe.[22]

Linkage and leverage encouraged democratization in Eastern Europe in at least three ways.[23] First, extensive monitoring and attention given to even minor

---

[17] Phinnemore (1999); Vachudova (2005b).

[18] Pridham (2002: 207).

[19] See Pridham (2002: 206; 2005: 44–5) and Vachudova (2005b: 129, 134). For example, the Venice Commission, under the umbrella of the Council of Europe, provided an explicit democratic "good housekeeping seal of approval" for constitutions and major legislation of countries across the region; and the OSCE, an outgrowth of the 1975 Helsinki Agreement, regularly monitored elections in Eurasia.

[20] Pridham (2005); Levitz and Pop-Eleches (forthcoming).

[21] Linden and Pohlman (2003); Pridham (2005: 84–96). The economic benefits of EU membership have been estimated at $25 billion to $50 billion (Moravcsik and Vachudova 2003: 47).

[22] Zielonka (2003: 1).

[23] It is important to note that democratic outcomes in Eastern Europe were a *product*, rather than a *cause*, of ties to the EU. The countries selected for potential EU membership were not necessarily more democratic than those that were excluded. In 1993–1994, for example, Freedom House placed Romania and Slovakia in the same "partly free" category as Armenia, Belarus, Georgia, Russia, and Ukraine. Indeed, Romania was scored as *less* democratic in 1993 than Armenia, Belarus, Russia, and Ukraine. Yet, Romania and Slovakia were declared eligible for EU membership, whereas Commonwealth of Independent States (CIS) countries were not. The logic behind these selections was more geographic and historical than meritocratic (Kopstein and Reilly 2000; Cameron 2007: 208). The EU took a fundamentally different approach to Eastern Europe than to CIS states. This was manifested in the different institutions of aid and cooperation (i.e., Europe Agreements and PHARE aid programs in Eastern Europe versus Partnership and Cooperation Agreements and the Technical Aid to the Commonwealth of Independent States [TACIS] program in the CIS) that were created for each region (Phinnemore 1999; Hillion 2005). This distinction proved critical, for only countries with Europe Agreements were given an opportunity to join the EU in 1993 (European Council 1993: 13; Smith 2004: 109).

abuse tied the hands of authoritarian governments. Although this scrutiny did not prevent all abuse,[24] it limited the range of tactics that could be used by incumbents, which gave opposition forces greater room to maneuver than in other parts of the world. Second, Western intervention helped to reshape domestic power balances. For example, Western military action weakened the Milošević government in Serbia, and European ostracism undermined public and political support for Mečiar in Slovakia. At the same time, Western assistance helped to strengthen and unify opposition forces.[25] Third, linkage and leverage created a web of constraints that discouraged most post-transition governments from abusing power, thereby ensuring that transitions led to stable democratic outcomes.

Two points merit attention regarding EU conditionality. First, recent studies have drawn skeptical conclusions about the EU's impact in Eastern Europe. In particular, scholars have highlighted the EU's failure to achieve ambitious reform objectives in areas such as corruption, judicial independence, and treatment of ethnic minorities.[26] In terms of the *core elements of democracy*, however, EU conditionality was remarkably effective. Beginning in the late 1990s, even the region's most autocratic leaders – with the exception of Milošević – refrained from serious violations of democratic procedure. Although leaders such as Vladimir Mečiar and Ion Iliescu (during his second term) were responsible for considerable abuse, they did not engage in the type of large-scale violence, arrests and media closures seen in Armenia, Belarus, Russia, and other post-Soviet regimes. Moreover, with the exception of Serbia (and possibly Albania in 1996), there were no instances of significant (i.e., outcome-changing) electoral fraud after 1992. By contrast, every post-Soviet competitive authoritarian regime (except Moldova) engaged in significant fraud at some point between 1992 and 2008. Placed in comparative perspective, then, authoritarian governments in Eastern European were remarkably restrained in the late 1990s and 2000s. As we demonstrate in this chapter, this outcome was rooted in ties to the West.

Second, although the EU played a central role in Eastern European democratization,[27] its effectiveness was not merely a product of formal conditionality. Rather, it was rooted in the fact that conditionality was embedded in widespread linkage – much of which was exogenous to (and predated) the formal EU accession process. In other words, the success of conditionality hinged on the penetration of Western media, NGOs, IOs, and party networks.[28] These ties at times encouraged Western intervention (e.g., Albania in 1997 and Serbia in 1999–2000) outside of the EU accession process. Indeed, linkage constrained autocrats in Romania and Slovakia before the formal accession process

---

[24] Vachudova (2005b); K. Krause (2003b).
[25] Vachudova (2005b); Fisher (2006).
[26] See, for example, Ciobanu (2007), Pridham (2007, 2008), and Schimmelfennig (2008). The EU was also said to fail to gain Balkan cooperation with the International Criminal Tribunal for Yugoslavia.
[27] Vachudova (2005b); Schimmelfennig and Sedelmeier (2005).
[28] Bunce and Wolchik (2006a, 2006b).

generated "active leverage" in 1995,[29] and it appears to have prevented serious authoritarian backsliding in the late 2000s *after* accession had reduced EU leverage.[30] Moreover, linkage encouraged democratic behavior even in Albania and Macedonia, where EU membership was "far more distant and less credible."[31] Hence, although EU conditionality was critical to democratization, its effectiveness was rooted at least partly in linkage.

Although ties to the West were critical in all six Eastern European countries, the mechanisms of external influence varied across cases. In Romania and Slovakia, democratization was driven primarily by the incentives created by the prospect of EU membership. In the Western Balkans, the mechanisms of international influence were more indirect and multifaceted. In Croatia and Serbia, security problems created by ethnic civil war initially sidelined efforts to promote democracy. Efforts to weaken authoritarianism and strengthen democratic oppositions were undertaken only after the 1995 Dayton Accords. Finally, in Albania and Macedonia, linkage and geographic proximity motivated Western engagement not only to promote democratization but also, initially, to address more fundamental problems of state collapse and (in Macedonia) severe ethnic tension. We examine these cases in the following sections.

LINKAGE, DEMOCRATIZATION, AND THE EU: SLOVAKIA AND ROMANIA

In Slovakia and Romania, linkage and EU enlargement played a central role in constraining authoritarian governments and strengthening otherwise weak and fragmented oppositions. As a result, both cases democratized – despite considerable domestic obstacles – in the late 1990s and 2000s.

Slovakia

Slovakia was a competitive authoritarian regime from 1993 until 1998, when Prime Minister Vladimir Mečiar's Movement for a Democratic Slovakia (HZDS) was defeated by a coalition of opposition parties. Despite the fact that Mečiar benefited from a relatively strong party, a healthy economy, and a weak and fragmented opposition, linkage significantly constrained his behavior and ultimately undermined his rule. Although EU pressure hardly transformed Mečiar into a democrat,[32] it discouraged serious abuse, strengthened the opposition, and undermined the governing coalition – all of which facilitated democratization.

Linkage, Leverage, and Organizational Power
Slovakia is a case of high leverage and high linkage. Slovakia was a small state that fell solidly into Western Europe's orbit. It enjoyed no black-knight

---

[29] Cameron (2007). The term *active leverage* is taken from Vachudova (2005b).

[30] Levitz and Pop-Eleches (forthcoming).

[31] Epstein and Sedelmeier (2008: 798).

[32] See Vachudova (2005b: 141).

support,[33] and no issue trumped democracy promotion on Western foreign-policy agendas. In terms of linkage, Slovakia's entry into the EU accession process – eventually formalized in a 1994-1995 Europe Agreement – was accompanied by a fundamental reorientation of social, economic, and political ties toward the West.[34] Whereas Czechoslovakia had been solidly in the Soviet orbit in the 1980s,[35] the Slovak economy was "radically" reoriented Westward and, by the mid-1990s, the vast bulk of its trade was with Western Europe.[36] In the political arena, Slovak parties established extensive ties to transnational party organizations, including the European Democratic Union, the European Union of Christian Democrats, and the Liberal International. Civic organizations gained considerable support from Western agencies such as USAID, the British Know-How Fund, and the Open Society Foundation.[37]

Organizational power was medium high. Party scope and cohesion were medium. Founded in 1991 in a context of nationalist mobilization, the Movement for Democratic Slovakia (HZDS) quickly built a "powerful network of regional and local party units."[38] Although it was not a mass party, the HZDS penetrated many NGOs and was the only party in Slovakia with a strong rural presence.[39] Despite its relative newness, the HZDS exhibited "a degree of party discipline unrivaled by any other party" in Slovakia or the Czech Republic.[40]

Coercive capacity was medium high. Scope was high, as Slovak governments inherited a vast internal-security apparatus from the communist regime.[41] Although Mečiar purged the coercive apparatus of personnel deemed too loyal to the Czechoslovak Federation,[42] "generous budgets" and leftover communist-era capacity allowed the security services to carry out "broad surveillance of political society," including much of the media, business, political parties, the church, trade unions, and "most major civil-society foundations."[43] Cohesion

33 Mečiar attempted to strengthen ties to Russia in the mid-1990s (Rhodes 2001: 4; Malova and Rybar 2003: 106), but he was unable to gain sufficient assistance to offset Slovakia's dependence on Europe.

34 See Bricke, Lukas, and Szomolányi (1995: 213), Pridham (1999), and Kopstein and Reilly (2000: 31).

35 Collins and Rodrik (1991: 39).

36 Winiecki (2002: 61–3). In 1997, the value of Slovakia's trade with Western Europe equaled 84 percent of GDP (International Monetary Fund, Direction of Trade Statistics database (CD-ROM).

37 Pridham (1999a: 1229–30); Reichardt (2002: 15–16); Bunce and Wolchik (2006a, 2006b).

38 K. Krause (2003a: 67). As Krause notes (2003a: 67), Mečiar "devoted an unusual degree of attention to party organiza-

tion." The party claimed to have 2,000 local party organizations, an average of 25 organizations per district (Krause 2006: 81–2).

39 On NGO penetration, see Malova (1997: 101) and Fisher (2006: 139). On the HZDS' extensive organization and rural penetration, see Obrman (1992: 14), Haughton (2001: 60), and Krause (2006: 81, 261).

40 Krause (2006: 88–9). See also Meseznikov (1997: 42) and Haughton (2001: 756; 2002: 1320). We score party cohesion as medium following the completion of two national election cycles in 1992 and 1994.

41 Pridham (1999a: 1227); Williams (2001a, 2001b).

42 Williams (2001b: 127).

43 Williams (2001b: 137–8). See also Rosenberger (1999: 34, 39–40) and Wehrle (1999: 169).

was medium. The security forces possessed no special source of cohesion, but they also showed no prior evidence of indiscipline.[44]

Origins and Evolution of the Regime

Competitive authoritarianism in Slovakia was closely linked to the political career of Prime Minister Vladimír Mečiar, who negotiated the breakup of Czechoslovakia in 1992 and helped found an independent Slovakia in January 1993.[45] After being ousted in March 1994, Mečiar returned to power following the HZDS's victory in the September-October 1994 parliamentary elections.[46] Once a "darling of Slovakia's anti-Communist dissident community,"[47] Mečiar governed in an authoritarian manner. Although elections were clean and opposition parties operated without fear of repression, Mečiar abused power in several ways. For example, the media playing field was skewed. State television, which accounted for 84 percent of viewers before 1996,[48] reported in a "biased and selective manner."[49] Moreover, the government withdrew licenses from independent media and launched numerous libel cases against journalists.[50] Consequently, most media were biased.[51] Mečiar also employed extralegal measures to undermine President Michal Kováč, who broke with Mečiar following Kováč's election by parliament in February 1993.[52] Mečiar limited Kováč's access to broadcast media and drew the Slovak Intelligence Service into a bizarre effort to embarrass Kováč by abducting his son.[53] In 1997, when Kováč and opposition forces added a proposal to introduce direct presidential elections to a Mečiar-sponsored referendum on NATO membership, the government – in violation of a Constitutional Court ruling – refused to distribute ballots with the question on it.[54]

Mečiar enjoyed several advantages in his effort to consolidate power. Not only did he possess a strong party and close ties to the business elite (rooted in a corrupt privatization process),[55] but the economy also was healthy and Mečiar enjoyed

---

[44] Goldman (1999: 62). Mečiar, who led the Slovak police in 1990, also maintained close ties to the security apparatus. A longtime loyalist, Ivan Lexa, served as head of internal security (Williams 2001b: 126, 130–2; Krause 2006: 34–5).

[45] Leff (1997: 126–45). Mečiar first became Prime Minister of Slovakia after elections in June 1990, was ousted in April 1991 and regained the premiership following legislative elections in June 1992.

[46] Fitzmaurice (1995).

[47] Rosenberger (1999: 36). Mečiar had been excluded from the Communist Party for his support of the 1968 reforms in Czechoslovakia.

[48] Goldman (1999: 74).

[49] Bricke, Lukas, and Szomolányi (1995: 201). See also Kalnyczky (1992: 68) and Obrman (1993).

[50] Obrman (1993); Buturova and Butura (1995: 121–2).

[51] See Buturova and Butura (1995: 121–2), Nivat (1997), Carpenter (1997), and Krause (2006: 24–5).

[52] Krause (2006: 35–8).

[53] The secret police reportedly kidnapped the President's son and drove him across the border to Austria, where he was arrested and extradited to Germany on fraud charges. The government was later accused of killing a witness in connection with the case. See Rosenberger (1999: 34), Williams (2001b: 136), and Krause (2006: 38, 49).

[54] See Henderson (2004: 134–5), Fisher (2006: 126), and Krause (2006: 53–4).

[55] Miklos (1997); Rhodes (2001: 4).

broad public support.[56] At the same time, opposition forces were "fragmented and weak,"[57] as well as divided along ideological (ex-communists versus market-oriented) and ethnic (Slovak versus Hungarian) lines.[58] No opposition party even remotely matched the HZDS's resources or grassroots organization.[59]

Yet Mečiar faced a hostile international environment. As a state in the middle of Europe, Slovakia received "far more international attention – and condemnation – than many other post-communist countries" and was subject to "somewhat exaggerated reactions of international organizations to the political situation."[60] Western media, the EU, the OSCE, and the Council of Europe closely monitored the government and provided the opposition with a "forum where it could [voice] its concerns to [an] international audience."[61] Indeed, even minor abuse – such as the violation of *informal* parliamentary norms of committee assignment – triggered criticism from Western powers.[62] The government was confronted with two series of demarches (in November 1994 and October 1995), a critical resolution by the European Parliament (in 1996), criticism from the chair of the Joint Inter-Parliamentary Committee, and warnings from the U.S. ambassador and numerous European politicians.[63] Such statements "were important signals to the Slovak public showing that the opposition's criticisms of the government were justified."[64] Finally, in 1997, the EU rejected Slovakia's request to begin accession negotiations, primarily due to its failure to meet the Copenhagen political criteria.[65]

The international reaction imposed important costs on the government. Because EU membership enjoyed broad public support, EU declarations citing the government as a barrier to accession were politically costly.[66] Mečiar's ostracism transformed relations with Europe into a "central theme of domestic politics."[67] Slovakia's pariah status appears to have discouraged investment,[68]

---

[56] Fisher (2006: 151). Between 1994 and 1997, annual GDP growth averaged 6.5 percent, which was higher than Hungary, the Czech Republic, or Poland (World Bank World Development Indicators (online: www.worldbank.org/data)).

[57] Baer (2001: 103).

[58] See Fisher (2006: 130, 153). Because there was initially "no focal point around which Mečiar's opponents could unite," their votes were "dispersed ineffectively across a wide range of parties" (Szomolanyi 2001: 165).

[59] Krause (2006: 125). Civic organizations, although "undeniably visible" by 1996 (Reichardt 2002: 13; Henderson 2004: 135–40), depended heavily on U.S. and EU assistance (Henderson 2001: 220; Reichardt 2002; Fisher 2006: 134–5).

[60] Skolkay (1997: 201). See also Kopstein and Reilly (2000: 30–1) and Malova and Rybar (2003: 98).

[61] Malova and Rybar (2003: 103). Thus, as early as 1993, *The New York Times* condemned Mečiar's interference in state-run media. See "Unshackle the Press in Slovakia," *The New York Times*, 18 September 1993 (online: http://www.nytimes.com/).

[62] Vachudova (2005b: 158); Krause (2006: 27–33).

[63] Malova and Rybar (2003: 104); Vachudova (2005b).

[64] Malova and Rybar (2003: 103).

[65] Pridham (1999a, 2002); Toma and Kováč (2001).

[66] Vachudova (2005b: 174); Fisher (2006: 127). EU integration was so popular that even Mečiar backed it (Haughton 2005: 122).

[67] Szomolanyi (2004: 19).

[68] During the mid-1990s, per capita foreign investment in Slovakia was less than half of that in the Czech Republic and barely one tenth of that in Hungary (Gould and Szomolanyi 2000: 57–8).

and it clearly undermined Mečiar's governing coalition. Several HZDS politicians with ties to the West moved into opposition, and foreign ministers – who were most likely to have contact with European officials – resigned repeatedly: Mečiar had six ministers in fewer than five years.[69] The "impossibility of selling Mečiar to the West combined with the weight of Western disapprobrium was apparently too much for any foreign minister to bear."[70]

Although the EU failed to prevent all government abuse,[71] external pressure clearly limited it. For example, Mečiar's move to expel 15 opposition legislators on dubious procedural grounds following the 1994 election was abandoned after "vehement...protests" from the Liberal International and other Western actors.[72] Likewise, the government softened legal penalties for public criticism of state officials and ceased financial pressure on newspapers after these measures triggered protest from journalists and "harsh criticism from the West."[73] In 1996, Mečiar permitted the emergence of Slovakia's first major private television station, *Markiza*, "in response to complaints from Western democracies about anti-democratic restrictions on freedom of the press."[74] Although the government restricted *Markiza*'s access in much of the country,[75] the station quickly became the most popular in Slovakia, and it played a major role in mobilizing opposition to Mečiar.[76]

International influence was most critical in the 1998 parliamentary election.[77] Linkage shaped the election's outcome in at least three ways. First, it helped strengthen and unite the opposition. Support from the EU and European party networks enhanced the organizational capacity of what had been a weak and fragmented opposition.[78] At the same time, "[r]eturning Slovakia to 'Europe' served as a focal point for cooperation," which encouraged ex-Communist, liberal, populist, and Hungarian parties to forge a broad "coalition of coalitions."[79] Foreign funding also helped sustain independent civic and media organizations.[80] U.S. and EU institutions provided extensive support for voter turnout (including a "Rock the Vote" campaign that sponsored pop concerts across the country), media monitoring, and electoral observation – all of which benefited the

---

[69] Toma and Kováč (2001: 314); Vachudova (2005b: 161–72).

[70] Vachudova (2005b: 172).

[71] See Malova and Rybar (2003: 105), Krause (2003b: 69–70), Vachudova (2005b: 109), and Haughton (2007: 241).

[72] Leff (1996: 46); Pridham (1999a: 1233). The parliamentarians were from the Democratic Union, which had close ties to the Liberal International. See also Goldman (1999), Henderson (2004: 134), and Krause (2006: 39–40).

[73] Bricke, Lukas, and Szomolányi (1995: 201); Krause (2006: 122). See also Rhodes (2001: 4) and International Press Institute "World

Press Freedom Review 1998: Slovakia." (online: http://www.ifex.org/).

[74] Goldman (1999: 74).

[75] Henderson (2004: 135).

[76] Goldman (1999: 74–5); Fisher (2006: 129). In addition, according to Wolchik (1997: 236), Western pressure may have limited Mečiar's ability to use overt or extralegal measures to oust Kováč from office.

[77] See Reichardt (2002: 17) and Vachudova (2005b).

[78] Pridham (1999a: 1229–39).

[79] Vachudova (2005b: 170). See also Malova and Rybar (2003: 98, 105–106).

[80] Fisher (2006: 132).

opposition.[81] Indeed, the most important civic campaign, led by OK '98, "could not have [been] sustained" without foreign financing and technical support.[82] Moreover, foreign-funded voter mobilization campaigns helped boost turnout, which was said to be critical to opposition success.[83]

Linkage also influenced the election itself. Western criticism "raised the electoral salience of government abuse."[84] In particular, the EU's 1997 decision not to begin accession negotiations generated a "heightened sense of isolation," which limited Mečiar's electoral appeal and transformed Slovakia's regional standing into a major campaign issue.[85] EU integration was a central focus of opposition campaigns, and there is some evidence that the issue had an impact on voters.[86] Thus, despite a campaign marked by restrictive media laws, harassment of journalists, state media bias, and skewed access to finance,[87] the opposition vote in 1998 increased markedly relative to 1994. The HZDS won only a narrow plurality, with 27 percent of the vote and 43 of 150 seats in parliament.[88]

Finally, linkage and leverage played a central role in postelection coalition-formation. Given the HZDS's parliamentary plurality in and substantial administrative resources, Mečiar very likely would have been able to form a new government coalition in the absence of strong external pressure.[89] By 1998, however, it was clear that any opposition politician who cooperated with Mečiar risked international isolation, which – given Slovakia's ties to Europe and widespread public support for integration – was viewed as political suicide.[90] Thus, all major opposition parties refused to enter into a coalition with the HZDS,[91]

---

[81] Reichardt (2002: 12–16); Butora, Butorova, and Meseznikov (2003: 57–8); Bunce and Wolchik (2006a); Fisher (2006: 140–2). The Open Society Foundation and EU-funded Civil Society Development Foundation provided 4 million euros to Slovak NGOs in 1998 (Henderson 2001: 220), and USAID provided $8 million in assistance (Reichardt 2002: 16).

[82] Reichardt (2002: 18); Fisher (2006: 140–1).

[83] Reichardt (2002: 12); Fisher (2006: 146). Turnout rose from 75 percent in 1994 to 84 percent in 1998. The increase was reportedly driven by first-time voters, who voted heavily for the opposition (Butora, Butorova, and Meseznikov 2003: 53). In a survey conducted shortly after the election, 9 percent of respondents reported that the get-out-the-vote campaign had influenced their decision to go to the polls (Reichardt 2002: 12). For a counterargument, see Krause (2003b).

[84] Butora, Butorova, and Meseznikov (2003: 59).

[85] Fisher (2006: 11, 158, 165).

[86] On the EU role in opposition campaigns, see Malova and Rybar (2003: 106) and Fisher

(2006: 163). On the EU's possible electoral impact, see Vachudova (2005b: 174–5) and Schimmelfennig, Engert, and Knobel (2005: 40).

[87] See ODIHR (1998c) and Fisher (2000a: 86). See also Committee to Protect Journalists, "Attacks on the Press in 1998: Slovakia" February 1999 (online: www.cpj.org).

[88] The Slovak Democratic Coalition finished second, with 26 percent of the vote and 42 seats.

[89] See Vachudova (2005b: 170). Viable coalition partners clearly existed. The Slovak National Party, which had aligned with the HZDS in the 1994–1998 period, won 14 seats, and the former communists (the Party of the Democratic Left) and the Party of Civic Understanding (SOP) – both of which had considered alliances with the HZDS in the past (Fisher 2006: 155; Krause 2006: 104–5) – won a combined 36 seats. With these parties, Mečiar would have had a 93-seat majority coalition.

[90] Pridham (2001); Vachudova (2005b: 170).

[91] Toma and Kováč (2001: 342); K. Krause (2003a).

and the government was replaced by an opposition coalition led by Mikuláš Dzurinda.

Slovakia was democratic after 1998. Elections were free and fair, restrictive media laws were overturned, and laws dictating balanced coverage on public television were enforced.[92] Because the political success of the Dzurinda government hinged on successful negotiations with the EU,[93] violations of democratic procedure would have been very costly. Ties to Europe also helped to prevent Mečiar's return to power – despite his strong support base – in the early 2000s. Thus, despite the fact that the Dzurinda government presided over a slowing economy and was "often on the verge of collapse," the "common aims of entry into the Euro-Atlantic clubs" helped keep the governing coalition together,[94] and the prospect of EU membership provided an important source of electoral support. EU integration was a "paramount domestic issue" in the 2002 parliamentary election, and Mečiar's perceived inability to advance EU membership appears to have limited his appeal.[95] The HZDS vote declined by nearly a third relative to 1998, and although it won a slim parliamentary plurality, Dzurinda's Slovak Democratic and Christian Union was able to forge a new governing coalition. Slovakia joined NATO and the EU in 2004.[96] Although EU accession eliminated the leverage created by positive conditionality, Slovakia's regime trajectory was unchanged. Indeed, even after the 2006 election brought to power a coalition that included the HZDS and the ultranationalist Slovak National Party, the regime remained fully democratic.[97]

In summary, the Slovak case highlights the constraints that high linkage and leverage imposed on post–Cold War autocrats. Despite a well-organized party, a weak and fragmented opposition, and a booming economy, linkage and EU conditionality effectively undermined Mečiar's rule. Thus, although he has been compared to autocrats like Alyaksandr Lukashenka,[98] Mečiar in fact was far more constrained by the international environment, which created ample opportunity for opposition groups to strengthen and win power.

Romania

Like Slovakia, Romania is a strikingly successful case of Western democracy promotion.[99] Conditions for democracy in Romania were unfavorable.[100] It was

92 ODIHR (1999b: 7, 16); Butora, Butorova, and Meseznikov (2003: 64).

93 European Commission President Romano Prodi once remarked that for Dzurinda, progress in EU negotiations was "more important than sex" (quoted in Toma and Kováč [2001: 355]). See also Pridham (2002) and Krause (2003).

94 Haughton (2003b: 71–3; 2003a). See also Rhodes (2001: 8) and Harris (2004: 190–1).

95 On the EU role in the campaign, see Henderson (2004: 194). On Mečiar's electoral vulnerability on this issue, see Mudde (2002) and K. Krause (2003a).

96 In a binding referendum held in 2003, an overwhelming 92 percent voted for EU membership.

97 See Haughton and Ryber (2008). See also Freedom House, "Freedom in the World 2008: Slovakia" (online: www.freedomhouse .org).

98 K. Krause (2003b: 80).

99 See Vachudova (2005b: 165).

100 See Crowther (2003: 87).

underdeveloped and, outside Albania, "no other Eastern European country experienced such an uninterrupted exercise of Stalinist repression."[101] Nevertheless,
intense Western engagement – including EU membership negotiations – raised
the cost of abuse, empowered a weak and fragmented opposition, and induced
autocratic elites to engage in increasingly democratic behavior.[102] Thus, although
Romania's path to democracy was rocky, and included a regression into competitive authoritarianism in the early 2000s, it was ultimately successful.

Linkage, Leverage, and Organizational Power

Romania is a case of high leverage and high linkage. A small state with an "acute
dependence on international aid" and weak ties to Russia,[103] Romania was highly
vulnerable to Western democratizing pressure. In terms of linkage, although the
Ceauşescu dictatorship left Romanians isolated from the West,[104] geographic
proximity and Western engagement brought a dramatic expansion of ties after
1989. Trade with the United States and EU (as a share of GDP) doubled between
1990 and 1995.[105] Travel to the United States tripled between 1985 and 1990,[106]
and Romania was among the top 20 most-covered countries in *The New York
Times* in the early 1990s.[107] Western powers reinforced these emerging ties by
encouraging integration. Due to geographic proximity and fears of instability in
neighboring states, Western actors opted to engage Romania, rather than isolate
it, in the early 1990s.[108] Thus, a 1993 Association Agreement opened up the
possibility of EU membership. Romania also was granted membership in the
Council of Europe, on the condition that rapporteurs produce biannual human-
rights reports.[109] Given the Romanian public's "almost unanimous enthusiasm
for integration into Europe,"[110] Europe's engagement created strong incentives
for democratic behavior.

Organizational power in Romania was medium. The ruling party was characterized by medium scope and low cohesion. The National Salvation Front
(FSN) was created in 1989 by a heterogeneous coalition of Ceauşescu opponents

---

[101] Tismaneanu (1993: 320, 315). These condi-
tions generated widespread pessimism about
Romania's prospects for democratization.
See, for example, Gallagher (1995: 234).

[102] See Mungiu-Pippidi (2006).

[103] Bing and Szajkowski (1994: 350). On Romania's weak ties to Russia, see Linden and
Pohlman (2003: 324) and Pascu (2004).

[104] Ceauşescu imposed tight controls on foreign travel and communication. No one was
given a personal passport, and any conversation with a foreigner had to be reported
within 24 hours. See Ionescu (1990: 28),
Linz and Stepan (1996: 360), and Deletant
(2001a: 186).

[105] International Monetary Fund Direction of
Trade Statistics database (CD-ROM).

[106] This figure refers to nonimmigrant visitors of all classes. See U.S. Department of
Homeland Security (2004).

[107] Hickman and Trapp (1998: 397). Romania's
proximity and ties to Western Europe thus
made isolation "impossible" (Agh 1998a:
275).

[108] See Papadimitriou (2001: 83–4) and Phinnemore (2001: 102–104).

[109] Deletant (1995). Such special monitoring
persisted until 1997. See *RFE/RL Newsline*,
25 April 1997 (online: http://www.rferl
.org/archive/en-newsline/latest/683/683.
html) .

[110] Crowther (2003: 91). See also Linden and
Pohlman (2003).

but later captured by ex-Communist officials.[111] Although the Communist Party "disappeared without a trace,"[112] the FSN appropriated much of its infrastructure and was thus able to establish an organized presence throughout the country.[113] When the FSN divided in 1992, the governing Ion Iliescu faction – which eventually became the Party of Democratic Socialists (PDSR) – retained most of the party's organization, resources, and vast patronage networks.[114] As a new organization without any special source of cohesion, the FSN and its successor parties are scored as low cohesion.

The coercive apparatus was high in scope and medium in cohesion. In terms of scope, much of the communist-era internal security structure remained intact after 1989.[115] The Romanian Intelligence Service (SRI) and the UM 0215 (considered the "dirty tricks" arm of the SRI) were built from Ceauşescu's notorious *Securitate* and demonstrated a clear capacity to monitor and penetrate society.[116] Cohesion was medium. Although the security forces lacked a strong ideology, a past history of conflict, or another special source of cohesion, they remained disciplined and under tight executive and ruling-party control in the early 1990s.[117]

Origins and Evolution of the Regime

The sudden and violent collapse of the Ceauşescu regime in 1989 brought only a partial break with the past.[118] The FSN government, led by Ion Iliescu, was composed of ex-communist officials with a limited commitment to democracy.[119] In May 1990, Iliescu won an unfair presidential election with 85 percent of the vote.[120] Elements of the old authoritarian state persisted under Iliescu. All national television stations were state-run through 1993, and the state media "maintained a strict allegiance to the government."[121] The electoral authorities were politicized,[122] and the security services functioned as a "handmaiden" of the

---

[111] Pilon (1990); Calinescu and Tismaneanu (1992: 21–4); Roper (1999: 177).
[112] Tismaneanu (1993: 329).
[113] See Ionescu (1992a; 1992c: 20), Pop-Eleches (1999; 2001: 162), Crowther (2003: 91), Gallagher (2005: 311), Stan (2005: 4), and Mungiu-Pippidi (2006: 19).
[114] Mungiu Pippidi (1999: 141); Roper (1999: 183). In 2001, the PDSR merged with the smaller Romanian Humanist Party and was renamed the Social Democratic Party (PSD).
[115] Deletant (1995).
[116] Deletant (1995; 2001b: 216; 2004: 505). In the mid-1990s, it was estimated that the SRI had 10,000 to 12,000 officers and troops (Deletant 1995). There were also between 200,000 and 300,000 active military personnel in Romania, a large number by European standards (Nelson 2002: 437).
[117] See Deletant (1995), Krause (1996), and Crowther (2003: 91).
[118] On the collapse of the Ceauşescu regime, see Siani-Davies (2005).
[119] Calinescu and Tismaneanu (1992: 23–4); Pop-Eleches (1999: 134); Mungiu-Pippidi (2006: 25).
[120] The election was marred by heavy media bias, abuse of state resources, and the use of secret police to harass opposition (Calinescu and Tismaneanu 1992: 29–30; Tismaneanu 1993; Carothers 1997c).
[121] Mollison (1998: 132–4). See also Human Rights Watch (1994: 8).
[122] See Shafir (1992), Human Rights Watch (1994: 9), Carey (1995), and ODIHR (1997b: 14).

ruling party.[123] The Iliescu government also engaged in considerable repression, including a series of high-profile thug attacks – coordinated by the security services – on critics.[124] On several occasions in 1990, coal miners were transported to Bucharest from Jiu Valley to attack opposition groups. In June, the most violent of these attacks – which were coordinated by the security services – left six people dead and more than five hundred injured.[125]

The domestic push for democracy was weak. Due to tight controls on society and a pervasive secret service, dissident activity during the Ceauşescu era had been lower than in other Eastern European cases.[126] As a result, after the collapse of communism, civil society was strikingly undeveloped, even by post-communist standards.[127] Opposition parties were "improvised, understaffed [and] plagued by inner factionalism."[128] None of them effectively penetrated the countryside. As one journalist noted, the opposition was "known better in Washington than in [Romanian] villages."[129] Finally, like Slovakia, opposition forces were weakened by ethno-national divisions (between Romanian and pro-Hungarian parties).[130]

Democratization thus was externally driven. Despite the fact that the Iliescu government was not initially committed to Western integration (indeed, it sought Russian support to balance the West),[131] Romania's increasingly dense web of relations with the West generated powerful constraints on autocratic behavior. The external cost of abuse was made manifest after the June 1990 miners' attacks, which were "regarded by the world media as a 'Tiananmen massacre' in Bucharest."[132] The EU responded by freezing aid, and Romania's application to join the Council of Europe was shelved.[133]

---

[123] Deletant (2001b: 221). In 1992, the security services provided office space for Iliescu's new ruling party following the breakup of the National Salvation Front (Ionescu 1992b: 19).

[124] Deletant (1995; 2004: 507); Gledhill (2005: 94–8).

[125] See Deletant (1995) and Gledhill (2005: 94–8). Miners "vandalized the headquarters of opposition parties, some university buildings, and several offices of media outlets, beating hundreds of Iliescu's opponents" (Amariei 2005). See also Vasi (2004) and Gledhill (2005).

[126] Under Ceauşescu, typewriters and copy machines were tightly regulated (Ionescu 1990: 28; Man 1993: 90) and large wedding parties in restaurants were banned (Deletant 2001a: 187). As many as one in seven adults worked for the security services in some capacity (Mungiu-Pippidi 1999: 135; Deletant 2001a: 199). A study of independent movements in June 1989 conducted by Radio Free Europe showed that Romania had far fewer independent organizations than any other Eastern European country (2, compared to 13 in Bulgaria) (Pehe 1989). Moreover, unlike most other communist countries, there appears to have been no regular *samizdat* publications (Linz and Stepan 1996: 353).

[127] See Tismaneanu (1993, 1996), Howard (2003), and Pralong (2004).

[128] Tismaneanu (1993: 313). See also Shafir (1995b) and Vachudova (2005b: 165).

[129] Quoted in Shafir (1992: 4).

[130] Shafir (1995a, 1995b).

[131] See Linden (1992: 213–14), Crowther (2003: 93–4), and Papadimitriou and Phinnemore (2008: 67).

[132] Agh (1998a: 275). See also Gallagher (1995: 105).

[133] See Ionescu (1993: 35), Zidaru-Barbalescu (1993: 11), Pridham (2001: 96), and Crowther (2003: 93). Likewise, U.S. President George Bush described the attacks as "government inspired vigilante violence" and refused to back reintroduction of Romania's favored nation trading status until it became more democratic (Harrington, Karns, and Karns 1995: 207–9; Gallagher 1995: 105).

Western pressure had an important impact. The Iliescu government's "acute dependence on international aid" and "fear of international isolation" led it to take several steps to soften the regime's authoritarian image.[134] Thus, the FSN-dominated parliament moved to assert greater control over the security agencies involved in the miners' attacks and government-sponsored miners' attacks ceased.[135] The level of overall repression declined. As early as 1991, a "strongly negative" external response discouraged the government from carrying out its threat to arrest Ceaușescu-era dissident Doina Cornea after he called for Iliescu's ouster.[136] Likewise, international criticism of media censorship induced Iliescu to "ease government control" over the electronic media.[137] Finally, in the face of strong U.S. pressure,[138] the government agreed to hold new elections in 1992. The elections were marred by uneven access to media and finance and irregularities in the vote count, but they marked a "significant improvement" over the 1990 election.[139] Although Iliescu was reelected, he required a runoff, and the governing party failed to win a parliamentary majority.[140]

Democratization was pushed forward by European integration. Beginning in 1992, the Iliescu government adopted a more pro-European position, presenting itself as a "potential bulwark against a tide of Balkan instability that was emerging as a core concern of the Western governments."[141] In 1993, Romania signed a European Agreement, which placed it on a path to EU accession. The move had a major impact on the regime. Democratic conditionality was now explicit,[142] and the level of external monitoring increased markedly.

European integration induced the Iliescu government to soften its behavior in important ways. For example, "constant attention" from international agencies appears to have discouraged Iliescu from cracking down on the private media.[143] Thus, the emerging private-television sector (including ProTV and Antena 1) operated "without serious interference from the government."[144]

---

[134] Bing and Szajkowski (1994: 350); see also Ionescu (1993: 34) and Harrington, Karns, and Karns (1995: 221).

[135] See Deletant (2001b: 220) and Vachudova (2005b: 102). Miners' attacks against incumbent governments occurred in 1991 and 1999, but they "showed no element of coordination by the central political authorities" (Gledhill 2005: 83). Indeed, in 1999, Iliescu – now in opposition – took a firm stand against a miners' offensive that threatened to topple the government (Pop-Eleches 2001: 162). We thank John Gledhill for his clarification of this point.

[136] Ionescu (1993: 37).

[137] Stefanescu (1991: 37).

[138] The U.S. Congress tied reintroduction of Most Favored Nation (MFN) trade status to the conduct of free and fair elections, delaying a vote on MFN until after September 1992 national elections (Harrington, Karns, and Karns 1995: 211–12).

[139] Crowther (2003: 95). See also Carey (1995, 2004: 561), Harrington, Karns, and Karns (1995: 212), Carothers (1997c: 3), and Pop-Eleches (2001: 161).

[140] The governing party won about 35 percent of seats in the Chamber of Deputies (lower house), down from 68 percent in 1990, which forced it to forge an alliance with small nationalist parties. In local elections held that year, the opposition Democratic Convention captured Bucharest and most other large cities.

[141] Crowther (2003: 97). The government's adoption of a pro-European position can be attributed, in part, to broad public support for European integration. See Papadimitriou and Phinnemore (2008: 75).

[142] Verheijen (1994: 164).

[143] Zidaru-Barbalescu (1993: 14).

[144] Pop-Eleches (1999: 137); see also Gallagher (2001: 26).

Although state-run television remained dominant in the mid-1990s, independent electronic media provided a "competent and capable competition to the public broadcaster."[145] Likewise, the easing up of repression permitted a proliferation of NGOs, which provided critical organizational resources to the opposition.[146]

International scrutiny also appears to have induced the Iliescu government to hold a clean election in 1996.[147] By 1996, "most of Romania's political actors were aware that the country could not afford to become the pariah of the international community."[148] Thus, electoral conditions were far better than they had been in 1990 and 1992. Although state television remained biased,[149] it was counterbalanced by private television.[150] Moreover, linkage and leverage strengthened the hand of opposition forces. The opposition benefited from technical and organizational support from international party networks,[151] and as in Slovakia, the EU enlargement process encouraged convergence around a pro-Europe platform, providing a focal point around which disparate members of the opposition could rally.[152] Indeed, whereas in 1992 the opposition had included a range of nondemocratic forces (including monarchists and anti-Hungarian nationalists), the leading opposition group in 1996, the Democratic Convention (CDR), embraced liberal democracy and alliance with Hungarian parties – two planks that were essential for EU entry.[153] In what was generally considered a clean election,[154] Iliescu was defeated in the second round by CDR candidate Emil Constantinescu. Iliescu left power peacefully. As one observer put it, "[i]n the existing international environment, a forceful resistance to the electorate's decision (if it was ever contemplated) was inconceivable."[155]

The Constantinescu government (1996–2000) was democratic. The new government's ties to (and dependence on) the West, as well as the political salience of the EU accession issue,[156] appear to have discouraged abuse. Thus, Constantinescu's election "had a nearly immediate effect" on civil liberties, as the media harassment and other abuse that occurred under Iliescu largely disappeared.[157] The 2000 election was considered free and fair,[158] and incumbent forces were

---

[145] ODIHR (1996c: 8).
[146] Carothers (1997c: 4). Strong diplomatic pressure also induced the government to abandon ties with ultranationalist and anti-Hungarian parties (Gallagher 1996; Shafir 1996a; Roper 1999: 187).
[147] See Shafir (1996b), Crowther (2003: 99), and Vachudova (2005b: 154).
[148] Tismaneanu (1997: 440).
[149] ODIHR (1997b: 8).
[150] Deletant and Siani-Davies (1998: 158).
[151] Carothers (1996); Stan (2000: 155–6).
[152] Vachudova (2005b: 166–7).
[153] Papadimitriou and Phinnemore (2008: 77).

[154] See ODIHR (1997b) and Deletant and Siani-Davies (1998: 158).
[155] Shafir (1996b). See also Gallagher (2001: 126).
[156] Demetropoulou (2002).
[157] Committee to Protect Journalists, "Attacks on the Press in 1996: Romania" (online: www.cpj.org). Although there were a number of libel suits against journalists, these occurred mainly at the local level. See Committee to Protect Journalists, "Attacks on the Press 2000: Romania" and "Attacks on the Press 1999: Romania" (online: www.cpj.org).
[158] ODIHR (2001d).

badly defeated. Iliescu returned to the presidency, and his PDSR won a solid plurality in the legislature.[159]

Under Iliescu (2000–2004), Romania fell back into competitive authoritarianism. State media was re-politicized and government pressure on private media increased.[160] However, following the launch of formal EU negotiations in 2000, external constraints were formidable. The goal of EU entry was universally embraced across the political spectrum,[161] and the Iliescu government was thus highly sensitive to Western criticism.[162] Under pressure from European officials, the governing party avoided alliances with illiberal parties such as the Greater Romania Party (PRM) and instead forged a minority coalition backed by Hungarian parties, which it had once spurned.[163] International monitoring helped to ensure relatively clean parliamentary and presidential elections in 2004. Although the first-round elections were plagued by media abuse and at least some fraud,[164] "[i]nternational pressure, especially from the United States, resulted in a clean second round."[165] The governing party's presidential candidate, Prime Minister Adrian Năstase, was defeated by Bucharest mayor, Traian Băsescu, the candidate of the opposition Justice and Truth Alliance. The subsequent transition was peaceful.

Romania was democratic after 2005. Although the regime suffered multiple crises, including severe conflict between President Băsescu and Prime Minister Călin Popescu-Tăriceanu, civil-liberties violations (e.g., government pressure on the media) ceased. Moreover, the 2008 parliamentary elections were considered free and fair.[166] Democratic Romania joined the EU in 2007.

---

[159] Iliescu defeated ultranationalist Vadim Tudor 67 to 33 percent in the second round, and Iliescu's PDSR won 155 of 345 seats in parliament. Paradoxically, the Constantinescu government's failure to gain early entry into the EU or NATO may have contributed to Iliescu's comeback in 2000 (Aligica 2001; Nelson 2004: 473).

[160] See Gallagher (2005: 311), ODIHR (2005a), and Amariei (2006). According to the Committee to Protect Journalists, major TV channels "carr[ied] virtually no criticism of the government." See Committee to Protect Journalists "Attacks on the Press: 2004: Romania" (online: www.cpj.org).

[161] Tismaneanu and Kligman (2001); Knaus and Cox (2005: 44).

[162] Mungiu-Pippidi (2006: 20).

[163] The PRM won almost a quarter of the seats in the Chamber of Deputies and slightly more than that in the Senatein 2000. Western diplomats warned the government that alliances with ultranationalist parties would harm Romania's bid to join the EU and NATO. See *RFE/RL Newsline*

3 November 2003 (online: http://www.rferl.org/archive/en-newsline/latest/683/683.html) and Smith (2004: 142). The Iliescu government also softened its treatment of the Hungarian minority and enacted a series of liberalizing laws pushed by EU officials. See *RFE/RL Newsline*, 25 May and 22 June 2001 (online: http://www.rferl.org/archive/en-newsline/latest/683/683.html).

[164] Public TVR1, the only station that operated in some rural areas, was "clearly biased in favor of the party in government" (Pârvulescu 2004: 11). There was also some evidence of multiple voting (Pârvulescu 2004: 17; ODIHR 2005a: 14–15; Ciobanu 2007: 1440).

[165] Gallagher (2005: 355).

[166] See Freedom House, "Freedom in the World 2006: Romania" (online: www.freedomhouse.org). See also International Press Institute "World Press Freedom Review 2005: Romania." (online: www.freemedia.at/)Dragomir (2005), and U.S. Department of State (2009g).

In summary, Romania is a case in which extensive linkage and leverage sharply constrained authoritarian behavior. Indeed, as in Guyana and Nicaragua (see Chapter 4), a high-linkage/high-leverage environment helped engender and sustain democracy despite highly unfavorable domestic conditions.

LINKAGE AND DEMOCRATIZATION AMID ETHNIC CIVIL WAR: SERBIA AND CROATIA

Serbia and Croatia are also cases of high linkage and high leverage. However, war and ethnic conflict in the early 1990s created security concerns that sidelined democratization efforts and initially created permissive conditions for autocratic rule.[167] Following the resolution of the Bosnian crisis in 1995, however, Western attention turned to weakening autocratic forces, which contributed to democratization in both countries.

Serbia

Serbia's post–Cold War regime trajectory was shaped in critical ways by shifts in Western policy. In the early and mid-1990s, competitive authoritarianism was bolstered by high organizational power and limited Western pressure, due to President Slobodan Milošević's perceived utility in resolving regional conflicts. Over time, however, Western policy shifted, culminating in NATO's 1999 military intervention. Military defeat and a severe economic crisis, generated by international sanctions, weakened the Serbian state and regime. When the Western-backed opposition united in the 2000 Yugoslav presidential election, the regime collapsed. By 2004, Serbia had democratized.

Linkage, Leverage, and Organizational Power
Serbia was a case of high linkage and high leverage. Linkage was rooted in the relative openness of communist-era Yugoslavia.[168] Thus, in the early 1990s, Serbian industry was characterized by a "relatively high degree of integration with Western markets."[169] Although Western sanctions beginning in 1992 affected linkage (making Serbia a case in which linkage was partially endogenous to regime behavior), they had only a minor impact on Serbia's overall ties to the West. Although sanctions reduced legal trade with the West, available data suggest that per capita Serbian migration to Western Europe was among the highest of the countries examined in this study.[170] Moreover, the plethora of social, media, and communication ties generated by geographic proximity made it difficult for

---

[167] See Tull (2003: 141).
[168] See Zimmerman (1987: 9) and Collins and Rodrick (1991: 40). In the 1970s, there were three to five times more Yugoslav students in the West per capita than any other communist country (calculated from data on "foreign students by country of origin,"

United Nations Educational, Scientific and Cultural Organization (UNESCO) (1972: table 4.8, 1977: table 5.7, 1983: table 3.16)).
[169] Thomas (1999: 163).
[170] Data calculated from European migration data obtained from Eurostat New Cronos database (CD-ROM). See Appendix III.

Western governments to ignore events in Serbia and their potential regional impact.

Leverage is scored as high, because Serbia possessed neither military or economic clout nor the support of a counter-hegemonic power. As discussed below, however, a competing foreign-policy goal – the need for Serbian cooperation in resolving the conflict in Bosnia – reduced Western democratizing pressure during much of the 1990s. Thus, only after the 1995 Dayton Accords, which ended the Bosnian war, did Western democratizing pressure take force.

Organizational power was high in the early 1990s. The Socialist Party of Serbia (SPS) was extremely well organized.[171] Created directly out of the Serbian League of Communists in 1990,[172] the SPS inherited the old party's assets, real estate, media, personnel, physical infrastructure, and "a structure of branches and membership extending across the whole country."[173] With a membership that reached 500,000 in the mid-1990s, the party built extensive patronage networks and established workplace organizations in major factories.[174] Cohesion also was high, due to the existence of a salient ideology. Under Milošević, the SPS abandoned its predecessor's long-standing commitment to Yugoslavism and "embraced the mantle of Serbian nationalism," an ideology that clearly shaped elite behavior.[175]

Coercive capacity was similarly high.[176] The central components of the coercive apparatus were the large and well-equipped Secret Service, which was inherited from the communist period,[177] and an increasingly potent police force.[178] By the mid-1990s, the police force had grown to 80,000 to 100,000 personnel, drawn in large part from veterans from Bosnia and Croatia.[179] Belgrade alone had 25,000 police, making the city "the most heavily policed capital in Europe."[180] The police were complemented by a "shadow state apparatus": football clubs and militias that, using arms and equipment from the army, were deployed to harass opponents.[181] As one opposition candidate put it, these shadow state organizations gave Milošević the "power to intimidate the voters in every village and town beyond the reach of Belgrade's opposition voices."[182] A final component of the coercive apparatus was the Yugoslav army, which at times was deployed to defend the regime.[183] State cohesion also was high in the early 1990s. Although the army's regime loyalty was considered

---

[171] Antonic (2002).
[172] Andrejevich (1990a); Thomas (1999: 64).
[173] Thomas (1999: 76); Cohen (2001a: 120). The SPS was also strengthened by its incorporation of the pro Communist mass organization, the Socialist Alliance of Working People of Serbia.
[174] Thomas (1999: 76) and Cohen (2001a: 121).
[175] Pavlakovic (2005: 17). See also Thomas (1999: 229); Glaurdic (2009: 89–90).
[176] As discussed below, however, sanctions and military defeat eroded organizational power in the late 1990s.

[177] Edmunds (2007: 87).
[178] According to Cohen (2001a: 132), the police were "[d]isciplined, generously financed, well-trained and equipped, including units with heavy mortars and heavy artillery."
[179] Cohen (2001a: 132); Pavlakovic (2005: 23).
[180] Thomas (1999: 161).
[181] Edmunds (2007: 154). See also Moore (1992a: 71), Gagnon (1994/1995: 161), Colovic (1996: 384), and Djukic (2001: 43).
[182] Quoted in Thomas (1999: 131).
[183] See Moore (1992a: 70), A. Remington (1996: 164–6), and Cohen (2001a: 132–3).

suspect,[184] the police – the main internal security force – were widely viewed as loyal.[185] The police shared the SPS's nationalist ideology and, crucially, its ranks included a large number of veterans from Serbian militias in Bosnia and Croatia.[186] Finally, it is worth noting that the government enjoyed considerable discretionary economic power.[187] In the early 1990s, Milošević reversed earlier privatizations and systematically appointed allies to head state, para-state, and even private enterprises.[188] Through these proxy arrangements and other policy instruments, Milošević and his wife gained control of an estimated 85 percent of the economy.[189]

Origins and Evolution of the Regime

Competitive authoritarianism in Serbia was the product of an incomplete transition from communist rule. Under Milošević's leadership, the League of Communists (renamed the SPS in 1990) used nationalism to mobilize public support and – assisted by effective state and party structures – to retain power through the transition to multiparty rule. Milošević eliminated potential rivals through a series of mass demonstrations – christened the "anti-bureaucratic revolution" – directed against opponents in various localities.[190] Riding a wave of nationalist sentiment, Milošević easily defeated anti-communist leader Vuk Drašković in the 1990 presidential election.[191]

The post-communist regime was authoritarian. The Milošević government engaged in frequent harassment of – and occasional violence against – domestic opponents. Opposition activists were attacked by government thugs, and opposition politicians occasionally suffered arrest and even violent attacks.[192] Moreover, the playing field was highly uneven. Milošević was "in control of virtually all elements of power in Serbia – media, money, army, and police."[193] State television and radio – the primary source of news in the countryside – were biased,[194] and the governing coalition's co-optation of business allowed it to nearly

---

[184] Cohen (2001a: 133).
[185] Thomas (1999: 124); Sell (2002: 52, 121, 135).
[186] Thomas (1999: 161); Cohen (2001a: 132); Edmunds (2007: 155).
[187] Palairet (2000); Dragović-Soso (2003b: 122–3).
[188] Bossom (1996: 519); Cohen (2001a: 131); Antonic (2002).
[189] Antonic (2002); Dragović-Soso (2003b: 122).
[190] Vladisavljevic (2008). Relying on transportation and other logistical support from the secret police and state-run factories, pro-Milošević forces mobilized as many as five million people (Silber and Little 1996: 59; Thomas 1999: 44–51; Cohen 2001a: 74–9). On the importance of organizational capacity in the pro-Milošević mobilization, see LeBor (2004: 121, 124, 141, 200–201).

[191] Serbia's institutional system was complex. Milošević's power was based in both Serbian institutions and federal Yugoslav institutions, both of which were controlled by loyalists. Milošević operated from Serbia's presidency through 1997, when he transferred the presidency to a loyalist and was elected Yugoslav president.
[192] Assassination attempts included a failed attack on Vuk Drašković in 1999 and the August 2000 assassination of Ivan Stambolic. See Moore (1999b), Thomas (1999: 304), LeBor (2004: 302), Pribicevic (2004: 107), and Pavlovic and Qirezi (2005). See also *RFE/RL Newsline* 18, October 1999 (online: http://www.rferl.org/archive/en-newsline/latest/683/683.html).
[193] Pribicevic (1996).
[194] Markotich (1994); ODIHR (1997c).

monopolize access to private-sector contributions, which "made the opposition even poorer."[195] Finally, elections were marred by fraud throughout the 1990s.[196]

Yet the Serbian regime was always competitive. No major parties were banned and, prior to the late 1990s, no major politicians were killed, imprisoned, exiled, or excluded from elections. Moreover, elections were not simply a façade. Outright fraud was relatively limited in scope,[197] which meant that Milošević had to attract significant popular support to win presidential elections. Legislative elections also were highly competitive. In fact, the SPS never won a majority of the legislative vote and, after 1992, it never held a parliamentary majority. Thus, Milošević at times struggled to control parliament and even to prevent votes of no confidence.[198] Finally, influential private media – such as Studio B television and Belgrade's Radio-B92 – provided an important degree of media pluralism in the major cities.[199] Indeed, one observer suggested in the early 1990s that Serbia had "the freest media environment of any of the former Yugoslav republics."[200]

REGIME SURVIVAL, 1990–1997. Milošević's hold on power was seriously contested throughout the 1990s. Government performance was disastrous. Facing Western sanctions beginning in 1992, Serbia's economy collapsed into hyperinflation and mass unemployment.[201] Moreover, opposition groups led massive and sustained protests throughout the decade.[202] During this period, Milošević's political survival hinged on several factors, including the government's organizational power, its manipulation of Serbian nationalism,[203] and opposition division.[204]

---

[195] Pribicevic (1996).

[196] See Schoen (1993), Thomas (1999: 352), and Cohen (2001a: 227–8).

[197] Even in the notorious 2000 election, fraud was estimated to be about 10 to 15 percent (Cohen 2001a: 417).

[198] Markotich (1993); Hislope (1996: 484); Gordy (2000: 99).

[199] Studio B reached up to 50 percent of Serbian territory in the early 1990s (Andrejevich and Bardos 1992: 88; Canak 1993: 83). See also Lebor 2004: 264–5) and Judah (2002: 264). In Belgrade, there were two independent TV stations and three independent radio stations (Dereta 1994: 23).

[200] Andrejevich and Bardos (1992: 86). See also Sell (2002: 193).

[201] The UN imposed sanctions against Serbia in May 1992 due to Milošević's support for Serb aggression in Bosnia and Croatia. International actors also maintained an "outer wall" of sanctions that barred Serbia from World Bank and IMF funding (Caplan 1998). In 1993, annual inflation reached 286 billion percent, surpassing that of Weimar Germany (Thomas 1999: 165–66). See also Lyon (1996: 321).

[202] Protest levels in Serbia during the 1990s were among the highest in the postcommunist world. On numerous occasions, the opposition mobilized between 50,000 and 100,000 demonstrators (and, on a few occasions, even more) in multiple cities across Serbia. These included protests of 50,000 to 70,000 in June 1990 (Andrejevich 1990b: 40); 80 thousand to 500 thousand in March 1991 (Andrejevich 1991c: 12; Doder and Branson 1999: 78; Thomas 1999: 82; LeBor 2004: 160–161); up to 100 thousand in June–July 1992 (Thomas 1999: 113; Bieber 2003: 83); and "millions of people nationwide" during 88 days in 1996–1997 (Brkic 1996–1997: 88; Thomas 1999: 285–318; Gordy 2000: 99).

[203] See Gordy (1999, 2000), Cohen (2001a), and Dragović-Soso (2003a).

[204] Moreover, Milošević's de facto control over the economy, which was enhanced by international sanctions (Dragović-Soso 2003b: 122), encouraged opposition defection by making it difficult to gain resources without cooperating with the authorities (Pribicevic 1996).

Crucially, however, the government also benefited from a permissive international environment. In the early and mid-1990s, the Bosnian conflict created a countervailing Western interest in regional stability that trumped democracy promotion. Milošević's control over Bosnian Serbian forces made him a valuable asset in peace negotiations and allowed him to offer cooperation in international peacekeeping efforts in exchange for Western tolerance of authoritarianism at home.[205]

Milošević faced strong opposition challenges beginning in the early 1990s. In the 1992 parliamentary election, the SPS captured only 29 percent of the vote and 101 of 250 seats, forcing it into a coalition with the far right Serbian Radical Party (SRS) in order to retain control of parliament. Later that year, when Serbia held presidential elections following the dissolution of the Yugoslav Federal Republic, Milošević was challenged by Yugoslav Prime Minister Milan Panić, an émigré businessman from California who ran on a pro-European and antiwar platform. With some polls showing Panić ahead, Milošević engaged in considerable fraud to secure reelection.[206] The Western response was muted; indeed, Panić "never secured any real support from the European Community or the United States."[207]

Opposition challenges continued in the mid-1990s, even as the U.S. led peace process helped to shield the regime from external pressure.[208] In November 1996, the opposition *Zajedno* (Together) won local elections in Belgrade and other major cities. The government responded by annulling the elections, which triggered massive protest. Despite widespread arrests, *Zajedno* mobilized hundreds of thousands of people in daily protests for almost three months.[209] Under pressure from the international community and the Serbian Orthodox Church, Milošević accepted the opposition victories.[210] However, state and governing-party structures remained intact and the protests failed to topple Milošević.

In 1997, Milošević opted to respect Serbia's presidential term limits and was elected, by the Yugoslav parliament, to the presidency of Yugoslavia. However, his effort to impose loyalist Zoran Lilić as his Serbian successor failed when – despite fraud – Lilić lost to ultranationalist candidate Vojislav Šešelj.[211] The election was annulled on the dubious grounds that turnout was below the 50 percent required by law, and new elections (again marred by fraud) were won by

---

[205] See Komlenovic (1997), Holbrooke (1999), Sell (2002: 209–10), and Dragović-Soso (2003b: 124–6).

[206] "How Milosevic Stole the Election" *The New York Times Magazine*, 14 February 1993 (online: www.nyt.com). By official count, Milošević won with 53 percent of the vote, compared to 32 percent for Panić.

[207] Sekelj (2000: 64).

[208] Pribicevic (1996); Holbrooke (1999: 231–312). In 1996, Milošević used Dayton as a

cover to close down the Studio B television station (Pribicevic 1996; Thomas 1999: 260).

[209] See Brkic (1996–1997: 88), Markotich (1998), Thomas (1999: 285–318), and Gordy (2000: 99).

[210] See de Krnjevic-Miskovic (2001: 98).

[211] Šešelj had been the leader of a notoriously violent paramilitary force in Bosnia. He was later indicted for crimes against humanity by the International Criminal Tribunal for the Former Yugoslavia.

another Milošević ally, Milan Milutinović,[212] Western powers – fearing a Šešelj victory – did not protest the fraud.[213]

LINKAGE, WAR, AND AUTHORITARIAN BREAKDOWN, 1998–2000. After the implementation of the 1995 Dayton Accords, international pressure weighed more heavily on the regime. Western sanctions took a heavy toll on the economy,[214] and crucially, linkage generated sustained international attention to government abuse, particularly in Kosovo. Extensive media coverage, large-scale refugee flows, and pressure by transnational human-rights networks made it difficult for Western powers to ignore the impact of violence and instability in the region. In particular, the 1995 Srebrenica massacre in Bosnia served as a "wake-up call" in the West,[215] triggering a "swelling demand for tough action against Serbia" among human-rights and other groups.[216] In 1998, Milošević's offensive in Kosovo "grabbed Western headlines... [and] the United States and its allies came under growing pressure to act."[217] Demands for action were rooted in moral concern that mass murder could not be allowed in what U.S. President Bill Clinton called "the heart of Europe."[218] Security interests also played a role; according to Daalder and O'Hanlan (2000), "traditional national self-interest argue[d] for quelling violence in the Balkans because instability there can affect key allies more directly than instability in most other parts of the world."[219] The perceived cost of inaction in Bosnia induced Western powers to move aggressively against the regime, including tightened international sanctions,[220] support for opposition groups, and – finally – NATO air strikes beginning in March 1999.[221] After 78 days of NATO bombing, Milošević abandoned Kosovo.

Although the NATO attack initially rallied public support behind Milošević,[222] it ultimately weakened the regime in several ways. In the first place, the humiliating loss of Kosovo, together with the economic devastation caused by tightened sanctions and war (the NATO bombings alone inflicted $30 billion to $40 billion in damage to the economy), eroded public support for the

---

[212] See Markotich (1998), Thomas (1999: 352), Cohen (2001a: 227–8), and de Krnjevic-Miskovic (2001: 99–103).
[213] Thomas (1999: 393).
[214] Thomas (1999: 163).
[215] Pond (2006: 30). See also Heinemann-Gruder (2001).
[216] Sell (2002: 237).
[217] Sell (2002: 285). See also Nye (1999: 30) and Macgregor (2001: 99).
[218] Carpenter (2002: 23). See also Daalder and O'Hanlon (2000: 13). As Pond (2006: 104) wrote, it was widely believed that "this kind of atrocity [should not] happen in Europe." Indeed, NATO chose to take action against Yugoslavia while doing far less to deal with humanitarian crises in Sudan, Afghanistan, Angola, and Ethiopia, where humanitarian emergencies were arguably

worse (Daalder and O'Hanlon 2000: 194).
[219] Daalder and O'Hanlan (2000: 12).
[220] The United States and EU froze the international assets of regime elites, banned new foreign investment, barred Yugoslav airlines from flying to Western countries, and imposed travel bans on top regime figures (Dragović-Soso 2003b: 127; Lebor 2004: 294).
[221] In response, Milošević sought Russian support and lobbied to join the Russian–Belarusian Union (Doder and Branson 1999: 70). However, the Yeltsin government did little to help Milošević and in fact provided passive consent for NATO's actions (Sell 2002: 308–9).
[222] Cohen (2001b: 99); Dragović-Soso (2003b: 127); Pavlakovic (2005: 25).

government.[223] Perhaps even more important, the conflict weakened the state's coercive capacity.[224] Sanctions and economic collapse left the government unable to dispense patronage and pay state salaries.[225] Increasingly, then, the Serbian army, police forces, and business elite "no longer believed Milošević could protect their interests."[226] In this context, the state that had bolstered Milošević's power for a decade began to crumble beneath him. Army and police command structures weakened, giving rise to unprecedented rebellion within their ranks.[227] Coup rumors abounded, and "hundreds of officers ordered to Kosovo...simply refused to deploy."[228] By mid-2000, even the Secret Service appears to have abandoned Milošević.[229]

In this context, Milošević's authoritarian coalition unraveled. Momčilo Perišić, a respected general, broke with Milošević in late 1998, complaining that Serbia "had no allies."[230] Ex-Yugoslav president Zoran Lilić also defected from the government in response to Serbia's growing international isolation.[231] Simultaneously, the West's asset freeze and travel ban "sowed dissent among the senior ranks of the Milošević regime, by hitting key figures in their pockets and humiliated them by refusing them visas."[232] As state discipline crumbled, Milošević relied increasingly on cronies who had little authority within the security forces.[233]

Milošević was thus in a very weak position in 2000. He presided over a ruined economy, he enjoyed little public support, and his control of the security forces was increasingly in question. Anticipating further economic deterioration,[234] and apparently believing the opposition too divided to pose a threat, Milošević called early presidential elections for October 2000.[235]

---

[223] See Bardos (2001: 419), LeBor (2004: 220), and Pavlakovic (2005: 25–6).

[224] Cohen (2001a: 316–17).

[225] Kearns (1999); Cohen (2001a: 321–2).

[226] Pavlakovic (2005: 26); see also Doder and Branson (1999: 281).

[227] See Cohen (2001a: 414–25), Sell (2002: 329), Bujosevic and Radovanovic (2003), and LeBor (2004: 279–83).

[228] Macgregor (2001: 97); Sell (2002: 313, 329). On coup rumors, see Judah (2002: 150, 167) and LeBor (2004: 279–83). Subsequently, as many as 80 percent of army officers voted for the opposition, Koštunica, in the 2000 elections (Cohen 2001a: 417).

[229] According to Vasic (2001), "the prevailing mood [in the secret service]...was that Milošević's sell-by date was nearing and that the service's corporate and professional interests should somehow be protected."

[230] Quoted in Cohen (2001a: 251).

[231] Doder and Branson (1999: 280); LeBor (2004: 278–9). In addition, longtime Secret

Service chief Jovica Stanišić was dismissed after questioning Milošević's Kosovo policy (Doder and Branson 1999: 248).

[232] LeBor (2004: 294). See also Doder and Branson (1999: 281).

[233] For example, Vlajko Stojiljković, who was primarily known for his police experience in Milošević's home town, was named head of the Interior Ministry (Cohen 2001a: 214; Bujosevic and Radovanovic 2003: 24; Lebor 2004: 272, 300).

[234] According to Damjan de Krnjevic-Miskovic (2001: 103), Milošević called early elections in 2000 because "the country's infrastructure was collapsing. [Milošević] knew, for example, that the electrical grid could not withstand another high-demand season."

[235] In July 2000, the Yugoslav constitution was reformed to allow for direct presidential elections. Milošević engineered this change to reduce the power of Montenegro, which was providing critical support to the Serbian opposition (Moore 2000d).

The political climate in the run-up to the 2000 election was repressive. Major independent media – including the influential B-92 radio station – were shut down in 1998 and 1999. The regime also grew increasingly violent, orchestrating a failed assassination attempt on opposition leader Vuk Drašković in 1999 and killing ex-communist (and potential rival) Ivan Stambolić in August 2000.[236] Yet opposition forces enjoyed important advantages. For example, much of the opposition – including Zoran Đinđić's influential Democratic Party – united into the Democratic Opposition of Serbia (DOS), which backed the presidential candidacy of Vojislav Koštunica, who quickly earned broad public support. Opposition forces also benefited from massive Western assistance. In the run-up to the election, the United States and EU provided the opposition with $40 million to $70 million, which was used to support independent media, activists' salaries, polling, and a massive get-out-the-vote campaign.[237] Coordinated, in part, from a satellite U.S. embassy in Budapest, opposition-party assistance reached every major area of Serbia.[238] Western officials also worked to encourage opposition unity. Opposition leaders frequently were brought to Berlin and given strong incentives to cooperate.[239]

Facing defeat, the government attempted to steal the 2000 election.[240] Although opposition counts showed Koštunica ahead with 52 percent of the vote, government officials gave him only 48.96 percent, thereby necessitating a runoff. In response to the fraud, opposition forces called a general strike. On October 5, more than 600 thousand demonstrators gathered in Belgrade and stormed parliament, SPS headquarters, and Radio-Television Serbia.[241] The weakened Serbian state met opposition protests with near-total passivity and even open disobedience.[242] The Interior Ministry's authority over the police "was nonexistent," as officers across the country refused orders to come to the capital to defend the regime.[243] In Belgrade, many of the police who were deployed against protesters seeking to storm parliament simply lay down their weapons.[244] Likewise, the Secret Service "didn't move a finger" to protect Milošević.[245] Left unprotected, Milošević resigned, and Koštunica took over as

---

[236] On these assassination cases, see Moore (1999b), Pribicevic (2004: 107), and Pavlovic and Qirezi (2005).

[237] Carothers (2001: 3), LeBor (2004: 304), and Pavlakovic (2005: 27). As one British diplomat remarked, "There was so much money pouring into the opposition that Milošević would have been justified in canceling the election on the grounds of outside interference" (quoted in Lebor 2004: 304).

[238] Carothers (2001: 2); LeBor (2004: 298–9).

[239] LeBor (2004: 301).

[240] On fraud in the 2000 election, see Cohen (2001a).

[241] See Cohen (2001a: 410–15), Bujosevic and Radovanovic (2003: 47–97), and Thompson and Kuntz (2004).

[242] See Sell (2002: 347–51) and Bujosevic and Radovanovic (2003: 9–11, 41, 55, 57, 98).

[243] Bujosevic and Radovanovic (2003: 24); "How Milosevic was Ousted," *The Observer* 8 October 2000 (online: www.guardian.co.uk/).

[244] Sell (2002: 347).

[245] Vasic (2001). Đinđić reportedly obtained assurances from the special forces that they would not intervene (Bujosevic and Radovanovic 2003). Thus, according to Pavlakovic (2005: 29), "the final push to topple Milošević was carried out by former army and paramilitary troops."

Yugoslav President.[246] DOS won special Serbian parliamentary elections held in December 2000, and opposition leader Zoran Đinđić became Prime Minister in January 2001.

Ultimately, then, Milošević's fall was a product of regime weakness. Opposition protest was massive and well organized[247]; however, by 2000, the regime had been transformed into a "straw house" that could very well have fallen in the face of even modest protest. As one account stated, "Milošević's defeat came suddenly.... The throne on which the regime sat was already rotten. When the first leg was kicked away, everything crashed to the ground."[248]

DEMOCRATIZATION AFTER MILOŠEVIĆ. The post-Milošević regime was crisis-ridden and, initially, not fully democratic. A fierce rivalry between President Koštunica and Prime Minister Đinđić resulted in a parliamentary boycott by Koštunica's Democratic Party of Serbia (DSS), followed by a Đinđić-led attempt to expel 21 DSS deputies from parliament.[249] The Đinđić government engaged in other abuse as well, including denial of licenses to – and occasional threats against – independent media.[250] Finally, after Đinđić was assassinated in 2003 by supporters of the old regime, a state of emergency brought harsh censorship laws and the closure of an opposition newspaper – dealing a "severe blow to the weak democracy in Serbia."[251]

Full democratization was facilitated by intense Western engagement. Serbia "remained firmly under the influence of the international community" in the early 2000s.[252] The EU provided five billion euros to Serbia and Montenegro between 2000 and 2004; in 2005, Serbia signed an EU Stabilization and Association Agreement.[253] In this context, Serbia's political elite considered the support of Western governments, institutions, and NGOs to be of "great importance" and thus sought to cultivate an image as "pro-European politicians."[254] Western officials closely scrutinized the new regime, at times playing a critical role in thwarting governmental abuse. As early as 2001, the Council of Europe chided Đinđić for denying licenses to opposition media.[255] In 2002, OSCE pressure helped convince the Đinđić government to reinstate pro-Koštunica deputies who had been expelled from parliament. In 2003, the repressive turn that began after the Đinđić assassination was reversed because of "strong pressure coming from Western diplomats."[256] By late 2003, Serbia had democratized: Elections in 2003

---

[246] For detailed accounts of Milošević's fall, see Bujosevic and Radovanovic (2003) and Thompson and Kuntz (2004).

[247] Thompson and Kuntz (2004).

[248] Bujosevic and Radovanovic (2003: 140).

[249] Moore (2002a); Stojkovic (2002).

[250] Committee to Protect Journalists "Attacks on the Press 2002: Yugoslavia" (www.cpj .org); Committee to Protect Journalists "Serbia: CPJ Concerned about Safety of Independent Journalist." 15 July, 2002 (www.cpj.org); *East European Constitutional Review* (2002).

[251] Antonic (2003). See also Mitic (2004) and Pavlakovic (2005: 39). Đinđić was apparently assassinated by former Secret Service members who feared prosecution (Edmunds 2007).

[252] Mitic (2004).

[253] Tocci (2004: 562); Mitic (2005); Jovanovic (2006).

[254] Antonic (2003: 118).

[255] See *East European Constitutional Review* (2002).

[256] Antonic (2003: 118).

and 2004 were "free and fair, with few (if any) irregularities," media abuse largely ceased, and state-run television became much more balanced.[257]

After 2003, ties to the West played an important role in keeping authoritarian and nationalist forces from power.[258] Although ultranationalist leader Vojislav Šešelj surrendered to international authorities in 2003, his Radical Party (SRS) remained a major political force, capturing a plurality of seats in the 2003 parliamentary election. Yet, there existed broad public support for EU integration, and progress in EU negotiations was widely considered important for government survival.[259] As a result, Šešelj's pariah status had an important impact at both the elite and mass levels. After the 2003 election, four pro-Western parties united to exclude the Radicals and elect Koštunica Prime Minister. In 2004, Boris Tadić, the presidential candidate of Đinđić's Democratic Party, defeated SRS candidate Tomislav Nikolić, in part by raising the specter of international isolation.[260] Four years later, Tadić again defeated Nikolić in an election that was viewed as a "referendum on Serbia's relations with Europe."[261] Tadić's second-round victory was attributed to the "widespread feeling . . . that Serbia was really choosing between a prosperous and stable future inside the EU and more of the nationalism and isolation of the past."[262] Importantly, nationalist parties moderated over the course of the decade. The SPS replaced Milošević with a more moderate leadership and applied for membership in the Socialist International.[263] Similarly, the SRS split in 2008 as Nikolić and 15 other SRS legislators embraced EU membership.[264]

In summary, Serbia, like Nicaragua (see Chapter 4), is a case of a relatively strong competitive authoritarian regime that was weakened by large-scale Western intervention. Sanctions and a NATO-led bombing attack eroded the organizational and economic bases of the regime, and Western assistance was critical to the opposition's victory in 2000. Continued Western engagement after 2000 helped to keep Serbia on a democratic path.

Croatia

In Croatia, as in Serbia, violent ethnic conflict contributed to the rise of competitive authoritarian rule in the 1990s. Broad public support, cohesive state and party structures, and a relatively permissive international context allowed Franjo Tuđman and his Croatian Democratic Union (HDZ) to remain in power for a decade (1990–2000). However, external pressure increased after the resolution of the Bosnian conflict and, following Tuđman's death in late 1999, the HDZ came

---

[257] Bieber (2006). See also ODIHR (2003a, 2004c, 2004e) and Pavlovic and Qirezi (2005).

[258] Pavlakovic (2005: 36).

[259] Jovanovic (2005, 2006).

[260] Grubanovic (2004).

[261] "Serbia election victory for Tadić." BBC online, 4 February 2008.

[262] Loza (2008).

[263] Jovanovic (2008). In the 2008 parliamentary elections, Tadić's staunchly pro-European Democratic Party won a plurality of seats and was able to form a coalition government.

[264] *Transitions Online* (2008).

under intense pressure to hold clean elections and, ultimately, to leave power. Croatia remained democratic after 2000.

Linkage, Leverage, and Organizational Power

Croatia is a case of high leverage and high linkage. A small state with no black-knight support, Croatia was vulnerable, under most circumstances, to Western democratizing pressure. As in Serbia, however, external pressure initially was limited due to Western powers' desire for Croatian cooperation in resolving the Balkan conflicts.[265] Thus, it was only in the late 1990s that Croatia felt the full impact of Western leverage.

High linkage was rooted in Tito's open-borders policy and Croatia's proximity to Western Europe.[266] Thus, even as military conflict discouraged investment and tourism in the early 1990s,[267] trade with the West constituted about half of Croatia's GDP.[268] Diaspora ties also were extensive: An estimated 4.5 million Croatians lived abroad, mostly in North America and Western Europe.[269] Indeed, Western émigré communities played a major role in founding and financing the HDZ.[270] Finally, the Croatian Catholic Church – which maintained extensive transnational ties – provided a powerful voice in favor of democracy and ethnic tolerance and in opposition to isolation from Europe.[271]

Organizational power was medium high. Party scope was medium. Founded in 1989 in a context of nationalist mobilization, the HDZ built a solid national structure by 1990.[272] We score party cohesion as medium because although the HDZ was a new party, it was rooted in a salient nationalist ideology.[273] Coercive capacity was medium high. The Croatian state was born weak. Serbia's inheritance of the Yugoslav army forced Croatia to build much of its coercive apparatus "from scratch,"[274] and as a result, it lost up to a third of its territory to Serbian forces in 1991–1992. However, wartime state-building – with large-scale Western training and assistance – allowed the army to retake control over most of Serb-held territory by the mid-1990s.[275] At the same time, the HDZ government built a vast internal security apparatus, which brought coercive scope to at least

---

[265] See Holbrooke (1999: 273) and Sell (2002).

[266] Zimmerman (1987); Moore (1992b: 82). Croatia experienced heavy flows of Western tourism under Tito (Moore 2000c); by 1973, more than 224,000 Croatian citizens – 18 percent of the active labor force – were employed abroad (Pickering and Baskin 2008: 522).

[267] Bacinic and Dominis (1992); Bacinic (1993: 34).

[268] International Monetary Fund Direction of Trade Statistics database (CD-ROM).

[269] Moore 2000c; Winland (2004: 76). As Moore (2000c) stated, "[a]lmost every Croatian family has some friend or relative working abroad."

[270] See Cohen (1997: 86), Sucic (1997), Wayland (2003), and Moore (1994: 10). In the

early 1990s, the HDZ had branches in 35 U.S. cities (Moore 1994: 10). By strengthening the HDZ, these particular ties to the West initially facilitated authoritarian rule. Overall, however, linkage clearly undermined Croatian authoritarianism after the Cold War.

[271] Moore (1999c); Bellamy (2001: 19–20).

[272] Pickering and Baskin (2008: 528). HDZ benefited enormously from Communist Party defections.

[273] Bellamy (2003).

[274] Edmunds (2007: 121–5); see also Zunec (1996: 216–22).

[275] On Western training and assistance, see Moore (1996: 116), Holbrooke (1999: 191), and Mueller (2000: 64–5).

medium.[276] Cohesion was high; born into a nationalist war, Croatia's security forces were infused with a strong nationalist identity.[277] Cohesion was reinforced by military victories over Serbian forces in 1995.[278]

Origins and Evolution of the Regime

Croatia's competitive authoritarian regime emerged in a context of nationalism and ethnic violence.[279] After sweeping to power in 1990 via a nationalist appeal, Tuđman and the HDZ led Croatia to independence in 1991. New elections in 1992 produced a landslide victory for Tuđman and a parliamentary majority for the HDZ. Taking advantage of a surge of nationalist support and the weakness of its opponents, the Tuđman government concentrated power and skewed the playing field. The HDZ abused state resources and used insider privatization to dominate access to private-sector finance.[280] With privatized stations in the hands of HDZ allies, television was "tightly controlled by the government."[281] Moreover, the government made widespread use of libel laws to bully independent media.[282] The HDZ also maintained tight control over the electoral authorities, which it used to repeatedly manipulate the rules of the game.[283] Elections were skewed by laws that allowed ethnic Croats living abroad – but not Croatian Serbs who had fled in the early 1990s – to vote, which gave the HDZ a critical advantage.[284] Under these conditions, the HDZ easily retained its majority in the 1995 parliamentary election. In 1997, Tuđman was reelected president in a race that "did not meet the minimum standards for a meaningful and democratic election."[285]

The regime initially faced only limited democratizing pressure. In part, this was due to Tuđman's popularity, which was reinforced by military success and the president's ability to manipulate nationalist appeals and security threats to sideline opposition challenges.[286] At the same time, opposition forces were fragmented and lacked mobilizational capacity.[287] Crucially, moreover, external pressure was limited by competing Western security objectives. Because Western

---

[276] See Milivojevic (1994) and Zunec (1996: 228).

[277] Edmunds (2007: 53–6).

[278] Soberg (2007: 46).

[279] See *Uncaptive Minds* (1993a: 77) and Cohen (1997: 73–4).

[280] Kearns (1998: 254); Fisher (2006: 83–100).

[281] Fisher (2006: 129).

[282] Fisher (2006: 129); see also Basom (1995), Cohen (1997: 88), and Bjelakovic and Tatic (1998: 185).

[283] See Bacinic and Dominis (1993: 17), Basom (1995), ODIHR (1997e), and Cular (2000: 33).

[284] Croatians in the diaspora were provided a special nongeographic district of 12 parliamentary seats, which grossly overrepresented them (Human Rights Watch 1999).

[285] ODIHR (1997e: 1).

[286] See Markovich (1998: 92), Fisher (2006: 125), Haughton and Fisher (2008), and Pickering and Baskin (2008: 531).

[287] Pusic (1998: 119); Markovich (1998: 90–1); Fisher (2006: 143, 151, 155–6); Haughton and Fisher (2008: 445). The only major opposition protest occurred in 1996, when opposition forces mobilized 100 thousand people against a government decision not to renew the license of the popular independent radio station, Radio 101 (Fisher 2006: 134). The Tuđman government routinely divided the opposition by co-opting its leaders at key moments (Sucic 1997; Fisher 2006: 151). In 1997, for example, Tuđman bribed opposition leaders in the Zagreb city council in order to deprive the opposition of control over the capital (Pusic 1998: 120).

powers endeavored to strengthen Croatian forces as a counterweight to the Serbs and then later sought Tuđman's cooperation in the Bosnian peace process, "the democratization agenda of the EU was often lost."[288] By cooperating with international peacemaking efforts, Tuđman gained the toleration, if not support, of Western powers.[289] Hence, the cost of government abuse remained low.[290]

Following the conclusion of the Dayton Accords, however, Croatia was exposed to greater external pressure.[291] For example, the failure to implement reforms required by Croatia's admission to the Council of Europe triggered increasing Western criticism and pushed Croatia toward "pariah status" in Europe.[292] In the late 1990s, the United States, EU, OSCE, and Council of Europe issued a series of joint declarations calling for fairer media access, an independent electoral authority, and other reforms.[293] In 1999, EU officials determined that Croatia had failed to meet the political conditions necessary for a Stabilization and Association Agreement. These actions imposed heavy costs on the government. Amid growing isolation, the Croatian economy fell into recession in the late 1990s, and key domestic actors, including the Church, grew critical of the country's detachment from Europe.[294]

Yet it was Tuđman's death in December 1999 that created a real opening for democracy.[295] Disoriented and divided following the loss of its founder, the HDZ grew more open to outside pressure.[296] Incentives to comply with regional democratic norms were strong. Croatia's access to external finance increasingly depended on its relations with Europe.[297] Moreover, a framework for conditionality was established in 1999, when the EU launched a Stabilization and Association Process (SAP) for the Balkan states. Although Croatia would not sign a Stabilization and Association Agreement until 2001, the SAP created a "formalized framework for political dialogue" aimed at setting "higher incentives and more demanding political . . . conditions," which would eventually set the country on a path toward EU membership.[298]

---

[288] Tull (2003: 132). See also Sucic (1997); Kearns (1998: 249); Zuzul (1998); *RFE/RL Newsline* July 28, 1997; *RFE/RL Newsline* August 19, 1997; and *RFE/RL Newsline* April 29, 1997 (Online: http://www.rferl.org/archive/en-newsline/latest/683/683.html).

[289] Power (1995).

[290] Although Croatia's application to join the Council of Europe was suspended in 1993 and 1995, it was later admitted, despite continued abuse, in 1996 (Moore 1993; Sucic 1997). Although Croatia was denied access to PHARE funding (*East European Constitutional Review* 1998), it continued to receive military and other assistance from the West.

[291] Kearns (1998: 248); Tull (2003: 145).

[292] Fisher (2000b). Due primarily to the ethnic cleansing of Serbs, Croatia was denied access

to EU PHARE assistance through the end of the decade.

[293] Human Rights Watch (1999). Simultaneously, Western assistance was increasingly directed toward democracy promotion and civil society rather than the government (Ottaway and Maltz 2001: 277; Fisher 2006: 135, 143–4).

[294] Moore (1999c, 2000a).

[295] Howard and Roessler (2006).

[296] Bellamy (2001: 26).

[297] In the early 2000s, Croatia's credit rating hinged on its fulfillment of European conditionality regarding the International Criminal Tribunal for the Former Yugoslavia (ICTY) (*Transitions Online* 2002).

[298] Fisher (2000b).

The international dimension was critical to the outcome of the 2000 parliamentary and presidential elections. Although opposition forces remained weak and divided in the run-up to the elections, they benefited from linkage and leverage in several ways. For example, as in Romania, Serbia, and Slovakia, Western aid agencies provided large-scale assistance, helping to fund independent media and get-out-the-vote efforts.[299] External assistance was particularly critical to the success of efforts to increase turnout among younger voters – who were most likely to be pro-European.[300] Western officials also worked, with some success, to unite the disparate opposition forces.[301] Moreover, in response to external pressure, Croatia for the first time permitted domestic observers to operate on election day.[302] Finally, the issue of isolation versus EU integration likely worked to the opposition's electoral advantage.[303]

The 2000 elections were considerably cleaner than previous elections because international pressure and monitoring by foreign-funded NGOs "prevented the HDZ from resorting to outright fraud despite earlier signals that it would."[304] Opposition parties won a majority of seats in the January 2000 parliamentary election, and a multiparty coalition led by the Social Democratic Party (SDP) formed a new government, electing SDP leader Ivica Račan as Prime Minister. The February 2000 presidential election was clean, and Stjepan Mesić of the opposition Croatian People's Party won it in a runoff.

The regime democratized after 2000. Croatia became the "jewel in the crown of the EU's strategy for South-East Europe,"[305] as the new government undertook a series of democratic reforms: It eased restrictions on civic associations; restructured the security services; dramatically reduced the power of the executive branch; strengthened the Constitutional Court; and transformed the state television and radio network into an independent, Western-style public institution.[306] Libel and defamation lawsuits largely ceased,[307] and elections in 2003 (parliamentary), 2005 (presidential), and 2007 (parliamentary) were free and fair.

Democratization was heavily shaped by Croatia's ties to the West. Ending Croatia's isolation was a top priority for the new government, which viewed cooperation with the EU and NATO as essential to attracting foreign investment.[308]

---

[299] Jasic (2000: 161); Pridham (2001: 79); Fisher (2006: 203).

[300] Fisher (2006: 46–7).

[301] Although the opposition went into the election divided into two main coalitions, external pressure helped ensure a critical degree of cooperation among them. Thus, according to Fisher (2006: 156), "prodding from the National Democratic Institute" produced a "postelection cooperation agreement" in which the various opposition parties pledged to create a common government and, crucially, not to form a coalition with the HDZ."

[302] Jasic (2000: 161).

[303] Pickering and Baskin (2008: 536). Although all major parties championed European integration during the 2000 campaign (Fisher 2006: 192–3), opposition parties were better positioned to credibly promise it.

[304] Ottaway and Maltz (2001: 377). On conditions in the 2000 elections, see ODIHR (2000f, 2000g).

[305] Field (2001: 135).

[306] See Edmunds (2007: 130–1) and U.S. Department of State (2001e).

[307] Dragomir (2005).

[308] See Moore (2000b); Vujcic (2004); and *RFE/RL Newsline*, 11 May and 10 August 2000 (online: http://www.rferl.org/archive/en-newsline/latest/683/683.html).

Thus, the government "staked its reputation, and arguably its survival, on the EU."[309] Western powers reinforced incentives to govern democratically by accelerating the integration process. Within months of the 2000 election, Croatia was declared a "potential member" of the EU and admitted into NATO's Partnership for Peace Program. In 2001, Croatia signed an EU Stabilization and Association Agreement and, two years later, it officially applied for EU membership. Among the political elite, a solid consensus emerged around EU membership, which reduced the likelihood of democratic-norms violations.[310] Crucially, this consensus extended to the HDZ, which remained the strongest party in Croatia.[311] The pull of Europe reshaped the balance of power within the HDZ, strengthening moderates and marginalizing extremists.[312] Thus, in the aftermath of the 2000 defeat, a pro-European faction led by Ivo Sanader defeated more nationalist and authoritarian opponents to gain control of the party.[313] Under Sanader, the HDZ joined the European People's Party (EPP) and became a staunch advocate of EU membership.[314]

The HDZ's transformation was made manifest in 2003, when it won a plurality in parliamentary elections and Sanader was elected prime minister.[315] The minority HDZ-led government maintained Croatia's pro-European orientation. The country became an official candidate for EU membership in 2004, and formal membership negotiations began in 2005. Sensitive to its image in Europe, the Sanader government behaved democratically. For example, despite its minority status, it refused to form a coalition with the ultranationalist Croatian Party of Rights (HSP) – treated as a pariah by Western European governments – due to fear of "international isolation."[316] Instead, it forged a tacit alliance with the Independent Democratic Serbian Party – an extraordinary development given the HDZ's origins as an anti-Serbian party.[317]

In summary, although the Balkan conflict blunted the impact of Western democratizing pressure in the early and mid-1990s, linkage and leverage ultimately had a powerful democratizing impact, particularly after Tuđman's death. Despite a relatively weak and fragmented opposition, Croatia democratized rapidly in 2000 and, in a context of extensive EU engagement, remained democratic through 2008.

---

309 Boduszynski and Balalovska (2004: 25).

310 Erceg (2005).

311 See *RFE/RL Newsline*, 22 May 2001 (online: http://www.rferl.org/archive/en-newsline/latest/683/683.html).

312 Haughton and Fisher (2008: 449); Pickering and Baskin (2008: 536–7).

313 Fish and Krickovic (2003). According to Haughton and Fisher (2008: 450), HDZ's reform was facilitated by "strong links forged with . . . parties in the [European People's Party], especially the German Christian Democrats and the Austrian People's Party."

314 See Fish and Krickovic (2003: 111), Longo (2006: 37), and Haughton and Fisher (2008: 449–50).

315 Longo (2006: 37). The HDZ also won a plurality in the 2007 parliamentary election, and Sanader was reelected Prime Minister.

316 *RFE/RL Newsline* 3 December 2003 (online: http://www.rferl.org/archive/en-newsline/latest/683/683.html). See also Fisher (2006: 195). The Sanader government also deepened security-sector reform and cooperated with the controversial International Criminal Tribunal – a key European demand (Peranic 2004; Edmunds 2007: 64).

317 Fisher (2006: 195).

LINKAGE AND DEMOCRATIZATION AMIDST STATE COLLAPSE: ALBANIA AND MACEDONIA

Although Albania and Macedonia avoided large-scale ethnic violence, under-development, state weakness, and (in Macedonia) serious ethnic tension posed important obstacles to democratization. Nevertheless, extensive Western engagement strengthened states, reduced polarization, and created strong incentives for democratic behavior. By 2008, Macedonia was a democracy and Albania was a near-democracy.

Albania

Albania was a case of unstable competitive authoritarianism in the 1990s that very nearly democratized during the 2000s. Structural conditions for democracy were highly unfavorable. One of the poorest and most isolated countries in Europe, Albania lacked virtually any civil-society or democratic tradition. Under longtime ruler Enver Hoxha (1944–1985), Albania had been one of the most closed and repressive communist regimes in the world.[318] Nevertheless, due to a combination of state weakness and intense international engagement, autocrats consistently failed to consolidate power after 1990. In the late 1990s and 2000s, increasing international intervention prevented state collapse, encouraged moderation between bitterly opposed partisan rivals, and curbed authoritarian abuse. Although Albania had not fully democratized by 2008, the regime was far more stable, open, and competitive than it would have been in the absence of Western engagement.

Linkage, Leverage, and Organizational Power

Albania is a case of high leverage and high linkage. In terms of leverage, Albania was among the weakest and most externally vulnerable states in Europe.[319] With few ties to Russia (Albania broke with the Soviet Union in 1961), it had no prospect of black-knight support. Linkage was historically low because Enver Hoxha closed Albania off from external influences, transforming it into one of the most isolated countries in the world.[320] However, Albania's proximity to the West (50 miles from Italy) led to the emergence of extensive – if somewhat uneven – linkage after 1989. For example, the loosening of central controls created a "migratory tidal wave" that "unleashed a demographic shift of an

---

[318] See Prifti (1978), Sjoberg and Wyzan (1991), and Rakipi (2002).

[319] In the early 1990s, foreign aid accounted for between 24 and 59 percent of Albania's gross national income (World Bank World Development Indicators. See www.worldbank.org/data), and the country was "totally dependent on humanitarian aid from abroad to feed its people" (Biberaj 1993: 381; Zanga 1993: 77).

[320] See O'Donnell (1995: 21) and Katzikas (2004). Under Hoxha, foreign travel and

even unsanctioned contact with foreigners were forbidden and could result in imprisonment. The constitution explicitly banned foreign credit and investment (Copani and Danopoulos 1995: 124), and Albania was the only European country not to sign the Helsinki Final Act or join the CSCE (Katzikas 2004: 99). For much of the post–World War II period, the UN was the only international organization to which Albania belonged (Johnson 2001: 173).

unprecedented pace."[321] Flows of people and money were extensive. Approximately 600 thousand Albanians (15 percent of the workforce) moved abroad, and remittances – at 14 percent of GDP – became the country's primary source of foreign exchange.[322] In turn, Albanian refugee flows triggered considerable international engagement, as fear of further migration induced EU states to provide large-scale assistance and, in 1997, international peacekeepers.[323]

In terms of organizational power, Albania scores low. Party strength was medium. The two parties that dominated politics after 1991, the (ex-communist) Socialist Party (PS) and the Democratic Party (PD), were well organized and possessed strong regional bases of support (the PS in the south, the PD in the north). The PS, which governed in 1991–1992, used the old communist party infrastructure to build a strong grassroots organization – although it did not reach mass proportions.[324] The PD (which won power in 1992) was somewhat weaker organizationally, but it nevertheless possessed a national structure.[325] Cohesion is scored as medium for the PS because it was an established party without a non-material source of cohesion.[326] PD cohesion is scored as medium because, although it was a new party, it was characterized by a salient anti-communist ideology.[327]

Coercive capacity was very low. Albania may have had the weakest state in Europe. Although it had been one of the most militarized societies in the world under Hoxha, with enormous armed forces and arms caches throughout the country, poverty and isolation "led to a serious breakdown in military discipline, affecting morale, preparedness, and operational efficiency" in the 1980s.[328] Coercive structures weakened further in the early 1990s, as post-communist governments slashed military spending, purged up to two thirds of the military officer corps, dissolved the old secret police, and dismissed 70 percent of its members.[329] By the mid-1990s, the army was "weak and unmotivated"

---

[321] Carletto et al. (2006: 770). See also Monzini (2007).

[322] Bala (2002); Carletto et al. (2006: 767–8). Emigration created particularly strong ties to Italy (Belloni and Morozzo della Rocca 2008: 180), which, along with Greece, was the largest recipient of Albanian refugees (Carletto et al. 2006: 771). Indeed, Albanians became Italy's largest immigrant community (Belloni and Morozzo della Rocca 2008: 182).

[323] Zanga (1992b: 22; 1993: 75); Schmidt (1997b); Bala (2001); Johnson (2001); Tripodi (2002: 92); O'Rourke (2003). According to Zanga (1992b: 23), "refugees succeeded where diplomacy had failed in prompting others to take notice of Albania."

[324] The PS had 3,720 local branches and 100 thousand members in the early 1990s (Zanga 1994: 10–11).

[325] Zanga (1991b: 1).

[326] Copani and Danopoulos (1995: 127); Imholz (2000: 83).

[327] See Zanga (1991b). The salience of anti-communism was evidenced, for example, by the DP's promulgation of major "Genocide" and "Verification" laws in the early 1990s, which were intended to purge communists from the state apparatus (Abrahams 1996).

[328] Copani and Danopoulos (1995: 122–4). After Hoxha's break with China in 1978, Albania had no major international allies (Johnson 2001: 181), which left its military with chronic fuel and ammunition shortages, inoperable equipment, straining deficits, and an ineffective command system. See Daci (1998: 49), Gashi (1998: 30), and Vickers and Pettifer (2000: 46, 211–12).

[329] See Imholz (1995: 58), Biberaj (1998: 324, 152–3), and Vickers and Pettifer (2000: 217).

and civilian control was limited, which resulted in periodic breakdowns in social order.[330]

Origins and Evolution of the Regime

Competitive authoritarianism emerged in Albania after the fall of communism, in a context of state weakness and external dependence. Under Hoxha's successor, Ramiz Alia, Albania abandoned isolationism and sought closer ties to the West. Desperate for external assistance in 1990, the Alia government sought membership in the Commission on Security and Cooperation in Europe (CSCE) and worked to establish diplomatic relations with Western states.[331] Western powers demanded political reform, and in a context of severe economic and state crisis, the regime had little choice but to liberalize. In December 1990, in the face of a surge of uncontrolled emigration and soldiers' refusal to crack down on student demonstrators, the Alia government legalized opposition and scheduled elections for early 1991.[332] In March 1991, the communists won a majority in parliamentary elections marred by abuse of state resources, skewed access to media and finance, and voter intimidation.[333] The ex-communists (now renamed the PS) could not maintain their power, however. Food shortages and a wave of strikes and riots triggered the collapse of the government.[334] In what was "essentially a struggle for outside aid," Alia called new parliamentary elections for March 1992.[335] The PD won in a landslide.[336] Alia resigned as president and was replaced in April by PD leader Sali Berisha.

The 1992 transition did not bring democratization. The Berisha government committed a range of abuses, including harassment and arrest of opposition leaders, banning of demonstrations, confiscation of independent newspapers, and widespread use of libel suits against opposition media.[337] In 1993, the government arrested PS leader Fatos Nano, despite Western protest,[338] and in 1995, it passed "Genocide" and "Verification" laws that effectively barred numerous PS members from running for office.[339] Finally, the 1996 parliamentary election was badly flawed. The government ignored Western calls for Nano's release, excluded a large number of PS candidates, enforced tight control over media, barred opposition parties from holding outdoor meetings, and arrested numerous PS activists – citing an opposition "plot" to disrupt the vote – just prior to the election.[340] There were also credible reports of voter intimidation and fraud.[341] The Democrats won overwhelmingly, capturing 122 of 140 seats.

---

[330] Gross (1998). See also Zanga (1991c, 1992a), Biberaj (1998: 93), and Vickers and Pettifer (2000: 62, 227).

[331] Zanga (1991a: 1).

[332] Copani and Danopoulos (1995: 128); Daci (1998: 36–7).

[333] National Republican Institute for International Affairs (NRIIA) (1991).

[334] Szajkowski (1992: 119); Zanga (1992a: 18).

[335] Austin (1993: 268).

[336] The DP won 92 of 140 parliamentary seats, compared to just 38 for the Socialists.

[337] See Duffy (1995), Abrahams (1996), ODIHR (1996c), and F. Schmidt (1999b: 229–30).

[338] Angjeli (1995: 37); F. Schmidt (1999b: 227).

[339] Abrahams (1996).

[340] ODIHR (1996c); Schmidt (1997a); F. Schmidt (1999b: 229–31).

[341] ODIHR (1996c); Schmidt (1997a); F. Schmidt (1999b: 231).

The Democrats also failed to consolidate power. Less than a year after its landslide victory, the PD government fell amid a dramatic state collapse. In early 1997, the failure of numerous financial pyramid schemes in which hundreds of thousands of Albanians had invested their savings triggered massive riots and a descent into anarchy. Entire territories lay outside state control as armed bandits roamed the countryside, robbing banks, destroying public buildings, and looting arms depots that had been abandoned by security forces.[342] The military largely disintegrated and, at one point, as many as eight separate armies operated in the country.[343] A state of emergency was widely ignored; in the ensuing disorder, Nano simply walked out of prison.[344]

The crisis triggered large-scale Western intervention. Due to a surge of Albanian refugees, "[t]he Albanian problem became an Italian problem," as "the Italian press kept Albanian events on the front page for months."[345] Prodded by Italy and Greece, the OSCE brokered a compromise in March 1997 that established a transitional government and called new parliamentary elections. In April, Italy led a seven-thousand–strong UN peacekeeping force to restore order and oversee the elections.[346] In the absence of a viable central state, international actors played a major role in administering the election.[347] The Socialists won, capturing almost two thirds of parliament.[348] Nano was elected Prime Minister, and Berisha resigned the presidency and was replaced by Socialist Rexhep Meidani.

Although the level of abuse declined after 1997, Albania remained competitive authoritarian. The Socialist government used libel suits to bully the media; opposition activists were occasionally attacked or arrested; and state media, courts, and electoral authorities were politicized and deployed on behalf of the governing party.[349] Moreover, polarization and state weakness continued to threaten regime stability. The Democrats boycotted Parliament for much of the late 1990s and, in 1998, riots – in which activists seized tanks and the Prime Minister's office – forced the resignation of Prime Minister Nano.[350]

Nevertheless, international engagement continued to expand. Motivated by the 1997 crisis and the 1999 war in Kosovo, the EU invested heavily in "aid provision and civil society programs aimed at reestablishing control over public utilities and policing."[351] In 2000, the EU began negotiations toward a Stabilization and Association Agreement, signaling the possibility of eventual EU membership.[352]

---

[342] Schmidt (1998a); Biberaj (1998: 323); Nicholson (1999).

[343] See Sullivan (1997), Daci (1998: 68), Gross (1998), and Tripodi (2002: 94–5).

[344] Biberaj (1998: 325–6); Johnson (2001: 179).

[345] Belloni and Morozzo della Rocca (2008: 182).

[346] Tripodi (2002: 97–8).

[347] ODIHR (1997d); Elbasani (2007: 20).

[348] Biberaj (1998: 326–7); Johnson (2001).

[349] See U.S. Department of State (1999b, 2002d, 2002g), ODIHR (2000d, 2001a), and Human Rights Watch (2002a). See also

Committee to Protect Journalists, "Attacks on the Press 2000: Albania." (online: www. cpj.org)

[350] See Schmidt (1999b: 241) and *RFE/RL Newsline*, 29 September 1998 (online: http://www.rferl.org/archive/en-newsline/latest/683/683.html).

[351] Johnson (2001: 175). See also F. Schmidt (1999a). Foreign aid increased markedly, from 29th highest (per capita) in the world in 1994 to 4th highest in 1999 (Johnson 2001: 175).

[352] Puto (2006).

U.S. and European officials also actively intervened to reduce polarization and encourage the major parties to work within democratic institutional norms.[353] Finally, international actors played a central role in elections. The OSCE sent large observer teams to Albania to monitor even local elections and referenda.[354] As a result, increasing care was given to legal and electoral norms, and elections that were deemed problematic were often repeated.[355]

Although the 2001 parliamentary elections – in which the Socialists retained their majority – were fairer than previous elections, they were marked by abuse of state resources and at least some fraud,[356] which led to the PD's rejection of the results and another parliamentary boycott. In response, the EU pressed the Socialists to underutilize their power and reincorporate the Democrats into the democratic process. In mid-2002, the European Parliament invited the rival party leaders to Brussels to negotiate a mutually acceptable choice for president. Thus, despite having the votes to impose a partisan ally, the Socialists voted with the Democrats to elect Alfred Moisiu, a nonpartisan technocrat, as president.[357]

International actors were heavily involved in the 2005 parliamentary election. The EU made the signing of a Stabilization and Association Agreement contingent on a successful election, and international actors pushed reform on several fronts.[358] The OSCE and USAID oversaw substantial improvements in the vote-counting process and, under pressure from EU officials, the Socialists created a more balanced electoral commission, revised the voter registry, and redrew what had been heavily gerrymandered district boundaries.[359] The elections were subject to intense scrutiny. International observers monitored 97 percent of the vote-counting centers.[360] Notwithstanding abuse of state resources and some multiple voting, the election was viewed as the cleanest yet.[361] The opposition Democrats won a parliamentary plurality and formed a coalition government, again headed by Sali Berisha.

By 2008, Albania was very nearly democratic. Radio and television were "diverse and competitive" and civil liberties were increasingly well protected.[362] The 2009 election (in which the Democrats eked out a victory over the Socialists) was free of serious violations.[363] Nevertheless, independent media continued to suffer financial pressure and periodic attacks: libel suits remained "common" and

[353] For example, U.S. pressure helped convince the PD to end its boycott of Parliament in 1999 (Schmidt 1999b).

[354] See, for example, ODIHR (1999a, 2000e).

[355] See ODIHR (2000e; 2001b: 16; 2004a: 22).

[356] ODIHR (2001b). Media access was relatively even, and opposition harassment virtually ceased.

[357] Moore (2002b); Elbasani (2004: 41–3).

[358] *RFERL Newsline* 2 February 2005 (online: http://www.rferl.org/archive/en-newsline/latest/683/683.html).

[359] See Elbasani (2007: 33–4) and Freedom House, "Freedom in the World 2006: Albania." (online: www.freedomhouse.org)

[360] ODIHR (2005b: 20).

[361] ODIHR (2005b); Elbasani (2007: 36). See also Freedom House, "Freedom in the World 2006: Albania." (online: www.freedomhouse.org)

[362] U.S. Department of State (2006a, 2008a, 2009a); Austin (2009).

[363] See ODIHR (2009a).

reporters were still subject to intimidation and physical attack.[364] Thus, although Albania was very nearly democratic (and was widely characterized as such) in 2008, we score it as competitive authoritarian.

In summary, Albania's proximity and ties to the West powerfully shaped its post–Cold War democratization. Western intervention and aid helped secure social order and strengthen the state at key moments.[365] Beginning in the late 1990s, growing Western involvement encouraged democratic behavior among the major parties. Hence, although EU membership remained a distant prospect in 2008, Albania was nearly democratic.

Macedonia

Like Albania, Macedonia was an unlikely democratizer. It was the poorest and most closed of the Yugoslav republics, with virtually no active dissident movement and a weak post-communist civil society.[366] Moreover, ethnic tension between the majority Slavic population and minority Albanians (roughly a quarter of the population) simmered throughout the post–Cold War period.[367] Nevertheless, Macedonia had democratized by the late 2000s, due in large part to intense Western engagement.

Linkage, Leverage, and Organizational Power
Macedonia is a case of high leverage and high linkage. On the one hand, it was small, aid-dependent, and lacked black-knight support.[368] On the other hand, ties to the West – particularly trade and migration ties – were extensive.[369] Although diplomatic tension with Greece delayed widespread international recognition until 1993–1994,[370] Macedonia's proximity to Western Europe and fears of ethnic violence motivated large-scale Western engagement in the early 1990s.

---

[364] Freedom House, "Freedom in the World 2009: Albania" (online: www.freedomhouse.org). In 2008, the independent News 24 was fined for broadcasting an ad that was critical of the government. The government also attempted to evict an independent newspaper, *Tema*, from its headquarters, and it may have been behind a physical attack on the newspaper's publisher. See Freedom House, "Freedom of the Press 2009: Albania" (online: www.freedomhouse.org); and Committee to Protect Journalists, "Albania: Police Block Newspaper Staff from Entering Offices." 9 January 2009 (online: www.cpj.org).

[365] See Guri (2005).

[366] Andrejevich (1991b: 28); Petkovski, Petreski, and Slaveski (1993: 35); Poulton (1993: 30).

[367] Macedonia was often described as an ethnic "tinder box" (cf. Braun 1992). The country

faced potential threats of irredentism coming from four neighbors: Albania, Bulgaria, Greece, and Serbia (Perry 1992: 13; Buechsenschuetz 2001b; Pond 2006: 169). The threat of conflict was further heightened by civil wars in Kosovo and Bosnia.

[368] Between 1998 and 2002, aid accounted for between 13 and 39 percent of gross capital formation, and between 3 and 8 percent of gross national income (World Bank World Development Indicators (online: www.worldbank.org/data).

[369] By 2000, trade with the United States and Western Europe equaled more than half of Macedonia's GDP. According to our estimates, per capita emigration to the West was about three times the average for our post-Soviet cases. (See Appendix III).

[370] Dion (1997: 97–8).

International organizations – including the UN, the OSCE, and the International Commission on Former Yugoslavia (ICFY) Working Group on Ethnic and National Communities and Minorities – established a strong presence in the country and remained there throughout the decade.[371]

Organizational power was low. Party strength was medium. The ex-communist Social Democratic Union of Macedonia (SDSM), which governed through 1998, was characterized by medium scope and cohesion. The SDSM drew on the old League of Communists of Macedonia's extensive infrastructure to build a relatively strong national organization.[372] It was not a mass party, however, and it lacked a clear ideology or other nonmaterial source of cohesion. The Internal Macedonian Revolutionary Organization (VMRO-DPMNE), which won power in 1998, was weaker in organizational terms,[373] but it had established offices in most major cities by the mid-1990s. Although a new party, VMRO-DPMNE had a salient nationalist ideology.[374] Hence, we score it as medium cohesion.

Coercive capacity was low. The Macedonian state was "weak and fragile" in the early 1990s, relying on external support for survival.[375] Macedonia's military was "the weakest by far of all the Balkan states."[376] Serbian control of the Yugoslav army deprived the Macedonian government of "virtually all equipment needed to run a modern military, including armor, artillery and air defenses."[377] Coercive capacity remained low throughout the 1990s, and the state maintained only limited control over Albanian-dominated northwest Macedonia.[378]

Origins and Evolution of the Regime

Competitive authoritarianism emerged soon after Macedonia's 1990 transition to multiparty rule. Although the nationalist VMRO-DPMNE won a plurality (37 of 120 seats) in the 1990 parliamentary election, the ex-communist SDSM (26 seats) cobbled together a multiparty coalition and thus retained control of the government.[379] In 1991, SDSM leader Kiro Gligorov was elected President and oversaw Macedonia's declaration of independence. The SDSM ruled in a competitive authoritarian manner. The government harassed opposition activists and "tightly control[led] public and certain private media."[380] State television and radio retained a monopoly on national broadcasting and, in 1995, more than 80 private radio and TV stations were shut down on the pretext that they were

---

[371] UN troops were sent in 1992 to prevent the spread of ethnic conflict from Serbia. See Dion (1997: 97–8), Ackermann (1999), and Zahariadis (2003). Indeed, Macedonia grew "highly dependent for its security on international organizations" (Ackermann 2003: 116). See also Liotta and Jeb (2002: 97), Boduszynski and Balalovska (2004: 20), and Pond (2006: 168–87).

[372] Perry (1998: 123); Schmidt (1998b).

[373] Avirovic (1995: 72).

[374] K. Brown (2001).

[375] Ackerman (2003: 111, 116).

[376] Perry (1994: 120).

[377] Perry (2000: 133).

[378] In 2001, Macedonian territorial integrity was seriously threatened by Albanian paramilitary forces (Krause 2001, 2002, 2004; Hislope 2004: 22).

[379] Andrejevich (1990c).

[380] Krause (2003); see also *Uncaptive Minds* (1993b: 86–7).

pirating frequencies of foreign stations.[381] Gligorov was reelected in 1994 in a vote marked by widespread reports of voter intimidation and fraud.[382] This prompted a VMRO-DPMNE boycott of the second round of parliamentary elections, which left the SDSM with 95 of 120 seats in the legislature.

Macedonia's regime trajectory was powerfully shaped by Western engagement. Beginning in 1992, when UN troops were sent to prevent the spread of ethnic conflict from Serbia,[383] Western actors – and particularly the EU – were heavily involved in Macedonian politics. In 1992–1993, the EU began to offer PHARE assistance, a program that targeted future EU candidates.[384] The European embrace had a major impact on the regime. A broad elite- and mass-level consensus emerged around the EU,[385] and both government and opposition adhered increasingly to regional norms. For example, the nationalist VMRO-DPMNE, which had made strong anti-Albanian appeals in the early 1990s,[386] began to forge alliances with Albanian groups out of fear that regional pariah status would hinder its efforts to win power.[387] For its part, the SDSM government permitted extensive international observation of elections, which improved their quality and fairness. In the late 1990s, flawed elections in particular districts were routinely re-run to ensure that they were deemed clean.[388] Partly as a result, the 1998 parliamentary elections were considered "a significant improvement on past elections."[389] The VMRO-DPMNE won a plurality and formed a new coalition government.

The removal of the ex-communists from power did not immediately bring democratization. The VMRO-DPMNE–led government bullied the media,[390] and the 1999 presidential election – won by VMRO-DPMNE candidate Boris Trajkovski – was marred by media bias and "a number of irregularities," particularly in the Albanian western regions.[391] Like its predecessor, however, the VMRO-DPMNE's ability to consolidate power was constrained by state weakness and the accelerating process of European integration. In 2001, clashes between the government and Albanian militias, in which the "small and ill-trained Macedonian security force" was nearly overcome by loosely organized paramilitaries,[392] appeared to bring Macedonia to the brink of civil war.[393] The conflict triggered large-scale Western intervention. NATO and EU envoys mediated the Ohrid Framework Agreement between the government and Albanian forces,[394] and NATO troops played a major role in disarming the population

---

[381] Geroski (1995).

[382] Glenny (1995: 149).

[383] Glenny (1995: 155).

[384] Schmidt (1998b).

[385] Stavrova (2004a, 2004b).

[386] Zahariadis (2003: 266).

[387] K. Brown (2001: 133).

[388] See ODIHR (1998a: 26, 2000a: 16, 2002: 16). See also *RFE/RL Newsline*, 26 November 1999 (online: http://www.rferl.org/archive/en-newsline/latest/683/683.html).

[389] ODIHR (1998a: 3).

[390] Journalists were subjected to libel suits and attacks by police and, in 2001, the government closed one of the country's few private newspapers, *Makadonija Denes* (Krause 2002, 2003).

[391] Georgievski and Skaric (2000: 94); Krause (2000); ODIHR (2000a: 22).

[392] Pond (2006: 172–3).

[393] On the conflict, see also O'Shea (2001) and Ackermann (2003).

[394] Fraser (2002: 361).

and ensuring the Accord's implementation.[395] Macedonia thus was transformed into a "de facto international protectorate."[396] Macedonia also signed an EU Stabilization and Association Agreement in 2001, which – by placing the country on track to be an EU candidate – heightened the level of external scrutiny and conditionality.[397]

Western engagement encouraged increasingly democratic behavior in the 2000s. Due in large part to EU pressure, national media were relatively free of interference after 2001.[398] State media grew less biased, and private media – which had grown exponentially by the end of the decade – offered voters a wide range of views.[399] In the 2002 parliamentary election – despite problems such as attacks on journalists and violence at some polling stations[400] – an SDSM-led opposition coalition (Together for Macedonia) was able to win 60 of 120 seats and gain control of the government, ushering in Macedonia's second turnover. Gradual democratization continued under the SDSM. Albanian armed rebels – confident of the protection provided by EU integration – disarmed, created a new political party, and joined the governing coalition in 2002.[401] At the same time, widespread public support for EU membership encouraged VMRO-DPMNE's further evolution into a moderate, pro-European party.[402] In 2004, Nikola Gruevski, who favored cooperation with the EU, defeated a more nationalist faction led by Ljubčo Georgievski for control of the party, in part because he was viewed as a more viable European partner.[403] In 2005, Macedonia formally became an EU candidate, and the launching of official membership negotiations was conditioned on free and fair elections.[404] From that point onward, elections in the ethnic Macedonian parts of the country improved significantly, and abuse was increasingly confined to (Albanian-dominated) northwest Macedonia.[405] The 2006 parliamentary elections were relatively clean, and a VMRO-DPMNE-led opposition coalition was returned to power.[406]

By 2008, Macedonia had democratized. There were few reported incidents of media harassment,[407] and there existed a robust private media – with national

---

[395] See *RFE/RL Newsline*, 16 and 24 August 2001 (online: http://www.rferl.org/archive/en-newsline/latest/683/683.html).

[396] Boduszynski and Balalovska (2004: 20).

[397] By the early 2000s, the EU was undertaking what was described as an "x-ray of the Macedonian state" (Knaus and Cox 2005: 45).

[398] See ODIHR (2004f); Tsekov (2005); and Freedom House, "Freedom of the Press 2007: Macedonia" (online: www.freedomhouse.org).

[399] ODIHR (2006c: 15–16).

[400] ODIHR (2002: 10–14).

[401] Pond (2006: 177).

[402] In 2007, VMRO-DPMNE became an official observer in the EPP. On public support

for EU integration, see ODIHR (2006c: 13) and Grozdanovska (2007).

[403] See Buechsenschuetz (2001a) and Stavrova (2004c). Georgievski subsequently formed a breakaway party that gained only marginal support in the 2006 elections.

[404] ODIHR (2008a: 4). See also *Transitions Online* (2006).

[405] ODIHR (2006c, 2008a).

[406] ODIHR (2006c).

[407] Although the government won a major libel suit against a former SDSM leader in 2008, international criticism led the VMRO-DPMNE to drop all remaining libel suits against journalists. See Freedom House (online: www.freedomhouse.org); U.S. Department of State (2009c).

TABLE 3.1. *Predicted and Actual Competitive Authoritarian Regime Outcomes in Eastern Europe*

Case	Linkage	Leverage	Organizational Power	Predicted Outcome	Actual Outcome
Albania	High	High	Low	Democracy	Unstable Authoritarianism
Croatia	High	High	Medium High	Democracy	Democracy
Macedonia	High	High	Low	Democracy	Democracy
Romania	High	High	Medium	Democracy	Democracy
Serbia	High	High	High	Democracy	Democracy
Slovakia	High	High	Medium High	Democracy	Democracy

reach – that "reflected a variety of viewpoints."[408] Although the 2008 parliamentary elections were crisis-ridden due to violence and manipulation in Albanian regions,[409] the VMRO-DPMNE–led government responded by re-running elections that were deemed unfair or fraudulent, sending a massive police contingent to the region and encouraging a large international-observer presence.[410] Consequently, conditions improved in the second round.[411] The 2009 presidential election, which was won by VMRO-DPMNE candidate Gjorge Ivanov, was characterized by an open media environment and no serious incidents of violence or fraud.[412]

CONCLUSION

As shown in Table 3.1, our theory correctly predicts regime outcomes in five of six Eastern European cases. The role of linkage and leverage – and particularly that of the EU – in these cases was striking. Despite unfavorable conditions for democratization, autocratic governments failed to consolidate power throughout the region. By 2008, Croatia, Macedonia, Romania, Serbia, and Slovakia had democratized, and Albania was very nearly democratic.

International factors operated differently across the cases. In Romania and Slovakia, extensive ties to the West, large-scale Western assistance, and the prospect of EU membership created strong incentives for autocratic governments to limit abuse while empowering weak and fragmented oppositions. In Croatia and Serbia, democracy promotion was initially sidelined by ethnic civil war, but starting in the late 1990s, linkage and external pressure played a major role in authoritarian breakdown and subsequent democratization. In Albania and

---

[408] U.S. Department of State (2009c).

[409] The Democratic Party of Albanians (DPA) reportedly attacked the opposition Democratic Union for Integration (DUI)'s offices and abducted DUI supporters (ODIHR 2008a: 10). At the same time, Albanian-

language state television was marked by greater pro-incumbent bias than Macedonian TV (ODIHR 2008a: 14).

[410] ODIHR (2008a: 22).

[411] ODIHR (2008a: 21–3).

[412] ODIHR (2009: 16, 20–3).

Macedonia, Western actors initially focused more on strengthening the state (and in Macedonia, on averting civil war) than on democratization. In both cases, however, external intervention prevented autocratic incumbents from consolidating power and increasingly pushed them to play by democratic rules.

Our framework provides a better explanation for these regime outcomes than other theories. For example, although modernization theory may explain democratization in Slovakia, it can hardly explain democratization in Macedonia and Romania (or near-democratization in Albania). Likewise, although a strong opposition helped bring down Milošević in Serbia, oppositions were weak in Croatia, Romania, and Slovakia. Indeed, ties to the West – and intervention by Western actors – helped strengthen and unify oppositions in all four of these cases.

Our theory also provides a more compelling explanation than institutionalist approaches. Scholars have suggested that constitutional design played a central role in Eastern European democratization, pointing to the fact that the region's legislatures were endowed with greater formal power than those in most of the former Soviet Union.[413] However, our cases provide little evidence that formal rules played a major role in democratization. Indeed, constitutional rules were widely ignored. Thus, while the Yugoslav constitution granted federal executives "very little formal power," Milošević's power was "almost unlimited" in the late 1990s.[414] Although the Prime Minister in Slovakia was formally "weak,"[415] Mečiar exercised near dictatorial control over parliament. Formal legislative powers also did little to constrain Tuđman in Croatia.[416] Finally, in Albania, Macedonia, and Romania, our case studies demonstrate that it was consistently *external* – rather than parliamentary – pressure that induced autocratic leaders to limit abuse and/or cede power.

Our analysis thus confirms scholarly claims that leverage provided by prospective EU membership played a central role in Eastern European democratization.[417] Yet as this chapter demonstrates, the effectiveness of EU conditionality was rooted, to a significant extent, in the vast network of social, economic, political, technocratic, and communication ties within which it was embedded. These ties increased the salience of abuse; encouraged Western intervention; enhanced the unity, organization, self-confidence, and even prestige of oppositions; and, crucially, gave elites – and, in some cases, voters – a greater stake in integration. Indeed, linkage's democratizing effects were evident even before EU conditionality was in place, and it appears to have helped prevent backsliding even after accession had reduced EU leverage.[418]

---

[413] Colton and Skach (2005: 123); Stepan (2005: 298); Fish (2006).

[414] Sekelj (2000); von Beyme (2001: 16).

[415] Malova (2001: 369).

[416] *Uncaptive Minds* (1994: 41).

[417] See Pridham (2005: 95), Schimmelfennig and Sedelmeier (2005), and Vachudova (2005b).

[418] Levitz and Pop-Eleches's (forthcoming) analysis finds that linkage is critical in explaining the absence of serious backsliding in post-accession Eastern Europe.

4

Linkage, Leverage, and Democratization in the Americas

"Elections are a risky business.... If you get into the game, you should be prepared to lose."

— Fidel Castro, to Nicaraguan President Daniel Ortega[1]

In the Americas, five of six competitive authoritarian regimes democratized in the post–Cold War period. As in Eastern Europe, domestic variables cannot easily explain these outcomes. Democratization occurred in the Dominican Republic, Guyana, Nicaragua, and Peru despite underdevelopment, extreme inequality, and presidentialism.[2] Moreover, although Latin America as a region had greater experience with democracy than other regions covered in this book, the cases examined here had little or no democratic experience prior to 1990.[3] Indeed, in all cases except Mexico, the domestic push for democracy was weak.

As in Eastern Europe, regime outcomes in the Americas were powerfully shaped by countries' ties to the West. Latin America – particularly Mexico, Central America, and the Caribbean – is characterized by extensive economic, diplomatic, technocratic, social, and communication linkage to the United States.[4] These ties raised the perceived cost of international isolation, which heightened governments' sensitivity to external pressure.[5] Leverage was also high. Long the region's dominant military and economic power, U.S. influence

---

[1] Quoted in Oppenheimer (1992: 207).

[2] Indeed, Guyana and Nicaragua were two of the poorest countries in the hemisphere. Mexico was more developed, but it was presidentialist and marked by high inequality.

[3] Peru had four brief democratic experiences (1945–1948, 1956–1962, 1963–1968, and 1980–1992), all of which ended in coups. The Dominican Republic had a failed democratic experiment in 1962–1963 and then democratized in 1978, but it decayed into com-

petitive authoritarianism after 1986 (Hartlyn 1998). Guyana had competitive elections under British colonial rule, but all post-independence elections were fraudulent. Mexico, Nicaragua, and Haiti had no real democratic experience in the twentieth century.

[4] See Lowenthal (1990; 1999: 110–35), Whitehead (1996e), and Arceneaux and Pion-Berlin (2005).

[5] Castañeda (1994); Whitehead (1996e).

peaked in the 1990s.[6] Unlike much of Asia and the former Soviet Union, where regional powers limited U.S. influence during the post–Cold War period, the United States exercised "uncontested and complete hegemony" in the Americas.[7] Few issues trumped democracy promotion on the U.S. foreign-policy agenda. Whereas anti-communism often led the U.S. government to tolerate or support Latin American dictatorships during the Cold War,[8] the "temptation to support... authoritarian regimes... virtually disappeared" after 1989.[9] The United States was a relatively consistent prodemocratic actor after 1989; as a result, regional democratizing pressure was intense.[10]

The mechanisms by which international forces shaped post–Cold War regime outcomes in the Americas are subject to some debate. Some scholars have highlighted the role of regional organizations such as the OAS.[11] Through the 1991 Santiago Declaration and the 1992 Washington Protocol, the OAS created a regional "defense of democracy" regime that facilitated collective responses to coups.[12] However, the OAS lacked the EU's fine-tuned monitoring and enforcement mechanisms. The organization's focus on full-scale ruptures with the constitutional order (i.e., coups) limited its capacity to respond to abuse that occurred *within* electoral regimes or to induce such hybrid regimes to democratize.[13] Overall, the OAS's record with respect to the defense of democracy after 1990 was – at best – mixed.[14] Among the cases examined in this chapter, OAS pressure was either absent (Mexico), ineffective (Haiti), or of secondary importance (the Dominican Republic, Guyana, Nicaragua, and Peru).

Other scholars have focused on the role of the United States in promoting democracy in the region.[15] Although U.S. pressure was indeed important, we argue that its effectiveness – like that of the EU – was rooted in linkage. As the case studies show, linkage both increased the likelihood of a U.S. response and magnified the impact of that response. In high-linkage/high-leverage cases such as the Dominican Republic, Guyana, and Nicaragua, even threatened or *rumored* sanctions induced elites to conform to regional democratic norms. Moreover, as the Mexican case demonstrates, linkage created incentives to avoid fraud and abuse even in the absence of direct U.S. pressure.

---

[6] See Lowenthal and Trevorton (1994) and Smith (1996, 2001). Western leverage was not uniformly high in Latin America. It was lower, for example, in Brazil, Mexico, and Venezuela.

[7] Smith (1996: 6–7).

[8] Carothers (1991); Smith (1996).

[9] Millett (1994: 19).

[10] See Mainwaring and Pérez Liñán (2005: 41–3). Thus, whereas Latin America was less democratic than established theories predict during the Cold War period, it was *more* democratic than expected during the post–Cold War era – an outcome that has been widely attributed to the regional environment (Mainwaring and Pérez Liñán 2005; Pevehouse 2005). There were, of course, important exceptions to the U.S. prodemocratic foreign policy, including its support for non-democratic regimes in Mexico and Peru during the 1990s and its support for the 2002 coup attempt in Venezuela.

[11] See Halperin (1993) and Pevehouse (2005).

[12] Halperin (1993); Farer (1993, 1996b).

[13] Valenzuela (1997: 45); Mainwaring and Pérez-Liñán (2005: 51).

[14] Farer (1993: 739–46; 1996b); Millett (1994). More recently, the OAS failed to roll back the 2009 coup in Honduras.

[15] See Smith (1994).

Variation in linkage and leverage is critical to explaining post–Cold War regime outcomes in the Americas. Where linkage and leverage were both high, as in the Dominican Republic, Guyana, and Nicaragua, external pressure was decisive. Although the domestic push for democracy was weak in all three countries, the perceived cost of international isolation induced autocrats to either hold clean elections (Guyana and Nicaragua) or leave power in the aftermath of a stolen election (the Dominican Republic). Moreover, international scrutiny discouraged democratic backsliding after transitions. In Mexico, where high linkage was combined with low leverage, democratization was slower and required a domestic push. Linkage induced regime elites to underutilize their coercive capacity and invest in credible electoral institutions. However, it took the emergence of a strong opposition to force the PRI from power. In Peru and Haiti, where high leverage was combined with medium linkage, external pressure was less consistent and governments were less responsive to such pressure. Although autocrats fell in both cases, regime change was rooted primarily in state (Haiti) or party (Peru) weakness.

HIGH LINKAGE, HIGH LEVERAGE, AND DEMOCRATIZATION: THE DOMINICAN REPUBLIC, NICARAGUA, AND GUYANA

The Dominican Republic, Nicaragua, and Guyana are cases of high linkage and high leverage. In many ways, their regime trajectories parallel those in Eastern Europe. As in Croatia, Romania, and Slovakia, ties to the West generated powerful and consistent international pressure that constrained autocratic incumbents and allowed relatively weak oppositions to contest successfully for power. In the Dominican Republic, intense international reaction to the stolen 1994 election undermined the authoritarian coalition and induced President Joaquín Balaguer to leave power and oversee key democratizing reforms. In Guyana and Nicaragua, the pursuit of international credibility induced autocrats to allow large-scale international scrutiny of elections, which they lost. All three regimes subsequently democratized.

Dominican Republic

The Dominican Republic was considered an "unlikely democratizer" in 1990.[16] It was a poor country with a small middle class, a weak civil society, and a history of patrimonialism and authoritarianism, and it lacked a strong domestic push for democracy.[17] Indeed, civic and opposition forces were viewed as too weak to topple President Balaguer.[18] Nevertheless, linkage and leverage raised the cost of autocratic abuse, and the threat of external punitive action after the fraudulent

---

[16] Conaghan and Espinal (1990: 54).

[17] Conaghan and Espinal (1990); Hartlyn (1998).

[18] See Conaghan and Espinal (1990), Hartlyn (1990: 96; 1994: 108), and Huber (1993: 87).

1994 election forced Balaguer to negotiate an early exit from power, ushering in democratization.

Linkage, Leverage, and Organizational Power

The Dominican Republic combined high leverage and high linkage with medium organizational power. In terms of leverage, U.S. influence was "deep and pervasive."[19] The Dominican Republic has been described as "a dependency, a satellite – almost a colony of the United States."[20] The United States occupied the country between 1916 and 1924, maintained it under financial tutelage until 1940, and then invaded it again in 1965.[21] Indeed, "[it] would be difficult to identify a single major development in twentieth-century Dominican history that could be explained in its entirety without reference to the ... United States."[22]

Linkage was very high. Although ties to the United States were always extensive,[23] they expanded and deepened in the 1970s and 1980s with the "transnationalization" of the Dominican economy, as agriculture gave way to tourism, remittances, and export processing.[24] In the 1980s, the United States provided nearly 70 percent of foreign investment and consumed 61 percent of Dominican exports.[25] Social ties were also extensive: up to 14 percent of Dominicans lived abroad in the 1990s, the vast majority in the United States.[26] Travel, communication, and remittance flows transformed the Dominican Republic into a "binational"[27] and even "northamericanized"[28] society.[29] The diasporic community in New York "became an important adjunct to the Dominican political process": Dominican parties opened offices in New York and politicians "found it necessary to visit" to campaign and raise money.[30]

---

[19] Lowenthal (1972: 17).
[20] Wiarda and Krysanek (1992: 76).
[21] On the 1916–1924 occupation, see Calder (1984). On the 1965 intervention, see Lowenthal (1972).
[22] Black (1986: 116).
[23] In his comparative analysis of military, economic, and elite educational ties to the West, Li (1993: 359) found the Dominican Republic to be among the most "penetrated" countries in the world. Between 1952 and 1997, the Dominican Republic was the leading recipient of U.S. military aid in the Caribbean; in 1995, it was the second largest recipient of U.S. military training in the world (Bobea 2002: 90–2). As one U.S. military attaché noted, "Even their uniforms are copies of ours" (Black 1986: 107).
[24] Ramírez Morillo (1997: 141–6). Tourism revenue increased from $16 million in 1970 to $1.1 billion in the 1990s, becoming the country's primary source of income (141). Entry into the Caribbean Basin Initiative in the 1980s "further tied [the Dominican] econ-

omy into that of the U.S." (Maingot and Lozano 2005: 46). The Dominican economy was so closely linked to that of the United States that economist Jeffrey Sachs recommended dollarization, or the replacement of the Dominican currency with the U.S. dollar (*Latin American Regional Reports: Caribbean and Central America Report*, May 6, 2003, p. 7.

[25] Kryzanek and Wiarda (1988: 145, 162); Ferguson (1992: 11). By the early 2000s, U.S.-Dominican trade was valued at $9 billion and 85 percent of Dominican exports went to the United States (*Latin American Regional Reports: Caribbean and Central America Report*, March 23, 2004, pp. 8–9.

[26] See Hartlyn (1998: 142), Grosfoguel (1998), and Maingot and Lozano (2005: 120). Annual remittances exceeded $1 billion during the 1990s (Maingot and Lozano 2005: 46).

[27] Maingot and Lozano (2005: 106).

[28] Moya Pons (1986: 360–1).

[29] On circular migration's impact on Dominican culture, see also Suarez-Orozco (1999: 236).

[30] Atkins and Wilson (1998: 163–4).

Elite linkage was also high. In the early 1990s, 90 percent of tertiary students attended school in the United States – one of the highest rates in the world.[31] Moreover, many opposition elites lived in exile in the United States in the 1960s, where they "learned U.S. techniques, procedures, and styles and applied them to Dominican politics."[32] Linkage powerfully shaped opposition behavior. Convinced that it needed "friends in Washington to make it to power,"[33] the leftist Dominican Revolutionary Party (PRD) "assiduously developed international contacts" in the 1970s, building close relationships with U.S. legislators, U.S. State Department officials, and the Socialist International.[34] As one PRD leader noted, "in a country as dominated by the United States as the Dominican Republic, [Senators] Frank Church and William Fulbright are much more effective allies than Fidel Castro or Mao."[35]

Organizational power was medium. The Dominican state had historically been weak,[36] and it nearly collapsed in the face of an insurrection in 1965.[37] However, subsequent U.S. military assistance strengthened the coercive apparatus and, by the 1970s, the state had developed a potent internal security force that consistently and effectively put down opposition protest.[38] Coercive scope was thus medium by the 1980s. Cohesion was also medium. Although the military lacked any special source of cohesion, there were no major instances of indiscipline during the 1980s.[39]

Party strength was similarly medium. Balaguer's Social Christian Reformist Party (PRSC) was an established political machine, organized around a mix of personalism and clientelism.[40] Although the PRSC was not a mass party, it was well organized and financed, and its clientelist networks penetrated the countryside.[41] The party lacked nonmaterial sources of cohesion, but it was based on established patronage networks.[42] Thus, although the Balaguer government lacked the organizational power of the PRI or the FSLN, it was unlikely to implode or collapse in the face of mild opposition protest.

Origins and Evolution of the Regime

Competitive authoritarianism in the Dominican Republic was a product of democratic decay. After more than a decade of neopatrimonial autocracy under Joaquín Balaguer, the country had democratized in 1978 after U.S. pressure forced

---

[31] Li (1993: 359).
[32] Atkins and Wilson (1998: 163). See also Justo (2004: 218).
[33] Lozano (2002a: 228).
[34] Hartlyn (1998: 124, 117–19). See also Oviedo and Espinal (1986: 166–8) and Sanchez (1992: 306–7).
[35] José Francisco Peña Gómez, quoted in Jiménez (1999: 354).
[36] See Corten (1993).
[37] Lowenthal (1972: 34–77).
[38] See Atkins (1981), Mariñez (1988: 365–7, 372–3), Rodríguez Beruff (1998: 188–9), and

Lozano (2002b). The police force tripled in size, becoming a "highly visible and brutal" force with specialized battalions that "could be deployed rapidly to any section of the country" (Atkins 1981: 21, 42).
[39] Lozano (2002b).
[40] See Jiménez (1999a: 384–92).
[41] See Espinal (1987: 127–30), Lozano (2002b: 230), and Justo (2004: 231).
[42] Lozano (1998a: 106); Espinal and Hartlyn (1999: 504). The PRSC was highly disciplined in the 1980s (Cedeño 1999: 74–6; 142).

Balaguer to recognize a PRD electoral victory.[43] Although the PRD governed democratically, state institutions – including the Central Elections Board (JCE) – remained weak and politicized[44]; after Balaguer regained the presidency in 1986, the regime slid back into competitive authoritarianism.[45]

Balaguer's post-1986 presidency was less repressive than his earlier terms. Because open authoritarianism "increasingly risked international opprobrium and economic crisis," Balaguer deemed it "better to seek to push the limits, while seemingly respecting the electoral rules of the game."[46] Thus, the government largely respected civil liberties,[47] but it politicized the JCE, the judiciary, and other state institutions and deployed them against opponents.[48] In the 1990 election, the PRSC-dominated JCE awarded Balaguer a "dubious" one-point victory over longtime rival Juan Bosch.[49] Although international observers found no convincing proof of fraud at the time,[50] subsequent investigation uncovered evidence of illicit military and police voting, multiple registration of PRSC supporters, purchase of electoral identification cards in opposition strongholds, and "probably some fraud."[51]

Opposition forces failed to block the slide into competitive authoritarianism. Civil society was weak,[52] and although the PRD was well organized,[53] its rivalry with Bosch's Dominican Liberation Party (PLD) undermined opposition capacity.[54] After the 1990 election, the PLD, unions, and other popular organizations organized a series of protests and general strikes, but they failed to mobilize large numbers and thus "proved incapable of forcing the government to give in."[55]

The failure of the 1990 protests convinced opposition leaders that "only international forces had the capacity to...compel Balaguer to relinquish power."[56] Thus, as the 1994 election approached, opposition parties actively sought external support.[57] The election came under intense international scrutiny, and the

---

[43] See Atkins (1981: 104–11) and Hartlyn (1998).

[44] Hartlyn (1998: 246–8).

[45] Hartlyn (1998: 228–9).

[46] Hartlyn (1998: 228).

[47] See Espinal (1996: 134) and Hartlyn (1998: 189–99).

[48] Hartlyn (1998); Justo (2004: 232). For example, the government used the judiciary to orchestrate a corruption investigation against ex-President Salvador Jorge Blanco (1982–1986), who was viewed as a potential challenger, forcing him into exile (Moya Pons 1998: 423–6; Lozano 2002a: 92).

[49] Espinal (1995: 75); see also Hartlyn (1998: 245–51).

[50] See Council of Freely Elected Heads of Government (1990a).

[51] Hartlyn (1998: 202, 249); see also Espinal (2000: 188).

[52] Organized labor was "weak and fragmented" (Hartlyn 1999: 199; see also Oviedo and Espinal 1986), popular sector organizations were "atomized and subject to control through clientelism" (Conaghan and Espinal 1990: 568), and business associations were "weak and politically inactive" (Espinal 1998b: 100).

[53] The PRD was a mass party. In the 1980s, it had 10 thousand grassroots committees and 500 thousand active members (Black 1986: 82; Jiménez 1999a: 92–3, 366).

[54] Espinal (1998b: 97); Hartlyn (1998: 124).

[55] Cassá (1995: 91); see also Espinal (1996: 75; 2000: 187).

[56] Espinal (2000: 199).

[57] Hartlyn (1998: 22).

OAS and the National Democratic Institute (NDI) sent high-level observer delegations.[58]

The 1994 election was stolen. Trailing PRD candidate José Francisco Peña Gómez in the polls, Balaguer packed the electoral authorities, filling a key JCE vacancy – over opposition objections – with ally Leonardo Matos Berrido, who transformed the JCE into a partisan tool.[59] The election was stolen via massive manipulation of the voter rolls.[60] The JCE distributed two different lists – one to the parties and another to the polling stations. Tens of thousands of voters were left off the latter list, and many of them were replaced with fictitious names.[61]

The opposition's response to the fraud centered on the international arena. The PRD abstained from mass mobilization; indeed, civil society "was largely absent" during the postelection crisis.[62] Instead, the PRD "internationalized" the crisis by mobilizing allies in the United States.[63] After the election, the OAS and NDI issued reports documenting the fraud, and NDI observers testified before the U.S. Congress. Fraud charges "were soon echoed by the mainstream U.S. press and by the U.S. government,"[64] and the Congressional Black and Hispanic Caucuses called on the Clinton Administration to not recognize the election.[65] U.S. officials called Balaguer's victory illegitimate and warned that bilateral relations could be damaged.[66] Soon afterward, rumors circulated that the United States was considering downgrading diplomatic relations, restricting visas, and imposing sanctions.[67]

Facing the specter of U.S. punitive action, Balaguer's coalition unraveled. Key business and church sectors broke with the regime and called for a negotiated settlement.[68] Within days, Balaguer was "looking for a way out."[69] Under pressure from U.S. and OAS officials, he agreed to OAS-mediated negotiations with Peña Gómez, which produced the Pact for Democracy.[70] The Pact called for an overhaul of the voter registry, creation of an independent elections board, and new elections in 1996 in which Balaguer would not participate.[71] By all accounts, U.S. pressure was critical in forcing these concessions.[72] Although regime hardliners called on Balaguer to cancel the 1996 election,[73] such a move would have brought "high international costs."[74] Moreover, it was opposed by

[58] Díaz Santana (1996: 142, 260); Espinal and Hartlyn (1998: 155).

[59] Díaz Santana (1996: 85–7, 122).

[60] National Democratic Institute for International Affairs (1998).

[61] National Democratic Institute for International Affairs (1998); Espinal (1999: 290–1).

[62] Díaz Santana (1996: 235); see also Espinal (2000: 194).

[63] Espinal (1998b: 104); see also Lozano (2002a: 119–22).

[64] Hartlyn (1998: 253).

[65] Díaz Santana (1996: 263).

[66] Ferguson (1994: 14); Diaz Santana (1996: 265); Espinal (2000: 194).

[67] Ferguson (1994: 14); Peña (1996: 312).

[68] Lozano (2002a: 123).

[69] *Latin American Weekly Report*, August 25, 1994, p. 377.

[70] Peña (1996: 316–17); Espinal (1999: 293).

[71] See Hartlyn (1998: 255), Espinal (2000: 195), and Lozano (2002a: 124).

[72] See, for example, Lozano (1998b: 262), Hartlyn (1998: 255), and Espinal (2000: 195).

[73] *Latin American Weekly Report*, July 27, 1995, p. 328; August 3, 1994, p. 337.

[74] Hartlyn (1994: 132).

business groups that – dependent on U.S. investment and tourism – now championed democratic reform.[75]

The 1996 election completed the transition. In a closely scrutinized vote that was widely deemed free and fair,[76] Peña Gómez won a first-round plurality, but PLD candidate Leonel Fernández won the runoff. The regime remained democratic after 1996. Presidential elections were free and fair, and incumbents lost in 2000 and 2004. Fernández, who grew up and studied in the United States,[77] governed democratically.[78] His successor, Hipólito Mejía of the PRD, governed in a more patrimonial manner and pushed through an unpopular constitutional reform allowing presidential reelection.[79] Mejia's abuse of public funds and efforts to politicize the JCE triggered some fear of fraud in the 2004 election[80]; yet, linkage effects remained strong. At the time of the election, negotiations for the Dominican Republic's entry into the U.S.–Central America Free Trade Agreement (CAFTA) were in the final stages; to solidify its international image, the Mejía government invited OAS observers to scrutinize the electoral process.[81] The election was clean and Mejía was easily defeated by ex-President Fernández. Fernández governed democratically after 2004.[82]

In summary, external pressure was decisive in the Dominican case. Although the domestic push for democratization was modest, the mere threat of U.S. punitive action following the 1994 fraud undermined Balaguer's authoritarian coalition, leaving him with little alternative but to reverse course.

Nicaragua

Nicaragua's democratization has been described as "one of the more extraordinary and puzzling developments in a remarkable era of global change and democratization."[83] Nicaragua "fit few of the 'requisites of democracy' that democratization theorists emphasize" and "seemed decades if not centuries away from their realization."[84] Moreover, the 1979 revolution had allowed the Sandinista National Liberation Front (FSLN) to gain hegemonic control over the state. The FSLN developed strong party and coercive structures, and it faced weak opposition. Nevertheless, in a context of high linkage and high leverage, it oversaw a democratic transition in 1990.

---

[75] See Espinal (1998a, 1998b). For example, the National Council of Businessmen, an erstwhile Balaguer ally, joined prodemocracy organizations in calling for clean elections (Espinal 1998b: 115–16).

[76] National Democratic Institute for International Affairs (1998); Espinal (2000: 197–8).

[77] See Atkins and Wilson (1998: 220) and Ozuna (2003: 87–104).

[78] Hartlyn (1998: 272–3).

[79] Justo (2004: 283, 332).

[80] *Latin American Weekly Report*, March 2, 2004, p. 10 and May 11, 2004, p. 13.

[81] See Freedom House, "Freedom in the World 2005: Dominican Republic" (http://www.freedomhouse.org).

[82] Freedom House, "Freedom in the World 2008: Dominican Republic" (http://www.freedomhouse.org).

[83] Anderson and Dodd (2005: 4).

[84] Anderson and Dodd (2005: 280, 4).

Linkage, Leverage, and Organizational Power

Nicaragua combined high leverage and high linkage with high organizational power. In terms of leverage, Nicaragua was among the most dependent states in the hemisphere. The U.S. military occupied Nicaragua intermittently between 1912 and 1933, and the Somoza dictatorship depended on U.S. support for its survival.[85] Massive Soviet assistance reduced U.S. leverage in the 1980s[86]; however, when Soviet aid was reduced beginning in 1987, external vulnerability increased dramatically.[87]

Linkage was also high. Historically, the United States was Nicaragua's leading trade partner,[88] and Nicaraguan elites traveled to the United States in large numbers.[89] Thus, most top opposition leaders – including leading presidential candidates Arturo Cruz (1984) and Violeta Chamorro (1990) – had lived or studied in the United States, as had much of the business elite.[90] Although economic and diplomatic ties were weakened by the 1979 revolution and subsequent U.S. trade embargo, other forms of linkage expanded. The revolution attracted widespread attention in U.S. policy circles. The U.S. media developed a "Nicaragua obsession"; indeed, "not since Vietnam [had] a small country attracted so much U.S. media attention."[91] The U.S. government developed strong ties to the opposition, providing assistance to numerous opposition politicians, as well as church, business, and civic groups and the newspaper *La Prensa*.[92] These ties were reinforced by a large exile community. More than 150,000 Nicaraguans – 5 percent of the population – lived in Florida in the 1980s.[93] Exile groups maintained extensive ties to the U.S. policy community and worked closely with the Nicaraguan opposition.[94] Finally, FSLN established its own ties

---

[85] Morley (1994).

[86] Nicaragua received $4.5 billion in Soviet-bloc aid between 1981 and 1989 (Orozco 2002: 54). During the mid-1980s, the Soviet Union supplied $500 million a year in military assistance (Vanden 1991: 312). The break with the United States came at great cost, however: a trade embargo and U.S.-sponsored civil war resulted in nearly 30 thousand deaths and more than $9 billion in damage (Conroy 1990: 48–9; Orozco 2002: 68).

[87] Roberts (1990).

[88] Conroy (1987: 182).

[89] Anderson and Dodd (2005: 303). Of the 31 Nicaraguan elites listed in Corke's *Who's Who in Latin American Politics and Government* (1984: 177–83), 18 had lived or studied in North America – the highest percentage of the cases examined in this chapter.

[90] See Spalding (1994). Cruz spent more than a decade living in the United States and maintained extensive ties in Washington (Reding 1991: 27). His presidential candidacy was

said to be "not so much for his appeal to Nicaraguan voters as for his attractiveness to the U.S. congress and public" (Reding 1991: 27).

[91] Leiken (1990: 12, 26). According to one study of U.S. media coverage, Nicaragua was the eighth most covered country in the world during the 1980s, ahead of Japan, Germany, and China (Leiken 2003: 13). At the same time, it was "bombarded with propaganda-laden radio and television signals transmitted by the ... foreign telecommunications system encircling [the] country" (Frederick 1987: 141). Nine television and seventy-five radio stations penetrated Nicaragua from Costa Rica and Honduras (Frederick 1987: 127–34; Linfield 1991: 282).

[92] Cohn and Hynds (1987: 114–15); Cruz (1989: 230); Robinson (1992: 68–76); Spalding (1998: 161).

[93] Schwartz (1992: 36).

[94] Robinson (1992: 119–31); Lacayo Oyanguren (2005: 55).

to the West. Both the INGO presence and travel to Nicaragua increased sharply in the 1980s.[95] Dozens of solidarity groups and more than 100 sister-city projects emerged in the United States.[96] Although Western *brigadistas* (solidarity activists) were sympathetic to the FSLN, they also constrained it. Most solidarity groups lobbied against U.S. policy toward Nicaragua on the grounds that the Sandinista regime was not a Cuban-style dictatorship; egregious violations of democratic procedure undermined such efforts.

Organizational power was high. The FSLN built a powerful security apparatus. Whereas ex-dictator Anastasio Somoza's National Guard had 7,500 troops in the 1970s,[97] the Soviet-backed Sandinista Popular Army (EPS) mobilized nearly 100,000, becoming the largest and best-equipped army in Central America.[98] The General Directorate of State Security – 10 times larger than Somoza's secret police – served as a "potent political police force."[99] It operated a vast surveillance system that tapped telephones, opened mail, and oversaw a network of informants and undercover agents that "went into all aspects of society."[100] The coercive apparatus was highly cohesive. Forged out of revolution, the security forces were "explicitly Sandinista."[101] All top army officials were ex-guerrilla leaders and most remained active in the FSLN leadership.[102] Thus:

Sandinista ideological influence in the ranks of the army was total. The cohesion and *esprit de corps* of the [army] ... were essentially political-partisan. The immense majority of officers were possessed by a genuine sense of mission that transcended the strictly military. They were defenders and guarantors of a revolutionary political project ... marked by history and a destiny of conflict with the greatest power on earth.[103]

Internal discipline was high. Despite a costly war, economic collapse, and an unpopular military draft, there were no revolts within the security forces during the 1980s.[104]

Party strength was also high. Born of a "mass movement without precedent in Nicaraguan history,"[105] the FSLN was "the largest and best organized party in

95 Orozco (2002: 61–2); Anderson and Dodd (2005: 303).
96 See Gosse (1995). These organizations sent up to $250 million a year in aid – nearly matching Nicaragua's export earnings – in the late 1980s (Membreño Idiáguez 1997).
97 Farhi (1990: 33).
98 See Walker (1991: 81–7); Premo (1997: 68). Taking into account militias and active duty reserves, the EPS had as many as 200,000 under arms during the late 1980s (Close 1988: 176; Walker 1991: 81–6; Miranda and Ratliff 1993: 199, 204).
99 Kinzer (1991: 179, 185).
100 Miranda and Ratliff (1993: 189–95).
101 Walker (1991: 81); see also Cajina (1997: 116–23).

102 Gilbert (1988: 63); Cajina (1997: 107). Army Chief Humberto Ortega was a guerrilla commander and a leading member of the FSLN's National Directorate (DN). The DN tightly controlled army promotions, and party membership was required in order to rise above the rank of captain (Miranda and Ratliff 1993: 206–7).
103 Cajina (1997: 125).
104 See Miranda and Ratliff (1993: 206–7, 244–8) and Cajina (1997: 11, 28). Efforts to trigger army revolts, such as that led by Eden Pastora in 1982, failed miserably (Christian 1985: 277–9).
105 Gilbert (1988: 13).

the country."[106] During the 1980s, the FSLN operated hundreds of base committees in neighborhoods and workplaces throughout the country, and Sandinista
youth, labor, peasant, and women's associations had a combined membership
of nearly 300,000.[107] The FSLN displayed "remarkable internal cohesion,"[108]
which can be traced to its revolutionary origins. All nine members of the FSLN
National Directorate had been revolutionary combatants, and most rank-and-file
activists had participated in the revolution.[109] The party maintained the military
command structure it developed as a guerrilla movement.[110] During the 1980s,
there were no schisms or defections within the FSLN leadership or legislative
bloc.[111]

Organizational power was reinforced by state control over the economy. Under the postrevolutionary mixed economy, the state monopolized
trade, finance, and foreign exchange, and land reform legislation and "anti-
decapitalization" laws gave state officials vast discretionary power over property
rights.[112]

Origins and Evolution of the Regime

Competitive authoritarianism emerged in Nicaragua in the late 1980s. The 1979
revolution allowed the FSLN to establish hegemonic control of the state and
much of the economy.[113] However, intense external pressure – including a U.S.-
sponsored counterrevolutionary ("Contra") movement – induced the Sandinistas
to "scrap much of the initial revolutionary state machinery and replace it with
the conventional structures of representative democracy," including multiparty
elections held in 1984.[114] Although electoral competition was overshadowed by
civil war during the mid-1980s,[115] the waning of the Cold War had a dramatic

---

[106] Robinson (1996: 240). The FSLN built
an "elaborate organization stretching from
the Managua headquarters to every corner of the nation" (Booth 1985: 201). During the 1984 election campaign, it operated
"thousands of community or neighborhood-
based organizing committees" (Latin American Studies Association [LASA] 1984: 7).
In 1990, the FSLN infrastructure included
4,500 branches and 60,000 full-time activists
(LASA 1990: 23; Kinzer 1991: 390).

[107] Prevost (1991: 112). On FSLN mass organizations, see Serra (1991) and Williams
(1994). The FSLN maintained strict membership criteria; in the 1980s, party membership never exceeded 30,000 (Vanden and
Prevost 1993: 114). When these criteria were
relaxed in 1990, FSLN membership rose to
350,000 (Prevost 1997: 36).

[108] Spalding (1994: 209).

[109] Gilbert (1988: 53); Cajina (1997: 183).

[110] Gilbert (1988: 49–55). As one activist put it,
"the party can send us wherever it wants and

say 'be there tomorrow'.... Whoever can't
meet these demands is out of the party."
Quoted in Gilbert (1988: 55).

[111] See Prevost (1991: 108), Miranda and Ratliff
(1993: 13–24), and Spalding (1994: 209).

[112] Weeks (1987); Gilbert (1988: 115–16);
Spalding (1994: 66–7; 1997: 251).

[113] Booth (1985).

[114] Close (2004a: 7–9). As FSLN leader Humberto Ortega later described, the Sandinistas
opted for multiparty elections "because we
began detecting that the Soviet Union was
not strong.... The elections were a tactical
tool. They were a bitter pill that had to be
swallowed" (quoted in Kagan (1996: 304)).

[115] During this period, a state of emergency
"effectively suspended all civil liberties"
(Leogrande 1992: 192). The leading opposition coalition, the Nicaraguan Democratic
Coordinator (CDN), boycotted the 1984
election, and much of its leadership subsequently joined the Contras (Weaver and
Barnes 1991: 128–9).

impact on the regime. After 1986, the withdrawal of Soviet assistance forced the FSLN to "submit to the realities of U.S. hegemony."[116] With the economy in ruin, the status quo became unsustainable.[117] Thus, the FSLN embraced the 1987 Esquipulas II peace process, in which it agreed to political liberalization in exchange for a "measure of international protection from U.S. coercion."[118] In 1988, the government lifted the state of emergency, released political prisoners, and allowed independent newspapers to circulate.[119] Exiled opposition leaders returned and entered the electoral arena; in 1989, 14 parties formed the National Opposition Union (UNO) and announced their participation in the 1990 election. Although opposition leaders were subject to occasional arrest or property expropriation and government-sponsored *turbas divinas* (divine mobs) disrupted opposition rallies,[120] the regime was clearly competitive.[121]

Going into the 1990 election, the domestic balance of power heavily favored the Sandinistas. Opposition forces were weak; independent associations existed but were limited to narrow elite circles.[122] Indeed, outside of the Catholic Church, the largest civic and social organizations were linked to the FSLN.[123] Political parties were also weak. During the 1980s, Nicaragua's traditional parties fragmented into a variety of "microparties," most of which lacked any organizational presence beyond the major cities.[124] Even in 1990, the UNO was a "feeble opponent," with virtually no grassroots organization or mobilizational capacity.[125]

The international dimension was thus critical to democratization. Internationally credible elections were central to the FSLN's post–Cold War survival strategy. Such elections "promised to unlock aid from Western Europe, lift the U.S. embargo, and end the contra war definitively."[126] For the Sandinistas, then, the electoral process "had to be as impeccable as possible so as to deny the United States, the contras, and the internal opposition the opportunity to claim fraud."[127] The government "went to extraordinary lengths to win international and American approbation of the electoral process."[128] For example, it agreed to international monitoring of "unprecedented scope," including official observers from the UN and the OAS and a high-profile team led by former U.S. President Jimmy Carter.[129] The FSLN also agreed – in an internationally sponsored

---

[116] Vanden and Prevost (1993: 106).
[117] Roberts (1990: 93).
[118] Roberts (1990: 96–7, 88).
[119] Linfield (1991: 280–2, 289); Leogrande (1992: 194).
[120] See Miranda and Ratliff (1993: 190–5), Kagan (1996: 550–551, 583), and Walker (2003: 147–9).
[121] By 1989, the press "flourished free of censorship, and political dissidents were allowed to protest without interference" (Kinzer 1991: 387–8).
[122] The largest business association, the Superior Council of Private Enterprise (COSEP), possessed "few institutional resources" and

operated with a "skeletal staff in rented facilities" (Spalding 1998: 161).
[123] Serra (1991); Williams (1994).
[124] See Leogrande (1992: 190), Cajina (1997: 42–5), and Walker (2003: 165). Many of these parties existed "only on paper" (Gilbert 1988: 122).
[125] Close (1999: 31); see also Latin American Studies Association (1990: 23) and Oquist (1992: 34).
[126] Pastor (1990); see also McCoy, Garber, and Pastor (1991: 108).
[127] Bendaña (1992: 168).
[128] Kagan (1996: 668).
[129] Richard and Booth (1995: 207).

National Dialogue – to repeal repressive internal-security laws, create a more balanced electoral authority, improve opposition access to state-owned media, and lift the ban on foreign financing of opposition parties.[130]

The 1990 election pitted President Daniel Ortega against UNO candidate Violeta Chamorro. The election was not fair. Both national television stations and 80 percent of radio stations remained Sandinista and biased,[131] and the FSLN's politicization of the bureaucracy and security forces created a "triangle of power" that seriously disadvantaged the opposition.[132] The FSLN enjoyed access to "seemingly unlimited funds" and made massive use of public buildings, employees, and vehicles.[133] By contrast, the UNO "seemed lacking in everything,"[134] and it was only able to open campaign offices in about half of the country's departments.[135] The Sandinistas "out-spent the opposition by a wide margin.... Even with the help of Washington, UNO had nothing comparable."[136]

Nevertheless, linkage helped to level the playing field in three ways. First, it provided the opposition with critical resources. UNO benefited from considerable U.S. assistance. A $7.7 million grant (channeled through the National Endowment for Democracy [NED]), together with $5 million in CIA "housekeeping" money, provided UNO with the "financial and material resources necessary to organize and sustain a nationwide electoral campaign."[137] This money allowed UNO to purchase 62 campaign vehicles, open offices across the country, pay campaign workers' salaries, and mobilize 15 thousand poll watchers.[138] U.S. agencies financed the leading independent newspaper (*La Prensa*) and four opposition radio stations, and CIA and United States Information Agency (USIA)-run radio stations worked to "inundate Nicaraguan airwaves" from neighboring Costa Rica and Honduras.[139]

Second, linkage induced the FSLN to underutilize its coercive capacity. The Sandinistas' behavior toward the domestic opposition was monitored closely by the U.S. Congress in 1988 and 1989,[140] and the 1990 election was subject to unprecedented external scrutiny.[141] The campaign received "extensive coverage" in the international media,[142] and it was watched "by more international

---

[130] Moreno (1995: 236); Nuzzi, Dodson, and Dodson (1999: 111).

[131] Council of Freely Elected Heads of Government (1990b: 75).

[132] Cajina (1997: 16); see also Gilbert (1988: 59–78).

[133] Kinzer (1991: 390). See also Council of Freely Elected Heads of Government (1990b), Leiken (1990: 27), and López Pintor (1998: 44).

[134] Pastor (1992: 182); Close (1999: 82).

[135] Kagan (1996: 667).

[136] Leogrande (1992: 197).

[137] Robinson (1996: 225); see also López Pintor (1998: 41). Most but not all of the NED funding went to opposition groups.

[138] See Council of Freely Elected Heads of Government (1990b: 23) and López Pintor (1998: 45). NED also sent consultants to train UNO leaders and help run their campaign (Robinson 1996: 232–3; Orozco 2002: 81–85; Lacayo Oyanguren 2005: 52–3, 64–7).

[139] Robinson (1996: 231–2, 1992: 81). This assistance is said to have "largely compensated" for the FSLN's control of state-run media (Kagan 1996: 701).

[140] See Kagan (1996: 604–617).

[141] Carothers (1991: 95).

[142] Booth (1998: 190).

observers than any previous election in an independent country."[143] Observers "closely monitored nearly all radio and television political programs," attended nearly 80 percent of opposition rallies, and visited 100 percent of polling stations.[144] This scrutiny limited the FSLN's capacity to harass the opposition. Because "repressive reaction, however mild or provoked, only tended to confirm Washington's portrayal of the Sandinistas as totalitarian," any reported abuse was costly for the FSLN.[145] Early in the campaign, Sandinista *turbas* broke up opposition rallies and attacked UNO activists.[146] However, international observers were present in December 1989 when a *turba* attack killed a UNO activist, creating a scandal.[147] Jimmy Carter intervened, and the UN reported no further incidents of violence.[148] Abuse declined sharply over the course of the campaign. Thus, "if the 'playing field' was not 'level,' the slope was reduced to where it was obvious neither from the box seats nor the press box."[149]

Third, linkage shaped voter preferences in ways that favored UNO. Surveys showed that most voters sought better relations with the United States, and Chamorro was widely viewed as the candidate best able to achieve this.[150] Thus, UNO could "claim with confidence that if it won the election, the United States would end its economic embargo... and open the floodgates of U.S. economic assistance."[151] The promise of an end to the war and the trade embargo became the centerpiece of UNO's campaign.[152] Indeed, Chamorro "went out of her way to appear to be President Bush's preferred candidate," even flying to Washington early in the campaign to be photographed with him.[153] Although Ortega derided UNO leaders as "political mercenaries of the United States,"[154] it is clear that U.S. intervention benefited rather than hurt Chamorro.[155]

---

[143] Pastor (1990: 18).

[144] López Pintor (1998: 44); also Council of Freely Elected Heads of Government (1990b: 12).

[145] Walker (2003: 164). An early example of this boomerang effect was the July 1988 crackdown in the town of Nandaime. The events "created scandal in the U.S. media" (Valdivia 1991: 360), and international pressure led the Sandinistas to grant the early release of the arrested politicians (Kinzer 1991: 386).

[146] One human-rights group documented 7 killings, 12 disappearances, 20 arrests, and 30 beatings of opposition activists through December 1989 (Leiken 1990: 31; Council of Freely Elected Heads of Government 1990b: 18).

[147] See Council of Freely Elected Heads of Government (1990b: 18) and Leiken (2003: 187).

[148] Pastor (1990: 20).

[149] Leiken (2003: 182–3). Indeed, "even opposition leaders had to admit that the Sandinistas behaved much better than they ever expected" (Kagan 1996: 705).

[150] Oquist (1992); Anderson and Dodd (2005: 152–4).

[151] Moreno (1995: 240). At the same time, most Nicaraguans believed that an FSLN victory would bring renewed conflict with the United States (Oquist 1992: 29–31). U.S. officials reinforced these perceptions by publicly backing Chamorro and linking a UNO victory to the end of the embargo (Reding 1991: 41; Robinson 1996: 237–8; Orozco 2002: 84).

[152] Williams (1990: 23–4); Tulchin and Walter (1991: 258).

[153] Kagan (1996: 697).

[154] Quoted in Moreno (1995: 239); also Kagan (1996: 696).

[155] Walker (2003: 196–7).

The 1990 election was clean, and Violeta Chamorro won it easily. [156] On election night, when the outcome became clear, Carter rushed to FSLN headquarters to ensure Ortega's acceptance of the results. [157] The subsequent transition was negotiated in The Carter Center offices, under close international supervision. [158]

Nicaragua's post-1990 regime was crisis-ridden but democratic. Presidential elections were free and fair, and incumbent forces were defeated in 1996 and 2006. Under Chamorro, civil liberties were respected and press freedom was "near absolute." [159] Chamorro's successor, Arnoldo Alemán of the Constitutional Liberal Party (PLC), governed in a more illiberal manner, packing the Supreme Court, using the tax authorities to harass opponents, and attempting to bully the media. [160] However, international pressure forced Alemán to back off from his most serious abuses, and civil liberties ultimately remained intact. [161] Alemán failed to overturn a constitutional ban on reelection, and the 2001 election was clean. [162] Alemán's successor, Enrique Bolaños, governed democratically. [163] In 2005, when a Sandinista–Liberal alliance sought to remove Bolaños from office via constitutionally dubious means, U.S. officials threatened to suspend economic assistance, exclude Nicaragua from CAFTA, and restrict visas to Liberal leaders and their families. [164] Because Liberal leaders maintained close ties to the United States (many lived in exile in the United States in the 1980s, shopped regularly in Miami, and had children in U.S. schools), the threat was effective: The Liberals quickly backed off. [165] In 2006, the governing party lost the presidency to FSLN leader Daniel Ortega.

Because Nicaragua was a democracy for three consecutive presidential terms (1990–2006), we score it as a case of democratization. [166] However, it is worth noting that the Ortega government moved in a competitive authoritarian direction, harassing media, using thugs to break up opposition protests and intimidate

---

[156] Chamorro defeated Ortega by 54 to 41 percent. For a detailed analysis of election conditions, see Council of Freely Elected Heads of Government (1990b).

[157] See Council of Freely Elected Heads of Government (1990b: 25–6) and Pastor (1990: 21).

[158] Pastor (2001: 266); Lacayo Oyanguren (2005: 105–9).

[159] Walker (2003: 168); Anderson and Dodd (2005: 87).

[160] See Anderson and Dodd (2002: 89–92), Orozco (2002: 113–15), Close (2004a: 4; 2004b: 172–3), and Anderson (2006: 155–6). Alemán's PLC forged a pact with the FSLN through which the two parties divided control over the electoral and judicial authorities and reformed the electoral law to make it difficult for other parties to compete (Orozco 2002: 113–17; Close 2004a: 11; Hoyt 2004).

[161] Anderson and Dodd (2005: 298). For example, after the government imprisoned

Comptroller Agustín Jarquín – who had been investigating corruption – in 1999, U.S. pressure forced Alemán to release Jarquín and restore him to the Comptroller's office (Walker 2003: 66; Hoyt 2004: 23).

[162] Anderson and Dodd (2002: 9, 82–3; 2005: 236).

[163] See Freedom House, "Freedom in the World 2006: Nicaragua" (http://www.free-domhouse.org). Bolaños oversaw Alemán's prosecution on corruption charges (Close 2004b: 167–8; Anderson and Dodd 2005: 241).

[164] U.S. official told business elites who backed the Liberals that economic opportunities would be "lost" if the maneuver went forward. See *The New York Times*, October 5, 2005, p. A3 and October 6, 2005, p. A7. *El Nuevo Diario*, October 5, 2005, p. 1, and *La Prensa*, October 5, 2005, p. 1.

[165] *El Nuevo Diario*, October 5, 2005, p. 1, *La Prensa*, October 5, 2005, p. 1.

[166] See Appendix I.

opposition activists, and possibly stealing the 2008 municipal elections in Managua.[167] In 2009, a group of Sandinista Supreme Court justices (in a secret vote taken without the knowledge of non-Sandinista jurists) illegally ruled that constitutional term limits could not be applied to Ortega. As predicted by our theory, linkage and leverage effects raised the cost of Ortega's autocratic turn. The United States and EU suspended aid, capital flight increased, and business leaders – dependent on U.S. markets and investment – grew increasingly critical of the government.[168] Moreover, Ortega's public approval rating fell sharply, a decline that was attributed, in part, to the government's growing international isolation.[169] In 2010, it remained unclear whether Western pressure would undermine Ortega's effort to consolidate power.

In summary, Nicaragua's democratization was externally driven. The FSLN possessed powerful party and coercive organizations and faced a feeble opposition. In the post–Cold War era, however, "the impressive military force of the state was of little use."[170] External vulnerability induced the FSLN to underutilize its coercive power and permit a successful opposition challenge that, in a different international context, it could have easily thwarted.

Guyana

Like the Dominican Republic and Nicaragua, Guyana is a case in which high linkage and high leverage contributed to democratization despite unfavorable domestic conditions. A poor country that was deeply divided between an East Indian majority (represented by the Progressive People's Party [PPP]) and a black minority (represented by the People's National Congress [PNC]), and in which the autocratic PNC regime had developed a powerful coercive apparatus, Guyana was an unlikely democratizer.[171] Yet strong external pressure induced the PNC to hold free elections in 1992, and the regime democratized.

Linkage, Leverage, and Organizational Power

Guyana is a case of high leverage and high linkage. Leverage was very high. A poor Caribbean state, Guyana was characterized by extreme "military, political, and economic vulnerability . . . to the foreign policy and security actions of the United States."[172] Between 1962 and 1990, it was the second leading U.S. aid recipient in

[167] See U.S. Department of State (2009f).

[168] *Latin American Caribbean and Central America Report*, March 2009, p. 4. One business leader called the aid freeze a "nuclear bomb on the economy" ("Nicaragua's Ortega Defiant after US, Europe Yank Aid," *Christian Science Monitor*, December 6, 2008 (Online edition: http://www.csmonitor.com/World/Americas/2008/1206/p25s08-woam.html.)).

[169] See Silva (2008). In late 2009, Ortega's public approval was among the lowest in Latin America, and nearly two thirds of Nicaraguans opposed his reelection ("Ortega entre los peores," *La Prensa*, November 20, 2009; "Total rechezo a la Reelección de Ortega," *La Prensa*, December 15, 2009 (Online edition: http://www.laprensa.com.ni)).

[170] Herrera Zúniga (1994: 122).

[171] Premdas (1995). Guyana was the second poorest country in the hemisphere (after Haiti) and one of the world's 20 poorest nations (Griffith 1993: 52; 1997a: 167).

[172] Griffith (1993: 4).

the Commonwealth Caribbean, and it was briefly the world's leading per capita recipient of U.S. aid.[173] After the Cold War, no issue trumped democracy on the U.S. foreign-policy agenda.[174]

Guyana's linkage score is the highest of all the cases examined in this book. A small Caribbean state, Guyana historically maintained an open economy, with extensive trade and investment ties to the United States and Britain.[175] In the 1980s, the United States and Britain consumed two thirds of Guyana's exports.[176] Social ties were also extensive; 10 percent of Guyana's population emigrated to the United States between 1968 and 1985.[177] By the 1990s, nearly a third of Guyanese lived abroad, mainly in the United States, and remittances constituted more than a quarter of GDP.[178]

As in Nicaragua, the domestic balance of power in Guyana favored the incumbents. Organizational power was high. The PNC built a vast security apparatus, transforming Guyana into one of the most militarized societies in the hemisphere.[179] The security forces – which included the Guyana Defense Forces (GDF), police, Peoples' Militia, and a vast intelligence apparatus – expanded from 2,135 soldiers in 1964 to 22,000 in the 1980s.[180] Among Caribbean states, Guyana's ratio of 8.1 soldiers per 1,000 people was second to Cuba.[181] The security forces were highly cohesive, due, in large part, to racial ties.[182] In a deeply divided society with a clear Indian majority, the security forces were "almost entirely black."[183] In the 1980s, 90 percent of the GDF officer corps and the police force were black.[184] The security forces were highly disciplined. Army and police loyalty were "never...in question" during the 1970s and 1980s, and police routinely carried out orders to repress protest.[185]

Party strength was medium high. PNC scope was medium: although never a mass party, it maintained an organized presence throughout the country.[186] Party cohesion – rooted in racial polarization – was high. Ethnicity was the dominant political cleavage in Guyana, and all elections were "decided along racial lines."[187] The PNC and the PPP were originally built on communal organizations[188]; as a result, the PNC was "intimately identified with the interests of a single ethnic community."[189] In a society where cross-ethnic voting was "virtually absent,"

[173] Griffith (1993: 73); Premdas (1995: 132).

[174] Premdas (1993a: 119–20).

[175] Stone (1986: 79).

[176] Jeffrey and Baber (1986: 136).

[177] Griffith (1993: 54). Guyanese are thus "culturally accustomed to the political values of the West" (Jeffrey and Baber 1986: 70).

[178] Watson and Craig (1992: 49).

[179] See Danns (1982, 1983), Griffith (1991b), and Phillips (2002).

[180] Danns (1982: 46, 156–7; 1983: 71–2, 80); Hintzen (1989: 92); Phillips (2002: 168).

[181] Stone (1986: 54).

[182] Enloe (1976); Danns 1982, 1983).

[183] Spinner (1984: 162).

[184] Danns (1983: 80–6). The security forces' "communally lopsided" character "ensured that...election results were not forcibly overturned by [East Indian] riots and demonstrations" (Premdas 1995: 119).

[185] Latin America Bureau (1984: 88); see also Hintzen (1989: 172) and Premdas (1995: 133–4).

[186] Jeffrey and Baber (1986: 58, 67, 83); Premdas (1995: 49, 103).

[187] Thomas (1990: 75); see also Premdas (1995).

[188] Premdas (1995: 50–3).

[189] Enloe (1976: 50).

party defection was costly; indeed, the PNC suffered few defections through the 1980s.[190]

Origins and Evolution of the Regime

Competitive authoritarianism emerged in Guyana in the 1960s, after the United States and Great Britain – viewing the PPP as a Marxist threat – helped install a PNC government led by Forbes Burnham.[191] Although the PNC retained the constitutional architecture of democracy after independence in 1966, it maintained power through a "succession of rigged elections."[192] Elections were marred by intimidation, padded voter rolls, ballot stuffing, and fictitious proxy and overseas votes.[193] Opposition parties were often denied permits for public meetings, and opposition activists were spied on, arrested, and occasionally killed.[194] Much of the violence was carried out by state-sponsored "goon squads" such as the House of Israel.[195] Independent media were "barely tolerated."[196] Television and radio remained in state hands into the 1990s,[197] and, although private newspapers were allowed to publish, the government used restrictions on newsprint and costly libel suits to squeeze them so that they "might seem to choke to death on their own accord."[198] Finally, interlocking party–state ties created an uneven playing field.[199] The Ministry of National Development was "at once an agency of the ruling party and a ministry of the government," financing PNC activities, mobilizing supporters, and organizing electoral campaigns.[200] Likewise, the GDF was "practically an arm of the ruling PNC," working for the party during elections,[201] and the courts were "used as an instrument of political harassment on a widespread scale."[202]

Guyana's democratization was rooted in the end of the Cold War.[203] The domestic push for democracy was limited. Repression had reduced the opposition PPP to a "skeleton body operating mainly at headquarters."[204] In the

[190] Premdas (1995: 50, 52–3); see also Jeffrey and Baber (1986: 73).

[191] Spinner (1984: 101–16).

[192] Premdas (1993b: 119).

[193] See Latin America Bureau (1984) and Americas Watch (1985).

[194] See Danns (1982: 30–3, 54–5; 1983: 80), Spinner (1984: 211; and Americas Watch (1985: 57). The most notorious killing was the 1980 assassination of WPA leader Walter Rodney.

[195] Danns (1982: 85). The House of Israel was a black religious cult that was used to break up strikes and demonstrations and to attack opposition activists (Singh 1988: 82–93; Hintzen 1989: 94).

[196] Americas Watch (1985: 52).

[197] Commonwealth Observer Group (1992: 24).

[198] Premdas (1994: 52; 1995: 55). Restrictions on newsprint reduced the *Mirror* to a weekly

and the *Catholic Standard* to a "short irregular stencil sheet" (Premdas 1994: 52; Americas Watch 1985: 52–5). Newspaper editors also faced costly lawsuits, in which they were "dragg[ed] before the politicized courts" and "fined exorbitant sums" (Premdas 1995: 55).

[199] Premdas (1993b: 111).

[200] See Americas Watch (1985: 39–40), Griffith (1991a: 145), and Rose (2002: 194–5).

[201] Griffith (1997b: 275); see also Singh (1988: 78–79).

[202] Rose (2002: 199); see also Hintzen (1989: 98).

[203] See Will (1997).

[204] Premdas (1993: 48). Moreover, government co-optation of East Indian civic groups served to "deny the PPP use of their organizations for anti-regime mobilization" (Hintzen 1989: 71).

late 1970s, a protest movement led by the leftist Working People's Alliance was heavily repressed, after which "public demonstrations against the regime came to an abrupt end."[205] Nevertheless, the geopolitical thaw of the 1980s left the PNC "shorn of its Cold War shield of protection."[206] Whereas the United States had once tolerated the regime as a "necessary evil,"[207] by the mid-1980s, "the need to maintain an illegitimate pro-Western government in power was no longer compelling."[208] Thus, the Reagan Administration "turned its wrath on Guyana," closing down USAID offices and blocking international loans, which triggered a steep economic decline.[209] When Desmond Hoyte became president after Burnham's death in 1985, the state was effectively bankrupt[210]; when donors began to condition assistance on free elections after 1989, the political status quo became "untenable."[211] Capital outflows left the economy "starved of investment resources," and businessmen seeking loans abroad were told that no further credit would be forthcoming until Guyana held free elections.[212]

As in Nicaragua, then, regime survival required that the PNC improve its international standing.[213] Seeking internationally credible elections, Hoyte invited Jimmy Carter to oversee electoral reforms and monitor elections to be held in 1992.[214] As the "international guarantor of free and fair elections," The Carter Center exerted enormous influence.[215] During Carter's first visit in 1990, he convinced Hoyte to create a new voter registry and permit vote-counting at local polling stations – demands he had rejected since 1985.[216] As the *Stabroek News* observed, Carter "managed to achieve in under 24 hours what opposition parties had not been able to rest from the ruling [PNC] in almost 23 years."[217] The Carter Center also successfully pressured Hoyte to create a more independent Electoral Commission (EC); after U.S. "arm twisting," Rudy Collins, a diplomat with a "reputation for integrity and independence," was appointed to chair it.[218] Assisted by The Carter Center and other international agencies, the EC "thoroughly sanitized" the electoral system, overhauling the voter registry and taking virtually every aspect of the electoral process (including the printing of ballots,

---

[205] Hintzen (1989: 172); Premdas (1995: 133–4).

[206] Premdas (1995: 142).

[207] Jeffrey and Baber (1986: 35–6).

[208] Premdas (1993a: 119–20).

[209] Premdas (1993b: 117); Rose (2002: 358). Guyana's GDP contracted by nearly a quarter, reaching a postcolonial low (Premdas 1993b: 122).

[210] Premdas (1993b: 117–18).

[211] Will (1997: 64). On donor conditionality, see Griffith (1993: 102) and Premdas (1993a: 115–20).

[212] *Latin American Monitor: Caribbean*, June 1991, p. 911; see also Will (1997: 65).

[213] See Will (1997) and Rose (2002: 360–1).

[214] Will (1997: 64–6).

[215] Ryan (1992: 74); Will (1997: 65–6).

[216] Council of Freely Elected Presidents (1993: 19); Premdas (1993a: 123–124); Will (1997: 64).

[217] *Stabroek News*, October 16, 1990, p. 1. Similarly, *The Mirror* wrote that Carter "breezed into Guyana...and within 24 hours... breezed out again, having achieved in that ultra-short time, what the combined opposition political and civic forces failed to achieve in two bone-jarring decades! Thank you President Carter! Do come again soon! (*The Mirror*, October 21, 1990. p. 1)

[218] *Latin American Regional Report: Caribbean*, May 16, 1991, p. 2; see also *Stabroek News*, April 7, 1991, p. 1, Council of Freely Elected Heads of Government (1993: 19–20), and Will (1997: 64).

which was done in Miami) out of the government's hands.[219] By 1992, the PNC had "lost control" of the electoral process, and Hoyte began to accuse the EC of pro-opposition bias.[220] By the time PNC leaders realized they were likely to lose, however, the cost of reversing course was prohibitively high.[221] The 1992 elections were free and fair,[222] and the PPP – led by longtime leader Cheddi Jagan – won them easily. The PNC left power peacefully.

The post-1992 regime was crisis-ridden but democratic. PPP governments scaled back the security apparatus and respected civil liberties.[223] Although politics remained polarized along racial lines, elections were deemed free and fair by observers.[224] When the PNC denounced fraud after the 1997 election, the government acceded to business leaders' calls for an international audit by the Caribbean Community, which concluded that the election was clean.[225] The 2001 election was monitored by a "small army" from The Carter Center, OAS, and EU, and it was again judged free and fair.[226]

MEXICO: LINKAGE WITHOUT LEVERAGE

Mexico differs from the previous cases in that leverage was low. Indeed, U.S. democratizing pressure was "conspicuous by its absence."[227] Hence, domestic forces played a more central role than in the Dominican Republic, Nicaragua, and Guyana. Nevertheless, linkage effects clearly facilitated – and likely accelerated – democratization. Linkage induced the Institutional Revolutionary Party (PRI) to underutilize its coercive power and create credible electoral institutions. Inertial power asymmetries enabled the PRI to remain in power throughout the 1990s. However, when the emergence of a strong opposition forced the PRI to choose between risking international scandal and risking defeat, it chose the latter – and lost power.

Linkage, Leverage, and Organizational Power

Mexico is a case of low leverage and high linkage. Low leverage was a product of size and strategic importance. The world's 11th largest economy in the early 1990s, Mexico did not depend on U.S. assistance. Moreover, Mexico's potential

---

[219] Premdas (1993a); Council of Freely Elected Heads of Government (1993: 23–32).

[220] Premdas (1994: 56); also Council of Freely Elected Heads of State (1993: 25, 29–30).

[221] Premdas (1993a: 113).

[222] Commonwealth Observer Group (1992); Council of Freely Elected Heads of Government (1993).

[223] See Griffith (1997a: 164–5), U.S. Department of State (2001b), and Rose (2002: 212).

[224] Erikson and Minson (2005b: 167); Freedom House, "Freedom in the World 2008: Guyana" (http://www.freedomhouse.org).

[225] Singh (1998: 110–16); *Central America and Caribbean Report*, March 31, 1998, p. 3 and July 21, 1998, p. 1.

[226] *The Economist*, April 14, 2001, p. 36; see also *Central America and Caribbean Report*, March 27, 2001, p. 1 and *Latin America Monitor: Caribbean*, May 2001, p. 10.

[227] Meyer (1991: 218).

impact on the United States in areas such as trade, finance, security, drugs, and immigration was "on a level with Japan, Germany, China, and Russia."[228] Given this level of mutual dependence, the United States was often unwilling to "bring the full range of its overall power capabilities to bear" on the PRI.[229] Indeed, the United States rarely sought to impose political outcomes in Mexico,[230] and Mexico's democratization "was never a major U.S. policy goal."[231]

Linkage was high on all dimensions. In the economic realm, the United States "was virtually Mexico's only real trading partner" in the 1980s, accounting for more than 80 percent of trade and 60 percent of foreign direct investment (FDI).[232] Economic integration – culminating in the 1994 North American Free Trade Agreement (NAFTA) – transformed Mexico into "a North American nation."[233] Mexico became the number-two trading partner of the United States, and the U.S. share of Mexican exports rose to 88 percent.[234] Intergovernmental contacts "multiplied at all levels," as some 50 bilateral commissions were set up to work on labor, health, environmental, customs, and transportation issues.[235] Social ties were extremely high. Mexico was the leading source of immigration to the United States in the late 1980s, sending three times more immigrants than any other country.[236] Mexicans maintained "personal links to the United States at a level unmatched by any other country with the possible exception of Israel."[237] In the early 1990s, one third of Mexicans had visited the United States and half had close relatives living there.[238] Moreover, tourism – nearly all of it from the United States – was Mexico's second largest source of foreign exchange, which heightened its dependence on U.S. perceptions of political stability.[239] Media penetration was also extensive. Most major U.S. newspapers had full-time correspondents in Mexico, and Mexicans paid such close attention

---

[228] Wiarda (1997: 51).
[229] Bagley and Tokatlian (1992: 221).
[230] Knight (1997: 8–11).
[231] Fox (2004: 471).
[232] Pastor and Castañeda (1988: 220); Smith (2001: 60). In the late 1980s, eight of the ten largest U.S. banks had more than a third of their primary equity capital at risk in Mexico (Lowenthal 1990: 70).
[233] Lowenthal (1990: 218). According to Wiarda (2003: 75), the "volume of private activities and transactions vis-à-vis Mexico is among the largest in the world, second only to U.S. business conducted with Canada. Be it the Ford Foundation, human rights groups, soldiers of fortune, the flood of tourists flocking into Mexico, investors, maquiladoras, coyotes carrying immigrants into the United States, drug runners, and so forth, the value of these private transactions ... is stupendous."

[234] Smith (2000: 95); González (2001: 259).
[235] Domínguez and Fernández de Castro (2001: 75, 31). According to Wiarda (2003: 74), "so many U.S. government programs operated in Mexico that it [was] impossible to keep track of them."
[236] Pastor (1993: 11–12).
[237] Camp (1999: 213).
[238] Pastor (1993: 11–12); Camp (1999: 213). In the 1990s, there were 750,000 *legal* border crossings each day (Pastor 1993: 11), and 1.1 million Mexican households received remittances from the United States (Fitzgerald 2004: 527).
[239] Pastor and Castañeda (1988: 224). The United States was the source of 80 percent of Mexico's tourism in the late 1980s, and more U.S. citizens visited Mexico than any other developing country (Lowenthal 1990: 82).

to events in the United States that one television station broadcasted *NBC Nightly News.*[240]

Technocratic linkage also was strikingly high.[241] A survey of Mexico's "power elite" found that 50 percent of those born after 1945 had studied in the United States.[242] Presidents Miguel De la Madrid (1982–1988), Carlos Salinas (1988–2004), and Ernesto Zedillo (1994–2000) all earned Ivy League graduate degrees, and each filled his government with PhDs from Harvard, Yale, Chicago, Stanford, and MIT.[243] PRI elites were "fluent in English [and] familiar with U.S. culture" and many of them had held, or aspired to hold, positions in U.S. universities or international organizations.[244] Hence, they closely followed developments abroad and were highly sensitive to international opinion.[245] Business and opposition elites also maintained close ties to the United States.[246]

Finally, U.S.–Mexican relations were characterized by an "increasingly dense bi-national civil society."[247] Mexican human-rights and prodemocracy NGOs proliferated during the 1980s, and many of them received "political, organizational, and financial support from allies in the United States."[248] These groups gained a solid foothold in U.S. media and policy circles,[249] which brought "increased visibility...to human-rights abuses" and created a "much more favorable environment for dissent than otherwise would have been the case."[250]

---

[240] Pastor and Castañeda (1988: 336); Oppenheimer (1996: 321). Social and communication ties appear to have shaped public attitudes. Surveys showed a convergence of U.S. and Mexican attitudes on many issues, including democracy (Pastor 1993: 30; 2001: 291). In a recent study, Pérez-Armendáriz and Crow (2010) found that Mexicans who had lived in or knew people who lived in the United States were more likely to hold democratic attitudes and to view the Mexican government critically.

[241] See Centeno (1994), Golob (1997), Babb (2001), and Camp (2002).

[242] Camp (2002: 159–60).

[243] See Babb (2001) and Camp (2002: 174–84). A survey of "top and medium economic policymakers" found that 70 percent had earned a graduate degree in the United States (Babb 2001: 187).

[244] Domínguez and Fernández de Castro (2001: 31). For example, Salinas aspired to be president of the World Trade Organization (Kaufman 1999: 185), and Zedillo became director of Yale's Center for the Study of Globalization after leaving office.

[245] Camp 1985: 52); Centeno (1994: 124–6).

[246] One survey found that 50 percent of business elites had studied in the United States (Camp 2002: 154). See also Mizrahi (2003: 72). Many leaders of the National Action Party, including Felipe Calderón, Manuel Clauthier, Vicente Fox, and Ernesto Ruffo, studied in the United States, as did democracy activists such as Sergio Aguayo, Jorge Castañeda, and Adolfo Aguilar Zinser. See Camp (2002: 189–90).

[247] Middlebrook (2004: 46); see also Dresser (1996b).

[248] Middlebrook (2004: 21). The number of Mexican human rights NGOs increased from 4 in 1984 to more than 200 in 1993 (Sikkink 1993: 430). Nearly half of NGO financing came from abroad (Chand 2001: 228–9).

[249] For example, Mexico's leading election observation group, Civic Alliance, received the bulk of its funding from abroad (Aguayo 1995a: 162), and its ties to the NED helped it "disseminate its views in Washington policymaking circles" (Dresser 1996b: 330).

[250] Camp (1995: 37); see also Dresser (1996b: 326–30).

Organizational power was high. The Mexican state possessed considerable coercive capacity.[251] Although relatively small,[252] the army developed impressive surveillance capacity and established a "pervasive presence" in the countryside.[253] Throughout the postrevolutionary period and into the 1980s, the security forces routed guerrilla movements and consistently put down strikes, peasant uprisings, postelection riots, and other protest.[254] The army was also highly cohesive – a phenomenon that has been widely attributed to its revolutionary origins.[255] For decades, all top military posts were held by officials with "revolutionary credentials."[256] Over time, revolutionary ties were replaced by partisan ties,[257] but military discipline remained impeccable.[258] There were no military rebellions after 1939, and security forces consistently carried out orders to repress – including high-intensity repression in 1968 and the early 1970s.[259]

Party strength was medium-high. Scope was high. The PRI maintained "roots in every corner of Mexican life."[260] The party's "gigantic human network of clientelist relations" thoroughly penetrated the countryside,[261] transforming it into "one of the world's most accomplished vote-getting machines."[262] Although the PRI's corporatist base eroded in the 1980s, it successfully reorganized along territorial lines.[263] In the early 1990s, the PRI had 8.3 million members and an "unmatched mobilizational capacity."[264] Party cohesion was medium. Originally a revolutionary party, the PRI was "phenomenally cohesive."[265] Its founding elite shared a revolutionary and military background.[266] Over time, the party evolved into a patronage-based machine with institutionalized procedures for career advancement and presidential succession.[267] The PRI remained disciplined

---

[251] Ronfeldt (1984b); Li (2004: 37–52).

[252] Historically, Mexico's army was among the smallest in Latin America (Ronfeldt 1986: 227; Camp 1992: 52). In the 1980s, however, perceived security threats (i.e., Central America and Chiapas) led to a major expansion of the coercive apparatus (Wager 1984: 160–9; Domínguez and Fernández de Castro 2001: 49–51).

[253] Wager (1984: 173); Williams (1986: 145).

[254] See Ronfeldt (1984a, 1984b), Wager (1984: 89–93), and Camp (1992: 89–91).

[255] On army cohesion and its origins, see Ronfeldt (1989: 446), Ackroyd (1991), Camp (1992, 2005), Serrano (1995, 1997), and Wager (1995).

[256] Camp (1992: 102–3; 2005: 42–5).

[257] See Piñeyro (1988) and Serrano (1997: 143). After 1952, all military officers with career ambitions had to work through the PRI (Piñeyro 1988: 284).

[258] Ackroyd (1991); Serrano (1995: 432–3).

[259] Camp (2005: 27–36, 59, 92–3).

[260] Li (2004: 5).

[261] Pacheco Mendez (1991: 255).

[262] Cornelius (1996: 57); see also Klesner (1994: 164–5).

[263] Molinar Horcasitas (1991: 159–70); Collier (1992); Klesner (1994). The PRI launched a "massive effort . . . to create a network of get-out-the-vote promoters . . . with connections down to the lowest level of Mexican society" (Klesner 1994: 186). The party mobilized a "staggering number" of activists, developing a capacity to visit millions of homes (Bruhn 1997: 281–3); see also Morris (1995: 97) and Calderón and Cazés (1996: 59).

[264] Cornelius (1996: 59); Langston (2001: 497).

[265] Ronfeldt (1989: 435).

[266] Kaufman Purcell (1973: 36); Camp (2005: 5–6). Between the 1910 revolution and 1946, all presidents were revolutionary generals (Camp 2005: 75). On PRI cohesion, see Knight (1992), Weldon (1997), and Langston (2001, 2006).

[267] See Langston (2006). Incentives for cooperation were reinforced by the executive's "near complete control over who could hold office under the official party label" (Weldon 1997: 247; see also Garrido 1989).

through the 1980s. There were no major defections between 1952 and 1987, and legislative discipline was nearly 100 percent.[268] However, because the revolutionary generation had died off by 1990, we score cohesion as medium.

Origins and Evolution of the Regime

Mexico maintained a stable electoral authoritarian regime between the 1920s and the mid-1980s.[269] Although the National Action Party (PAN) and other opposition parties competed in elections, PRI hegemony – rooted in a combination of co-optation, repression, and government performance – reduced electoral uncertainty to almost zero.[270] The 1982 debt crisis brought an end to PRI hegemony.[271] In 1983, a string of PAN victories in northern municipal elections "altered the terms of political competition,"[272] and beginning with the 1985 legislative race, elections "ceased to be mere rituals."[273] The 1988 presidential race was "the most vigorously contested in Mexican history."[274] Facing an unprecedented challenge by Cuauhtemoc Cárdenas, a popular politician who had left the party in 1987, the PRI resorted to a "fraud of major proportions."[275] Although PRI candidate Carlos Salinas was officially declared the winner with 50 percent of the vote, the fraud triggered massive protest, and only a divided opposition and strong U.S. support allowed Salinas to ride out the crisis.[276]

Mexico thus entered the post–Cold War era with a competitive authoritarian regime. Fraud and repression persisted into the 1990s,[277] and the persistence of an "umbilical cord" linking the PRI to the state skewed the playing field.[278] Thus, the PRI used its control over licensing, credit, and subsidies to mobilize

---

[268] Weldon (1997, 2004); Langston (2006).

[269] On the sources of authoritarian stability under the PRI, see Magaloni (2006) and Greene (2007).

[270] Before the 1980s, elections were "untainted by...uncertainty of outcomes" (Bruhn 1997: 39). Through 1988, the PRI won a *carro completo* (clean sweep) in each election, including all governorships and nearly all municipalities. On the sources of authoritarian stability under the PRI, see Magaloni (2006) and Greene (2007).

[271] Collier (1992, 1999b); Greene (2007).

[272] Loaeza (1994: 111).

[273] Becarra, Salazar, and Woldenberg (2000: 147). Although the PRI won the 1985 legislative election easily, PAN leaders took it very seriously, publicly aiming for a legislative majority (Loaeza 1999: 375; 2000: 105).

[274] Middlebrook (1988: 133).

[275] Chand (2001: 48). The fraud included multiple voting, ballot stuffing, and manipulation of the vote count. When early returns

showed Cárdenas ahead in Mexico City, a "breakdown" of the computer system led to a six-day delay in the results (Cornelius, Gentleman, and Smith 1989: 20–1; Bruhn 1997: 140–2; Preston and Dillon (2004: 172–5). According to Eisenstadt (2004: 203), the PRI "may well have lost" the 1988 election.

[276] See Bruhn (1997: 146–53) and Eisenstadt (2004: 175–93). The Reagan Administration gave Salinas a "bye" after the 1988 fraud (Eisenstadt 2003: 247). Indeed, on election night, President Reagan telephoned his congratulations to Salinas before the official results had been tabulated (Domínguez and Fernández de Castro 2001: 107).

[277] At least 152 PRD activists were killed between 1988 and 1994 (Eisenstadt 2004: 121–2). In a practice known as "selective democracy," the PRI tolerated PAN victories in some states but used fraud to block PRD victories in others (Gómez Tagle 1994a, 1994b; Crespo 1995: 181–6; Eisenstadt 2004).

[278] Castañeda (1995: 131).

support and punish opponents,[279] and it "enjoyed virtually unlimited access to government funds."[280] During the early 1990s, the PRI reportedly siphoned off $1 billion a year in state money.[281] Although state reform led the PRI to privatize much of its fundraising in the 1990s, lax campaign-finance laws allowed it to raise hundreds of millions of dollars in illicit donations from business tycoons with ties to the state.[282] The media playing field was also skewed: Virtually all major media outlets were in the hands of "sympathetic private owners."[283] Mexico's dominant television network, *Televisa*, was "deeply intertwined" with the PRI, providing the government with "strikingly sympathetic coverage" while blacklisting opponents.[284] Radio also was concentrated in the friendly hands, and media owners "lived under constant threat that their licenses... [would] be suspended" if they fell out of favor with the government.[285] Finally, newspapers were co-opted via subsidies, paid news stories (*gacetillas*), and cash bribes (*chayotes*).[286]

The PRI faced little direct pressure to democratize in the early 1990s. Opposition forces were relatively weak.[287] The most established opposition party, the PAN, "posed no threat to either the PRI or the state,"[288] and Cárdenas' embryonic Party of the Democratic Revolution (PRD) lacked resources and infrastructure in much of the country.[289] At the same time, external pressure was minimal. The U.S. foreign-policy establishment "closed ranks as one to assist in the consolidation of the Salinas administration,"[290] and the Bush and Clinton Administrations "remained mum" on issues of democracy throughout the 1990s.[291] Indeed, when NAFTA negotiations were launched in 1990, U.S. officials stated explicitly that democracy "is not on our agenda."[292]

Nevertheless, linkage generated powerful *indirect* pressure for reform. The technocrats who led the PRI shared a belief in "the importance of insertion, as

---

[279] Teichman (1997); Greene (2007).

[280] Cornelius (1996: 58).

[281] Oppenheimer (1996: 88). A secret presidential budget provided a "major source of campaign finance" (Cornelius 2004: 61) and the National Lottery was a source of "petty cash" (Oppenheimer 1996: 88).

[282] See Oppenheimer (1996: 85–110), De Swaan, Martorelli, and Molinar Horcasitas (1998: 157–8), and Philip (1999: 80–1).

[283] Lawson (2002: 26–8).

[284] Lawson (2004c: 377–9, 385–7).

[285] Cornelius (1996: 56); see also Camp 1985: 189).

[286] See Oppenheimer (1996: 136–7) and Lawson (2002: 31–3). State subsidies kept hundreds of newspapers afloat, converting them into "government propaganda sheets" (Oppenheimer 1996: 136; Lawson 2002: 32–3). The "vast majority" of journalists "accepted regular cash payments from the government agencies they covered" (Lawson 2004c: 379).

[287] The PRI's control over state resources and co-optation of labor, peasant, and business organizations left opposition groups without resources or a mass base (Middlebrook 1995; Greene 2007).

[288] Loaeza (1999: 197); see also Shirk (2001: 101–2). The PAN had not "penetrated into isolated rural areas and impoverished urban neighborhoods" (Cornelius 1996: 71) and thus "did not have... sufficient political and organizational infrastructure to mount an all-out attack against the PRI" (Mizrahi 2003: 26).

[289] Bruhn (1997). In 1994, the PRD had only 50 full-time employees (Bruhn 1997: 189). Opposition weakness was exacerbated by ideological division between the conservative PAN and the left-of-center PRD (Eisenstadt 2003; Magaloni 2005).

[290] Whitehead (1991: 246).

[291] Domínguez and Fernández de Castro (2001: 107).

[292] Quoted in Mazza (2001: 75).

opposed to isolation, as a means of advancing the national interest."²⁹³ Convinced
that "Mexico could only hope to prosper... by aligning itself closely with the
United States," they made NAFTA the centerpiece of their program, betting the
PRI's political future on economic integration.²⁹⁴ Although NAFTA entailed
no political conditionality, it brought intense international scrutiny. NAFTA
"expanded U.S. public interest in... Mexican affairs,"²⁹⁵ to the point where "every
detail of Mexican life... became an object of attention from abroad."²⁹⁶ It also
increased "the number of groups in the United States who came to believe that
their interests could be adversely affected by Mexico."²⁹⁷ Democracy and human-
rights issues were central to the NAFTA debate in the U.S. Congress.²⁹⁸ Critics
of the treaty brought Mexican opposition leaders to testify before Congress,
providing them with an important platform.²⁹⁹ In effect, then, NAFTA forced
the PRI to "accept the scrutiny of the U.S. Congress, public interest groups, and
a myriad of committees and commissions."³⁰⁰

NAFTA also created new forms of linkage-based constraint. For example,
greater dependence on capital flows heightened the government's sensitivity to
the "image it project[ed] to key opinion leaders and fund managers in external
capital markets" and to be "more sensitive than ever to currents of opinion in the
U.S. executive and Congress."³⁰¹ Foreign investors sought stability, and in the
1990s, Wall Street came to view electoral fraud as a greater threat to stability than
a PRI defeat.³⁰² NAFTA also accelerated the "flow of communication, people, and
ideas."³⁰³ U.S. media and NGO penetration increased dramatically,³⁰⁴ bringing
unprecedented attention to cases of fraud and abuse.³⁰⁵ International exposure
"strengthened the clout of Mexican opposition organizations" and helped "magnify domestic demands for democracy."³⁰⁶ Even without conditionality, then,
linkage "limit[ed] the range of choices that might be made by Mexican policy

---

²⁹³ Golob (1997: 99).
²⁹⁴ Gentleman and Zubek (1992: 76–7).
²⁹⁵ Domínguez and Fernández de Castro (2001: 92).
²⁹⁶ Castañeda (1995: 1).
²⁹⁷ Kaufman Purcell (1997: 142).
²⁹⁸ Mazza (2001: 71–7).
²⁹⁹ Oppenheimer (1996: 321); Mazza (2001: 100).
³⁰⁰ Centeno (1994: 240).
³⁰¹ Coatsworth (1999: 151). As one Mexican analyst noted, the PRI "transferred its politi-cal nerve center to the United States, because it is so dependent on foreign investment. As a result, public opinion in the United States matters to the government whereas in Mexico it doesn't" (quoted in Dresser [1996b: 333]).
³⁰² Domínguez and Fernández de Castro (2001: 109).
³⁰³ Dresser (1996b: 341).

³⁰⁴ See Dresser (1996b) and Chand (1997). With NAFTA, "the impact of U.S. non-governmental actors from private founda-tions, think tanks and universities to var-ious NGOs, lobbyists and interest groups on Mexico...increased dramatically.... The number of Mexican organizations from cultural institutions to all manner of NGOs supported by U.S. foundations, the 'stock' of human capital represented by Mexicans edu-cated in U.S. universities, the cross-border cooperation between labor and environmen-tal groups, have all grown larger and more important" (Coatsworth 1999: 151).
³⁰⁵ Thus, the U.S. media "began to report elec-tion irregularities as a main theme of Mexico coverage" during the early 1990s (Eisenstadt 2004: 47). Even fraud in gubernatorial elec-tions gained widespread U.S. media coverage (Dresser 1996b: 332).
³⁰⁶ Dresser (1996b: 329).

makers."[307] Having bet on integration, PRI leaders were "willing to accept the constraints" that integration entailed.[308] Henceforth, they would seek to retain power by internationally acceptable means.

The pursuit of international credibility led the PRI to undertake two strategic changes. First, it underutilized its coercive capacity. Under Salinas, the PRI was "more sensitive to outside human-rights accusations than ever before in its history."[309] Human-rights issues were highly salient at the onset of NAFTA negotiations. The May 1990 killing of human-rights activist Norma Corona "put the Mexican human-rights situation on the front pages" of U.S. newspapers,[310] and a 1990 Americas Watch report on Mexican human rights "attracted significant attention in Washington."[311] That year, the U.S. Congress held its first-ever hearings on Mexico's human-rights situation. Aware that human rights "could become a powerful tool for sectors in the United States that opposed the trade agreement," Salinas created the National Commission on Human Rights and named a respected jurist, Jorge Carpizo, to head it.[312] Although created for international consumption, the Commission "won the respect of broad sectors of society" by documenting hundreds of abuses.[313]

The PRI's coercive restraint was clearly seen in its response to the 1994 Zapatista National Liberation Army (EZLN) uprising. Militarily, the Zapatistas were no match for the government: The army quickly surrounded the rebels and drove them into the countryside.[314] However, the uprising received "intense public attention" in the United States.[315] The Zapatistas made "sophisticated use of the...international media,"[316] and their "extensive use of the Internet" allowed them to "diffuse information...throughout the world instantly."[317] The rebels also drew on an "extensive transnational network," composed of hundreds of human-rights, religious, and solidarity groups.[318] Within weeks of the uprising, more than 100 international NGO delegations were in Chiapas.[319] The internationalization of the conflict – one official dubbed it a "war of ink and the Internet"[320] – precluded the use of coercion. Thus, initial repression:

> ... spurred international concern and led to an influx of human-rights organizations from abroad. CNN dissemination of events in Chiapas undoubtedly raised the costs of the government's initial military response.[321]

---

[307] Cornelius (1996: 23). As a former U.S. ambassador observed, "the prospect of being branded as a noncooperating pariah state, with all that might mean for Mexico's international image and ability to attract investment, tourism, and American goodwill, meant a lot" (Davidow 2004: 49).

[308] Centeno (1994: 240).

[309] Radu (2000: 52); see also Aguayo (1993: 123).

[310] Mazza (2001: 69).

[311] Sikkink (1993: 430–2).

[312] Aguayo (1995b: 367). The Commission published reports in English and shipped

them by express mail to major international human-rights organizations (Sikkink 1993: 433).

[313] Aguayo (1995b: 367).

[314] Wager and Schulz (1995: 172–3, 182).

[315] Schultz and Williams (1995: 12).

[316] Chand (2001: 240).

[317] Castells (1997: 80).

[318] Kumar (2000: 115–18).

[319] Dresser (1996b: 334) and Kumar (2000: 118–25).

[320] Quoted in Fox (2004: 193).

[321] Dresser (1996b: 334).

Because U.S. officials and investors "were unenthusiastic about the prospect of their new NAFTA partner becoming engaged in a televised bloodbath,"[322] it became "impossible for the...government to use repression on a large scale."[323] Concerned that repression would "frighten away investors" and "create a backlash that could destroy NAFTA," the government opted for peace talks.[324]

The PRI's second strategy was to develop credible electoral institutions.[325] Facing heavy scrutiny by the U.S. media and Congress, PRI leaders grew "increasingly sensitive to charges of pervasive electoral fraud from abroad."[326] Here, opposition strength played an important role. Although the PAN and PRD lacked strong national organizations in the early 1990s, they developed the capacity to mobilize massive protest in their regional strongholds.[327] In several states, opposition parties "immobilized PRI governments by filling the streets and government buildings with protesters."[328] International scrutiny and opposition protest interacted in an important way: "messy protests against fraud" could be expected to "sully [the PRI's] image in the United States" and give "ammunition to congressional critics of NAFTA."[329]

The cost of fraud induced the PRI to undertake electoral reform. For the first time, the government began to recognize PAN victories in gubernatorial elections.[330] In addition, reforms in 1989 and 1990 created a new electoral authority, the Federal Electoral Institute (IFE), and endowed it with a generous budget, sophisticated technology, and a large professional staff.[331] Reforms in 1993 and 1994 revamped the voter registry, introduced "fraud-proof" photo ID cards, expanded IFE autonomy (by requiring that its Governing Council be elected by a two-thirds majority in Congress), and created a new Federal Electoral Tribunal to serve as an independent arbiter of electoral disputes.[332] The reforms dramatically improved the quality of national elections, virtually eliminating fraud by 1994.[333]

The reform strategy initially paid off. An uneven playing field and a divided opposition allowed the PRI to win elections without substantial fraud or repression. In the 1991 legislative race, for example, the PRI abused state resources

---

[322] Fox (2004: 505).

[323] Castells (1997: 80). Likewise, Kaufman Purcell (1997: 149) writes that the PRI "found itself hampered in using force to...suppress [the Zapatistas], as it had frequently done with earlier such movements, by its concern that such action would hurt its image and strengthen the hand of NAFTA's opponents in the United States."

[324] Schulz and Williams (1995: 12); see also Dresser (1996b: 334).

[325] See Eisenstadt (2004).

[326] Camp (1999: 188).

[327] Between 1989 and 2000, there were 1,300 postelectoral conflicts over mayoral races alone (Eisenstadt 2004: 115). See also Chand (2001: 236–7) and Magaloni (2005: 134–5).

[328] Cornelius (1994: 59).

[329] Chand (2001: 61).

[330] The first PAN victories took place in Baja California in 1989 and Chihuahua in 1991.

[331] See Crespo (1995: 93–4) and Prud'homme (1998: 148–9).

[332] See Alcocer (1995); Becarra, Salazar, and Woldenberg (2000: 302–3); and Eisenstadt (1999: 88; 2004: 48, 67–8). Overall, the government invested more than $1 billion – that is, more than 1 percent of the federal budget – on electoral reform between 1989 and 1994 (Cornelius 1996: 61; Eisenstadt 2004: 8).

[333] As Magaloni wrote, the PRI "credibly tied its hands not to commit electoral fraud" (2005: 122). See also Eisenstadt (2004).

and dominated access to finance and media,[334] but the election itself was "unusually clean."[335] The PRI won easily, with nearly 60 percent of the vote.

The 1994 presidential election constituted the high-water mark of the PRI's reform strategy. The election was closely scrutinized by the U.S. media and Congress.[336] Moreover, the Zapatista uprising and the March 1994 assassination of PRI candidate Luis Donaldo Colosio "shook investor confidence deeply," triggering $11 billion in capital flight.[337] In this context, PRI technocrats feared a "nightmare scenario," in which a contested victory would "unleash civil violence and prolonged political instability that would.... drive away foreign investors, and jeopardize the country's ... relationship with the United States."[338] Seeking a "certificate of 'good democratic conduct' from the outside world,"[339] the PRI placed Jorge Carpizo – the internationally respected head of the National Commission on Human Rights – in charge of the IFE.[340] For the first time, it also permitted international observers, transforming the race into "the most 'watched' elections in Mexican history."[341]

The 1994 election was "clean but not fair."[342] Although the PRI did not commit fraud,[343] it massively abused state resources and raised hundreds of millions of dollars in illicit contributions,[344] which allowed it to vastly outspend all other parties combined.[345] Moreover, analyses of media coverage found a "clear bias in favor of the PRI."[346] In an election that was "deemed transparent by most observers,"[347] PRI candidate Ernesto Zedillo won 49 percent of the vote, well ahead of both Cárdenas and PAN candidate Diego Fernández.

The PRI's strategy of retaining power via internationally credible elections was eventually undermined by a changing domestic balance of power. By the 1980s, socioeconomic modernization had engendered a "large and diverse middle class

---

334 Gómez Tagle (1993: 18–19).

335 Bruhn (1997: 255); see also Crespo (1999: 90) and Kaufman (1999: 183).

336 Mazza (2001: 111–16).

337 Starr (1999: 40). Foreign investors "clearly wanted a credible election" (Chand 2001: 238).

338 Chand (2001: 240).

339 Aguayo (1995a: 162).

340 Carpizo's role was deemed so critical that his threat to resign in April 1994 triggered more than $1 billion in capital flight (Salinas 2002: 1034).

341 Chand (1997: 543); see also Aguayo (1995a). In addition to more than 900 international observers (Chand 1997: 556–7), Civic Alliance mobilized 20 thousand observers in a "civic action without precedent" in Mexico (Olvera 2003a: 310); see also Dresser (1996b: 329).

342 Dresser (1996a: 163).

343 By virtually all accounts, the registration, voting, and vote-counting processes were

clean (Becarra, Salazar, and Woldenberg 2000; Woldenberg 2002; Eisenstadt 2004; Magaloni 2005).

344 The PRI made extensive use of state funds, agencies, transportation, and personnel (Camp 1999: 200; Cornelius 2004: 61; Gómez Tagle 2004: 92). On illicit private finance, see Oppenheimer (1996: 110) and Philip (1999: 80–1).

345 Campaign finance laws "proved ridiculously irrelevant" (Bruhn 1997: 283–4). The PRI reportedly raised $700 million – 20 times beyond the legal limit (Oppenheimer 1996: 89). Even using the official figure of $105 million, PRI spending more than doubled all other parties combined (Bruhn 1997: 283–4). In the legislative election, PRI spent up to 20 times more than any other party (De Swaan, Martorelli, and Molinar Horcastitas 1998: 165).

346 Aguayo (1995a: 164).

347 Eisenstadt (2004: 48).

and business community,"[348] which laid the foundation for a robust opposition. As the private sector gained strength and autonomy, leading entrepreneurs and business associations increasingly backed the PAN.[349] By the 1990s, the PAN was a "comparatively rich" party with extensive ties to the private sector.[350] Yet, modernization alone does not explain the opposition's rapid growth: Coercive self-restraint also allowed civic and opposition forces to flourish. As repression eased, independent media and human-rights and prodemocracy NGOs proliferated[351]; the PRI's toleration of PAN gubernatorial victories allowed it to use its control of state governments to strengthen its organization and reputation.[352] By the mid-1990s, the PAN was an "electoral force to be reckoned with."[353] Likewise, the PRD expanded its membership from 70 thousand members to 2 million over the course of the 1990s.[354] At the same time, the PRI weakened. Mexico's 1994–1995 financial crisis delivered the "final blows to PRI hegemony."[355] The PRI's public support declined,[356] and it lost a string of state and local elections in 1995 and 1996.

The changing balance of power left the PRI in a bind. To avoid defeat, it would have had to engage in a level of fraud not seen since 1988. Yet, unlike 1988, fraud would require repression of a well-organized opposition and the dismantling of prestigious electoral institutions. Moreover, such a move would trigger international criticism, putting foreign investment and even NAFTA at risk. Unwilling to pay these costs, President Zedillo launched multiparty negotiations that culminated in a 1996 pact called the National Accord. The pact leveled the playing field in several critical respects. First, electoral authorities were made fully independent. Not only would the IFE General Council be selected by a legislative supermajority, but also the IFE President would be selected from within the Council.[357] Second, strict limits were imposed on campaign contributions and spending, and the IFE was given considerable power to enforce them.[358] Moreover, a new public finance system made resource distribution more equitable by providing "the most generous (per capita) public campaign funding in world"[359] Finally, opposition parties also were

---

[348] Chand (2001: 23).

[349] Chand (2001); Mizrahi (2003).

[350] Wuhs (2001: 151–2); Middlebrook (2001: 23–4). For detailed analyses of the PAN's growth, see Mizrahi (2003) and Shirk (2005).

[351] Chand (2001); Lawson (2002); Olvera (2003a, 2003b). The number of human-rights groups more than tripled between 1985 and 1994 (Lawson 2002: 133). The Civic Alliance, an election-observer group, grew into a "gigantic animal" that was "capable of tracking elections in every corner of the country" (Preston and Dillon 2004: 236).

[352] See Lujambio (2001) and Shirk (2005). PAN membership increased from 58 thousand in 1989 to 150 thousand in 1996; after

relaxing its membership criteria, the party's membership reached 600 thousand in 2000 (Mizrahi 2003: 98; Shirk 2005: 242–3). See also Calderón and Cazés (1996: 56–8) and Lujambio (2001: 89–91).

[353] Dresser (1998: 229).

[354] Borjas Benavente (2003: 239–52).

[355] Klesner (2004: 92); Magaloni 2005: 143–4).

[356] Magaloni and Poire (2004).

[357] Prud'homme (1998: 150–1).

[358] See De Swaan, Martorelli, and Molinar Horcasitas (1998: 164–5) and Becarra, Salazar, and Woldenberg (2000: 444).

[359] Brinegar, Morgenstern, and Nielson (2006: 81). See also De Swaan, Martorelli, and Molinar Horcasitas (1998); Becarra, Salazar, and Woldenberg (2000: 456–9).

guaranteed hundreds of hours of free television and radio time during campaigns, and the IFE was given extensive power to monitor media coverage to ensure equity.[360]

The National Accord democratized Mexico. After 1996, electoral institutions were independent and effective. Under the leadership of José Woldenberg, a respected academic, the IFE "devised registration, voting, and tabulation schemes perhaps unparalleled anywhere in the world for their completeness and impenetrability."[361] By the late 1990s, the IFE had earned the "full confidence of the major opposition parties."[362] Indeed, as the body began to rule against the PRI and investigate government abuse, ruling-party officials came to view it as biased toward the opposition.[363] Yet the need for credible elections left the PRI little choice but to comply with its rulings.[364] The PRI had "created an electoral institution 'monster,'" whose professionalism, prestige, and autonomy became very costly to reverse.[365]

Post-1996 elections were democratic. The 1997 midterm elections – in which the PRI lost its legislative majority – were free and fair,[366] and the 2000 election was "Mexico's first presidential campaign in which opposition candidates were able to present themselves on roughly equal footing with the PRI."[367] Media coverage was balanced and the parties competed under "extraordinarily even financial conditions."[368] Moreover, the IFE's controls over the voting and vote-counting processes "probably have no parallel in world history."[369] PAN candidate Vicente Fox won the election and the PRI left power peacefully. Mexico was fully democratic after 2000.[370]

In summary, Mexico's democratization was rooted in both linkage and opposition strength. This analysis differs from recent work on Mexico's transition, such as that of Magaloni and Greene,[371] which focuses exclusively on changing domestic conditions. Indeed, the domestic push for democracy was stronger than

---

[360] Chand (2001: 243–4); Aziz Nassif and Sanchez (2003: 71).

[361] Davidow (2004: 138). According to Schedler (2000: 8), the voter registry ranked "among the world's best in terms of coverage and reliability," and ballots were "harder to forge than U.S. dollars."

[362] Schedler (2000: 8).

[363] In 1998, PRI representatives launched a four-month boycott of the body. See De Swaan, Martorelli, and Molinar Horcasitas (1998: 169) and Gómez Tagle (2004: 96–9).

[364] As one PRI official said, "we don't want to shoot our own foot by discrediting the IFE." Quoted in Eisenstadt (2004: 251).

[365] Eisenstadt (2004: 237); see also Magaloni (2005: 136).

[366] Resource distribution was equitable (Becarra, Salazar, and Woldenberg 2000: 456–9), media access was balanced (Trejo Delarbre 1999; Lawson 2004c: 396), and voting and vote-counting processes were clean.

[367] Lawson (2004b: 187–8).

[368] Schedler (2000: 12); also Becarra, Salazar, and Woldenberg (2000: 47). On media coverage, see Lawson (2004b: 199). Although the PRI government did commit some campaign finance violations (Lawson 2004a), these abuses were not seen to skew the playing field as in past elections.

[369] Elizondo (2003: 30).

[370] Although the 2006 election – narrowly won by PAN candidate Felipe Calderón – triggered accusations of fraud, no evidence of fraud was uncovered (Schedler 2007).

[371] See Magaloni (2006) and Greene (2007).

in the Dominican Republic, Guyana, and Nicaragua. Yet the transition was initiated "from above," by PRI elites, at a time when opposition forces were still relatively weak.[372] The key to understanding why they did so lies in the interplay of domestic and international factors. In their pursuit of international credibility, PRI governments underutilized their coercive capacity and invested in strong electoral institutions. When opposition parties gained sufficient strength to win elections, the PRI was trapped in its own institutional framework. Reversing course would have generated domestic and international costs that PRI technocrats were unwilling to pay.

MEDIUM LINKAGE AND HIGH LEVERAGE: PERU AND HAITI

Peru and Haiti differ from the other cases examined in this chapter in that linkage was medium rather than high.[373] Although external factors at times were critical in each case, helping to soften (Peru) or reverse (Haiti) coups, the international environment had a less consistent democratizing impact. Although competitive authoritarian regimes broke down in both countries, domestic factors such as weak state (Haiti) and party (Peru) structures played a central role in the transitions. Ultimately, regime outcomes diverged: Whereas Peru democratized after 2000, Haiti remained nondemocratic.

Peru

The dynamics of the competitive authoritarian regime that emerged under President Alberto Fujimori (1992–2000) differed from those of others examined in this chapter. In a context of medium linkage, external pressure was uneven and the regime was less responsive to such pressure. Indeed, regime breakdown was primarily a domestic process, triggered by the revelation of a massive state mafia network – operated by Fujimori's "intelligence advisor," Vladimiro Montesinos – constructed in lieu of a governing party. Peru's subsequent democratization is not predicted by our theory.

Linkage, Leverage, and Organizational Power
Peru is a case of medium linkage, high leverage, and low organizational power. Ties to the West were weaker than in the other cases examined in this chapter. Although the United States was Peru's primary economic partner,[374] trade and foreign-capital flows were lower than in the Dominican Republic or Mexico.[375] Technocratic ties also were more limited,[376] and, although civic and opposition

---

[372] Kaufman (1999: 174).
[373] Linkage scores for Peru and Haiti are 0.59 and 0.63, respectively, which is just below the threshold for high linkage (see Appendix III).
[374] McClintock and Vallas (2003: 97–100).

[375] World Bank World Development Indicators (www.worldbank.org/data/).
[376] Conaghan (2005: 151–3). Between 1978 and 1995, for example, only three of Peru's 15 economic ministers were U.S.-educated (Conaghan 1998: 151).

groups were well connected abroad,[377] these ties were weaker than in Mexico or the Caribbean Basin.[378] Thus, "no significant domestic political constituency... became activated over the U.S. role in Peru,"[379] and Peru "rarely appeared on the radar screen of American policymakers."[380] Leverage is scored as high because Peru lacked substantial economic or military power, black-knight support, or strategic importance to the United States. [381] In practice, however, U.S. democratizing pressure was limited in the 1990s by a competing policy objective: drug interdiction.[382] Cooperation in the drug war "delivered Fujimori important political credit... in Washington"[383]; as a result, U.S. officials placed a fairly low priority on democracy.[384] Unlike the Dominican Republic, Guyana, and Nicaragua, then, external pressure exerted only a "modest and sporadic effect" in Peru.[385]

Organizational power was low. Coercive scope and cohesion were at best medium. Peru's state had historically been weak,[386] and it was further weakened in the 1980s by economic collapse and the Shining Path insurgency.[387] Beginning in 1990, however, the Fujimori government strengthened the coercive apparatus, expanded its presence in the countryside, and defeated the guerrillas.[388] At the same time, the National Intelligence Service (SIN) grew into an "immense apparatus,"[389] operating a "vast espionage network" with 15 thousand agents and informers.[390] By 1992, then, coercive scope was medium. We score state cohesion as medium because – although Peru had a long history of military coups – there were no coup attempts in the 1980s.[391]

---

[377] Opposition candidates such as former UN General Secretary Javier Pérez de Cuellar and Alejandro Toledo (a Stanford Ph.D. and World Bank economist) maintained strong international ties. NGOs were well connected to transnational human-rights networks (Basombrio 2000), and journalists and media organizations were well connected to international press organizations (Conaghan 2005: 152, 221).

[378] Roberts and Peceny (1997: 220–2).

[379] Roberts and Peceny (1997: 220–1).

[380] Conaghan (2005: 162).

[381] See Palmer (2006).

[382] See Roberts and Peceny (1997: 213–14) and Palmer (2006).

[383] Cotler (2000: 39).

[384] Cotler (2000: 39); McClintock and Vallas (2003: 21). These priorities were reflected in a 1995 U.S. embassy cable, which acknowledged Fujimori's poor human-rights record but stated, "It is a reality – albeit uncomfortable – that we have a massive national security problem – drugs – which at this point requires his cooperation" (quoted in Conaghan [2005: 106–7]).

[385] Roberts and Peceny (1997: 221); see also Palmer (2006).

[386] See Mauceri (1996, 1997) and Soifer (2006).

[387] In the late 1980s, the Shining Path gained control of more than a quarter of Peru's municipalities (McClintock 1999: 329), and the state lost its "capacity to provide... basic levels of social order and security" (Burt 1997: 290). See also Obando (1993: 77–82), Mauceri (1996, 1997), and Burt (1997: 282–4).

[388] Obando (1994b); Mauceri (1996, 1997).

[389] Rospigliosi (2000: 156).

[390] Mauceri (1995: 24); Rospigliosi (2000: 197–201); Loayza (1998: 154–7). With a 50-fold budget increase and sophisticated intelligence equipment, the SIN became "one of the most powerful intelligence services in Latin America" (Degregori 2000: 51). See also Obando (1994a: 373; 1994b: 114–15) and Mauceri (1997: 160–1; 2004: 157).

[391] Fujimori's security advisor, Vladimiro Montesinos, packed the army hierarchy with loyalists (Obando 1993, 1994b). By the mid-1990s, all top army posts were held by Montesinos allies, most of whom were from his graduating class in the military academy (Cameron 1997: 53–4; Loayza 1998: 188).

Party strength was low. Elected as a political outsider, Fujimori "did not build a real party."[392] Instead, he created a series of "empty vessels" that "did not have national organizations with local branches, central bureaucracies... or affiliated members" and were "incapable of fielding candidates in most municipal districts."[393] Fujimori closed the headquarters of his first party, Change 90, on winning the presidency[394]; his second party, New Majority, had no members and "scarcely any organizational presence outside the national congress."[395] A third party, Let's Go Neighbor, was "left to rot" after the 1998 municipal elections[396]; a fourth, Peru 2000, was created "out of thin air" before the 2000 election.[397] Cohesion was low. Cobbled together prior to each election, Fujimori's parties lacked stable organizations, a clear ideology, or a shared history of struggle.

Lacking a real party, Fujimori turned to the state as an organizational substitute. Basic party activities, such as fundraising, candidate selection, and campaigning, were done illicitly by the SIN and other state agencies[398]; state corruption served as the regime's primary source of cohesion.[399] Numerous cabinet members, legislators, and other state officials received bribes from Montesinos and thus were subject to blackmail.[400] Although corruption and state patronage helped to substitute for a party machine in the 1990s, they were a fragile source of cohesion because cooperation hinged on an array of illicit activities that, if exposed, would threaten regime legitimacy.

Origins and Evolution of the Regime

Competitive authoritarianism in Peru emerged out of democratic breakdown. Facing a guerrilla insurgency, hyperinflation, and a hostile legislature, President Fujimori carried out a "self-coup" (*autogolpe*) in 1992, dissolving Congress and the Constitution with the aim of establishing a full-blown dictatorship.[401] The coup triggered a "swift and universally unfavorable" response from the international community.[402] U.S., World Bank, and IMF assistance was suspended and the OAS threatened sanctions.[403] The specter of international isolation triggered resistance among Fujimori's technocratic and business

---

392 Tanaka (2005: 278–80).
393 Roberts (2006a: 139–40). On the weakness of Fujimori's parties, see Roberts (1995, 2006b), Tanaka (1998), Planas (2000), and Levitsky and Cameron (2003).
394 Planas (2000: 251).
395 Roberts (2006b: 94–5). Indeed, after Fujimori was reelected with New Majority in 1995, "there wasn't even... a party headquarters where the president could celebrate" (Degregori 2000: 62).
396 Barr and Dietz (2006: 74).
397 Cameron (2000: 10).
398 Thus, the SIN became "Fujimori's political party" (Rospigliosi 1995: 332; 2000: 202). Also see Roberts (1995), Planas (2000:

357–8), and Bowen and Holligan (2003: 344–72).
399 Rospigliosi (2000); Cameron (2006).
400 Conaghan (2005: 105); Cameron (2006).
401 See Cotler (1994: 208–10), Rospigliosi (2000: 84, 96–7), and Kenney (2003).
402 Ferrero (1993: 34). President George H. W. Bush called the coup "unacceptable" and telephoned Fujimori to insist on a return to democracy (Conaghan 2005: 9, 36–7). U.S. State Department officials reportedly told Peruvian diplomats, "We will not allow this. We will close you down." Quoted in Cameron (1997: 65).
403 Ferrero Costa (1993: 34–6).

allies.[404] To "cover his international flank," Fujimori called constituent assembly elections for November 1992.[405] *Fujimorista* forces won a majority and wrote a new constitution, which was approved, via referendum, in 1993.[406]

Although the return to electoral rule allowed Fujimori to meet the "minimal democratic conditions demanded by the developed countries and the OAS,"[407] the new regime was not democratic. Behind the new constitutional façade emerged a "clandestine government" through which state institutions were systematically corrupted and deployed against opponents.[408] Using the SIN, Fujimori's shadowy advisor, Vladimiro Montesinos, operated a "vast telephone espionage network" that monitored politicians and media figures.[409] As videotapes later documented, Montesinos also constructed a vast mafia network by bribing and blackmailing hundreds of government officials, legislators, judges, military commanders, media owners, journalists, and opposition politicians.[410]

The SIN's mafia network allowed the Fujimori government to abuse its authority in several ways. First, it gained illicit control over judicial and electoral authorities. Fujimori purged the judiciary in 1992, sacking 80 percent of sitting judges – including 13 Supreme Court justices – and replacing most of them with "provisional" appointees who could be removed at any time.[411] Moreover, a "staggering" number of judges – including several Supreme Court justices – received payments or favors from the SIN.[412] The politicized courts served as a "shield for friends of the regime and a weapon against its enemies."[413] Judicial and tax authorities targeted opposition politicians, businessmen, and media, forcing some of them into exile.[414] The National Elections Board was also

---

[404] Mauceri (1995: 29–30). Among business elites, "a growing fear soon set in about the implications of the international aid cutoff" (Mauceri 1996: 69). The coup triggered a run on Peru's currency and raised the specter of massive capital flight (Cameron 1997: 66). Finance Minister Carlos Boloña threatened to resign if democratic institutions were not restored (Cameron 1994: 154) and he was backed by business elites (Durand 2003: 380–1).

[405] Ferrero Costa (1993: 36).

[406] The constituent assembly election was marred by biased electoral authorities and abuse of state resources (Rospigliosi 1994: 49–50; LASA 1995: 10; Conaghan 2005: 51–4). The 1993 constitutional referendum suffered "serious denunciations of fraud and irregularities" (Tanaka 2005: 280), which led one electoral official to publicly call for an annulment of the results. See LASA (1995: 7) and Rospigliosi (1995: 327).

[407] Durand (2003: 381).

[408] Rospigliosi (2000); Conaghan (2005).

[409] Mauceri (1995: 24). See also Bowen and Holligan (2003: 290–1). The SIN placed cameras and microphones in Congress, courthouses, government ministries, and brothels frequented by leading politicians (Rospigliosi 2000: 157–8, 202; Bresani 2003: 39–40, 216).

[410] At least 1,600 Peruvians – including at least four Supreme Court justices, a majority of the National Elections Board, two attorney generals, and dozens of legislators – were implicated by the videos. See Moreno Ocampo (ND), Rospigliosi (2000), Conaghan (2005), and Cameron (2006). The mafia network was reinforced through surveillance and blackmail (Cameron 2006).

[411] Rospigliosi (2000: 103–4); Youngers (2000: 26–32); Pease (2003: 286–90, 300–301).

[412] Conaghan (2005: 167); see also Cameron (2006: 280).

[413] Durand (2003: 459).

[414] The most notorious of these cases was that of Channel 2 owner, Barch Ivcher. See Youngers (2000: 17, 43), Avendaño (2001), Comisión Andina de Juristas (2001: 361), and Durand (2003: 459–61).

packed.[415] Consequently, complaints of electoral abuse were routinely buried and "enforcement of campaign regulations was almost nonexistent."[416]

The Fujimori government also skewed access to resources and the media. At least $164 million was transferred illicitly from various state agencies into Fujimori's campaign coffers between 1992 and 2000.[417] Moreover, the SIN organized and financed Fujimori's election campaigns, and the army was mobilized to campaign for Fujimori.[418] The government controlled much of the private media through manipulation of debt and judicial favors, strategic use of state advertising, and massive bribery.[419] By the late 1990s, four of Peru's five private television networks were receiving monthly payments from the SIN (the fifth received judicial favors) and more than a dozen tabloid newspapers were on the SIN payroll.[420] Finally, although the regime was not highly repressive, journalists and human-rights activists were often harassed or threatened.[421]

Fujimori's authoritarianism initially met few serious challenges. After the return to constitutional rule, the OAS declared the Peru case "closed,"[422] and due to its cooperation in the drug war, Peru became the leading recipient of U.S. aid in Latin America.[423] At home, economic stabilization and the defeat of the Shining Path insurgency earned Fujimori broad public support.[424] Moreover, opposition forces were weak. Peruvian parties collapsed in the early 1990s, giving way to dozens of personalistic vehicles that were "too disorganized to deserve the label party."[425] At the same time, civil society was decimated by economic crisis and penetration by the Shining Path, leaving the democracy movement without

---

[415] After the 1992 coup, Fujimori fired two of five National Elections Board members and appointed a new president who was widely viewed as biased (Conaghan 2005: 53–4). In 1997, Congress passed legislation – dubbed the "Fraud Law" – that modified the National Elections Board selection process to facilitate its packing (Pease 2003: 311–13; Conaghan 2005: 133).

[416] Schmidt (2000: 110); Conaghan (2005: 92–3, 168).

[417] Conaghan (2005: 164).

[418] See Rospigliosi (1994: 49; 2000: 202), Planas (2000: 357–8), and Bowen and Holligan (2003: 344–72).

[419] The government used state advertising and television and newspaper owners' debts and judicial problems as sources of leverage, providing advertising, debt relief, and judicial favors in exchange for sympathetic coverage (Ames et al. 2001: 229, 232; Bowen and Holligan 2003: 340–4, 361–2). When advertising revenues fell during the economic slowdown of the late 1990s, the government more than doubled its spending on state advertising,

becoming the leading advertiser in the country (Degregori 2000: 12; Youngers (2000: 54).

[420] See Fowks (2000: 68–72), Bowen and Holligan (2003: 361–2), Bresani (2003), Pease (2003: 338–9), Felch (2004: 44), and MacMillan and Zoido (2004: 8–9).

[421] See Youngers (2000: 41–2) and Conaghan (2005: 71). There were a few cases of state-sponsored violence, such as the 1992 killing of nine students at La Cantuta University by the Colina Group, a death squad linked to the army. When General Rodolfo Robles went public with information about the Colina Group in 1993, death threats forced him into exile (Rospigliosi 2000: 129–33).

[422] Millet (1994: 15).

[423] Roberts and Peceny (1997: 220).

[424] Between April 1992 and May 1996, Fujimori's public-approval rating hovered between 60 and 80 percent (Tanaka 2001: 74; Carrión 2006: 129).

[425] Weyland (2006: 33); see also Tanaka (1998), Planas (2000), and Levitsky and Cameron (2003).

"broad-based organization."[426] Fujimori was easily reelected in 1995, defeating former UN General Secretary Javier Pérez de Cuellar by a nearly three-to-one margin and capturing a legislative majority. Although the election was marred by abuse of state resources, phone-tapping of opposition candidates, and irregularities in the legislative vote count,[427] it was accepted by the international community.[428]

Despite Fujimori's success, however, party weakness left the regime vulnerable on several fronts. First, substitution of the state for party organization was risky because public exposure of corruption and other illicit activities could be politically costly.[429] Second, party weakness created succession problems. The 1993 constitution limited presidents to two terms in office, and Fujimori lacked a viable successor. No other government official enjoyed Fujimori's popularity, and *Fujimorismo* fared poorly in elections whenever Fujimori himself was not a candidate.[430] The failure of Fujimori ally Jaime Yoshiyama in the 1995 Lima mayoral race made it clear that "there could be no *Fujimorismo* without Fujimori."[431]

Unwilling to leave power and unable to find a viable successor, the government adopted a strategy of "reelection at any cost" during Fujimori's second term.[432] In August 1996, Congress passed the Law of Authentic Interpretation, which declared that because Fujimori's first term began under the old constitution, it did not count under the new one, leaving him free to seek reelection in 2000.[433] When the Constitutional Tribunal voted to declare the law "inapplicable," the government ignored the ruling; in May 1997, Congress impeached the three members of the court who voted for it.[434] Opposition groups launched a petition drive to call a referendum on the reelection issue; yet this, too, was derailed via institutional manipulation.[435] Finally, the government packed the National

---

[426] Conaghan (2005: 134–5). See Roberts (1998); and Schonwalder (2002: 81–3). Thus, the opposition was reduced to "a small group of intellectuals, politicians displaced by the coup, [and] union and popular leaders, most of whom had little public following" (Arias 2001: 60).

[427] See Degregori (2000: 51–2), Conaghan (2005: 91–2), and McClintock (2006a: 248–50). More than 40 percent of legislative ballots were declared invalid, a figure that was four times greater than that of the presidential election and more than three times that of previous legislative elections (McClintock 2006a: 249). *Fujimorismo's* legislative majority ran "contrary to the predictions of almost every pollster" (Conaghan 2005: 99; see also McClintock 2006a: 249). Postelection complaints were buried by electoral and judicial authorities (Schmidt 2000: 110; Conaghan 2005: 92–3).

[428] McClintock and Vallas (2003: 42–3).

[429] Cameron (2006); Roberts (2006b: 97).

[430] Tanaka (2005: 280).

[431] Roberts (2006b: 93).

[432] Cotler (2000: 53).

[433] See Conaghan (2005: 121–2). The law was "considered absurd by most constitutional experts" (McClintock and Vallas 2003: 144).

[434] Conaghan (2005: 126–30).

[435] In 1996, Congress passed a law requiring that referenda be approved by 40 percent of Congress, which "ensured that no referendum could pass without *Fujimorista* support (Conaghan 2005: 124). After the National Election Board ruled that the new law could not be applied in the reelection case, the Board was packed. The new Board reversed the earlier ruling and the referendum project died in Congress (Pease 2003: 311–13; Conaghan 2005: 133–6).

Elections Board and modified its governing rules to ensure that Fujimori's candidacy would not be disqualified. [436]

The regime also tightened its grip on the media. Thus, after Channel 2 ran a series of critical news stories in 1997, the government revoked owner Baruch Ivcher's citizenship and forced him into exile on tax charges.[437] Channel 2 was taken over by Fujimori allies, leaving all television stations in progovernment hands. Montesinos then signed a "contract" with each television owner that ensured pro-Fujimori coverage in exchange for a monthly payment.[438] Likewise, tabloid newspapers received as much as $2 million a month to publish articles faxed from the SIN.[439] Remaining independent media were harassed: 136 media attacks were reported between 1998 and 2000.[440]

The government got away with this abuse for two reasons. First, the opposition remained weak, and prodemocracy protest was "anemic and unsustained."[441] Second, external pressure was limited. The United States took no punitive action against Fujimori,[442] and the government was largely unresponsive to linkage-based pressure. Government abuse *did* reverberate in the international community.[443] For example, exiled media owner Baruch Ivcher "mounted an effective lobby" in Washington, which – together with campaigns by international press and human-rights groups – eroded Fujimori's image in the U.S. Congress.[444] Despite the costs,[445] however, Fujimori largely defied international criticism. He rejected international demands to reverse course on the Constitutional Tribunal and Ivcher cases, and when the Inter-American Human Rights Court ruled against him on another case, he pulled Peru out of the Court.[446] These actions triggered little opposition from business and other pro-regime elites.[447]

---

[436] The Election Board's voting rules were modified so that four of five votes were required for candidate disqualification. Because Fujimori had two allies on the Board, the change ensured that his candidacy would remain legal (Avendaño 2001: 131–3; Conaghan 2005: 133, 153).

[437] The government cited "irregularities" in the procedure through which Ivcher had immigrated from Israel. Under Peruvian law, Ivcher was forced to cede control of Channel 2. See Conaghan (2005: 141–53).

[438] Bowen and Holligan (2003: 390); MacMillan and Zoido (2004: 8); Conaghan (2005: 154–6). In a 1999 videotape, Montesinos declared that the television stations were "all lined up now.... Every day, I have a meeting with them here ... and we plan the evening news." Quoted in Conaghan (2005: 156).

[439] See Fowks (2001: 71–2), Bowen and Holligan (2003: 355, 366), Bresani (2003: 189), and Felch (2004: 44).

[440] Youngers (2000); Ames et al. (2001: 236).

[441] Roberts (2006b: 98).

[442] McClintock and Vallas 2003: (143–57).

[443] See McClintock and Vallas (2003: 63–5).

[444] McClintock and Vallas (2003: 146). U.S. Senator Jesse Helms, an Ivcher ally, helped "whip up a bipartisan anti-Fujimori mood in Congress" and orchestrated passage of a 1999 Senate resolution expressing "concern" over media abuse in Peru (Conaghan 2001: 9–12). See also Conaghan (2005: 152).

[445] Foreign Minister Francisco Tudela, who was one of the most internationally connected officials in the government, resigned in 1997 – due, in part, to the Ivcher scandal (McClintock and Vallas 2003: 60).

[446] McClintock and Vallas (2003: 143).

[447] Durand (2003).

The limits of external pressure were made manifest in the 2000 election, when Fujimori faced a serious electoral challenge by former World Bank official Alejandro Toledo. Unlike 1995, Fujimori was quite vulnerable in 2000. He trailed in the polls throughout much of 1998 and 1999, and his new party, Peru 2000, lacked the infrastructure to perform even the most basic party activities, which forced the government to use state agencies to carry them out illicitly.[448] The election was unfair. Opposition parties "faced a steeply tilted playing field – indeed, a virtual cliff."[449] Their candidates were spied on and their campaigns were disrupted by SIN-orchestrated mob attacks and power outages.[450] Media coverage was biased and the SIN-controlled media launched a "dirty war" against opposition candidates, accusing them of everything from terrorism to homosexuality.[451] Moreover, millions of dollars in state funds were diverted to Fujimori's campaign, the security forces worked for Fujimori, and at least three of five National Elections Board members were linked to the SIN.[452] On election night, the government appeared to manipulate the results to avoid a runoff against Toledo.[453] International pressure and a massive protest led by Toledo forced Fujimori to accept a runoff.[454] However, the government rejected calls – by Toledo and international observers – to level the playing field for the second round.[455] Toledo dropped out of the race and the OAS and The Carter Center withdrew, calling the election "fatally flawed."[456] Uncontested, Fujimori won easily.

Following the election, Toledo launched a protest campaign that culminated in a massive mobilization on Inauguration Day.[457] Nevertheless, the mobilization

---

[448] Roberts (2006b: 95–7). In 2000, *El Comercio* revealed that the 1.2 million signatures required to register Peru 2000 as a party had been forged in government-run "signature factories" (Conaghan 2005: 181). Although the judiciary shelved the case, it triggered a costly scandal (Roberts 2006b: 96).

[449] McClintock (2006a: 255).

[450] Reportedly, some 400 SIN agents spied on the opposition during the campaign (Youngers 2000: 63–4; Bowen and Holligan 2003: 296; Conaghan 2005: 172–6).

[451] Studies found that Fujimori received more than twice as much coverage as all other candidates combined (García Calderon 2001: 52; Boas 2005: 36). Television networks generally ignored opposition candidates and often refused to run their ads (Ames et al. 2001: 78; Dammert 2001: 49–50). On the media "dirty war," see Degregori (2000: 151–68), Fowks (2000: 69–70), and Bowen and Holligan (2003: 377–8).

[452] On the diversion of state funds, see Bowen and Holligan (2003: 359). On the role of the security apparatus, see Conaghan (2005:

165). On SIN ties to the electoral authorities, see Moreno Ocampo (ND: 2); Conaghan (2005: 132–3).

[453] Credible "quick counts" showed Fujimori ahead of Toledo but short of the 50 percent needed to avoid a runoff (Ames et al. 2001: 139). As the evening progressed, Fujimori's vote share inexplicably rose, leading OAS representative Eduardo Stein to declare that he had "no idea where these results [were] coming from" and that "something sinister [was] going on" (Bowen and Holligan 2003: 384). See also Conaghan (2001: 14).

[454] See McClintock and Vallas (2003: 150) and Conaghan (2005: 192–3). OAS representatives, The Carter Center, and U.S. Secretary of State Madeleine Albright all made "forceful and unequivocal public statements" that a first-round Fujimori victory would be "unacceptable" (Balbi and Palmer 2001: 67). Official results ultimately gave Fujimori 49.9 percent of the vote.

[455] Conaghan (2005: 195–200).

[456] Balbi and Palmer (2001: 67).

[457] See Conaghan (2005: 216).

could not be sustained,[458] and the international response was tepid. Opposition groups lobbied for a "Balaguer solution," in which the United States and the OAS would force Fujimori to call new elections.[459] However, the United States took no punitive action; indeed, U.S. officials "seemed to have resigned themselves to a third Fujimori term."[460] The OAS sent a High Level Mission to Peru to foster a "national dialogue" and "strengthen democracy," but the Mission was not authorized to impose conditionality.[461] Although refusing to cooperate with the OAS Mission "ran the risk of being isolated from the international community,"[462] Fujimori ignored its recommendations – and most business, technocratic, and military elites continued to back him.[463]

After surviving the 2000 election, the government turned to a key area of vulnerability: Congress. Peru 2000 had won only 52 of 120 legislative seats, leaving Fujimori vulnerable to impeachment.[464] To prevent such an outcome, Montesinos "bribed his way to a congressional majority."[465] As many as 18 opposition legislators were induced to defect via monthly payments of $10,000 to $20,000, allowing pro-Fujimori forces to gain control of Congress.[466]

Competitive authoritarianism collapsed in late 2000, but the roots of regime change were largely endogenous.[467] In many respects, Fujimori's fall was a contingent outcome: It was triggered by the September 2000 release of a videotape showing Montesinos bribing an opposition legislator. After the tape's release, Fujimori sacked Montesinos (who fled the country) and called new elections in which he would not participate. Yet party weakness played a major role in the transition. The system of organized corruption that was revealed by the videotapes had been – at least partially – a substitute for a strong party.[468] In the absence of a party, moreover, the governing coalition quickly disintegrated. As the crisis deepened, "the rats jumped the sinking ship."[469] Erstwhile allies – including Vice President Francisco Tudela and several legislators – defected, thereby depriving Fujimori of a parliamentary majority.[470] Facing impeachment, Fujimori fled to Japan.

Peru democratized after 2000. Interim President Valentin Paniagua dismantled the SIN and overhauled the electoral authorities. In 2001, Toledo won what was "probably the cleanest and fairest [election] in Peruvian history."[471] Toledo governed democratically and subsequent elections were free and fair. Although

---

[458] See Tanaka (2001: 99–100). According to López (2001: 78), opposition protest "did not reach the mass proportions necessary to produce the collapse of the regime, as occurred in Yugoslavia."

[459] Conaghan (2001: 29; 2005: 210). Protesters chanted "Clinton, listen, join the fight" (Conaghan 2001: 29).

[460] Wise (2003: 215); McClintock and Vallas (2003: 5, 151–3).

[461] McClintock (2001: 138).

[462] Cotler (2000: 65).

[463] López (2001: 70–1).

[464] Roberts (2006b: 93).

[465] Roberts (2006b: 98).

[466] See Tanaka (2001: 99), Bowen and Holligan (2003: 386–7), and Conaghan (2005: 212–13).

[467] See Cameron (2006).

[468] Cameron (2006); Roberts (2006a: 140).

[469] Weyland (2006: 34).

[470] Cameron (2006: 279–80).

[471] López (2001: 85).

this outcome is not predicted by our theory, it is worth noting that Peru's linkage was relatively high. Toledo was a Stanford-educated technocrat with extensive U.S. ties. He relied heavily on INGOs while in opposition, and he filled his government with U.S-oriented technocrats.[472] Still, democracy remained fragile after 2000. Ollanta Humala, a populist outsider with ties to Hugo Chavez, nearly captured the presidency in 2006. Had he won, Peru might well have shifted back in a competitive authoritarian direction.[473]

In summary, external factors played only a secondary role in the collapse of competitive authoritarianism in Peru. International pressure prevented outright authoritarianism in 1992, but it was insufficient to re-democratize Peru or prevent Fujimori's illegal reelection in 2000. Although the regime's international legitimacy was eroded by the 2000 election,[474] it likely would have survived had it not been for the videotape scandal.[475] Party weakness contributed to authoritarian breakdown in at least four ways. First, it forced Fujimori to rely on illicit activities to maintain cohesion, which generated the scandals that ultimately undermined the regime. Second, party weakness increased Fujimori's electoral and legislative vulnerability. Fujimori may have needed fraud to obtain a legislative majority in 1995, and he required massive bribery to achieve one in 2000. Third, party weakness made it difficult for the regime to perpetuate itself in power. Without a viable successor, the regime "depended on Fujimori's personal continuity in power,"[476] which pushed it in an autocratic direction. Fourth, party weakness undermined elite cohesion. Fujimori's coalition disintegrated after the video scandal, ensuring his fall.

Haiti

Haiti is the only one of our cases in the Americas that failed to democratize – an outcome that is hardly surprising given the country's unfavorable structural conditions.[477] Due to Haiti's relatively limited economic and technocratic ties to the United States, external incentives for democratic behavior were weaker than in the Dominican Republic, Guyana, and Nicaragua. Nevertheless, extreme state weakness prevented autocrats from consolidating power. The governments of Jean Bertrand Aristide and his ally, René Préval, survived in the 1990s due to U.S. tolerance and the protection of UN forces. After 2000, however, international isolation led to state collapse, which permitted Aristide's overthrow by armed thugs.

---

[472] McClintock and Vallas (2003: 161, 167).
[473] See McClintock (2006b).
[474] Cotler (2001: 195–7).
[475] Cameron (2006).
[476] Tanaka (2005: 278).
[477] With a per capita GDP of $300, Haiti ranked 150th on the UN's Human Develop-

ment Index (below Bangladesh and Sudan) (Erikson 2004: 292). Given Haiti's predominantly rural and illiterate society, small middle class, and weak civil society, "the likelihood of a successful transition to democracy...was very remote" (Dupuy 1997: 104).

Linkage, Leverage, and Organizational Power

Haiti is a case of high leverage and medium linkage. The poorest and most aid-dependent country in the hemisphere,[478] Haiti had long been vulnerable to U.S. pressure. The United States occupied Haiti between 1915 and 1934, and subsequent Haitian governments could not survive "without the recognition or at least benign indifference of the United States."[479] Indeed, U.S. military intervention restored Aristide to power in 1994, and the Aristide government depended on foreign aid for two thirds of its budget.[480] After 1990, few U.S. interests rivaled democracy promotion.[481]

Linkage was medium. Ties to the West were uneven. Social ties were extensive. Between 1970 and 1990, as much as 15 percent of Haiti's population emigrated, mostly to the United States.[482] By the 1990s, one million people of Haitian descent lived in the United States.[483] The diaspora "transnationalized" Haitian politics.[484] Haitian radio stations connected diasporic communities to events in Haiti and diaspora newspapers "competed with the local papers in Haiti."[485] Diasporic organizations possessed considerable resources, which they used to finance Haitian political parties. Haitian politicians set up offices in New York and Miami and did much of their fundraising and campaigning there.[486] Haitian–American organizations such as the Washington Office on Haiti, the National Coalition for Haitian refugees, and the Haiti Support Committee created a "constituency for Haiti in the United States."[487] Due to these ties, as well as sheer geographic proximity, Haiti received attention in the United States that was "highly disproportionate to its size."[488] In the 1980s and early 1990s, for example, the impact of refugee flows – magnified by U.S. television images of Haitian "boat people" – heightened U.S. politicians' sensitivity to developments in Haiti.[489]

In other areas, however, linkage was lower. For example, the paucity of communication technology in Haiti limited information flows. Few Haitians had

---

[478] Foreign assistance accounted for up to 25 percent of Haiti's GDP during the mid-1990s (Preeg 1996: 77).

[479] Laguerre (1993: 68–71, 178).

[480] Gros (1997: 106); Schulz (1997–1998: 77). As Aristide himself declared, "If the international community is not for us, one thing is sure: we will fail." Quoted in Orenstein 2001: 23).

[481] Preeg (1996: 82).

[482] Weinstein and Segal (1992: 138).

[483] Weinstein and Segal (1992: 122–3); Preeg (1996: 64–5); Catanese (1999: 89).

[484] Laguerre (1997: 173–4).

[485] Laguerre (1997: 178); see also Jean-Pierre (1994: 58).

[486] Laguerre (1997: 172–5; 1999: 645).

[487] Weinstein and Segal (1992: 120).

[488] Maguire (2003: 3). According to Preeg (1996: 10), the ease of travel between Miami and Haiti "reduces the cost of television and other media coverage compared with more distant troubled countries. Interaction between direct reporting out of Haiti and political activities of the Haitian diaspora in prominent American cities adds to the media impact linking US and Haitian interests." See also Preeg (1993) and von Hippel (2002: 102–3).

[489] Preeg (1993: 2–3; 1995: 57–8); Perusse (1995: 93); Ballard (1998: 77–8); von Hippel (2000: 102–3).

access to television,[490] and the number of telephone lines was far lower than in the Dominican Republic, Guyana, or Nicaragua.[491] In the economic realm, the predominance of subsistence agriculture and informal commerce meant that relatively few Haitian businesses had ties to the United States that could be disrupted by sanctions.[492] Finally, relatively few elites were educated in the United States or maintained close ties to Western universities and international organizations.[493] Thus, although both pro- and anti-Aristide forces received assistance from allies in the United States,[494] international pressure often failed to resonate broadly within the elite. As Carey wrote:

> Would-be mediators find that one instrument that serves them well in other countries – that is, observers' ability to publicize internationally any irregularities they witness – is of little use in Haiti. With few exceptions, Haitian political parties and election authorities care little about outsiders' accusations of improper conduct.[495]

Organizational power was low. The coercive apparatus was strikingly weak. The Haitian state "always had a short reach, its writ seldom running beyond Port-au-Prince and a few provincial towns."[496] Even before the 1994 U.S. invasion, Haiti had a lower percentage of its population under arms (0.1 percent) than Costa Rica.[497] The army was underfinanced and ill-equipped, and the intelligence service was so dysfunctional that files on opposition leaders often were stolen.[498] After the fall of Duvalier, much of the coercive apparatus – including the paramilitary *Tontons Macoutes* – was dismantled, leading to a breakdown in public order and the spread of vigilante groups.[499] By 1990, the coercive apparatus was in an "advanced state of decomposition" and was unable to "perform even the most elementary of . . . tasks."[500]

The 1994 U.S. intervention destroyed what remained of the coercive apparatus. The army collapsed. On returning to power, Aristide eliminated its funding, vacated its headquarters, and dismissed nearly all of its members, effectively

---

[490] Weinstein and Segal (1992: 162). In the mid-1990s, there were only 5 televisions per 1,000 people in Haiti, compared to 62 in Nicaragua and 72 in Honduras (Rotberg 1997: x).

[491] World Bank World Development Indicators (www.worldbank.org/data/).

[492] Maingot (1996a: 149).

[493] Fauriol (1993: 55). In Corke's *Who's Who in Politics and Government in Latin America* (1984: 134–7), 12 of 30 Haitian elites are listed as having lived or studied in North America – easily the lowest of the 6 Latin American/Caribbean countries examined in this study.

[494] President Aristide was well connected to human-rights NGOs, African American groups, and liberals in the Democratic Party (I. Martin 1999: 726; Kumar 2000: 129–33). Opposition groups developed strong

ties to the International Republican Institute (Fatton 2002: 178; Maguire 2004).

[495] Carey (1998: 154).

[496] Gros (1997: 105).

[497] Rodríguez Beruff (1998: 187); see also Maingot (1994: 7). Historically, presidents relied on personal militias – such as the Duvaliers' notorious *Tontons Macoutes* – rather than the army and police. Indeed, under the Duvalier dictatorship, the *Tontons Macoutes* dwarfed the army (Girault 1991: 196; Laguerre 1993: 115–21). In rural areas, order was maintained by military "Section Chiefs" and private militias (Maguire 1997: 184; Nield 2002: 286).

[498] Laguerre (1993: 135); Maingot (1994: 7).

[499] Laguerre (1993: 135–6, 173); Dupuy (1997: 117).

[500] Maingot (1992: 67; 1996: 208).

reducing it to a "fifty-man presidential band."[501] The old police force was dissolved and the new Haitian National Police (HNP) was undersized. Although U.S. and UN officials estimated that Haiti needed a minimum of 12,000 police to maintain security,[502] the HNP never had more than 5,200, making it one of the smallest police forces – per capita – in the world.[503] The HNP failed to penetrate the countryside and "often lack[ed] the means to conduct basic operations."[504] Frequently unpaid and without ammunition, the police were "simply not capable of maintaining law and order."[505] Cohesion was also low. The fall of Duvalier in 1986 triggered a "collapse of military discipline," giving rise to a series of coups and rebellions.[506] The post-1994 security forces – cobbled together quickly, with little training, by international peacekeepers – were marked by widespread absenteeism, desertion, and indiscipline.[507]

Party strength was medium-low. We score party scope as medium. Aristide's Lavalas movement was a "fluid and loosely knit organization" with "no formal structure."[508] However, Lavalas' ties to peasant groups and Christian-based communities provided it with a significant, if uneven, grassroots presence.[509] Party cohesion was low, as Aristide repeatedly disrupted and abandoned his own organizations.[510] After being elected president, he jettisoned his first party, the National Front for Change and Democracy, to form the Lavalas Political Organization (OPL), only to abandon later the OPL for Lavalas Family (FL).[511] In this context of constant disorganization, it was often "difficult to know ... who spoke for the movement and with what authority."[512]

Origins and Evolution of the Regime

Haiti's regime trajectory was shaped by state weakness and uneven Western intervention. Competitive authoritarianism was partly a product of U.S. intervention. After elected President Jean Bertrand Aristide was overthrown by the

---

[501] Stotzky (1997: 180). See also Schulz (1997b: 5), Ballard (1998: 145–6, 216), and von Hippel (2000: 111).

[502] *The New York Times*, March 7, 2004 Online edition (http://www.nytimes.com/2004/03/07/world/facing-new-crisis-haiti-again-relies-on-us-military-to-keep-order.html), January 29, 2006, p. 10. See also Schulz (1996: 20).

[503] See U.S. Department of State (2001c: 1; 2002a: 1) and Erikson and Minson (2005a: 4).

[504] Schulz (1997–1998: 85); see also Schulz (1996: 20), McCoy (1997: 18), and Malone (1998: 138).

[505] Schulz (1997b: 17, 12); Human Rights Watch (1997: 4–5).

[506] Maingot (1992: 66–7); Fatton (2002).

[507] See Human Rights Watch (1995: 15), Schulz (1996: 13, 1997–1998: 89), and Malone

(1998: 128–38). HNP officers were "rushed onto the job with insufficient training" (Schulz 1997–1998: 89) and the state could not pay sufficiently high salaries to ensure officers' loyalty (Schulz 1996: 13).

[508] Dupuy (2007: 92–3).

[509] Dupuy (1997: 86–91, 172); Mozaffar (2001: 8).

[510] See Schultz (1997b: 8; 1997–1998: 81) and Dupuy (1997; 2007: 145–6).

[511] Dupuy (2007: 86–92, 136–7).

[512] Dupuy (2003: 92). According to Dupuy (2007: 145–6), neither Lavalas leaders nor its base organizations were "accountable to anyone." At one point during the mid-1990s, Lavalas' parliamentary leader claimed he did not even know how many legislators belonged to his bloc (Schulz 1997b: 8).

military in 1991, pressure by human-rights NGOs, Haitian diaspora organizations, and the Congressional Black Caucus, together with massive refugee flows, induced the Clinton Administration to use force to restore Aristide to power in 1994.[513]

The U.S. invasion did not bring democracy, however. From the outset, the Aristide government created a "climate of intimidation," in which media and opposition figures were subject to threats and attacks.[514] Unable to rely on the security forces, Aristide turned to informal repression, particularly "armed thugs" known as *chiméres*.[515] *Chiméres* "did the government's dirty work," disrupting opposition meetings, ransacking their offices, and attacking (and sometimes killing) their activists.[516] The government also packed the Provisional Electoral Council (CEP), and the 1995 parliamentary election – won easily by Lavalas – was marred by violence, intimidation, and fraud.[517] After U.S. officials blocked Aristide's effort to extend his presidential term, his chosen successor, Prime Minister René Préval, won the 1995 presidential election in an unfair campaign that was boycotted by much of the opposition.[518]

Aristide initially got away with this abuse for two reasons. First, the domestic opposition was weak.[519] Haiti's civil society was "the weakest in the Americas,"[520] and opposition parties lacked even a minimum of organization or presence outside the capital.[521] Thus, the opposition "lacked the means to generate any form of 'people's power' with which to challenge seriously the... regime."[522] Second, the government initially faced a permissive international environment. Having invested heavily in Aristide's return, the Clinton Administration "could not afford a failure" in Haiti.[523] Consequently, it largely ignored human-rights violations and accepted the 1995 elections, despite widespread evidence of fraud.[524] Finally, the impact of state weakness was blunted by the presence – through 1997 – of

[513] More than 60,000 Haitians set sail for Florida between 1991 and 1994 (Dupuy 1997: 139), gaining widespread media attention and threatening to "overwhelm the U.S. Coast Guard" (Perusse 1995: 27–30; Preeg 1996: 85–9; Dupuy 1997: 158). As refugee flows peaked, "alarm bells began to ring in Florida and Washington." Eventually, "the impact of seeing so many small boats on the television screens of average homes in the United States became too stark for Washington to ignore" (Ballard 1998: 77–8). On transnational pressure for U.S. intervention, see Perusse (1995: 70–7), Dupuy (1997: 156–7), I. Martin (1999: 725–6), and Kumar (2000: 129–33).
[514] Schulz (1997a: 98). See especially Neild (2002) and Dupuy (2007: 144–5).
[515] Schulz (1996: 5); Dupuy (2007: 144–5).
[516] Dupuy (2003: 3); see also Schulz (1996: 5) and U.S. Department of State (1999a:

7; 2002a: 3). According to one report, 20 political murders occurred between 1994 and 1996 (General Accounting Office 1996: 13).
[517] Observer Robert Pastor described the election as the worst he had ever witnessed (Carey 1998: 149). See Pastor (1997) and Carey (1998).
[518] Pastor (1997: 132–3); Carey (1998). Préval won with 87 percent of the vote.
[519] Dupuy (1997: 47–9); Fatton (2002: 149).
[520] Carey (1998: 163).
[521] Weinstein and Segal (1992: 160, 163), Schulz (1996: 8), and Gros (1997: 100).
[522] Fatton (2002: 149).
[523] McCoy (1998: 76–8); Carey (1998: 159).
[524] Pastor (1997: 126–7, 132–4), Carey (1998), and Malone (1998: 130–1); see also *Latin American Weekly Report*, April 8, 1997, p. 159 and December 9, 1997, p. 581.

international peacekeepers. In effect, the regime was "protected by U.S. and multinational troops."[525]

Competitive authoritarianism persisted under President Préval. The 1997 senate election was marred by intimidation and ballot stuffing.[526] After the OLP – now abandoned by Aristide – moved into opposition, undermining the government's legislative majority,[527] Préval dissolved parliament, creating a "constitutionally irregular situation."[528] Thugs routinely broke up OLP meetings and threatened opposition politicians. In 1999, OLP Senator Yves Toussaint was assassinated and death threats forced several other legislators into exile.[529]

Authoritarianism eventually proved costly. U.S. assistance slowed to a trickle in the late 1990s,[530] and, following the dissolution of parliament, Western donors insisted that Préval "restore some semblance of democratic government before their programs could go ahead."[531] For the first time, external assistance was made conditional on the holding of credible elections in 2000.[532]

The government was largely unresponsive to external pressure. The 2000 parliamentary elections were marred by violence and fraud. Pro-Lavalas mobs burned opposition headquarters and forced many opposition candidates into hiding, and there were numerous attacks on the media, including the assassination of prominent radio journalist Jean Dominique.[533] The election itself was marred by irregularities, particularly an illegal vote-counting system in which votes for candidates below the top four were tossed out, inflating the percentages of the leading candidates. This increased – from 6 to 16 – the number of FL candidates who won a first-round majority, thereby assuring Lavalas a lock on the 27-seat senate.[534] Three Electoral Council members, including President Leon Manus, resigned in protest (Manus fled the country amid death threats).[535] OAS observers demanded that the 10 disputed senate seats go to a second-round vote; when the government refused, the OAS pulled out.[536] The government responded to postelection protest by arresting 35 opposition leaders.[537] In November 2000, Aristide returned to the presidency in a

---

[525] Maingot (1996: 157); Ballard (1998: 131).
[526] Schulz (1997–1998: 76–7), Carey (1998: 151), and U.S. Department of State (1998a).
[527] Schulz (1997b: 8–9); Fatton (2002: 112–13).
[528] U.S. Department of State (2000a: 1). See also Mobekk (2001: 177); Fatton (2002: 114).
[529] U.S. Department of State (1999a: 7); see also *Latin American Weekly Report*, March 2, 1999, p. 108 and *Latin American Regional Report/Caribbean and Central American Report*, May 11, 1999, p. 8.
[530] Malone (1998: 160).
[531] *Latin American Regional Report/Caribbean and Central American Report*, November 2, 1999, p. 1.

[532] *Latin American Weekly Report*, April 18, 2000, p. 192 and *Latin American Regional Report/Caribbean and Central American Report*, June 13, 2000, p. 2.
[533] *Latin American Regional Report/Caribbean and Central American Report*, June 13, 2000: p. 2; see also U.S. Department of State (2001c: 8); Dupuy (2007: 144).
[534] See Mobekk (2001: 183), Mozaffar (2001: 1), and Fatton (2002: 116–19).
[535] U.S. Department of State (2001c: 1, 11); Mobekk (2001: 184).
[536] *Latin American Regional Report/Caribbean and Central American Report*, July 18, 2000, p. 1 and August 22, 2000, p. 3. See also Fatton (2002: 118).
[537] Wucker (2004: 46).

"farcical" election that the OAS refused to monitor and all major opposition parties boycotted.[538]

The flawed 2000 elections marked the breaking point in Haiti's relations with the international community. The U.S., IMF, World Bank, and European governments froze assistance, resulting in the suspension of $500 million in aid.[539] Thus, after having received more than $2.5 billion in assistance between 1994 and 2000, Haiti was cut off after 2000.[540] Moreover, beginning in 2001, the Bush Administration adopted a more anti-Aristide position, ending high-level diplomatic contact and ceasing efforts to mediate the crisis.[541]

The Aristide government remained unresponsive to external pressure, however. OAS efforts to broker a settlement failed.[542] Aristide's "scant effort... to comply with [OAS] demands" made the body look "toothless."[543] Indeed, the government responded to rising protest by stepping up repression. Opposition leaders faced a "constant threat of arrest" after 2000, and many fled the country.[544] In 2001, a wave of mob attacks forced several radio stations to close and forced 20 journalists into exile.[545]

The failure to respond to external pressure proved fatal to the regime. Deepening isolation eroded state capacity to the point of collapse.[546] Without external assistance, the security forces "deteriorated rapidly."[547] Decimated by desertion, the police force disappeared in much of the country.[548] The state lost control of the Dominican border, allowing former army officers to enter the country and organize an insurgency.[549] Aristide eventually fell prey to armed rebellion. In early 2004, a *chiméres* gang called the Cannibal Army rebelled and took the city of Gonaives.[550] Police units sent to retake the town were ambushed and defeated.[551] As the rebels advanced, the security forces melted away. The police had "neither the weapons nor the stomach to defend their president" and, as a result, "what began... as an episode of gang warfare... turned into a coup in slow motion."[552] By mid-February, rebels had driven the police out of more than a dozen towns and captured much of northern Haiti.[553] As the rebels approached

---

[538] Orenstein (2001: 21); Fatton (2002: 141); Erikson (2005: 83). Aristide won 92 percent of the vote.

[539] Dupuy (2003: 5); Erikson (2004: 288; 2005: 84); see also *Latin American Regional Report/Caribbean and Central American Report*, August 22, 2000, p. 3.

[540] Erikson (2004: 293) and Maguire (2004). The regime's isolation was exacerbated by the ascent of the Bush Administration, which was far more anti-Aristide (Mozaffar 2001: 11; Maguire 2003: 4–5).

[541] Mozaffar (2001: 11); Fatton (2002: 185); Maguire (2003: 4–5).

[542] Maguire (2002: 33); Erikson (2004: 288).

[543] Foreign observer quoted in *Latin American Regional Report/Caribbean and Central American Report*, June 17, 2003, p. 6.

[544] U.S. Department of State (2003a: 3, 11).

[545] U.S. Department of State (2002a: 3, 10; 2003a: 8). In 2002, Reporters without Borders named Aristide to its list of "Predators against Press Freedom" (*Latin American Regional Report/Caribbean and Central American Report*, June 11, 2002, p. 8).

[546] On his own, Aristide "did not have the...military means to...sustain a dictatorship" (Dupuy 2007: 146).

[547] Erikson (2004: 292).

[548] U.S. Department of State (2000a: 4; 2001a: 1).

[549] Erikson (2005: 85).

[550] On the Cannibal Army, see Human Rights Watch (2004a: 3) and Packer (2004: 33).

[551] Dudley (2004: 24).

[552] *The Economist*, February 28, 2004, p. 35.

[553] Erikson (2005: 85).

the capital, U.S. officials notified Aristide that they would not protect him, and he fled the country. Aristide was thus "toppled by a rag-tag army of as few as 200 rebels."[554] The rebels "did not fight a single battle. The police simply changed out of their uniforms, grabbed bottles of rum, and headed for the hills."[555]

Haiti did not democratize after 2004. UN peacekeeping forces occupied the country for two years, during which an interim government repressed Lavalas supporters.[556] In 2006, ex-President Préval won an internationally sponsored presidential election. Although the Préval Administration was less abusive than earlier Lavalas governments, it was not fully democratic.[557]

In summary, the collapse of competitive authoritarianism in Haiti was rooted in a combination of high leverage and low organizational power. The Aristide government's insensitivity to external pressure led to deepening international isolation, which triggered a collapse of the state's already weak coercive apparatus. Without a minimum of coercive capacity, Aristide "could not... prevent a ragtag band of not more than 200 rebels from overcoming the government... in a matter of weeks."[558]

CONCLUSION

As shown in Table 4.1, regime outcomes match those predicted by our theory in five cases: the Dominican Republic, Guyana, Haiti, Mexico, and Nicaragua. In Peru, our theory correctly predicts Fujimori's fall from power but fails to predict subsequent democratization. Alternative approaches have difficulty explaining these outcomes. Democratization occurred despite presidentialist constitutions, extreme inequality, and – outside of Mexico – low levels of economic development. Although economic crises weakened regimes in Haiti, Guyana, Nicaragua, and Mexico, crises cannot explain why turnover led to democratization rather then new competitive authoritarian governments, as in much of the former Soviet Union and Africa (see Chapters 5 and 6).

By contrast, the Latin American/Caribbean cases provide strong support for our theory of linkage and democratization. High linkage and high leverage generated strong external democratizing pressure. In all four high-linkage cases, authoritarian governments faced intense and persistent international pressure. In all four cases, incumbents eventually fell from power and regimes subsequently democratized. Indeed, democratization occurred even where organizational power was high (i.e., Mexico and Nicaragua) and/or domestic

---

554 *The Economist*, March 6, 2004, pp. 13–14. Our account of Aristide's fall differs from those that center on the role of the U.S. government, which both supported groups seeking Aristide's ouster and failed to protect Aristide (Dupuy 2007: 148–78). Such an explanation understates the role of incumbent weakness. Thus, we argue that it was international *isolation* – which exacerbated state weakness – that contributed most forcefully to Aristide's ouster.

555 Dudley (2004: 27).

556 Erikson and Minson (2005a: 3–4); Dupuy (2007: 179–94).

557 For example, journalists continued to suffer frequent harassment. See Freedom House, "Freedom in the World 2008: Haiti" (http://www.freedomhouse.org) and U.S. Department of State (2009b).

558 Wucker (2004: 42).

TABLE 4.1. *Predicted and Actual Competitive Authoritarian Regime Outcomes in the Americas*

Case	Linkage	Leverage	Organizational Power	Predicted Outcome	Actual Outcome
Dominican Republic	High	High	Medium	Democracy	Democracy
Guyana	High	High	High	Democracy	Democracy
Haiti	Medium	High	Low	Unstable Authoritarianism	Unstable Authoritarianism
Mexico	High	Low	High	Democracy	Democracy
Nicaragua	High	High	High	Democracy	Democracy
Peru	Medium	High	Low	Unstable Authoritarianism	Democracy

pressure was weak (i.e., Guyana and Nicaragua). In the Dominican Republic, Guyana, and Nicaragua, where both linkage and leverage were high, autocrats fell quickly from power and regimes democratized, despite unfavorable domestic conditions. In Mexico, where linkage was high but leverage was low, democratization required a domestic push. Although linkage induced the PRI to underutilize its coercive capacity and create credible electoral institutions, it took a strong opposition movement to level the playing field and defeat the PRI at the polls. Where linkage was lower, organizational power weighed more heavily. In Peru, it was ultimately governing-party weakness and a historically contingent event – the video scandal – that brought down the regime. In Haiti, extreme state weakness limited incumbents' ability to thwart even modest opposition challenges.

Competitive authoritarianism did not disappear from the Americas in the 2000s. In Venezuela, Hugo Chavez politicized state institutions and used them – together with massive oil revenue – to skew the playing field against opponents.[559] Although elections were relatively clean, the Chavez government increasingly violated civil liberties in the mid- and late 2000s, closing down a major television station (RCTV) and arresting or exiling several government critics.[560] The Venezuelan regime proved durable. Due to oil exports, Western leverage is low. Although linkage is relatively high, the Chavez government used its discretionary economic power – enhanced by soaring oil prices – to weaken civic and opposition forces.[561] As of 2010, Chavez had been in power for more than a decade. Venezuela was not alone in its competitive authoritarian turn. In Ecuador and Bolivia, governments engaged in mildly competitive authoritarian behavior in the late 2000s,[562] and, as noted previously, Nicaragua slid back toward competitive

---

[559] See Corrales and Penfold (2007).

[560] For example, Manuel Rosales, the main opposition presidential candidate in 2006, was forced into exile.

[561] Corrales and Penfold (2007).

[562] The governments of Rafael Correa in Ecuador and Evo Morales in Bolivia expanded and politicized the state media

authoritarian after Daniel Ortega's return to the presidency in 2006.[563] These governments received substantial aid from Venezuela, which used its oil wealth to engage in black-knight–like behavior.

Outside of Venezuela, the obstacles to stable competitive authoritarianism remain considerable. Linkage is high in Ecuador and Nicaragua, and indeed, the external costs of abuse in Nicaragua were already manifest by 2008. In Bolivia, the government of Evo Morales faces a more permissive environment: Linkage in Bolivia is only medium, and massive Venezuelan support may help blunt the impact of external pressure. Nevertheless, the Bolivian state is notoriously weak – a fact that has consistently undermined regime stability in the past.

Whatever the fate of these new regimes, their emergence in the 2000s highlights an important point: Authoritarian regimes faced a hostile international environment in post–Cold War Latin America, but the conditions that give rise to such regimes – recurring economic crises; extreme inequality; and weak states, parties, and democratic institutions – persist in much of the region.

---

and occasionally used state-sponsored mobs to intimidate journalists or opposition parties. The Correa government used dubiously constitutional means – including the sacking of 57 of 100 legislators – to dissolve Congress and impose a new constitution. The Morales government sought to arrest (on corruption charges) presidential candidate Manfred Reyes in the wake of Morales's reelection in 2009. On Ecuador, see Conaghan (2008); on Bolivia, see Lehoucq (2008).

[563] Honduran president Manuel Zelaya also showed signs of competitive authoritarian behavior, but he was toppled by a military coup in 2009.

III

The Dynamics of Competitive Authoritarianism in Low-Linkage Regions

The Former Soviet Union, Africa, and Asia

In the cases examined in Chapter 3 (Eastern Europe) and Chapter 4 (the Americas), extensive linkage generated strong external pressure for democratization in the post–Cold War era. As a result, even powerful autocrats fell and nearly all competitive authoritarian regimes democratized. The remaining chapters of the book focus on regions that were characterized by lower linkage (the former Soviet Union, sub-Saharan Africa, and Asia). With the exception of Taiwan, countries in these regions had weaker social, economic, technocratic, and intergovernmental ties to the United States and Western Europe. As a result, external democratizing pressure was weaker and more uneven. Because most of these lower-linkage cases lacked a strong domestic push for democracy, the vast majority (18 of 22) remained nondemocratic through 2008. These cases differed, however, in terms of authoritarian stability: In several cases, authoritarian incumbents or their chosen successors survived in power through 2008; in many other cases, leaders fell from power and were replaced by new autocrats. This variation is largely explained by differences in leverage and domestic organizational power. Where state and party structures were strong, and/or where Western leverage was medium or low, autocrats were able to hold onto power even in the face of highly mobilized opposition. By contrast, where organizational power was low and leverage was high, incumbents were often unable to thwart even modest opposition challenges. In such cases, authoritarian incumbents routinely fell from power – often two (e.g., Georgia, Moldova, and Ukraine) or more (e.g., Benin and Madagascar) times.

5

The Evolution of Post-Soviet Competitive Authoritarianism

This chapter examines the trajectory of six competitive authoritarian regimes that emerged from the collapse of the Soviet Union: Armenia, Belarus, Georgia, Moldova, Russia, and Ukraine. By 2008, two patterns had emerged. First, with the exception of Ukraine, competitive authoritarian regimes in the former Soviet Union failed to democratize. Second, whereas regimes broke down repeatedly in some countries (Georgia, Moldova, and Ukraine), they were relatively stable in others (Armenia, Russia, and post-1994 Belarus). This chapter explains these outcomes.

The recent literature on regime change in the former Soviet Union has been dominated by two approaches: those that focus on constitutional design and, more recently, those that focus on opposition tactics and mobilization. The fall of communism generated a vast literature exploring the effects of institutional design.[1] For example, scholars linked presidentialism or semi-presidentialism to democratic failure in the region.[2] Our analysis highlights two problems with this approach. First, as Gerald Easter shows, presidential power is often a *product*, rather than a cause, of authoritarianism.[3] In Russia and Belarus, for example, super-presidentialist constitutions were imposed *after* Boris Yeltsin and Alyaksandr Lukashenka had suppressed parliament. More generally, constitutions often did not constrain politicians' behavior sufficiently to determine regime outcomes. As the case studies show, constitutional rules such as executive term limits were frequently changed (Belarus in 2004), sidestepped (Ukraine in 2003–2004), or divorced from de facto power distributions (Russia in 2008).

Second, authoritarian breakdown in Serbia (2000), Georgia (2003), and Ukraine (2004) gave rise to a literature that focused on the role of opposition tactics – and their diffusion across the region – in organizing protest movements

---

[1] See McFaul (2001), Moser (2001b), Colton and Skach (2005), Fish (2005, 2006), and Stepan (2005).

[2] On presidentialism, see Fish (2005, 2006). On semi-presidentialism, see Colton and Skach (2005).

[3] Easter (1997).

that toppled non-democratic governments (the so-called color revolutions).[4] Our study raises questions about the utility of such approaches in explaining post-Soviet regime outcomes.[5] Among our cases, the relationship between mass protest and authoritarian stability was weak. With the exception of Armenia in the 1990s and Ukraine in the early 2000s, the size and frequency of opposition mobilization were relatively limited. Nevertheless, four of the six regimes experienced at least one breakdown during the post–Cold War period. Moreover, Armenia, which arguably had the highest overall level of opposition mobilization, was stable, whereas Moldova, which experienced little opposition mobilization, was unstable.[6] Thus, although opposition protest was important in certain cases (e.g., Ukraine in 2004), it is insufficient to explain the success or failure of post-Soviet authoritarianism.

Linkage, leverage, and organizational power account for both the relative lack of democratization and the variation in authoritarian stability among our six post-Soviet cases. First, external democratizing pressure was limited by low linkage, which was a legacy of Soviet communism. The Soviet regime restricted flows of people and information to and from the West, isolating the country from global cultural, economic, and ideational trends.[7] Although cultural flows increased over time, they remained limited compared to other parts of the world.[8] Travel and emigration restrictions were even more severe than in Eastern Europe.[9] In general, "contact with the West was an option ... only for the most loyal and reliable of the Communist Party's allies."[10] Access to Western books, newspapers, and scientific journals was strictly controlled by the Communist Party, and the regime invested heavily in jamming Western broadcasts.[11] Hence, the Soviet elite and public had few contacts in – and little familiarity with – the West.

---

[4] See McFaul (2005a), Bunce and Wolchik (2006a, 2006b), Beissinger (2007), and Tucker (2007).

[5] For a more extended critique of this literature, see Way (2008a, 2009a).

[6] Armenia witnessed demonstrations of up to 100 thousand in 1993 (Goldenberg 1994: 149), of 150,000 to 200,000 in 1996 (Danielian 1996–1997: 128), and of 25,000 to 100,000 in 2003–2008 (Petrosian 2003a; Fuller 2003b, 2003c; Hakobyan 2004a, 2004b; Karapetian 2004; *RFE/RL Newsline*, 25 February 2008 (online: http://www.rferl .org/archive/en-newsline/latest/683/683 .html). In Moldova between 1992 and 2008, the largest opposition demonstration was a 2002 protest against education policy, which mobilized just over 20–30 thousand people (*RFE/RL Newsline*, 15 February 2002 (online: http://www.rferl.org/archive/ en-newsline/latest/683/683.html)).

[7] See Kneen (1984), Jowitt (1992: 171), and Chandler (1998). Thus, globalization "was

not in fact global: It took sides during the Cold War" (Njølstad 2004: 91). Westerners were required to stay only in official hotels and could not travel beyond certain cities. In 1976, visitors could only enter 135 of the USSR's more than 2,000 cities (Radio Free Europe 1978: 10).

[8] Through the late 1980s, student exchanges with the West rarely exceeded 50 a year, and the Soviet Union imported only 4 or 5 U.S. movies a year (Richmond 2008: 213).

[9] See Radio Free Europe (1978: 1, 10–11) and Chandler (1998: 71, 84).

[10] Chandler (1998: 6–7).

[11] According to an estimate from the 1980s, the Soviet Union spent $900 million to block radio broadcasts from the West. See Motyl (1986: 146–7), "In a Crisis, Who to Turn in? In the Soviet Bloc, Probably Western Radio." *The New York Times*, 3 May 1986 (online: www.nyt.com), and Mickiewicz (1988: 20–1). On party control over publications, see Kneen (1984) and Richmond (2008).

The Soviet collapse brought an expansion of linkage. In the 1990s, former Soviet states were the object of considerable attention and resources from Western governments, IOs, and NGOs.[12] They also were actively monitored by a range of European organizations, including the European Institute for the Media, Venice Commission, OSCE, and Council of Europe. Nevertheless, ties to the West remained considerably lower than in the Americas or in Eastern Europe.[13] For example, immigration and trade flows were much more limited.[14] Moreover, the EU did not embrace the former Soviet states as it did Eastern European states. In part because the region was viewed as part of Russia's sphere of influence, the EU created a distinct set of aid structures (e.g., Partnership and Cooperation Agreements and the TACIS program) to deal with CIS countries and never offered them an opportunity to join the EU.[15] As a result, the kind of linkage-based democratizing pressure seen in Eastern Europe and the Americas was largely absent in the post-Soviet cases. Although Western actors periodically influenced the course of events (as in Ukraine's Orange Revolution), they never fundamentally altered the domestic balance of power as they did in Eastern Europe and the Americas.

Western influence was further blunted by Russia's role as a regional power. Russia's military and economic strength not only reduced Western leverage within its own borders, it also allowed Russia to aspire to black-knight status in the region.[16] However, Russia's actual influence varied across cases. In Belarus, Russia acted as a black knight. Russian assistance, which constituted between 20 and 30 percent of GDP,[17] clearly blunted the impact of Western pressure. Armenia and Ukraine also received considerable Russian assistance, but unlike Belarus, they also relied heavily on Western aid. Hence, although Russia was a major player in these countries, it was not a black knight – and consequently, Western leverage was high. Finally, Georgia and Moldova, which experienced military conflict with Russia and thus received no black-knight assistance, were particularly vulnerable to Western pressure.

---

[12] Thus, "a virtual army" of Western NGOs descended on Russia and other post-Soviet states (Mendelson 2001: 68). USAID spent more than $1 billion on democracy promotion in Eastern Europe during the 1990s (Carothers 1999: 51; Henderson 2003: 6) and Western foundations contributed tens of millions of dollars to NGOs in the region (Henderson 2003: 7). According to Bunce and Wolchik (2006b: 13), the post-Communist region as a whole received greater Western democratization assistance than any other region in the world.

[13] Kopstein and Reilly (2000); Lobjakas (2009).

[14] In the 1990s, the average annual share of immigrants to the West from the former Soviet Union was only one fourth that of our Eastern European cases and less than a

tenth that of cases in the Americas. Likewise, among our post-Soviet cases, average annual trade with the United States and Western Europe constituted 17 percent of the GDP, compared to 38 percent among our Eastern European cases in the 1990s. See Appendix III for description of data sources.

[15] Bojcun (2001); Hillion (2005: 53–4).

[16] By the late 2000s, Russia's position as a regional power allowed it to even soften Western assessments of elections in other former Soviet states. Thus, Russian lobbying within the OSCE appears to have resulted in milder OSCE criticism of elections in Armenia, Azerbaijan, and Moldova in 2008–2009 (Whitmore 2009).

[17] Aslund (2002: 182); Karol (2006); Belarusian Institute for Strategic Studies (2008).

Organizational power and leverage were central to explaining variation in post-Soviet regime stability. Where incumbents possessed relatively strong states and/or governing parties, as in Armenia and Putin's Russia, regimes were stable. By contrast, where organizational power was low, incumbents were more vulnerable. In these latter cases, Western leverage was critical. Where leverage was low, due to either strategic importance (Russia) or support from a regional black knight (Belarus), even relatively weak incumbents tended to survive. Where leverage was high (Georgia, Moldova, and Ukraine), incumbents with low organizational power were likely to fall.

LEVERAGE, ORGANIZATIONAL POWER, AND AUTHORITARIAN STABILITY: RUSSIA, BELARUS, AND ARMENIA

Russia, Belarus, and Armenia illustrate how low leverage and high organizational power contributed to authoritarian stability in the post–Cold War period. In Russia, relatively low organizational power in the early 1990s gave rise to a series of regime crises; however, in the absence of Western pressure, President Yeltsin enjoyed broad room for maneuver in cracking down on challenges. After 2000, stronger state and party structures – and the absence of any real external pressure – allowed President Putin to eliminate key sources of opposition and consolidate authoritarian rule. In Belarus, state control over the economy allowed President Lukashenka to starve opponents of resources, and black-knight support from Russia limited the regime's vulnerability to Western democratizing pressure. Armenia was more dependent on Western assistance, but a powerful coercive apparatus – forged out of war with Azerbaijan – allowed incumbents to repeatedly thwart opposition protest.

Russia

Russia was a stable competitive authoritarian regime through 2008. During the 1990s, limited state and party capacity threatened regime stability, but low leverage and a divided opposition facilitated Boris Yeltsin's survival. Under Vladimir Putin (1999–2008), increased state and party capacity helped eliminate many potential sources of regime instability, and the regime – largely immune from outside pressure – consolidated.

Linkage, Leverage, and Organizational Power
Russia is a case of low linkage and low leverage. Although an economic crisis and Yeltsin's opening to the West facilitated U.S. and EU engagement in the early 1990s,[18] ties to the West remained limited.[19] For example, no major

---

[18] See Goldgeier and McFaul (2003). In the immediate post-communist period, "Western advisors were invited to 'occupy' virtually every branch of the Russian government" (Goldgeier and McFaul 2003: 59). Yeltsin

himself placed great value on his relations with Western leaders. See Yeltsin (2000: 149–165).

[19] See Kopstein and Reilly (2000).

official in Yeltsin's initial reformist government had studied in the West.[20] Leverage was low. Despite the external vulnerability – and opportunities for Western influence – created by the post-Soviet economic collapse,[21] Russia's economic and strategic importance inhibited Western democratizing pressure. Even at its weakest, Russia was a big state with vast military capacity. It possessed about 10,000 strategic nuclear warheads and "the world's largest stockpile of weapons-usable plutonium and highly enriched uranium."[22] In addition, Russia possessed massive oil reserves and was the world's largest supplier of natural gas.[23] Rising energy prices in the 2000s thus further reduced leverage.[24] If vulnerability to external democratizing pressure was low in the 1990s, it was almost nonexistent in the 2000s. As one European analyst observed, "We don't have influence with Russia.... We have no levers."[25]

Organizational power in Russia increased over time. In the early 1990s, organizational power was low. Party strength was low.[26] After the Communist Party was banned in 1991, President Yeltsin chose not to build a party.[27] Although he was backed by several parties, including Democratic Russia in 1991, the Party of Russian Unity and Concord (PRES) and Russia's Choice in 1993–1994, and Our Home Is Russia and Russia's Democratic Choice in 1995, Yeltsin did little to strengthen these organizations.[28] Indeed, he often circumvented them, adopting a strategy of "enhancing his personal authority to the neglect of institution building."[29] Under Yeltsin, therefore, party scope and cohesion were low.

---

[20] Vronskaya and Chuguev (1994: 119, 561, 596); Gaidar (1999).

[21] Goldgeier and McFaul (2003: 60).

[22] Collina and Wolfsthal (2002). Figures for nuclear warheads (from 1992) are taken from "Table of USSR/Russian Nuclear Warheads," the National Resource Defense Council (online: www.nrdc.org).

[23] Russia possessed roughly 6 percent of the world's proven oil reserves and about a quarter of its natural gas (Rutland 2006: 19). Europe was particularly dependent on Russian gas. As one EU official stated, "You know what happens when [EU leaders] get in the same room with Vladimir Putin?.... [they] say 'I love you, Vladimir.'" Quoted in "The Really Cold War," *New York Times*, 25 October 2006 (online: www.nyt.com).

[24] Oil revenue allowed the government to pay off much of its foreign debt (M. Goldman 2008: 81).

[25] Quoted in *The International Herald Tribune*, 7–8 October 2006: 7.

[26] See Fish (1995).

[27] Yeltsin reportedly did not want to be constrained by a party and believed, in the words of his former chief of staff, that "because

he had been elected on a nonparty basis [in 1991]... he should act as president of the entire population" (Gennady Burbulis, quoted in McFaul 2001: 155). Yeltsin's press secretary, Viacheslav Kostikov (1997: 299), argued that Yeltsin also did not want to tie his fate to weak and unpopular organizations (also Shevtsova 1999: 36). Moreover, government technocrats apparently believed that strengthening pro-Yeltsin groups such as Democratic Russia would hamper policy implementation (McFaul 2001: 155). Finally, like his counterparts in Moldova and Ukraine, Yeltsin apparently believed that his popularity and formal executive powers were sufficient to maintain control (Way 2009b).

[28] Democratic Russia eschewed party status and opposed political parties in its platform (Ponomarev 1993).

[29] Urban (1992: 193). See also Gaidar (1999: 263), Filatov (2001: 41), and McFaul (2001: 172). Prior to the 1995 parliamentary election, Yeltsin openly disparaged the government's achievements and predicted a weak showing for the "party of power" – a move that was seen as a betrayal by "Our Home Is Russia" supporters (Shevtsova 1999: 140).

Progovernment parties lacked extensive national structures,[30] and in the absence of any stable organization, cohesion was minimal.

Coercive capacity was initially medium. On the one hand, coercive scope was high. The Russian army, successor to the Soviet army, retained approximately three million troops in the early 1990s, making it the largest army in Europe and one of the largest in the world.[31] Moreover, the internal security apparatus remained largely intact. The Committee for State Security (KGB) "was virtually the only Soviet institution unscathed by perestroika."[32] Although Yeltsin pledged to abolish it after the failed August 1991 coup, he later reversed course.[33] The KGB was formally dismantled, but many of its functions – and much of its infrastructure and personnel – were inherited by its eventual successor, the Federal Security Service (FSB).[34] Yeltsin made little effort to purge the intelligence services of Soviet-era officials; indeed, all but a few top officials retained their positions.[35] Yeltsin also endowed the FSB with broad, intrusive powers that paralleled those of the Gorbachev-era KGB.[36] In effect, "the KGB was re-formed . . . without being reformed."[37] In the early 2000s, the FSB had an estimated 269,000 troops and continued to penetrate the army, the media, and major societal organizations.[38]

On the other hand, state cohesion was low in the early 1990s. The collapse of the Soviet state, economy, and Communist Party – the primary source of central control during the Soviet period – triggered bureaucratic chaos.[39] Elements of the state apparatus were "completely outside any control and acted each according to its own plan."[40] Regional leaders ignored central directives, gained de facto control over natural resources in their territories, and dictated policy in areas

---

[30] As Yeltsin's press secretary noted, pro-Yeltsin forces consisted only of supporters in the capital and a "conglomerate of small regional organizations" (Kostikov 1997: 264).

[31] Kramer (1992: 329, 330).

[32] Waller (1994: 2).

[33] According to Yeltsin's chief of staff at the time, Yeltsin believed that "the [Communist Party] had been the country's brain and the KGB its spinal cord: And he clearly did not want to rupture the spinal cord now that the head had been lopped off." Quoted in Colton (2008: 259). See also Knight (1993, 2000), Albats (1994), and Waller (1994).

[34] Following the 1991 coup, the KGB was divided into several agencies, including the Ministry of Security (MB), the Foreign Intelligence Service (SVR), the Federal Agency for Government Communications and Information (FAPSI), and the Federal Border Service. The MB was responsible for domestic security and was viewed as the KGB's main successor. In 1993, the MB was reorganized into the

Federal Counter-Intelligence Service (FSK); in 1995, it was strengthened and transformed into the Federal Security Service (FSB). In 2003, the Border Service and FAPSI were incorporated into the FSB.

[35] Pringle (2001–2002); Mlechin (2002: 786); Mukhin (2002: 158).

[36] See Knight (1993: 47), Knight (2000), Pringle (2001–2002), and Mlechin (2002: 744).

[37] Waller (1994: 100). See also Murawiec and Gaddy (2002: 34–5).

[38] Mlechin (2002: 786); Mukhin (2002: 158); Staar and Tacosa (2004: 45). Overall, the armed services – including the FSB, police, army, foreign intelligence, and the Federal Protective Service – had an estimated 1.8 million troops in the early 2000s (Staar and Tacosa 2004: 45).

[39] See Treisman (1999), Baturin et al. (2001: 118), Kahn (2002), and Stoner-Weiss (2006: 36, 38).

[40] Kryshtanovskaia (2005: 230); see also (Huskey 1999).

that were officially the realm of the central government (e.g., citizenship, tax collection, and privatization).[41] Enforcement of military conscription declined precipitously, and the disappearance of the Soviet center and mounting wage arrears generated a "dangerous vacuum in the administration of military and security structures."[42]

Organizational power increased in the late 1990s and early 2000s. For one, Vladimir Putin helped build a stronger governing party: United Russia.[43] Unlike earlier parties, United Russia provided an organizational hub for progovernment forces, incorporating smaller parties and regional leaders into a well-financed "dominant party" by the mid-2000s.[44] It also gave Putin an effective presence in parliament.[45] Although United Russia was not a mass party, it developed a solid structure that penetrated the national territory.[46] By the mid-2000s, the party had established an extensive patronage-based organization.[47] Built on existing regional machines,[48] and incorporating politicians from across the ideological spectrum, the party lacked an identifiable ideology or other nonmaterial source of cohesion.[49] Yet in contrast to Yeltsin's loosely organized "parties of power," it became a "disciplined and centralized organization,"[50] with parliamentary discipline that "rivaled the Communists."[51]

Coercive capacity also increased in the 2000s. Toward the end of his presidency, Yeltsin adopted a strategy of appointing a large number of security and military officials to positions throughout the state.[52] Due to their discipline, organizational *esprit de corps*, and sense of elite status and mission, the security forces

---

[41] See Kahn (2002: 284–7) and Stoner-Weiss (2006: 57–8). As Stoner-Weiss (2006: 42) notes, "the Russian central state only weakly penetrated regional politics and faced strong resistance to many of its policies in the heartland." Many regions periodically refused to send up tax monies to Moscow (Kahn 2002: 151, 152, 186; Stoner-Weiss 2006: 88), and regional governments often ignored central constitutional court rulings on the illegality of laws and local executive actions (Kahn 2002: 154, 178–9). According to one 1997 estimate, "22,000 regional laws and executive orders contradicted the federal constitution" (Kahn 2002: 173). For a thorough analysis of subnational noncompliance, see Stoner-Weiss (2006: 59–76).

[42] Gaidar (1999: 124). In the early 1990s, Russian military commanders often acted "without the full control of Moscow" in ways that contributed to the escalation of conflicts in Moldova and Georgia (King 2000: 195). On military conscription, see Moran (1999: 61).

[43] United Russia was built out of Unity, which had been created by pro Yeltsin forces in 1999 (Hale 2004, 2006).

[44] Reuter and Remington (2009: 502). See also Smyth (2002), Hale (2004), and Smyth, Wilkening, and Urasova (2008).

[45] Remington (2003c).

[46] As of 2004, the party had 89 regional, 2,582 local, and 27,320 primary party organizations (Ivanov 2008: 187). See also Reuter and Remington (2009: 502). Official party membership increased from a reported 220,000 in 2000 to more than 1.7 million in 2007 (Ivanov 2008: 66, 331).

[47] See Ivanov (2008: 128, 232, 277); Reuter and Remington (2009). We score Unity/United as low cohesion in 2000 because it was a new party and medium by 2003 following its second election.

[48] See Chebankova (2008: 998), Gelman (2008b: 21), and Ivanov (2008: 128, 232, 277).

[49] On ideological heterogeneity within United Russia, see Ivanov (2008: 194–5).

[50] Gelman (2008a: 921).

[51] Remington (2003b: 36).

[52] Kryshtanovskaia (2005: 270).

were well placed to be the "steel rod" that Yeltsin hoped would bring order to the state.[53] In a sense, the KGB provided an alternative to rebuilding state structures from scratch. The process of state-rebuilding accelerated under Putin. Improved fiscal health (due in large part to rising energy prices) allowed Putin to strengthen central state authority.[54] Bureaucratic discipline increased[55]; subnational rebellion declined sharply; and Putin reasserted central control over tax, agencies, police, and other state agencies.[56] By the early 2000s, state cohesion was clearly medium.[57]

Organizational power was enhanced by increased discretionary control over the economy.[58] The Putin government renationalized or reasserted state control over key sectors of the economy, including transportation, communication, and – crucially – energy.[59] Between 2000 and 2007, the state's share of oil production rose from 16 to 50 percent, which – combined with the massive revenue generated by higher energy prices – dramatically increased the government's economic power.[60]

In summary, organizational power in Russia increased from medium low in the early 1990s to medium high in the early 2000s. As we shall see, increased state and party capacity helps to explain Russia's transformation from a relatively fragile regime under Yeltsin to an increasingly stable and closed one under Putin.

Origins and Evolution of the Regime under Yeltsin (1992–1999)
Russia's competitive authoritarian regime emerged in the wake of the communist collapse. Following Mikhail Gorbachev's introduction of multicandidate legislative elections in the Soviet republics in 1990, Boris Yeltsin – a former Moscow Communist Party boss whose reformist challenge had earned him broad public support – was elected chair of the Russian legislature.[61] In June 1991, Yeltsin was elected President of the Russian Federation, and when the Union of Soviet Socialist Republics (USSR) collapsed in December 1991, he became president of an independent Russia.

---

[53] Yeltsin (2000: 253–254). Bringing into government officials who were "accustomed to military discipline … seemed like a quick and simple way of reviving functionally effective government" (Kryshtanovskaia 2005: 267).

[54] For example, increased energy revenue allowed the government to eliminate most public wage arrears (World Bank 2003; M. Goldman 2008: 15).

[55] See Huskey (2001), Kryshtanovskaia (2005: 238–43), and Gelman (2006).

[56] Petrov and Slider (2005); Stoner-Weiss (2006: 62); Gelman (2006).

[57] At the same time, Russia does not merit a score of "high." Russia did not experience large-scale military conflict (the war in Chechnya was costly in terms of lives lost but

remained localized). Although Putin's ties to the security services may have increased cohesion, the evidence is not clear. See Kryshtanovskaia (2008: 18).

[58] See, in particular, Fish (2005) and M. Goldman (2008).

[59] M. Goldman (2008); Kryshtanovskaia (2008: 22).

[60] See *The Financial Times*, 4 May, 2007 (online: www.ft.com). In 2005, energy products accounted for more than 60 percent of Russian exports (World Bank World Development Indicators (online: www.worldbank.org/data)).

[61] On Yeltsin's rise, see Morrison (1991), Zlotnik (2003), and Colton (2008).

Post-Soviet Russia was never a democracy. Yeltsin illegally closed parliament in 1993 and retained power via flawed elections.[62] Moreover, close ties between the state and emerging entrepreneurs and media barons gave Yeltsin enormous media and resource advantages.[63] Nevertheless, the regime was quite open in the early and mid-1990s. Elections were highly competitive, the legislature wielded considerable power, and private mass media – most notably, Vladimir Gusinsky's NTV – regularly criticized Yeltsin and provided a platform for opposition.[64]

The relative pluralism of the 1990s may be attributed, in part, to Yeltsin's personal tolerance and support for it.[65] However, it was also "pluralism by default," in that the government lacked the organizational tools to suppress opposition or prevent challenges from within.[66] The Russian state was at its weakest in the early and mid-1990s. The central Soviet state had just collapsed, and a severe economic crisis left the government unable to regularly pay public-sector salaries.[67] Agencies of coercion were so unreliable that they sometimes failed to carry out orders to suppress extremists. Thus, Yeltsin's advisor complained that the president:

... gave orders to stop the extremist behavior, to close openly fascist publications. But after his orders, nothing changed... he could not do anything. His strict orders to the power ministries... did nothing but disturb the air.[68]

Yeltsin also lacked a party. After ignoring his original party movement, Democratic Russia, during the 1991 presidential campaign, Yeltsin governed by relying on multiple and competing organizations and political cliques.[69]

Organizational weakness posed a serious challenge to regime stability. Despite Yeltsin's initially broad public support,[70] his government was challenged repeatedly in the early 1990s. The first challenge, the 1992–1993 parliamentary rebellion led by Speaker Ruslan Khasbulatov,[71] was a clear product of incumbent weakness. As recently as late 1991, a majority of parliament had been pro-Yeltsin,

---

[62] On fraud and abuse in Russian elections during the 1990s, see Fish (2001b, 2005). As McFaul and Petrov (1998: 319) write, "Direct falsification and various forms of interference... [were] integral characteristics of Russian elections."

[63] See European Institute for the Media (1996), McFaul (1997), and Hoffman (2003). For example, three major national television stations existed in the 1990s: the state-run ORT and RTR and the private NTV (launched in 1993), whose owner, Vladimir Gusinsky, frequently aligned himself with the government.

[64] Opposition forces won pluralities in the 1993 and 1995 parliamentary elections and nearly won the presidency in 1996 (Belin et al. 1997; McFaul 1997; Colton and Hough 1998). On the power of the legislature, see T. Remington (1996) and Troxel (2003). On media pluralism, see Mickiewicz (1999) and Lipmann and McFaul (2001).

[65] The emergence of independent media outlets such as NTV may be traced to Yeltsin's willingness to allow open media criticism "as long as the situation did not become mortally dangerous for him and his power" (Baturin et al. 2001: 504). On the importance of Yeltsin's political tolerance and anti-communism in the evolution of Russian politics, see Aron (2000: 500), McFaul (2001: 128), and Colton (2008).

[66] Way (2005a).

[67] Russia's economy shrank by 24 percent in 1992–1993 alone and by at least 40 percent between 1990 and 1996. See World Bank World Development Indicators (online: www.worldbank.org/data); and Ellman (2000).

[68] Kostikov (1997: 115–16).

[69] Urban (1992); McFaul (2001).

[70] See McFaul (2001: 155).

[71] For detailed analyses of the crisis, see Baturin et al. (2001: 219–373), Filatov (2001), McFaul (2001: 161–204), Andrews (2002), and Colton (2008).

and Khasbulatov was a Yeltsin ally who owed his position to the president.[72] Yeltsin possessed vast power resources with which to influence the legislature, including control over the security forces, all major TV stations, key economic ministries, and a plethora of patronage appointments.[73] Yet, without a party, he lacked the means to manage intra-elite rivalries or maintain legislative control.[74] Consequently, the ruling coalition quickly fell apart. Yeltsin's parliamentary support evaporated within months of the Soviet collapse, as "a number of deputies felt themselves cut off or removed from power."[75] In early 1992, Khasbulatov and Vice President Alexander Rutskoi moved into opposition.[76] Led by Khasbulatov, parliament forced Yeltsin to replace Acting Prime Minister Yegor Gaidar in December 1992 and nearly impeached Yeltsin – falling 72 votes shy of the necessary 689 – in March 1993.[77] Conflict came to a head in late 1993. In September, unable to secure legislative approval of a new constitution (and seeking to prevent passage of a pro-parliamentary constitution), Yeltsin dissolved parliament by decree and called a constitutional referendum and new parliamentary elections for December.[78] The Constitutional Court declared the decree unconstitutional, and hundreds of legislators – camped out in the parliament building – voted to impeach Yeltsin and elected Rutskoi in as president.[79] In response, Yeltsin cut off parliament's electricity and telephone service. On October 3, Rutskoi called on supporters – including armed paramilitaries – to seize control of the state. Supporters occupied the mayor's office and stormed the Ostankino television station. Yeltsin responded by ordering military units to storm the legislature.[80]

   Yeltsin confronted important obstacles in assaulting the legislature. Given the high-intensity nature of the conflict (it was covered live on CNN) and the government's limited control over the coercive apparatus, the move was fraught with uncertainty and risk. Security officials – fearful of taking the blame for repression – were reluctant to be drawn into the crisis.[81] Special combat units openly resisted Yeltsin's entreaties to put down the parliamentary rebellion,[82] and Defense

---

[72] Filatov (2001: 170); Andrews (2002: 237).

[73] See Hahn (1996: 18); Huskey (1999: 63), Baturin et al. (2001: 250, 291), and Mukhin (2002: 148). Although most accounts portray the conflict between Yeltsin and the legislature as one between two relatively equal forces (T. Remington 1996: 121–3; McFaul 2001), Yeltsin enjoyed far greater access to patronage and other power resources. Khasbulatov attempted to create a military force and assert control over the regions (Filatov 2001: 168, 185; Baturin et al. 2001: 281) but these efforts failed.

[74] Kryshtanovskaia (2005: 160).

[75] Sobyanin (1994: 188).

[76] On Yeltsin's loss of parliamentary support, see also Remington et al. (1994) and Filatov (2001: 70). Khasbulatov's defection was reportedly due in part to frustration over not being named Prime Minister (Shevtsova 1999: 38; Aron 2000: 497; Filatov 2001: 171).

Vice President Rutskoi publicly opposed Yeltsin's economic policies, calling them an "economic genocide" ("Yeltsin Deputy Calls Reforms, 'Economic Genocide'" *The New York Times*, 9 February 1992 (online: www.nyt.com)).

[77] Dunlop (1995: 311); Baturin et al. (2001: 304–14).

[78] McFaul (2001: 194).

[79] McFaul (2001: 195).

[80] Kulikov (2002: 164–7).

[81] The media played up such fears. *Rosiiskaia gazeta* wrote that officers participating in an assault on parliament could "spend the rest of their life in prison after Russia revives constitutional government" (quoted in Kostikov 1997: 220). Many security officials believed that they had been unfairly held responsible for past repression, including the 1991 Soviet crackdown in Lithuania (Krickus 1997: 154).

[82] See Yeltsin (1994: 11–12).

Minister Pavel Grachev repeatedly told Yeltsin that troops were entering Moscow when in fact they had stopped at the edge of the city.[83] On October 4, after Yeltsin put his orders in writing,[84] military forces shelled the parliament: Hundreds were killed, and Khasbulatov, Rutskoi, and other parliamentary opposition leaders were arrested.

Yeltsin's willingness to personally sanction high-intensity coercive action against parliament can be explained, in part, by low leverage. Although concern over international reaction discouraged many post–Cold War autocrats from engaging in high-intensity repression (and encouraged the use of informal mechanisms, such as thugs and oral commands, which provide greater plausible deniability),[85] Western support allowed Yeltsin to take open responsibility for the crackdown. Despite Russia's relative weakness, any potential for Western democratizing pressure was outweighed by fears that Russia – and its nuclear weapons – would fall into the wrong hands. Thus, in March 1993, Yeltsin obtained support from German leader Helmut Kohl to use "extreme measures" against parliament. Kohl, in turn, sent a letter to other Western leaders calling on them to back Yeltsin.[86] Unambiguous Western support allowed Yeltsin to publicly back the use of force, which was critical to gaining the compliance of the security forces in a context of low cohesion.[87]

The success of the October 1993 crackdown allowed Yeltsin to impose a new super-presidentialist constitution and elect a new parliament. Parliamentary elections were held jointly with a constitutional referendum in December 1993. However, Yeltsin's limited organizational power was again made manifest in these elections. Despite unfair conditions and apparent manipulation of the results of the constitutional referendum,[88] Yeltsin – according to some accounts – had to bargain extensively with regional officials to guarantee victory.[89] In the parliamentary election, despite massive resource advantages, pro-Yeltsin forces fared poorly. Two new pro-Yeltsin parties were created prior to the 1993 election: Russia's Choice and PRES. However, Yeltsin remained aloof from them, which hurt their performance.[90] In the absence of a single governing party, pro-Yeltsin candidates competed against one another in many districts, costing the

---

[83] Korzhakov (1997: 168).

[84] Fearing that he would be held personally responsible for storming the legislature, Grachev resisted taking action until Yeltsin provided him explicit written orders to attack the parliament building (Yeltsin 1994: 386). For discussions of military and security efforts to avoid involvement in the crisis, see Yeltsin (1994), Korzhakov (1997: 168–93), and Kulikov (2002: 160–70).

[85] In Ukraine, for example, concern over potential international condemnation may have discouraged President Leonid Kuchma and Prime Minister Viktor Yanukovych from ordering violent suppression of protests in 2004 (Kuzio 2006b).

[86] Yeltsin (1994: 176); Baturin et al. (2001: 276).

[87] Yeltsin (1994: 386).

[88] Yeltsin's press secretary reports witnessing Yeltsin alter the final vote tallies in the referendum (Kostikov 1997: 268). The referendum also was marred by substantial media bias and reports of pressure within the military and by state employers to vote for the constitution (Urban 1994: 138; Skillen 1995: 102, 122).

[89] *Izvestiia*, 4 May 1994: 4; Sobianin and Sukhovol'skii (1995); Dunlop (1999).

[90] See also T. Remington (1996: 110). Aron (2000: 561) cites estimates that Yeltsin's failure to back a party cost pro-Yeltsin forces 10 to 15 percent of the vote.

government seats.[91] Ultimately, Russia's Choice and PRES captured less than 30 percent of parliament. Pro-Yeltsin forces also performed poorly in the 1995 legislative elections. In an effort to eliminate (in Yeltsin's words) "the political hullabaloo that makes it difficult to sort things out,"[92] Yeltsin promoted two competing "centrist" parties in 1995: Prime Minister Viktor Chernomyrdin's Our Home Is Russia and the Rybkin bloc. Yet, despite widespread access to state resources and media, the two parties won a combined 58 seats, which was far fewer than the 157 seats of the Communist Party of the Russian Federation (KPRF).

Yeltsin faced another serious challenge in the 1996 presidential election, this time from KPRF candidate Gennady Zyuganov.[93] Yeltsin's falling popularity amid continued economic crisis and an unpopular war in Chechnya generated considerable uncertainty around the vote. With presidential approval ratings in single digits, Yeltsin was widely expected to lose.[94] Indeed, fear of a Zyuganov victory nearly led Yeltsin to cancel the election.[95]

Yeltsin possessed several advantages, however. First, his opponents were deeply divided between communist and anti-communist forces; thus, although the KPRF was well organized and possessed a solid base of support,[96] widespread fear of a return to Soviet rule placed a ceiling on that support.[97] Second, the 1996 election was markedly unfair. Two of Russia's three major television stations, ORT and RTR, were in state hands; the third, Vladimir Gusinsky's NTV, was so close to the government that its director, Igor Malashenko, served as media director for the Yeltsin campaign. Opposition access to the airwaves was thus limited.[98] Access to finance was similarly skewed. Tens of millions of dollars in government bonds were diverted to Yeltsin's campaign,[99] and in a highly dubious "loans for shares" arrangement, the government obtained millions of dollars in loans – never expected to be repaid – in exchange for shares in key petroleum firms that had yet to be privatized.[100] Yeltsin's campaign was thus able to spend between 30 and 150 times the amount permitted the Communists.[101] Finally,

---

[91] McFaul (1994: 315).

[92] Quoted in McFaul (2001: 242).

[93] On the 1996 election, see McFaul (1997) and Shevtsova (1999).

[94] See Colton (1996: 371) and McFaul (1997: ix–x). Rose (1996: 381) described Yeltsin's approval rating as "so low it can hardly fall further," and several polls showed Zyuganov ahead (White, Rose, and McAllister 1996).

[95] Yeltsin (2000: 23–5); Kulikov (2002: 394–402).

[96] See March (2002).

[97] McFaul (1997).

[98] European Institute for the Media (1996); Mickiewicz (1999: 185–6). Private media refused to sell advertising to the KPRF (McFaul 1997: 47), and the media covered up Yeltsin's heart attack in the run-up to the second round (Mickiewicz 1999: 185–6).

The government also pressured the media to marginalize liberal candidate Grigorii Yavlinsky, whose campaign it feared would split the anti-communist vote (McFaul 1997: 26).

[99] Hoffman (2003: 348–51).

[100] According to Yeltsin ally Yegor Gaidar, the "loans-for-shares" program "created a political pact" that "helped ensure that Zyuganov did not come to the Kremlin" (quoted in Freeland 2000: 171; Hoffman 2003). The deal allowed a number of bankers to gain ownership of valuable oil reserves for virtually nothing. For example, Mikhail Khodorkovsky paid just $309 million for Yukos, which had a market value of $15 billion (M. Goldman 2008: 64).

[101] McFaul (1997: 13).

there was extensive fraud in some regions.[102] These advantages allowed Yeltsin to defeat Zyuganov – with 54 percent of the vote – in a runoff.

Western powers again played an important supporting role. Yeltsin's claim that opposition success would harm Western interests was strengthened by the communists' emergence as the leading opposition force.[103] Thus, the United States strongly backed Yeltsin during 1996, working to ensure a $10.2 billion IMF loan in the run-up to the election.[104] Although the Clinton Administration apparently discouraged Yeltsin from canceling the election,[105] it turned a blind eye to fraud and abuse committed during the campaign.[106]

The Yeltsin government continued to face crises through the end of the decade. Despite efforts to control parliament through ad hoc patronage deals with opposition parties,[107] Yeltsin's legislative support remained precarious.[108] In the wake of the August 1998 financial crisis, Yeltsin's erstwhile parliamentary allies blocked his reappointment of Viktor Chernomyrdin as Prime Minister and forced him to select Evgenii Primakov.[109] Primakov emerged as a likely successor to Yeltsin, who – due to ill health and unpopularity – was almost certain to leave office when his term ended in 2000.[110] Many of Yeltsin's powerful former supporters – including Moscow Mayor Iurii Luzhkov and several regional leaders – abandoned him for Primakov.[111] In 1999, these politicians formed what would become the Fatherland-All Russia (OVR) coalition, an alternative "party of power" that would eventually oppose the Kremlin. Backed by powerful oligarchs, OVR emerged as the favorite in the run-up to the 1999 parliamentary election, which was expected to foreshadow the 2000 presidential election.[112]

Primakov's rise – and the succession issue more generally – posed a serious dilemma for Yeltsin. Given the considerable corruption that existed within his inner circle (then dominated by Yeltsin's daughter Tatyana), leaving the presidency in the wrong hands was potentially risky. And given Primakov's independence from Yeltsin, he was unlikely to protect the president's entourage.[113] Yet, lacking a strong party, Yeltsin's ability to find a successor who was both loyal and electorally viable appeared limited.

---

[102] See McFaul (1997: 63), McFaul and Petrov (1998: 222, 241–2), and Myagkov, Ordeshook, and Shakin (2009: 77–8).

[103] Goldgeier and McFaul (2003: 54).

[104] "Russia and IMF Agree on a Loan for $10.2 billion," *New York Times*, February 23, 1996 (online: www.nyt.com); Talbott (2002).

[105] McFaul (2005b).

[106] According to Sarah Mendelson (2001: 86), "the U.S. embassy warned the USAID staff in Moscow to keep their distance from [electoral] monitoring efforts. Unofficially, they were told of worries that fraud benefiting Yeltsin might be uncovered."

[107] Huskey (2001); Colton (2008: 410).

[108] Troxel (2003).

[109] See Shevtsova (1999: 258–9), Yeltsin (2000: 266–268), and Colton (2008: 416–17).

[110] Shvetsova (2003: 219–20).

[111] See Yeltsin (2000: 298–300) and Shvetsova (2003: 217–24). For an insightful discussion of the governors' decision to back Primakov, see Shvetsova (2003: 217–23).

[112] Hale (2004); Shvetsova (2003: 223).

[113] Primakov's relationship with Yeltsin's daughter was tense (Primakov 2007: 231–2, 314, 320–1; Ostrow, Saratov, and Khakamada 2007: 86). Moreover, as Prime Minister, Primakov had begun to prosecute oligarchs tied to Yeltsin and warned of future prosecutions (Yeltsin 2000: 298; Hoffman 2003: 459; Shevtsova 2005: 22–3; Primakov 2007: 324–33).

It was at this point that Yeltsin pulled a political rabbit out of his hat. In May 1999, Yeltsin dismissed Primakov and, three months later, named his virtually unknown intelligence chief, Vladimir Putin, as Prime Minister and designated successor.[114] Putin proved to be an effective politician. In September 1999, following a series of bombings in Moscow that killed nearly 300 people, Russian forces invaded Chechnya and regained effective control of the breakaway region. Military success and economic growth generated a surge in public support,[115] which – together with Putin's embrace of a new pro-Kremlin party, Unity – improved the prospects of pro-Yeltsin forces in the 1999 parliamentary elections.[116] Putin's popularity, as well as manipulation of the electronic media,[117] allowed Unity to finish a close second (with 23 percent of the party list vote) in the 1999 legislative election, just behind the KPRF (24 percent) and well ahead of OVR (13 percent).[118]

Unity's strong performance paved the way for Putin's successful presidential bid in 2000. In December 1999, Yeltsin resigned and called early elections for March 2000. Putin became acting President and incumbent. Moreover, OVR's poor performance in the parliamentary vote triggered a massive defection of national and regional politicians back to the pro-Kremlin camp.[119] Primakov opted not to run and OVR backed Putin, leaving the now weakened KPRF as the only significant opposition. In an election marked by media bias, abuse of state resources, and fraud in several regions,[120] Putin won an easy first-round victory with 53 percent of the vote.

Under Yeltsin, then, the Russian regime was highly competitive, but this competitiveness was rooted, to a considerable extent, in incumbent weakness. Most accounts of this period point to Yeltsin's failure to build a party as a cause of democratic breakdown, rather than authoritarian failure.[121] Such accounts rest

---

[114] Putin had helped to block efforts to prosecute members of Yeltsin's inner circle (Baker and Glasser 2005: 45–52; Colton 2008: 431), and his demonstrated loyalty to his previous political patron, St. Petersburg Mayor Anatolii Sobchak, amid corruption scandals (Putin organized a covert operation to smuggle Sobchak out of the country) apparently convinced those close to Yeltsin that Putin could be trusted (Sakwa 2004: 11; Baker and Glasser 2005: 45–54). Yeltsin confidante Valentin Yumashev reportedly felt that since "[Putin] didn't give up Sobchak, he won't give us up" (See "The Rollback of Democracy In Vladimir Putin's Russia," *The Washington Post*, 7 June 2005 (online: www.washingtonpost.com)). Indeed, Putin's second decree as acting president provided Yeltsin lifetime immunity from criminal prosecution (Sakwa 2004: 24; Colton 2008: 587).

[115] Sakwa (2004: 18–19); Colton (2008: 433–4).

[116] Hale (2004).

[117] See Colton and McFaul (2003) and White, Oates, and McAllister (2005). Although NTV supported OVR, state-owned television stations – the only ones with full national coverage – were biased toward Unity (ODIHR 2000h). For a comprehensive analysis of media in the 1999–2000 elections, see Oates (2003).

[118] Although there was fraud in the election, the defection of many regional leaders to the OVR undermined the Kremlin's control over electoral manipulation and resulted in what Fish (2001a) called "pluralism of falsification."

[119] Hanson (2003: 164); Shvetsova (2003); Ivanov (2008: 62–4).

[120] ODIHR (2000i); Myagkov and Ordershook (2001).

[121] See, for example, McFaul (1994, 2001), Remington et al. (1994), and Colton and Skach (2005). Indeed, the conflict with

on the assumption that a strong governing party could have provided a bulwark against autocratic forces. However, given the weakness of civic or pro-democracy forces, any party created by Yeltsin almost certainly would have been dominated by the executive. As this book makes clear, such parties can facilitate authoritarian consolidation, particularly where other sources of political competition – such as civil society and the private sector – are weak. Indeed, as we demonstrate below, the emergence of a stronger governing party after 1999 hardly contributed to democracy. Russia's subsequent authoritarian turn was caused not by the triumph of Yeltsin's opponents but rather by the victory of his *allies*.

Authoritarian Consolidation under Putin: 2000–2008

After 2000, external and domestic constraints on autocratic behavior largely disappeared. On the external front, economic growth and skyrocketing oil prices made Russia virtually immune to Western pressure. In the domestic arena, the balance of power shifted in Putin's favor. Putin strengthened party and state organizations. He invested heavily in the ruling Unity, which absorbed OVR and became United Russia in 2001. A more institutionalized ruling party effectively eliminated parliament as a site for opposition challenges.[122] Indeed, the legislative defections and rebellions that had plagued Yeltsin disappeared under Putin. United Russia became the dominant force in the Duma,[123] which spelled "the end of the independence of legislative power from the executive."[124] Putin also undermined regional power centers. He consolidated Russia's 89 provinces into seven regional districts, effectively barred regional parties from parliamentary elections,[125] and emasculated the upper legislative chamber (Federation Council), which governors had used to lobby for regional interests.[126]

In addition, Putin reasserted state control over the economy. He nationalized key economic sectors – including much of the energy sector – and tightened the Kremlin's grip over the monopoly gas company, Gazprom.[127] Whereas Gazprom (a joint stock company) had operated semi-autonomously under Yeltsin, Putin established full control over it, transforming it into an instrument of political patronage and punishment.[128] Putin also weakened leading business "oligarchs" by prosecuting and/or exiling them and stripping them of their assets.[129] In

---

parliament might have been avoided had Yeltsin been backed by a well-organized party.

[122] See Gelman (2008a), Ivanov (2008: 183–4), and Reuter and Remington (2009).

[123] Remington (2003c: 233).

[124] Kryshtanovskaia (2005: 253).

[125] A new law required that parties participating in parliamentary elections have a minimum of 50 members in each of Russia's 89 regions (Sakwa 2007: 104).

[126] See Kryshtanovskaya and White (2003: 300), Remington (2003a), and Chebankova (2008:

1003). Under Yeltsin, the Federation Council had been composed of provincial governors. After Putin's reforms, more than three quarters of nominations for Council seats were recommended or cleared by the executive (Remington 2003a: 674); as a result, the Chamber "effectively ceased its independent functioning" (Chebankova 2008: 995).

[127] M. Goldman (2008).

[128] M. Goldman (2008: 136–43). As Goldman (2008: 143) noted, "[i]t is hard to tell where Putin begins and Gazprom ends."

[129] M. Goldman (2008).

2003, Putin took on Mikhail Khodorkovsky, the head of the giant Yukos oil company (and Russia's wealthiest man), who not only challenged the government but also began to finance the opposition, "buying" an estimated 100 members of parliament.[130] In late 2003, Khodorkovsky was arrested (and later imprisoned) for tax fraud and other crimes, and Yukos was broken up and sold off to various Kremlin-controlled companies.[131]

Finally, Putin assaulted the oligarch-controlled media. In 2001, business tycoon Boris Berezovsky, who ran the influential television station, ORT,[132] was forced into exile on fraud charges and stripped of his control of ORT after the station aired critical coverage of the government.[133] That year, the Kremlin utilized Vladimir Gusinsky's $473 million debt to Gazprom to engineer a Gazprom-led takeover of NTV.[134] In 2002, the government took over Berezovsky's TV-6, leaving Russia without independent television.[135]

The elimination of regional and oligarchic power centers and independent mass media crippled the opposition. Opposition access to television was largely curtailed by the early 2000s, and Khodorkovsky's imprisonment served as a "warning to other oligarchs against involvement in political affairs or . . . financial support to independent civil society."[136] Civic and opposition groups thus were starved of resources; as a result, many of them either collapsed or were co-opted by the government.[137] At the same time, public support for the largest and best organized opposition party, the KPRF, declined considerably.[138]

As the domestic balance of power shifted, elections became less competitive. The 2003 parliamentary election was characterized by media bias, massive abuse of state resources, and at least some electoral manipulation.[139] United Russia won 223 of 450 parliamentary seats, which – when combined with small allied parties and independents – gave Putin a two-thirds majority.

The post-2003 period saw the "destruction without exception of all opposition parties" and elimination of "meaningful alternatives to incumbent power."[140] As the 2004 presidential election approached, several major candidates – including Gennady Zyuganov – opted not to run. Facing only minor opposition,

---

[130] Yukos produced 20 percent of Russia's oil exports (Rutland 2006: 11; M. Goldman 2008: 106). In addition to defying the government politically, Khodorkovsky made major economic decisions – such as negotiating with China and planning the sale of vast oil reserves to Exxon-Mobil – without consulting the government (M. Goldman 2004, 2008: 111–13; Baker and Glasser 2005: 280–3).

[131] Goldman (2004); Baker and Glasser (2005: 272–92); Pazderka (2005).

[132] ORT was majority state-owned but Berezovskii, who owned 49 percent, controlled it.

[133] M. Goldman (2008: 104, 123).

[134] Gazprom also took over two independent publications owned by Gusinskii: *Segodnya*

and *Itogi*. See Lipman and McFaul (2001) and Hoffman (2003: 482).

[135] Ostrow, Saratov, and Khakamada (2007: 118).

[136] U.S. Department of State (2006c).

[137] McFaul and Petrov (2004: 24, 27); Gelman (2007: 69). For example, Yabloko, which been supported by Yukos and had been the most significant liberal opposition party in the 1990s, fell to 4.3 percent of the vote in the 2003 parliamentary elections and to just 1.6 percent in 2007. Likewise, the once-powerful Union of Right Forces fell to just 1 percent of the vote in 2007.

[138] Clark (2006).

[139] See ODIHR (2004b: 12) and Gelman (2007: 73, 80).

[140] Gelman (2007: 69).

Putin was overwhelmingly reelected with 71 percent of the vote in the first round.[141]

Putin's authoritarian turn did not go unnoticed by Western powers. U.S. officials – including President Bush – criticized Putin's attack on Yukos and his "failure to pursue democratic reforms."[142] External criticism had little impact, however. Western governments were "hardly prepared to do anything about Khodorkovsky's arrest."[143] Indeed, U.S. policy toward Russia did not change significantly, and Western investment continued largely unabated.[144] In effect, Russia's strategic and economic importance made Putin "impervious to the criticism."[145]

Authoritarian consolidation continued during Putin's second term. In late 2004, Putin increased the barriers to creating political parties and pushed through a law that eliminated elections for regional governors.[146] Harsh restrictions were imposed on NGOs, and censorship, harassment, and violence against journalists transformed Russia into "one of the most dangerous countries in the world for the media."[147] Elections became increasingly noncompetitive. In the 2007 parliamentary election, the government strictly limited opposition access to the media and used a highly restrictive political-parties law to bar several liberal parties from running.[148] United Russia won overwhelmingly, capturing 64 percent of the vote and 315 of 450 parliamentary seats.

In 2008, Putin orchestrated a presidential succession that allowed him to abide by constitutional term limits while retaining effective power. Following the 2007 Duma election, he announced his support for Dmitri Medvedev, a close associate, to succeed him. Simultaneously, Medvedev announced that he would pick Putin as Prime Minister. At the same time, the government imposed onerous administrative requirements for opposition candidates seeking access to the ballot.[149] Former Prime Minister Mikhail Kasyanov, the only potentially viable

---

[141] The election was characterized by media bias, abuse of state resources, and some fraud (ODIHR 2004d).

[142] Maynes (2004).

[143] Baker and Glasser (2005: 291–2).

[144] "Putin's Assertive Diplomacy Is Seldom Challenged," *The New York Times*, 27 December 2006 (online: www.nyt.com); M. Goldman (2008).

[145] "Putin's Assertive Diplomacy Is Seldom Challenged," *The New York Times*, 27 December 2006 (online: www.nyt.com); *RFE/RL Newsline*, 12 July 2006 (online: http://www.rferl.org/archive/en-newsline/latest/683/683.html).

[146] Remington (2008: 974–5).

[147] Freedom House, "Freedom of the Press, 2008: Russia" (online: www.freedomhouse.org); U.S. Department of State (2009h). According to the Glasnost Defense Fund, 87 investigative journalists were murdered between 2000 and 2006 (Ostrow, Saratov, and Khakamada 2007: 116–17). Perhaps the

best known case of repression was the October 2006 killing of influential journalist Anna Politkovskaia. On NGO restrictions, see Ostrow, Saratov, and Khakamada (2007: 122) and Stoner-Weiss (2008: 317).

[148] Among the most important parties barred from participation in 2007 were former Prime Minister Mikhail Kasyanov's Russian Popular Democratic Union Party (S. Goldman 2008).

[149] Candidates from parties without representation in the Duma or in fewer than a third of regional assemblies were required to collect 2 million signatures within a three-week period that overlapped with the Russian holiday season (Sakwa forthcoming: Chapter 8). Given the paucity of significant opposition in the Duma, heavy restrictions on opposition activity, and Russia's highly uneven playing field, these requirements made it virtually impossible for viable opposition candidates to get on the ballot.

opposition candidate to overcome these hurdles, was subsequently disqualified on the grounds that too many signatures had been forged.[150] In an election marred by media bias and widespread manipulation, Medvedev won with 71 percent of the vote.[151] Putin was then named Prime Minister and remained the effective head of state through 2008.[152] Thus, although the transition nominally adhered to constitutional rules, it had virtually no effect on the balance of power in Russia.

Authoritarian consolidation in Russia may be attributed, in part, to economic recovery, which heightened Putin's popularity.[153] Yet, autocrats in Georgia and Ukraine fell from power during the 2000s despite high levels of growth. Russia differed from these cases in two ways. First, due to low leverage, Putin faced few external constraints. Second, Putin possessed stronger state and party institutions. Greater economic control and a relatively cohesive ruling party helped to prevent elite defection and starved the opposition of critical resources, which resulted in a more stable – and closed – authoritarian regime.

In summary, due to state and party weakness, the Russian regime was precarious in the 1990s, but low Western leverage facilitated its survival. Putin succeeded in consolidating authoritarian rule mainly by eliminating key organizational sources of vulnerability. In a context of very low leverage and a weak opposition, he met virtually no resistance as he eliminated the last vestiges of democracy.

The absence of nonmaterial bases of cohesion may eventually be a source of regime vulnerability. Recent scholarship has highlighted United Russia's strength, describing it as "a true dominant party" comparable to ZANU–PF

---

[150] *RFE/RL Newsline*, 2 March 2008 (online: http://www.rferl.org/archive/en-newsline/latest/683/683.html and Stoner-Weiss 2008. According to Sakwa (forthcoming: Chapter 8), Kasyanov might have successfully challenged this ruling but chose not to because his poll numbers were very low. Former chess champion Garri Kasparov, facing heavy harassment and unable to even rent a meeting space for his party, also dropped out. The remaining candidates, Gennadii Zyuganov, Vladimir Zhirinovsky, and Andrei Bogdanov were either unknown (Bogdanov) or widely considered incapable of winning (Zyuganov and Zhirinovsky). One observer dismissed them as "a has-been, a clown, and a nobody" ("Russia's Presidential Election," *Times Online*, 29 February 2008 (www.timesonline.co.uk). Many observers felt that Bogdanov's candidacy had been promoted by the Kremlin to provide the appearance of competition (Whitmore 2008).

[151] See *Moscow Times*, 4 March 2008: 1-2 Stoner-Weiss (2008); Sakwa (forthcoming: Chapter 8).

[152] Although formally in a weaker position, Putin's strong ties to the security services and broad popularity allowed him to effectively run the country through the end of 2008 (Stoner-Weiss 2008). It remains unclear why Putin chose to abide by the constitutional two-term limit. However, there is little evidence that the constitution per se posed a serious constraint. Given Putin's domination of the Duma and regional governments, he could have easily changed the constitution. It also seems unlikely that Putin left the presidency to avoid "criticism from abroad" (Bush 2005). After all, he shut down independent television stations, jailed major critics, and even invaded Georgia in the face of serious Western criticism.

[153] Economic growth averaged 6 percent annually between 2000 and 2008 (World Bank World Development Indicators (online: www.worldbank.org/data)).

in Zimbabwe.[154] As this book demonstrates, however, pure patronage-based machines are often vulnerable to defection during periods of crisis. Although dominant in terms of size and resources, United Russia lacks the critical sources of cohesion – such as ideology or past history of conflict – that held ruling parties in Nicaragua, Mozambique, and Zimbabwe together during periods of crisis. Putin did not face such a crisis in the 2000s, but United Russia's heavy reliance on patronage may leave it vulnerable in the future.[155]

Belarus

The Belarusian case highlights the importance of black-knight support and discretionary economic power in stabilizing authoritarian rule. Although state and party weakness contributed to the fall of Viacheslau Kebich in 1994, vast state control over the economy – combined with external assistance from Russia – allowed his successor, Alyaksandr Lukashenka, to consolidate authoritarian rule.

Linkage, Leverage, and Organizational Power
Belarus is a case of low linkage and medium leverage. Despite its proximity to Western Europe, trade, migration, and communication ties to the West were weak.[156] EU contacts were "limited," and EU membership thus was "not seen as a credible prospect by most Belarusian citizens and elites."[157] In terms of leverage, Belarus benefited from Russian black-knight support. Russian assistance, which included heavily subsidized natural gas and vast revenues via the resale of Russian oil and arms,[158] accounted for an estimated 20 to 30 percent of GDP and one third of government revenue.[159]

Organizational power increased from low in the early 1990s to medium high in the late 1990s. Party strength was low. Neither Kebich (1992–1994) nor Lukashenka (1994–) built a stable ruling party. Kebich created a "Belarus" parliamentary faction in 1992, but it had no presence outside the legislature and

---

154 Reuter and Remington (2009: 521, 504). See also Smyth, Wilkening, and Urasova (2008).

155 In 2004–2005, for example, United Russia suffered "unusually widespread defection" in parliament when the government's attempt to reform the system of housing subsidies generated relatively small-scale demonstrations across the country (Remington 2008: 976). On United Russia's reliance on patronage, see Ivanov (2008: 295–6) and Remington (2008).

156 In the 1990s, average annual Belarusian trade to the United States and the EU, as a percentage of GDP, was half that of Croatia and Bulgaria (IMF, Direction of Trade Statistics). Albania and Croatia produced 26 and 18 times more migrants, respectively, than Belarus (See Appendix III).

157 Lynch (2006: 157).

158 Through the mid-2000s, Belarusian industry paid the lowest price for Russian gas of any post-Soviet country – less than in Ukraine and up to five times lower than in Western Europe ("Sochins"kyj hazavat," *Ukrainska Pravda* 16 October 2000 (online: www.Pravda.com.ua); Silitski 2003b, 2004b; Grigoriev and Salikhov 2006; "Russia Threatens Cut in Belarus Gas Supply," *The New York Times*, 2 August 2007). The resale of Russian oil generated up to $5 billion in annual export revenue – about 15 percent of Belarus' GDP. See Suzdaltsev (2007) and *The Economist*, 3 January 2007: 44–5. The resale of Russian arms generated $1.1 billion in revenue in the late 1990s (Silitski 2004c: 159; Feduta 2005: 407–11).

159 Aslund (2002: 182); Karol (2006); Belarusian Institute for Strategic Studies (2008).

did not survive a single term.[160] After experimenting with a small parliamentary faction, Lukashenka opted to govern without a party.[161] In terms of coercive capacity, the Belarusian state retained the high scope of the Soviet era. The armed forces were among the largest, per capita, in the former Soviet Union,[162] and the internal security apparatus remained largely intact. The security apparatus thus included the old KGB, which engaged in widespread surveillance and had "hundreds of thousands" of informants spread throughout virtually every population center,[163] more than 100,000 paramilitary forces (including the special police, or OMON), a powerful SWAT team (*Alma*), and a rapid reaction detachment (SOBR).[164] As in Russia, however, cohesion was initially low. In the wake of the Soviet state's collapse, security agencies – including the KGB – retained considerable autonomy (and competing ties to Moscow),[165] and economic crisis and wage arrears undermined central control over regional governments and local state enterprises.[166]

Coercive capacity increased under Lukashenka. Improved state finances and the reestablishment of central control over the security forces and regional governments eliminated open disobedience by lower-level officials.[167] Hence, not only were the security services vast and well financed,[168] but their cohesion also increased. In the absence of a military threat or conflict, however, post-1994 state cohesion is scored as medium.

Organizational power was enhanced by discretionary economic control. Unlike other governments in the region, Lukashenka did not engage in large-scale privatization. Thus, as of 1998, the private sector accounted for only 20 percent of GDP, compared to 50 to 70 percent in Armenia, Georgia, Moldova, and Ukraine.[169] Energy, property, and even employment remained

---

[160] Lucan Way interview with Pavel Kazlauskii, Minister of Defense under Kebich, Minsk, 23 June 2004. See also *Narodnaya hazeta*, 5–7 November 1994: 2.

[161] Shushkevich (2002: 94).

[162] Following the collapse of the Soviet Union, Belarus retained an army of approximately 90,000 (Kramer (1992: 330). According to Parliamentary Speaker Stanislau Shushkevich, Belarus had "the greatest concentration of servicemen anywhere in the world. For every 43 citizens, there is one serviceman." Quoted in Zaprudnik (1993: 206).

[163] Lucan Way interview with Sergei Anis'ko, former counterintelligence official, Minsk, 14 July 2004. See also Sannikov and Kuley (2006: 58–9).

[164] Burger and Minchuk (2006: 34–5).

[165] See Kharitonov (2003) *Narodnaia hazeta* 18 May 1991: 1.

[166] See Way (2008b: 19–21). Due to the lack of central-state control, we do not score Belarus as having high discretionary economic power

in the early 1990s, despite the persistence of a statist economy.

[167] Feduta (2005: 309).

[168] Lucan Way interviews with Vladimir Alekseevich Reznikov, KGB official, Minsk, July 13, 2004, and Sergei Anis'ko, former counterintelligence official, Minsk, July 14, 2004. In 1995, according to one observer, the budget for the KGB matched "all the outlays needed for the government, the Supreme Soviet, the prosecutor's office, and the president's administration taken together" (quoted in Knight 1996: 155).

[169] Data are taken from European Bank for Reconstruction and Development "Structural Change Indicators" (online: www.ebrd.com). A major source of state control was the Presidential Business Administration. Reportedly the largest commercial structure in the country, the Presidential Business Administration enjoyed a monopoly over the import and export of a wide range of consumer products (Silitski 2004c: 158; Feduta 2005: 401–2).

concentrated in state hands, which meant that the government could easily affect the livelihood of numerous businesses, groups, and individuals. Hence, individuals "faced immediate dismissal from state jobs,"[170] and civic organizations could be "condemned to financial ruin" if they were deemed to oppose the government.[171]

Origins and Evolution of the Regime

Competitive authoritarianism in Belarus emerged under Prime Minister Viacheslau Kebich in the wake of the Soviet collapse. The post-communist playing field was highly skewed: Television and radio were concentrated in state hands and biased, and the Kebich government enjoyed disproportionate access to state resources.[172] The Kebich government also committed numerous abuses, including the closure of the country's only private television station and several independent radio programs.[173] Kebich failed to consolidate power, however. After reforming the constitution to introduce presidentialism,[174] Kebich called elections in 1994. Despite media harassment and abuse of state resources,[175] as well as substantial Russian aid, Kebich suffered a stunning defeat at the hands of Alyaksandr Lukashenka, a little-known parliamentary deputy.[176] Although Kebich's defeat is partly explained by economic crisis,[177] it was also rooted in widespread noncompliance and defection within the state: KGB officials reportedly worked for Lukashenka,[178] and state agencies and officials throughout the country ignored orders to deliver the vote for Kebich.[179]

Unlike his predecessor, Lukashenka consolidated authoritarian rule. He censored state media, closed Belarus's only independent radio station and several

---

[170] Silitski (2006c: 22).
[171] Sannikov and Kuley (2006: 58).
[172] On media access, see Feduta (2005: 157). On state resources, see *Narodnaia hazeta*, 17 June 1994: 2.
[173] Silitski (2004c: 76).
[174] Silitski (2004c: 76).
[175] Several radio and television programs critical of Kebich were taken off the air during the campaign (*Narodnaia hazeta* 1 June 1994: 1; 9 June 1994: 1; 10 June 1991: 1). On abuse of state resources, see *Narodnaia hazeta*, 17 June 1994: 2.
[176] Lukashenka won 45 percent of the first-round vote compared to 17 percent for Kebich, and he won the runoff with a stunning 80 percent of the vote.
[177] The economy contracted by 18 percent in 1992–1993 (World Bank World Development Indicators (online: www.worldbank .org/data)).
[178] KGB agents reportedly fed Lukashenka material that undermined Kebich's reputation and enhanced his own image as a fighter against corruption (Lucan Way interviews

with Vladimir Alekseevich Reznikov, KGB official, July 13, 2004, Minsk, and Sergei Anis'ko, former counterintelligence official, July 14, 2004, Minsk).
[179] Lucan Way interviews with Valerii Fadeev, former Council of Ministers, official in charge of local government relations, June 28, 2004, Minsk; Nikolai Voitenkov, former head of Gomel' province, July 9, 2004, Gomel'; and Aleksandr Kornienko, June 30, 2004, Minsk. According to Silitski (2005: 86), Lukashenka won because "incumbents had not yet learned the finer points of manipulation and rigging." Kebich had assumed that nominal control of the state was sufficient to ensure victory, but he was mistaken. A former local official from Mogilev reported that officials from his region would "go to [the capital] and report to Kebich, 'we support you 100 percent,' but then fail to do the most basic activities to support his candidacy" (Lucan Way interview with Vladimir Novosiad, July 8, 2004, Minsk). For an analysis of failed authoritarianism under Kebich, see Way (2009b).

independent newspapers, and imposed an "information blockade" on opponents in the 1995 parliamentary election.[180] By late 1996, the Constitutional Court had declared 16 of Lukashenka's executive decrees unconstitutional, but he ignored these rulings.[181] Lacking a party, Lukashenka also met strong legislative opposition,[182] and in mid-1996, opposition parties began to call for his impeachment.[183] Lukashenka responded by organizing a referendum in November to dissolve parliament and approve a new constitution that reduced parliament to a "rubber stamp for presidential decrees."[184] Lukashenka ignored a Constitutional Court ruling that the referendum was nonbinding; when Election Commission head Victor Hanchar questioned the referendum's legality, he was illegally sacked.[185] In November, 70 legislators, led by Semyon Sharetskii, began formal impeachment proceedings against the president.[186]

Russian intervention helped resolve the conflict in Lukashenka's favor. Top Russian officials, including Prime Minister Chernomyrden, traveled to Belarus and convinced the head of parliament, Sharetskii, to allow the referendum to go ahead.[187] Russian leaders maintained close ties to Sharetskii, dating back to their days in the Soviet Communist Party. According to an ex-government official close to the events, when the Russians insisted that the referendum go ahead, "Sharetskii had a hard time refusing."[188] Under Russian pressure, Sharetskii agreed to halt impeachment proceedings and told thousands of demonstrators gathered outside parliament to go home.[189] The referendum, which was marred by "massive violations of election law," including widespread fraud, passed overwhelmingly.[190] Parliament was disbanded and replaced by a body filled with "hand-picked Lukashenka supporters,"[191] and the Constitutional Court, under intense pressure (including blackmail) from the government, halted

---

[180] *RFE/RL Newsline*, 23 October 1996; 4 September 1996 (online: http://www.rferl.org/archive/en-newsline/latest/683/683.html); Silitski (2005: 86).

[181] "Parliament deputy chairman says election preparations to continue," *Belapan*, 19 August 1996 (online: www.lexisnexis.com); *RFE/RL Newsline*, 23 October 1996 (online: http://www.rferl.org/archive/en-newsline/latest/683/683.html); Silitski (2005: 87).

[182] Silitski (2005: 87).

[183] "Parliament deputy chairman says election preparations to continue" Belapan, 19 August 1996 (online: www.lexisnexis.com); *RFE/RL Newsline*, 23 October 1996 (online: http://www.rferl.org/archive/en-newsline/latest/683/683.html); "How Would You Say "Impeachment" In Belorussian?" *Literaturnaia gazeta*, 31 July 1996 (online: www.lexisnexis.com).

[184] Silitski (2004c: 94). See also Feduta (2005: 283); Sannikov (2005).

[185] *RFE/RL Newsline*, 15 November 1996 (online: http://www.rferl.org/archive/en-newsline/latest/683/683.html); Silitski (2005: 87).

[186] Feduta (2005: 286–8).

[187] Silitski (2004c: 96–7).

[188] According to the official, Sharetskii was "awestruck" by such high-level Soviet-era officials (Lucan Way interview with Andrei Sannikov, former official in the Belarusian Foreign Ministry, Minsk, July 3, 2004). This version of events was confirmed by Mikhail Pastukhov, a Constitutional Court Justice with intimate knowledge of the negotiations (Lucan Way interview, July 6, 2004). See also Feduta (2005: 312–21).

[189] Lucan Way interview with Vincuk Viacorka, leader of the Belarusian Popular Front, Minsk June 29, 2004.

[190] Silitski (2004c: 95).

[191] Silitski (2005: 87–8).

impeachment proceedings.[192] Western powers – including the United States, EU, and OSCE – criticized the referendum, but Lukashenka, backed by Russia, ignored them.[193]

The regime grew increasingly closed after 1996. In 1999, four major opposition figures – including former Election Commissioner Viktor Hanchar, who had emerged as a leader of the prodemocracy movement – disappeared, apparently at the hands of government-sponsored death squads.[194] In the 2000 parliamentary election, nearly half of all opposition candidates were denied registration, and only three opposition candidates were elected.[195] In 2001, Lukashenka retained the presidency – with 76 percent of the official vote – in an election marred by near-total media censorship and massive fraud.[196] Although opposition forces sought to "mimic Serbia's electoral revolution," postelection protests were small and quickly fizzled.[197]

Lukashenka faced several obstacles to authoritarian consolidation after 2001, including declining public support and a constitutional ban on a third presidential term.[198] He overcame these obstacles via repression. The government restricted street protest and imprisoned several major opposition figures, including some presidential contenders.[199] In 2003, it launched a "massive 'cleanup' of Belarusian civil society,"[200] imposing restrictions that forced more than 100 NGOs to "close down or self-liquidate."[201] The following year, Lukashenka called a referendum to eliminate presidential term limits. In a fraudulent vote, the referendum passed with nearly 80 percent support.[202] Two years later, Lukashenka was easily reelected – with 83 percent – in a vote marred by fraud and heavy restrictions on opposition campaigns.[203] Inspired by events in Georgia, Ukraine, and Kyrgyzstan, opposition groups mobilized an estimated 10,000 people in postelection demonstrations, but security forces easily contained the protest, beating and arresting demonstrators en masse.[204] By the mid-2000s, the regime

---

[192] Lucan Way interview with Mikhail Pastukhov, former Constitutional Court Judge, Minsk, July 6, 2004. See also Silitski (2005: 87).

[193] *RFE/RL Newsline*, 26 November 1996, 27 November 1996, 4 December 1996, 13 December 1996 (online: http://www.rferl.org/archive/en-newsline/latest/683/683.html).

[194] See Silitski (2004c: 151; 2005b: 88), Feduta (2005), and Burger and Minchuk (2006: 30).

[195] Freedom House, "Freedom in the World 2008: Belarus" (online:www.freedomhouse.org).

[196] Independent observers estimated that 20 to 25 percent of the vote was stolen (ODIHR 2001c: 24). See also Silitski (2005: 90).

[197] Silitski (2005: 90).

[198] Silitski (2005: 91).

[199] Silitski (2005: 91, 94).

[200] Jarábik (2006: 88).

[201] Silitski (2005: 91); see also Jarábik (2006: 88).

[202] During the campaign, opposition activists faced arrest and intimidation and opposition headquarters were raided by police. See ODIHR (2004i), Sannikov (2005), and Silitski (2005: 93).

[203] See ODIHR (2006a). In a polling station visited by one of the authors, officials used a system of early voting to steal roughly 30 to 40 percent of the votes in favor of Lukashenka. Opposition parties also had virtually no access to the media.

[204] See ODIHR (2006a: 10, 25), Marples (2006: 99–100), and Silitski (2006c: 24–5). Crowd size based on the estimate of one of the authors who was present at the protest. Marples (2006: 99) puts the number of protesters at 15,000.

was hegemonic and opposition was "effectively silenced."[205] Indeed, opposition parties failed to win a single seat in the 2004 and 2008 parliamentary elections.

Two factors facilitated authoritarian consolidation in Belarus. First, state control over the economy left opposition forces enfeebled even by post-Soviet standards. The weakness of the private sector deprived the opposition of an important source of funding, and Lukashenka used his discretionary economic power to discourage business elites from backing the opposition.[206] As a result, the type of semi-autonomous business elite that funded opposition forces in Ukraine (see below) never emerged.[207] Economic control also raised the cost of protest. Individuals faced dismissal from state jobs or universities for participating in opposition activity or failing to attend progovernment rallies.[208]

Second, low linkage and black-knight support shielded the regime from external pressure. Western powers repeatedly condemned Lukashenka's abuses and took action to isolate him. After 1996, Belarus lost its observer status in the Council of Europe,[209] Western governments imposed visa restrictions on Belarusian officials, and U.S. and European aid fell dramatically[210]; after the 2004 referendum, the United States ended all bilateral assistance.[211] However, Russian subsidies and diplomatic support blunted the impact of Western pressure.[212] As one observer noted, "[a]s long as Russia continues to support his regime economically, Lukashenka does not seem to care much about his isolation in the international arena."[213]

Key points of regime vulnerability remained in the late 2000s. For one, black-knight support was precarious. Russia's reduction in energy subsidies after 2006

[205] Burger and Minchuk (2006: 33).

[206] See Center for Political Education (2006). An estimated 16 state agencies were empowered to investigate abuse in business and finance (Silitski 2004a; Silitski 2004c: 116). Indeed, businesses faced significant harassment. One human-rights organization estimated that 20 percent of prison inmates in Belarus are former heads of state and private enterprises. See "Samyi bol'shoi strakh belorusov – tiur'ma," www.charter97.org/rus/news/2006/10/24/turma. We thank Serhyi Kudelia for pointing us to this site.

[207] See Lukashuk (1998) and Silitski (2004c: 158). Thus, Belarus "has no private businessmen remotely as wealthy as those in Ukraine (or Russia)" (Kudrytski 2005).

[208] Silitski (2006b; 2006a: 22); Lucan Way interview with Alexandr Dobravolskii, leader of United Civic Party, March 20, 2006, Minsk.

[209] *RFE/RL Newsline* 10 June 1997, 30 September 1997 (online: http://www.rferl.org/archive/en-newsline/latest/683/683.html); Silitski (2004c: 181–2); Feduta (2005: 351); Shephard (2006: 75–96).

[210] *RFE/RL Newsline*, 13 December 1996 (online: http://www.rferl.org/archive/en-newsline/latest/683/683.html); Levy (1998: 35).

[211] See Shephard (2006: 75–6). In 2005, U.S. Secretary of State Condoleezza Rice named Belarus as one of six "outposts of tyranny" – along with Cuba, Zimbabwe, Myanmar, Iran, and North Korea.

[212] Due in part to Russian assistance, Belarus suffered a less severe economic contraction and fewer wage and pension arrears than most other post-Soviet states in the 1990s (Nesvetailova 2002). Russia accepted Belarusian elections as free and fair and publicly criticized international observers as biased (Trenin 2006: 81). By the 2000s, the EU policy toward Belarus was characterized as one of "learned helplessness" (Lynch 2006: 161).

[213] Maksymiuk (2004); see also Silitski (2004c: 181). As one observer noted in 2006, "it is not easy to see what more the United States could do to promote democratic change in Belarus" (Shephard 2006: 77).

cast doubt about its reliability as a patron and exposed Belarus to greater Western leverage.[214] Second, the absence of a ruling party left Lukashenka vulnerable to elite defection, particularly in the event of a crisis.[215] Whether such a crisis would create an opening for democratization or bring a new autocrat to power is uncertain.

Armenia

The Armenian case illustrates the role of state coercive capacity in maintaining autocratic stability. Despite facing a profound economic crisis and several waves of opposition protest, Presidents Levon Ter-Petrosian (1991–1998), Robert Kocharian (1998–2008), and Serzh Sarkisian (2008) survived, winning or stealing elections in 1991, 1996, 1998, 2003, and 2008.[216] Although party weakness permitted internal conflict that at times threatened regime stability, a powerful coercive apparatus – forged out of a successful war with Azerbaijan – helped to consistently fend off external challenges.

Linkage, Leverage, and Organizational Power

Armenia is a case of medium linkage and high leverage. In terms of linkage, although Armenia had a large diaspora community in the West,[217] émigré ties existed largely in isolation from other types of linkage. Economic, political, and technocratic ties were weak,[218] and whereas Western media penetration was limited, Russian television was widely available.[219] Western leverage was high. Although Armenia benefited from Russian assistance, particularly military aid and subsidized natural gas,[220] this support was far less extensive than in Belarus.[221] Russian influence was also limited by the fact that Armenia was a major recipient of

---

[214] A steep increase in Russian gas prices in 2006–2008 forced Lukashenka to devalue the Belarusian ruble (Silitski 2009) and apparently was behind Lukashenka's overtures to the IMF and EU for aid ("Belarus counts on Czechia's aid in expanding cooperation with EU," *BelTa* (news agency), January 20, 2009 (online: www.belta.by); "Belarus raises gas price for consumers by 9.8 pct," *Reuters*, January 20, 2009). Indeed, heightened external vulnerability also may have been behind Lukashenka's decision to release several political prisoners in 2007 and 2008 (Bluff 2008).

[215] Way (2008a).

[216] Although Ter-Petrosian fell from power in 1998, he was replaced by his Prime Minister. After two presidential terms, Kocharian handed power to his chosen successor.

[217] Bakalian (1992: 12–13); Masih and Krikorian (1999: 12–13).

[218] Trade with Western Europe and the United States was half that of the Eastern European countries in our sample in the 1990s (See Appendix III). Opposition parties had few ties to the West (Bremmer and Welt 1997: 86). Per capita immigration to Western Europe and the United States in the 1990s was about half that of the Eastern European countries in our sample (See Appendix III).

[219] Grigorian (1997).

[220] Fuller (1998d); Horowitz (2005: 82).

[221] As of mid-2006, Armenia paid about three times as much for Russian gas as did Belarus (Whitmore 2006). In addition, because Armenia did not serve as an energy transit point for high-priced European markets, it could not benefit from the resale of gas that benefited the Belarusian regime.

U.S. aid.[222] Armenia's dependence on the West was further heightened by an economic blockade from Turkey and Azerbaijan.[223]

Organizational power was high. Armenia combined a relatively weak governing party with effective coercive institutions. The Armenian National Movement (ANM) emerged in 1989 from the nationalist Karabakh Committee, which had spearheaded a series of massive strikes and demonstrations calling for Armenian control over the ethnically Armenian Nagorno-Karabakh territory in Azerbaijan.[224] A new party that incorporated a diverse array of communist-era dissidents, former communist establishment figures, and younger activists, the ANM was never very disciplined.[225] Due to a shared nationalist ideology, however, we score cohesion as medium. The ANM was not a mass party, but given its demonstrated mobilizational capacity in the late 1980s, we score scope as medium. Party strength declined after 1998. Following the ANM's 1998 collapse, President Kocharian avoided ruling through a single party and instead operated through a coalition of three – often competing – parties. Although one of these parties, the Dashniaks, was well organized across the national territory,[226] party cohesion was clearly low.[227]

Coercive capacity was high. After a breakdown in state authority in 1989–1990, the Ter-Petrosian government brought rogue paramilitary forces under state control,[228] and in the context of a successful war against Azerbaijan, it built a strong military and internal security apparatus. With Russian assistance, Armenia developed a large and well-funded army.[229] Rapid state-building helped Armenia to conquer Nagorno-Karabakh (and gain control of 20 percent of Azerbaijani territory) and transformed the army into "the most powerful institution in Armenia."[230] Armenia also maintained a vast internal security apparatus. The National Security Services, which succeeded the local KGB, "retained the Soviet-era function of secret police," extensively monitoring opposition activity and "suppressing any activity that threatened the regime's grip on power."[231] Coercive capacity was augmented by Yerkrapah (Defenders of the Land), a

---

[222] See Henderson (2002: 152) and Goldgeier and McFaul (2003: 118). In the late 1990s, external aid accounted for 58 percent of Armenia's gross capital formation (World Bank World Development Indicators (online: www.worldbank.org/data)); in 2002, Armenia was the world's third largest per capita recipient of U.S. aid (Giragosian 2003).

[223] Burke (2001).

[224] See Sarafyan (1994), Malkasian (1996: 37–47), and Dudwick (1997: 77–81).

[225] See Sarafyan (1994: 30), Aves (1996), and Malkasian (1996: 199).

[226] Sarafyan (1994: 31); Mitiaev (1998: 108).

[227] The Dashniaks in the early 1990s had opposed the regime but joined the governing coalition under Kocharian.

[228] On state breakdown in 1989–1990, see Dudwick (1997: 83–4) and De Waal (2003: 111). On the state's successful reincorporation of paramilitary groups, see Goldenberg (1994: 144), Aves (1996), Mitiaev (1998: 77–8), Masih and Krikorian (1999: 20–2), and De Waal (2003: 111).

[229] Russian military aid led to a "doubl[ing] of [Armenia's] defense capacity" in the mid-1990s (Fuller 1998d). See also Fairbanks (1995) and de Waal (2003: 162–3). According to *Military Balance* (2006: 398–9), Armenia had the highest level of military expenditure (7.7 percent of GDP) in Europe in the early 2000s.

[230] De Waal (2003: 257).

[231] Danielyan (2005, 2007a).

paramilitary organization that incorporated thousands of battle-hardened Karabakh veterans.[232] Created and financed by the Defense Ministry, Yerkrapah played a key role in suppressing regime opposition.[233] State cohesion – rooted in a strong national identity and reinforced by military victory – was high. The army demonstrated considerable *esprit de corps*, and it successfully instituted conscription in the early 1990s.[234]

In summary, party weakness made Armenian governments vulnerable to internal conflict. However, the powerful coercive apparatus that emerged from the Nagorno-Karabakh conflict enabled the governments to thwart a series of large-scale opposition challenges.

Origins and Evolution of the Regime

As in other post-Soviet cases, competitive authoritarianism in Armenia emerged in the wake of the Soviet Union's demise. The ANM, which spearheaded the drive for independence, won the May 1990 legislative elections and installed Ter-Petrosian as head of parliament.[235] In September 1991, Armenia declared independence; in October, Ter-Petrosian was elected president with 83 percent of the vote.

The Ter-Petrosian government was authoritarian. It harassed and prosecuted journalists, and shut down 11 major media outlets, including the country's largest newspaper.[236] In 1994, following a series of opposition protests, the government banned the most popular opposition party, the nationalist Armenian Revolutionary Party (Dashniaks).[237] Finally, the playing field was skewed. State television – the only national source of television news – was biased,[238] and extensive ties between the government and the emerging economic elite made it "virtually impossible for opposition parties to secure financial backing."[239]

The Ter-Petrosian government was vulnerable in the early 1990s. The economy contracted by 60 percent between 1990 and 1993, which eroded public support and triggered a series of mass protests in 1993 and 1994.[240] At the same time, the governing ANM suffered several high-level defections, including former Prime Minister and Defense Minister Vazgen Manukian.[241]

---

[232] Yerkrapah mobilized between 5,000 and 30,000 veterans (Fuller 1998a; Abrahamyan 2008).

[233] Fuller (1998a); Minasian (1999); Zakarian (2005); Abrahamyan (2008). Yerkrapah was described as a "state within a state" (Abrahamyan 2008; Cheterian 2000).

[234] De Waal (2003: 257, 122). On conscription, see Aves (1995: 223; 1996). The central state also maintained firm control over regional governments (Hakobyan 2004a).

[235] Suny (1995: 145); Dudwick (1997: 80–1).

[236] Fuller (1995); U.S. Department of State (1996); Mitiaev (1998: 99).

[237] See Bremmer and Welt (1997: 85–6), Dudwick (1997), and Mitiaev (1998: 99).

[238] U.S. Department of State (1996).

[239] Bremmer and Welt (1997: 83, 86).

[240] In February 1993, for example, 100,000 protesters called for Ter-Petrosian's resignation (Mitiaev 1998: 86; Masih and Krikorian 1999: vii). Economic data taken from World Bank World Development Indicators (online: www.worldbank.org/data).

[241] See Libaridian (1999: 10, 23–4) and Masih and Krikorian (1999: 45–6).

The government responded to these challenges with abuse and fraud. In the 1995 parliamentary election, nine parties – including the Dashniaks – and more than a third of all candidates were disqualified.[242] Remaining opposition parties were "denied financial backing" and had "next to no access to the press."[243] Finally, the vote itself was marred by fraud.[244] The flawed election enabled the ruling party to forge a legislative majority.[245]

In the 1996 presidential election, Ter-Petrosian was challenged by ex-Prime Minister Vazgen Manukian, who had left the government to form the National Democratic Union. Despite massive incumbent abuse of state resources and a virtual monopoly over the electronic media, Manukian may have won the election[246]; only fraud allowed Ter-Petrosian to claim a first-round victory.[247] The fraud triggered massive opposition protest: At least 120,000 Manukian supporters rallied in front of the Central Election Committee and stormed the parliament.[248] The regime's coercive structures were critical in suppressing this challenge. Ter-Petrosian declared a state of emergency and security forces encircled and barred protesters from the capital, Yerevan; public plazas were closed, demonstrations were banned, and opposition headquarters were shut down; at least 250 opposition activists were arrested; and Manukian was forced into hiding.[249] Yerkrapah's paramilitary wing – whose members patrolled the streets with machine guns and grenade launchers – enforced the state of emergency.[250] The Western reaction was tepid. Although the United States condemned the election, it soon softened its stance, and U.S. assistance fell only slightly.[251]

Having thwarted several opposition challenges, the regime fell into internal crisis in the late 1990s. The ANM fractured in late 1997 when Ter-Petrosian's adoption of a relatively moderate position on Nagorno-Karabakh triggered intense intra-governmental conflict and a slew of parliamentary defections. In early 1998, Ter-Petrosian resigned in favor of his Prime Minister, Robert

---

[242] Bremmer and Welt (1997: 87).

[243] Bremmer and Welt (1997: 87).

[244] Dudwick (1997: 94–5).

[245] Bremmer and Welt (1997: 87).

[246] Mkrtchian (1999); Astourian (2000–2001: 45). Preelection surveys showed Manukian ahead (Bremmer and Welt 1997: 88). On abuse of state resources and media, see ODIHR (1996a, 1998b).

[247] Opposition representatives were thrown out of polling places, soldiers were forced to vote in front of their unit commanders, and more than 20,000 ballots disappeared (ODIHR 1996a; Bremmer and Welt 1997: 88). Interior Minister Vano Siradeghian later admitted that top government officials met after receiving "distressing news" of Ter-Petrosian's failure and decided to falsify the results in order to give Ter-Petrosian a first-round victory (Bremmer and Welt 1997:

88–9; Danielyan 1998b). Official results gave Ter-Petrosian 52 percent, compared to 41 percent for Manukian.

[248] See Danielian (1996–1997: 128) and *RFE/RL Newsline*, 25–26 September 1996 (online: http://www.rferl.org/archive/en-newsline/latest/683/683.html).

[249] See Danielian (1996–1997: 129), Bremmer and Welt (1997: 88), Mkrtchian (1999), and Human Rights Watch (2003b: 5).

[250] See Fuller (1998a), Minasian (1999), and Zakarian (2005).

[251] See Mitiaev (1998: 119–21). U.S. assistance declined from $135 million in 1996 to $98.72 million in 1997, and then rose to $116 million in 1998. On a per capita basis, this was considerably higher than that received by most other post-communist countries (Bureau of European and Eurasian Affairs 2009).

Kocharian. New presidential elections were called, and Kocharian was challenged by Karen Demirchian, a former communist who ran as an independent. In an election characterized by uneven media access, voter intimidation, and ballot-box stuffing,[252] Kocharian defeated Demirchian in a runoff.

Party weakness initially hindered Kocharian's efforts to consolidate power. Kocharian governed without a party, aligning instead with several parties, including the previously oppositionist Dashniaks and the Republican Party, a Yerkrapah-based party created by Defense Minister Vazgen Sarkisian.[253] In the 1999 parliamentary election, the Republican Party aligned with Karen Demirchian's People's Party to form the Unity Bloc, which won a large plurality.[254] Sarkisian was named Prime Minister and Demirchian became Speaker of Parliament. In late 1999, however, gunmen stormed the parliament building and assassinated Sarkisian, Demirchian, and 6 other officials, ushering in another round of instability.[255] The rump ANM and other groups – alleging that members of Kocharian's inner circle were involved in the killings – sought Kocharian's impeachment. However, the president – who retained the backing of the security forces – eventually reconsolidated power.[256]

Like his predecessor, Kocharian governed autocratically, assaulting independent media and persecuting opposition activists.[257] The 2003 presidential and parliamentary elections were marred by intimidation, media bias, and large-scale ballot-box stuffing.[258] Kocharian won 49.5 percent of the first-round vote, which placed him in a runoff against Stepan Demirchian, the son of assassinated Parliamentary Speaker Karen Demirchian. The fraud triggered considerable protest, with opposition demonstrations mobilizing between 25,000 and 100,000 people.[259] Again, however, security forces beat back the protest movement through a ban on demonstrations and the "prophylactic" arrest of hundreds of opposition leaders.[260] During the runoff campaign, police blocked or disrupted pro-Demirchian campaign rallies and arrested more than 200 Demirchian supporters.[261] Kocharian won the runoff with 67 percent of the vote. Two months later, progovernment forces captured a majority in fraud-filled parliamentary

[252] See (ODIHR 1998b) and Wheatley (2003).

[253] See "Political Equilibrium Crumbling in Armenia," *Eurasia Daily Monitor*, 2 November 1998; "Ruling Party Emerges in Armenia," *Eurasia Daily Monitor*, 1 February 1999 (online: www.jamestown.org).

[254] The Unity Bloc captured 62 of 131 seats in parliament, whereas no other party won more than 10.

[255] Krikorian (2000).

[256] Simonian (2001).

[257] See Grigorian (2000a; 2000b), Petrosian (2003a, 2003b), and Danielyan (2004b, 2004c). In 2002, two independent television stations – including the largest and most watched, A1+ TV – were denied frequencies and taken off the air (Committee to Protect Journalists, "Attacks on the Press 2002: Armenia" (online: www.cpj.org); U.S. Department of State 2003f).

[258] Fuller (2003a); ODIHR (2003b, 2003c); Giragosian (2004).

[259] See Fuller (2003b), Hoel (2003), Human Rights Watch (2003b), and Petrosian (2003a).

[260] Human Rights Watch (2003b, 2004b); Stepanian and Kalantarian (2005).

[261] Human Rights Watch (2003b) and Freedom House, "Freedom in the World 2008: Armenia" (online: www.freedomhouse.org).

elections.[262] Again, the United States criticized the elections but took no real punitive action.[263]

The government continued to fend off opposition protest after 2003. In April 2004, opposition forces – seeking to replicate Georgia's Rose Revolution – organized demonstrations of as many as 25,000 people.[264] However, the opposition faced a far more effective coercive apparatus than its Georgian counterparts. Unlike Georgia (and Ukraine in 2004), the government was able to prevent demonstrators from entering the capital.[265] Security forces and pro-government thugs broke up protests, ransacked opposition headquarters, and launched a sweeping campaign in which hundreds of activists across the country were arrested.[266] The crackdown succeeded, and protest soon diminished.[267]

The regime remained competitive authoritarian through 2008. Much of the private media remained in the hands of government allies,[268] opposition parties were largely denied access to finance,[269] and government critics were harassed and arrested.[270] The 2007 parliamentary election again was marred by fraud and abuse,[271] and progovernment forces captured 106 of 131 seats. Lacking a stable ruling party, however, the regime continued to be plagued by internal conflict. [272] The various progovernment parties competed constantly,[273] "do[ing] everything to boost their standing by discrediting each other."[274] Facing difficulty getting bills through parliament, the government at times resorted to police harassment and threats of prosecution to keep its legislative allies in line.[275]

The 2008 presidential election brought succession within the ruling party, as Kocharian, adhering to constitutional term limits, chose Prime Minister and Republican Party leader Serzh Sarkisian – an ally – to succeed him. Sarkisian was challenged by ex-President Ter-Petrosian, now an independent. The election was marred by media bias, abuse of state resources (including mobilization of police,

[262] ODIHR (2003c).
[263] Danielyan (2007b).
[264] Hakobyan (2004a); Karapetian (2004).
[265] See Hakobyan (2004a), Danielyan (2004b), and Human Rights Watch (2004b).
[266] See Danielyan (2004b) and Freedom House, "Freedom in the World 2005: Armenia" (online: www.freedomhouse.org). As one observer noted, "just about everyone challenging the regime [was] on the police watch list" (Danielyan 2004b).
[267] Freedom House, "Freedom in the World 2005: Armenia" (online: www.freedomhouse.org).
[268] As one journalist put it, "frequencies are never given to a company if the owner is not loyal." Quoted in USAID (2005: 31). See also ODIHR (2007a: 18).
[269] See USAID (2005). As one legislator put it, "you cannot be a leader of an opposition party and have a businessman as a partner –

he would be eliminated as a businessman." Quoted in USAID (2005: 32).
[270] Freedom House, "Freedom in the World 2008: Armenia" (online: www.freedomhouse.org).
[271] ODIHR (2007a).
[272] Danielyan (2004a).
[273] Initially, the progovernment coalition was composed of the Republicans, the Dashniaks, and Country of Law. In 2006, Country of Law left the governing coalition and was replaced by the United Labor Party.
[274] Bedevian (2006). After a widely criticized 2005 constitutional reform referendum, for example, several government officials and progovernment legislators denounced the election and blamed other progovernment parties for the fraud (Khachatrian 2005; Saghabalian 2005; Grigoryan and Abrahamyan 2008).
[275] Khachatrian (2006a, 2006b).

teachers, and other public employees on behalf of the Republican Party), and at least some fraud.[276] Official results gave Sarkisian a first-round victory, with 53 percent of the vote, compared to 22 percent for Ter-Petrosian. Ter-Petrosian denounced fraud and called on supporters to mobilize in the capital.[277] Although the regime suffered several defections,[278] opposition protest was again effectively repressed. Kocharian declared a state of emergency, banned public gatherings, and imposed widespread media censorship. More than 100 opposition supporters were arrested and at least 8 were killed.[279] Again, Western reaction was muted.[280]

In summary, Armenia is a case of regime stability amid repeated challenge. The absence of a strong party contributed to periodic internal crises. At the same time, the regime faced repeated waves of opposition protest. Indeed, despite the fact that Armenia has the smallest population of the countries examined in this chapter, the opposition was more mobilized *in absolute terms* than in any other case except Ukraine in 2004. Yet, the regime survived, for two main reasons. First, it possessed a powerful and cohesive coercive apparatus, which meant that unlike Georgia and Ukraine, governments could repeatedly thwart opposition protest by arresting its leaders, closing down its offices, and sealing off the capital. Second, in the absence of extensive linkage, electoral fraud and other abuse triggered little response from the West.[281]

ORGANIZATIONAL WEAKNESS AND AUTHORITARIAN INSTABILITY: UKRAINE, GEORGIA, AND MOLDOVA

Competitive authoritarian regimes in Ukraine, Georgia, and Moldova faced greater obstacles to consolidation than those in Russia, Belarus, and Armenia. In each case, weak ruling parties suffered high levels of elite defection, and limited coercive capacity undermined efforts to crack down on opposition challenges.[282] High leverage resulted in greater external pressure than in Belarus and Russia. In a context of low linkage, however, such pressure was insufficient to bring about full democratization. Neither Georgia nor Moldova democratized through 2008 and, although Ukraine democratized, this outcome was rooted more in domestic processes than in external pressure.

Ukraine

Ukraine provides a clear illustration of how limited organizational power – particularly weak ruling parties – can undermine authoritarianism. Lacking

---

[276] ODIHR (2008b).

[277] ODIHR (2008b: 27); *RFE/RL Newsline*, 25 February 2008 (online: http://www.rferl. org/archive/en-newsline/latest/683/683. html).

[278] Grigoryan and Abrahamyan (2008).

[279] ODIHR (2008b: 28); "Emergency Order Empties Armenian Capital's Streets," *The*

New York Times, 3 March 2008 (online: www. nyt.com).

[280] Danielyan (2007b, 2008).

[281] Indeed, Western support remained strong (Mitiaev 1998: 119–21; Giragosian 2003; Danielyan 2007b, 2008).

[282] In post-2000 Moldova, the strength of the ruling Communist Party enhanced authoritarian stability.

institutionalized party support, Presidents Leonid Kravchuk (1992–1994) and Leonid Kuchma (1994–2004) suffered large-scale defections and lost power to former allies. Contrary to our theory, Ukraine democratized in 2005.

Linkage, Leverage, and Organizational Power

Ukraine is a case of low linkage and high leverage. In terms of linkage, Ukraine had a relatively large diaspora in the United States and Canada; as in Armenia, however, these ties were not accompanied by the strong economic, political, technocratic, and diplomatic ties found in Eastern Europe. Ukraine was not offered the possibility of EU membership, and levels of trade with the West were about half that of our Eastern European cases in the 1990s.[283] In terms of leverage, Ukraine never had effective control over nuclear weapons,[284] and it was not a major energy exporter. Although Ukraine benefited from Russian energy subsidies,[285] it nevertheless relied heavily on Western aid, which prevented Russia from achieving black knight status.[286]

Organizational power evolved from low under Kravchuk to medium low under Kuchma. Party strength was consistently low. Kravchuk made little effort to build a party after the communist collapse and thus had "no political team."[287] Kuchma also failed to build a party. Like Yeltsin, he drew support from competing parties organized by different government officials and oligarchic factions.[288]

Coercive capacity evolved from medium low to medium high over the course of the 1990s. Coercive scope was consistently high: The regime inherited a vast coercive apparatus from the Soviet era, including a 700,000–strong army and a largely unreformed KGB structure.[289] However, Communist Party

---

[283] CIS countries were Ukraine's largest trading partners during the 1990s (Molchanov 2004: 464; Youngs 2006: 102). Although trade shifted toward Western Europe in the 2000s (Wilson 2010), Ukraine's overall linkage score remained well below the threshold for high linkage.

[284] Although Ukraine retained a vast nuclear arsenal on its territory in the early 1990s, it remained under central command in Moscow ("Ukraine Wants Voice in Use of Atomic Arms," *The New York Times*, 25 October 1991(online: www.nyt.com)). By 1996, all nuclear warheads had either been destroyed or transferred to Russia (Dyczok 2000: 113; Powaski 2000: 130–1, 167–8).

[285] These subsidies were more modest than those provided to Belarus. Through the mid-2000s, Ukraine paid nearly twice as much for Russian natural gas as did Belarus ("Sochins"kyj hazavat," *Ukrainska Pravda* October 16, 2000 (online: www.pravda.com.ua); Silitski 2003b; Grigoriev and Salikhov 2006; "Russia Threatens Cut in Belarus Gas Supply," *The New York Times*, 2 August

2007 (online: www.nyt.com)). On Ukraine's energy sector, see Pollier (2008).

[286] Ukraine was one of the leading recipients of U.S. aid in the world in the 1990s. Between 1992 and 2007, the United States provided approximately $3 billion in aid (U.S. State Department 2008d). In addition, the EU provided 4 billion euros in aid during the 1990s (Youngs 2006: 102).

[287] Markov (1993: 34).

[288] Way (2005b: 137).

[289] On the army, see Kramer (1992: 330) and Olynyk (1994: 5–6). Although the KGB successor, the Committee on Security in Ukraine (SBU), was reportedly cut in half, it still retained an estimated 9,000 employees in the early 1990s (Strekal 1995; Knight 1996: 149), which is roughly equivalent, in per capita terms, to the size of the U.S. CIA and FBI. The SBU retained the KGB's top personnel and organizational structure as well as a special subdivision charged with protecting Ukraine against "political instability" and "anti-constitutional" activity (Knight 1996: 150–3).

collapse, economic crisis, and wage arrears resulted in low cohesion in the early 1990s.[290] There were initially fears of a military coup,[291] and at times, central government appointees in eastern and southern Ukraine rebelled, openly backing antigovernment strikes in 1993.[292] Cohesion within the security forces was undermined by the fact that military officers were predominantly Russian, and many (ex-KGB) intelligence officials maintained strong ties to Moscow.[293]

Coercive capacity increased under Kuchma. Scope remained high. The internal security forces were expanded to the point where they were larger than the army,[294] and they included an array of specialized anti-terrorist and crowd-control units (e.g., Alfa, Berkut, Sokil, and Tytan). Indeed, recorded conversations of Kuchma released in 2000 revealed the existence of a vast surveillance network extending across the country.[295] Cohesion increased to medium. Although the state possessed no special source of cohesion, Kuchma centralized control over regional and local governments and ended wage arrears; by the late 1990s, regional rebellions had ceased.[296]

In summary, the Kuchma government possessed a relatively effective coercive apparatus by the late 1990s. As discussed later in this chapter, however, persistent party weakness left the regime vulnerable to challenges from within.

Origins and Evolution of the Regime

Ukraine emerged from the Soviet collapse with a relatively mild competitive authoritarian regime. Leonid Kravchuk, a former member of the Politburo of the Ukrainian Communist Party, became the head of the Ukrainian legislature in July 1990, backed by a loose pro-Communist majority. On December 1, 1991, the day that Ukrainians voted for independence, Kravchuk was overwhelmingly elected president.

Kravchuk failed to consolidate power – a failure that can be attributed, in part, to party weakness. The new president "did not have the support of any political force in parliament."[297] Like Yeltsin, he never effectively controlled parliament even though an ally, Ivan Plyushch, headed it.[298] Parliament rejected many of Kravchuk's cabinet appointments, forcing him to name ministers with independent support bases and weak presidential allegiances.[299] Some of Kravchuk's ministers joined opposition parties, and in 1992, he was forced to accept Leonid

[290] Bubnova and Way (1998); Boichenko (2004).
[291] Kuzio (1993).
[292] See Wilson (1993), *Nezavisimost'* 11 August 1993, p. 3, Solchanyk (1994), and Kubicek (2000: 77–8).
[293] Olynyk (1994); Knight (1996: 152).
[294] Kuzio (2000: 29).
[295] Darden (2001).
[296] *Nezavisimost'* 17 August 1994, pp. 1–2; 10 February 1995, p. 5; Boichenko (2004); Sasse (2007: 175–80).
[297] Kravchuk (2002: 248).

[298] Markov (1993). In 1992, the deputy head of parliament, Vladimir Grinev, complained that the legislature lacked any structure and was victim to constantly shifting whims of deputies. "It is always impossible to predict when the legislature will vote 'yes' or vote 'no'" (*Nezavisimost'* 12 June 1992, p. 8).
[299] For example, Kravchuk was forced to accept the appointment of a head of security services with few ties to the president (Matviiuk 1994).

Kuchma, who was "barely known" to him, as Prime Minister.[300] At the same time, a severe economic crisis eroded public support and gave rise to social protest,[301] which – although smaller than protests in Armenia – threatened Kravchuk's hold on power. In 1993, following a miners' strike in Donetsk and large demonstrations in Kiev, Kravchuk agreed to hold early presidential elections in June 1994.[302] In early 1994, he changed his mind and, following Yeltsin's example, sought to close the legislature and postpone elections.[303] Unlike Yeltsin, however, Kravchuk could not draw on Western support, and key security officials – including the Interior Minister – refused to cooperate, leaving Kravchuk with little choice but to leave parliament intact and go ahead with the elections.[304]

In the 1994 election, Kravchuk was challenged by Kuchma, who had resigned as Prime Minister in late 1993. The election was unfair. Media coverage was biased; Kravchuk harassed independent media and temporarily closed a pro-Kuchma TV station.[305] Due in part to state weakness, however, the election was free of serious fraud.[306] Kravchuk appears to have assumed that he could manipulate the election in his favor,[307] but many public officials – especially in eastern Ukraine – worked for Kuchma.[308] Indeed, Kravchuk complained that the security service "shut its eyes" to violations committed by his opponents.[309] Kuchma won a runoff election with 52 percent of the vote.

Regime stability increased under Kuchma. Kuchma built a support base among business oligarchs with close ties to the state.[310] His governing coalition was based on several competing oligarchic parties, including the Party of Regions (led by Mykola Azarov and Viktor Yanukovich), Yulia Tymoshenko's Fatherland, and the Social Democratic Party (United).[311] Pro-Kuchma oligarchs also controlled the major media. Kuchma's ally, Viktor Medvedchuk, ran the three largest television stations: UT-1, Inter, and 1+1; his son-in-law, Viktor Pinchuk, controlled three others: STB, ICTV, and New Channel.[312] Media coverage thus was heavily biased. In 2002, Medvedchuk became head of the Presidential Administration, where he distributed detailed directives on how to cover the news and which events to ignore.[313] Kuchma also used the tax administration and surveillance to develop an elaborate system of blackmail to control elites (many of whom

[300] Kravchuk (2002: 198); on ministers joining opposition parties, see *Nezavisimost'*, 1 July 1992, p. 3.
[301] Ukraine's GDP declined by 24 percent in 1992–1993.
[302] See Borisov and Clarke (1994).
[303] Kravchuk (2002: 227).
[304] Kravchuk (2002: 228).
[305] *Nezavisimost'*, 22 December 1993, p. 1; 6 July 1994, p. 2; European Institute for the Media (1994: 190, 224, 227–8); Dyczok (2006).
[306] See Democratic Elections in Ukraine (1994); Kuzio (1996).
[307] Kuzio (1996: 132).
[308] See Democratic Elections in Ukraine (1994: 14) and Kravchuk (2002: 230).
[309] Kravchuk (2002: 229).
[310] Thus, "exemptions from the anti-monopoly legislation, privileged access to privatization, budget subsidies, quotas and licenses for the import and export of oil, gas, wheat, vodka and tobacco were all used by Kuchma and his entourage as currency to win the economic elite's support" (Puglisi 2003: 836). See also Wilson (2005a: 116–17; 2005b).
[311] Wilson (2005a: 133–42).
[312] See Kuzio (2004), Nikolayenko (2004), and Dyczok (2006: 222–3).
[313] See Human Rights Watch (2003c), Kipiani (2005), and Dyczok (2006: 223, 226).

potentially could be prosecuted for illicit behavior) throughout the administration – an informal apparatus that was critical to orchestrating electoral fraud.[314]

Despite relatively low levels of public support, Kuchma was reelected in 1999. Although he won only 36 percent of the first-round vote, Kuchma used a combination of patronage, harassment, media bias, and fraud to prevent the most viable electoral contenders – most notably, former head of parliament Oleksandr Moroz – from qualifying for the runoff.[315] Instead, he faced hard-line Communist candidate Petro Symonenko, "who never really stood a chance."[316] The second-round campaign was marred by media bias, and the government used its greater control over the state to commit "widespread, systematic and coordinated" fraud.[317] Kuchma won with 56 percent of the vote.

Kuchma ultimately failed to consolidate power, however. Ukraine was more vulnerable to external pressure than its counterparts in Belarus and Russia. Thus, soon after his reelection, Kuchma faced ballooning debt payments[318]; following a meeting with U.S. Vice President Al Gore, he replaced loyalist Prime Minister Valerii Pustovoitenko with Viktor Yushchenko, a technocrat who was widely respected in the West.[319] Lacking a strong party, the government also was vulnerable to elite defection in the event of crisis. Such a crisis emerged in late 2000, after the release of tapes by Kuchma's former bodyguard that suggested that Kuchma had ordered the murder of journalist Georgii Gongadze – and which revealed a striking level of presidential corruption and abuse.[320] A wave of protest ensued, and Prime Minister Yushchenko, who was now one of the country's most popular politicians,[321] emerged as a threat to Kuchma and was dismissed in April 2001.

Although the 2000–2001 protests failed to oust Kuchma, the tapes crisis triggered a hemorrhaging of elite support that culminated in the 2004 Orange Revolution. In the absence of a coherent ruling party, the persistence of semi-autonomous progovernmental groups with independent economic bases provided politicians with the resources to launch serious opposition challenges.[322] Thus, beginning in 2001, Yulia Tymoshenko transformed her Fatherland party into a major opposition force. At the same time, Yushchenko's "Our Ukraine" bloc gained the support of leading financial figures (such as Petro Poroshenko) in the 2002 legislative elections.[323] In this way, Yushchenko was able to gain a "share of 'administrative resources' and some shelter from negative campaigning."[324] These resources, together with Yushchenko's popularity, enabled Our Ukraine to finish first (with 24 percent of the vote) in the 2002 election.[325]

---

[314] Darden (2001, 2008).

[315] Birch (2002); Wilson (2005b: 42–3).

[316] Birch (2002: 340); see also Wilson (2005b: 42).

[317] ODIHR (2000b: 18, 21); see also Nikolayenko (2004).

[318] Nikitchenko (2000).

[319] Pikhovshek (1998: 244–5); Yurchuk (1999); *Holos Ukrainy*, 24 December 1999, pp. 1, 7; Wilson (2005b: 44–5).

[320] See Darden (2001), Karatnycky (2001), and Kuzio (2005).

[321] A 2001 poll found that 36 percent of Ukrainians would vote for Yushchenko in the next election (Kudelia 2008: 158).

[322] Way (2005b).

[323] Birch (2003); Wilson (2005b: 62–3).

[324] Wilson (2005b: 65).

[325] Birch (2003).

Kuchma thus faced a major challenge in the 2004 presidential race. Constitutional term limits were not a serious obstacle; Kuchma successfully pressured the Constitutional Court into ruling that he could run for a third term.[326] Yet Kuchma was so unpopular that he opted not to run,[327] thereby opening the search for a successor. Yushchenko was an obvious possibility. Our Ukraine's 2002 victory had established Yushchenko as a presidential front-runner and, despite his firing, he had consistently backed Kuchma through early 2002.[328] Yet, Yushchenko's popularity and ties to the West limited his dependence on Kuchma, which reduced his attractiveness as a successor. Given Yushchenko's independent support base, Kuchma assumed that he would defect – and potentially prosecute him and his inner circle – after the election.[329] By contrast, Prime Minister Viktor Yanukovych, a twice-convicted felon with weak ties to the West,[330] appears to have been more attractive to Kuchma because he was less likely to investigate past corruption.[331] Thus, party weakness led Kuchma to reject a potentially winning candidate in favor of someone with severe electoral liabilities.

Kuchma's succession gambit failed. The 2004 presidential election was stolen. Following a campaign marred by media bias, harassment of journalists and opposition activists, an attempted assassination of Yushchenko, and massive election-day fraud in parts of eastern Ukraine,[332] Yanukovych was awarded a narrow second-round victory.[333] In response to the fraud, protest quickly spread across the country, and hundreds of thousands of demonstrators – organized in a massive tent city in the center of Kiev – mobilized in the capital for more than three weeks.[334] Eventually, EU-brokered negotiations led to a new election, which Yushchenko won with 52 percent of the vote.

Although the 2004 Orange Revolution is widely viewed as a case of successful mobilization from below, it was driven, to a significant extent, by elite defection.[335] Virtually the entire leadership of the "orange coalition" – including top leaders such as Tymoshenko and Yushchenko – had been Kuchma's allies

---

[326] Danilochkin (2003).

[327] In a March 2001 poll, only 7 percent of Ukrainians expressed trust in Kuchma (Kudelia 2008: 158).

[328] Yushchenko, who had once referred to Kuchma as a "father" figure (Way 2005b: 139), had condemned the early 2001 anti-Kuchma protests and refrained from publicly attacking Kuchma in the months following his dismissal (Kuzio 2007; Kudelia 2008: 156).

[329] Kudelia (2008: 168).

[330] Kupchinsky (2006).

[331] Yanukovych also ran a powerful regional machine in Donetsk and, given the weakness of the ruling coalition, there was no guarantee that another candidate would gain the machine's backing.

[332] On election night, one of the authors witnessed policemen carrying falsified election material from the mayor's office to a regional election commission in central Ukraine at 3 a.m. When asked what he had under his arm, an apparently drunk officer responded, "Ballots, you idiot! What do you think?!"

[333] See Karatnycky (2005), Kuzio (2005c), Way (2005b), and Wilson (2005b). Officially, Yanukovych won 49 percent of the second-round vote compared to 47 percent for Yushchenko. Yushchenko had won a narrow plurality in the first round, with 40 percent of the vote, compared to 39 percent for Yanukovych.

[334] On the crisis, see Karatnycky (2005), Kuzio (2005c), Way (2005b), and Wilson (2005b).

[335] Way (2005b).

within the previous three years.[336] Moreover, leading oligarchs who had once backed Kuchma now played a major role in financing the protest movement. They helped transport protesters to Kiev and provided camp kitchens, food, tents, bio-toilets, and giant television screens to sustain the tent city that came to symbolize the Orange Revolution.[337] Former Kuchma ally Petro Poroshenko financed Channel 5, which spread information about the fraud and mobilized protest during the crisis.[338] Crucially, Parliamentary Speaker Volodymyr Lytvyn – a former Kuchma aide who had aspired to succeed him – forged a coalition behind a legislative resolution declaring the official results invalid.[339] Thus, former regime insiders both led the opposition and provided it with critical assistance during the 2004 crisis, which facilitated the regime's overthrow.

Enormous attention has also been given to the role of international factors in shaping the Orange Revolution.[340] The United States and the EU provided considerable assistance to the opposition,[341] Western governments unambiguously rejected the fraudulent election,[342] and an EU delegation brokered the accord that brought new elections.[343] This intervention likely tipped the balance in favor of the opposition, both by encouraging protest and by raising the cost of a high-intensity crackdown.[344] Yet the role of external factors should not be overstated. Western pressure never seriously constrained autocratic behavior or fundamentally altered the domestic balance of power, as in much of Eastern Europe and the Americas. Indeed, the Ukrainian opposition had emerged as a major threat long before Western assistance became an issue,[345] and it was sufficiently well financed by domestic elites that it did not necessarily require such

---

[336] At least two thirds of the Committee of National Salvation that was created in response to the 2004 fraud were former Kuchma allies, including nearly all of its most prominent leaders (Way 2005b: 145).

[337] See Silina, Rakhmanin, and Dmitricheva (2004), Amchuk (2005), and Sledz (2005). Before the election, David Zhvania, an industrialist, purchased camping equipment to be used in the protests. The Kiev city government also provided critical assistance. See also Way (2005b: 143) and Wilson (2005b: 123, 126). On the causes of mass protest during the Orange Revolution, see Way (2009b).

[338] Wilson (2005b: 131); McFaul (2007: 62–3).

[339] Wilson (2005b: 142).

[340] Indeed, Jonathan Steele wrote that the West "orchestrated" the Orange Revolution. See "The Untold Story," *The Nation*, 2 December 2004 (online: www.thenation.com). For more nuanced treatments of Western influences, see Youngs (2006), Sushko and Prystayko (2006), and McFaul (2007).

[341] The United States and other Western governments reportedly provided $65 million in assistance (Wilson 2005b: 183), although much of this funding went to nonpartisan activities. The most direct form of U.S. support was party training and financing of civil-society groups, such as *Znayu*. In addition, George Soros gave $1.3 million to NGOs to carry out election-related projects (Sushko and Prystayko 2006: 135). See also Wilson (2005b: 183–8), Youngs (2006: 106–8), and McFaul (2007).

[342] Sushko and Prystayko (2006: 134); McFaul (2007: 77).

[343] Wilson (2005b: 138–40).

[344] Kuzio (2006b); McFaul (2007).

[345] As early as mid-2002 – nearly two-and-a-half years before the Orange Revolution – Yushchenko was widely considered to be "Ukraine's most popular politician" and the likely winner of the 2004 presidential election (Krushelnycky 2002).

assistance.[346] Finally, Ukraine was never offered the possibility of EU membership that both strengthened opposition and constrained incumbents in Eastern
Europe.[347]

Ukraine democratized after 2004. Despite repeated internal crises, President
Yushchenko governed democratically, and parliamentary elections in 2006 and
2007 were free and fair.[348] In 2010, Yanukovych defeated Tymoshenko and
Yushchenko in presidential elections that were widely considered free and fair.
Ukraine's democratization – an outcome that is not predicted by our theory –
thus remained quite fragile in 2010.

In summary, authoritarian instability in Ukraine was rooted in high leverage and weak ruling-party structures. Unlike their counterparts in Russia and
Belarus, Ukrainian governments were vulnerable to Western pressure. Moreover, incumbents were repeatedly challenged from within, as former allies used
patronage, media, and other resources garnered while in government to contest seriously for power. Indeed, the Ukrainian case is a striking example of how
opposition strength can be endogenous to incumbent weakness. Such autocratic
failure created an opening for democratization.

Georgia

Georgia is another case of unstable competitive authoritarianism in a context of
low organizational power. In the absence of effective state and party structures,
Zviad Gamsakhurdia (1991–1992) and Eduard Shevardnadze (1992–2003) not

---

[346] According to one source, foreign funding
accounted for just 2 percent of the budget
of the Pora youth movement, which was
critical in organizing street protests in late
2004 (Kaskiv et al. 2007: 134). On a per
capita basis, the estimated $65 million in
U.S. financing was three to five times lower
than the $40 million to $70 million provided
in Serbia (Carothers 2001: 3; Lebor 2004:
304). Further, the Yushchenko campaign
appears to have had significant resources.
David Zhvania, a Yushchenko fundraiser,
boasted, "I don't know of a financial group in
Ukraine...which doesn't want Yushchenko
to become president. Yushchenko has no
problem with money" ("Davyd Zhvaniya:
Vid moho pomichnyka na dopytax vyma-
haly: 'Ty ziznajsya, shho vbyty Rybkina tobi
doruchyv Yushhenko'," *Ukrainska Pravda*, 7
March 2004 (online: www.pravda.com.ua)).

[347] Prior to 2004, Western powers were divided
in their willingness to put pressure on
Kuchma. As Youngs (2006: 103) noted, "EU
documents and statements routinely suggested that Ukraine was making progress

towards democratic consolidation, when
events on the ground did not in any obvious
sense confirm such optimism. Kuchma was
seen by both the United States and European governments as having usefully steered
Ukraine away from Russia and towards a
European orientation, while still providing
a useful bridge to Moscow." See also Sushko
and Prystayko (2006: 131–3).

[348] The OSCE noted that by 2007, "The systematic intimidation and harassment of the
media by state agencies as well as the practice of editorial guidelines imposed by the
State on broadcast media outlets after the
2002 elections have disappeared" (ODIHR
2006b; 2007b: 14). The most serious threat
to Ukrainian democracy occurred in 2007,
when Yushchenko dissolved parliament on
suspect constitutional grounds (Way 2008b;
Freedom House, "Freedom in the World:
2008 Ukraine" (online: www.freedomhouse.
org)). However, the 2007 elections were free
and fair (ODIHR 2007b: 2). For a discussion
of the sources of democracy in post-2004
Ukraine, see Way (2008b, 2009b).

only failed to consolidate power but also fell in the face of only modest opposition challenges. At the same time, ties to the West were insufficient to induce full democratization. Thus, Mikheil Saakashvili, who took power in 2003 after a so-called democratic revolution, governed in a competitive authoritarian manner.

Linkage, Leverage, and Organizational Power

Like Armenia and Ukraine, Georgia is a case of high leverage and low linkage. A small, weak, and regionally isolated state, Georgia was highly dependent on the West.[349] Not only did it not enjoy black-knight support from Russia, but it also faced Russian hostility. Russian governments closed off access to key energy resources and actively supported the separatist regions of Abkhazia and Ossetia.[350] In terms of linkage, Georgia possessed weak economic, political, technocratic, and communication ties to the West.[351] Like the other cases in this chapter, Georgia was never offered the prospect of EU membership, which weakened the impact of external democratizing pressure.

Organizational power in Georgia was low. Party strength was initially very low. The "Round Table" created by Gamsakhurdia prior to the 1990 legislative elections was an ad hoc formation with little cohesion and virtually no organizational structure.[352] Party strength increased somewhat under Shevardnadze. Unlike many of his regional counterparts, Shevardnadze created a single governing party, the Citizen's Union of Georgia (CUG), which brought together old *nomenklatura* networks, members of the intelligentsia, and numerous mayors and lower-level state officials.[353] The CUG was a heterogeneous coalition of "uneasy bedfellows,"[354] and it lacked a clear ideology or other source of cohesion.[355] However, it developed a national organization and relatively stable patronage networks.[356] By the late 1990s, then, it could be scored as medium strength.

Coercive capacity was low. Due to conflict with Russia in the wake of the Soviet collapse, Georgia's post-communist elite could not draw on preexisting Soviet force structures and thus had to effectively create an army from scratch.[357]

---

[349] See Helly and Gogia (2005) and de Waal (2005). Foreign aid accounted for between 50 and 80 percent of Georgia's state budget in the 1990s (World Bank World Development Indicators (online: www.worldbank.org/data)). Georgia also received far greater U.S. military assistance than any other country discussed in this chapter (Helly and Gogia 2005).

[350] Collier and Way (2004); Coppieters and Legvold (2005).

[351] In the 1990s, Georgia's trade with the United States and Western Europe was between a third and a quarter that of our countries in the Americas and Eastern Europe. (See Appendix III). Likewise, per capita immigration to the West was several times lower than in Eastern Europe (see Appendix III).

[352] Aves (1992: 165–6); Slider (1997: 177).

[353] Slider (1997: 164–5); Wheatley (2005: 85–6).

[354] Wheatley (2004); see also Dragaze (1994: 183) and Jones (1999).

[355] See Wheatley (2005: Chapter 5). Indeed, the CUG lacked discipline (Jones 1999, 2000: 53; Fuller 2001a).

[356] Wheatley (2005: 132).

[357] Due to President Gamsakhurdia's anti-Ossetian mobilization (Aves 1992: 166–72), early state-building efforts were opposed by powerful forces in Moscow, many of which backed separatist claims within Georgia. Soviet military bases on Georgian territory remained outside Georgian control (Zürcher 2007: 137). See also Coppieters and Legvold (2005).

The military consisted mainly of "weekend fighters and volunteers," who had to feed and arm themselves and were never "under the control of the state."[358] In the early 1990s, the embryonic security forces coexisted with a variety of autonomous paramilitaries – most notably, Jaba Ioseliani's *Mkhedrioni* (Knights) – that contested central power over many parts of the country.[359] The security forces also lost battles for control over the regions of Ossetia and Abkhazia.[360] Although the Shevardnadze government consolidated power over paramilitaries and gained a minimum of control over the police,[361] the state remained strikingly weak. It failed to impose order across the national territory,[362] police often went unpaid for months at a time,[363] and the country was plagued by coup attempts and assassination plots throughout the 1990s.[364]

Origins and Evolution of the Regime

Georgia's competitive authoritarian regime was unstable from the outset. The initial post-communist government was led by Zviad Gamsakhurdia, a nationalist dissident who gained control of parliament in late 1990 and led Georgia to independence in 1991.[365] In May 1991, Gamsakhurdia was overwhelmingly elected president, with 87 percent of the vote.

The Gamsakhurdia government is a striking case of failed authoritarianism.[366] The new president governed in an autocratic manner, attempting to impose media censorship and arrest opponents.[367] However, his rule quickly disintegrated. Following the failed August 1991 Soviet coup, the head of the National Guard, Tengiz Kitovani, broke with the government, "leaving the president without an effective military force."[368] In September, the ruling coalition collapsed amid opposition protest.[369] As demonstrations escalated, the president attempted to crack down, closing an opposition newspaper and a major television station (Channel 2) and arresting opposition leader Giorgi Chanturia.[370] On December 21, however, Kitovani's paramilitary forces attacked the capital.[371] Warlord Ioseliani escaped from prison, and his *Mkhedrioni* forces joined the assault. Defended by "young, untrained and ill-disciplined gunmen,"[372] Gamsakhurdia was forced into a bunker, and in early 1992, he fled into exile.[373] Although

---

[358] Zürcher (2007: 137–9). Soldiers were recruited from various criminal-based "clannish" paramilitary groups (Jones 1996: 36).

[359] Jones (1996); Zürcher (2007: 137–8).

[360] Suny (1994: 325–31); Zürcher (2007: 140–3).

[361] Ekedahl and Goodman (1997: 279); Wheatley (2005: 86–7).

[362] See Mitchell (2008: 76). In addition to Abkhazia and Ossetia, "brown areas" included Pankisi Gorge, Ajaria, and, to a lesser extent, Kodori Gorge and Mingrelia (Welt 2000).

[363] See Fuller (1998b, 1998c) and Devdariani (2003).

[364] See Jones (1999), Welt (2000), Devdariani (2002), and Fuller (2003d); see also

RFE/RL Newsline, 1 June 2001 (online: http://www.rferl.org/archive/en-newsline/latest/683/683.html).

[365] Suny (1995: 154–7).

[366] Suny (1994: 322–8).

[367] Jones (1997: 516–23); Slider (1997: 162–4).

[368] Zürcher (2007: 127).

[369] Jones (1997: 517); Wheatley (2004: 3).

[370] Suny (1994: 327); Bokeria, Targamadze, and Ramishvili (1997: 10).

[371] Slider (1997: 166).

[372] "Stunned, Georgians Reckon the Cost of Independence," *The New York Times*, 10 January 1992 (online: www.nyt.com).

[373] Suny (1995: 158).

Gamsakhurdia's fall is often attributed to his own erratic behavior,[374] it was also a product of coercive weakness. Lacking a minimally cohesive military force, Gamsakhurdia was toppled by small militias – just seven months after his landslide election.[375] As Jonathan Wheatley observed, Gamsakhurdia:

…had no institutionalized societal organization to support him.… His political future was dependent entirely on the day-to-day vicissitudes of public opinion and was not rooted in any stable social or political structure. Once public opinion began to slip away from him, he had no institutional levers to maintain his grip on power.[376]

THE RISE AND FALL OF SHEVARDNADZE. Unable to control the chaos that followed Gamsakhurdia's exit, victorious warlords invited Eduard Shevardnadze, a former Georgian Communist Party Secretary (and former Soviet Foreign Minister), to lead the country.[377] For the next two years, Georgia effectively lacked a regime as rival militias battled for control.[378] By 1995, however, Shevardnadze had arrested Kitovani and Ioseliani, weakened the militias, and established a modicum of central-state control.[379]

Shevardnadze abused power in a variety of ways.[380] Journalists and opposition activists suffered police harassment, persecution by tax authorities, and occasional arrest.[381] Most influential media were biased.[382] The only significant private television station, Rustavi-2, suffered violent attacks, libel lawsuits, and harassment by tax authorities; in 1996, the government temporarily revoked its license.[383] Elections were also unfair. The 1995 presidential election – won by Shevardnadze with 74 percent of the vote – was marred by widespread reports of manipulation as authorities sought to ensure a convincing victory over former Communist leader Jumber Patiashvili.[384] In the 1995 legislative election, vote tallies for pro-Gamsakhurdia parties appear to have been "massaged" to fall below the 5 percent threshold for parliamentary representation.[385] Shevardnadze's CUG won 107 of 235 seats, which enabled it to forge a majority coalition in parliament. Four years

---

[374] See, for example, Suny (1994: 326) and Cornell (2001: 168).

[375] Suny (1994: 327–8).

[376] Wheatley (2004: 3).

[377] Suny (1995: 153–4, 159).

[378] Wheatley (2005: 77). One of the authors was delayed in his effort to leave Georgia in April 1992 when a militia group absconded with fuel intended for a flight from Tbilisi to Moscow.

[379] See Ekedahl and Goodman (1997: 279), Wheatley (2005: 86–7), and Mitchell (2008: 24–6).

[380] See especially King (2001) and Mitchell (2008: 26–42).

[381] Supporters of ex-President Gamsakhurdia were frequently blocked from holding rallies and, in 1998, security forces responded to a Traditionalist Party petition drive to demand a referendum calling for President Shevardnadze's resignation by arresting and intimidating party members (U.S. Department of State 1998b, 1999c). See also Jones (2000: 57–8), ODIHR 2000c: 26), and *RFE/RL Newsline*, 1 April 2003 (online: http://www.rferl.org/archive/en-newsline/latest/683/683.html).

[382] See Fuller (1996b), Jones (2000: 59), and ODIHR (2000c, 2000d).

[383] See U.S. Department of State (1998b), Jones (2000: 59), Devdariani (2001b), and Committee to Protect Journalists "Attacks on the Press 2001: Georgia" (online: www.cpj.org); Committee to Protect Journalists "Attacks on the Press 2003: Georgia" (online: www.cpj.org).

[384] Patiashvili finished second with 19 percent of the vote. See Slider (1997: 189) and Wheatley (2004).

[385] Slider (1997: 189); Wheatley (2004).

later, the CUG won parliamentary elections marred by media bias, attacks on opposition candidates, and fraud.[386] Likewise, the 2000 presidential election was characterized by media bias and fraud, and Patiashvili, the leading opposition candidate, was effectively blocked from campaigning in parts of the country.[387] Shevardnadze was reelected with nearly 80 percent of the vote.

Shevardnadze faced few serious challenges during the 1990s. On the external front, Western powers tolerated government abuse and provided considerable assistance throughout the decade.[388] At home, the economy boomed, and state and governing-party structures – although still weak – were more effective than they had been earlier in the decade. Moreover, opposition forces were weak. Civil society was underdeveloped,[389] and the political opposition was fragmented among dissidents in the capital and disparate regional patronage networks.[390] Thus, no opposition group "figured to pose a serious threat" to the regime.[391]

Nevertheless, Shevardnadze lacked the organizational tools to sustain competitive authoritarian rule, and despite a healthy economy,[392] the regime collapsed in 2003. As in Ukraine, regime change came largely from within. The transition was rooted in a combination of party and state weakness. As public support for Shevardnadze eroded in the early 2000s, the CUG disintegrated.[393] In late 2000, a group of businessmen abandoned the CUG to form the New Rights Party. In mid-2001, major regime officials – including Justice Minister Mikheil Saakashvili, Parliamentary Speaker Zurab Zhvania, and Nino Burjanadze (who succeeded Zhvania as Parliamentary Speaker) – broke with the government and moved to "the forefront of the mounting popular opposition to . . . Shevardnadze."[394] Large-scale elite defection ensued, leaving the ruling coalition "in shambles, torn apart by defecting factions."[395] By the end of 2001, only 41 of the CUG's 109 deputies remained in the party, and "Shevardnadze's top protégés were now leading many of the major opposition parties."[396] A decimated CUG performed poorly in the 2002 local elections, winning less than 4 percent of the vote in Tbilisi. With the ruling party in a state of collapse, Shevardnadze resigned as leader of the CUG and was subsequently backed by a reconfigured alliance, "For a New Georgia!"[397]

---

[386] ODIHR (2000d). The government also inflated turnout figures to ensure that a major opposition party did not pass the minimum threshold to enter parliament (ODIHR 2000c: 27). The CUG won 42 percent of the vote and 121 of 235 parliamentary seats. The All-Georgia Union of Revival finished second with 58 seats.

[387] ODIHR (2000c).

[388] King (2001). The U.S. Congress earmarked or allocated more than $1 billion in aid between 1992 and 2002, making Georgia one of the highest per capita recipients of U.S. aid in Eurasia (Nichols 2003: 5).

[389] Stefes (2005).

[390] See Jones (1998), ODIHR (2000c), Wheatley (2004), and Mitchell (2008: 35–6).

[391] Mitchell (2008: 36).

[392] GDP growth was 5.5 percent in 2002 and 11.1 percent in 2003 (World Bank World Development Indicators (online: www.worldbank.org/data)).

[393] Mitchell (2008: 36–8).

[394] Fuller (2001c). See also Fuller (2001b).

[395] Fairbanks (2004: 113); see also Mitchell (2008: 36–7).

[396] Wheatley (2005: 128); and Mitchell (2008: 38).

[397] Anjaparidze (2002); and Mitchell (2008: 49–50).

Shevardnadze faced a serious threat in the 2003 legislative election. His public-approval rating was in the single digits,[398] and he confronted potent challenges by parties led by former regime insiders, including the New Rights Party, Saakashvili's National Movement, and the Burjanadze-Democrats, which was led by Burjanadze and Zhvania.[399] Although sometimes derided as representatives of a "new CUG,"[400] Burjanadze, Zhvania, and Saakashvili all enjoyed connections, resources, and name recognition that – given Georgia's weak civil society and private media – would have been difficult to achieve from outside the regime.

Flawed elections in 2003 triggered a regime crisis. Despite considerable Western pressure, the Shevardnadze government rejected calls for more balanced electoral authorities and a cleanup of the registration and voting processes.[401] In an election marred by "massive fraud," including ballot-box stuffing, multiple voting, and falsification of the results,[402] Shevardnadze's "For a New Georgia!" coalition won a narrow plurality. Led by Saakashvili, opposition groups organized demonstrations in the capital calling for Shevardnadze's resignation and culminating in the storming of parliament by protestors on November 22 and Shevardnadze's resignation the following day.

The success of the Rose Revolution led many observers to highlight the role of "people power" in the 2003 transition.[403] Yet observers on the ground reported that the demonstrations were "small" and "undersized."[404] Postelection efforts to organize strikes against the regime appear to have fizzled.[405] During the initial week of protests, there were never more than five thousand demonstrators in front of parliament[406]; according to most accounts, the largest demonstration – on November 22 – numbered in the "tens of thousands."[407]

Saakashvili's successful storming of the legislature was rooted less in the scale of mass protest than in the decomposition of the coercive apparatus.[408] The

[398] Fairbanks (2004: 113).
[399] Wheatley (2005: 181).
[400] Mitchell (2008: 48).
[401] See ODIHR (2003c), Fairbanks (2004: 114–15), and Mitchell (2008: 47–8).
[402] Fairbanks (2004: 114–15); see also ODIHR (2003c).
[403] See, for example, *The Economist*, 10 November 2007, p. 66.
[404] Mitchell (2004: 345; 2008b: 63–4); Welt (2006: 14) calls the demonstrations "not that large or sustained."
[405] Wheatley (2005: 184).
[406] Mitchell (2004: 345).
[407] "Caucasus after The Fall, Georgia After Shevardnadze," *The Financial Times*, July 10, 2004 (online: www.ft.com); See also *RFE/RL Newsline*, 24 November 2003 (online: http://www.rferl.org/archive/en-newsline/latest/683/683.html); "Power Struggle Breaks Out in Georgia" *Independent on Sunday*, November 23, 2003 (online: www.lexisnexis.com); One Georgian news source that had overestimated the size of earlier protests reported 60,000 (Welt 2006: 14) – a figure cited by Saakashvili himself (Karumidze and Wertsch 2005: 25). Some observers (Fairbanks 2004: 116; Wheatley 2005: 184) reported numbers as high as 100 thousand. This figure may come from the celebrations on the streets *after* Shevardnadze's resignation (televised worldwide), which were considerably larger than the demonstrations that led to his downfall. See Welt (2006: 14).
[408] As opposition leader David Zurabishvili said, "Thanks to typical Georgian negligence, no one was watching the sides of the entrance to the parliament. Only the police were there, but they couldn't stop the demonstrators

police who were guarding the parliament building simply "stepped aside and let [the protesters] through."[409] As Shevardnadze's Interior Minister put it, the police "had not been paid . . . for three months. So why should they have obeyed Shevardnadze?"[410] Shevardnadze declared a state of emergency, but he "no longer controlled the . . . security forces," and military and police units refused to cooperate.[411] On November 23, key army units declared loyalty to Parliamentary Speaker Nino Burjanadze (who became acting President).[412] As Charles Fairbanks observed, "the army, police, and presidential guard . . . never moved. There was little Shevardnadze could do but resign."[413]

Leverage played an important secondary role in Shevardnadze's fall. Lacking significant support from Russia, the Shevardnadze government relied heavily on Western assistance.[414] The United States initially backed Shevardnadze but, by the 2000s, it no longer invested importance in his political survival and chose instead to push for free and fair elections.[415] Isolated from both Russia and the West, Shevardnadze had little choice but to resign.[416]

COMPETITIVE AUTHORITARIANISM AFTER THE ROSE REVOLUTION. Georgia remained competitive authoritarian after 2003. With pro-Saakashvili forces in control of the state, new presidential and parliamentary elections were held in early 2004. Although cleaner than previous races, the elections were characterized by abuse of state resources, media bias, and at least some fraud.[417] Saakashvili won the presidency with 96 percent of the vote and his National Movement captured nearly two thirds of parliament.

---

from going in." Quoted in Karumidze and Wertsch (2005: 15).

[409] Opposition leader David Zurabishvili, quoted in Karumidze and Wertsch (2005: 15).

[410] Quoted in Karumidze and Wertsch (2005: 39).

[411] Mitchell (2004: 348). Thus, there was no repression because the president was "too politically weak to command it" (Mitchell 2004: 348). Shevardnadze later complained that "the Georgian state apparatus did not stand up to the challenge before it." Quoted in Karumidze and Wertsch (2005: 15).

[412] Karumidze and Wertsch (2005: 54).

[413] Fairbanks (2004: 117).

[414] The U.S. Congress earmarked or allocated more than $1 billion in aid between 1992 and 2002, making Georgia "among the highest" per capita recipients of aid in Eurasia (Nichols 2003: 5).

[415] See Fairbanks (2004) and Karumidze and Wertsch (2005: 36–8). In mid-2003, President Bush sent Shevardnadze a letter expressing hope that he would cede power to a "new generation of leaders" (Devdariani 2004a). On November 20, as postelection protest escalated, the U.S. State Department denounced "massive fraud" – reportedly the first time that the United States had openly accused a former Soviet republic of rigging an election (Fairbanks 2004: 116).

[416] As one commentator noted, "What was decisive for Shevardnadze in terms of his decision to resign was the realization that neither the Russians nor the Americans were going to view developments at the time as a coup . . . [if] either the Russians or the Americans had decided that what was going on was a coup, he probably would not have resigned." Quoted in Karumidze and Wertsch (2005: 64).

[417] See ODIHR (2004g: 1–2). In the partial repeat parliamentary elections in March, the OSCE cited problems of implausible voter turnout, vote fraud, selective cancellation of election results, and "clear bias" in the media (ODIHR 2004h: 1–2).

Notwithstanding important successes in state-building,[418] the Saakashvili government was not democratic.[419] Media harassment persisted, including tax raids of independent television stations, prosecution of journalists, and government pressure to cancel programs critical of Saakashvili.[420] The Rustavi 2 TV station was "effectively taken over by the state through government-controlled interests" and began "cheering rather than scrutinizing" government activities.[421] The judiciary was packed, and government critics were occasionally arrested and, in a few cases, charged with treason.[422] For example, the government enforced anticorruption laws selectively, "arresting and punishing political enemies while leaving supporters untouched."[423] In late 2007, Irakli Okruashvili – a former defense minister who was viewed as a potential challenger to Saakashvili – was arrested and charged with corruption (he later fled into exile).[424] The arrest triggered a wave of opposition protest, and in November, the government responded by violently breaking up demonstrations and declaring a state of emergency in which demonstrations were banned, private news-broadcasting was suspended, and several television stations – including the most influential opposition station, Imedi – were taken off the air.[425] Saakashvili then called early presidential elections for January 2008. The election was marred by abuse of state resources, media bias, harassment and intimidation of opposition supporters, at least some restrictions on opposition campaigning, and numerous irregularities in voting and vote-counting.[426] Saakashvili won easily.[427]

---

[418] The Saakashvili government jailed numerous corrupt officials, undertook police reform, and subordinated the breakaway region of Ajaria (Khutsidze 2004; Mitchell 2008: 85–6).

[419] See Dolidze (2007), "Viewing Georgia, Without the Rose-Colored Glasses," *The New York Times*, 25 September 2008 (online: www.nyt.com), and Ognianova (2009). As Nodia (2005: 1) stated, "strengthening the state was accompanied by certain setbacks in democratic freedoms."

[420] See Peuch (2004), Fuller (2005), Corso (2006b), and Dolidze (2007). In the 2005 Reporters Without Borders media freedom report, Georgia fell five places, from 94th to 99th of 167 countries surveyed (Corso 2006a).

[421] After reportedly resisting government efforts to interfere in editorial policy, Rustavi 2's director was fired in July 2006 and replaced with a close associate of the president's chief of staff (Ognianova 2009).

[422] In 2005, several "rebel judges" critical of the regime were forced out of the Supreme Court under government pressure (Dolidze

2007). On civil-liberties abuses, see Corso (2004), *RFE/RL Newsline*, 31 July 2006 (online: http://www.rferl.org/archive/en-newsline/latest/683/683.html), Dolidze (2007), U.S. Department of State (2008b), and Freedom House, "Freedom in the World 2008: Georgia." In 2004, the OSCE noted "a noticeable increase" in human-rights complaints since the inauguration of Saakashvili as president. Quoted in Van Der Schriek (2004).

[423] Devdariani (2004b).

[424] Freedom House, "Freedom in the World 2008: Georgia" (online: www.freedomhouse .org).

[425] Faced with government prosecution, Imedi owner Badri Patarkatsishvili fled into exile. See Freedom House, "Freedom in the World 2008: Georgia" (online: www.free domhouse.org) and U.S. Department of State (2008b).

[426] ODIHR (2008c).

[427] Saakashvili defeated opposition MP Levan Gachechiladze, 53 to 26 percent. His United National Movement captured 59 percent of the vote and 119 of 150 seats in parliament.

Saakashvili's survival through 2008 can be attributed to several factors, including a growing economy and broad public support. However, "unconditional" Western support was also critical.[428] Like other postauthoritarian turnover cases (e.g., Zambia, Malawi, and Kenya), the post-2003 regime received a virtual free pass from the international community, particularly the United States.[429] Thus, despite widespread abuse, "criticism from the U.S. was muted,"[430] U.S.-backed programs to promote electoral oversight were shut down, and U.S. support for independent media "all but disappeared."[431] The United States also provided large-scale military and economic assistance.[432] Despite the West's embrace, however, Georgia's overall ties to the West remained modest and its prospects for joining the EU were remote. Hence, external incentives for democratic behavior were limited.[433]

In summary, Georgia represents a striking case of state weakness and authoritarian instability. Despite a weak opposition and civil society, both Gamsakhurdia and Shevardnadze fell from power – largely because they lacked the organizational capacity to fend off even mild opposition challenges. In the absence of strong ties to the West, however, external incentives for democratic behavior were limited; indeed, Georgia failed to democratize despite two turnovers.

Moldova

Moldova is another case of low organizational power and unstable competitive authoritarianism. Presidents Mircea Snegur (1991–1996) and Petru Lucinschi (1997–2001) lacked effective coercive or ruling-party structures and fell quickly from power. Although the regime stabilized somewhat with the rise to power of the Communist Party in 2001, the communists also failed to consolidate power.

Linkage, Leverage, and Organizational Power
Moldova is a case of borderline medium-low linkage and high leverage. Moldova had only weak economic, technocratic, social, and communication ties to the West. The Moldovan economy was "overwhelmingly oriented towards the east" in the 1990s.[434] In terms of leverage, Moldova, like Georgia, was a small,

---

[428] Mitchell (2008: 131).

[429] In May 2005, for example, President Bush praised Georgia as a "beacon of liberty for this region and the world." "President Addresses and Thanks Citizens in Tbilisi, Georgia, Office of the Press Secretary, 10 May 2005." (online: www.whitehouse.gov).

[430] "Viewing Georgia, Without the Rose-Colored Glasses," *The New York Times*, 25 September 2008 (online: www.nyt.com).

[431] Mitchell (2008: 130, 92).

[432] Mitchell (2008: 131). Georgia received more than $1.5 billion in external assis-

tance between 2003 and 2007 (World Bank World Development Indicators (online: www.worldbank.org/data)) and, according to one estimate, it received $150 million in security aid between 2004 and 2006 (Sawyer 2006).

[433] Rochowanski (2004).

[434] King (2000: 165). In the 1990s, trade with the West accounted for an annual average of only 20 percent of the country's GDP, compared to 50 percent for Croatia and 77 percent for Slovakia (IMF, Direction of Trade Statistics, 1992–2000).

aid-dependent country,[435] and conflict with Russia deprived it of the type of economic assistance that benefited other post-Soviet republics.[436] The conflict increased Moldova's reliance on Western support, which heightened the regime's vulnerability to Western pressure.[437]

Organizational power was low. The Moldovan state was exceptionally weak in the early 1990s. Due to Moldova's postindependence dispute with Russia over Moldova's Eastern Transnistria territory, the country's coercive structures had to be effectively rebuilt from scratch. Thus, coercive scope was initially very low. In the fall of 1991, the only regular armed forces in Moldova were the Russian 14th Army, which was based in the Transnistria region, outside of Moldovan control.[438] Moldova's own security forces consisted of only a ragtag collection of underpaid police officers, a "hastily assembled" army, and nationalist volunteers, some of whom were armed with farm implements.[439] The KGB was disbanded; much of the old KGB staff were ethnic Russians who abandoned the state after the start of hostilities with Russia.[440] Overall, per capita military expenditure was the lowest in Europe, and the police were so ill-equipped that officers were "forced to borrow helmets and shields" from one another.[441] Cohesion also was low. Control over the military and police was limited, and discipline within the security forces was undermined by wage arrears and low morale.[442]

Party strength increased over time. In the 1990s, governing parties were merely loose coalitions of independent politicians that lacked a shared ideology or partisan identity.[443] Early party-building efforts failed. Thus, the Moldovan Popular Front, a nationalist party that performed well in the 1990 parliamentary election,[444] might have emerged as a ruling party. However, the Front broke

---

435 Foreign aid accounted for about a third of government expenditure in the late 1990s (World Bank World Development Indicators (online: www.worldbank.org/data)).

436 In 1990–1992, conflict erupted between nationalist politicians in the Moldovan government who sought reunification with Romania and separatists in the eastern region of Transnistria, who were backed by Russian troops based in the territory (Crowther 1996; King 2000: 178–207). In the spring of 1992, fighting broke out briefly between the Moldovan police and Russian-backed separatists, resulting in an estimated 300 deaths (Crowther 1996: 37; King 2000:178).

437 See Freire (2003: 236–40), March and Herd (2006: 360, 369), Crowther (2007: 289), and Dura (2007).

438 Helsinki Watch (1993: 18).

439 Helsinki Watch (1993: 18–19); Lucan Way interviews with Viorel Cibatoru, former military advisor, Chişinău, Moldova, February

7, 2002, and with Nicolai Chirtoaca, former national security advisor, February 5, 2002.

440 Lucan Way interview with Nicolai Chirtoaca, former KGB official, February 5, 2002.

441 "Moldova Professors Charged With Instigating Student Unrest," *Basapress*, 26 April 2000 (online: wnc.fedworld.gov). On military spending, see Military Balance (2006: 398–9).

442 See "Moldova: 3bn Backlog in Unpaid Wages," *Radio Mayak* (Russia) 17 August 1993 (online: wnc.fedworld.gov), King (2000: 192–3), and March and Herd (2006: 365).

443 Way (2002a, 2003).

444 See Crowther (1997b: 293). The Popular Front emerged out of a movement for Moldovan linguistic rights in 1989–1990. The Front developed a "vast grassroots network in the countryside" and, in 1990, it captured 140 of 380 seats in parliament (King 1994: 295–6).

with President Mircea Snegur and collapsed soon thereafter. Snegur won the 1991 election as an independent;[445] he later aligned with the Agrarian Democratic Party (ADP), a group of rural parliamentarians, but the ADP fractured prior to the 1996 election.[446] President Petru Lucinschi (1996–2001) governed without a party, relying instead on the support of multiple and competing political forces.[447] Party strength increased with the victory of the Communist Party of Moldova (PCRM) in the 2001 election. Reestablished in 1993,[448] the PCRM scored medium in scope and high in cohesion. The PCRM was far better organized than its predecessors. It had an extensive national structure with an organized presence in villages across the entire country.[449] Because the party maintained a clear communist ideology in a context of a deep communist–anticommunist cleavage, we score party cohesion as high after 2001.[450]

Origins and Evolution of the Regime
Competitive authoritarianism emerged in Moldova in the wake of the Soviet collapse. Snegur, a former Communist boss who broke with the Soviet leadership and led Moldova to independence, used harassment and manipulation of the electoral rules to exclude his main rivals (most notably, former Prime Minister Mircea Druc) from the 1991 presidential race and was elected unopposed.[451] The post-1991 regime – although more open than many regimes in the region – was not democratic. Most of the media remained in state hands, and the Snegur government imposed steep fines and prison terms for "slandering" the President.[452]

Like his counterparts in Belarus, Georgia, and Ukraine, Snegur failed to consolidate power. His initial alliance with the Moldovan Popular Front collapsed in 1991 over his opposition to unification with Romania, leaving him "without a secure base of support in the legislature."[453] The president allied with the ADP, which won the 1994 parliamentary elections in a context of a skewed

---

445 See Socor (1992: 42), Crowther (1997b: 308–9), and King (2000: 153).

446 King (1994: 299); Horowitz (2005: 119–20); Crowther (2007: 275, 277).

447 Way (2003).

448 Sorokin (2008).

449 Crowther (2007: 290). In 2001, the PCRM had 10,362 dues-paying members (www. pcrm.md, accessed April 28, 2001) and representatives in 1,000 of Moldova's 1,004 villages (March 2005: 13). In 2009, it reported 30,000 members and more than 1,400 local party organizations across the country ("Novosti Politcheskikh partii Rossii i stran SNG," 20 March 2009, available at www.qwas.ru). See data on party organization from the description of the 6th Party

Congress of the PCRM, available at www. kprf.ru/international/55790.html.

450 Its ideology clearly distinguished it from other parties and – particularly in the early 2000s – motivated party behavior. See March (2005: 1–3, 23).

451 See Fane (1993: 126). Another less prominent candidate withdrew after claiming to be the victim of harassment by pro-Snegur local authorities (*Izvestiia*, 29 November 1991, p. 4).

452 TASS, 9 January 1992 available from *Foreign Broadcast Information Service – Soviet Union*. 14 January 1992: 62.; U.S. Department of State (1995a).

453 Crowther (1997b: 308); see also King (2000: 152, 160).

playing field and harassment of opposition.[454] However, the ADP fractured in advance of the 1996 presidential election. Snegur broke with the ADP, which backed the presidential candidacy of Prime Minister Andrei Sangheli.[455] The head of Parliament, Petru Lucinschi, also sought the presidency, which meant that Snegur was opposed by his own Prime Minister and the head of parliament – both of whom were former allies in the governing ADP. These internal divisions undermined Snegur's incumbent status, as he was unable to monopolize control over state resources. Indeed, with local governments under the control of the Prime Minister and much of the state media controlled by the head of parliament,[456] President Snegur arguably enjoyed the fewest incumbent advantages of the three candidates. Although some observers speculated that Snegur would try to steal the election,[457] his limited control over state coercive agencies appears to have precluded such an option. Snegur lost in the second round to Lucinschi.[458]

Party weakness also prevented Lucinschi from consolidating power. Although backed by For a Democratic and Prosperous Moldova (FDPM), Lucinschi refused to align closely with any party and instead governed with multiple and competing parties. As in Russia, this strategy failed. The progovernment FDPM finished third in the 1998 parliamentary election, winning just 24 of 101 seats (compared to 40 for the opposition Communists). Although noncommunist parties forged a majority coalition in parliament, electing Lucinschi ally Dumitru Diacov as Speaker, the president quickly alienated his own parliamentary allies and lost control of the body.[459] Thus, when Lucinschi attempted to expand executive powers, Diacov – in alliance with the communists – pushed through a 2000 constitutional reform that strengthened parliament by creating a system in which the president would be elected by parliament rather than by popular vote.[460] Early parliamentary elections in 2001 were won handily by the communists, whose powerful ground organization helped them capture 50 percent of the vote and more than two thirds of parliament.[461]

The emergence of a stronger governing party eliminated key sources of pluralism and competition. The PCRM used its disciplined parliamentary

[454] International Foundation for Electoral Systems (IFES) (1994); Carothers et al. (1994: 31–2).

[455] Horowitz (2005: 119–20); Crowther (2007: 275).

[456] See "Teleradio-Moldova Head Backs Lucinschi in Elections," *Infotag* 11 October 1996; "Presidential Candidates Comment on 17 Nov Elections," *Basapress*, 18 November 1996, "'Last Year Parliament Encouraged Disobedience, Now Fights It," *Basapress* 30 July 1997; "Moldova: Snegur To Run for Presidency on Behalf of PRAM," *Infotag*, 26 June 1996, "Sangheli Has 'More Chances to Win'," *Infotag* 8 November 1996 (online: wnc.fedworld.gov); ODIHR (1997a: 6).

[457] "Daily Fears Snegur Might 'Take Power by Force'," *Basapress*, 23 November 1996 (online: wnc.fedworld.gov).

[458] Snegur won a plurality (39 percent compared to 28 percent for Lucinschi) in the first round, but Lucinschi won the runoff with 54 percent.

[459] Way (2003: 475).

[460] Way (2003: 476); Crowther (2007: 278).

[461] Hill (2001: 133).

majority to establish control over all major state institutions.[462] The judiciary
and the electoral authorities were packed,[463] and the state media (still the dominant source of news), which had been relatively pluralist in the 1990s due to the
fragmentation of parliamentary power,[464] fell under full PCRM control. State-
run television was censored and grew increasingly biased, and independent talk
shows were taken off the air.[465] By 2004, Freedom House categorized Moldova's
media as "not free."[466]

The communists retained their majority in the 2005 parliamentary election,
marking the first time since the introduction of multiparty rule that an incumbent had been reelected. Although the election was marred by media bias, abuse
of state resources, and some harassment of opposition,[467] the PCRM's victory
was clearly facilitated by its extensive organization and tight control over local
governments.[468]

Although the regime remained competitive authoritarian through 2008,[469] the
communists suffered a surprising defeat in 2009. After winning 60 of 101 seats in
the April 2009 parliamentary election, they failed to secure the 61 votes needed to
elect the president. New elections were called, and an opposition coalition won
a majority and removed the communists from power. Moldova thus experienced
its third incumbent turnover in less than two decades. The prospects for full
democratization, however, remained uncertain.

CONCLUSION

Three sets of factors shaped the trajectories of post-Soviet competitive authoritarian regimes. First, low linkage meant that Western pressure played only a
peripheral role in shaping regime dynamics. This was particularly the case where
military and economic power (Russia) or Russian black knight assistance (Belarus)
reduced Western leverage. At most, Western actors helped to tip the balance in

[462] By the mid-2000s, the communists had
"become omnipresent in all public institutions, which ma[de] it difficult to speak about
effective checks and balances on the power of
the ruling party" (Dura 2007).

[463] See Way (2002a: 131) and ODIHR (2005c).
Due to court packing, the government did
not lose a single libel case against journalists between 2002 and mid-2004 (Lucan Way
interview with Vladislav Gribincea, lawyer,
Chisinau, 29 July 2004).

[464] Lucan Way interview with Viorel Cibotaru,
in charge of media for the military in the
mid-1990s, 11 February 2002.

[465] EIM Media Report from the CIS, No. 10
(19), October 2001 (online: www.internews.

ru/eim/october2001/mde.html). In 2002,
journalists at the state TV channel went
on strike in response to censorship efforts
(Way 2002a: 131). See also "Moldovan journalists' unions protest against ban on TV
programme," *Basapress*, 4 June 2001 (online:
wnc.fedworld.gov).

[466] See Freedom House "Freedom of the
Press 2004: Moldova" (online: www.freedom
house.org).

[467] See ODIHR (2005c) and Freedom House,
"Freedom in the World 2006: Moldova"
(online: www.freedomhouse.org).

[468] Crowther (2007: 290).

[469] See Kennedy (2007) and U.S. Department
of State (2008e).

favor of an already powerful opposition challenge (e.g., Ukraine). Nowhere, however, did Western engagement play a decisive role in either toppling authoritarian governments (as in Serbia and Slovakia) or inducing them to behave democratically (as in Romania). Consequently, post-Soviet regime outcomes hinged primarily on the domestic balance of power, and because civic and opposition forces were generally weak, few regimes democratized.

Second, the stability of post-Soviet authoritarian regimes was rooted primarily in incumbent organizational power. Where state and/or governing-party organizations were relatively strong, as in Armenia and Putin's Russia, incumbents were better able to thwart opposition challenges. Where state and party structures were weak, outcomes were often shaped by Western leverage. Where leverage was high, as in Georgia, Moldova, and Ukraine, weak incumbents often fell. Where leverage was low, as in Russia under Yeltsin, even relatively weak incumbents tended to survive.

Table 5.1 summarizes the six post-Soviet cases. As the table shows, our framework correctly predicts regime outcomes in Armenia, Georgia, Moldova, and Russia. The two other cases, Belarus and Ukraine, are "near misses." In Belarus, we expected authoritarian stability due to black-knight support from Russia. Although Kebich's defeat in 1994 runs counter to our theory, the regime was replaced by a stable nondemocratic regime. In Ukraine, we expected unstable competitive authoritarianism, and indeed, neither Kravchuk nor Kuchma was able to consolidate power. However, the regime's democratization after 2004 was not predicted by our theory.

Other theoretical approaches do less well in explaining these outcomes. For example, modernization explains little: Belarus and Russia are among the most developed cases examined in the book. The impact of economic performance was also limited: Regimes in Armenia and Russia survived despite extraordinary economic collapse, whereas Kuchma and Shevardnadze fell despite relatively robust economic growth. The impact of constitutional design also was limited. Far from facilitating authoritarian rule, Russia's super-presidentialist constitution was imposed by Yeltsin *after* he had illegally and violently closed down the parliament. Likewise, in Belarus, the problem was not the president's constitutional authority but rather that Lukashenka ignored constitutional limits on executive power and then imposed a highly presidentialist constitution *after* parliamentary opposition had been suppressed.

Finally, variation in regime outcomes had little to do with the strength, unity, or tactics of opposition forces. First, opposition unity does not explain outcomes across the cases. In Georgia in 1991–1992 and 2003, autocrats fell despite facing highly fractious opposition challenges. In Belarus in 2006, a unified opposition posed little threat to Lukashenka. Mobilizational strength also correlates poorly with our outcomes. In Moldova and Georgia, where organizational power was low, incumbents fell at least two times despite facing relatively weak oppositions. In Armenia, where state coercive capacity was much higher, governments successfully thwarted repeated – and much larger – waves of protest. Even in Ukraine, where opposition protest was decisive in 2004, the opposition's

TABLE 5.1. *Predicted and Actual Competitive Authoritarian Regime Outcomes in the Former Soviet Union*

Case	Linkage	Leverage	Organizational Power	Predicted Outcome	Actual Outcome
Armenia	Medium	High	High	Stable Authoritarianism	Stable Authoritarianism
Belarus	Low	Medium	Low	Stable Authoritarianism	Unstable Authoritarianism
Georgia	Low	High	Low	Unstable Authoritarianism	Unstable Authoritarianism
Moldova	Medium	High	Low	Unstable Authoritarianism	Unstable Authoritarianism
Russia	Low	Low	Low	Stable Authoritarianism	Stable Authoritarianism
Ukraine	Low	High	Low	Unstable Authoritarianism	Democratization

mobilizational capacity was partly endogenous to incumbent party weakness, as the most powerful opposition leaders were recent defectors from the government. The post-Soviet cases thus demonstrate the need to pay attention not only to opposition mobilization but also to the character of the regime it mobilizes against.

6

Africa

Transitions without Democratization

"It is better to be President in a nondemocratic country than not to be President in a democratic one."

– Advisor to Frederick Chiluba, President of Zambia[1]

This chapter examines 14 competitive authoritarian regimes in Africa. The African cases share several features in common. First, they lacked favorable conditions for democracy. Nearly all of them were poor, rural, and had small middle classes and weak civil societies.[2] Notwithstanding episodes of mass protest in some cases,[3] large or sustained democracy movements were rare.[4] Second, most African states faced an external environment characterized by high leverage and low linkage. Sub-Saharan African states were among the weakest and most dependent in the world,[5] and the disappearance of competing Western security interests after the Cold War brought a sharp increase in external democratizing pressure.[6] In 1990, the United States, United Kingdom, and France announced that future aid to Africa would be linked to democratic and human-rights performance.[7] The new political conditionality had a major impact: The number of *de jure* single-party regimes in the region fell from 29 in 1989 to zero in 1994.[8]

---

[1] Quoted in Rakner (2003: 103).

[2] In 1993, GDP per capita (at purchasing-power parity) in sub-Saharan Africa ($1,161) was close to five times lower than in the Americas ($5,301) and Europe and Central Asia ($5,735). In 1990, adult literacy in sub-Saharan Africa averaged 54 percent compared to 87 percent in Europe and Central Asia and 70 percent in the Americas (World Bank World Development Indicators (online: www.worldbank.org/data); see also Bratton and van de Walle 1997: 237–8).

[3] Bratton and van de Walle (1997).

[4] Olukoshi (1998).

[5] See Jackson and Rosberg (1982), Callaghy (1991), Jackman (1993), and Clapham (1996). In 1991, external assistance constituted 9.3 percent of GDP in Africa, compared to less than 1 percent in Latin America and Southeast Asia (Clapham 1996: 182–3; Chazan et al. 1999).

[6] See Moss (1995) and Alden (2000: 237–356). As Michaels (1993: 94) wrote, the end of the Cold War left the United States "free to pursue its own interests in Africa – and it found that it did not have any."

[7] Clapham (1996: 191–7).

[8] Bratton and van de Walle (1997: 8).

TABLE 6.1. *Organizational Power and Leverage in Africa*

	High Leverage	Medium/Low Leverage
High Organizational Power	Zimbabwe, Mozambique, Botswana, Tanzania	Gabon
Medium Organizational Power	Kenya, Senegal, Ghana	Cameroon
Low Organizational Power	Madagascar, Malawi, Benin, Mali, Zambia	

At the same time, transitions took place in a context of low linkage. Africa's economic ties to the West were minimal,[9] and information flows to and from the region were limited. In the early 1990s, Africa had the lowest density of telephone lines in the world, lacked virtually any internet connections, and was "severely underrepresented" in transnational human-rights networks.[10] Consequently, global events such as the fall of the Berlin Wall "mostly affected urban elites,"[11] and even large-scale human-rights abuses in Africa often "manage[d] to slip almost completely beneath the radar of the international media."[12] In the absence of strong ties, U.S. policy toward Africa was "marked by indifference ... and neglect."[13] Hence, external democratizing pressure was thin. The international community set a low threshold for democracy, routinely accepting elections that "fell far short of 'free and fair.'"[14] Between elections, government abuse often "met with little or no response" from donors.[15]

Within this common environment, cases varied on two key dimensions: organizational power and Western leverage (Table 6.1). Where incumbents possessed strong party and/or coercive structures (Mozambique, Tanzania, and Zimbabwe), enjoyed vast discretionary economic power (Botswana and Gabon), and/or benefited from black knight support (Cameroon and Gabon), competitive authoritarian regimes were stable. Where leverage was high and organizational power was either medium (Kenya and Senegal) or low (Benin, Madagascar, Malawi, Mali, and Zambia), regimes were unstable. In each of these cases, incumbents fell from power at least once. Turnover created an opportunity for democratization, and indeed, Benin and Mali democratized. More frequently, however, it brought another authoritarian government to power. Ghana, which democratized despite low linkage and a relatively strong incumbent, is an outlier.

[9] In the early 1990s, Africa received barely 1 percent of total U.S. exports and less than 0.5 percent of U.S. investment abroad (Michaels 1993: 95).

[10] Florini and Simmons (2000: 7).

[11] Bratton and van de Walle (1997: 136).

[12] Joseph (2003: 160); see also Schraeder (1994: 4–5).

[13] Schraeder (1996: 188). See also Herbst (1991a). Africa "consistently ranked last"

in terms of U.S. foreign-policy attention (Schraeder 1994: 2, 13–14); see also Moss 1995: 197–8). Thus, African states were "transformed from Cold War pawns ... into irrelevant international clutter" (Decalo 1998: 283).

[14] Lawson (1999: 6–7); see also Carothers (1997a), Joseph (1997, 1999a), and Diamond (1999: 55–6).

[15] Lawson (1999: 6–7).

ORGANIZATIONAL POWER AND AUTHORITARIAN STABILITY: ZIMBABWE, MOZAMBIQUE, BOTSWANA, AND TANZANIA

Four African cases are characterized by high or medium-high organizational power. In Mozambique and Zimbabwe, cohesive parties emerged from violent liberation struggles; in Tanzania, an extensive party organization developed under the tutelage of founding leader Julius Nyerere; and in Botswana, the ruling Botswana Democratic Party (BDP) benefited from discretionary economic power based on mineral wealth. In all four cases, competitive authoritarian regimes remained stable through 2008.

Zimbabwe

Conditions for democratization in Zimbabwe were more favorable than elsewhere in the region.[16] Zimbabwe possessed a history of electoral competition and judicial independence, a relatively strong civil society, and – beginning in the late 1990s – a well-organized and unified opposition. Nevertheless, competitive authoritarianism persisted through 2008. Although this outcome is often attributed to President Robert Mugabe's autocratic leadership,[17] it also was facilitated by the organizational tools that Mugabe had at his disposal, particularly an effective coercive apparatus and a strong governing party: the Zimbabwe African National Union (ZANU).

Linkage, Leverage, and Organizational Power

Zimbabwe combined high leverage and low linkage. In terms of leverage, the regime did not benefit from either black knight assistance or competing Western security issues.[18] In terms of linkage, years of international isolation had eroded Rhodesia's ties to the West. Zimbabwe's primary economic partner was South Africa,[19] international media and NGO penetration was limited,[20] and ZANU elites had few connections to the West.[21]

Organizational power was high. ZANU inherited a "remarkably efficient and brutal state."[22] The Rhodesian settler state was among the strongest in

---

[16] In the 1980s, Zimbabwe was one of the wealthiest countries in Africa, with a literacy rate of nearly 80 percent (Stoneman and Cliffe 1989: xv, 8).

[17] See Meredith (2002) and Chan (2003).

[18] Our leverage score requires a caveat. Although South Africa does not meet our criteria for black knight status (see Appendix II), it may have played such a role in Zimbabwe. As Zimbabwe's primary source of trade, investment, and energy (Herbst 1990: 129–30), South Africa possessed "immeasurably greater leverage than the U.S. or Britain"

(Blair 2002: 138–9). Hence, Western leverage may have been lower than our scoring suggests.

[19] Bowman (1973: 111–17); Stoneman and Cliffe (1989: xv); and Herbst (1990: 129–30).

[20] Due to weak media and NGO ties, massive repression in Matabeleland during the early 1980s was largely unreported in the West (Alexander and McGregor 1999: 258–61).

[21] See Stoneman and Cliffe (1989: 35) and Sylvester (1991: 166).

[22] Herbst (2000: 17).

Africa.[23] It penetrated the countryside and developed a "strong...capacity for controlling society."[24] During the 1970s counterinsurgency, the state developed a vast surveillance capacity and "formidable" military power.[25] The coercive apparatus was preserved – and expanded – after the end of white rule in 1980.[26] The Zimbabwe National Army (ZNA) was one of the largest and best equipped in Africa,[27] and the Central Intelligence Organization (CIO) was "even more formidable than under settler rule," penetrating civil society and operating spy networks throughout the country.[28] ZANU also created new coercive structures, including the notorious (North Korean-trained) Fifth Brigade and paramilitary groups such as the ZANU Youth Brigades.[29]

State cohesion was high. By most accounts, this cohesion was rooted in ZANU's guerrilla origins.[30] The ZNA "evolved out of a national struggle...in which the distinction between politicians and soldiers...was blurred."[31] Army commanders were drawn "primarily from the ranks of ex-guerrillas who fought against the settler regime," and security agencies were led by "war-hardened" ex-combatants who had shared the bush life together during the 1970s.[32] As late as 2000, the army, police, and CIO were led by ex-combatants.[33] The security forces demonstrated considerable discipline during the 1980s, surviving "a number of testing situations without fracturing."[34]

Party strength also was high. During the liberation struggle, ZANU established organizations throughout the countryside, which gave it a "stronger presence in rural areas than most African parties had at independence."[35] Building on

---

[23] See Weitzer (1984a, 1990), Herbst (1990, 2000), Du Toit (1995: 108–9), and Lodge (1998: 21, 29).

[24] Du Toit (1995: 108–9); see also Bowman (1973: 145–54), Weitzer (1984a, 1990), and Herbst (1990: 26).

[25] Evans (1992: 232–3). On the Rhodesian state's surveillance capacity, see Weitzer (1990: 145–6) and Ellert (1995). The Central Intelligence Organization (CIO) kept "lists of thousands of recruits" into the guerrilla movement (Ellert 1995: 94) and "was able to account for virtually every guerrilla coming into Rhodesia" (Flower 1987: 105).

[26] Weitzer (1984a, 1984b, 1990).

[27] See Weitzer (1990: 146) and Evans (1992: 236–40, 247). The 50,000-strong ZNA merged the Rhodesian and guerrilla armies. The army's professional capabilities were "probably unequalled in Southern Africa" (Evans: 1992: 240; MacBruce 1992: 235). Military intervention in Mozambique in the 1980s brought a "quantum leap in professionalization" (Evans 1992: 239, 245–6; Alao 1995: 114).

[28] Weitzer (1990: 145–6); see also Hatchard (1993: 31), Sithole (1998: 116–18), and Makumbe and Compagnon (2000: 6, 14, 290–1).

[29] See Evans (1992: 241–2), MacBruce (1992: 214–15), and Sithole (1993: 37).

[30] See Weitzer (1990), Alao (1995), and Chitiyo and Rupiya (2005). Also Herbst (2007).

[31] Alao (1995: 115). Although the ZNA hierarchy initially included ex-Rhodesian army officials and commanders from ZIPRA, a rival guerrilla army, by 1983 only ZANU-affiliated senior officials remained (Chitiyo and Rupiya 2005: 340–1). See also Weitzer (1984b: 113–14; 1990: 147).

[32] Weitzer (1990: 142, 143); see also Alao (1995: 112–16).

[33] Kriger (2000: 446).

[34] Evans (1992: 248) and Kriger (2003c: 199). According to Chitiyo and Rupiya (2005: 350), the liberation struggle explains "the general absence of coups and military indiscipline in Zimbabwe."

[35] Herbst (1990: 34); see also Cokorinos (1984: 35).

its guerrilla networks,[36] ZANU created party structures "at cell, branch, district, and province levels"; by 1984, it had developed a "nation-wide organizational structure ... from the village up to the national level."[37] Cohesion was high. Like the security forces, ZANU was dominated by ex-combatants who spent years together in the bush or in prison.[38] Indeed, unlike other ruling parties in the region, ZANU suffered "virtually no defections" during the late 1980s.[39]

Origins and Evolution of the Regime

Zimbabwe's competitive authoritarian regime emerged out of the 1979 Lancaster House Agreement that ended white rule. After winning the 1980 election, ZANU violently repressed the rival Zimbabwe African People's Union (ZAPU).[40] Following a "forced merger" between ZANU and ZAPU in 1987,[41] Zimbabwe appeared to be evolving into a "de facto one-party state."[42] However, proposals for formal single-party rule were abandoned in 1990 in the face of both domestic opposition – from civic and business associations and the embryonic Zimbabwe Unity Movement (ZUM) – and Western pressure.[43]

Zimbabwe thus entered the post–Cold War era with a competitive authoritarian regime. The playing field was highly uneven. ZANU was the sole recipient of public finance in the 1990s,[44] and the government punished businesses that sought to privately finance opposition.[45] Television and radio were state-owned and biased.[46] Opposition activity also was hindered by the Law and Order (Maintenance) Act, which restricted public meetings and banned speech deemed to "excite disaffection," and the Private Voluntary Organizations Act, under which NGOs could be "de-registered" in the "public interest."[47] Finally, the president appointed – directly or indirectly – 30 of 150 members of parliament, which meant that ZANU needed to win only 46 of 120 contested seats to gain a majority.[48]

ZANU was largely unchallenged during the 1990s.[49] External democratizing pressure was "virtually nonexistent,"[50] and domestic opposition forces lacked

[36] Stoneman and Cliffe (1989: 25) and Kriger (1991: 213–15).

[37] Nordlund (1996: 148). See also Nkiwane (1998: 105–6).

[38] Stoneman and Cliffe (1989: 35) and Meredith (2002: 34); see also *Africa Confidential*, February 17, 1995, p. 4 and November 10, 2000, p. 1).

[39] Nordlund (1996: 287); see also Makumbe and Compagnon (2000: 41).

[40] ZAPU leaders were exiled or imprisoned, and, in 1982, security forces launched a massive campaign of violence (Operation Gukurahundi) in the ZAPU stronghold of Matabeleland. See Weitzer (1990: 174), MacBruce (1992: 212–14), Nordlund (1996: 146–7), and Meredith (2002: 68–75).

[41] Nordlund (1996: 153–4).

[42] Kriger (2003a: 308); see also Makumbe and Compagnon (2000: 166). After the merger, ZANU held 99 of 100 seats in parliament.

[43] Makumbe (1991: 187), Sachikoyne (1991), Nordlund (1996: 161–3, 170–2), and Raftopoulos (2001: 10–11). According to Sithole (1993), there was also much opposition to single-party rule within ZANU.

[44] See Makumbe (1995: 184–9), Makumbe and Compagnon (2000); and National Democratic Institute (2000: 10). ZANU also financed itself through a party-run conglomerate, ZIDCO (Makumbe 1995: 186–7).

[45] Makumbe and Compagnon (2000: 14).

[46] Ronning (2003).

[47] Weitzer (1990: 72), Makumbe and Compagnon (2000: 95), and Raftopoulos (2000: 35–6).

[48] Chikuhwa (2004: 40).

[49] Laakso (2002a: 336).

[50] Clapham (1996: 204); see also Laakso (2002b: 444–5).

organization, resources, and even a minimal rural presence.[51] Although ZUM seriously contested the presidency in 1990,[52] violence, intimidation, and skewed access to media and finance allowed Mugabe to win 78 percent of the vote.[53] In the 1995 parliamentary and 1996 presidential elections, the playing field was so skewed that much of the opposition boycotted.[54] Thus, ZANU won a parliamentary majority in 1995 before a single vote was cast,[55] and Mugabe was reelected in 1996 with 93 percent of the vote.

CONTESTATION AND REPRESSION: 1997–2002. The first serious challenge to ZANU emerged in the late 1990s. Economic stagnation and an unpopular war in Congo generated broad public discontent manifested by a wave of strikes, student and veteran protests, and food riots in 1997 and 1998.[56] At the same time, civic and opposition forces strengthened. There was "an explosion in the number, variety, and geographical spread of civic groups."[57] The Zimbabwe Congress of Trade Unions (ZCTU), which had been "little more than a government appendage" in the 1980s,[58] evolved into a potent force.[59]

The ZCTU spearheaded a wave of social protest, including five successful "stay-aways" (general strikes) in 1997–1998.[60] In 1998, the ZCTU joined with church and civic groups to form the National Constitutional Assembly (NCA), which launched a constitutional-reform movement.[61] In 1999, NCA and ZCTU leaders created the Movement for Democratic Change (MDC).[62] Led by unionist Morgan Tsvangirai, the MDC united the opposition and built a national organization with considerable mobilizational capacity.[63] At the same time, the independent *Daily News* emerged as Zimbabwe's leading newspaper,[64] giving the opposition an important platform.

ZANU's electoral vulnerability was manifested in 2000. Seeking to preempt the NCA-led campaign for constitutional reform, the government drew up its

---

[51] Sylvester (1995), Makumbe (1995: 189–90), and Nkiwane (1998). The largest opposition party in the early 1990s, ZUM, had "no intelligible structures, no headquarters anywhere" (Sithole 1998: 117).

[52] Laakso (2002a: 335–6).

[53] Opposition parties were often denied permits to hold rallies, ZANU Youth broke up opposition rallies and attacked ZUM activists, and several ZUM candidates withdrew or went into hiding due to intimidation. See Makumbe (1991: 184), Quantin (1992: 35), Laakso (2002a: 335–6), and Meredith (2002: 91–3). On access to media and resources, see Makumbe (1991: 182–3) and Makumbe and Compagnon (2000: 197).

[54] Makumbe (1995: 184–9), Sithole (1997: 138), and Makumbe and Compagnon (2000). Opposition candidates Ndabaningi Sithole and Bishop Abel Muzorewa dropped out just prior to the 1996 presidential election. Sithole had earlier been arrested and spent part of the campaign in prison (Chan 2003: 208–9).

[55] See Laakso (2002a: 338). ZANU won 117 of 120 contested seats.

[56] Sithole (1998: 31; 1999: 85), Saunders (2001; 2007: 178–83), Meredith (2002: 148), and Blair (2002: 40).

[57] Saunders (2007: 179).

[58] Nordlund (1996: 216).

[59] Alexander (2000) and Saunders (2001).

[60] See Saunders (2001: 160–2, 2007: 180–3) and Sachikoyne (2001: 100). The December 1997 stay-away "brought the country to a standstill" (Saunders 2001: 160–2) and was described as the most successful strike in Zimbabwe's history (Raftopoulos 2001: 12). Overall, the number of labor actions increased fivefold between 1992 and 1997 (Saunders 2007: 176).

[61] Raftopoulos (2000: 39–40).

[62] Alexander (2000).

[63] Alexander (2000) and Raftopoulos (2001: 171).

[64] Ronning (2003: 209).

own reform proposal and put it to a referendum in February 2000.[65] The NCA and MDC launched a campaign for a "No" vote. Despite highly uneven access to media and resources,[66] nearly 55 percent of Zimbabweans voted "No," marking ZANU's first-ever electoral defeat.

The referendum defeat "shook ZANU-PF to the core."[67] With parliamentary (2000) and presidential (2002) elections approaching, the ruling party faced a "real possibility of losing power."[68] The Mugabe government responded with a massive land-reform program, accompanied by a wave of violent, state-sponsored land invasions carried out by war veterans and unemployed youth.[69] By June 2000, nearly 1,500 farms had been invaded.[70] Although the land reform was partly aimed at shoring up ZANU's rural support base, it also had clear repressive goals.[71] Government-backed war veterans "terrorized, raped, intimidated and killed alleged supporters of the MDC."[72] The land invasions thus become a "frontal assault" on the opposition, "effectively cordoning off large areas of the rural constituency from opposition politicians."[73]

The 2000 parliamentary election was marred by violence. Opposition meetings were blocked by police, MDC supporters were terrorized by war veterans and ZANU "youth brigades," and at least 10 districts were considered "no-go" areas for the MDC.[74] A monopoly over public finance, media bias, and voter intimidation allowed ZANU to win narrowly, capturing 48 percent of the vote (compared to 47 percent for the MDC) and 62 of 120 contested seats.[75] To preempt protest, the government unleashed a wave of repression in which MDC supporters "took a terrible beating."[76] The repression "sent a clear message to the MDC" about what would occur in the event of mass protest.[77] Indeed, a late-2000 mass-action campaign, inspired by the fall of Milošević in Serbia, was aborted after police mobilization made it clear that "the risk of being gunned down" was far greater than in Serbia.[78] The repression triggered a harsh international response,

[65] Cheater (2001).
[66] The government's advantages were such that "to call [the] referendum a David and Goliath contest does not go nearly far enough. It was a fight between an elephant and a mouse" (Blair 2002: 53–4).
[67] Meredith (2002: 165–6).
[68] Makumbe (2002: 89).
[69] See Kriger (2000b: 446; 2003c: 197), Laakso (2002b: 448), and Meredith (2002: 167–9).
[70] Meredith (2002: 183).
[71] Kriger (2003b).
[72] Laakso (2002b: 449). The war veterans also set up "reeducation camps" where suspected opposition supporters were beaten and tortured. See National Democratic Institute (2000: 25), Cheater (2001: 25–6), and Meredith (2002: 172).
[73] Raftopoulos (2001: 17)
[74] International Crisis Group (2000); National Democratic Institute (2000), and Stiff (2000: 303, 377, 404–6); Blair (2002: 149); Meredith (2002: 173–80). In April, the *Daily News* was firebombed (Stiff 2000: 277). Overall, human-rights groups reported 37 deaths and 5,000 incidents of political violence (Blair 2002: 158; Meredith 2002: 183).
[75] See National Democratic Institute (2000), Commonwealth Observer Group (2000), and Meredith (2002: 187–8). According to one study, ZANU received 29 times more television coverage than the MDC (Zaffiro 2002: 139).
[76] Chan (2003: 171).
[77] Raftopoulos (2001: 23).
[78] *Africa Today*, November 2000, p. 23–25, Raftopoulos (2001: 23), and Blair (2002: 193–6).

including U.S. sanctions.[79] However, the South African government refused to cooperate with the sanctions, providing the government a "crucial lifeline."[80]

The 2002 presidential election posed another serious challenge. Surveys showed MDC candidate Morgan Tsvangirai with a large lead.[81] Indeed, MDC leaders were "confident of victory,"[82] believing that the "enormous groundswell of anti-Mugabe sentiment . . . would translate into an election deluge that would submerge all attempts at electoral fraud."[83] Despite growing rank-and-file disaffection,[84] however, ZANU and the security forces closed ranks behind Mugabe,[85] which facilitated a repressive response.

Mugabe's survival strategy had several prongs. First, he assaulted the judiciary. The courts had remained relatively independent in the 1980s and 1990s[86]; however, in 2000, they began to threaten Mugabe's rule. The Supreme Court declared the government's land reform illegal and, in 2001, the High Court threw out the results of three parliamentary races due to violence.[87] In response, Mugabe moved against the courts. In late 2000, war veterans invaded the Supreme Court building and threatened to kill the justices if they did not resign.[88] Chief Justice Anthony Gubbay eventually stepped down, and by 2002, five Supreme Court and High Court justices had been purged.[89] The government also clamped down on media and opposition. The 2002 Access to Information and Protection of Privacy Act permitted a withdrawal of journalists' licenses for a wide range of "offenses."[90] The 2002 Public Order and Security Act required police permits for all political gatherings and banned speech that provoked "feelings of hostility" toward the president.[91] Finally, ZANU increased its use of violence. During the 2002 campaign, a paramilitary youth group known as the "Green Bombers" manned roadblocks in the countryside, broke up opposition rallies, and abducted and tortured hundreds of MDC supporters.[92] In parts of the countryside, the MDC was "effectively a banned organization."[93] Late in the campaign, Tsvangirai was arrested on trumped up charges of plotting to kill Mugabe.[94]

---

[79] See Raftopoulos (2002: 417) and Laakso (2002b: 449–56).
[80] Kriger (2003a: 312) and Chimanikire (2003: 187).
[81] *Africa Confidential*, August 10, 2001, p. 4 and *Africa Today*, January 2002, p. 15. See also Hill (2003: 160).
[82] Blair (2003: 254).
[83] Raftopoulos (2002: 418).
[84] *Africa Today*, December 2000, pp. 20–22 and February 2001, p. 29, *Africa Report*, January 2001, p. 25.
[85] See Kriger (2003c: 199) and Bauer and Taylor (2005: 200).
[86] Weitzer (1984b: 94–100) and Ncube (2001: 114–18). As late as 2000, the courts struck down parts of the Law and Order (Maintenance) Act as unconstitutional and voided the

arrests of *Standard* editor Mark Chavunduka and MDC leader Morgan Tsvangirai (Meredith 2002: 155–6; Chikuhwa 2004: 43, 53).
[87] Meredith (2002: 197–8, 217).
[88] Chan (2003: 166–7).
[89] Makumbe (2002: 95) and Meredith (2002: 206–7).
[90] Ronning (2003: 219–22) and Chikuhwa (2004: 122–3). More than 70 journalists were arrested under this law during 2002 and 2003 (Chikuhwa 2004: 123).
[91] Human Rights Watch (2003a: 2, 7).
[92] Blair (2003: 249). Overall, at least 33 people were killed in 2002 (Blair 2003: 257; Chikuhwa 2004: 130).
[93] *Africa Today*, January 2002, p. 15.
[94] Raftopoulos (2002: 419). Tsvangirai was acquitted in 2004.

The 2002 presidential election was rigged. New laws made it difficult for opposition supporters to register and vote,[95] and, on election eve, the government reduced the number of polling places in Harare, Bulawayo, and other MDC strongholds.[96] The resulting delays prevented at least 350,000 urban residents from voting.[97] Mugabe's victory – with 56 percent of the vote – was rejected by "virtually the entire Western world."[98]

Although opposition forces called a stay-away and announced plans for "indefinite mass action,"[99] protest again fizzled in the face of repression.[100] Security forces attacked MDC members, militias "ranged the countryside assaulting known and suspected MDC supporters,"[101] riot police "invaded campuses... beating students to a pulp," and "the dreaded Central Intelligence Organization [was] everywhere."[102] The stay-away was a "dismal failure,"[103] and later efforts to "kick-start mass action" were "met with instant arrest and torture in prison."[104] In mid-2003, the MDC launched a "final push" – including a week-long stay-away – that generated talk of a "Milošević moment."[105] However, the arrest of hundreds of opposition activists, heavy deployment of riot police, and armed roadblocks on all roads leading into Harare defused the protest.[106] By late 2003, MDC leaders admitted that the party "had tried but been incapable of organizing a mass action."[107]

REGIME SURVIVAL AMID ECONOMIC COLLAPSE, 2003–2008. After 2002, Zimbabwe fell into an extraordinary crisis. Western sanctions were tightened and the country became an international pariah.[108] At the same time, Zimbabwe suffered an "economic collapse of an almost unprecedented scale."[109] By 2007, GDP had contracted by 40 percent, inflation had surpassed 1,500 percent, and the country was suffering widespread hunger.[110] Nevertheless, ZANU remained intact.[111] Despite internal conflict over the looming presidential succession, "party leaders... rallied around Mugabe."[112] Top military officials – nearly all of them ex-liberation fighters – gained influence as decision making shifted to a Joint Operation Command (JOC) dominated by security officials.[113]

---

[95] See Makumbe (2002: 96), Raftopoulos (2002: 417), and Blair (2003: 246).
[96] Blair (2003: 258) and Hill (2003: 180).
[97] *Africa Today*, March-April 2002, p. 24 and Makumbe (2002: 97).
[98] Hill (2003: 182). See also Chikuhwa (2004: 126–7).
[99] *Africa Confidential*, March 22, 2002, p. 1. See also Raftopoulos (2002: 423–4).
[100] Raftopoulos (2002: 424).
[101] Makumbe (2002: 99).
[102] *Africa Today*, February 2003, p. 27.
[103] *Africa Today*, April-May 2002, p. 25 and Raftopoulos (2002: 424). Failure was rooted partly in the fact that MDC leaders were "unwilling to consider" mass action "given the vast repressive machinery that would confront them" (Raftopoulos 2002: 418).
[104] *Africa Today*, April 2003, p. 21.

[105] *Africa Confidential*, May 30, 2003, p. 3, June 13, 2003, p. 1, and July 25, 2003, p. 3; See also LeBas (2006: 419–20).
[106] LeBas (2006: 420).
[107] LeBas (2006: 433).
[108] Raftopoulos (2002: 422–3) and Chikuhwa (2004: 126–7).
[109] Moss (2007: 134).
[110] Moss (2007: 134–5).
[111] *Africa Confidential* observed in late 2002 that "in 22 years of independence, no more than a handful of [ZANU] politicians have defected" (December 20, 2002, p. 1).
[112] *Africa Today*, April-May 2002, p. 21; see also International Crisis Group (2005: 10–12) and LeBas (2006: 431).
[113] Ndlovu-Gatsheni (2006) and Human Rights Watch (2008b).

Repression intensified after 2002. The MDC was "treated as if it were a banned organization," and 48 of its 55 MPs were arrested between 2000 and 2004.[114] In 2004, *The Daily News* was closed down, leaving all major media outlets in pro-government hands.[115] The government also employed high-intensity coercion, such as the 2005 Operation Murambatsvina ("Drive out Rubbish"), a violent sweep of informal traders – aimed at "cleansing" MDC urban strongholds – in which some 30 thousand people were detained and hundreds of thousands were displaced.[116] The operation cost ZANU public support but it "appears to have met the government's primary objective of preempting an anti-state uprising."[117] Repression weakened the opposition.[118] The MDC's rural structures "disintegrated" and the party suffered a schism in 2005.[119] The ZCTU also weakened, and the NCA's capacity to mobilize was "all but eliminated."[120] Thus, despite Archbishop Pius Ncube's call for a Ukrainian-style uprising after ZANU won fraud-ridden legislative elections in 2005,[121] mass protest "predictably did not materialize."[122]

ZANU failed to reconsolidate power, however. After 2005, Zimbabwe's economy descended into hyperinflation and the basic capacities of the state eroded.[123] In this context, support for ZANU evaporated, even in its rural strongholds.[124] Moreover, the looming issue of succession – Mugabe was 84 years old in 2008 – generated intraparty tension.[125] Although Mugabe's decision to seek reelection in 2008 may have prevented a more serious conflict, it nevertheless triggered the defection of ex-Finance Minister Simba Makoni, who launched an independent presidential bid backed by a handful of ZANU defectors.[126]

The first round of 2008 parliamentary and presidential elections were less violent than those of 2002. Tsvangirai and Makoni were able to campaign throughout the country, which – given the level of public discontent – allowed them to mount a serious challenge.[127] The MDC won the parliamentary race,[128] and when early presidential returns showed Tsvangirai ahead, state officials undertook a

---

[114] *Africa Today*, February 2004, p. 21.

[115] *New York Times*, December 10, 2004, p. A5 and *Africa Confidential*, March 18, 2005, p. 1.

[116] See International Crisis Group (2005: 14–15) and Bratton and Masunungure (2006).

[117] Bratton and Masunungure (2006: 41–4).

[118] LeBas (2006); Saunders (2007).

[119] LeBas (2006: 433). The MDC organization weakened considerably (Blair 2002: 246; International Crisis Group 2005: 13). As of 2004, the party lacked resources to pay its employees or telephone bills. See *Africa Confidential*, April 16, 2004, p. 2.

[120] Saunders (2007: 187–8). According to Blair (2003: 281), the ZCTU was transformed into a "penniless, drifting shambles."

[121] *Africa Confidential*, April 1, 2005, p. 8 and Bratton and Masunungure (2006: 26).

[122] *Africa Today*, May 2005, p. 33. MDC leaders shied away from protest "because they would be bloodily suppressed" (*The Economist*, April 9, 2005, p. 39). Consequently, "the situation did not evolve as in Georgia, Ukraine and Kyrgyzstan" (International Crisis Group 2005: 1).

[123] Moss (2007).

[124] Human Rights Watch (2008b).

[125] International Crisis Group (2005).

[126] *Africa Research Bulletin*, February 2008, p. 17422.

[127] *Africa Research Bulletin*, April 2008, p. 17484; see also Human Rights Watch (2008a).

[128] Tsvangirai's MDC won 100 seats and a breakaway MDC faction won an additional 10. ZANU won 99 seats. The ruling party retained control of the senate, however.

large-scale falsification of the results.[129] Thus, although Tsvangirai is widely believed to have won a first-round majority, official results gave him only 47.9 percent (compared to 43.2 percent for Mugabe), sending the election to a runoff.[130] During the second round, ZANU orchestrated a massive wave of violence in which at least 36 MDC activists were killed.[131] In the face of this repression, the MDC withdrew from the race. Despite widespread international calls for Mugabe's resignation, including from neighboring Botswana and Zambia, ZANU held firm.

In 2009, after months of internationally sponsored negotiations, Mugabe and Tsvangirai agreed to a "unity government" in which Tsvangirai would serve as prime minister and the MDC gained several important ministries. Nevertheless, Mugabe remained president and the coercive apparatus remained under ZANU control.

In summary, the 2000–2008 period was one of striking regime durability.[132] Despite nearly a decade of international isolation and a historic economic collapse, the Mugabe government was able to use coercive force to systematically preempt or thwart protest. Indeed, despite considerable rank-and-file disaffection, the security forces – led by veterans from the liberation struggle – remained sufficiently disciplined to carry out high-intensity coercion. In contrast to other cases in the region, where economic (Zambia) or succession (Kenya) crises triggered large-scale defection, ZANU suffered few defections. Given the depth of Zimbabwe's economic collapse and the looming succession crisis, ZANU's future remained uncertain in 2010. Nevertheless, the regime proved more far robust than other regimes in the region, including many that faced less severe crises.

Mozambique

Like Zimbabwe, Mozambique is a case of competitive authoritarian stability, rooted in cohesive state and party structures that emerged from a violent anticolonial struggle and civil war. A cohesive ruling party, the Front for the Liberation of Mozambique (Frelimo), limited elite defection and facilitated incumbent control over state institutions. Regime cohesion, together with a decline in international attention after the first post-conflict elections in 1994, allowed Frelimo to reconsolidate power in the late 1990s and 2000s.

Linkage, Leverage, and Organizational Power
Mozambique is a case of high leverage and low linkage. A small and impoverished state, Mozambique was a proxy in Cold War geopolitical competition

---

[129] *Africa Research Bulletin*, March 2008, pp. 17448–9 and April 2008, p. 17484. See also Human Rights Watch (2008a, 2008b).

[130] *Africa Research Bulletin*, April 2008, p. 17484. Makoni won 8.3 percent of the vote.

[131] In a campaign known as Operation Where Did You Put Your Vote?, security forces and war veterans engaged in large-scale abduction, beating, torture, and killing. MDC offices were raided and political rallies were banned. Hundreds of MDC leaders and activists were arrested, and more than 2,000 people were beaten and tortured in "reeducation" meetings. See Human Rights Watch (2008b) and *Africa Research Bulletin*, April 2008, pp. 17484–17486.

[132] The regime survived three terms since the end of the Cold War and five terms overall.

in the 1980s. Locked in a civil war against the South African–backed Mozambican National Resistance (Renamo), the government relied heavily on Soviet military and economic assistance.[133] When this aid ended, the regime became heavily dependent on the West.[134] By the early 1990s, international assistance constituted as much as three quarters of Mozambique's GDP.[135] Thus, the regime was highly vulnerable to external pressure; indeed, the 1990–1994 UN-led peace process subjected Mozambique to heavy international intervention.[136]

Organizational power in Mozambique was medium high. State coercive structures were low in scope. The security forces, which had expanded rapidly after independence,[137] were devastated by civil war and economic crisis in the 1980s. Indeed, the state lost control over much of Central Mozambique to Renamo.[138] The 1992 Rome Peace Accords allowed Frelimo to reassert a minimum of territorial control.[139] However, they also mandated a military restructuring that left the army small and poorly equipped.[140] Indeed, the security forces were widely viewed as ineffective in the 1980s.[141]

By contrast, state cohesion was high. The security forces were forged out of a violent liberation struggle, and Frelimo subsequently penetrated the state's coercive agencies at all levels.[142] Although army cohesion was undermined by the post-1992 restructuring,[143] the police force – which served as the regime's main internal security force – remained intact.[144] Dominated by Frelimo, the police hierarchy maintained "a strong *esprit de corps*," with a "sense of solidarity rooted in a history of political struggle."[145]

Party strength was medium high. Scope was medium. Under single-party rule, Frelimo was largely fused with the state.[146] Although it never took on the mass character of the CCM in Tanzania, the party maintained a grassroots infrastructure with mass labor, youth, women's organizations, and its cells were found – at least nominally – "in the most remote rural areas and in every enterprise."[147]

---

[133] Ayisi (1991: 25), Seeger (1996: 132, 146), and Lala and Ostheimer (2004: 5).

[134] The withdrawal of Soviet Bloc assistance cost Mozambique an estimated $150 million annually (Plank 1993: 410). See also Finnegan (1992: 130), Simpson (1993: 332–3), and Alden (2001: 94).

[135] See Ayisi (1991: 24), Plank (1993: 407, 411), and Lloyd (1995: 152).

[136] Meldrum (1993a, 1993b), Alden (2001), and Manning (2002b).

[137] With Soviet support, the army expanded from 10,000 in the mid-1970s to as many as 70,000 by the early 1980s (Malache, Macaringue, and Borges Coelho 2005: 165, 172).

[138] Finnegan (1992: 60, 77) and Malache, Macaringue, and Borges Coelho (2005: 175–6).

[139] Monteiro (2000: 40) and Lodge, Kadima, and Pottie (2002: 206).

[140] Malache et al. (2005: 179–83); see also Young (1996). It is worth noting that many of the army's troops, supplies, and budgetary allocations were transferred to the Frelimo-dominated police force, which expanded in size. See Chachiua (2000) and Leao (2004).

[141] US. Department of State (1995b), Chachiua (2000), Alden (2001: 61), and Leao (2004).

[142] Malache Macaringue, and Borges Coelho (2005: 162–3, 169). The party exercised considerable control over the army and police (Seeger 1996: 145; Baker 2003: 149), and there were no major rebellions or coup attempts between 1975 and 1990 (Lala and Ostheimer 2004: 50).

[143] As part of the restructuring, Renamo officials were incorporated into the army (Young 1996; Leao 2004).

[144] Chachiua (2000) and Leao (2004).

[145] Rauch and Van DerSpuy (2006: 112).

[146] Carbone (2003) and Manning (2005).

[147] Manning (2005: 230).

With the formal separation of state and party in 1990, Frelimo's grassroots structures languished somewhat, particularly in the hinterlands.[148] However, Frelimo used its control over the state to rebuild an effective party structure, which eventually encompassed 30 thousand *celulas* and more than 1 million members. Thus it remained the "dominant organization" in Mozambique.[149]

Party cohesion was high. Like ZANU, Frelimo was "profoundly influenced by the experience of the independence struggle."[150] The violent struggle against Portuguese rule transformed Frelimo from a broad anticolonial movement into a disciplined, ideologically committed vanguard party.[151] Frelimo thus "inherited a military ethos" from the liberation war,[152] and this ethos was reinforced by civil war in the 1980s.[153] The impact of the liberation struggle was seen in the predominance of ex-guerrilla fighters (*antigos combatentes*) in the Frelimo leadership: In 1989, 9 of 10 politburo members were veterans of the liberation struggle.[154] Viewed as "guarantors of superior ethics ... in the face of the new and allegedly more corruptible politicians brought to the fore by multiparty politics,"[155] the *antigos combatentes* were "accorded unquestioned leadership and privileges" and they remained influential in the party leadership throughout the 1990s.[156] A final sign of cohesion was Frelimo's two successful leadership successions before 1990: after the 1969 assassination of founder Eduardo Mondlane and after the 1986 death of President Samora Machel.[157]

Origins and Evolution of the Regime

Like Cambodia (Chapter 7) and Nicaragua (Chapter 4), Mozambique's transition to competitive authoritarianism was rooted in an international settlement of a Cold War conflict. Soon after independence in 1975, Mozambique had been plunged into a civil war between the Soviet-backed Frelimo government and the Rhodesian/South African–backed Renamo. By the late 1980s, the civil war had crippled the economy and left an estimated 700,000 dead.[158] Desperate for assistance in the wake of Soviet withdrawal, Frelimo had little choice but to turn to the West.[159] Under "immense pressure" from the international community,[160] the government adopted a multiparty constitution and entered internationally sponsored peace negotiations with Renamo, which culminated in the 1992 Rome Accords.[161] Under the Accords, Renamo was legalized and presidential and parliamentary elections were held in 1994.

---

[148] Manning (2002b: 130–1; 2005: 230–1).
[149] Carbone (2003: 9–10; 2005: 430) and The Carter Center (2005: 30–1).
[150] Carbone (2003: 5). See also Henriksen (1978).
[151] See Henriksen (1978), Munslow (1983: 82), Simpson (1993), and Alden (2001: 115).
[152] Alexander (1997: 3).
[153] According to Finnegan (1992: 111), 10 years of fighting "produced a powerfully disciplined, unusually mature political movement with a leadership deeply committed to the idea of unity."

[154] Finnegan (1992: 111). Through 1995, all Frelimo general secretaries were *antigos combatentes* (Manning 2005: 231).
[155] Carbone (2005: 430).
[156] Carbone (2003: 5). See also Manning (2005: 234).
[157] Sidaway and Simon (1993: 17).
[158] Austin (1994).
[159] Bowen (1992: 272), Plank (1993), Simpson (1993), and Harrison (1996: 20).
[160] Harrison (1996: 20).
[161] Alden and Simpson (1993) and Simpson (1993).

The 1992–1994 transition was characterized by large-scale international intervention, including the presence of more than 7,000 UN peacekeepers.[162] International actors closely scrutinized the 1994 electoral process,[163] ensuring the selection of a nonpartisan head of the electoral commission and guarantees of equal access to the media.[164] Foreign intervention also helped level the financial playing field: Renamo received millions of dollars in external financing to compensate for Frelimo's huge advantage in business contributions.[165] Finally, 2,500 foreign observers monitored the election, and the UN worked to place "at least four trained observers" at virtually every polling station.[166] In elections that were widely considered free,[167] President Joaquim Chissano defeated Renamo leader Afonso Dhlakama by a margin of 53 to 34 percent. Frelimo won a narrow parliamentary majority.[168]

Although the UN intervention brought an unprecedented level of pluralism, Mozambique nevertheless remained competitive authoritarian. As in Cambodia (see Chapter 7), international actors failed to dislodge Frelimo from the state.[169] Although state and party were formally delinked after 1990, the separation was "largely an artificial one," as key elements of the old party-state remained intact.[170] Thus, Frelimo retained tight control over the courts and the police, which they routinely wielded against the opposition.[171] Frelimo also deployed public buildings, employees, and other resources for partisan ends,[172] and it used its control of the state to maintain a near-monopoly over private-sector finance.[173] For example, the government routinely allocated licenses, subsidies, and credit to friendly entrepreneurs, who in turn financed Frelimo.[174] Entrepreneurs who backed the opposition were said to "commit economic suicide" in the form of licensing delays and loss of subsidized credits.[175] Finally, the government violated civil liberties. Renamo protests were often broken up, at times violently,[176] and although the post-1994 media environment was considered relatively free

---

[162] See Meldrum (1993a, 1993b), Alden and Simpson (1993), and Alden (2001).
[163] On external financing of the election, see Turner, Nelson, and Mahling-Clark (1998: 156) and Alden (2001: 62).
[164] Alden (2001: 46) and Manning (2002b: 168).
[165] Synge (1997: 60). See also Isaacs (1993: 42) and Turner, Nelson, and Mahling-Clark (1998: 160). In addition, such financing was used to encourage Renamo to participate in the peace process.
[166] Turner, Nelson, and Mahling-Clark (1998: 157); see also Lloyd (1995: 154) and Manning (2002b: 169–70). The vote-counting process was particularly well scrutinized. Ballots were counted at the local and provincial levels and were then flown to Maputo to be "scrutinized for a third time" (Isaacs 1995: 21, also Turner, Nelson, and Mahling-Clark 1998: 162).
[167] Manning (2002b).

[168] Frelimo won 129 of 250 seats, Renamo gained 112, and the Democratic Union gained 9.
[169] The Chissano government rejected Western calls for full-scale power-sharing. See Alden (2001: 63), Manning (2002b: 176), and Weinstein (2002: 152).
[170] Carbone (2003: 10); see also Harrison (1994).
[171] Leao (2004).
[172] Hanlon (2000: 595), Carbone (2003: 10), and Lala and Ostheimer (2004: 13).
[173] See Meldrum (1993b: 48–9), Harrison (1994: 433), Alden (2001: 75–6), and The Carter Center (2005: 31–2).
[174] The Carter Center (2005: 31).
[175] The Carter Center (2005: 31–2). See also Lala and Ostheimer (2004: 13).
[176] U.S. Department of State (1998c). See also Human Rights Watch, "World Report 1998: Mozambique" (http://www.hrw.org).

by African standards,[177] journalists occasionally faced arrest or libel suits, which encouraged self-censorship.[178]

Two factors facilitated Frelimo's reconsolidation of power after 1994. First, international involvement "dropped off dramatically," largely because Mozambique was viewed as having entered a period of "normal politics."[179] Renamo continued to seek foreign intervention, viewing the international community as a critical "third force"; however, these appeals never induced external punitive action.[180] Second, Frelimo remained cohesive in the face of Renamo challenges.[181] Despite holding only a narrow legislative majority, iron-clad discipline – reinforced by the predominance of the "historic generation" – allowed Frelimo to retain control of parliament.[182] Thus, unlike Benin, Madagascar, and Malawi, where weak parties cost presidents control of the legislature, Frelimo's internal discipline meant that "parliament's oversight function on government [was] almost nonexistent."[183] Party discipline and firm legislative control allowed Frelimo to weaken nominally independent institutions and prevent them from serving – as they did, at times, in Benin and Malawi – as effective checks on executive power. For example, although the National Elections Commission included opposition representatives, much of the Commission's authority – including day-to-day management of elections – was transferred to a Technical Secretariat for Election Administration that was "staffed entirely by government employees" and clearly biased.[184]

Elections after 1994 were less clean. The government imposed onerous registration requirements for the 1998 municipal elections, leaving Frelimo unopposed in 19 of 33 municipalities.[185] Renamo boycotted the election, allowing Frelimo to win every race.[186] The 1999 elections were badly flawed – and possibly stolen.[187] The presidential race, which again pitted Chissano against Dhlakama, received far less international attention than the 1994 election,[188] thereby expanding the government's room to maneuver. Frelimo massively abused state resources, and independent observers raised "serious doubts... regarding the probity of the [vote] counting process."[189] Chissano was declared the winner by a small margin, and Frelimo captured a narrow parliamentary majority.[190] Although Western donors "gloss[ed] over poll irregularities" and accepted the results,[191] Renamo rejected the election and boycotted parliament. In November

[177] See MISA (1998). Although most media remained in state hands, the most important news source, the state-owned Radio Mozambique, was not heavily biased (U.S. Department of State 1998c, 2005f).

[178] See Seleti (2000: 357), Hanlon (2002), and Lala and Ostheimer (2004: 13).

[179] Manning (2001b: 6; 2002b: 185–91); see also Hanlon (2000: 593) and Alden (2001: 65).

[180] Manning (2005: 240).

[181] Alden (2001: 115).

[182] Manning (2002a: 67–9; 2005: 234–5).

[183] Lala and Ostheimer (2004: 33).

[184] Manning (2001a: 154).

[185] Manning (2002b: 191–2).

[186] Wood (1999: 163).

[187] See Manning (2002b: 194–199) and de Brito (2007: 1); see also *Africa Confidential*, February 4, 2000, p. 5.

[188] Mondlane (2003: 200).

[189] Manning (2005: 241).

[190] Chissano won 52 percent of the vote compared to 48 percent for Dhlakama, and Frelimo captured 133 of 250 seats in parliament.

[191] *Africa Confidential*, February 4, 2000, p. 5; see also Manning (2005: 421).

2000, opposition street demonstrations were violently repressed by police, resulting in more than 40 deaths.[192] That month, Carlos Cardoso, a prominent journalist, was killed – an event that had a chilling effect on local journalism.[193]

Frelimo's strength was again manifested after 2001, when Chissano decided not to seek reelection in 2004. In 2002, the Frelimo Central Committee selected Armando Guebuza, a member of the "historic generation," as the party's 2004 presidential candidate. Unlike Kenya, Malawi, and Zambia, where presidential succession threw weaker parties into crisis, Frelimo's succession was remarkably smooth, as the party quickly rallied behind Guebuza.[194]

The 2004 presidential election was marred by uneven access to finance, abuse of state resources, and "serious irregularities," including ballot-box stuffing and manipulation of the vote count.[195] Frelimo won easily: Guebuza defeated Dhlakama with 64 percent of the vote, and Frelimo won 160 of 250 seats in parliament. In 2009, Guebuza was reelected in a landslide (defeating Dhlakama by a margin of 75 to 16 percent).[196]

In summary, Frelimo's continued domination under competitive authoritarian rule after 1990 can be attributed to two main factors. First, international pressure, which was decisive in the 1992–1994 political opening, largely disappeared after 1994. Second, high party cohesion – rooted in the liberation struggle – allowed Frelimo to hang together in the face of both strong electoral challenges and the challenge of leadership succession.

Tanzania

Tanzania is another case of competitive authoritarian stability rooted in governing party strength. Tanzania combined low linkage and high leverage: It was poor and aid-dependent, and it lacked black knight support.[197] Organizational power was medium high. Coercive capacity was medium. Although Tanzania never developed an extensive internal security apparatus comparable to Zimbabwe, there were no significant territories outside the control of the national government.[198] The coercive apparatus was not forged out a liberation struggle or large-scale military conflict, but it demonstrated a history of internal discipline prior to 1990.[199] Hence, we score cohesion as medium.

---

[192] Manning (2002c: 79).

[193] Committee to Protect Journalists (CPJ), "Attacks on the Press 2001: Mozambique" (http://www.cpj.org). See also Manning (2005: 245).

[194] See de Brito (2007).

[195] The Carter Center (2005: 12, 31–9, 51–2).

[196] The election led *Africa Confidential* to observe that "Frelimo's grip over the country is now total." See "Mozambique: A Dominant Party – Not a One Party State," *Africa Confidential* November 6, 2009 (online: www.africa-confidential.com).

[197] In 1990, foreign assistance constituted 48 percent of GNP – one of the highest figures in the world (Vener 2000: 134).

[198] The military was also relatively strong. In 1978, Tanzania successfully invaded Uganda in response to a military incursion on its northern border (Mambo and Schofield 2007).

[199] Indeed, Tanzania was one of the few African states to have maintained civilian rule throughout the post-independence period (Zirker 1992).

Party strength was medium high. The ruling Chama Cha Mapinduzi (CCM) was an unusually strong party.[200] Founding President Julius Nyerere invested heavily in party-building, both during and after colonial rule.[201] The Tanganyika African National Union (TANU) mobilized one million members – nearly one in five adults – in the early 1960s.[202] After independence, TANU built "one of the most extensive party organizations in Africa,"[203] with a grassroots structure based on thousands of neighborhood-level "10 House Party Cells" (or "10 Cells").[204] The party penetrated society down to the village and workplace levels.[205] TANU 10 Cells played a central role in the life of many villages, settling disputes between neighbors and punishing husbands who beat their wives.[206] Renamed CCM in 1977 after a merger with Zanzibar's Afro-Shirazi Party, the party maintained a powerful grassroots organization into the 1990s.[207] The 10-cell structure remained active in communities across the country, giving the CCM a permanent village-level presence that no opposition party could match.[208] Party cohesion was medium. The CCM was an established machine with a track record of internal discipline, but it lacked the history of violent struggle that characterized ruling parties in Mozambique and Zimbabwe.

Tanzania's transition to competitive authoritarianism was externally driven. The country had maintained *de jure* single-party rule since shortly after independence in 1961, and it underwent a smooth succession in 1985 when President Nyerere retired and was replaced by Ali Hassan Mwinyi as President.[209] The domestic push for democracy was limited.[210] Opposition parties were small and inconsequential,[211] and after decades of party control over associational life, civil society was "quite weak, even by African standards."[212] Thus, the transition was largely a preemptive response to changing international conditions, driven by a desire to "stay in the good graces of international donors."[213] In early 1990, shortly after a CCM delegation witnessed "first hand" the fall of Ceaușescu in Romania, Nyerere called for a move toward multiparty rule.[214]

[200] See Okumu and Holmquist (1984), Barkan (1994), and Mihyo (2003).
[201] Bienen (1967).
[202] Iliffe (1979: 536) and Coulson (1982: 115).
[203] Okumu and Holmquist (1984: 50).
[204] Ingle (1972) and O'Barr (1972).
[205] Mihyo (2003).
[206] Ingle (1972: 214–18) and O'Barr (1972: 446–7).
[207] See Pinkney (1997: 205), Gros (1998b: 108), and Mihyo (2003).
[208] Lucan Way interview with Bashiru Ally, researcher in the Political Science Department, University of Dar es Salaam, 20 November 2007.
[209] Nyerere remained head of the CCM until 1990 when Mwinyi took over.
[210] As one observer noted, "[t]he mass stirrings and protests for change that marked other

African transitions in the 1990s were conspicuously absent in Tanzania" (ARD, Inc. 2003: 3). See also Hyden (1999) and Tripp (2000).
[211] Hyden (1999).
[212] Hyden (1999: 149). On party control over associational life, see Barkan (1994: 20), Mmuya and Chaligha (1994: 37), Pinkney (1997: 112), and Mihyo (2003: 66).
[213] Tripp (2000: 197). See also Hyden (1999). Recalling an old Swahili saying, Nyerere noted that "When you see your neighbor being shaved, you should wet your beard. Otherwise you could get a rough shave." Quoted in Morna (1990: 24).
[214] "Tanzanian leader suggests multi-party state." *United Press International* 22 February 1990 (online: www.lexisnexis.com).

Two years later, encouraged by donors,[215] the government ended one-party rule and scheduled multiparty elections for 1995.

The regime liberalized considerably in the early 1990s. Opposition activity was largely unfettered on the mainland and media frequently criticized the government.[216] Nevertheless, the persistence of de facto state-party ties skewed the playing field.[217] The CCM continued to receive state subsidies, and it retained control over much of the state's infrastructure, including buildings, stadiums, and vehicles.[218] As one opposition activist complained, "In many areas, every open space is owned by the CCM. There are simply no places that we can hold meetings other than on the road side."[219] Moreover, close state–business ties – as well as the CCM's own business holdings – gave the party a virtual monopoly over private-sector finance, creating enormous resource advantages.[220] The media playing field also was skewed. Although private radio and television stations were permitted beginning in 1994, their reach was largely limited to the capital, which meant that the CCM received "far more media exposure than opposition parties."[221] In addition, draconian media laws allowed the government to "arrest, harass, and detain journalists, editors, and publishers, and to close down newspapers."[222] Finally, the CCM retained tight partisan control over the electoral authorities.[223] In the context of such an uneven playing field, CCM leaders could boast that the party did not "need to cheat" because victory was assured in any case.[224]

The 1995 elections were described as "hotly contested."[225] The CCM had suffered several defections,[226] and one of them, ex–Deputy Prime Minister Augustine Mrema, emerged as a serious presidential contender. The elections were marred by "serious irregularities," including arbitrary disqualification of opposition candidates and manipulation of the vote count.[227] In the semi-autonomous island of Zanzibar, opposition leaders were arrested, protesters were repressed, and local elections were fraudulent.[228] CCM candidate Benjamin

[215] Vener (2000: 139). See also Chege (1994).
[216] On media conditions, see Ngaiza (1999) and Tripp (2000: 207–11). Also see Committee to Protect Journalists (2000) and Freedom House, "Freedom of the Press 2003: Tanzania" (http://www.freedomhouse.org).
[217] ARD, Inc. (2003: 2) and Hoffman and Robinson (2009).
[218] Mihyo (2003: 87).
[219] Lucan Way interview with Wilbrod Slaa, Arusha, 29 November 2007.
[220] The CCM used its control of the state to develop a range of businesses – including paid parking lots, mining enterprises, and food-processing plants – that served as an important source of party income (Mwase and Raphael 2001: 259; Bryan and Baer 2005: 129). Also Lucan Way interview with Max Mmuya, professor of Political Science, University of Dar es Salaam, 19 November

2007. The financial playing field was further skewed in 2000 with the elimination of state funding for parties (Electoral Institute of Southern Africa [EISA] 2006: 3, 21–2).
[221] Hoffman and Robinson (2009: 130). See Tripp (2000: 209) and EISA (2006); see also Freedom House, "Freedom in the World 2002: Tanzania" (http://www.freedomhouse.org).
[222] Tripp (2000: 209).
[223] Mwase and Raphael (2001: 255) and Karume (2005: 9–10).
[224] Hoffman and Robinson (2009: 123).
[225] Mwase and Raphael (2001: 264).
[226] Maliyamkono (1995: 19) and Snoeks and McKendy (1996: 15–16).
[227] Gros (1998b: 107) and Mwase and Raphael (2001).
[228] *Africa Confidential*, November 3, 1995, p. 5.

William Mkapa – Mwinyi's successor – won easily, with 62 percent of the vote, and the CCM captured about 80 percent of parliament.[229]

The CCM was not seriously challenged after 1995, despite relatively low levels of repression. This outcome was rooted in a combination of CCM strength and a skewed playing field. The CCM's mass organization allowed it to distribute patronage and effectively mobilized votes throughout the country. The party was said to know "every voter by name,"[230] as well as "what his or her political position is and material needs are."[231] At the same time, the CCM's virtual monopoly over resources and media access hindered the development of a viable opposition. Thus, the opposition remained a "smattering of small parties that [did] not constitute a real or potential threat to [CCM] hegemony."[232] CCM dominance was reinforced by a relatively permissive international environment. As in Mozambique, Western donors applied little democratizing pressure once multiparty rule was in place.[233]

The 2000 and 2005 elections were landslides. The results of the 2000 race were viewed as a "foregone conclusion."[234] President Mkapa was reelected with 72 percent of the vote, and the CCM captured 258 of 295 seats in parliament. The Zanzibar election was again marred by fraud, and postelection protest was repressed.[235] In 2005, Mkapa's successor, Jakaya Kikwete, was elected with 80 percent of the vote.[236] Although the elections were deemed cleaner than in the past, the unevenness of the playing field remained "striking."[237]

Although a skewed playing field and the CCM's vast organizational scope helped to eliminate nearly all viable opposition in the 1990s and 2000s, it is worth noting that Tanzania's economy was fairly healthy during this period. Thus, the CCM remained relatively untested. In the face of a serious economic or other crisis, the regime's modest coercive capacity and lack of nonmaterial sources of cohesion may prove to be important sources of vulnerability.

Botswana

Botswana is another case of competitive authoritarian stability rooted in high organizational power. Botswana has long been viewed as a democracy.[238]

---

[229] Mrema finished second with 28 percent of the vote in the Presidential election.

[230] Lucan Way interview with Bashiru Ally, researcher in the Political Science Department, University of Dar es Salaam, Dar es Salaam, 20 November 2007.

[231] Lucan Way interview with Wilbrod Slaa, chair of CHADEMA party, Arusha, 29 November 2007.

[232] Hyden (1999: 148). In 2000, opposition parties were unable to field candidates in 13 percent of mainland constituencies (ARD, Inc. 2003: 5). The only exception to this pattern of weakness was in Zanzibar and Kilimanjaro, where opposition groups tapped into regional and ethnic identities (Kaiser 1996: 235).

[233] Tripp (2000: 198–9); ARD, Inc. (2003: 4).

[234] EISA (2006: 3).

[235] *Africa Today*, February 2002, pp. 24–25. See also ARD, Inc. (2003: 12).

[236] The CCM captured about 85 percent of parliament. The election was again marred by abuse of state resources, highly uneven access to media and resources, and at least some election day irregularities (Karume 2005, Morck 2006, and National Democratic Institute 2006).

[237] Morck (2006: 27).

[238] See Holm and Molutsi (1990), Wiseman (1998), Samatar (1999), and Leith (2005).

Freedom House has rated it as "Free" since 1973, and *The Economist* has described it as "Africa's Prize Democracy."[239] Yet such characterizations obscure important authoritarian features of the regime. The ruling Botswana Democratic Party (BDP), which has overwhelmingly won every election since independence in 1966, benefited from an uneven playing field, in which extreme resource and media disparities undermined the opposition's ability to compete.[240]

Botswana combined high leverage and low linkage with high organizational power rooted in discretionary economic power.[241] State and party strength were medium. The Botswanan state was underdeveloped at independence, and it did not create an army until 1977.[242] By the 1980s, however, the military was relatively well funded,[243] and a well-equipped police force penetrated "all towns and major villages."[244] Nevertheless, the state never developed the type of vast internal security apparatus seen in Zimbabwe, so we score coercive scope as medium. State cohesion also was medium. Although the state lacked any special source of cohesion, they never experienced coups, internal rebellions, or other episodes of serious indiscipline.[245]

Party strength likewise was medium. The BDP maintained a "well-established party apparatus" with a clear presence throughout country,[246] but it was more a "collection of local notables" than a mass party.[247] In terms of cohesion, the BDP was a patronage-based machine that, although institutionalized, lacked a salient ideology or history of violent struggle.[248] Unlike Mozambique and Zimbabwe, the overthrow of white rule in Botswana was marked by "smoothness and brevity," as the British actively facilitated the transfer of power to Seretse Khama and the BDP.[249]

The regime's modest organizational and coercive capacity was complemented by discretionary state control over mineral wealth. Diamond exports constituted 80 percent of foreign-exchange earnings and more than 50 percent of government revenue in the 1990s.[250] The Debswana mining company, jointly owned by the state and De Beers, maintained a monopoly over the diamond industry.[251] Debswana's ties to the BDP government were so close that former President Festus Mogae described the two as "Siamese twins."[252] Diamond wealth gave the

---

[239] *The Economist*, November 6, 2004, p. 50. See also Holm and Molutsi (1990), Samatar (1999), and Leith (2005).

[240] Holm and Darnolf (2000), Taylor (2003), Sebudubudu and Osei-Hwedie (2005), Molomo and Sebudubudu (2006: 149), Good (2008), and *Mmegi Online*, July 24, 2009 (http://www.mmegi.bw).

[241] In terms of leverage, Botswana was wealthier and far less aid-dependent than Mozambique and Tanzania (Holm and Darnolf 2000: 143), but it remained a small and militarily weak state without black knight support.

[242] Dale (1978), Somelakae (1993: 118), and Du Toit (1995).

[243] Good (2008: 12).

[244] Bouman (1987: 286).

[245] Molomo (2001).

[246] Polhemus (1983: 414, 402); see also Charlton (1993: 346) and Holm (1993: 107).

[247] Holm (1987: 22); see also Wiseman (1998).

[248] Polhemus (1983: 402), Charlton (1993: 349), and *Mmegi Online*, July 24, 2009 (http://www.mmegi.bw).

[249] Good (1992: 84); see also Polhemus (1983: 401), Picard (1987: 138–40), and Good and Taylor (2008: 253).

[250] Wiseman (1998: 243) and Good (2005: 28).

[251] See Good (2005, 2008).

[252] Quoted in Good (2005: 28). Mogae was himself a former director of Debswana. See *Africa Research Bulletin*, April 1998, p. 13066.

BDP government access to vast resources, dwarfing the private sector.[253] Hence, although the BDP lacked ZANU's cohesion or repressive capacity, discretionary economic power provided it with potent tools for preempting or thwarting opposition challenges.

Botswana has been a stable competitive authoritarian regime since independence. Under founding President Seretse Khama, the BDP overwhelmingly won elections in 1969, 1974, and 1979; after his death, his successor, Quett Masire, led the BDP to landslide victories in 1984 and 1989. In all five elections, the BDP won at least 65 percent of the vote and three quarters of parliament. Although this electoral dominance is partly explained by high growth rates and the BDP's reputation for good governance,[254] it also was rooted in the ruling party's vast resource advantages, which inhibited the emergence of serious opposition challenges.[255]

Botswana thus entered the post–Cold War era with an institutionalized competitive authoritarian regime. To be sure, it was one of the least repressive regimes examined in this book. Elections were generally free of vote-rigging, intimidation, or violence.[256] Although the BDP government occasionally violated civil liberties by shutting down independent radio programs, using the allocation of state advertising to pressure private media, and using the 1986 National Security Act to prosecute (and deport) critics,[257] such abuse was neither as frequent nor as severe as in other countries in the region.[258]

Nevertheless, the playing field was highly uneven. The BDP "tower[ed] over the political scene," enjoying a level of access to financial and infrastructural resources that was "unmatched by any of the other parties."[259] Although the Botswanan state was less politicized than others in the region,[260] the BDP nevertheless made considerable use of state resources, and it routinely mobilized public employees – approximately 40 percent of the workforce – for partisan ends.[261] Moreover, close state–business ties brought the party "generous donations from various sources."[262] By contrast, the opposition enjoyed no access to public funding and received "virtually no donations" from the private sector.[263] Indeed, dependence on the state made it "extremely risky for business entities

---

[253] Holm (1987: 25), Holm and Darnolf (2000), and Rabobank (2007: 2–3).

[254] See Matsheka and Boltlhomilwe (2000) and Leith (2005).

[255] Molomo and Sebudubudu (2006) and *Mmegi Online*, July 24, 2009 (http://www.mmegi. bw).

[256] Sebudubudu and Osei-Hwedie (2005: 13, 41); see also Molutsi and Holm (1990: 323).

[257] See Fombad (2002: 663), Taylor (2003: 220), Sebudubudu and Osie-Hwedie (2005: 24), U.S. Department of State (2006b), Good and Taylor (2007: 277), and Freedom House, "Freedom of the Press 2007: Botswana" (http://www.freedomhouse.org). In 2005, the government invoked the National Security Act to deport Kenneth

Good, a leading academic who had been critical of Botswana's democracy record (Taylor 2006).

[258] Indeed, most of these abuses occurred prior to 1990 and largely ceased after the Cold War.

[259] Taylor (2003: 216, 218); see also Good (1996: 53), Wiseman (1998: 248, 253), and Sebudubudu and Osei-Hwedie (2005: x, 17).

[260] Du Toit (1995); Leith (2005).

[261] Picard (1987: 148–66), Holm and Darnolf (2000: 122), Taylor (2003: 218), Molomo and Sebudubudu (2006: 153), and Good (2008: 12).

[262] Taylor (2003: 218); see also Molomo and Sebudubudu (2006: 149).

[263] Taylor (2003: 218).

to fund ... opposition parties."[264] The BDP's financial advantages seriously hindered the opposition's ability to compete. For example, opposition parties lacked the resources to effectively penetrate the countryside. Whereas the BDP provided each of its parliamentary candidates with a four-by-four vehicle, which greatly enhanced their mobility, opposition parties "had no such support," which "gravely reduc[ed]" their capacity to campaign outside large cities.[265] As one newspaper editorialized prior to the 2004 election, "only the [BDP] enters the race with resources to reach every voter."[266]

Media access also was skewed.[267] Prior to 1999, private television and radio stations were banned and the only national daily newspaper was state-owned.[268] State-run radio, which was the primary national-news source, was "predominantly one-sided."[269] Although a more diverse media emerged in the 2000s, private radio programming was mainly local, and private newspapers' "narrow ... circulation and use of the English language" limited their influence.[270] The state-run Radio Botswana and Botswana TV remained the dominant news sources, and they consistently favored the ruling party.[271]

With a virtual monopoly over resources and electronic media, as well as a relatively robust economy, the BDP retained power with relative ease between 1990 and 2008. The only real challenge occurred in the early 1990s, when an economic slowdown and rising unemployment eroded ruling-party support and the Botswana National Front (BNF) emerged as a serious rival, particularly in the urban centers.[272] The 1994 parliamentary election was the closest ever. Although the BDP won with 53 percent of the vote and 27 of 40 elected parliamentary seats, the BNF's unprecedented performance – 38 percent of the vote and 13 seats – led many to believe that it would be "strong enough to replace the ruling BDP" in the 1999 election.[273]

Yet unlike cases such as Kenya and Senegal, where ruling patronage machines weakened over the course of the 1990s (see below), economic recovery and mineral wealth enabled the BDP to reestablish its dominance. Extreme resource disparities continued to obstruct opposition party-building and in 1998, the BNF divided, partly over suspicions that its leader, Kenneth Koma, had been secretly co-opted by the government.[274] After a dissidents left to form the Botswana

---

[264] "Have patronage and paternalism been shaken in the BDP?" *Mmegi Online*, July 24, 2009 (http://www.mmegi.bw).

[265] Holm and Darnolf (2000: 121–2); see also Osei-Hwedie (2001: 60–1), Molomo and Sebudubudu (2006: 157), and *Mmegi Online*, July 24, 2009 (http://www.mmegi.bw). The BDP's access to resources thus gave it "high and active visibility which the opposition manifestly does not have" (Taylor 2003: 218).

[266] "Botswana Elections: Free But Not Fair," *Mmegi Online* June 23, 2004 (http://www.mmegi.bw).

[267] Malila (1997: 23–4).

[268] Fombad (2002: 652).

[269] Zaffiro (2000: 91) and Fombad (2002: 662, 663).

[270] Sebudubudu and Osei-Hwedie (2005: 24); see also Fombad (2002: 652), Molomo and Sebudubudu (2006: 48), and Freedom House, Freedom of the Press 2008: Botswana" (http://www.freedomhouse.org).

[271] Fombad (2002: 652), Sebudubudu and Osei-Hwedie (2005: 23), and U.S. Department of State (2009i).

[272] Wiseman and Charlton (1995: 323) and Wiseman (1998: 257).

[273] Makgala (2003: 51).

[274] Dissidents accused Koma of having been "completely disarm[ed] by his close ties to

Congress Party, BNF structures "collapsed throughout the country."[275] Led by new President Festus Mogae,[276] the BDP easily won the 1999 parliamentary elections, capturing 57 percent of the vote and 33 of 40 seats. The BNF suffered an "electoral pounding," winning only six seats.[277]

The BDP dominated politics throughout the 2000s. Opposition parties remained "poor and demoralized,"[278] with "limited financial and other campaign resources."[279] Koma, who had been the most prominent opposition politician in the 1990s, was now derided as the leader of an "official opposition" that did not challenge the government.[280] The BDP won the 2004 elections, capturing 44 of 57 seats. Five years later, the ruling party – now led by Ian Khama – won its ninth consecutive election. As in Tanzania, the patronage-based BDP remained vulnerable to economic or other crises. Through 2010, however, the party coffers remained sufficiently full to ensure stability.

BLACK KNIGHTS AND REGIME SURVIVAL: CAMEROON AND GABON

Cameroon and Gabon followed a distinct path to competitive authoritarian stability. In these cases, state and party strength was only medium (although in Gabon, oil rents enhanced the regime's organizational power) and large-scale opposition protest nearly toppled autocrats in the early 1990s. However, external support from France was decisive in fending off these challenges and, in both cases, autocrats reconsolidated power during the late 1990s and 2000s.

Cameroon

Cameroon is a case of a ruling-party machine that faced growing public discontent amid economic crisis in the early 1990s. Unlike many other African cases, however, the government of President Paul Biya enjoyed black knight support from France, which – together with a divided opposition – allowed it to survive massive protest and a stolen election before reconsolidating power in the late 1990s.

Linkage, Leverage, and Organizational Power
Cameroon combined low linkage with medium leverage, rooted in black knight support from France. Franco–Cameroonian ties remained strong throughout the postcolonial period.[281] In 1990, France was Cameroon's leading trade and investment partner and accounted for more than 50 percent of bilateral assistance[282]; consequently, France was "*the* singular influence" in Cameroon.[283]

Organizational power was medium. In terms of coercive scope, founding President Ahmadou Ahidjo built a powerful security apparatus that defeated

---

the BDP leadership" (Makgala 2005: 311–12); see also Good (2008: 56).

[275] Makgala (2003: 60).
[276] Mogae, who had been vice president, succeeded to the presidency in 1998 after Masire resigned.
[277] *Africa Confidential*, December 22, 1999, p. 4.
[278] Molomo and Sebudubudu (2006: 153).
[279] Good (2008: 56).

[280] Taylor (2003: 221) and Makgala (2005: 312, 315, 317).
[281] See Joseph (1978a), DeLancey (1986, 1989), Takougang (1993b), and Amin (2004).
[282] Takougang (1993b: 136–9); Organisation for Economic Co-operation and Development, "Aid Statistics" (available at www.oecd .org/dac/stats/data).
[283] Takougang and Krieger (1998: 242).

an insurgency in the early 1960s.[284] By the 1970s, Cameroon had the largest military establishment in francophone Africa, including a vast internal security apparatus.[285] However, economic crisis eroded state capacity in the 1980s;[286] we therefore score coercive scope as medium. Cohesion also was medium. Cameroon had a history of stable civilian rule, never suffering a military coup,[287] but the state lacked any special source of cohesion.[288]

Party strength likewise was medium. The Cameroon People's Democratic Movement (CPDM) was a patronage-based machine. Although it was never a mass party, it maintained an organized presence throughout the country.[289] In terms of cohesion, the CPDM was an established party that maintained a complex ethno-regional coalition via an institutionalized system of patronage.[290] However, it lacked nonmaterial sources of cohesion,[291] so we score it as medium.

Origins and Evolution of the Regime

Cameroonian authoritarianism dates back to the single-party regime established by Ahidjo in the 1960s and inherited by his chosen successor, Paul Biya, in 1982.[292] The Biya government oversaw a transition to competitive authoritarian rule in the early 1990s. Facing a severe economic crisis and growing domestic and international pressure for reform, Biya legalized opposition in 1990.[293] However, the transition left party–state ties remained virtually intact.[294] Thus, the CPDM enjoyed "unlimited access to the government treasury"[295]; deployed state infrastructure and employees for partisan ends[296]; and retained full control over electronic media, the electoral authorities, and the courts.[297] The government also continued to repress opposition protest, arrest prodemocracy activists, and seize, ban, and censor independent newspapers.[298]

OPPOSITION CHALLENGE AND REGIME SURVIVAL, 1991–1992. The CPDM regime faced a major opposition challenge in the early 1990s. In June 1991,

[284] Joseph (1978a: 29) and Gros (1995: 121).

[285] See Eyinga (1978: 106–8), Joseph (1978b: 182–5), DeLancey (1989: 63–4), and Takougang (1993a; 2004a: 74–86).

[286] Takougang and Krieger (1998: 244–5).

[287] Decalo (1998). The 1982 succession from Ahidjo to Biya triggered internal conflict, including a 1984 coup attempt (Le Vine 1986: 40–7 and Takougang 2004b: 102–4), but Biya later consolidated control by packing the army hierarchy with allies from his Beti ethnic group (Torimiro 1992: 99–101, and Decalo 1998: 27, 37).

[288] We do not count the successful counterinsurgency of the early 1960s because the generation that fought the insurgency was no longer present in the military hierarchy after the 1982–1985 purge (Torimiro 1992: 99–101 and Decalo 1998: 27, 37).

[289] See GERDDES-Cameroon (1995) and Takougang and Krieger (1998: 104).

[290] See Nyamnjoh (1999), Mbuagbo and Akoko (2004), and Takougang (2004b: 104).

[291] See GERDDES-Cameroon (1995) and Takougang and Krieger (1998: 199).

[292] Takougang and Krieger (1998: 42–50).

[293] Cameroon's GDP declined by 25 percent between 1985 and 1992 (van de Walle 1993: 358). On the initial liberalization, see Azevedo (1995: 273), Fonchingong (1998: 120–1), Takougang and Krieger (1998: 103–5), Mentan (1998: 45), and Konings and Nyamnjoh (2003: 77–8).

[294] See GERDDES-Cameroon (1995) and Fombad (2004: 371–3).

[295] Fombad (2004: 372–3).

[296] GERDDES-Cameroon (1995) and Fombad (2004: 372–4). Public employees belonged to the CPDM and contributed a portion of their salary to the party coffers (GERDDES-Cameroon 1995: 89).

[297] National Democratic Institute (1993), Krieger (1994: 605), Mentan (1998: 48–9), Mbaku (2004a: 37–8).

[298] See Derrick (1992), Breitinger (1993), Krieger (1994: 610–11), and Konings (2002).

Biya's rejection of demands for a National Conference triggered massive protest, which evolved into an indefinite general strike – called Operation Ghost Town – in which as many as two million people closed their businesses, boycotted schools, and refused to pay taxes.[299] Operation Ghost Town was one of the largest and most sustained prodemocracy protests in Africa in the 1990s. The protests continued for several months. Several cities were taken over by protesters,[300] and state revenue declined by 85 percent.[301]

Biya survived Operation Ghost Town for at least two reasons. First, the security forces remained loyal and effective.[302] Although the coercive apparatus was "stretched,"[303] it

... never broke down altogether. ... [T]he police were always on duty, always able to break up demonstrations, raid houses and newspaper offices, and fire on crowds. ... Repressive actions never ceased. ... The police could lose control of the streets but remained intact, under discipline, and able to act.[304]

Second, French assistance helped avert a fiscal collapse.[305] With French support, the Biya government met IMF obligations and ensured payment of military and civil-servants' salaries.[306] Confident of military and French support, Biya refused to yield, and the Ghost Towns eventually "ran out of steam."[307] In November 1991, all major opposition parties except the Social Democratic Front (SDF) signed the Yaoundé Declaration, in which they agreed to end the Ghost Towns in exchange for the release of political prisoners, the return of exiles, and a commitment to future constitutional reform.[308]

The 1992 parliamentary and presidential elections posed another major challenge. Economic decline had eroded public support for the government,[309] and although opposition forces were divided along linguistic (francophone–anglophone) and ethno-regional lines,[310] the anglophone SDF had emerged as a potent opposition force.[311] Indeed, SDF leader John Fru Ndi was considered the most popular politician in the country.[312] The CPDM performed poorly in the March 1992 legislative election. Despite an uneven playing field and the

---

[299] See van de Walle (1993: 381), Krieger (1994: 611), and Takougang and Krieger 1998: 126–39).

[300] Breitlinger (1993: 560) and Takougang and Krieger (1998: 126–8). The capital, Yaoundé, was "effectively cut off from the rest of the country" for two months (*Africa Confidential* July 26, 1991, p. 4).

[301] van de Walle (1994: 146).

[302] Derrick (1992: 174–5) and Gros (1995: 120).

[303] Takougang and Krieger (1998: 126–7).

[304] Derrick (1992: 175).

[305] van de Walle (1993: 381–3); Gros (1995).

[306] See van de Walle (1993, 1994: 147), Gros (1995: 120), and Mbaku (2002: 159).

[307] Fonchingong (1998: 124).

[308] Takougang and Krieger (1998: 141–2).

[309] van de Walle (1993: 358, 372).

[310] On the weakness of civil society, see van de Walle (1994: 388) and Dicklitch (2002). On the ethno-linguistic cleavages, see Kofele-Kale (1986), Konings and Nyamnjoh (1997, 2003), and Nyamnjoh (1999).

[311] The SDF exhibited "tremendous ... organizational capacity" (Jua 2003: 101) and in 1992, its membership reportedly surpassed that of the CPDM (*Africa Confidential*, September 25, 1992, p. 2). The SDF gained considerable support among the Bamileke, Cameroon's largest and wealthiest ethnic group (Konings and Nyamnjoh 2003: 79; Fru Awason 2004: 272–3). See also Takougang (1997: 170) and Jua (2003: 89).

[312] Gros (1995: 119) and Mbaku (2002: 153).

SDF's ill-advised boycott,[313] the CPDM won only 88 of 180 seats, compared to 68 for the National Union for Democracy and Progress (UNDP) and 18 for the Cameroon People's Union (UPC).

The SDF participated in the October 1992 presidential election and, despite the CPDM's overwhelming media and resource advantages,[314] SDF candidate John Fru Ndi "almost certainly won."[315] Nevertheless, the ruling party stole the election via massive fraud, declaring Biya the winner with 40 percent of the vote, compared to 36 percent for Fru Ndi.[316] The fraud triggered riots in SDF strongholds.[317] However, protest did not extend into francophone regions, and the largest francophone opposition party, the UNDP, failed to back Fru Ndi.[318] The government cracked down hard on the protests, arresting Fru Ndi and hundreds of supporters.[319] French support was again critical. Whereas the United States rejected the election results and cut assistance in half,[320] France accepted the election, blocked efforts to mobilize international opposition, and sent an additional $100 million in aid.[321]

AUTHORITARIAN RECONSOLIDATION, 1993–2008. Biya reconsolidated power after 1992. French support continued unabated and, in 1993, Cameroon became its leading recipient of development aid.[322] At the same time, U.S. policy shifted from criticism to "indifference."[323] Domestic opposition also diminished. The government forged a legislative majority by co-opting small parties and inducing several UNDP leaders to defect.[324] At the same time, the rise of a militant anglophone movement – which heightened ethno-regional polarization – eroded the SDF's national appeal.[325]

In the absence of significant external or domestic pressure, the Biya government refused to undertake the type of reform seen in Ghana, Kenya, and Senegal in the 1990s (see below). Although a new constitution was drafted in 1996, it brought little change.[326] The CPDM tightly controlled the new

---

[313] See National Democratic Institute (NDI) (1993), Krieger (1994: 614), and Takougang and Krieger (1998: 143–5). Conditions were so unfair that NDI declined to observe the elections (Takougang and Krieger 1998: 149).

[314] See National Democratic Institute (1993). A U.S. embassy study found that Biya received nearly three times as much television coverage as all opposition candidates combined (National Democratic Institute 1993: 32). Civil servants and security forces were mobilized for partisan ends and the government engaged in intimidation of opposition activists (National Democratic Institute 1993: 34, Asuagbor 1998: 135, and Gros and Mentan 2003: 144–5).

[315] *Africa Confidential*, August 30, 2002, p. 2. See also Krieger (1994: 416) and Jua (2003: 98).

[316] National Democratic Institute (1993) and Jua (2003: 98).

[317] Ngoh (2004: 442).

[318] Dicklitch (2002: 172) and Ihonvbere, Mbaku, and Takougang (2003: 387).

[319] Takougang (1997: 175–6).

[320] Krieger (1994: 627) and Mbaku (2004a: 35).

[321] Takougang (1997: 168–9; 2004a: 86–7), Dicklitch (2002: 169), and Amin (2004: 162).

[322] Fonchingong (1998: 122).

[323] *Africa Confidential*, November 1, 1996, p. 5. On the easing of U.S. pressure, see Tangwa (1998: 69).

[324] Takougang (1997: 171–2; 2003a: 430).

[325] Takougang and Krieger (1998: 162–7).

[326] Takougang and Krieger (1998: 192–3).

Constitutional Council and the nominally independent electoral authority.[327] Repression (including the arrest and occasional killing of opposition activists) continued and elections remained unfair.[328] The 1997 legislative elections were marred by fraud, allowing the CPDM to capture nearly two thirds of parliament.[329] All major opposition candidates either boycotted or were excluded from the 1997 presidential election, and Biya won with 92.5 percent of the vote.[330] Western powers took no punitive action. Thus, Biya could "rely on the support of Paris and the indifference of Washington... to sustain a flawed victory."[331]

The regime grew increasingly hegemonic after 1997. External pressure largely ceased.[332] At home, the UNDP joined the government and the SDF became increasingly marginal.[333] Other critics were arrested or exiled.[334] As a result, opposition forces gradually weakened. By the early 2000s, SDF was in "disarray" and the UNDP was "all but wiped out."[335] In the 2002 legislative election, no opposition party could field candidates in all constituencies.[336] The CPDM thus "reestablished itself as the dominant political party," capturing 149 of 180 seats.[337] Fru Ndi ran for president in 2004, but the SDF was a "shadow of its former self" and Biya was easily reelected, with 72 percent of the vote.[338] Despite serious irregularities, the election attracted little international attention, demonstrating "how anonymous and marginal Biya's Cameroon had become."[339]

By the mid-2000s, then, Cameroon seemed "once more to be adopting all the trappings of a one-party state."[340] In January 2008, Biya's announcement of plans to eliminate presidential term limits triggered riots, which the government met with repression.[341] A few months later, parliament abolished term limits, paving the way for Biya to run again in 2011.

In summary, although the Biya government confronted massive protest and a strong electoral challenge in the early 1990s, it survived for two reasons. First, black knight assistance from France allowed it to pay soldiers and civil servants

[327] Fombad (1998: 186) and Tangwa (1998). An "independent" National Observatory of Elections was created in 2001, but the body was packed – its president was a longtime CPDM member – and was "never really in charge" of elections (Nyamnjoh 2005: 119–20).

[328] On repression during this period, see Mentan (1998: 51–2).

[329] See Gros and Mentan (1998: 146–7), Mentan (1998: 46), and Jua (2003: 102).

[330] Fombad (2004: 382) and Ngoh (2004: 444).

[331] *Africa Confidential*, November 1, 1996, p. 5.

[332] *Africa Confidential*, October 8, 2004, p. 7.

[333] Dicklitch (2002: 172) and Takougang (2003a: 424, 431).

[334] U.S. Department of State (2000b; 2002c: 9; 2003c: 15; 2004c; 2005c) and Jua (2003: 105–6).

[335] *Africa Confidential*, August 30, 2002, pp. 1–2.

[336] *Africa Confidential*, October 8, 2004, p. 7.

[337] Takougang (2003a: 423). Five years later, in 2007, the CPDM won 153 of 180 parliamentary seats.

[338] *Africa Confidential*, November 5, 2004, p. 7. See also *Africa Today*, May 2004, p. 19. Fru Ndi won just 17 percent of the vote. Another challenger, CPDM defector Pierre Mila Assoute, was disqualified by the electoral authorities (*Africa Confidential*, October 8, 2004, p. 7).

[339] *Africa Confidential*, November 5, 2004, p. 6.

[340] Takougang (2003a: 433).

[341] *Africa Research Bulletin*, April 2008, p. 17495. Independent radio stations were closed, hundreds of opposition activists and journalists were arrested, and security forces fired on protesters, killing at least 40. See *U.S. Department of State (2008f)*.

throughout the 1991 crisis. Second, civil society was weak and a deep ethno-regional cleavage inhibited the formation of a national opposition coalition. The CPDM was not stronger or more cohesive than Zambia's UNIP, Kenya's KANU, or Senegal's PS, and a severe fiscal crisis might have triggered the type of elite defection that contributed to those parties' defeat. However, French support was sufficient to prevent such an outcome.

Gabon

Gabon's regime trajectory parallels that of Cameroon's in several ways. Western leverage in Gabon was medium. Black knight assistance from France,[342] as well as Gabon's role as a secondary oil producer, provided President Omar Bongo with considerable room to maneuver in thwarting opposition challenges.

Organizational power was high, due, in large part, to oil resources. State and party strength were at best medium. The army was small and poorly equipped, but the French-trained Presidential Guard was sufficiently effective to score coercive scope as medium.[343] Cohesion was medium: Gabon had a history of stable civilian rule,[344] but the state lacked any special source of cohesion.[345] Party strength also was medium. The Gabonese Democratic Party (PDG) was an established patronage-based machine with an organized presence throughout the country,[346] but it lacked a mass organization and nonmaterial sources of cohesion.[347] Organizational power was enhanced, however, by oil revenue, which provided Bongo with vast discretionary resources.[348] In the early 1990s, oil accounted for more than 80 percent of Gabon's exports.[349] The rentier economy gave Bongo "control of opportunities for lucrative public employment," which made it possible for him to "incorporate the bulk of the educated elite into the system and to obtain their ... acquiescence to his policies."[350]

Competitive authoritarianism emerged from the single-party regime led by Omar Bongo since 1967. In the late 1980s, an economic crisis – rooted in falling oil prices – eroded the regime's support base and triggered massive protest, including a January 1990 general strike that "shook the foundations" of the regime.[351] Bongo responded by calling a National Conference to draft a multiparty constitution.[352] Unlike Benin (see below), however, the National Conference's autonomy was limited by Bongo's control over the coercive apparatus.[353]

---

[342] France provided 85 percent of Gabon's development assistance in the early 1990s (Barnes 1992: 75, Tordoff and Young 1999: 275, and Gardinier 2000: 226). It also played a dominant role in training, supplying, and even commanding Gabonese security forces (Reed 1987: 307 and Decalo 1998: 156–7). Simultaneously, hundreds of French troops were stationed outside the capital (Neher and Bakary 1993: 6–7).

[343] See Barnes (1992: 54–5) and Decalo (1998: 156–8).

[344] Decalo (1998: 17).

[345] Yates (1996: 96–7).

[346] Yates (1996: 119) and Decalo (1998: 163).

[347] Neher and Bakary (1993: 14).

[348] Yates (1996: 119–20).

[349] World Bank World Development Indicators (online: www.worldbank.org/data/).

[350] Gardinier (1997: 147).

[351] Decalo (1998: 165–7). See also Gardinier (1994: 23), Yates (1996: 126–8).

[352] Messone and Gros (1998: 137).

[353] Gardinier (1997: 152).

As a result, the 1990 constitution failed to loosen the president's grip on the security forces, oil revenue, or the electoral machinery.[354]

Like Biya in Cameroon, President Bongo faced a series of opposition challenges in the early 1990s. However, oil revenue and French support left the government better positioned than most African governments to survive these challenges. Oil revenue helped ensure that the security forces were paid,[355] and the threat of French military intervention – reinforced by the stationing of hundreds of French troops outside the capital – helped "discourage... outbursts of popular discontent"[356] and made opposition challenges seem "dangerous and futile."[357] Thus, in May 1990, when massive riots – triggered by the mysterious death of an opposition leader – threatened Bongo's hold on power, order was restored by five hundred French troops.[358] Although the intervention aimed primarily to protect French citizens and oil operations, it "had the effect of propping [Bongo] up and enabling the Presidential Guard to regain control of the situation."[359]

Bongo also faced challenges in the electoral arena. Only fraud enabled the PDG to win a majority in the 1990 legislative election,[360] and as the 1993 presidential election approached, several high-level officials abandoned the PDG to run against Bongo.[361] The president faced a particularly strong challenge from Paul Mba Abessole, a longtime opposition leader.[362] Thus, despite the ruling party's virtual monopoly over media and resources, Bongo still needed "massive fraud" to claim the 51 percent necessary to avoid a runoff.[363] The fraud triggered another round of violent protest,[364] but France backed the result and the international community took no punitive action.[365] Several months later, France brokered a pact in which Bongo agreed to a set of nominal reforms, including the creation of an independent electoral commission.[366] Confident of French support, however, Bongo failed to implement the reforms.[367] Thus, the electoral commission "proved neither autonomous nor competent," and Bongo later transferred many of its functions back to the interior ministry.[368] Fraud allowed

---

[354] Messone and Gros (1998: 138–41).

[355] Gardinier (1997: 154–5); Messone and Gros (1998: 138). Increased oil revenue following the 1991 Persian Gulf War allowed Bongo to double the national budget and expand military and internal-security spending (Yates 1996: 132 and Gardinier 2000: 227).

[356] Yates (1996: 113–14).

[357] Gardinier (1994: 27).

[358] Yates (1996: 128–30). The May riots brought 10 days of "total anarchy" and left the oil-refining center of Port-Gentil "for all practical purposes in insurgent hands" (Decalo 1998: 165).

[359] Gardinier (2000: 227); see also Decalo (1998: 165).

[360] Barnes (1992: 66–7) and Gardinier (1997: 153–4).

[361] Gardinier (1997: 156).

[362] Preelection surveys showed Mba Abessole and Bongo in a dead heat (Gardinier 1997: 156; 2000: 228).

[363] Gardinier (2000: 228); see also Messone and Gros (1998: 141).

[364] See Yates (1996: 135), Decalo (1998: 167), and Gardinier (2000: 229).

[365] Gardinier (1997: 156); see also *Africa Confidential*, March 4, 1994, p. 6.

[366] Decalo (1998: 167) and Gardinier (2000: 229).

[367] Gardinier (2000: 229–31, 236).

[368] Freedom House, "Freedom in the World 2004: Gabon" (http://www.freedomhouse.org). See also Tordoff and Young (1999: 271) and Gardinier (2000: 230, 236).

the PDG and its allies to capture 100 of 120 seats in the 1996 legislative election and helped Bongo win easy reelection in 1998.[369] Despite the fraud, the election was accepted by the international community.[370]

The regime grew increasingly hegemonic after 1998, as Bongo used oil rents to co-opt erstwhile opponents into a "Presidential Majority" coalition.[371] Even Mba Abessole joined the government, becoming Deputy Prime Minister.[372] By the mid-2000s, 29 of Gabon's 35 registered parties belonged to the Presidential Majority; those that remained in opposition did so "at the cost of losing money, and therefore supporters."[373] Other opposition politicians were arrested or exiled.[374] In 2003, the PDG-dominated parliament eliminated presidential term limits.[375] The move "barely caused an outcry inside or outside of Gabon,"[376] and Bongo was reelected with 79 percent of the vote in 2005. By the mid-2000s, then, Gabon "look[ed] much the one-party state that emerged when Bongo took over" during the 1960s.[377]

In 2009, the regime survived a presidential succession triggered by Bongo's death. New presidential elections were held, and Bongo's son, Ali-Ben, won a plurality of the vote amidst widespread charges of fraud.[378] Although the election triggered riots, it was endorsed by France and accepted by the international community.[379]

POLITICAL MACHINES, CRISIS, AND TURNOVER WITHOUT DEMOCRATIZATION: KENYA AND SENEGAL

In Kenya and Senegal, regimes possessed minimally effective coercive structures and established patronage parties not unlike those in Cameroon and Gabon. However, in the absence of black knight assistance, governments were vulnerable to external democratizing pressure. Although relatively stable during normal times, the Kenya African National Union (KANU) government in Kenya and the Socialist Party (PS) government in Senegal were prone to elite defection during periods of crisis. In Kenya, a succession crisis triggered by President Daniel arap Moi's retirement led to KANU's implosion and defeat in 2002; in Senegal, patronage scarcity due to economic crisis and adjustment led to a string of defections that culminated in the Socialists' defeat in 2000. In a context of low linkage, however, successor governments were not democratic.

---

[369] Gardinier (2000: 231–7).
[370] Gardinier (2000: 236–7).
[371] *Africa Confidential*, December 20, 2002, pp. 6–7.
[372] *Africa Confidential*, December 20, 2002, p. 7.
[373] *Africa Confidential*, January 21, 2005, p. 5.
[374] See U.S. Department of State (2004f: 2).
[375] U.S. Department of State (2003d: 1, 2004f: 5).

[376] Freedom House, "Freedom in the World 2004: Gabon" (http://www.freedomhouse.org).
[377] *Africa Confidential*, January 7, 2005, p. 5.
[378] Bongo won 42 percent of the vote, compared to 26 percent for ex Interior Minister André Mba Obame.
[379] "Old French Nightmare Brewing in Gabon after President Ali Bongo is elected," *Times Online*, September 4, 2009 (www.timesonline.uk).

Kenya

Kenya is a case of high leverage and medium organizational power that experienced turnover without democratization. Although an effective coercive apparatus and a divided opposition allowed autocrat Daniel arap Moi to remain in power through 2002, civic mobilization and external pressure prevented him from reconsolidating power as ruling parties did in Botswana, Cameroon, and Gabon. Instead, the patronage-based KANU broke apart amid the succession crisis triggered by Moi's retirement, leading to electoral turnover but not democratization.

Linkage, Leverage, and Organizational Power

Kenya was characterized by high leverage and low linkage. An aid-dependent state without black knight support or an alternative issue that trumped democracy on Western foreign-policy agendas,[380] Kenya was considered highly vulnerable to international pressure.[381]

Organizational power was medium. Historically, the Kenyan state was among the strongest in Africa.[382] State structures such as the Provincial Administration (PA) penetrated the national territory, and the security forces were effective in maintaining internal order.[383] Notwithstanding signs of state deterioration in the late 1980s,[384] coercive scope was clearly medium. Cohesion also was medium. Although the state lacked any special source of cohesion, civilian rule was stable – that is, there were no coups – throughout the postcolonial period.[385] Party strength was medium as well. KANU was a patronage-based machine.[386] After languishing under founding President Jomo Kenyatta,[387] KANU strengthened under Moi.[388] Moi rebuilt KANU's local structures and enhanced its "police functions," transforming the party Youth Wing into an instrument of surveillance and control.[389] Thus, although KANU was never a mass party like the CCM in Tanzania,[390] it maintained active branches across the territory.[391] In the 1990s, it was the only party in Kenya with the "networks and wherewithal to reach

[380] Widner (1992b: 217).
[381] Clinkenbeard (2004). Development assistance constituted more than 10 percent of Kenya's GDP in the early 1990s (Miller and Yeager 1994: 172–5 and Clinkenbeard 2004: 162).
[382] See Jackson and Rosberg (1982: 12), Berg-Schlosser and Siegler (1990: 140), Widner (1992a: 14), Holmquist and Ford (1998: 245), and Hanmer et al. (2003: 185).
[383] See Tamarkin (1978: 301–306), Moeller (1984), Berg-Schlosser and Siegler (1990), Decalo (1998: 20, 238, 253), and Throup and Hornsby (1998: 3–11).
[384] Grindle (1996: 33) and Barkan (2004: 97).
[385] Decalo (1998). Although the 1978 succession triggered instability within the armed

forces, including a failed 1982 coup attempt, Moi subsequently packed the security forces with loyalists from his Kalenjin ethnic group (Goldsworthy 1986: 112–14 and Decalo 1998: 243–5). By the early 1990s, the armed forces were "well controlled by the President" (Holmquist and Ford 1994: 24).
[386] See Widner (1992a) and Throup and Hornsby (1998).
[387] Widner (1992a: 56–7).
[388] On party building under Moi, see Widner (1992a, 1992b: 216).
[389] Widner (1992a: 170, 143–54) and Adar (2000: 105).
[390] Barkan (1994: 25).
[391] See Widner (1992a; 1992b: 216), Barkan (1994: 25), and Throup and Hornsby (1998: 36–8, 179).

every nook and cranny of the country."[392] Cohesion was medium. Although it was an established patronage-based machine,[393] KANU was essentially a "party of notables," without any nonmaterial source of cohesion.[394]

In summary, a relatively effective coercive apparatus and a stable patronage machine provided the Moi government with more effective tools for political survival than those available to incumbents in Benin, Madagascar, Malawi, and Mali. However, its reliance on patronage as the sole source of cohesion left KANU vulnerable during periods of crisis.

Origins and Evolution of the Regime

Kenya had maintained a stable civilian regime since independence in 1963. Although founding leader Jomo Kenyatta consolidated de facto single-party rule, intraparty electoral competition gave rise to a class of politicians with independent support bases,[395] and an open economy permitted the rise of a robust private sector and civil society.[396] Although Moi established *de jure* single-party rule and cracked down on civil society after succeeding Kenyatta in 1978,[397] private associations remained strong,[398] and Moi's displacement of Kikuyu elites pushed many wealthy and well-connected politicians into opposition.[399] Hence, solid bases existed for opposition organization.

Single-party rule was seriously challenged in 1989–1990. With the end of the Cold War, the United States "downgraded Kenya's strategic importance" and Moi became a target of Western pressure.[400] At home, Moi faced calls for multipartyism from churches and an emerging opposition; ex-KANU barons such as Charles Rubia and Kenneth Matiba joined longtime opposition leader Oginga Odinga to launch the Forum for the Restoration of Democracy (FORD).[401] Moi met calls for multiparty rule with repression. In July 1990, Matiba and Rubia were arrested and subsequent protest (known as "Saba Saba") was met with an "orgy of violence" that left at least 28 dead.[402] However, repression triggered unprecedented political conditionality.[403] In November 1991, donors suspended $350 million in assistance and tied future aid to political reform.[404] Moi responded "almost immediately,"[405] announcing – just days later – a constitutional reform legalizing opposition and permitting multiparty elections in late 1992.[406]

The 1991–1992 transition revealed the vulnerability of KANU's patronage-based coalition. Given Moi's unpopularity, "all predictions were that [KANU]

[392] Mutua (2008: 84).
[393] Throup and Hornsby (1998: 45).
[394] Beinin (1978: 83) and Throup (1993: 377–9).
[395] Widner (1994: 69–71).
[396] Barkan (1992: 175–6; 1994: 18–19), Widner (1992a: 35–7; 1994), and House-Midamba (1996: 292–3).
[397] See Kanyinga (2003: 104–5), and Mutua (2008: 77).
[398] Widner (1992a: 177) and Ndegwa (1998: 195–6).

[399] Himbara (1994: 27–8), Clinkenbeard (2004: 252–3), Hulterstrom (2004: 116–17), and Mutua (2008: 77).
[400] Mutua (2008: 78); see also Schmitz (1999: 51–6) and Clinkenbeard (2004: 254–8).
[401] On church opposition, see Sabar (2002: 210–14). On FORD, see Throup and Hornsby (1998: 61–79).
[402] Decalo (1998: 256–8).
[403] Schmitz (1999); Clinkenbeard (2004).
[404] Throup and Hornsby (1998: 84).
[405] Clinkenbeard (2004: 22–3).
[406] Throup and Hornsby (1998: 87–8).

would lose" a multiparty election,[407] and, with the emergence of FORD as a viable alternative, numerous KANU bigwigs jumped to the opposition.[408]

Moi survived, however, for several reasons. First, the coercive apparatus remained intact,[409] which meant that unlike Banda in Malawi, Kaunda in Zambia, or Kérékou in Benin, Moi could continue to use repression against his opponents. Second, the playing field remained uneven. Because Western demands were limited to elections, the 1991–1992 transition left intact a range of authoritarian institutions.[410] KANU continued to finance itself via the state, and it maintained a monopoly over television and radio.[411] Moreover, a host of repressive laws – giving governments sweeping authority to block public meetings, deny registration to parties and NGOs, arrest without warrant, and censor or close down media – remained in force.[412] Third, the opposition divided, largely along ethnic lines.[413] Thus, Moi faced three major challengers in the 1992 election: FORD-Kenya, a predominantly Luo party led by Oginga Odinga; FORD-Asili, led by Kikuyu politician Kenneth Matiba; and the Democratic Party, a Kikuyu-based party led by Mwai Kibaki.

The 1992 election was unfair. The government engaged in heavy repression, including sponsorship of paramilitary "ethnic warriors" that attacked Kikuyu, Luo, and other potential opponents in KANU strongholds.[414] State-sponsored "ethnic clashes" left at least 1,000 people dead and 250,000 displaced.[415] During the campaign, parts of the countryside were declared "KANU Zones" in which "opposition organizers...were simply refused entry."[416] KANU also abused state resources,[417] packed the electoral commission,[418] dominated access to television and radio,[419] and engaged in at least some fraud.[420] In what was described as a "C-Minus" election," Moi won narrowly with 36 percent of the vote.[421] KANU won only 30 percent of the legislative vote – although

[407] Holmquist and Ford (1994: 7).
[408] Late 1991 and early 1992 saw a "continuous flow of present and former MPs, local KANU officials and other prominent Kenyans into the opposition parties" (Throup and Hornsby 1998: 96). It was KANU's "darkest hour. No one knew who was loyal or who was about to defect to the opposition" (Throup and Hornsby 1998: 105).
[409] Throup and Hornsby (1998: 105).
[410] Adar (2000); Clinkenbeard (2004).
[411] See Holmquist and Ford (1994: 14), Holmquist, Weaver, and Ford. (1994: 95), and Throup and Hornsby (1998: 372–7).
[412] Ndegwa (1998: 198–201), Mutua (2001: 99–100), Mwagiru (2002: 33), and Odhiambo-Mbai (2003: 52). Thus, Moi enjoyed "a formidable arsenal of repressive tools with which to stall democratization" (Mutua 2008: 84).
[413] Oyugi (1997) and Jonyo (2002: 96–7).

[414] See Kirschke (2000), Klopp (2001), Human Rights Watch (2002b), and S. Brown (2003).
[415] Human Rights Watch (2002b: 20) and Kioko (2002: 323–4).
[416] Barkan (1993: 93); Adar (2000: 108).
[417] See Wanjala (2002: 107). KANU reportedly channeled at least $300 million in illicit funds toward the campaign (Grignon, Rutten, and Mazrui 2001: 15, Cowen and Kanyinga 2002: 153, and CSIS 2002: 3).
[418] Electoral Commission Chair Zacchaeus Chesoni was "widely regarded as a puppet of President Moi" (Foeken and Dietz 2000: 131). See also Ajulu (1998: 275–7) and Throup and Hornsby (1998: 244–6).
[419] Kiai (1998: 187).
[420] Geisler (1993) and Throup and Hornsby (1998: 454–62).
[421] Barkan (1993: 95). Matiba finished second with 26 percent of the vote compared to 19.5 percent won by Kibaki.

gerrymandering and fraud helped secure a parliamentary majority.[422] Western donors accepted the election.[423] Foreign aid was restored and external pressure subsided.[424]

After 1992, Moi attempted to use repression – including widespread arrest of opposition politicians and state-sponsored "ethnic violence" – to reconsolidate power, as autocrats did in Cameroon and Gabon.[425] However, two factors precluded such an outcome. First, due to high leverage, the specter of conditionality remained; thus, heavy repression risked a punitive external response. Second, civic and opposition forces were much stronger than in Cameroon and Gabon. Under the umbrella of the Citizen Coalition for Constitutional Change (the "Four Cs") and later the National Convention Executive Council (NCEC), legal, human-rights, and religious NGOs launched a large and sustained movement for political reform.[426] In mid-1997, the NCEC spearheaded a wave of protests that were "unprecedented in their scope and intensity."[427] In July, the government responded with repression, turning Nairobi into a "war zone" in which at least 10 people were killed.[428] Again, however, repression triggered external punitive action; donors suspended more than $400 million in assistance.[429] The new round of sanctions, together with mass mobilization, forced Moi to negotiate modest political reforms via the Inter-Party Parliamentary Group (IPPG) before the 1997 election.[430] Although the reforms – including the repeal of several repressive laws, a more balanced electoral commission, and creation of a Constitutional Review Commission – were not fully implemented,[431] they made the 1997 election "somewhat more even-handed."[432]

The 1997 election posed a serious threat to KANU. Moi remained unpopular, and Mwai Kibaki's emergence as a major candidate gave the opposition a "serious ... chance to secure a victory."[433] However, KANU "cheated, bribed, intimidated and finally rigged its way to [victory]."[434] Facing a divided opposition, Moi

---

[422] Barkan (1998: 213) and S. Brown (2001: 728).

[423] Geisler (1993: 626–9) and Throup and Hornsby (1998: 520–3).

[424] Brown (2003a) and Clinkenbeard (2004).

[425] Throup and Hornsby (1998: 539–40), Schmitz (1999: 62–3), and Adar (2000: 114–15). The Kenya Human Rights Commission documented 233 extrajudicial killings between 1994 and 1996 (Adar 2000: 114). Moreover, nearly 50 opposition MPs were arrested in 1993–1994 (Mutua 1994: 52 and Clinkenbeard 2004: 280).

[426] See Barkan and Ng'ethe (1999), Mutunga (1999), Akivaga (2002), and Mutua (2008: 102–6).

[427] Harbeson (1998: 171). The protests mobilized as many as 100 thousand people (Clinkenbeard 2004: 286); in July, they spread across 56 cities (Peters 2001: 42).

[428] Steeves (1999: 73).

[429] Barkan (1998: 218) and Clinkenbeard (2004: 287).

[430] See Schmitz (1999: 66) and Adar (2000: 123–4). On the IPPG reforms, see Barkan (1998: 220–1), Ndegwa (1998: 203–5), Barkan and Ng'ethe (1999: 190–1), and Ng'ethe and Kutamanga (2003: 330–1).

[431] Mutua (2008: 109).

[432] Steeves (1999: 73) and Mwagiru (2002: 40–1).

[433] Southall (1998: 103) and Ajulu (2003: 5).

[434] Hornsby (2001: 201). Opposition parties faced police harassment (Kagwanja 2001: 85–7), a biased electoral commission (Aywa and Grignon 2001), and an electronic media "blackout" (Omukada 2002: 81–4).

won with 41 percent of the vote, and fraud in a handful of districts gave KANU a slim parliamentary majority.[435] Western donors again accepted the results.[436]

SUCCESSION, PARTY CRISIS, AND INCUMBENT TURNOVER, 1998–2002. Moi again sought to reconsolidate power after 1997. The government stymied efforts at constitutional reform,[437] harassed media and other critics, and sponsored a wave of "ethnic violence" against Kibaki supporters in the Rift Valley in January 1998.[438] It also co-opted powerful opposition leader Raila Odinga, whose National Development Party (NDP) gave KANU the legislative votes it needed to block constitutional reform.[439] The NDP joined KANU in 2002 and Odinga became KANU general secretary.

Nevertheless, the regime continued to weaken. Moi's "lousy reputation in Washington"[440] made him a target of conditionality.[441] Periodic aid freezes exerted "tremendous pressure" on the government, denying it "resources and legitimacy."[442] Civic mobilization for constitutional reform continued,[443] and as the economy stagnated, KANU's public support eroded.[444] As the balance of forces shifted against Moi, KANU discipline began to break down. KANU MPs grew increasingly independent, transforming parliament into a "real center of power."[445] For the first time, opposition parties were able to "thwart the government in parliament on several key occasions."[446] Moi's weakness was manifested when despite efforts to reform the constitution to permit him a third term in office,[447] KANU could not secure the necessary two-thirds parliamentary majority; in June 2002, he announced his retirement.[448]

Moi's retirement triggered a debilitating succession crisis for KANU. After Moi chose Uhuru Kenyatta, the inexperienced son of Jomo Kenyatta, as the ruling party's presidential candidate, KANU imploded as Odinga, Vice President George Saitoti, Kalonzo Musyoka, and other powerful barons abandoned the party and formed the Liberal Democratic Party (LDP).[449] The defections "broke KANU in two."[450] In October 2002, the LDP joined forces with an existing opposition coalition to form the National Alliance Rainbow Coalition

435 Rutten (2000) and S. Brown (2001: 728). Kibaki finished second with 31 percent and Raila Odinga of the Luo-based National Development Party won 11 percent.

436 S. Brown (2001).

437 Ng'ethe and Katumanga (2003) and Mutua (2008: 111–38).

438 Amnesty International (2001, 2002b), Klopp (2001: 504), Wanjala (2002: 117), U.S. Department of State (2002e, 2004e), and S. Brown (2003: 72).

439 The NDP officially joined the government in 2001. See Munene (2001: 89–90), Mutunga (2002: 60–2), and Kanyinga (2003: 111–13).

440 *Africa Confidential*, May 29, 1998, p. 7.

441 Clinkenbeard (2004: 316–22).

442 Clinkenbeard (2004: 316–22, 343).

443 Kanyinga (2003: 120).

444 Throup (2001: 2).

445 *Africa Today*, Jan 2000, p. 18 and February 2001, pp. 35–36, Kibwana (2002: 275–6), and Barkan (2003: 2–3).

446 Clinkenbeard (2004: 208).

447 See Ajulu (2001: 205–6). In 2001, KANU MPs introduced a constitutional reform bill to permit a third term (*Africa Confidential*, March 9, 2001, p. 2), and, as late as 2002, Moi was "widely expected to circumvent the [term limits] rule" (Brown 2004: 329).

448 Brown (2004: 330).

449 See Ajulu (2003: 8), Kanyinga (2003: 118–19), Odhiambo-Mbai (2003: 72–80), and Brown (2004: 331–3).

450 *Africa Confidential*, April 4, 2003, p. 4.

(NARC), which backed the presidential candidacy of Mwai Kibaki. In the face of a united opposition, KANU members "began to defect to the new party in droves"; by 2002, at least half of the 1990s-era KANU elite had joined the NARC.[451]

The defections "crippled KANU,"[452] leaving it without tools to win or steal the 2002 election. The defectors delivered much of the electorate to NARC.[453] Because Odinga, Musyoka, and other ex-KANU barons possessed large ethno-regional support bases, their departure cost KANU much of the Luo, Luhya, and Kamba vote "in one fell swoop."[454] The ex-KANU barons also controlled vast financial and organizational resources, which they put at the disposal of the opposition.[455] Indeed, by the time of the election, NARC's mobilizational capacity exceeded KANU's, which helped to ensure a relatively clean election.[456] Finally, KANU's implosion crippled the government's machinery of repression and fraud. Because several KANU defectors controlled militias that were responsible for much of the state-sponsored "ethnic conflict" in the 1990s, KANU effectively lost its monopoly over violence.[457] Moreover, given the uncertainty generated by Moi's retirement and the KANU defections, state officials were reluctant to engage in rigging and abuse.[458] Thus, "KANU did bribe; it did rig; it did intimidate voters; but in a spasmodic, half-hearted manner."[459] Consequently, even with the "dice loaded heavily in its favor,"[460] KANU lost the election in a landslide. Kibaki defeated Uhuru Kenyatta by a two-to-one margin and, in the face of Odinga's threats to lead a million-person march on the state house, KANU ceded power peacefully.[461]

Although opposition unity was widely viewed as critical to the 2002 transition,[462] two other factors were at least as important. The first was a "persistent and ultimately irrepressible" push by civil society, which prevented authoritarian retrenchment.[463] Second, the defections triggered by KANU's succession crisis were "probably the single most important" set of factors shaping the transition.[464] Although the KANU machine was relatively effective during normal times, it lacked the cohesion to prevent Moi's succession from triggering a fatal string of defections.

---

[451] Odhiambo-Mbai (2003: 80–81); see also *Africa Confidential*, December 20, 2002, p. 1.

[452] Brown (2004: 331).

[453] Ajulu (2001: 200–1).

[454] Ajulu (2003: 14).

[455] Brown (2003: 333) and Odhiambo-Mbai (2003: 80, 88).

[456] Anderson (2003: 333). Because NARC was able to monitor results at the precinct level, the party "knew it had won hours before the national radio broadcast the results.... There was simply no opportunity for anyone to 'retool' the count" (Ndegwa 2003: 154).

[457] Klopp (2001: 490–1) and Brown (2004: 333).

[458] Ajulu (2003: 5–6).

[459] Throup (2003a: 4).

[460] Ajulu (2003: 6). KANU outspent NARC "by at least fivefold" during the campaign (CSIS 2002: 3; Throup 2003a: 4) and state television and radio were heavily biased (Ajulu 2003: 6–7).

[461] Brown (2004: 333).

[462] See Odhiambo-Mbai (2003: 57), Hulterstrom (2004), and Howard and Roessler (2006).

[463] Ndegwa (2003: 158); see also Kibwana (2002: 274–5).

[464] Ndegwa (2003: 150). See also Throup (2003b: 2) and Brown (2004: 331).

THE POST-2002 REGIME. The 2002 transition did not democratize Kenya. Although NARC had campaigned for constitutional reform,[465] President Kibaki proved "loathe to give up the despotic powers vested in the executive by the constitution" and thus stalled efforts at far-reaching reform.[466] The Kibaki government packed the judiciary and the electoral commision (EC), and attacks on journalists and government critics – although less frequent – continued.[467]

Kibaki's capacity to consolidate power was limited by party weakness, however. NARC, which had been a "coalition of parties with no party structures," collapsed almost immediately.[468] Kibaki did not build a new party but instead governed with a clique known as the Mount Kenya Mafia.[469] Consequently, the government fragmented into competing personal and ethno-regional factions, at times appearing "like a political madhouse with no one in charge."[470] Odinga's LDP moved into opposition, undermining Kibaki's legislative majority.[471] Party weakness was manifested in 2005, when the government's draft constitution – which retained a powerful executive – was put up for a referendum. Although pro-Kibaki "Yes" forces (known as Bananas) enjoyed numerous incumbent advantages, the "No" movement (known as Oranges), led by Odinga and other ex-NARC members, prevailed with 57 percent of the vote.[472]

Party weakness hindered Kibaki's reelection bid in 2007. Kibaki did not create a new party until two months before the 2007 election, and his Party of National Unity was an "empty vessel" that could not even field candidates in all constituencies.[473] Without a strong party, Kibaki was unable to maintain a broad ethno-regional coalition.[474] Consequently, despite a booming economy, Kibaki found a wide array of political forces lined up against him. The opposition Orange Democratic Movement (ODM), which backed the presidential candidacy of Raila Odinga, was the "largest collection of ethnic barons...in the land."[475]

The 2007 election was tragically crisis-ridden. Despite abuse of state resources, media bias, and a packed electoral commission, pro-Kibaki forces captured a mere 43 of 210 seats in parliament, compared to 99 for the ODM.[476] The presidential election apparently was stolen.[477] Falsification of the results in

[465] Oyugi (2003: 374–5).

[466] Mutua (2008: 4, 201–2).

[467] In 2003, Crispin Odhiambo-Mbai, a constitutional reform advocate, was murdered. In 2005, death threats forced anticorruption czar John Githongo to resign and flee the country (Clinkenbeard 2004: 342); see also U.S. Department of State (2007d). On court packing, see *Africa Confidential*, November 7, 2003, p. 2.

[468] Mutua (2008: 148–9).

[469] Throup (2003a: 9) and Barkan (2008: 2).

[470] Mutua (2008: 149) and Barkan (2008: 2).

[471] Holmquist (2003: 203) and Throup (2003a:9).

[472] *The New York Times*, October 16, 2005, p. 2 and November 3, 2005, p. A3; and Mutua (2008: 226–9).

[473] Mutua (2008: 242).

[474] Brown (2003: 334) and Barkan (2008: 2).

[475] Mutua (2008: 241).

[476] See Commonwealth Observer Group (2007) and European Union Election Observer Mission (2008a, 2008b). See also Mutua (2008: 244).

[477] Odinga held a slight lead in most preelection polls (Mutua 2008: 243) and one exit poll – commissioned by the IRI – showed him with an eight-point lead ("A Chaotic Kenya Vote and a Secret U.S. Exit Poll," *The New York Times* Online Edition, January 30, 2009; available at http://www.nytimes.com.

numerous districts – documented by domestic and international observers – allowed Kibaki to claim a narrow victory.[478] The ODM rejected the results and Western donors refused to endorse the election.[479] Kibaki's rushed inauguration – in defiance of calls for a new election or an independent audit of the results – triggered massive riots, and the government responded with repression. Live media broadcasts were suspended; protest was banned; and police fired on crowds, killing dozens.[480] Kenya descended into large-scale ethno-political violence that cost as many as a thousand lives.[481]

Kibaki survived the crisis. Pro-Kibaki forces closed ranks in the face of severe ethnic conflict and, crucially, the coercive apparatus remained intact. Eventually, government and opposition forged a power-sharing deal (in which Odinga became Prime Minister) that allowed Kibaki to remain in power.

In summary, the KANU government possessed sufficient organizational power to survive for more than a decade after the transition to multiparty rule. An effective coercive apparatus allowed Moi to fend off opposition protest and two serious electoral challenges. Moi failed to reconsolidate power, however, for three reasons. First, the external cost of repression was higher than in states with black knight support. Second, opposition forces were stronger than in Cameroon and Gabon. Third, because KANU lacked the cohesion of ruling parties in Mozambique and Zimbabwe, it was more vulnerable to internal crisis – a vulnerability that became manifest with Moi's retirement.

Senegal

Like Kenya, Senegal is a case of a patronage-based regime whose clientelist networks unraveled, resulting in turnover but not democratization. Senegal combined high leverage and medium organizational power. Notwithstanding historic ties to France, Senegal's external ties diversified in the 1980s; by the early 1990s, French assistance was far less significant than in Cameroon and Gabon.[482]

---

[478] According to domestic observers, there were serious problems in 75 of 210 constituencies ("Disputed Vote Plunges Kenya into Bloodshed," *The New York Times* Online Edition, December 31, 2007; available at http://www.nytimes.com. In several districts, there were discrepancies between results reported by EU observers and those later reported by the EC (European Union Election Observer Mission 2008a, 2008b). EC Chair Samuel Kivuitu later declared that he was pressured into declaring Kibaki the winner and that he did not know who actually won (Mutua 2008: 246–7).

[479] *Africa Research Bulletin*, December 2007, p. 17731 and Schaefer and Groves (2008).

[480] See European Union Election Observer Mission (2008a: 9) and "Kenyan Riot Police Turn Back Rallying Protesters," *The New York Times* Online Edition, January 4, 2008 (http://www.nytimes.com) and "Signs in Kenya that Killings were Planned," *New York Times* Online Edition, January 21, 2008 (available at http://www.nytimes.com).

[481] Barkan (2008: 1).

[482] See (Coulon 1988: 171) and Gellar (1995: 104). French assistance constituted less than 20 percent of overall development assistance between 1990 and 1995 (OECD "Aid Statistics"; available at www.oecd.org/dac/stats/data).

State and party strength were medium. Although the state was relatively strong and the army was "among the best trained in Africa,"[483] Senegal never possessed a developed internal security apparatus, and state effectiveness was clearly eroded by economic crisis in the 1980s.[484] In terms of cohesion, Senegal had a history of stable civilian rule,[485] but the state possessed no special source of cohesion.

Party strength also was medium. The Socialist Party (PS) was a patronage-based machine. Although Socialist patronage networks penetrated the national territory,[486] the party never developed a mass structure.[487] Indeed, it relied on Sufi Muslim brotherhoods, particularly Mourides, to deliver rural votes.[488] In exchange for patronage, Mouride leaders (*marabouts*) issued religious edicts (*ndigals*) to vote for the PS.[489] This dependence on maraboutic support would be a key source of vulnerability.[490] In terms of cohesion, the PS was a classic "party of barons."[491] Although the party was institutionalized, it lacked nonmaterial sources of cohesion.[492]

Senegal's competitive authoritarian regime emerged out of a liberalization process that began under founding President Léopold Sédar Senghor in 1976 – when two opposition parties were legalized – and continued under Senghor's successor, Abdou Diouf, who legalized all opposition in 1981.[493] Although elections were marred by extreme resource inequalities, an "optional" secret ballot, and at least some fraud,[494] Senegal's multiparty regime was seen as one of Africa's most democratic.[495] The regime fell into crisis in the late 1980s, however, as economic stagnation and austerity measures eroded the PS's patronage networks.[496] Diouf's flawed reelection in 1988 triggered mass protest, which was met with martial law and the arrest of opposition leaders.[497] The crisis tarnished the regime's international image, generating external pressure for Senegal to "legitimize its alleged democracy."[498] Thus, in 1991, the Diouf government agreed to a set of electoral reforms that included an obligatory secret ballot and various measures – most

[483] Gellar (1995: 48). On state capacity, see Cruise O'Brien (1978: 187), Villalón (1995: 83–4), and Villalón and Kane (1998: 145, 164).
[484] Boone (1990: 352–3).
[485] Decalo (1998: 17).
[486] See Gellar (1982: 29), Fatton (1987: 15–16), and Coulon and Cruise O'Brien (1989: 145).
[487] See Cruise O'Brien (1978: 186) and Gellar (1982: 29; 2005: 96–7).
[488] See Behrman (1970), Cruise O'Brien (1971, 1975), Fatton (1987), Beck (2001), and Galvan (2001).
[489] See Behrman (1970), Villalón (1995), Beck (2001: 612), and Galvan (2001: 58–9).
[490] Beck (2001) and Galvan (2001).

[491] Fatton (1987: 115), Coulon (1988: 512), Coulon and Cruise O'Brien (1989: 149), and Boone (1992: 95–8).
[492] Mozaffar and Vengroff (2002: 603), Creevey, Ngomo, and Vengroff (2005: 486), and Beck (2008).
[493] Fatton (1987: 14–16).
[494] Young and Kante (1992: 66–8) and Beck (2008: 60).
[495] Fatton (1987).
[496] See Boone (1990: 349–53), Villalón (1994: 172), Thioub, Diop, and Boone. (1998: 71–3), and Beck (2008: 62).
[497] Young and Kante (1992), Villalón (1994: 173–4), and Diaw and Diouf (1998: 136).
[498] Villalón (1994: 173) and Beck (1997: 18, 2008: 63).

notably, the allowing of foreign election monitors – to reduce fraud.[499] The pact also gave rise to a coalition government – the Enlarged Presidential Majority – in which the main opposition, Abdoulaye Wade's Senegalese Democratic Party (PDS), gained four cabinet posts.[500]

Although the 1991 reforms made an opposition victory a "real possibility,"[501] the playing field remained uneven.[502] The intent of the new electoral code was "frequently thwarted" during the 1993 presidential campaign: The PS abused state resources, and the electoral authorities and electronic media – still a state monopoly – were biased.[503] Diouf easily defeated Wade, winning 58 percent of the vote. After the election, Wade and other PDS leaders were arrested, political meetings were restricted, and the opposition Moustarchidine movement was banned (and its leader, Moustapha Sy, was jailed).[504]

Like KANU, the PS failed to reconsolidate power after 1993. "Patronage decompression," caused by years of fiscal retrenchment and economic reform, undermined the Socialists' capacity to contain elite defection.[505] By the late 1990s, the party "could no longer hold its ranks together," and barons such as ex–Interior Minister Djibo Ka and ex–Foreign Minister Moustapha Niasse defected.[506] Economic liberalization also undermined the Socialists' clientelist ties to Sufi brotherhoods; as a result, Mouride support "dramatically declined."[507] Most marabouts remained neutral in 1993, and many of them backed Wade in the 2000 election.[508]

The breakup of the ruling-party coalition led to the Socialists' defeat, at the hands of Wade and the PDS, in 2000. The loss of marabouts' support eroded the PS vote in the countryside,[509] and presidential candidacies by PS defectors Ka and Niasse siphoned off enough votes to prevent Diouf from winning a first-round victory.[510] Niasse backed Wade in the runoff, ensuring his victory.[511]

---

[499] National Democratic Institute (1991); Guerin, Morris, and Tessier (1992); Beck (2008: 63–4). According to Beck (2008: 64), the reforms "read like a checklist of the complaints lodged by the opposition in the aftermath of the 1988 elections."

[500] Beck (1999: 198–204).

[501] Villalón and Kane (1998: 162).

[502] Villalón (1994) and Beck (1997, 1999, 2008: 64).

[503] Beck (2008: 64; 1997: 21–7); see also Guerin, Morris, and Tessier (1992), Gueye (1995), and Gellar (2005: 84–5).

[504] Vengroff and Creevey (1997: 209), Villalón and Kane (1998: 143–4, 150–1), and Villalón (1999: 143).

[505] Galvan (2001: 54, 59); see also Boone (1990: 350–353).

[506] Galvan (2001: 54–5).

[507] Vengroff and Magala (2001: 149). See especially Boone (1990: 350–3) and Beck (2001).

[508] Villalón (1995: 138) and Beck (2001: 617; 2008: 98, 103–5).

[509] Villalón (1999: 136), Galvan (2001: 59–60), and Vengroff and Magala (2001: 150).

[510] Mozaffar and Vengroff (2002).

[511] Vengroff and Magala (2001: 139). Diouf finished first in the first round, with 41 percent of the vote, but Wade won the second-round election with 58.5 percent of the vote. It is widely believed that in the absence of these defections, Diouf would have won the election (Galvan 2001: 55, 59–60 and Vengroff and Magala 2001: 139).

The 2000 turnover did not bring democratization. The PDS emerged as a new dominant party.[512] Long-standing PDS proposals to weaken the presidency and liberalize media laws were shelved, and Wade packed key state institutions – including the courts and electoral authorities – and deployed them against opponents.[513] Opposition protest was occasionally banned, several radio stations were closed, and journalists and government critics were "harassed, intimidated, interrogated, and jailed."[514] In 2005, ex–Prime Minister Idrissa Seck – seen as a threat to Wade's reelection – was jailed for threatening state security; in 2006, opposition leader Amath Dansokho was arrested for accusing the government of "gagging the press."[515] Wade was reelected in 2007 amidst fraud allegations, which led opposition parties to boycott that year's legislative election. Wade was subsequently believed to be grooming his son to succeed him.[516]

Senegal is thus another case of turnover without democratization. Like KANU in Kenya and UNIP in Zambia, the Socialist Party's patronage-based machine was vulnerable in the absence of black knight support. Although the PS did not face a severe economic (e.g., Zambia) or succession (e.g., Kenya) crisis, economic liberalization eroded its patronage base, which led to a politically fatal string of elite defections.

LOW ORGANIZATIONAL POWER AND REGIME INSTABILITY

Five cases (Benin, Madagascar, Mali, Malawi, and Zambia) combined low linkage, high leverage, and low organizational power. In all five cases, external dependence and the absence of black knight support left governments exposed to Western democratizing pressure. At the same time, weak party and/or state structures left regimes vulnerable to both internal crisis and opposition challenge. The result was frequent turnover and relatively contingent regime outcomes. In Benin and Mali, turnover brought a fragile democratization; in Madagascar, Malawi, and Zambia, it did not.

Madagascar

Madagascar is a case of unstable competitive authoritarianism rooted in low organizational power. Although transitions in 1992, 2002, and 2009 were

---

[512] See Creevey et al. (2005: 487–9) and Mbow (2008). In a process known as *transhumance*, PS leaders and cadres defected en masse to the PDS (Creevey, Diop, and Vengroff 2005: 487–9 and Gellar 2005: 158).

[513] See Ottaway (2003: 105), Creevey, Diop, and Vengroff (2005: 487–8), and Mbow (2008). The police Criminal Investigation Division was transformed into a "political force" and the "Damoclean Sword of public audits" was used to compel public officials to work for the PDS (Mbow 2008: 163, 159).

[514] Mbow (2008: 162–3) and Beck (2008: 228–9). See also U.S. Department of State (2003e: 4; 2004g: 4).

[515] Beck (2008: 228) and Mbow (2008: 164). In early 2007, Wade banned an opposition demonstration and detained several opposition leaders, including three presidential aspirants (Beck 2008: 228).

[516] *Africa Research Bulletin*, December 2007, pp. 17304–17305.

accompanied by massive protest, they were driven by extreme state weakness that left governments unable to repress opposition forces. Turnover did not result in democratization.

Linkage, Leverage, and Organizational Power

Madagascar is an extreme case of high leverage and low linkage. It was one of the poorest, most aid-dependent states in the world, and it did not benefit from black knight support or issues that trumped democracy on Western policy agendas.[517] Ties to the West were minimal.[518]

Organizational power in Madagascar was low. The state was very weak.[519] It never penetrated the countryside and the coercive apparatus was "primarily decorative."[520] Even the Leninist regime installed by Didier Ratsiraka in the 1970s failed to establish control over society.[521] As the economy deteriorated in the 1980s, the state "seemed perpetually on the verge of dissolution."[522] The capital, Antananarivo, was "barely in contact with much of the country,"[523] and the security forces failed to prevent the emergence of armed groups such as "Kung Fu" self-defense societies.[524] In 1984, Kung Fu groups attacked and weakened Ratsiraka's main paramilitary force, Youth Aware of Responsibilities (TTS).[525] Cohesion was also low. The state always had "difficulty...controlling its own agents."[526] During the 1970s, conflict within the armed forces brought the country to the brink of anarchy.[527] In the 1980s, the army suffered several instances of disobedience or mutiny, including the army's refusal to intervene during the Kung Fu attacks on the TTS in 1984.[528]

Party strength was at best medium. The Vanguard of the Malagasy Revolution (AREMA) was a "confederation of notables" held together by patronage.[529] Although AREMA's clientelist networks penetrated the countryside,[530] the party was "weakly rooted in society."[531] Because AREMA was an established patronage-based party, we score cohesion as medium.

In summary, organizational power was low, which permitted considerable pluralism by default. Although civil society was weak,[532] autonomous associational life persisted throughout Ratsiraka's rule,[533] which facilitated periodic, large-scale mobilization. At the same time, low cohesion within the military limited the government's capacity to engage in the high-intensity coercion needed to thwart mass mobilization.

---

517 Randrianja (2003: 309, 329).
518 Allen (1995: 1, 38).
519 Covell (1987).
520 Covell (1987: 85, 42) and Allen (1995: 57).
521 Covell (1987) and Allen (1995).
522 Allen (1995: 194) and Raison-Jourde (1995: 296).
523 *Africa Confidential*, April 28, 1995, p. 7. See also Covell (1987: 88).
524 Covell (1987: 70, 133).
525 Covell (1987: 71–5) and Allen (1995: 96).
526 Covell (1987: 7).
527 Allen (1995: 72–3).
528 See Covell (1987: 74) and Allen (1995: 96).
529 Marcus and Razafindrakoto (2005: 497, 501); see also Covell (1987: 120).
530 See Covell (1987: 120), Allen (1995: 83), Randrianja (2003: 312), and Marcus (2005: 162–3).
531 Marcus and Razafindrakoto (2005: 501–2).
532 Marcus (2001: 231).
533 Covell (1987: 76–8).

Origins and Evolution of the Regime

The origins of competitive authoritarianism in Madagascar lie in incumbent weakness. Efforts to establish single-party rule after Ratsiraka's 1975 seizure of power failed, giving rise to a "semi-single-party" regime in which six opposition parties joined AREMA in a National Front for the Defense of the Revolution (FNDR) but competed against it in elections.[534] In the 1980s, the withdrawal of Soviet assistance generated a severe economic crisis.[535] Isolated, Ratsiraka legalized opposition in 1989.[536] Presidential elections held that year were competitive but badly flawed.[537] Ratsiraka officially won 62 percent, but he reportedly stole up to 15 percent of the vote.[538]

DEMOCRATIZATION BY DEFAULT, 1991–1996. Ratsiraka was unable to thwart pressure for further reform, however. In 1990, a broad civic opposition – the Vital Forces (*Forces Vives*) – emerged under the aegis of Christian churches.[539] In mid-1991, the Vital Forces led a general strike and massive street protests that mobilized hundreds of thousands of people.[540] Ratsiraka declared a state of emergency but security forces could not put down the protest.[541] Opposition activists took over state office buildings and the Vital Forces formed a parallel government.[542] After the Presidential Guard fired on a crowd of 400,000 people, killing 31, Ratsiraka's remaining authority evaporated.[543] In 1991, he accepted a pact that transferred most authority to an independent prime minister, replaced parliament with a High State Authority dominated by the Vital Forces, and scheduled a constitutional convention and presidential elections for 1992.[544] Extreme fragmentation of power – the presidency, cabinet, and legislature were controlled by three distinct forces – resulted in considerable pluralism, which permitted far-reaching institutional change.[545] The Constitutional Convention, led by the Christian Council of Churches, created a semi-presidential regime with a weak president and powerful prime minister,[546] and media liberalization brought a "proliferation of private radio and television stations."[547] The 1992–1993 elections were clean, and Vital Forces leader Albert Zafy easily defeated Ratsiraka.[548]

Although Madagascar was briefly democratic after 1993,[549] this outcome was largely by default.[550] President Zafy inherited a weak state and virtually no party. The Vital Forces quickly fragmented, and as a result, Zafy's governing coalition

534 Kuhn, Massicotte, and Owen (1992: 29) and Allen (1995: 82–6).
535 Covell (1987) and Allen (1995).
536 Allen (1995: 101–3).
537 Kuhn, Massicotte, and Owen (1992: 29).
538 Randrianja (1999: 186–7).
539 See Raison-Jourde (1995: 298) and Randrianja (1999: 184–9).
540 Allen (1995: 105–7) and Randrianja (1999: 188).
541 Marcus (2001: 226).
542 Lippman and Blue (1999: 5) and Marcus (2001: 226).

543 Allen (1995: 92, 106–7).
544 Kuhn, Massicotte, and Owen (1992: 13, 17), Allen (1995: 107–8), and Marcus (2001: 226).
545 Kuhn, Massicotte, and Owen et al. (1992: 17–21) and Allen (1995: 107–11).
546 Allen (1995: 110) and Marcus (2001: 227).
547 Lippman and Blue (1999: 6).
548 Marcus and Razafindrakoto (2003a: 216).
549 Randrianja (2003: 311).
550 Marcus (2005).

was unstable.[551] Zafy's "Vital Forces" won only 47 of 138 seats in the 1993 legislative election and, although Zafy pushed through a constitutional reform strengthening the executive, he never gained control of parliament.[552] In 1996, Zafy was impeached on corruption charges, with half the progovernment bloc voting for impeachment.[553] The resulting power vacuum allowed Ratsiraka to make a comeback, defeating (the now-impeached) Zafy in the 1996 presidential elections[554]

UNSTABLE COMPETITIVE AUTHORITARIANISM: 1997–2009. Madagascar slid back into competitive authoritarianism under Ratsiraka. The Ratsiraka government re-politicized state-owned media and packed the Constitutional Court and the National Election Commission.[555] Subsequent elections were marked by "credible complaints of . . . fraud."[556] The government also pushed through a constitutional reform – via a dubious referendum – that expanded executive power,[557] and it harassed and occasionally arrested opponents.[558]

Although a combination of fraud and opposition weakness allowed AREMA to gain control of parliament in 1998,[559] the state's limited coercive capacity left the regime vulnerable to protest, and Ratsiraka's unpopularity left AREMA vulnerable to electoral challenge. Such a challenge emerged in 2001, when Antananarivo Mayor Marc Ravalomanana launched a presidential bid. Ravalomanana was well positioned to compete on an uneven playing field. As owner of Tiko, Madagascar's leading producer of dairy goods, he could finance a national campaign and "win a foothold in the countryside."[560] Tiko's 10,000 employees and its 14 stores and distribution networks reached into the "remotest areas" of the country,[561] and Ravalomanana contracted a fleet of helicopters and four-wheel-drive vehicles to "ferry him and his colleagues from village to village."[562] Ravalomanana's party, "I Love Madagascar," drew its infrastructure, cadres, and symbols from Tiko.[563]

---

[551] Allen (1995: 105–13, 221).

[552] Allen (1995: 113) and Marcus (2001: 227).

[553] Lippman and Blue (1999: 5), Marcus (2001: 227), and Randrianja (2003: 311).

[554] Ratsiraka barely defeated Zafy 51 to 49 percent in the second round. See Marcus (2005: 159) and Marcus and Razafindrakoto (2005: 503).

[555] Marcus and Razafindrakoto (2003a: 218, 2003b: 31), Randrianja (2003: 316), and Marcus (2004: 162; 2005: 168).

[556] U.S. Department of State (2000c: 1; 2002d: 4), Randrianja (2003: 312), Marcus (2005: 163).

[557] See Marcus (2001: 227–9; 2005: 164–6) and Randrianja (2003: 312).

[558] In 2001, for example, opposition leader (and Assembly Vice President) Jean Eugene Voninahitsy was imprisoned on corruption charges (U.S. Department of State 2002d: 3 and Randrianja 2003: 313).

[559] Marcus (2001: 227), Marcus and Razafindrakoto (2003a: 216; 2005), and Randrianja (2003: 312–14).

[560] Marcus (2005: 169); see also Randrianja (2003: 328).

[561] Marcus and Razafindrakoto (2005: 508); see also Marcus and Razafindrakoto (2003b: 35).

[562] Marcus and Razafindrakoto (2003a: 218).

[563] Marcus and Razafindrakoto (2003b: 35; 2005: 508) and Randrianja (2003: 314). Ravalomana's campaign "flooded the country" with Tiko hats and t-shirts. He also created a corporate slogan ("Love Tiko, Madagascar") that was nearly identical to the new party label ("I Love Madagascar") and "emblazoned his yogurt and milk containers" with it (Marcus and Razafindrakoto 2005: 508).

Ravalomanana was also Vice President of the Church of Jesus Christ in Madagascar (FJKM), which was "Madagascar's most important religious association."[564] With three thousand churches and nearly one million members, the FJKM provided a national infrastructure and activist base.[565] Finally, as owner of the Malagasy Broadcasting System, Ravalomanana possessed a media empire that could compete with state-run media.[566]

Ratsiraka tried but failed to steal the 2001 presidential election. The election was marred by fraud.[567] Whereas independent counts gave Ravalomanana a first-round victory, the electoral authorities announced that Ravalomanana had won only 46.6 percent, which required a runoff.[568] Ratsiraka could not enforce the fraud, however. In January 2002, Ravalomanana called a general strike and, backed by the FJKM, mobilized hundreds of thousands of protesters.[569] After a "half-hearted attempt at repression," the army declared itself "neutral," effectively eliminating Ratsiraka's coercive capacity.[570] When Ravalomanana declared himself president,[571] Ratsiraka tried to impose martial law, but his military governor was "unable to maintain security, persuade his troops to clamp down on protesters, or restore order."[572] As Ravalomanana's followers stormed government ministries, the security forces "made no effort to confront... the demonstrators,"[573] and the cabinet fled the capital. Madagascar was "split in two," as Ravalomanana supporters occupied the capital and pro-Ratsiraka forces retreated to the provinces.[574] By April, Ravalomanana had won over a "substantial part of the army."[575] Responding to the changing balance of forces, the courts declared him the election winner.[576] Ratsiraka fled to France.

The 2002 transition did not bring democracy. The fusion of Ravalomanana's business and media empires and Madagascar's neopatrimonial state created a highly uneven playing field.[577] The new president controlled both the state treasury *and* Madagascar's largest private company, and he controlled both the state media *and* the largest private media company.[578] In one of the world's poorest countries, this concentration of financial and media resources made it extremely difficult for opposition parties to compete. Most opposition parties joined the government, leaving only AREMA and Zafy's National Reconciliation Committee (CRN) in opposition.[579] Ravalomanana also repressed

---

[564] Marcus and Razafindrakoto (2003a: 217).
[565] Raison-Jourde (1995: 295–6).
[566] Marcus and Razafindrakoto (2003a: 218; 2003b: 37)
[567] Marcus and Razafindrakoto (2003b: 37–8).
[568] Randrianja (2003: 316).
[569] Marcus and Razafindrakoto (2003a: 215–19), Randrianja (2003: 317), Marcus (2004: 5).
[570] Randrianja (2003: 317).
[571] Marcus and Razafindrakoto (2003a: 219).

[572] Marcus (2004: 6).
[573] Cornwell (2003: 43–4).
[574] Marcus (2004: 6).
[575] Randrianja (2003: 324).
[576] Marcus and Razafindrakoto (2003a: 219, 220; 2003b: 40–1) and Randrianja (2003: 324).
[577] Marcus (2004).
[578] See Marcus (2004: 9) and U.S. Department of State (2004d: 5).
[579] Marcus (2004: 10–11).

opponents. AREMA and CRN leaders were imprisoned or exiled,[580] opposition rallies were banned or broken up, and libel suits were used to bully the media.[581] In 2006, Ravalomanana was reelected in a race from which four presidential candidates were excluded.[582]

Yet Ravalomanana also fell victim to state weakness. In 2008, 34-year-old Antananarivo Mayor Andry Rajoelina emerged as a high-profile critic of the president. After the government closed down Rajoelina's television and radio stations, Rajoelina responded by leading a series of protests that turned violent, killing dozens. Rajoelina demanded Ravalomanana's resignation, and in January 2009, he declared himself president.[583] Ravalomanana responded by sacking Rajoelina and cracking down on protest, but the regime soon began to break apart. In mid-February, protesters took over four government ministries; in early March, a sector of the army launched a mutiny, declaring that soldiers would disobey orders to repress.[584] The army command then declared itself neutral, and two days later, the military police abandoned the president.[585] Rajoelina pronounced himself head of state and soldiers stormed the presidential palace, forcing Ravalomanana into exile.[586] Despite widespread international criticism, the army installed Rajoelina as president – even though he was constitutionally too young to assume the office.[587]

In summary, Madagascar is a case of unstable competitive authoritarianism. Governments repeatedly failed to consolidate power after 1989, resulting in four turnovers. This instability was rooted primarily in low organizational power. Although economic crisis contributed to the 1992–1993 transition, governments fell under better economic conditions in 1996, 2002, and 2009. Although mass protest played an important role in the 1992, 2002, and 2009 transitions,

---

[580] These included ex–Prime Minister Tantely Andrianarivo, Toamasina Mayor Roland Ratsiraka, AREMA National Secretary Pierrot Rajaonarivelo, and a Vice Chair of Rafy's CRN. Other opposition activists – including Liva Ramahazomanana and Victor Wing Hong – were imprisoned as well. See Amnesty International (2002a, 2003), Marcus (2004: 11), and U.S. Department of State (2004d: 3–7).

[581] U.S. Department of State (2004d, 2007b). In 2004, the government closed a radio station and seized the equipment of three others for "insulting President Ravalomanana" (U.S. Department of State 2005d: 4–5).

[582] The most important of these, exiled AREMA leader Pierrot Rajaonarivelo, was barred from returning to the country. See Freedom House, "Freedom in the World 2007: Madagascar" (http://www.freedomhouse.org). Ravalomanana won 55 percent of the vote. His nearest competitor, ex-

Assembly Speaker Jean Lahiniriko, won less than 12 percent.

[583] *The New York Times*, March 10, 2009, p. A10.

[584] "Madagascan Forces Retake Ministries," *Independent Online*, February 20, 2009 (www.independent.co.uk) and *The New York Times*, March 10, 2009, p. A10.

[585] "Madagascar Army's Crisis Deadline," *BBC Online*, March 10, 2009 (bbc.co.uk) and "'Civil War Looms' in Madagascar," *BBC Online*, March 12, 2009 (bbc.co.uk).

[586] "Madagascar Soldiers Seize Palace," *BBC Online*, March 16, 2009 (bbc.co.uk); "Madagascar Leader Defies Troops," *BBC Online*, March 17, 2009 (bbc.co.uk); and "Madagascar Court Backs Handover," *BBC Online*, March 18, 2009 (bbc.co.uk).

[587] "Island of Instability," *The New York Times Online*, March 18, 2009 (www.nytimes.com) and "Madagascar Court Backs Handover," *BBC Online*, March 18, 2009 (bbc.co.uk).

these protests were accompanied – indeed, facilitated – by the decomposition of the coercive apparatus, which undermined incumbents' capacity to repress them.

Malawi

Malawi is another case of unstable authoritarianism rooted in low organizational power. The disintegration of state and governing-party structures undermined the neopatrimonial dictatorship of Hastings Kamuzu Banda and made it difficult for successors to consolidate power. Due to low linkage and opposition weakness, however, turnover did not bring democracy.

Linkage, Leverage, and Organizational Power

Malawi is a case of high leverage and low linkage. One of the poorest and most aid-dependent countries in the world,[588] Malawi had no access to black knight support, and no competing interests trumped democracy on Western policy agendas.[589] Ties to the West were minimal. Indeed, Banda kept Malawi so "hermetically sealed" that it became known as the "Albania of Africa."[590]

Organizational power was low. In the 1960s and 1970s, Banda maintained effective state and party structures under tight patrimonial control.[591] Although the army was small and weak,[592] a larger paramilitary force – the Malawi Young Pioneers (MYP) – served as a fearsome agent of repression.[593] Over time, however, Banda's advancing age – he was older than 90 in 1990 – undermined the neopatrimonial state. Banda's effort to name his right-hand man, John Tembo, as his successor triggered military resistance.[594] Discipline eroded and by the early 1990s, Banda had lost control of the army.[595] An army mutiny in 1993 – Operation Bwezani – disarmed the MYP, closed its bases, and forced at least 2,000 MYP members to flee the country.[596] By destroying Banda's primary instrument of repression, the mutiny severely eroded the regime's coercive capacity.[597] Likewise, Banda's Malawi Congress Party (MCP), which was once considered

---

[588] External assistance constituted nearly 30 percent of Malawi's GDP in 1990 (Clinkenbeard 2004: 162).

[589] Sindima (2002: 170–83) and Clinkenbeard (2004: 235).

[590] van Dijk (2000: 186). Foreign journalists were "virtually barred...from the country," there were few international flights, and Western tourism was negligible (Decalo 1998: 49, 84).

[591] See Williams (1978: 236), Nyong'o (1992: 3), and Decalo (1998: 64–8, 86–9). Indeed, Malawi was described as "the best-run police state in Africa" (Nyong'o 1992: 3; Ihonvbere 1997: 225).

[592] Lwanda (1996: 27, 179–82).

[593] Lwanda (1996: 180), Wiseman 1996: 39), and Decalo (1998: 85–6).

[594] See Newell (1995: 245; 1999: 218), Mchombo (1998: 35), and Clinkenbeard (2004: 213).

[595] See Lwanda (1993: 290, 295), Carver (1994: 56–7), Decalo (1998: 90), and Newell (1999: 217).

[596] See Cullen (1994: 92), Lwanda (1996: 186–8), and Schoffeleers (1999: 326).

[597] See Posner (1995: 142), Lwanda (1996: 187), Mchombo (1998: 36–8), and Roessler (2005: 221–2).

"one of the most powerful parties in Africa,"[598] weakened to the point where it "had, functionally, almost evaporated" and its patronage networks "had, for all intents and purposes, collapsed."[599] By the early 1990s, then, organizational power was low.

Origins and Evolution of the Regime

Malawi's transition to multiparty rule is often characterized in society-centered terms. Civil-society groups – particularly churches – are said to have played a "central role" in forcing a referendum on multiparty rule in 1993 and competitive elections in 1994.[600] Yet civil society in Malawi was strikingly weak.[601] Prior to 1992, social protest was "unknown in Malawi," and the country had no political parties and virtually no NGOs.[602] Thus, the transition began with "no preexisting political organizations except the one to be deposed."[603]

The 1992–1994 transition was rooted in a combination of external pressure and incumbent weakness. Western powers – which had backed Banda during the Cold War – came to view him as an "embarrassment" after 1989, which exposed the regime to political conditionality.[604] At the same time, a succession crisis triggered by Banda's advancing age undermined regime cohesion.[605] Tembo's emergence as Banda's chosen successor generated unrest within the security forces and, in 1992, army commanders vetoed Tembo's appointment as vice president.[606]

With the regime crumbling from within, it took only a small opposition push to set the transition in motion. This occurred in March 1992, when Catholic bishops issued a Pastoral Letter – read aloud in churches – criticizing corruption and human-rights abuse.[607] The Pastoral Letter triggered a wave of public opposition, including unprecedented strikes and student protest.[608] Two opposition parties emerged: (1) the United Democratic Front (UDF), a party of ex-regime "insiders" and businessmen who had fallen out with Banda[609]; and

---

[598] Lwanda (1993: 97).

[599] Venter (1995: 167, 172). Outside of Banda's stronghold in Central Region, MCP structures were reported to be "virtually nonexistent" (*Africa Confidential*, October 22, 1993, p. 7).

[600] See VonDoepp (2002: 123); see also Nzunda and Ross (1995) and (Ross 1995).

[601] Posner (1995), Ihonvbere (2003: 245), Clinkenbeard (2004: 363), and Bauer and Taylor (2005: 37). The few prodemocracy NGOs that emerged during the early 1990s were "based only on a couple of volunteers or [were] one-man/woman organizations" (Lohmann 1997: 53).

[602] Decalo (1998: 94–5). See also Cullen (1994: 16) and Ham and Hall (1994: 59). Indeed, there were no strikes in Malawi between 1964 and 1991 (Chipeta 1992: 44, Cullen 1994: 59).

[603] Kaspin (1995: 611).

[604] Newell (1999: 205) and Clinkenbeard (2004).

[605] Lwanda (1993: 106, 243) and Decalo (1998: 720).

[606] See Lwanda (1993: 290; 1996: 103), Newell (1995: 245; 1999: 217–18), and Posner (1995: 137).

[607] Ross (1995: 98–9) and Lwanda (1996: 103–4).

[608] See Lwanda (1993: 295), Cullen (1994: 60–1, 87), and Venter (1995: 158–9).

[609] Described as a "party of political recycles" or the "MCP Team B," the UDF was led mainly by "dismissed or disgraced ministers of the previous Banda cabinets" (Ihonvbere 1997: 232); see also Posner (1995: 137–41) and Lwanda (1996: 147–9).

(2) the Alliance for Democracy (AFORD), a northern-based party of regime out-siders led by Chakufwa Chihana. Attempts to crack down on emerging opposition failed.[610] Military officials refused to repress prodemocracy protesters and army troops intervened to protect them from police and MYP attacks.[611] At the same time, acts of repression – most notably, Chihana's arrest – triggered international sanction.[612] In May, donors suspended nonhumanitarian aid and conditioned future aid on political reform.[613] The aid suspension "deprived the regime of financial liquidity" and left it unable to pay public employees.[614] Banda had "no choice ... but to cave in," and a referendum on multiparty rule was scheduled for June 1993.[615]

The Banda government was too weak to win or steal the 1993 referendum. The MCP had "almost evaporated" and was unable to organize even modest progovernment rallies.[616] Thus, despite the ruling party's virtual monopoly over finance and the media,[617] opposition forces won easily. Because a refusal to accept the results would have generated army resistance and "seriously affected the flow of Western financial aid,"[618] Banda had little choice but to legalize opposition and call elections for 1994.

Banda also lacked the organizational tools to survive the transition to mul-tiparty rule. In December 1993, an army revolt dismantled the MYP.[619] The operation "destroyed Banda's last meaningful influence on the security machin-ery," leaving "no way for the regime to disrupt the transition using force."[620] Thus, although Banda benefited from several advantages in the 1994 election, including a monopoly over electronic media and vast economic power,[621] he could not control the election. The government's inability to use coercion allowed the Electoral Commission (EC), chaired by Anastazia Msosa, to emerge as an inde-pendent actor.[622] The election was clean and UDF candidate Bakili Muluzi won the presidency.[623]

Although Malawi's 1994 transition is widely characterized as a case of democratization,[624] it actually brought little institutional change. A new

---

[610] Lwanda (1996: 106–9).

[611] Carver (1994: 57), Venter (1995: 159), and Newell (1999: 216).

[612] Newell (1995: 254–5).

[613] Venter (1995: 160–1) and Clinkenbeard (2004: 359–70).

[614] Mchombo (1998: 38); see also Cullen (1994: 63–4) and Clinkenbeard (2004: 360).

[615] Decalo (1998: 96). See also Cullen (1994: 63–4) and van Donge (1995a: 231).

[616] Venter (1995: 167); see also Nzunda and Ross (1995: 8).

[617] Venter (1995: 165–8), Lwanda (1996: 131–5), and Ng'ong'ola (1996: 93–6).

[618] Meinhardt and Patel (2003: 11–12).

[619] Lwanda (1996: 186–8) and Sindima (2002: 226–7).

[620] Mchombo (1998: 36–8) and Meinhardt and Patel (2003: 12, 67).

[621] See Ihonvbere (1997: 235) and Chipanyula (2003: 24). The Press Trust, a private "chae-bol" owned by Banda (van Donge 2002), controlled nearly half of the formal economy (Posner 1995: 134, Harrigan 2001: 35–7, van Donge 2002: 656–7).

[622] van Donge (1995a: 237) and Lwanda (1996: 209).

[623] Muluzi won 47 percent compared to 33 per-cent for Banda. The UDF won 84 of 177 seats in parliament.

[624] See Kaspin (1995), Decalo (1998: 99), Reynolds (1999: 142), and VonDoepp (2005: 177).

constitution was hurriedly written,[625] and although civic groups pushed for new mechanisms to limit executive power, UDF leaders – nearly all of them ex-MCP barons – preferred to "inherit Banda's machinery intact."[626] Muluzi also inherited a near-monopoly over electronic media.[627] Indeed, state radio – the only news source for most Malawians – continued to function "more or less the way it had done under Banda," refusing to cover opposition.[628]

The Muluzi government had little incentive to govern democratically. Opposition forces were weak and Western donors, viewing Malawi as a new democracy, were "generous and supportive."[629] Facing weak domestic and external constraints, Muluzi deployed Malawi's weak and politicized state institutions to "tilt the playing field in [his] favor and cripple the capacity of other players to effectively compete."[630] Discretionary use of licenses and contracts enabled the UDF government to co-opt business and "financially enfeeble the opposition, thus limiting its capacity to effectively compete."[631] The government also employed the UDF youth wing – the Young Democrats – to harass government critics and break up opposition rallies.[632] Opposition leaders were occasionally arrested and newspapers suffered thug attacks, defamation suits, and occasional bans.[633]

Muluzi's 1999 reelection was flawed. Muluzi packed the EC, replacing its independent chair, Anastazia Msosa, with a partisan ally.[634] The new EC was biased.[635] After a campaign marred by media bias, abuse of state resources, intimidation, and numerous election day irregularities,[636] Muluzi was reelected with 52 percent of the vote. Experienced observers described the election as a "sham," but it was accepted by the international community.[637]

The UDF lacked the organizational tools to entrench itself in power, however. Muluzi took office "with much of the state's repressive apparatus dismantled,"[638] and the patronage-based UDF lacked cohesion. Incumbent weakness was

[625] Reynolds (1999: 145). As Ng'ong'ola (2002: 65) wrote, the new constitution had the "dubious distinction . . . of being enacted in one day". See also Sindima (2002: 231).

[626] Lwanda (1996: 191–2, 197).

[627] Chirwa (2000). Television was state-owned and private radio did not reach the countryside (Meinhardt and Patel 2003: 17–18).

[628] Ihonvbere (1997: 244); see also Chirwa (2000: 113) and Englund (2002b: 175). As one journalist noted, "Before it was Banda, Banda, Banda – every day. Now it is Muluzi, Muluzi, Muluzi" (*Africa Report*, November-December 1994, p. 57).

[629] Clinkenbeard (2004: 74, 353–4, 403–11).

[630] VonDoepp (2001: 233–4).

[631] VonDoepp (2005: 181); also Von Doepp (2001: 233–4).

[632] Englund (2002a: 13) and VonDoepp (2005: 194–5).

[633] Chirwa (2000: 113), Patel (2000b: 168), Chipanyula (2003: 18), and Clinkenbeard (2004: 373–4, 380–1).

[634] Patel (2002: 157) and Clinkenbeard (2004: 373, 383).

[635] After the MCP and AFORD united behind the candidacy of Gwanda Chakuamba, the EC barred the coalition. When the ruling was struck down by the High Court, the EC removed the AFORD party symbol – critical in a country with high illiteracy – from the ballot (Patel 2000a: 26–8).

[636] See Kadzamira (2000: 58), Patel (2000b: 174–81; 2002: 149), and Clinkenbeard (2004: 380). According to one study, the UDF received as much as 80 percent of state radio and television coverage (Patel 2000b: 179).

[637] *Africa Confidential*, June 25, 1999, p. 6. Post-election protest was repressed (Patel 2000a: 41–2, VonDoepp 2001: 236–7, and Meinhardt and Patel 2003: 26–7).

[638] Venter (1995: 181).

manifested by Muluzi's abortive effort to eliminate presidential term limits. The so-called Open Terms Bill faced strong public opposition, especially from churches[639]; crucially, it divided the UDF.[640] Several UDF leaders, including Deputy Leader Brown Mpinganjira and party financier James Makhumula, left to form the National Democratic Alliance (NDA), which cost the UDF its parliamentary majority.[641] The government attempted to impose the Open Terms Bill via repression: It broke up opposition rallies, orchestrated thug attacks on reform opponents, arrested journalists and opposition leaders, and finally banned public protest.[642] Nevertheless, the project failed. Repression triggered criticism from Western governments, raising the specter of sanctions.[643] Moreover, key UDF leaders – including Vice President Justin Malewezi – continued to oppose the Open Terms Bill.[644] The bill fell three votes short – with three UDF MPs voting against it.[645]

Three months later, the government drafted a new bill that would permit three presidential terms.[646] Despite a crackdown on opposition rallies and the arrest of some opposition leaders,[647] however, the bill failed. The U.S. and EU diplomatic missions issued a communiqué warning against a revival of the reelection issue,[648] and civic and church groups mobilized considerable opposition.[649] Key UDF leaders continued to oppose the reform, and the High Court struck down the ban on antireform demonstrations.[650] The bill was eventually withdrawn, and Muluzi named Bingu wa Mutharika as the UDF presidential candidate.[651]

Succession weakened the UDF. Mutharika's nomination triggered "an exodus of senior officials" from the ruling party,[652] and as a result, Mutharika faced a crowded field of opponents – including Vice President Malewezi – in the 2004 election. The election was marred by media bias, a biased EC, abuse of state resources, thug attacks on opposition parties, and irregularities in the vote count.[653] Official results gave Mutharika a narrow victory with 36 percent of the

---

[639] Ross (2004).

[640] VonDoepp (2005: 192).

[641] VonDoepp (2003: 11–12).

[642] Baker (2002: 295), VonDoepp (2003: 12–13; 2005: 194–5), and Clinkenbeard (2004: 395–7); Ross (2004: 94, 101). See also *Africa Confidential*, April 6, 2001, p. 4 and May 2, 2003, *Africa Research Bulletin*, October 2001, p. 14599 and October 2002, p. 15037; and Freedom House, "Freedom in the World 2001–2002: Malawi" (http://www.freedomhouse.org).

[643] Clinkenbeard (2004: 397); see also *Africa Research Bulletin*, June 2002, p. 14888 and October 2002, p. 15036, *Africa Today*, December 2002, p. 19.

[644] VonDoepp (2003: 13–14).

[645] See VonDoepp (2003: 16; 2005: 194) and Clinkenbeard (2004: 397).

[646] *Africa Research Bulletin*, October 2002, p. 15036.

[647] *Africa Research Bulletin*, August 2002, p. 14965 and October 2002, p. 15037; U.S. Department of State (2002b).

[648] *Africa Research Bulletin*, October 2002, p. 15036; *Africa Today*, November–December 2002, p. 19.

[649] Meinhardt and Patel (2003: 37).

[650] VonDoepp (2003: 16–17, 41).

[651] Ross (2004: 92).

[652] *Africa Confidential*, April 30, 2004, p. 4, May 2, 2003, p. 6; See also Clinkenbeard (2004: 398–400).

[653] Clinkenbeard (2004: 401–3, 418–19), Bauer and Taylor (2005: 36), and U.S. Department of State (2005a: 7). The EC was "so widely and plausibly accused of political bias that it [pled] incompetence in its own defense" (*Africa Confidential*, June 11, 2004, p. 5). Muluzi aides later claimed to have rigged the election (*Africa Confidential*, December 3, 2004, p. 8).

vote, and the UDF captured less than a third of Congress.[654] Again, however, Western donors accepted the election.

The regime remained unstable and competitive authoritarian after 2004. Soon after taking office, Mutharika broke with the UDF and formed the Democratic Progressive Party (DPP).[655] The new president ruled in an autocratic manner. UDF leaders were targeted in corruption investigations, and several – including Muluzi – were arrested.[656] Other opposition leaders were arrested for sedition or insulting the president.[657] In 2006, Mutharika illegally dismissed Vice President Cassim Chilumpha and then arrested Chilumpha and 13 opposition leaders for treason.[658]

Like its predecessor, however, the Mutharika government was weak. The security forces remained "inefficient, poorly trained, and inadequately funded,"[659] and the DPP was a hastily created coalition of patronage-seekers from other parties. The governing party suffered numerous defections, including two vice presidents, and as the 2009 election approached, Mutharika faced serious challenges from Muluzi and MCP leader John Tembo. Muluzi was arrested in May 2008 (on treason charges) and February 2009 (on corruption charges).[660] In March 2009, in a questionable ruling, the EC barred Muluzi from the election on grounds that he had already served two presidential terms.[661] Mutharika won an unfair election in May 2009.

In summary, Malawi experienced turnover but did not democratize. Given the absence of linkage and the weakness of civic and opposition groups, post–Cold War governments could abuse power and tilt the playing field against opponents at relatively low cost. However, weak state and ruling-party structures limited governments' capacity to consolidate authoritarian rule. The result was a pattern of unstable authoritarianism.

---

[654] *Africa Confidential*, May 28, 2004, p. 8. After some initial protest, several opposition parties joined the governing coalition, giving Mutharika a parliamentary majority (*Africa Confidential*, June 11, 2004, p. 4, June 25, 2004, p. 8, November 19, 2004, p. 4).

[655] Opposition MPs flocked to the new ruling party and, by 2006, the DPP claimed between 70 and 90 of 177 MPs (*Africa Confidential*, December 3, 2004, p. 8; February 18, 2005, p. 8; *Africa Research Bulletin*, November 2006, p. 16853).

[656] *Africa Confidential*, August 6, 2004, pp. 6–7, November 19, 2004, p. 4, December 3, 2004, p. 8, and January 21, 2005, p. 8. See also U.S. Department of State (2007a: 3, 4–5, 8–9).

[657] *Africa Research Bulletin*, January 2007, p. 16929. See also U.S. Department of State (2007a: 4–5).

[658] The government also broke up opposition rallies, prosecuted independent newspapers for libel or "false information," and ordered the closure of a television station owned by Muluzi. See Committee to Protect Journalists, "Attacks on the Press 2006: Africa" (online: http://www.cpj.org), U.S. Department of State (2007a: 5–6), and Freedom House, "Freedom in the World 2008: Malawi" (http://www.freedomhouse.org).

[659] U.S. Department of State (2004a: 3).

[660] U.S. Department of State (2009d); "Ex-Malawi Leader on Theft Charges," BBC News Online, February 27, 2009 (http://news.bbc.co.uk).

[661] "Bakili Muluzi Vows to Fight Axing as Malawi's Candidate," *Mail & Guardian*, 21 March 2009 (www.mg.ca.za).

Zambia

Zambia is a third case of low organizational power and unstable competitive authoritarianism. A poor, aid-dependent state with neither black knight support nor strategic value to the West, Zambia was highly vulnerable to Western pressure.[662] Organizational power was medium low. Coercive scope was medium: The repressive apparatus, though relatively undeveloped, penetrated the national territory.[663] Cohesion was low: President Kenneth Kaunda faced five coup attempts between 1964 and 1990, including uprisings in 1987 and 1988.[664]

Party strength was medium. The ruling United National Independent Party (UNIP) maintained a national structure and a substantial urban presence, but it lacked a mass organization and was weakly organized in much of the countryside.[665] Cohesion also was medium. UNIP was an established patronage-based machine. Unlike its counterparts in Mozambique and Zimbabwe, it achieved independence in 1964 largely without a violent struggle.[666] Thus, rather than developing an ideologically committed cadre, UNIP emerged as a "coalition of factional interests."[667] Lacking alternative sources of cohesion, President Kaunda relied heavily on patronage to prevent elite defection.[668]

Competitive authoritarianism in Zambia emerged out of the demise of the *de jure* single-party regime established by Kaunda, the country's founding president, in 1972. Like others in the region, the Kaunda government fell into crisis in the late 1980s amid a steep economic decline.[669] Bankrupt and facing rising social protest, the government grew dependent on international financial institutions.[670] In mid-1990, internationally sponsored structural adjustment triggered massive urban riots, followed by an attempted coup.[671] Protest quickly evolved into a democracy movement, and civil-society groups, led by the Zambian Congress of Trade Unions (ZCTU), called for multiparty elections.[672] In this context of rising protest, the regime imploded. Zambia's underdeveloped security apparatus faced difficulty putting down unrest,[673] and lacking resources, UNIP's patronage machine unraveled.[674] Party and government officials defected in large numbers; in July 1990, several prominent UNIP leaders joined ZCTU leader Frederick Chiluba to create the Movement for Multiparty Democracy (MMD). The MMD's emergence triggered a massive "bandwagon effect," in which local and national UNIP leaders throughout the country defected.[675]

---

[662] Baylies and Szeftel (1992: 82), Lodge (1998: 32), and Burnell (2001b: 208).

[663] Pettman (1974: 232) and Lodge (1998).

[664] Mwanakatwe (1994: 176) and Ihonvbere (1996: 88–9).

[665] Scott (1976: 12, 14) and Lodge (1998: 32).

[666] Mulford (1967).

[667] Tordoff (1988: 9); see also Baylies and Szeftel (1992: 78), Ihonvbere (1996: 51), and Momba (2003: 39).

[668] Baylies and Szeftel (1992: 78), Mwanakatwe (1994: 53), and van Donge (1995b: 196).

[669] Bratton (1992) and Ihonvbere (2003b).

[670] Bratton and van de Walle (1997: 104).

[671] Bratton (1992: 85–6) and Ihonvbere (1996: 90).

[672] Bratton (1992); Momba (2003: 44–5).

[673] Mwanakatwe (1994: 151, 175) and Bartlett (2000: 444).

[674] Bratton (1994: 123–4).

[675] Overall, 20 MMD candidates for parliament in 1991 were former or sitting UNIP deputies (Baylies and Szeftel 1992: 83). See also van Donge (1995b: 199) and Ihonvbere (1996: 69–70).

Facing a strong opposition challenge and unable to contain internal dissent, Kaunda announced in late 1990 that multiparty elections would be held in 1991.[676] The regime liberalized considerably: Press freedom expanded and opposition groups were allowed to organize freely.[677]

The 1990 reforms fell short of democratization, however. Kaunda enjoyed numerous advantages in his 1991 reelection bid. A state of emergency – which restricted a range of civil liberties – was in effect for much of the campaign; UNIP controlled the electoral authorities; and the electronic media remained state-owned and biased.[678] Nevertheless, Kaunda was unable to translate these advantages into an electoral victory. Crucially, UNIP's patronage machine "ran out of fuel,"[679] and large-scale defection strengthened the MMD. UNIP defectors brought their experience, constituencies, and financial resources to the opposition.[680] At the same time, in the absence of black knight support, the regime was vulnerable to external pressure. IMF conditionality forced Kaunda to maintain unpopular austerity measures – despite large-scale rioting – throughout the election campaign, which further eroded public support for the governing party.[681] MMD candidate Frederick Chiluba overwhelmingly defeated Kaunda – with 76 percent of the vote – in the 1991 election.

The 1991 turnover did not bring democratization. The Chiluba government engaged in widespread abuse, including a 1993 state of emergency that restricted civil liberties, occasional arrest or expulsion of opponents, restrictions on protest, and numerous attacks on the media, including police raids and the arrest of newspaper editors.[682] Moreover, the government abused state resources and packed the electoral authorities, and the bulk of the media remained state-owned and biased.[683] The 1996 election was unfair. When Kaunda reentered politics in 1995, reinvigorating UNIP, the government "reacted with panic" and passed a dubious constitutional reform that excluded Kaunda from running.[684] Due to a UNIP boycott, Chiluba was overwhelmingly reelected, and the MMD won 131 of 150 seats in parliament.[685] In 1997, after a failed coup attempt, Kaunda and other major opposition leaders were arrested.[686]

Chiluba's authoritarian behavior triggered little external reaction. Widely viewed as a "new democracy" after 1991, Zambia was subject to little political conditionality.[687] Thus, whereas the 1991 election gained widespread

[676] Ihonvbere (1996: 90) and Momba (2003: 47–9).
[677] Bratton (1992) and van Donge (1995b).
[678] See Mwanakatwe (1994: 230–1), Panter-Brick (1994: 241), and Ihonvbere (1996: 120).
[679] Bratton (1994: 123–4); see also Joseph (1992: 200).
[680] Ihonvbere (1996: 65; 2003b: 56–9).
[681] The IMF rejected Kaunda's request to freeze prices until after the election (Baylies and Szeftel 1992: 81). See also Bratton (1994: 113).
[682] See Ham (1993), Bratton and Posner (1999), Phiri (1999), Ihonvbere (2003b:

77–8), Rakner and Svåsand (2005: 94), and Simon (2005).
[683] In the mid-1990s, the only television station, most radio stations, and two of three major newspapers were state-owned (Bratton and Posner 1999: 397, Rakner and Svåsand 2005: 95–100, and Simon 2005: 208–9).
[684] Ihonvbere (2003b: 73–4).
[685] Chiluba won 73 percent of the vote compared to just 13 percent for his nearest competitor.
[686] Burnell (2001a: 242).
[687] Simon (2005: 214).

international scrutiny, virtually no Western observers monitored the 1996 election.[688] Although some donors froze aid after Kaunda was barred from the 1996 election, IMF and World Bank assistance continued.[689] Consequently, the government was able to deflect external pressure without much domestic consequence.[690]

Chiluba failed to consolidate power, due, in large part, to party weakness. The MMD was an "agglomeration of disparate opposition elements and interests, alienated businessmen, and disgraced or displaced politicians."[691] Lacking any "ideological glue to hold the party together," MMD governments relied exclusively on patronage[692]; as a result, they were riddled with internal conflict and defection throughout the 1990s.[693] In this context, Chiluba's effort to perpetuate his own rule failed.[694] Toward the end of his second term, Chiluba's supporters began to push for a constitutional reform to allow him to run for a third term. The MMD fractured over the reelection bid, with several government officials defecting to the opposition.[695] When Chiluba backers organized a party convention to endorse the third term, internal critics boycotted and initiated impeachment procedures in parliament.[696] With much of his own party lined up against him,[697] Chiluba abandoned his reelection bid and named Levy Mwanawasa as the MMD's presidential candidate in 2001.

The MMD barely survived the 2001 election. The presidential succession triggered another round of defections. Several politicians who had sought the MMD nomination left the party to launch presidential bids, and numerous MMD deputies followed them out of the party.[698] Four major ex-MMD politicians ran against Mwanawasa.[699] Those defections, in a context of widespread economic disaffection, created a "real possibility that the [MMD] would lose" the election.[700] A fragmented opposition, a skewed playing field (including abuse of state resources, uneven media access, biased electoral authorities, and some restrictions on opposition campaigning), and at least some fraud allowed Mwanawasa to narrowly win, with just 29 percent of the vote.[701] Although EU and other observers judged the election "unfree and unfair,"[702] the international community took little punitive action.[703]

---

[688] Human Rights Watch (1998).

[689] Rakner (2003: 150–1).

[690] Simon (2005: 214).

[691] Ihonvbere (2003b: 66); see also Momba (1992: 17).

[692] Simon (2005: 211); see also Burnell (2001a: 247, 253).

[693] Ihonvbere (1996: 178; 2003b: 71–2) and Rakner and Svåsand (2004).

[694] See Foundation for Democratic Process (2001: 32) and Larmer and Fraser (2007: 617).

[695] "Zambia: MMD dissidents threaten to 'remove' Chiluba from party," AFP 30 April 2001 (online: wnc.fedworld.gov); see also "More, Higher Hurdles Ahead for Zambian President," Beijing Xinhua 2 May 2001

(online: wnc.fedworld.gov); Simon (2005: 205).

[696] Simon (2005: 205).

[697] Simon (2005: 205).

[698] Burnell (2003: 392) and Rakner and Svåsand (2004: 53–4, 63).

[699] Burnell (2003).

[700] Rakner and Svåsand (2004: 59). On the economic crisis, see Larmer and Fraser (2007).

[701] The MMD won only 69 of 150 seats in parliament. On fraud and abuse in the 2001 election, see Burnell (2003: 394), Rakner and Svåsand (2005), Simon (2005), and *Africa Confidential* 4 February 2005, p. 6.

[702] Larmer and Fraser (2007: 617).

[703] Rakner (2003: 150–3, 162).

After 2001, economic recovery – fueled by a copper boom – and the consolidation of MMD patronage networks improved conditions for the ruling party.[704] Thus, despite the MMD's having won only 69 of 150 seats in parliament in 2001, Mwanawasa used state resources to "buy a working parliamentary majority."[705] The government also continued to suppress independent media, making widespread use of libel and defamation laws.[706] In 2006, opposition efforts to form a unified front faltered when opposition candidate Anderson Mazoka – who had just barely lost to Mwanawasa in 2001 – died three months before the election. Although the election was fairer than those in 1996 and 2001,[707] the bulk of the media remained state-owned and biased, and opposition parties faced harassment, intimidation, and occasional arrest.[708] Mwanawasa won with 43 percent of the vote, compared to 29 percent for Michael Sata, who had earlier defected from the MMD. Sata claimed fraud and led large-scale protests, which led to his arrest and a ban on opposition political gatherings.[709]

Zambia remained competitive authoritarian through 2008. The MMD barely survived the presidential succession triggered by Mwanawasa's death in 2008. New elections were held, and Mwanawasa's vice president and successor, Rupiah Banda, narrowly defeated Sata, 40 to 38 percent, in an election marred by harassment and media censorship.[710]

In summary, Zambia is a case of unstable competitive authoritarianism. Following the 1991 turnover, the MMD managed to remain in power for more than three consecutive terms. Nevertheless, President Chiluba failed to secure reelection in 2001, and the MMD barely won elections in 2001 and 2008. The MMD's survival was rooted in several contingent factors, including a relatively healthy economy and a fragmented opposition. However, the highly contested elections of 2001, 2006, and 2008 suggest that the regime remained far from consolidated.

Benin

Benin is often characterized as a case of civil-society–driven democratization.[711] However, it is better understood as a case of unstable competitive authoritarianism rooted in incumbent weakness. Neither Mathieu Kérékou (1972–1991) nor his successor, Nicéphore Soglo (1991–1996), governed in a fully democratic

---

[704] Gould (2002: 310) and Larmer and Fraser (2007: 618).

[705] Larmer and Fraser (2007: 618, 634).

[706] Freedom House labeled Zambia's media as "Not Free" during this period. See Habasonda (2002: 8–9), Chanda (2003: 57), and U.S. Department of State (2004i).

[707] Larmer and Fraser (2007: 620) and Freedom House, "Freedom in the World 2007: Zambia" (http://www.freedomhouse.org).

[708] Sata was arrested in February 2006 for defaming the president. See Freedom House, "Freedom in the World 2007: Zambia" (http://www.freedomhouse.org). See also *Africa Confidential*, September 8 2006, p. 8 and October 20 2006, p. 4.

[709] See Larmer and Fraser (2007: 634–5) and Freedom House, "Freedom in the World 2008: Zambia" (http://www.freedomhouse.org).

[710] MISA (2008) and Baldwin (2009).

[711] Heilbrunn (1993) and Bratton and van de Walle (1997).

manner. However, the weakness of state and ruling-party structures limited their capacity to manipulate state institutions and thwart opposition challenges. The result was considerable pluralism by default, which permitted a fragile democratization after 2006.

Linkage, Leverage, and Organizational Power

Benin is a case of low linkage and high leverage. Benin (called Dahomey until 1975) was a "typical client state," characterized by extreme dependence.[712] Colonial ties to France eroded considerably during the 1970s, and French assistance never approached black knight levels in the 1990s.[713] Moreover, no issue trumped democracy promotion on Western foreign-policy agendas.[714]

Organizational power in Benin was low. The state never effectively penetrated the countryside and exhibited little capacity for social control.[715] The army was "quite small even by African standards," and Kérékou's Presidential Guard numbered no more than two thousand.[716] State weakness permitted considerable de facto pluralism, even under the nominally Marxist regime established in the 1970s.[717] Thus, the regime was characterized by "widespread . . . by-passing of official institutions,"[718] and Leninist organs such as the Committees for the Defense of the Revolution were little more than "paper structures."[719] In the late 1980s, a severe economic crisis bankrupted the state, which eliminated its remaining capacity for social control.[720] Cohesion was also low. The army was "the least cohesive in francophone Africa."[721] Benin suffered six coups during the 1960s and 1970s,[722] and the army was "bubbling with plots and power-grabs" – including three coup attempts – in the second half of the 1980s.[723]

Party strength was low. Kérékou's People's Party of the Revolution (PRPB) was small and lacked mobilizational capacity,[724] and it disintegrated in the late 1980s.[725] After 1990, no party in Benin possessed a national organization.[726] Party cohesion also was low. Presidents Soglo (1991–1996), Kérékou (1996–2006), and Boni (2006–) all took office without a party, governing instead through loose,

[712] Decalo (1997: 45); see also Allen (1992a: 49).

[713] Houngnikpo (2002: 153–6). French assistance constituted less than 20 percent of overall development assistance between 1990 and 1995 (OECD "Aid Statistics," available at www.oecd.org/dac/stats/data).

[714] Omitoogun and Onigo-Itite (1996: 33).

[715] Amuwo (2003); Bierschenk and Olivier de Sardan (2003). The state enjoyed "only a minimal presence in the village" (Bierschenk and Olivier de Sardan 2003: 164), and governments never effectively controlled students and other civil-society groups (Decalo 1997: 51; Houngnikpo 2002: 130).

[716] Decalo (1997: 47).

[717] See Decalo (1990: 124–36), Nwajiaku (1994), and Amuwo (2003).

[718] Allen (1992a: 56).

[719] Decalo (1990: 124).

[720] Allen (1992b: 76), Nwajiaku (1994) and Amuwo (2003: 150–1).

[721] Decalo (1990: 99–101).

[722] Ronen (1987: 93) and Decalo (1990: 89).

[723] Decalo (1997: 44); see also Allen (1992a: 47), Eades and Allen (1996: xxxix), and Decalo (1998: 50).

[724] In 1985, Kérékou complained that the PRPB's "very small number of members" had "not yet allowed the setting up of the proper party structures at all levels." Quoted in Allen (1992b: 67).

[725] Allen (1992b: 67, 72) and Decalo (1997: 54).

[726] Omitoogun and Onigo-Itite (1996: 18) and Bierschenk and Olivier de Sardan (2003: 164).

shifting coalitions of parties that "were not bound together by any shared interest in . . . any grand national ideals beyond the . . . sharing of spoils of office."[727]

Origins and Evolution of the Regime

Benin's transition to competitive authoritarianism was rooted in state weakness.[728] Like other peripheral Soviet client states in Africa, the Marxist regime established by Kérékou in the 1970s grew vulnerable at the end of the Cold War.[729] In 1988, Benin suffered "fiscal collapse of unprecedented depth and scope," leaving the government unable to pay public-sector salaries.[730] As government patronage networks unraveled, nominally state-controlled labor, merchant, and student associations "declare[d] their autonomy," and teachers, civil servants, and students protested massively, defying a formal ban.[731] To a considerable extent, then, social protest was rooted in state weakness.[732] The security forces could not be relied on to repress protest; in fact, military leaders "let it be known that they would not intervene to prop up the regime."[733]

With Kérékou unable to rely on either the army or external support, the balance of forces shifted markedly. In early 1990, Kérékou called a National Conference.[734] The president expected to control the Conference, but when delegates realized that he lacked army support, they declared sovereignty, named a transitional government headed by opponent Nicéphore Soglo, and called elections for 1991.[735] They also launched a constitutional reform process that gave rise to a range of new democratic institutions, including a Constitutional Court.[736] Hardliners pressed Kérékou to dissolve the Conference, but the military "could not be relied upon" to enforce such a move.[737] Indeed, the army "stood by and did nothing while the conference usurped Kérékou's powers."[738]

Although Kérékou stood for reelection in 1991, he effectively lost his incumbent status. Most state agencies were controlled by his main rival, Prime Minister Soglo.[739] Moreover, the collapse of the PRPB in 1990 left Kérékou without a party. In this context, several leading regional barons defected,[740] and Soglo won the election easily.

The post-1991 regime was among the most open in the region. Violent repression ceased and levels of incumbent abuse were lower than in post-transition

---

727 Amuwo (2003: 163).

728 Allen (1992a) and Decalo (1997).

729 Nwajiaku (1994).

730 Heilbrunn (1997: 475); see also Allen (1992a: 46–7). The treasury "literally ran out of banknotes" (Decalo 1990: 130).

731 Omitoogun and Onigo-Itite (1996: 15); see also Allen (1992b: 70).

732 See especially Nwajiaku (1994). As Allen (1992a: 54) wrote, "It might still have been possible to contain [popular protest] . . . had not the political structures that supported the regime been themselves collapsing. The army had already withdrawn active support."

733 *Africa Report*, January–February 1991, p. 24; see also Omitoogun and Onigo-Itite (1996: 16); Decalo (1997: 51–3).

734 See Heilbrunn (1993), Nwajiaku (1994), and Omitoogun and Onigo-Itite (1996).

735 See Omitoogun and Onigo-Itite (1996) and Houngnikpo (2002: 94–5).

736 Magnusson (1999: 221–5).

737 Decalo (1997: 54–55); see also Omitoogun and Onigo-Itite (1996: 16).

738 Omitoogun and Onigo-Itite (1996: 35).

739 Allen (1992a: 52) and Englebert (1996: 164–5).

740 Decalo (1997: 56–7).

Malawi or Zambia.[741] Nevertheless, the regime was not fully democratic. Protest at times was restricted or repressed, critics were occasionally threatened or arrested, and journalists were frequently charged with libel.[742] Media access also remained skewed.[743] Finally, the 1996 and 2001 presidential elections were marred by at least some abuse.[744]

Incumbents repeatedly failed to consolidate power after 1991. Without effective coercive or party structures, governments had a difficult time skewing the playing field. Party weakness made it difficult for presidents to win legislative majorities or bring ethno-regional barons into a stable patronage-based coalition. In turn, legislative weakness limited presidents' capacity to control other regime institutions, such as the judiciary. As a result, their efforts to abuse power or weaken opponents were frequently thwarted.

THE SOGLO GOVERNMENT (1991–1996). Notwithstanding a growing economy and strong international support,[745] the Soglo government was weak. Elected without a party,[746] Soglo's administration suffered from a "severe lack of internal cohesion."[747] Although Soglo's wife, Rosine, created Benin Renaissance (RB) in 1993, the new party never gained control over progovernment forces.[748] Party weakness limited Soglo's control over parliament. Having won only 12 of 64 seats in 1991, pro-Soglo forces lacked a legislative majority.[749] This legislative weakness resulted in the de facto empowerment of other democratic institutions. Parliament created – against Soglo's will – an independent electoral commission,[750] and the Constitutional Court – also elected by parliament – intervened on several occasions to block government abuse, including an attempt to pack the Supreme Court.[751] Soglo sought to improve his parliamentary standing in the 1995 legislative elections. Rosine Soglo ran for a National Assembly seat with the goal

---

[741] Magnusson (1999, 2005).

[742] According to Decalo (1997: 59), "anti-regime opposition...came to be equated a priori with treason, especially if mounted by strata regarded by definition as suspect – youth, students, and unions." See also Englebert (1996: 166) and Amuwo (2003: 164). In 1996, Maurice Kouandété, a Kérékou ally, was arrested (*Africa Research Bulletin*, March 1996, p. 12155). On media repression, see Englebert (1996: 165), Palmer (1997: 254), Freedom House, "Freedom in the World 1999–2000: Benin" (http://www.freedomhouse.org), Committee to Protect Journalists, "Africa 1999: Country Report: Benin" (http://www.cpj.org). In 1991, the Soglo government imposed new rules on the media that "came to be applied to any kind of critical attacks on state authority" (Decalo 1997: 58).

[743] Newspapers reached only a tiny fraction of the population (Bratton and van de Walle

1997: 254), and most radio programming remained in state hands (U.S. Department of State 2001d: 4).

[744] See Amuwo (2003: 166, 171), U.S. Department of State (2004b: 6), and Magnusson and Clark (2005: 560).

[745] Magnusson (2001: 219, 224) and Gazibo (2005).

[746] Englebert (1996: 166).

[747] Amuwo (2003: 163).

[748] *Africa Research Bulletin*, November 1993, p. 11185 and Africa Report, May-June 1995, p. 5

[749] Englebert (1996: 165) and Decalo (1997: 57). A loose majority coalition forged in 1992 collapsed within a year. See *Africa Report*, May-June 1995, p. 5, Eades and Allen (1996: xli), and Amuwo (2003: 163).

[750] See *Africa Report*, May-June 1995, p. 5.

[751] Decalo (1997: 59), Magnusson (1999: 223–225; 2001: 225–6), and Amuwo (2003: 164–5).

of becoming the body's president.[752] Yet, despite some electoral manipulation, RB won only 21 of 83 parliamentary seats.[753] When the Constitutional Court annulled 13 of the races – including Rosine Soglo's – due to ballot-box stuffing,[754] Soglo threatened Court President Elisabeth Pognon with legal action for "offense against the head of state."[755] The annulment stood, however, and parliament remained in opposition hands.

Soglo's weakness was manifested by his loss to ex-President Kérékou in the 1996 presidential election. Notwithstanding some electoral abuse,[756] the government was unable to tilt the playing field heavily in its favor.[757] It also failed to contain elite defection. Thus, although Soglo won a narrow first-round plurality, regional barons including Adrien Houngbédji, Bruno Amoussou, and Albert Tevoedjre backed Kérékou in the second round.[758] Facing defeat, the President attempted to postpone the runoff but was blocked by the Constitutional Court.[759] Soglo – the incumbent – later complained of fraud and pressed the Court to annul the election.[760] Ultimately, however, he was forced to accept defeat.

THE SECOND KÉRÉKOU PRESIDENCY: 1996–2006. Like Soglo, Kérékou had no real party structure. His main partisan ally, the Action Front for Renewal and Development (FARD)-Alafia, was a regional party that had won only 14 seats in the 1995 election. Pro-Kérékou forces fared poorly in the 1999 elections, winning barely a third of parliament. Like his predecessor, then, Kérékou was forced to govern with a fluid coalition of small parties.[761]

Kérékou was a more skillful coalition-builder than Soglo. Soon after taking office, he brought leading regional barons and their parties into the government, naming Adrien Houngbédji – who finished third in the election – as prime minister.[762] Kérékou also used state resources to buy off opposition parties, NGOs, and private media,[763] which helped him win reelection in 2001. Described by observers as "free but not entirely fair," the election was marred by intimidation, abuse of state resources, irregularities in the voter registry, and possible manipulation of the vote count.[764] After Kérékou captured a first-round plurality,

---

[752] *Africa Report*, May-June 1995, pp. 5–6 and *Africa Research Bulletin*, April 1995, p. 11818.

[753] Eades and Allen (1996: xlii); Amuwo (2003: 164).

[754] Magnusson (1999: 229–230). See also *Africa Report*, May-June 1995, p. 6 and *Africa Research Bulletin*, April 1995, p. 11818.

[755] *Africa Research Bulletin*, July 1995, p. 11876–7.

[756] The government politicized the electoral commission, detained some Kérékou supporters, and engaged in at least some intimidation and fraud (Amuwo 2003: 166) and Magnusson and Clark 2005: 560). See also *West Africa*, April 1–7, 1996, p. 497 and *Africa Research Bulletin*, March 1996, p. 12155.

[757] For example, Soglo did not monopolize the means of coercion: Both sides spon-

sored militias and engaged in intimidation (Amuwo 2003: 166); also see *West Africa*, April 1–7, 1996, p. 497.

[758] Amuwo (2003: 166) and Creevey, Ngomo, and Vengroff (2005: 478).

[759] *West Africa*, April 1–7, 1996, p. 497

[760] Amuwo (2003: 166); see also *West Africa*, April 17–23, 1996, p. 946. CC officials were threatened and attacked (*Africa Confidential*, February 18, 2000, p. 8).

[761] *Africa Confidential*, December 6, 2002, p. 7.

[762] *Africa Research Bulletin*, May 1996, p. 12223–4).

[763] Bierschenk, Thioléron, and Bako-Arifari (2003: 163).

[764] See U.S. Department of State (2004b: 6); see also Amuwo (2003: 171).

several members of the electoral commission resigned in protest.[765] Soglo and Houngbédji, who finished second and third, respectively, boycotted the second round, calling it a "masquerade."[766] Kérékou won with 84 percent of the vote. Two years later, pro-Kérékou forces won a parliamentary majority in legislative elections marred by media harassment, intimidation, and a government ban on opposition "anti-fraud" brigades.[767]

Kérékou also failed to consolidate power, however. Like Soglo, many of Kérékou's efforts to manipulate state institutions – including an attempt to pack the electoral authorities – were blocked by the Constitutional Court.[768] After 2001, Kérékou faced two constitutional obstacles: presidential term limits and a 70-year-old age limit in the presidency.[769] Similar institutional constraints were dismantled in Cameroon, Gabon, and elsewhere. As the 2006 election approached, there were "ominous signs" that Kérékou would pursue this option as well.[770] In 2005, he called for a suspension of the elections on the grounds that Benin lacked resources to finance them.[771] The government cut funding for the electoral commission, leaving it unable to function.[772] However, Kérékou's behavior triggered opposition at home and abroad. After the EU threatened to suspend aid, he backed down and the election proceeded as scheduled.[773]

CONTINGENT DEMOCRATIZATION, 2006–2008. Because Kérékou lacked a party and refused to name a successor, the 2006 presidential race was wide open.[774] Yayi Boni, a well-financed technocrat, won a clean election.[775] Post-2006 Benin qualified as a democracy. Governments had suspended the practice of arresting journalists for libel in 2004, and a more liberal broadcasting law permitted greater pluralism in the electronic media.[776] Through 2008, there was no evidence of systematic abuse under Boni.

In summary, although Benin's post-2006 democratization technically makes it an outlier, the case fits our theory well. The regime was unstable and competitive authoritarian from 1991 until 2006. Relatively high levels of pluralism and competitiveness were rooted in incumbent weakness. Both Soglo and Kérékou sought to abuse power, but lacking effective coercive and organizational tools, they often failed. Although institutions such as the Constitutional Court

---

[765] Amuwo (2003: 170–1).

[766] *Africa Research Bulletin*, May 2001, p. 14332 and Freedom House Freedom in the World 2002: Benin" (http://www.freedomhouse. org).

[767] See Freedom House, "Freedom in the World 2004: Benin" (http://www.freedom house.org). In 2002 and 2003, the government arrested journalists for libel and occasionally broke up – or denied permits for – rallies. See Freedom House, "Freedom in the World 2004: Benin" (http://www. freedomhouse.org) and U.S. Department of State (2003b: 4; 2004b: 4; 2005b: 4).

[768] Amuwo (2003: 170).

[769] Seely (2007: 196–7).

[770] *Africa Confidential*, March 31, 2006, p. 7. See also Seely (2007).

[771] Seely (2007: 198).

[772] *Africa Confidential*, March 31, 2006, p. 7.

[773] Seely (2007). See also *Africa Confidential*, March 31, 2006, p. 7.

[774] Seely (2007: 197).

[775] Seely (2007: 197–9).

[776] See Reporters without Borders, "Benin: Annual Report 2007" (http://www.rsf.org), Freedom House, "Freedom in the World 2001: Benin" (http://www.freedomhouse. org), and U.S. Department of State (2004b: 4).

constrained incumbents,[777] it was not these formal institutions per se that produced a democratic outcome.[778] Rather, democratic institutions gained authority in a context in which weak coercive capacity and political–organizational fragmentation prevented governments from imposing their will. In other words, compliance with the rules was at least as much a product of incumbent weakness as it was of institutional strength. Democratization was a highly continent outcome and the specter of competitive authoritarian remains.

Mali

Like Benin, Mali is a low-linkage/high-leverage case in which low organizational power permitted pluralism, turnover, and fragile democratization. Weak state and party structures prevented the Alliance for Democracy in Mali (ADEMA) from consolidating power after easily winning elections in 1992 and 1997.

Mali is an extreme case of high leverage and low linkage. Like Benin, it was poor and aid-dependent,[779] and it lacked oil or black knight support from France.[780] State and party structures were weak. Coercive scope was low. The state's penetration of the national territory was among the most limited in Africa.[781] The army and police force were small,[782] and the country was characterized by vast stateless areas, particularly in the northern Tuareg-dominated regions.[783] In 1991, the army was so weak that in the days following a bloody crackdown on protesters, "soldiers, fearing assault by civilians, remained confined to their barracks."[784] State cohesion also was low. Mali had a long history of successful and failed coup attempts, and the army was deeply divided prior to the 1991 coup that toppled dictator Moussa Traoré.[785] Party strength was medium low. The governing ADEMA (1992–2002) possessed a national structure, based on anti-Traoré networks built up during the dictatorship.[786] Cohesion was low, however. Created in 1990, ADEMA was a coalition of diverse political groups, with no coherent ideology or history of violent struggle.[787]

Competitive authoritarianism emerged in Mali after a 1991 military uprising toppled longtime autocrat Moussa Traoré. Surprising many, the coup leader,

[777] Magnusson (1999, 2005).

[778] Similar institutions were trampled on in other cases examined in this study.

[779] Foreign aid constituted nearly 30 percent of Mali's gross national income in the early 1990s (Bergamaschi 2008: 223).

[780] Mali "was never a priority for France" (Bergamaschi 2008: 218). France refused to intervene on behalf of dictator Moussa Traoré in 1991 (Ola-Davies 1991: 8).

[781] Herbst (2000: 145–68).

[782] The army had fewer than 7,000 troops in the 1990s and the police, gendarmes, and Republican Guard numbered an additional 4,800 (Ayissa and Sangaré 2006: 124).

[783] An armed insurgency emerged in these regions in the early 1990s. See *Africa Confidential*, 21 February 1992, p. 5 and *Africa Research Bulletin*, 30 September 2007, p. 17201A; 4 July 2008, pp. 17539A–40A.

[784] Villalón and Idrissa (2005: 56).

[785] Imperato (1989: 66–73) and Villalón and Idrissa (2005: 54–5).

[786] See Vengroff and Kone (1995: 51) and Smith (2001: 74). See also *Africa Confidential*, 15 September 2000, p. 5.

[787] Smith (2001: 74). In 2002, Amadou Toumani Touré was elected president without a party, and he declared that he did not have "the slightest intention" of creating one (Villalón and Idrissa 2005: 69–70).

Amadou Toumani Touré (known as ATT), not only oversaw clean elections in 1992 but also opted not to participate in them.[788] ADEMA leader Alpha Oumar Konaré won the presidency and ADEMA captured 76 of 116 seats in parliament.

Mali's transition was widely viewed as a democratic success story, and the Konaré government was strongly backed by donors.[789] Yet the post-1992 regime was competitive authoritarian. The government at times attacked the independent media, repeatedly closing Radio Kayira and occasionally arresting journalists and editors.[790] Moreover, the 1997 legislative elections were marred by numerous irregularities.[791] After opposition parties rejected the election as fraudulent, the government banned demonstrations and beat, arrested, and tortured opposition activists.[792] The Constitutional Court annulled the results; however, opposition parties boycotted a new round of elections held three months later, leaving ADEMA with 128 of 147 seats in parliament.[793] Much of the opposition also boycotted the May 1997 presidential race, allowing Konaré to win reelection with 96 percent of the vote.

Although Mali's winner-take-all electoral system and a weak opposition favored ruling-party hegemony,[794] intra-elite conflict prevented ADEMA from consolidating power.[795] ADEMA was "hopelessly factionalized" during Konaré's second term.[796] Konaré lacked support within ADEMA to overturn presidential term limits.[797] However, his departure triggered a succession crisis that "fatally splintered" the party.[798] The nomination of Finance Minister Soumaïla Cissé as ADEMA's 2002 presidential candidate led to the defection of two party barons: Prime Minister Mandé Sidibé and ex–Prime Minister Ibrahim Boubacar Keïta, who – together with 38 legislators – left to form Rally for Mali.[799] ADEMA decomposed further after ATT, the leader of the 1991 coup that ended single party rule, entered the race. Although ATT ran as an independent, many ADEMA politicians (including Konaré) quietly backed him, creating "an extraordinary

[788] See Boyer (1992), Clark (2000), and Smith (2001). The 1992 elections were generally considered free and fair (Vengroff 1993: 552–60); see also *West Africa*, 11–17 May, 1992, p. 787.

[789] Scholars who described Mali viewed it as a "model transition" (Villalón and Idrissa 2005: 49, 55) and a "democratic role model for Francophone Africa" (Martin, Martin, and Weil 2002: 87). See also Le Vine (2004).

[790] Myers (1998: 205) and Stamm, Bastian, and Myers (1998: xxxiv).

[791] Villalón and Idrissa (2005: 64–65). See also *Africa Confidential*, 25 April 1997, p. 6, *Africa Research Bulletin*, April 1–31, 1997, p. 12645.

[792] Amnesty International (1997); Villalón and Idrissa (2005: 64–5).

[793] Villalón and Idrissa (2005: 65).

[794] Smith (2001: 76) and Villalón and Idrissa (2005: 57–60).

[795] Villalón and Idrissa (2005).

[796] *Africa Confidential* 23 July 1999, p. 5; *Africa Today*, March 2002, p. 31. Different ADEMA factions competed against one another in many localities – including the capital of Bamako – in the 1998 local elections (*Africa Confidential* 22 January 1999, p. 5).

[797] *Africa Today*, March 2002, p. 31; *Africa Confidential* 5 November 1999, p. 8.

[798] Villalón and Idrissa (2005: 68).

[799] *Africa Research Bulletin* March 1–31, 2002, p. 14779 and *Africa Confidential*, June 15 2001, p. 8 and May 3, 2002, p. 8. See also Villalón and Idrissa (2005: 68).

situation for a party in power," in which Cissé lacked many incumbent advantages.[800] The election was marred by "bold and blatant… rigging" to ensure that Cissé finished ahead of Keïta to qualify for the second round.[801] However, ATT won the runoff.

Mali appears to have democratized after 2002. Private media proliferated and arrests, libel suits, and other forms of harassment against opposition and the media largely ceased.[802] However, the new democracy was fragile. ATT's "consensus" politics – in which opposition parties were encouraged to join the Presidential Bloc – resulted in the co-optation of most major parties, thereby virtually depriving the country of an opposition.[803] Indeed, there were signs of authoritarian backsliding in the late 2000s.[804] The 2007 presidential and parliamentary elections were marked by opposition charges of manipulation of the voter registry, pre-circulation of marked ballots, and government abuse of state resources.[805] However, these claims were not confirmed by independent observers, rendering them difficult to assess.[806] ATT was reelected with 71 percent of the vote and pro-ATT forces captured more than three quarters of parliament.

Mali is clearly a borderline case. Due to the lack of independent confirmation of abuse in the 2007 election, as well as the absence of reports of major abuse in 2008, we score it as a democracy. However, the likelihood of backsliding into competitive authoritarianism seems high.

GHANA: LESSONS FROM AN OUTLIER

Ghana's post–Cold War regime trajectory is not explained by our theoretical framework. Despite low linkage and considerable organizational power, Ghana democratized after 2000 – an outcome that may be attributed to both leadership choice and opposition strength. Autocrat Jerry Rawlings bet heavily on ties to the West, positioning his government as a model economic reformer in the 1980s. To retain this status during the 1990s, Rawlings invested in credible democratic institutions and retained power via those institutions throughout the decade. Like incumbents in Mexico and Taiwan, however, Rawlings was eventually trapped by

---

[800] *Africa Today, March* 2002, p. 31; *West Africa* 27 May-2 June 2002, p. 15. In addition, there are more than 100 private radio stations in Mali. The government controlled the country's sole national television station. However, this station was generally balanced in its coverage (Freedom House, "Freedom of the Press 2008: Mali" (http://www.freedomhouse.org)).

[801] *Africa Research Bulletin* (2002c: 14964); *Africa Confidential*, 13 May 2005: 8; *Africa Research Bulletin*, August 1–31, 2002, p. 14964. See also The Carter Center (2002) and Villalón and Idrissa (2005: 68).

[802] Moreover, state-owned media was fairly balanced. See U.S. Department of State (2003g,

2004h, 2005e, 2007c) and Freedom House, "Freedom of the Press 2008: Mali."

[803] Baudais and Chauzal (2006: 71). See also Villalón and Idrissa (2005: 69–71), Baudaisa and Sborgib (2008), and Wing (2008: 94).

[804] In March 2007, a provincial radio station was evicted from a state-owned building following critical coverage of the president. See Freedom House, "Freedom of the Press 2008: Mali" (http://www.freedomhouse.org). See also U.S. Department of State (2008c, 2009e).

[805] Baudaisa and Sborgib (2008: 772).

[806] See Baudaisa and Sborgib (2008: 772). See also *Africa Research Bulletin*, 29 June 2007, pp. 17076–17077.

the transition he initiated. Institutions and opposition forces strengthened over time; in 2000, Rawlings's chosen successor was defeated in an election, ushering in democracy.

Linkage, Leverage, and Organizational Power

Ghana is a case of high leverage and low linkage. A poor, aid-dependent country without black knight support, Ghana was vulnerable to external democratizing pressure.[807] Organizational power – scored as medium – increased over time. Historically, the Ghanaian state was weak and, during the 1970s, economic crisis brought it to the brink of collapse.[808] State cohesion was very low: There were four military coups between 1957 and 1981, and Rawlings – who seized power in 1981 – faced five coup attempts between 1981 and 1983.[809] However, state capacity increased during the 1980s.[810] The Rawlings government built a "formidable array" of security agencies,[811] thereby enhancing its "capacity to coerce."[812] Moreover, military rebellions ceased.[813] Hence, we score coercive scope and cohesion as medium.

Party strength is difficult to assess. In the 1980s, Rawlings ruled without a party, relying instead on state-sponsored mass organizations such as Committees for the Defense of the Revolution and the 31 December Women's Movement.[814] These organizations penetrated the countryside and possessed considerable mobilization capacity.[815] When the National Democratic Congress (NDC) was created in 1992, it was built on these structures,[816] which allowed the party to develop quickly into a powerful machine with a "full array of regional and district branches" and clientelist networks "that extend[ed] right down to the grassroots."[817] Hence, although the NDC was a new party, it was said to "operate like a former national-liberation movement."[818] Because the NDC possessed a

---

[807] Haynes (1995) and Boafo-Arthur (1998b, 1999).

[808] On state weakness, see Chazan (1983). The crisis of the 1970s eroded "what little control [the state] held over the population" (Chazan 1983: 319–20) and led to a "breakdown in the command and control of the military" (Luckham 1996c: 231); also Hutchful 1997: 254–6).

[809] Shillington (1992: 104–36) and Nugent (1995: 96–125).

[810] Green (1998) and Hutchful (2002).

[811] Luckham (1996a: 155). This included a large intelligence service, well-trained Forces Reserve Battalions, and paramilitary forces such as the Civil Defense Organizations and Mobisquads (Luckham 1996a and Hutchful 1997: 256–8).

[812] Luckham (1998: 151).

[813] Hutchful (1997: 258).

[814] Other mass organizations included the June 4 Movement and the Ghana Private Road Transport Union (GPRTU) (Bluwey 1998 and Crook 1999).

[815] Haynes (1993: 460–1) and Bawumia (1998: 69). Committees for the Defense of the Revolution operated in villages throughout the country, and the Women's Movement had at least 750,000 members and maintained active branches in every district in Ghana (Shillington 1992: 155, Sandbrook and Oelbaum 1997: 624; 1999: 20–2, and Ninsin 1998b: 53).

[816] Anebo (1997: 50–1) and Crook (1999: 130–1).

[817] Sandbrook and Oelbaum (1999: 20). See also Anebo (1997: 50–1), Ayee (1997a: 20), Bawumia (1998: 69), and Boafo-Arthur (2003: 220).

[818] Gyimah-Boadi (1999: 178–9).

national structure and was based on networks that had been in place since the 1980s, we score party strength as medium.

Origins and Evolution of the Regime

Competitive authoritarianism in Ghana emerged from the "no party" Provisional National Defense Council (PNDC) regime installed when Jerry Rawlings seized power in 1981. The transition to multiparty rule was a "top-down affair."[819] Unlike most African cases, the Rawlings government was in a relatively strong international position at the end of the Cold War.[820] Originally leftist, the government had responded to economic crisis by embracing the West and adopting market-oriented economic reforms.[821] Ghana "became a favorite of many Western governments and international donor agencies,"[822] and consequently, donors were "notably relaxed in their application of political conditionality."[823] At the same time, Rawlings faced little domestic pressure. Civil society had been effectively suppressed in the 1980s,[824] and opposition forces – divided between the liberal New Patriotic Party (NPP) and the fragmented Nkruhamist left – lacked the mobilizational capacity to force a transition.[825] Moreover, a growing economy provided Rawlings with resources to sustain his rule.[826] Thus, the democracy movement – led by the Movement for Freedom and Justice – that emerged in 1990 "never posed a direct threat to the security of the regime."[827]

International factors played an important if indirect role in the decision to liberalize. By 1990, the Rawlings government had developed a clear stake in its international status as a model reformer. Adherence to international economic norms paid off handsomely during the 1980s; after 1989, however, regime elites calculated that political reform was essential if Ghana were to retain its international standing.[828] In effect, then, reform was a strategic move undertaken in an effort to "conform with global and regional trends."[829]

The terms of the transition were imposed by the Rawlings government.[830] In 1991, Rawlings unilaterally appointed a Committee of Experts and a Consultative Assembly to design a new multiparty constitution.[831] Both bodies were packed with government allies.[832] Opposition parties called for an elected constituent

[819] Herbst (1994: 185) and Haynes (1999: 114)

[820] Pinkney (1997: 165).

[821] See Jeffries (1989), Herbst (1991b: 176; 1993: 29), and Green (1998).

[822] Saaka (1997: 143). Ghana received more than $3 billion in assistance between 1983 and 1990 (Gyimah-Boadi 1994a: 140 and Jebuni and Oduro 1998: 39–41).

[823] Gyimah-Boadi (1994b: 84) and Herbst (1994: 188).

[824] Chazan (1991: 25–6) and Ninsin (1998a: 8).

[825] See Gyimah-Boadi (1994b: 78), Herbst (1994: 187–90), and Karikari (1998: 197).

[826] Herbst (1993, 1994).

[827] Nugent (1995: 201). On the rise of the Movement for Freedom and Justice, see Ninsin (1996: 10–16).

[828] Oquaye (1995: 161) and Saaka (1997: 150). Indeed, Rawlings referred to political reform as "political structural adjustment" (Lyons 1999: 161).

[829] Gyimah-Boadi (1994b: 78); see also Herbst (1994: 185).

[830] Abdulai (1992: 71) and Nugent (1995: 216–18).

[831] Nugent (1995: 198–9) and Ninsin (1996: 80–102).

[832] Gyimah-Boadi (1991a: 37–8, 1991b).

assembly, but the government "ignored such faint voices of protest because they were not loud enough to compel it to make drastic changes."[833] Despite the opposition's exclusion,[834] the Assembly produced a constitution with an impressive array of – nominally independent – institutions, including a powerful Supreme Court and autonomous Media, Human Rights, and Electoral Commissions.[835]

The new regime was hardly democratic. Television and radio remained state-owned and biased.[836] Moreover, the NDC abused state resources and restricted opposition access to finance, using state contracts and other policy instruments to punish businesses that backed opposition parties.[837] Government contractors "had their businesses crippled" if they did not support the NDC,[838] and pro-NPP entrepreneurs were "blacklisted, denied government contracts, and [had] their businesses openly sabotaged."[839] Finally, paramilitary organs were deployed to intimidate opposition activists, and independent newspapers were targets of libel suits and occasional violent attacks.[840]

The 1992 presidential and legislative elections were unfair.[841] Whereas NDC candidates "used the state to underwrite their electoral expenses,"[842] opposition parties were "starved of funds."[843] In an election marred by intimidation and ballot-box stuffing,[844] Rawlings won easily with 58 percent of the vote. Major opposition boycotted the subsequent legislative election, allowing the NDC to win 189 of 200 seats.[845] Nevertheless, the elections were accepted by the international community.[846]

The 1991–1992 transition thus installed a competitive authoritarian regime.[847] Compared to other regimes in the region, the Ghanaian regime faced relatively little pressure for further reform. It retained strong international support,[848] and with a growing economy and a solid resource base, Rawlings enjoyed considerable support at home.[849]

Yet Ghana's post-1992 trajectory differed markedly from that of other surviving authoritarian regimes in the region. Rather than seeking to reconsolidate

---

[833] Abdulai (1992: 71).

[834] Ninsin (1996: 109–13).

[835] Gyimah-Boadi (1998a, 1998b), Debrah (2001), and Oquaye (2001: 22–49).

[836] Gadzekpo (1997: 64–5) and Smith and Temin (2001: 163).

[837] Boafo-Arthur (1998a: 85–6), Oquaye (2001: 56), and Morrison (2004: 436).

[838] Boafo-Arthur (1998a: 86).

[839] Oquaye (1998: 109).

[840] See Oquaye (1995: 263), Luckham (1996a: 167), Gyimah-Boadi (1998a: 106), and Karikari (1998: 206).

[841] Abdulai (1992) and Oquaye (1995).

[842] Saaka (1997: 159).

[843] Rothchild (1995: 61).

[844] See Haynes (1993: 462), Nugent (1995: 236–42), Oquaye (1995: 267), and Gyimah-Boadi (1998a: 106).

[845] Ayee (1998c: 160).

[846] Saaka 1997: 165) and Boafo-Arthur (1998b: 180–1).

[847] Media and opposition figures continued to be harassed and threatened after 1992 (Green 1995: 582; Anokwa 1997: 24–5; Clauson 1998: 192), and access to media and resources remained skewed (Oquaye 1995, 2000; Morrison 2004). Private television and radio were not legalized until 1995 (Morrison 2004: 433), and as late as 1996, there existed only a handful of private radio stations, concentrated in the urban centers (Gadzekpo 1997: 57–8 and Clauson 1998: 191).

[848] Following the 1992 election, Western donors pledged $2.1 billion in aid (Boafo-Arthur 1998b: 180–1; 1999: 64). See also Green (1995: 583).

[849] Green (1998: 203) and Panford (1998: 120–2).

power, as in Cameroon, Gabon, and Kenya, Rawlings acted more like the Mexican PRI, underutilizing his coercive capacity and investing in democratic institutions. Given its control over parliament and the coercive apparatus, the NDC government had the power to subordinate, emasculate, or dismantle the democratic institutions created by the 1991 Constitution – as occurred in numerous other cases examined in this book. Nevertheless, it worked to strengthen them. Two factors appear to have motivated this strategy. First, the NDC remained concerned about international legitimacy.[850] Thus, the government's support for "measures designed to ensure technically free and fair elections" was rooted in its desire to "shore up its position vis-à-vis donors" by "presenting itself...as a model democratic reformer."[851] Second, the NDC acted from a position of strength. Given Rawlings's public support and relative opposition weakness, the NDC could reasonably expect to retain power through democratic institutions. In other words, credible democratic institutions offered the NDC the best of both worlds: It would retain power *and* enhance its international legitimacy.

The Rawlings government invested heavily in democratic institutions.[852] The Electoral Commission (EC) was professionalized, upgraded technically, and infused with resources.[853] Thus, whereas electoral authorities elsewhere in the region (e.g., Benin and Malawi) were starved of human and financial resources, Ghana's EC had a thousand full-time professional staff by 1996.[854] Crucially, the government also consistently abided by institutional outcomes, even when they favored the opposition.[855] The new institutions grew increasingly independent.[856] The Supreme Court ruled against the government on several occasions, striking down a requirement that opposition parties obtain permits for public rallies and mandating that the state media provide equal access for opposition parties in future elections.[857] Similarly, the EC was transformed "from a perceived tool of NDC governments into a completely independent...electoral authority."[858] It undertook a thorough overhaul of the electoral system, creating a new voter registry and adopting a series of other measures to enhance electoral transparency.[859] The EC often ruled against the government; indeed, many of its reforms were opposed by the NDC.[860] These actions "lent legitimacy to the electoral process" and established the EC as a credible independent actor.[861] Surveys showed widespread public trust in the EC,[862] and by the late 1990s, it "was viewed by virtually all stakeholders as a credible independent agency."[863]

[850] Ayee (1997a: 12) and Boafo-Arthur (1998b).
[851] Jeffries (1998: 197).
[852] Jeffries (1998).
[853] Gyimah-Boadi (1998a, 1998b), Jeffries (1998), and Lyons (1999).
[854] *Africa Confidential*, December 13, 1996, p. 2.
[855] Gyimah-Boadi (1994b: 81) and Green (1998: 205).
[856] Green (1998: 205).
[857] See Gyimah-Boadi (1994b: 91), Luckham (1996a: 168–70), and Oquaye (2000: 63–4).

[858] Debrah (2001: 76).
[859] See Ayee (1997a: 7–9; 1998c: 162–4) and Gyimah-Boadi (1999: 109).
[860] Ayee (1998c: 162–4), Gyimah-Boadi (1998a: 111–12), Debrah (2001: 76), and Oquaye (2001: 4–5). Indeed, the NDC accused the EC of pro-opposition bias (Ayee 1998c: 162).
[861] Sandbrook and Oelbaum (1999: 15); see also Debrah (2001) and Aubynn (2002).
[862] Aubynn (2002: 83).
[863] Smith (2002: 645).

The 1996 election was more competitive than that of 1992. Due to a cleaner electoral process and the rise of NPP candidate John Kufuor,[864] Rawlings "found himself compelled to campaign seriously."[865] Nevertheless, the playing field remained skewed.[866] The NDC maintained an "enormous financial advantage,"[867] due, in part, to its "unbridled exploitation of state resources."[868] At the same time, opposition parties confronted "severe financial and organizational handicaps."[869] Faced with government blacklisting, business leaders "avoided... Kufuor like the plague," leaving the NPP with less access to finance than in 1992.[870] Television remained state-owned and biased, and private radio was confined to the capital.[871] Rawlings won with 57 percent of the vote, and the NDC won 133 of 200 seats in parliament. The election gained wide international acclaim,[872] and unlike in 1992, it was accepted by the opposition.[873]

The regime remained mildly competitive authoritarian after 1996. The NDC continued to abuse state resources and dominate media access.[874] Independent media continued to be targets of lawsuits and other harassment.[875] Although term limits prevented Rawlings from seeking reelection in 2000, rumors persisted that he would stay on as president.[876]

Two developments prevented this outcome. First, additional reforms made the playing field more level. Restrictions on campaign finance were eased,[877] and private radio, which had been only embryonic in 1996, "proliferated throughout the country," breaking the NDC's effective monopoly over electronic media.[878] The result was a "crude equity in media coverage," as state media bias was "offset by the ample and often positive coverage received by the opposition parties in the burgeoning private media."[879] Second, opposition forces strengthened. As in Mexico and Taiwan, the NDC government's decision to underutilize its coercive capacity allowed civic and opposition groups to thrive. Civic associations proliferated in the 1990s.[880] By 2000, NGO-based election-monitoring networks were "far more extensive" than in previous elections.[881] NGOs recruited more than 15,000 observers, covering every electoral district and more than half of Ghana's 20,000 polling stations.[882] The NPP also grew steadily. By the late 1990s, it penetrated the countryside and was one of the "strongest legal opposition parties in

[864] Ayee (1997a).
[865] Gyimah-Boadi (1999: 172).
[866] Ayee (1998b: 70–1).
[867] Sandbrook and Oelbaum (1999: 14).
[868] Aubynn (2002: 102).
[869] Panford (1998: 123). See also Ayee (1997a: 15–16), Aubynn (2002: 96–7), and Morrison (2004: 435–6).
[870] Oquaye 2001: 62). See also Boafo-Arthur (1998a: 86).
[871] Gadzekpo (1997) and Temin and Smith (2002: 589).
[872] Haynes (1999: 116) and Gyimah-Boadi (1999: 114).
[873] Ayee (1997a: 13).
[874] Gyimah-Boadi (2001a: 60) and Temin and Smith (2002: 572, 605).
[875] Clauson (1998: 192).
[876] Lyons (1999: 167) and Gyimah-Boadi (2001a: 57).
[877] Debrah (2001: 77).
[878] Gyimah-Boadi (2001a: 61).
[879] Gyimah-Boadi (2001a: 61).
[880] Denkabe (1996: 137) and Gyimah-Boadi 1999: 171–3).
[881] Gyimah-Boadi (2001a: 65).
[882] In 1996, electoral observation NGOs had 4,200 people to monitor 3,100 polling places (only 21 percent of the total) (Gyimah-Boadi 1998a: 113; 2001a: 54; 2001b: 103, Boafo-Arthur 2001: 95–9, and Oquaye 2001: 6–7).

Africa."[883] The NPP competed on more or less equal footing with the NDC in 2000, fielding candidates in all but one district and deploying agents in all polling stations.[884]

The 2000 election came down to a contest between Rawlings's chosen successor, Vice President John Atta Mills, and NPP candidate John Kufuor. The election was relatively fair.[885] Media coverage was balanced, the EC was widely viewed as independent, and "the secrecy of the ballot box was beyond question."[886] Kufuor defeated Atta-Mills in a runoff and the NDC left power peacefully.

The post-2000 regime was democratic. Civil liberties and press freedom were broadly protected, and the harsh libel laws of the Rawlings era were repealed.[887] In 2004, Kufuor again defeated Atta-Mills in elections that were widely viewed as fair.[888] In 2008, Atta-Mills narrowly defeated NPP candidate Nana Akufo-Addo in a tense runoff election,[889] ushering in Ghana's second democratic turnover.

In summary, Ghana underwent a top-down transition that resembled those in Mexico and Taiwan. The initial transition was rooted not in heavy-handed external pressure or incumbent weakness but rather in the strategic choice of a government that sought the international prestige of clean elections – and was confident it could win such elections. Thus, the NDC underutilized its coercive capacity and invested in credible electoral institutions. In 1996, the NDC won clean (but not fair) elections, much like Mexico in 1994 and Taiwan in 1996. However, like Mexico and Taiwan, the NDC's underutilization of power permitted the emergence of an opposition that was eventually strong enough to defeat it. Hence, Rawlings's behavior – essentially acting as if Ghana were a high-linkage case – and opposition strength were both decisive in Ghana's democratization.

CONCLUSION

The 14 African cases are summarized in Table 6.2. Outcomes may be divided into three clusters. The first cluster includes six cases of high organizational power and/or black knight support. As our theory predicts, all six of these regimes remained stable between 1990 and 2008. Two of the high organizational-power cases (Mozambique and Zimbabwe) emerged from liberation movements; a third (Tanzania) had an unusually strong governing party; and the fourth (Botswana) benefited from discretionary economic power. All four of these regimes survived despite high Western leverage. In Zimbabwe, the ZANU government survived despite a well-organized and unified opposition, eight years of international sanctions, and economic collapse. In the other two cases, regimes with medium coercive and organizational power (Cameroon and Gabon) were buttressed by black knight support from France. In these latter cases, patronage-based governing

---

[883] Lyons (1999: 167) and Ayee (2002: 52, 171).

[884] Boafo-Arthur (2001: 98) and Gyimah-Boadi (2001a: 62).

[885] Ayee (2001: 44).

[886] Ayee (2002: 152); see also Boafo-Arthur (2001: 98) and Debrah (2001).

[887] Freedom House, "Freedom in the World 2005: Ghana" (http://www.freedomhouse.org).

[888] Freedom House, "Freedom in the World 2006: Ghana" (http://www.freedomhouse.org).

[889] Atta-Mills won 50.2 percent of the vote.

TABLE 6.2. *Predicted and Actual Regime Outcomes in Sub-Saharan Africa, 1990–2008*

Case	Linkage	Organizational Power	Leverage	Predicted Outcome	Actual Outcome
Benin	Low	Low	High	Unstable Authoritarianism	Democratization
Botswana	Low	High	High	Stable Authoritarianism	Stable Authoritarianism
Cameroon	Low	Medium	Medium	Stable Authoritarianism	Stable Authoritarianism
Gabon	Low	High	Medium	Stable Authoritarianism	Stable Authoritarianism
Ghana	Low	Medium	High	Unstable Authoritarianism	Democratization
Kenya	Low	Medium	High	Unstable Authoritarianism	Unstable Authoritarianism
Madagascar	Low	Low	High	Unstable Authoritarianism	Unstable Authoritarianism
Malawi	Low	Low	High	Unstable Authoritarianism	Unstable Authoritarianism
Mali	Low	Low	High	Unstable Authoritarianism	Democratization
Mozambique	Low	Medium High	High	Stable Authoritarianism	Stable Authoritarianism
Senegal	Low	Medium	High	Unstable Authoritarianism	Unstable Authoritarianism
Tanzania	Low	Medium High	High	Stable Authoritarianism	Stable Authoritarianism
Zambia	Low	Medium Low	High	Unstable Authoritarianism	Unstable Authoritarianism
Zimbabwe	Low	High	High	Stable Authoritarianism	Stable Authoritarianism

parties were more vulnerable to crisis, but timely assistance from France helped governments survive stolen elections and large-scale protest. Indeed, French aid allowed the Biya government in Cameroon to fend off one of the largest and most sustained protests in the region in 1991.

A second cluster includes two cases of high leverage and medium organizational power (Kenya and Senegal). In these cases, established patronage-based parties and minimally effective coercive structures were sufficient to ensure regime stability during normal times but – in the absence of black knight support or nonmaterial sources of cohesion – made regimes vulnerable to elite defection during periods of crisis. In line with our theory, each regime experienced turnover during the 1990–2008 period. In Kenya, the KANU government survived an initial crisis in 1991–1992, but the succession crisis triggered by Moi's retirement led to its defeat in 2002. In Senegal, the unraveling of the PS patronage coalition led to turnover in 2000. In both cases, successor governments were not fully democratic.

In a third cluster of cases (Benin, Madagascar, Malawi, Mali, and Zambia), organizational power was low, which invariably brought regime instability. In these cases, weak party and coercive structures prevented incumbents from consolidating power and left them vulnerable to even modest opposition challenges. In Benin (1990–1991), Malawi (1992–1994), and Madagascar (1992, 2002, and 2009), regimes imploded as their coercive structures decomposed. In Zambia (1990–1991), UNIP's patronage coalition unraveled in the context of severe economic crisis. In Mali (2002), a presidential succession crisis triggered ADEMA's collapse. In these cases, regime outcomes were rather fluid and open to contingency. Thus, although our theory correctly predicts regime instability in all five cases, it fails to account for democratization in Benin and Mali. In an important sense, these democratic outcomes were "by default," as incumbents – lacking the organizational tools to consolidate power – were constrained by weak formal democratic institutions.

Ghana's democratization is not explained by our theory. Rather, it was a product of Rawlings's leadership (and, specifically, his investment in credible democratic institutions) and opposition strength.

Alternative theories do less well at explaining these outcomes. For example, the African cases highlight the limited explanatory power of institutional design. Autocratic incumbents frequently modified or manipulated constitutional rules and trampled on nominally independent electoral and judicial authorities. Rather than a taken-for-granted assumption, then, the strength of formal rules is an outcome to be explained. Formal rules and authorities gained strength in two scenarios: (1) where organizational weakness prevented incumbents from dominating parliament or repressing opponents, as in Benin; and (2) where incumbents' pursuit of greater (often international) credibility induced them to invest in independent institutions, as in Ghana. Whether either scenario will result in long-term institutional strength is uncertain.

Opposition cohesion also fails to explain longer-term regime patterns. Although unified oppositions shaped electoral outcomes in a few cases (e.g., Kenya in 2002),[890] the relationship between opposition unity and regime outcomes was weak. A united opposition failed in Zimbabwe, where organizational power was high, and divided oppositions defeated autocrats in several regimes in which organizational power was low (e.g., Benin, Madagascar, Malawi, and Mali). Moreover, as the case of Botswana shows, powerful incumbents may directly undermine opposition unity at critical moments. Indeed, as van de Walle argues, opposition cohesion is often endogenous to regime strength.[891] Oppositions are more likely to unite when incumbents are deemed vulnerable (e.g., Zambia in 1991 and Kenya in 2002) than when they are strong (e.g., Gabon, and Tanzania).

The impact of several other factors, including economic crisis and protest, was mediated by organizational power. For example, economic crisis was more likely to undermine regimes where organizational power was low. When states and parties lacked cohesion (e.g., Benin, Madagascar, Malawi, and Zambia in the early 1990s), fiscal crises often triggered elite defection or military insubordination. However, when organizational power was high – and particularly where states and parties possessed nonmaterial bases of cohesion – governments often survived severe economic crises. A clear example is Zimbabwe, where despite nearly a decade of economic collapse, the security forces remained disciplined and ZANU remained largely intact. Likewise, opposition protest was more likely to emerge – and succeed – where organizational power was low. When incumbents could not control civil society or crack down effectively on strikes and demonstrations, protest often escalated to regime-threatening levels (e.g., Benin in 1990, Zambia in 1990–1991, and Madagascar in 2001–2002). However, when incumbents possessed effective state and party structures or black knight assistance, they were generally able to ride out large-scale protest or riots (e.g., Cameroon, Gabon, and Kenya) or use low-intensity coercion to prevent mass protest from erupting in the first place (e.g., Zimbabwe).

Placed in broader comparative perspective, the African cases experienced more turnover than democratization. Autocratic incumbents fell from power 12 times between 1990 and 2008, but only 3 regimes democratized. By contrast, autocrats fell six times in the Americas and all but one transition (Haiti) led to democracy. This difference can be attributed to variation in linkage. Where linkage was low, international pressure often faded in the aftermath of electoral turnover, which meant that unless civic and opposition forces were strong (as they were, to some degree, in Ghana and Kenya), successor governments had a weaker incentive to rule democratically. Indeed, many African transitions were by default, driven by external pressure and incumbent weakness, rather than democracy movements from below. As we discuss in the conclusion, such transitions rarely result in democratization.

---

[890] Likewise, opposition fragmentation may have helped autocrats win elections in Kenya in 1992 and 1997, Zambia in 2001, and Malawi in 2004.

[891] van de Walle (2006).

7

Diverging Outcomes in Asia

Our three Asian cases – Cambodia, Malaysia, and Taiwan – are diverse. Unlike the Americas or Eastern Europe, they did not share a common international environment. Western leverage was high in Cambodia but lower in Malaysia and Taiwan.[1] Linkage ranged from low in Cambodia to medium in Malaysia to high in Taiwan. These differences had an important impact on regime trajectories. In Malaysia and Taiwan, ruling parties possessed considerable organizational power. However, whereas the Malaysian government used its coercive capacity to thwart opposition challenges at relatively low external cost, Taiwan's high linkage – and distinctive need to retain its international standing with the United States – induced the KMT government to underutilize its coercive capacity, which eventually led to democratization. In Cambodia, where state and party structures were weaker and Western leverage was higher, external intervention nearly dislodged the former communists from power in 1993. Over time, however, international attention faded, and within this more permissive international environment, effective state- and party-building permitted authoritarian reconsolidation.

TAIWAN

Taiwan's democratization was, in part, a story of modernization. Industrialization under the Kuomintang (KMT) led to the growth of a large middle class and a vigorous civil society, which eventually undermined single-party rule.[2] Yet Taiwan's democratization also had a top-down character. Indeed, many scholars have highlighted the role of Presidents Chiang Ching-kuo and Lee Teng-hui

---

[1] Western leverage was generally lower in Asia than in other regions (Chu, Hu, and Moon 1997) because security issues remained higher on the U.S. foreign-policy agenda (Inoguchi 2000) and because many states could gain black-knight assistance from China or Japan (Neher 2002: 13).

[2] See Cheng (1989), Chu (1992, 1994a), Tien and Cheng (1999), and Gold (2000).

in initiating and carrying out political reform.[3] According to this latter view, Taiwan was "unique in that the ruling party tolerated the evolution of a political opposition and . . . [risked losing control] when it had the power to control society indefinitely."[4] We view this top-down dynamic as rooted not in leadership but rather in Taiwan's distinctive international position. High linkage – and the perceived importance of maintaining Taiwan's standing in the West – heightened the KMT's sensitivity to changing international conditions. During the 1980s, the KMT's effort to maintain Taiwan's status as the "good" China induced it to underutilize its coercive capacity and launch reforms from above. Inertial resource asymmetries allowed the ruling party to retain power throughout the 1990s, but when the opposition grew strong enough to win elections, the KMT's technocratic elite – unwilling to pay the external cost of repression – opted to accept defeat.

Linkage, Leverage, and Organizational Power

Like Mexico, Taiwan is a case of low leverage and high linkage. Coding leverage is somewhat difficult. A score of low leverage, which we assign due to the size of the Taiwanese economy,[5] may seem inappropriate given Taiwan's geopolitical isolation and extreme military dependence on the United States.[6] However, geopolitical interests always trumped democracy in U.S. foreign policy toward Taiwan.[7] Even as U.S.–China relations improved in the late 1970s and 1980s, U.S. governments prioritized stability over democratization in Taiwan.[8] Hence, the regime's exposure to Western democratizing pressure was relatively low.

Linkage, by contrast, was unambiguously high. Taiwan's ties to the West were among the most extensive in the world.[9] Massive U.S. military and economic assistance in the 1950s and 1960s created strong ties on a variety of fronts.[10] In the decades that followed, extensive travel, trade, and media penetration brought a "major influx of foreign ideas and practices."[11] In the late 1980s, the United

---

[3] See Moody (1991: 87, 90), Chao and Myers (1997; 1998: 115–19), and Tsang (1999: 7).

[4] Chao and Myers (1998: 296).

[5] Taiwan's economy exceeded $100 billion in 1990, which, by our operationalization, qualified it as low leverage (see Appendix II).

[6] See Cheng (1989: 484), Chu, Hu, and Moon (1997: 273–4, 282), and Copper (1998: 27, 30).

[7] Tucker (1994); Chu, Hu, and Chung-in Moon et al. (1997).

[8] Chu, Hu, and Moon (1997: 271, 289); Ooi (2009: 71).

[9] Gold (1986); Li (1993: 359).

[10] See Tucker (1994: 59–67). The KMT created a Department of North American Affairs

(Copper 1995: 107) and many early government meetings were held in English so that U.S. advisors could understand (Berman 1992: 207).

[11] Gold (1986: 94). According to Clough (1998: 26), "[f]ew developing countries have been as open to outside influence as Taiwan. . . . By the 1990s foreign influences were pouring into Taiwan through innumerable channels: books and magazines, satellite television transmissions, films and compact discs, travel abroad each year by hundreds of thousands of people from Taiwan, visits to Taiwan by hundreds of thousands of foreigners, the return to Taiwan of thousands of those educated in the United States."

States was Taiwan's leading trading and investment partner, and Taiwan was the sixth leading trading partner of the United States.[12] Telecommunication ties rivaled those of Western Europe,[13] and a stunning 70 percent of Taiwanese traveled abroad in the 1980s.[14] Moreover, Taiwan experienced a surge of emigration to the United States in the late 1970s and 1980s, giving rise to a large diasporic community.[15] Affluent and organized,[16] the diaspora hosted a range of exile-based opposition groups and was closely tied to the domestic opposition movement that emerged in the 1970s and 1980s.[17] In the 1980s, both the KMT and the opposition operated branches in the United States and recruited candidates within the overseas community.[18]

Technocratic linkage also was high. The number of U.S.-educated officials in Taiwan "probably surpassed . . . any other government in the world."[19] Two thirds of Taiwanese university students attended college in the United States and, in the 1980s, Taiwan was the leading source of foreign students in the United States.[20] Returning graduates ascended to high-level state positions; by the late 1980s, there was a "stupendifying number of PhDs" in the government.[21] In 1988, two thirds of the cabinet had U.S. degrees and 17 of 31 KMT Central Committee members held foreign graduate degrees – nearly all from the United States.[22] KMT technocrats tended to be particularly sensitive to Taiwan's international standing.[23] Opposition elites also maintained strong ties to the United States. In the 1980s, most opposition leaders had lived or studied in the United States, and many of them were U.S. citizens.[24]

In the political realm, both the KMT and the opposition maintained a strong presence in Washington.[25] The KMT spent "hundreds of millions of dollars, and perhaps several billion," in lobbying efforts; in the 1980s, the "China Lobby" was considered the second largest foreign lobby (after the Israel lobby) in

---

[12] Healey (1991); Chu (1992: 163).

[13] On *The Economist*'s Information and Communications Technology Index, which measures per capita telephone lines, mobile phones, personal computers, and Internet use, Taiwan ranked ahead of Britain, France, Germany, and Japan in 2006 (*The Economist* 2006: 60).

[14] Shiau (1999: 110). Much of this travel was to the United States (Tucker 1994: 186–7).

[15] Overall, more than 145,000 Taiwanese emigrated to the United States between 1972 and 1990 (Ooi 2009: 68). On the diaspora community, see Shefferer (2003: 18–19) and Ooi (2009: 67–69).

[16] Tucker (1994: 182, 189); Shefferer (2003: 18–19); Ooi (2009: 67–9).

[17] Exile-based opposition groups included the World United Formosans for Independence, Taiwan Revolutionary Party, Taiwanese Democratic Movement Overseas, Formosan Christians for Self-Determination, Formosa Club in America, and Formosan

Association for Political Affairs (Tucker 1994: 141, 151). On diasporic ties to the Taiwanese opposition, see Arrigo (1994) and Ooi (2009: 67–9).

[18] Tucker (1994: 190); Liu (1999: 73).

[19] Tucker (1994: 189).

[20] Li (1993: 359); Wu (1995: 56–7).

[21] Moody (1991: 185); Dickson (1996: 52–8).

[22] Tien (1989: 122–4); Cheng and White (1990: 8). In 1990, President Lee Teng-hui, Vice President Li Yuan-Zu, Vice Premier Lien Chan, KMT General Secretary James Soong, and KMT Deputy General Secretaries Ch'en Lu-an and Ma Ying-jeou all held degrees from Western universities (Cheng and White 1990: 20; Baum 1994: 62).

[23] Gold (2000: 106–8).

[24] Cheng (1989: 483); Copper (1989: 16); Chao and Myers (1997: 231).

[25] Cheng (1989: 492–3); Schafferer (2003: 18–19).

Washington.[26] Yet opposition forces developed a powerful countervailing presence in the United States. Civic and opposition groups were well connected to the diaspora community and built strong ties to the transnational human-rights network, through which they gained access to the U.S. media and policymaking circles.[27] The result was what Su-Mei Ooi calls a "transnational protection regime," in which opposition ties to the United States "raised the international visibility of the ... regime's authoritarian practices" and heightened the cost of repression.[28]

Organizational power was high. The Taiwanese state was exceptionally strong.[29] Under the threat of Chinese aggression, the KMT developed a "vast military-security apparatus"[30] with a clear capacity to "monitor, control, and deactivate potential opposition."[31] The military's secret police, or Garrison Command, exercised vast powers of surveillance and detention,[32] and the National Security Bureau operated a surveillance network with 50 thousand full-time and 500 thousand part-time informants.[33] These agencies were complemented by KMT "security offices" in firms, schools, and social organizations.[34] Citizens were thus "closely monitored at school, work ... and in much of social life,"[35] and the KMT exerted "influence, if not outright control" over most civic organizations.[36] The state also was highly cohesive.[37] Forged in a context of intense military threat,[38] the coercive apparatus was highly disciplined: There is no evidence of rebellion within the security forces between 1950 and 1990.[39]

Party strength was medium high. Scope was high. The KMT possessed a "huge party apparatus,"[40] with a membership that exceeded 2.5 million – nearly 20 percent of the adult population – in the late 1980s.[41] The party "deeply penetrated the local society,"[42] operating cells in schools, businesses, and "social groups at all levels."[43] Moreover, the KMT's business empire, valued at more than $2.4 billion, gave it an "independent financial base which operated on an unheard-of scale in any representative democracy."[44] Historically, party cohesion was high.

---

[26] Tucker (1994: 186); Robinson (1998: 198–299).

[27] Ooi (2009).

[28] Ooi (2009: 70, 72–8).

[29] See Gold (1986, 2000).

[30] Chu, Hu, and Moon (1997: 274–5).

[31] Huang (1996: 108). During the 1980s, Taiwan had nearly half a million soldiers in the army (Chu 1992: 21) and its defense budget was the second largest in Asia (Copper 1997: 527).

[32] Chu (1992: 21–2); Hood (1997: 35).

[33] Shambaugh (1998: 245–6); Roy (2003: 91).

[34] Gold (1986: 60).

[35] Hood (1997: 45).

[36] Roy (2003: 152). The coercive apparatus was highly effective in maintaining social order. When protest arose, as in the 1970s, it was

effectively repressed (Chu 1992: 51; Gold 2000: 106; Roy 2003: 168–9).

[37] See Gold (2000: 90–3).

[38] Chu, Hu, and Moon (1997: 274–5).

[39] Cohesion was reinforced by the KMT's Leninist-style penetration of the security forces: KMT cells and commissars operated in all military units (Cheng 1989: 477; Fields 2002: 118–19).

[40] Tien and Chu (1998: 112).

[41] Chu (1992: 27); Huang (1996: 114–15); Dickson (1997: 61); Hood (1997: 125).

[42] Rigger (2000: 134).

[43] Kau (1996: 289); see also Dickson (1996: 46) and Rigger (2000: 137).

[44] Chu (1992: 150–1); Tien (1997: 147); Rigger (2001a: 949–50); Fields (2002: 123, 138).

Re-founded in Taiwan amid a civil war, the KMT developed a militarized structure modeled on the Chinese Communist Party, with cadres who were "socialized as revolutionary vanguards."[45] Described as a "political sect,"[46] the KMT was highly disciplined through the 1980s.[47] By 1990, however, the party's founding generation had died off and it had evolved into a patronage-based machine.[48] Hence, we score party cohesion as medium.

Origins and Evolution of the Regime

Taiwan's competitive authoritarian regime evolved out of the "quasi-Leninist" dictatorship established by Chiang Kai-shek in the late 1940s.[49] After its defeat on the mainland, the KMT imposed martial law, banned opposition, and suspended elections. In the four decades that followed, a set of "Temporary Provisions" overrode the constitution and granted the president an unlimited term in office.[50] Although the Legislative Yuan and the National Assembly (the body responsible for selecting the president) remained operational, their members – elected in 1947 – enjoyed lifetime mandates.[51] Prior to the 1970s, organized opposition "did not exist."[52] Nevertheless, Taiwan's status as the "good" China ensured the regime strong U.S. support.[53]

Beginning in the 1970s, the KMT was challenged on two fronts. On the domestic front, industrialization gave rise to a large middle class, a robust civil society, and eventually a potent opposition.[54] Civic, social, and economic associations proliferated in the 1970s and 1980s, triggering an "explosion of autonomous social mobilization,"[55] which, together with a burgeoning private sector,[56] lay the bases for "one of the most vibrant oppositions in East Asia."[57] Opposition began with the *Tangwai* (outside the party) movement in the late 1970s.[58] In 1986, activists founded the Democratic Progressive Party (DPP), which would emerge as a major opposition force in the 1990s.[59]

On the international front, the end of the Cold War came early to Taiwan. The West's rapprochement with China triggered a process of international "de-recognition" that culminated in the 1979 rupture of formal diplomatic relations with the United States.[60] Taiwan was isolated diplomatically, and as U.S.–China relations improved, its strategic importance waned. Although the KMT

---

45 Cheng (1989: 475–7); see also Dickson (1993).
46 Chao and Myers (1998: 33).
47 Chu (1992: 17); Dickson (1993: 70–7).
48 Bosco (1994); Hood (1997: 154–5).
49 Cheng (1989).
50 Chu (1992: 23–4); Roy (2003: 83–4).
51 Cheng (1989: 475).
52 Liu (1999: 68).
53 Tucker (1994).
54 Arrigo (1994); Rigger (2001b).
55 Chu (1994a: 99); see also Tien (1992, 1997), Rigger (1996), and Tien and Cheng (1999: 44).

56 Chu (1992: 137–42); Hing (1997: 224–7).
57 Rigger (1996: 300).
58 On the rise of the *Tangwai* and opposition protest in the late 1970s, see Fan and Feigert (1988), Chao and Myers (1998), and Rigger (2001b).
59 See Rigger (1996, 2001b).
60 Taiwan lost its UN seat in 1971 and lost diplomatic relations with 55 countries in the 1970s and 1980s (Tien 1996a: 9–10).

faced no direct U.S. government pressure for democracy,[61] it experienced substantial indirect pressure in the form of negative U.S. media coverage and growing
criticism from the U.S. Congress.[62] Indeed, as the domestic opposition established ties to the transnational human-rights network and gained a foothold in
U.S. media and policy circles, the international salience of the KMT's authoritarianism increased markedly.[63]

Although the KMT's initial response to the emerging opposition was to crack
down, as it did in 1979,[64] repression came at "an increasingly higher cost to
[its] already shaky international standing."[65] This cost was manifested after the
1984 murder – by KMT agents, on U.S. soil – of Taiwanese-American journalist
Henry Liu.[66] The killing "hurt the government's reputation both at home and
abroad," triggering critical U.S. media coverage and U.S. congressional hearings
that generated calls for an end to martial law.[67] These developments convinced
KMT elites that political reform was necessary to improve Taiwan's international
standing.[68] Because anti-communism was no longer sufficient to maintain U.S.
support and because human-rights abuses had "seriously damaged the island's
reputation as the 'good' China,"[69] KMT leaders viewed it as "imperative to be
seen as the . . . 'democratic China' in the eyes of the United States."[70] In this
context, President Chiang Ching-kuo initiated a political opening that continued
following his death in 1988 under his successor, Lee Teng-hui. Between 1986
and 1989, martial law ended, opposition parties were legalized, and most press
restrictions were lifted.[71]

The transition was pushed forward by a combination of linkage and opposition strength. The political opening triggered an explosion of social and
political protest.[72] Prodemocracy protest peaked in March 1990, with a massive student demonstration calling for direct presidential elections.[73] With tens
of thousands of riot police mobilized to confront the protest,[74] the government's capacity to repress was clear. Yet, whereas the Mahathir government
in Malaysia cracked down on rising protest in the late 1980s (see below), the
KMT, facing an international environment that was "unpropitious for a turn to
repression," opted for restraint.[75] Unwilling to pay the cost of a Malaysia-style

---

[61] Cheng and Haggard (1992: 16); Ooi (2009:
71). U.S. governments never demanded political reform during the 1970s and 1980s, and
neither arms sales nor Taiwan's Most Favored
Nation status was subject to conditionality
(Cheng 1989: 492; Tucker 1994: 159; Chu,
Hu, and Moon 1997: 271).

[62] See Cheng (1989: 487–92), Copper (1998:
27–30), Schafferer (2003: 14–17), and Ooi
(2009: 72–8).

[63] Ooi (2009).

[64] In December 1979, the regime cracked down
on opposition, arresting dozens of *dangwei*
leaders and closing independent magazines
(Chu 1992: 51; Rigger 2000: 140; Yang and
Engbarth 2000: 211).

[65] Gold (2000: 106); see also Ooi (2009: 75–8).

[66] Ooi (2009: 77–8).

[67] Copper (1997: 47); see also Tucker (1994:
183), Wu (1995: 39–40), and Ooi (2009: 78).

[68] Cheng (1989: 494); Dickson (1997: 205–11).

[69] Rigger (2000: 139).

[70] Copper (1998: 31).

[71] Berman (1992: 161); Hood (1997: 82); Chao
and Myers (1998: 5, 178).

[72] The number of protest incidents rose nearly
sevenfold between 1983 and 1988 (Chu 1992:
102–4). See also Chao and Myers (1998:
141–2).

[73] Wright (1999: 1004).

[74] Chu (1992: 120); Chu (1993: 178).

[75] Moody (1991: 89).

crackdown, the Lee government convened a multiparty National Affairs Conference (NAC). The conference abolished the Temporary Provisions and agreed to hold direct elections for the National Assembly (in 1991) and the Legislative Yuan (in 1992), thereby completing the transition to a competitive regime.[76] Although the president would not be directly elected, as the opposition demanded, the National Assembly, which selected the president, would be.[77]

The introduction of national elections did not democratize Taiwan, however. The persistence of interlocking KMT–state ties created a highly uneven playing field.[78] Media access, for example, was badly skewed: All three television networks, most radio stations, and Taiwan's two leading newspapers were in the hands of the state, the KMT, or allies.[79] In addition, overlapping state, party, and business ties gave the KMT a "huge financial advantage."[80] The government distributed state credit, licenses, and concessions to friendly businesses,[81] which contributed "huge sums" to the party in return,[82] and tax audits were used to punish businesses that backed the opposition DPP.[83] The KMT also maintained its own business empire, which was worth at least $2.4 billion.[84] Party-owned enterprises "enjoyed privileges denied other private firms,"[85] and much of their profits – estimated at up to $500 million a year – were channeled into KMT coffers.[86] Finally, in a practice known as "black-gold" politics, local KMT factions were granted contracts or oligopolistic concessions in sectors such as transportation, construction, utilities, and banking; in exchange, they channeled a portion of their profits back into party coffers.[87] The result was an "extraordinarily unequal" distribution of resources.[88] Whereas the KMT raised and spent at least $450 million a year in the mid-1990s,[89] the DPP raised only $7.7 million in 1996; the following year, it ran out of money and was unable to pay its staff.[90]

The KMT thus "entered the 1990s with a supremacy over domestic politics achieved by few authoritarian regimes."[91] Although elections were clean, unequal access to media and finance made it "extremely difficult for the opposition to defeat the ruling party."[92] Indeed, the DPP failed to meet even its modest

---

[76] Chao and Myers (1994: 224); Higley, Huang, and Lin (2001).

[77] See Tien (1996a: 13–14) and Chao and Myers (1998: 226–58).

[78] See Chu (1992), Chu, Hu, and Moon (1997: 286), and Rigger (2001b: 148–50).

[79] See Berman (1992), Chen (1998), and Rawnsley and Rawnsley (1998, 2003). Although cable television spread rapidly in the 1990s (Chin 1997: 81–2), the three KMT-dominated networks remained dominant. In 1995, 95 percent of Taiwanese obtained their news from one of the major networks (Rawnsley and Rawnsley 1998: 110).

[80] Rigger (2001a: 949).

[81] See Chu (1994b: 116) and Kau (1996: 289).

[82] Guo, Huang, and Chiang (1998: 212); Fields (2002: 120).

[83] Wu (1995: 79).

[84] Chu (1992: 150–1); Tien and Cheng (1999: 40); Fields (2002: 121–6, 138).

[85] Baum (1994: 62).

[86] See Chu (1992: 150), Shiau (1996), and Fields (2002: 127).

[87] See Wang (1994: 185), Tien (1996a: 15–19), Chu (1998: 141), and Rigger (2000: 146).

[88] Rigger (2000: 137).

[89] Baum (1994: 62).

[90] Guo, Huang, and Chiang (1998: 211).

[91] Roy (2003: 152).

[92] Rigger (2000: 137).

goal of winning a quarter of the seats in the 1991 National Assembly election,[93] and the KMT captured nearly two thirds of the seats in the 1992 legislative election.

Nevertheless, several factors conspired to loosen the KMT's grip on power. First, China's continued rise exacerbated Taiwan's problems of isolation. Taiwanese traveling abroad for business or tourism increasingly felt the impact of the country's lack of international standing, and surveys showed broad public support for government efforts to improve that standing.[94] Democratization was central to that effort.[95] A second factor was growing opposition strength. As in Mexico, the KMT's strategy of coercive restraint allowed civic and opposition forces to flourish. During the 1990s, the DPP evolved into a "formidable" organization.[96] The KMT thus "found itself at the mercy of a competitive system it had allowed to emerge but was unable to control."[97] Demands for reform mounted. In 1992, civic groups collected one million signatures calling for direct presidential elections.[98] Given the level of opposition strength, these demands were backed by a "credible threat" of mass protest.[99]

The KMT again opted for concessions rather than a crackdown. After defeating hardliners in the 1993 party congress, Lee pushed through a 1994 constitutional reform to establish direct presidential elections, which would be held in 1996.[100] The government also took additional steps to delink state and party, for example, by formally eliminating the KMT's presence in the military and state-run universities, and it opened the door for new private television stations (although none would appear until 1997).[101] Elections grew more competitive. In 1994, the DPP won the Taipei mayoral race, despite being outspent by more than 50 to 1.[102] In 1995, the KMT's massive media and resource advantages produced only a "razor-thin" legislative majority.[103]

Taiwan's 1996 presidential election was much like that of Mexico's in 1994. The election was "full of uncertainties," as President Lee was challenged not only by the DPP but also by two KMT defectors.[104] As in Mexico, however, the ruling party enjoyed massive inertial advantages.[105] The KMT retained a "tight grip on the electronic media,"[106] civil servants were mobilized massively on the KMT's

[93] See Arrigo (1994: 171–2) and Chao and Myers (1997: 229–35).

[94] Roy (2003: 212).

[95] Hood (1997: 120, 134); Copper (1998: 25).

[96] Rigger (2000: 147). DPP membership increased from 20,000 in 1990 to 160,000 at decade's end, and it established branches throughout the island. See Tien (1992: 34), Liu (1999: 73), and Rigger (2001b: 65).

[97] Wachman (1994: 158).

[98] Chao and Myers (1998: 264).

[99] Tien and Cheng (1999: 25).

[100] Tien and Chu (1998: 97, 107). In response, hardliners left the KMT to form the New Party (NP).

[101] See Chin (1997: 84–9), Tien (1997: 134), and Gobel (2001: 12).

[102] Wu (1995: 79).

[103] Cheng (1997: 46); Copper (1998: 86). The KMT won 46 percent of the vote and 85 of 164 legislative seats.

[104] Pao-Min (1996: 230–1). The KMT defectors were Taiwan provincial governor Lin Yang-kang, who was backed by the New Party, and Chen Li-an, who ran as an independent.

[105] See Hood (1997: 164), Tien and Chu (1998: 113), and Chu (1998: 140; 1999: 76–7).

[106] Chu (1999: 76–7).

behalf, and the resource gap remained enormous.[107] Due to an uneven playing field, a strong economy, and Chinese saber-rattling, Lee was easily reelected, with 54 percent of the vote.[108]

Although the 1996 election is often said to mark the completion of Taiwan's democratic transition,[109] the regime remained competitive authoritarian in the late 1990s due to persistent resource and media disparities.[110] Several factors contributed to the KMT's eventual defeat. First, the DPP grew strong enough to win elections despite resource asymmetries. Opposition strength was enhanced by media liberalization. The appearance of the independent Formosa Television in 1997, the extension of cable television to nearly the entire population, and the elimination of remaining press restrictions transformed Taiwan's media into "one of Asia's freest."[111]

Ultimately, the KMT fell victim to two contingent developments. First, James Soong, a popular governor of Taiwan province, abandoned the ruling party after failing to secure its 2000 presidential nomination. Soong's defection split the nationalist vote and "broke" the KMT organization, as much of the party machine was "hijacked by Soong."[112] A second and related development was the emergence of corruption as an electoral issue. Black-gold politics had become an increasingly salient electoral issue in the 1990s.[113] Soong's defection led to a mutually damaging exchange of corruption allegations that benefited the DPP.[114] Voter backlash against black-gold politics was such that "traditional KMT advantages – party wealth, machine politics, and administrative, judicial, and media bias – backfired."[115] DPP candidate Chen Shui-bian won a narrow victory,[116] and the KMT left power peacefully.

Taiwan was democratic after 2000. Elections were clean and civil liberties were respected.[117] Although the DPP government engaged in some minor abuse, including unlawful surveillance, selective tax audits, and discretionary use of credit and contracts in exchange for business donations,[118] the KMT retained such vast financial and media resources that this abuse did not seriously hinder its ability to

---

[107] Chu (1998: 140; 1999: 76–8); Myers (1998: 37–8); Tien and Cheng (1999: 40, 44). Whereas the DPP raised $7.7 million for the election (Guo, Huang, and Chiang 1998: 211), the profits generated by KMT firms in 1996 exceeded that figure by more than 60 times (Fields 2002: 127).

[108] DPP candidate Peng Ming-min won 21 percent.

[109] See Chu and Diamond (1999: 808), Tien and Cheng (1999: 45), and Rigger (2000: 137).

[110] The KMT continued to dominate the media until the late 1990s (Hong 2000: 22; Yang and Engbarth 2000: 212). As late as 2000, the *Taipei Times* reported that KMT assets were worth $6.7 billion compared to $7.3 mil-

lion for the DPP (Rigger 2001a: 950; 2001b: 67). On the uneven playing field after 1996, see Chu (1998: 139–40; 1999: 76–7), Guo, Huang, and Chiang (1998: 215), Alagappa (2001b: 14), and Rigger (2001b: 9–10).

[111] Schafferer (2003: 131).

[112] Stainton (2000: 23).

[113] Bosco (1994: 61); Copper (1998: 150).

[114] Rigger (2001a: 956–7).

[115] Rigger (2001a: 957).

[116] Chen won 39 percent of the vote compared to 37 percent for Soong and 23 percent for KMT candidate Lien Chan.

[117] Freedom House, "Freedom in the World 2008: Taiwan" (http://www.freedomhouse.org).

[118] Chu (2005: 49).

compete.[119] Chen was narrowly reelected in 2004; however, the KMT decisively won the 2008 presidential election, ushering in Taiwan's second turnover.

In summary, the KMT entered the 1990s with overwhelming organizational advantages. However, it was constrained by extensive linkage and Taiwan's distinctive problem of international recognition. Western powers never directly pushed for democratization, but the KMT's technocratic leadership viewed reform as necessary to retain Taiwan's status as the "good China." Thus, whereas the Malaysian government cracked down on opposition challenges, the KMT underutilized its coercive capacity, which allowed opposition activity to flourish. Although media and resource disparities persisted throughout the 1990s, the major obstacles to opposition victory were dismantled; in 2000, a corruption scandal and KMT schism permitted such a victory.

As in Mexico, Taiwan's democratization had an important domestic component. However, the timing of democratization cannot be explained without reference to international factors. The initiation of political reforms in 1986 was clearly motivated by changes in the international environment. Although the KMT possessed the organizational power to slow or even reverse the liberalization process, linkage made the cost of such a move prohibitive.

MALAYSIA

Like Taiwan, Malaysia is one of the most developed countries examined in this study. Yet, despite appearing to "satisfy the preconditions for democracy posed by modernization theorists,"[120] Malaysia remained competitive authoritarian throughout the 1990–2008 period. Two factors explain this outcome: (1) organizational power was high; and (2) the absence of high linkage or leverage allowed United Malays National Organization (UMNO) governments to use their coercive and organizational power to thwart opposition challenges.

Linkage, Leverage, and Organizational Power

Malaysia is a case of medium leverage and medium linkage. With respect to leverage, Malaysia's economy was the fourth largest in this study and it was not dependent on foreign aid.[121] In terms of linkage, although economic development and integration created substantial ties to the West, these ties were nevertheless weaker than in Taiwan and other high-linkage cases. Due in part to the government's "Look East Policy" in the 1980s, Malaysia had stronger trade and investment ties to Asia than to the United States and Europe.[122] Levels of

---

[119] See Wong (2003) and Chu (2005: 49).

[120] Case (2001a: 44).

[121] Malaysia's GDP increased from $44 billion in 1990 to $88.8 billion in 1995 (current dollars, see World Bank World Development Indicators (www.worldbank.org/data/), which qualifies it as a case of

medium leverage (see Appendix II). On aid dependence, see Thompson (1993: 480).

[122] Means (1991: 92–4); Milne and Mauzy (1999: 123–43); Khalid (2004: 325–30). In 1990, the United States accounted for 17 percent of Malaysian exports compared to 29 percent for ASEAN (Mohammad 2005),

Internet use and emigration to the West in the 1990s were about one third of Taiwan's.[123] Although study in the United States rose sharply in the 1980s,[124] there were few U.S.-educated technocrats in the UMNO government in the 1990s.[125] Moreover, ties to the West coexisted with non-Western linkage, particularly to the international Muslim community.[126] Between 1964 and 1988, more Malaysians traveled to Saudi Arabia to perform the *Hajj* than to the United States for tourism.[127] The UMNO government was active in the Organization of the Islamic Conference, and the Islamic Party of Malaysia (PAS) and the Malaysian Islamic Youth Movement (ABIM) maintained close ties to the Middle East.[128] Unlike Taiwan, therefore, where the United States was the primary international audience, Malaysia's elite played to multiple audiences, which may have blunted the impact of Western pressure.

Organizational power in Malaysia was high. Coercive capacity was very high. The Malaysian state possessed "highly developed coercive institutions" dating back to colonial rule.[129] The 1948–1960 British-led counterinsurgency gave rise to a powerful internal security apparatus.[130] Thus, UMNO inherited a "sophisticated coercive machine,"[131] including a "strong and reliable" army,[132] a "highly effective" police force,[133] and "one of the most efficient Special Branch [intelligence] forces in the region."[134] Security agencies monitored political activity throughout the country and their capacity to put down protest was "beyond question."[135] State cohesion was high, due, at least in part, to ethnic ties.[136] Malaysian society was divided between a Malay majority and Chinese (roughly

and Japan and Taiwan surpassed the United States as a source of foreign investment (Munro-Kua 1996: 114).

[123] See Appendix III. In the late 1990s, 6 percent of Malaysians used the Internet compared to 22 percent of Taiwanese (Abbott 2001b: 108).

[124] Welsh (2004: 356–7).

[125] Jomo and Cheek (1992: 89); Salleh (1999: 195); Derichs (2004); Rodan (2004: 116).

[126] See Nair (1997), Savananamuttu (2004), and Welsh (2004).

[127] Nair (1997: 69, 143–4).

[128] Nair (1997).

[129] Slater (2003: 83); see also Slater (2010).

[130] Stubbs (1997); Slater (2010). The British developed an "extensive police force, a well-trained army and ... an intelligence unit [Special Branch] that was considered one of the best in the world" (Munro-Kua 1996: 27; see also Stubbs 1997: 67–8). The colonial state successfully resettled more than 500 thousand rural Chinese into "new villages" (Bedlington 1978: 80; Stubbs 1997: 61), and the Special Branch "achieved remarkable success" in penetrating the insurgency

(Bedlington 1978: 81). Intelligence agents were reportedly "able virtually to pin-point every known communist ... in the jungle" (Zakaria 1987: 116).

[131] Barraclough (1985: 800).

[132] Means (1991: 143).

[133] Slater (2003: 89).

[134] Barraclough (1985: 800). The security apparatus also included a highly trained Federal Reserve Unit and a 21-battalion paramilitary Field Force. See Barraclough (1985), Stubbs (1997), and Slater (2003, forthcoming).

[135] Barraclough (1985: 800). UMNO governments established a record of "nipping opposition in the bud" (Slater 2003: 82). Thus, a 1974 crackdown on the student demonstrations "effectively ended campus-based political activism" (Barraclough 1985: 814) and, in 1987, a crackdown known as Operation Lallang effectively demobilized the emerging NGO movement (Santiago and Nadarajah 1999: 165; Abbott 2004: 96).

[136] See Enloe (1976, 1980), Zakaria (1985), and Mauzy (1992: 233–6).

30 percent) and Indian (roughly 10 percent) minorities.[137] Communalism had long pervaded Malaysian politics,[138] and UMNO and the security forces were closely bound by ethnic ties.[139] Thus, the army and police hierarchies were "solidly Malay."[140] The most important army unit, the Malay Royal Regiment, was a "rigidly Malay preserve."[141] The security forces developed an impeccable record of discipline: There were no coups or internal rebellions, and orders to carry out high-intensity repression were routinely carried out.[142]

Party strength also was high. UMNO was a mass party with more than 2 million members (roughly a quarter of adult Malays) and 16,500 branch organizations that "reach[ed] into every corner in Malaysia."[143] Under UMNO's *"Kepala 10"* system, party cadres each monitored 10 households in rural villages throughout the country.[144] Party cohesion was also high, due to shared ethnicity.[145] From its founding, UMNO was "intimately identified with the interests of a single ethnic community,"[146] and it viewed itself "first and foremost as a protector of the Malays."[147] Through 1990, elite defection was infrequent and unsuccessful.[148]

Origins and Evolution of the Regime

UMNO rule dates back to Malaysia's independence in 1957. Although UMNO was a Malay-based party, its *Barisan Nasional* (BN) coalition was multiethnic, including the Malaysian Chinese Association (MCA) and Malaysian Indian Congress (MIC).[149] With the exception of 1969–1971, when constitutional rule was suspended,[150] Malaysia maintained a stable parliamentary regime in which UMNO and its allies were regularly returned to power – with a two-thirds majority – via elections.

---

[137] Searle (1999: 27).
[138] See Enloe (1976) Case (1996: 39–40), Crouch (1996a: 39–40), and Guan (2002).
[139] Zakaria (1985); Mauzy (1992).
[140] Mauzy (1992: 234–5); see also Zakaria 1985: 125, 130) and Pepinsky (2007: 117–18).
[141] Bedlington (1978: 168); see also Zakaria (1985: 125, 130).
[142] Zakaria (1985: 131); Slater (2003).
[143] Liow (1999: 51). See also Gomez and Jomo (1999: 11), Case (2001a: 52), and Slater (2003: 90). Slater described UMNO as an "organizational colossus" (2003: 85).
[144] Gomez (1995: 22–3); Case (2001b: 37); Slater (2003: 90); Pepinsky (2007: 116). UMNO was also extraordinary wealthy, with corporate holdings valued at more than $1 billion (Gomez 1996, 1998; Crouch 1996a: 211–16; Searle 1999: 103). Thus, UMNO was "more than a political party. It [was] a huge business conglomerate with numerous banks" (Neher and Marlay 1995: 103).

[145] Enloe (1976); Zakaria (1985: 121). On UMNO cohesion in general, see Case (1995: 17–19; 1996), Crouch (1996a: 65), and Brownlee (2007a).
[146] Enloe (1976: 67).
[147] Thirkill-White (2006: 424). Cohesion was reinforced by an institutionalized patronage system and a successful party label (Crouch 1996a: 43; Case 2004a: 90–1).
[148] Case (1995: 16–18); Brownlee (2007a). On the rare occasions when elite defection occurred (e.g., founder Datuk Onn Jafar in 1951 and Tengku Razaleigh in 1987), the new parties created by the defectors quickly foundered (Crouch 1996a: 121–7; Hwang 2003: 170–1).
[149] Mauzy (1983); Case (1996: 83–103).
[150] In 1969, Malay rioting in the aftermath of a poor UMNO election led to the suspension of parliament, a ban on political activity, and rule by an unelected National Operations Council until 1971 (Means 1991: 6–11; Munro-Kua 1996: 56–9).

Notwithstanding its democratic appearance,[151] the Malaysian regime was marked by a highly uneven playing field.[152] Opposition activity was restricted by a range of authoritarian laws, including the Internal Security Act (ISA), which allowed the preventative detention of anyone deemed a threat to security, communal peace, or the economy[153]; the Societies Act, which permitted the banning of groups deemed to threaten national security[154]; the University and University Colleges Act, which banned campus protest and student party membership[155]; the Sedition Act, which banned speech promoting "disaffection" or "feelings of ill-will" between races or classes"[156]; the Printing Presses and Publications Act, which allowed the banning of publications deemed "prejudicial to public order, morality, [or] security"[157]; and severe restrictions on political meetings.[158] Although not enforced as systematically as in Singapore,[159] these laws made Malaysia one of the most *formally* authoritarian cases examined in this book.

UMNO also enjoyed massive *informal* advantages.[160] For example, resources were "overwhelmingly in the hands of the governing coalition."[161] UMNO used its control of the state to build a "sprawling corporate empire."[162] With privileged access to credit, licenses, and contracts, UMNO-linked firms grew spectacularly[163]; by the early 1990s, UMNO's business empire encompassed 16 thousand companies and was worth at least $1 billion.[164] UMNO also maintained a virtual lock on private-sector finance.[165] The government used its vast discretionary power over licensing and contracts to favor allied businesses, which in turn channeled money into UMNO coffers.[166] By contrast, opposition parties lacked any meaningful access to corporate finance.[167]

UMNO also enjoyed a near-monopoly on media ownership. Virtually all private media were owned by individuals or firms with ties to the governing coalition.[168] UMNO controlled Malaysia's leading English- and Malay-language newspapers, and firms linked to the BN owned all major Chinese- and

---

[151] Malaysia was said to have the "most consistently democratic record in Asia" outside of India and Japan (Case 1996: 251).

[152] See Gomez (1990, 1996), Jesudason (1995, 1996), Crouch (1996a, 1996b), and Case (1996, 2001a, 2004b).

[153] Barraclough (1985: 807); Crouch (1996a: 79). Although use of the ISA declined during the 1980s, it nevertheless "installed a general atmosphere of fear sufficient to keep people silent and passive" (Santiago and Nadarajah 1999: 165).

[154] Jesudason (1995: 338); Munro-Kua (1996: 121).

[155] Means (1991: 37); Gomez (1998: 279).

[156] Crouch (1992: 24).

[157] Crouch (1996a: 85); Nain 2002: (128–9).

[158] Neher and Marlay (1995: 106); Crouch (1996a: 60).

[159] Rodan (2004: 111–12).

[160] These informal advantages are widely known as the "Three M's": money, media, and (state) machinery (Gomez 1998: 264–5).

[161] Funston (2000: 21).

[162] Searle (1999: 103).

[163] Gomez (1990: 171–2).

[164] Milne and Mauzy (1999: 60–1); Searle (1999: 103).

[165] Beginning in the 1970s, the statist New Economic Policy (NEP) granted UMNO "overwhelming influence over the corporate sector" (Gomez 2002b: 111). See Jesudason (1989), Gomez and Jomo (1999), and Searle (1999).

[166] Searle (1999); Gomez (2002b: 3–4; 2002c).

[167] Gomez (1996: 92; 1998: 260–1).

[168] See Gomez (1990), Crouch (1996a: 86–7), Wong (2000), Nain (2002), and Rodan (2004: 25–6).

Tamil-language dailies.[169] All radio broadcasting and two of three television stations were controlled by the state; the only private television station (TV3) was controlled by UMNO allies.[170] Described as "the most supine in non-communist Asia,"[171] the mainstream media offered "no programming critical of the government" and was largely inaccessible to the opposition.[172]

Finally, state institutions were politicized.[173] Although the judiciary was relatively independent during the 1960s and 1970s,[174] Mahathir's 1988 packing of the Supreme Court led to an "enormous erosion of judicial powers,"[175] transforming the courts into "a powerful fist at the end of [Mahathir's] executive arm."[176] UMNO also dominated the Electoral Commission,[177] and it made "uninhibited use of state facilities and government workers" in elections.[178] Public agencies such as the Community Development Agency were "effectively transformed into political machines for the ruling BN."[179] Thus, even though elections were generally free of overt fraud,[180] extreme disparities in access to resources, media, and the state ensured that they were "heavily loaded in favor of the UMNO."[181]

Opposition forces were weakened by ethnic cleavage.[182] They were divided between the Islamic- and Malay-based PAS and the secular- and Chinese-based Democratic Action Party (DAP), which made it difficult to sustain a broad-based coalition.[183] Whereas the DAP was confined to Chinese constituencies and thus never developed a mass base or fielded a full slate of parliamentary candidates,[184] the PAS was limited mainly to the Malay heartland; on its own, the party "did not have adequate resources to capture political power."[185]

Notwithstanding these vast asymmetries, the Malaysian regime was competitive in the 1980s. Elections were "vigorously contested," and opposition parties viewed them as the only viable route to power.[186] Indeed, the opposition routinely won at least 40 percent of the parliamentary vote. Thus, even though UMNO victories were "virtually assured," elections "allowed the opposition to

---

[169] Vanden Heuvel and Dennis (1993: 153–8); Rodan (2004: 25–6). The only independent periodicals were party papers and weekly or monthly magazines with limited readership (Crouch 1992: 25; 1996a: 85).

[170] Vanden Heuvel and Dennis (1993: 157); Case (1996: 162); Rodan (2004: 26). Privatization in the 1990s simply "extend[ed] the tentacles of the ruling coalition," as the new private television and cable networks were all owned by government allies (Nain 2002: 119–23; Rodan 2004: 26).

[171] *The Economist*, April 5, 2003, "Survey of Malaysia," p. 8.

[172] Vanden Heuvel and Dennis (1993: 157); see also Crouch (1996a: 60–1) and Gomez (1998: 265).

[173] Crouch (1996a: 132–4).

[174] Lee (1995: 73–4).

[175] Munro-Kua (1996: 139–40).

[176] Slater (2003: 89).

[177] Case (2001a); Moten and Mokhtar (2006).

[178] Case (2001a: 48); see also Lim (2002: 189).

[179] Jomo (1996: 95); see also Case (1994: 922–3).

[180] According to Case (2001b: 38), there was "little evidence of systematic ballot-box stuffing, deliberate miscounting, or false reporting." See also Crouch (1996a: 57).

[181] Case (1996: 117); see also Crouch (1996a: 58–9).

[182] Jesudason (1989, 1995).

[183] Crouch (1996a: 56–72); Jesudason (1996: 140–1); Gomez (1998); Guan (2002); Verma (2002: 114–15).

[184] Jesudason (1996: 142); Khoo (2000: 4).

[185] Verma (2002: 92); see also Slater (2004) and Moten and Mokhtar (2006: 322).

[186] Crouch (1996a: 75). See also Jomo (1996: 112), Case (2001b: 53: 85–6), and Ufen (2009: 608–9).

mount a serious challenge to the government,"[187] and it was "not completely impossible...to envisage the government's defeat."[188]

When Mahathir Mohamad was elected Prime Minister in 1981, he thus inherited an institutionalized competitive authoritarian regime. Nevertheless, Mahathir confronted a series of challenges in the two decades that followed. These challenges were partially rooted in modernization. Industrialization gave rise to a large urban middle class, which served as a foundation for a vibrant civil society.[189] As a result, urban prodemocracy NGOs proliferated in the 1980s and 1990s.[190] Islamic political organizations such as the Malaysian Islamic Youth Movement (ABIM) and the PAS also strengthened.[191] The PAS became the best organized opposition party in the country, with a powerful grassroots network and a "steady following in the rural hinterlands."[192] Thus, although communal divisions undermined opposition strength in the 1980s, the potential for a serious opposition challenge clearly existed.

One such challenge emerged in the late 1980s, when an economic downturn and government austerity measures triggered a wave of social protest and a schism within UMNO.[193] During its 1987 General Assembly, UMNO split into "Team A" led by Mahathir and "Team B" led by ex–Finance Minister Tengku Razaleigh. After Team A won disputed leadership elections, Team B filed a lawsuit claiming fraud, leaving UMNO "in disarray."[194] The government responded with repression, arresting more than 100 civic and opposition leaders in late 1987 (Operation Lallang),[195] and then sacking Supreme Court President Salleh Abbas and two other justices in 1988.[196] The packed Court granted Mahathir's Team A control over UMNO's name and assets, forcing Team B to create an alternative party: Semangat '46 (Spirit of '46).[197]

Semangat '46 posed an "unprecedented challenge" to UMNO in the 1990 elections.[198] Team B had initially included as much as half of UMNO's rank-and-file base,[199] and Razaleigh enjoyed a large national following.[200] Opposition leaders believed they could deny the BN a two-thirds majority in parliament and many "seemed to believe that victory was not completely out of reach."[201]

---

[187] Crouch (1996a: 30–1).

[188] Crouch (1993: 136–7).

[189] See Crouch (1993: 141–3), Rahman (2002), and Thirkill-White (2006: 42).

[190] See Santiago and Nadarajah (1999), Weiss (2000, 2004), and Hassan (2002).

[191] Mutalib (1990); Verma (2002). ABIM became the "biggest and most influential Islamic NGO" in Malaysia (Hassan 2002: 205), with 100 branches and 40 thousand members in the mid-1980s (Mutalib 1990: 77).

[192] Singh (1991: 723); see also Mutalib (2000: 65), Nathan (2002: 162–3), and Verma (2002: 194–5).

[193] Means (1991: 173–99).

[194] Crouch (1992: 39); see also Means (1991: 201–6), Khoo (1992: 44–5), and Case 1996: 193–4).

[195] See Means (1991: 212–13) and Hwang 2003: (153–4). Although aimed primarily at civic opposition, the crackdown also targeted Team B (Case 1996: 199; Hwang (2003: 153–4).

[196] See Lee (1995: 52–3), Case (1996: 202–4), Crouch (1996a: 140–1), and Hwang (2003: 164–7).

[197] Means (1991: 229, 241); Crouch (1996a: 118–20).

[198] Crouch (1992: 35).

[199] Crouch (1992: 33, 39); Khoo (1992: 45).

[200] Singh (1991: 721).

[201] Crouch (1992: 36; 1996a: 125).

UMNO survived the challenge. Buoyed by economic recovery, the Mahathir government used patronage and a variety of threats (e.g., tax audits and calling in of outstanding loans) to persuade Team B members to rejoin Mahathir's "New UMNO."[202] Thus, "dissidents at all levels gradually moved back to UMNO" in 1989 and 1990.[203] Benefiting from an "extremely large war chest" and a divided opposition,[204] the BN won easily and retained its two-thirds parliamentary majority.[205] UMNO was not seriously challenged in the 1995 election,[206] and shortly thereafter, Semangat '46 dissolved and Razaleigh rejoined UMNO.[207]

The regime faced a more serious crisis in the late 1990s. The crisis was rooted in two interrelated developments. The first was the rise of Anwar Ibrahim. Described as "the most charismatic young politician of his generation,"[208] Anwar rose quickly through UMNO's ranks to become Finance Minister in 1991 and Deputy Prime Minister in 1993. Along the way, he won considerable grassroots support and built powerful patronage networks in the business community and the media.[209] By the mid-1990s, Anwar had emerged as a serious rival to Mahathir. The second development was the 1997 Asian financial crisis,[210] which eroded Mahathir's public support and brought him into conflict with the West. Adopting a nationalist discourse, Mahathir rejected IMF assistance and publicly blamed the United States and Jews for the crisis, which triggered international calls for his resignation.[211] U.S.–Malaysian relations reached an "all-time low,"[212] and in late 1997, the U.S. Congress called on Mahathir to apologize or resign.[213]

Anwar's ascent and the economic crisis converged in 1998. After Anwar challenged Mahathir in the 1998 UMNO Assembly, Mahathir purged Anwar's allies from the government and used the media to launch a "Blitzkrieg-like campaign of character assassination" against him.[214] On September 2, 1998, Anwar was sacked on charges of corruption and "homosexual conduct." Anwar led rallies in cities across the country, culminating in a massive protest in Kuala Lumpur.[215] The protest was broken up by police, and Anwar and 17 supporters were arrested.[216] Anwar was convicted of sodomy and corruption and he spent the next seven years in prison.

---

[202] Crouch (1992: 33–4, 39–40).
[203] Crouch (1996a: 127); see also Brownlee (2007a: 140–3).
[204] von der Mehden (1991: 165). UMNO reportedly spent as much as $500 million during the campaign (von der Mehden 1991: 165). On opposition division, see Means (1991: 263–4).
[205] See Crouch (1996: 230–1). Semangat '46 won only 17 percent of the vote.
[206] Kiat (1996: 218–20). The BN won 65 percent of the vote and secured 162 of 192 seats in parliament.
[207] Jesudason (1999: 149); Verma (2002: 146).

[208] *The Economist*, April 5, 2005, "Survey of Malaysia," p. 9.
[209] Case (1997: 399); Gomez and Jomo (1999: 124–6, 202).
[210] GDP contracted by 7 percent in 1998 (World Bank World Development Indicators, available at www.worldbank.org/data).
[211] Chin (1998: 186–9).
[212] Malaysian government official, quoted in Chin (1998: 189).
[213] Hilley (2001: 101–2); Hwang (2003: 294).
[214] Slater (2003: 93); see also Felker (1999: 44–5).
[215] Felker (1999: 44); Funston (1999: 170).
[216] Felker (1999: 46).

Anwar's arrest triggered massive protest.[217] Demonstrations rocked Kuala Lumpur in late 1998, giving rise to a broad-based *Reformasi* movement.[218] Prodemocracy groups attracted "unprecedented numbers of new members,"[219] mobilizing heretofore politically inactive citizens – students and Chinese and Malay professionals – behind demands for a repeal of the ISA, an independent electoral commission, and other reforms.[220] Islamic groups also grew dramatically.[221] PAS membership doubled from 400,000 to 800,000,[222] and the party spearheaded a "new social movement for reform,"[223] using political-religious meetings (*ceramah*) to mobilize thousands in a "continuous political campaign against UMNO."[224] The *Reformasi* movement united the opposition. The DAP and PAS cooperated to an unprecedented degree, and new multiethnic organizations such as the Movement for Social Justice (Adil) served as a "lynchpin" for Islamic and secular opposition groups.[225]

The Anwar crisis constituted "the most severe test in Mahathir's eighteen-year rule."[226] With its public support ebbing, the regime was "as vulnerable as it had ever been."[227] Moreover, Anwar's arrest was widely condemned by the international community[228]; at the 1998 Asia–Pacific Economic Cooperation (APEC) meeting in Kuala Lumpur, U.S. Vice President Al Gore publicly championed the Reformasi.[229]

In contrast to Lee in Taiwan, Mahathir responded to the *Reformasi* challenge with repression. The security forces "turned their considerable firepower against Anwar ... and his supporters."[230] Protest was "met forcefully" by police,[231] and opposition meetings were "subject to various forms of harassment, ranging from close surveillance to violent dispersal."[232] The government expelled student protesters, cracked down on *ceramah*, and arrested hundreds of opposition activists.[233] The crackdown succeeded in dampening protest.[234] Ultimately, the *Reformasi* movement "did ... not develop into a large-scale country-wide demand for reforms."[235]

---

[217] Verma (2002: 110–13).
[218] Hwang (2003: 315); see also Funston (1999: 172–3).
[219] Weiss (2000: 420, 424–5).
[220] Santiago and Nadarajah (1999).
[221] Anwar's arrest triggered unprecedented opposition among Malay Muslims (Verma 2002: 107–11).
[222] Weiss (2000: 420, 432); Thirkill-White (2006: 434). The PAS's *Harakah* newspaper tripled its circulation (Funston 1999: 173).
[223] Case (2004a: 88).
[224] Salleh (1999: 198); see also Rodan (2004: 166–7).
[225] Case (2004a: 89); see also Santiago and Nadarajah (1999: 168, 177).
[226] Funston (1999: 176).
[227] Case (2001a: 51); see also Verma (2002: 156–7).

[228] See Gomez and Jomo (1999: 200) and Singh (2000: 534). The IMF, World Bank, and UN condemned the arrest, and financier George Soros called for Mahathir's overthrow (Funston 1999: 174; Hilley 2001: 154).
[229] Felker (1999: 53); Liow (1999: 61).
[230] Slater (2003: 97).
[231] Hilley (2001: 151).
[232] Funston (1999: 174).
[233] See Felker (1999: 46l), Hilley (2001: 110, 151–7), and Pepinsky (2009b: 206). As Slater (2003: 95) wrote, "violent crackdowns on peaceful demonstrations quickly became the norm, and detention of Mahathir's opponents ... became so routine that the Kamunting Prison ... became colloquially known as the 'Mahathir Marriot.'"
[234] Hwang (2003: 315).
[235] Salleh (1999: 185). See also Felker (1999: 46).

Mahathir's defeat of the *Reformasi* movement was rooted in two main factors. First, UMNO closed ranks, suffering no major defections.[236] Despite considerable rank-and-file support for Anwar within the security forces,[237] Mahathir retained the "absolute loyalty of the police and other institutions of political control."[238] Although many security officials disliked Mahathir's course of action, "they did not disobey his orders.... [T]he cogs in the party–state continued obediently to work in their place."[239] Second, external pressure was limited. Notwithstanding broad international sympathy for Anwar, Western powers took no real punitive action.[240] Due to the size of Malaysia's economy and $3 billion in Japanese loan guarantees, Mahathir could pursue economic recovery without turning to the United States or the IMF.[241] Linkage effects also were weak. Unlike high-linkage cases such as Nicaragua and Slovakia, Malaysia's opposition "was hardly helped" by U.S. officials' embrace of the *Reformasi*.[242] Instead, Gore's intervention "sparked a chorus of objections to foreign interference from across Malaysia's political spectrum that ... strengthened the government's position."[243]

Having prevailed on the streets, UMNO still faced a difficult electoral challenge in 1999. Reformasi leaders created the multiethnic National Justice Party (later, the People's Justice Party), which brought the DAP and PAS into a "rainbow coalition" called the Alternative Front (BA).[244] The BA posed a serious electoral threat, and the campaign "took on an air of great competitiveness."[245] Although vast media and resource advantages (and some electoral shenanigans) allowed the BN to retain its two-thirds parliamentary majority,[246] the election was viewed as a "great setback" for UMNO.[247] UMNO lost 16 parliamentary seats, and opposition leaders began to think seriously about winning the next election.[248]

Mahathir quickly reasserted control, however. The government revived its "war against the *Reformasi*," stepping up surveillance, banning political

---

[236] Hwang (2003: 307–9); Brownlee (2007a).
[237] Jeshuran (2004: 340).
[238] Slater (2003: 91).
[239] Slater (2003: 83–4).
[240] Singh (2000: 534).
[241] Felker (2000: 55, 59).
[242] Liow (1999: 61).
[243] Felker (1999: 53).
[244] Santiago and Nadarajah (1999: 176–7); Weiss (2000: 420–5). Whereas the PAS and DAP represented "permanent political minorities," the National Justice Party's cross-communal appeal made it a "potential political majority" (Slater 2004: 5); see also Santiago and Nadarajah (1999: 176).
[245] Case (2001b: 46). Opposition leaders "aspired to an outright electoral victory" (Case 2001b: 36). See also Weiss (2000).
[246] See Felker (2000: 54), Weiss (2000: 421, 430–2), and Martinez (2001: 189). Nearly

700 thousand new voters were effectively disenfranchised because their registrations were not approved prior to the snap election (Pepinsky 2009b: 217). Moreover, media controls were extensive. According to Pepinsky (2009b: 217), "the mainstream Malay, English, Chinese, and Tamil presses did not print a single pro-BA editorial, letter, or opinion" during the 1999 campaign. The BN won 56 percent of the vote and 148 of 193 parliamentary seats.
[247] Case (2004b: 4). The PAS made substantial inroads among UMNO's traditional Malay electorate (Case 2004a: 89–90), increasing its parliamentary representation from 7 to 27 seats. Anwar's National Justice Party won 5 seats.
[248] Case (2004a: 90; 2004b: 35).

meetings, and sending police to block dozens of *ceramah*.[249] In late 2000, for example, police thwarted an opposition demonstration near the capital that was expected to draw 100,000 people.[250] Scores of opposition figures were arrested and the government cracked down on the media, banning two major weeklies and restricting the PAS newspaper, *Harakah*, to two issues a month.[251] Again, repression was effective. Protest waned, and the National Justice Party's embryonic organization was decimated.[252] Mahathir's crackdown was reinforced by the September 11, 2001, attack in the United States. Malaysia became a strategic player in the U.S.-led "war on terror" and consequently, security issues trumped democracy on the U.S. agenda.[253] Thus, Mahathir was able to repress Islamic opposition – including the PAS – "without a peep of protest from the West,"[254] while the *Reformasi* movement, which had "struggled to keep the international dimension of its campaign going" after 1999, found that its task had become "all the more difficult."[255]

UMNO's recovery facilitated a smooth succession in 2003–2004. Mahathir retired in October 2003 and was succeeded as prime minister by his deputy, Abdullah Badawi, who led the party to a landslide victory in the 2004 parliamentary election. With the *Reformasi* movement divided and weakened by repression,[256] the BN won an overwhelming 199 of 219 seats in parliament.

The 2004 election did not bring regime reequilibration, however. Antigovernment protest increased again after 2006. In late 2007, *Bersih* (Coalition for Clean and Fair Elections) – a coalition of 70 political parties and NGOs – mobilized tens of thousands of protesters calling for free elections.[257] At the same time, the release of Anwar Ibrahim from prison in late 2004 – after being cleared of sodomy charges – helped reenergize and unify the opposition.[258]

The 2008 election was described as a political "tsunami."[259] The BN captured only 140 of 222 seats in parliament – the first time since 1969 that the ruling

---

[249] Khoo (2000: 2). See also Martinez (2002: 134), Nathan (2002: 162), and Rodan (2004: 166–7).

[250] Ufen (2009: 612–13).

[251] Guan (2002: 191); Verma (2002: 112, 175); Slater (2003: 94); Rodan (2004: 166–7).

[252] Rodan (2004: 166; Slater (2004).

[253] Almost overnight, Mahathir became an "ally and a force for Islamic moderation," which generated a "new appreciation of his authoritarian rule ... in Washington" (Rodan 2004: 169).

[254] *The Economist*, April 5, 2003, p. 7. Calling the PAS the "Taliban of Malaysia," the government arrested dozens of PAS activists in 2001 and 2002 (Rodan 2004: 167–9). See also Nathan (2002: 162–3).

[255] Abbott (2004: 96). Post–September 11 events also undermined opposition unity.

The PAS radicalized in 2001, declaring a "holy war" against the United States and "vigorously resum[ing] its quest for an Islamic state" (Case 2004a: 99), which led the DAP to abandon the BA (Verma 2002: 212; Liow 2005: 922).

[256] Slater (2004). Due to UMNO's continued media and resource advantages, opposition parties faced an "uphill battle extraordinaire" (Slater 2004: 4); see also Moten and Mokhtar (2006).

[257] Case (2008: 25); Ufen (2009: 615–16). Also in 2007, an estimated 10 thousand to 30 thousand Indians protested discrimination and the destruction of Hindu temples. See Pepinsky (2009a: 90–1); Ufen (2009: 615–16).

[258] Ufen (2009: 615).

[259] Pepinsky (2009a: 87).

coalition had failed to win a two-thirds majority.[260] After the election, the PAS, DAP, and Anwar's People's Justice Party created a new opposition coalition, Pakatan Rakyat. Anwar, who was elected to parliament after his ban on holding public office was lifted in April 2008, launched a campaign to convince UMNO MPs to defect, with the goal of bringing down the government via a no-confidence vote.[261] Although these efforts failed, a weakened Abdullah resigned in April 2009 and was succeeded by Deputy Prime Minister Najib Razak.

The surprising vigor of the opposition challenge in the late 2000s was rooted, in part, in the growing strength of civic, ethnic, and opposition groups, as well as the rapid spread of communications technology.[262] However, it also was rooted in the behavior of the Abdullah government. Whereas Mahathir had systematically deployed coercive and other state institutions to put down protest and weaken opponents,[263] Abdullah *underutilized* his coercive power.[264] As Welsh observed, Abdullah's permissive approach to civil society and the right of assembly "created conditions for more mobilization by [government] critics."[265] Thus, it is not surprising that the Abdullah government "reverted to coercion" in 2008, filing new sexual-misconduct charges against Anwar.[266]

In summary, UMNO successfully thwarted opposition challenges throughout the 1990–2008 period, remaining in power for four parliamentary terms. Repression "served as a winning strategy" because powerful state and ruling-party organizations allowed UMNO governments to crack down on opposition challenges.[267] In the absence of high linkage or leverage, Western criticism never translated into effective external pressure.

Regime change remained a real possibility in Malaysia in the late 2000s. Indeed, due to its level of development and the growing strength of civic and opposition forces,[268] Malaysia's medium-term prospects for democracy were probably better than any other stable authoritarian regime examined in this book. As of 2009, however, the end of UMNO's 52-year rule was not in immediate sight.

CAMBODIA

Unlike Malaysia and Taiwan, Cambodia lacked favorable conditions for democracy. It was a poor, rural country with a tiny middle class and a weak civil society,[269] and its domestic push for democracy was limited. In the early 1990s, state weakness and extreme external vulnerability brought a political opening that nearly resulted in the removal of the Cambodian People's Party (CPP) from power.

---

[260] Opposition parties won 82 seats. They also won control of 5 of 13 state legislatures.
[261] Case (2008: 28).
[262] See Brown (2008: 742) and Ufen (2009). Between 2000 and 2008, the number of Internet users increased from 3.7 million to 14 million, reaching 60 percent coverage (Ufen 2009: 616).
[263] Slater (2003).
[264] Pepinsky (2009a: 109–10). Unlike Taiwan and Mexico, the decision to underutilize

the government's coercive power cannot be easily traced to linkage-based pressure; rather, it is best understood in voluntarist terms.
[265] Welsh (2008).
[266] Case (2008: 33).
[267] Slater (2003: 98).
[268] Ufen (2009).
[269] Heder and Ledgerwood (1996: 17–18).

After 1993, however, international pressure diminished, and effective state- and party-building allowed the CPP to reconsolidate power.

Linkage, Leverage, and Organizational Power

Cambodia is an extreme case of high leverage and low linkage. It was one of the most externally vulnerable states in the world.[270] During the 1980s, the state was propped up by Soviet Bloc assistance and 100,000 Vietnamese troops.[271] After 1989, the Soviet collapse and Vietnam's withdrawal dramatically increased the regime's dependence on the West.[272] Linkage was very low. The Khmer Rouge regime (1975–1979) cut off Cambodia from the world and decimated its small Western-educated elite. Vietnam's post-1979 occupation brought another decade of isolation.[273] Thus, economic and technocratic ties to the West were minimal[274]; communication ties were among the lowest in the world[275]; and international NGO penetration was limited to the cities, rarely reaching the 80 percent of Cambodians who lived in the countryside.[276]

Organizational power increased over time, from medium low to medium high. When the communist Kampuchean People's Revolutionary Party (the precursor to the CPP) took power in 1979, Cambodia had "one of the world's weakest states."[277] The Khmer Rouge had "dismantled all existing state structures,"[278] forcing the new government to rebuild the state "almost from scratch."[279] The new state had a limited "capacity . . . to project power,"[280] and the army – outmanned by the Khmer Rouge and plagued by desertion – depended on Vietnamese troops to maintain order.[281] The ruling party also was weak. Installed from above by Vietnam, the communists lacked an effective organization in the 1980s,[282] and internal discipline was "almost nonexistent."[283]

---

[270] D. Chandler (1998: 38–42).

[271] Hughes (2003: 31).

[272] Brown and Zasloff (1998: 53–6); Roberts (2001: 17–28). International assistance accounted for nearly 50 percent of the government's budget during the 1990s (Doyle 1998: 86; Hughes 2003: 39).

[273] Heder and Ledgerwood (1998: 6–8); Peou (2000: 268–70). Thus, "aside from a handful of humanitarian relief workers, almost no Westerners were in Cambodia" in the 1980s (Gottesman 2003: 206).

[274] In 1990, only three thousand Cambodians inside the country had more than a secondary education (Peou 2000: 96). See also Neher (2002: 254–5) and Hughes (2003: 124–5). On economic ties, see Neher (2002: 19) and Peou (2000: 268–70).

[275] In 2003, for example, Cambodia had only three telephones per thousand, which is fewer than in Benin and Malawi and less than a tenth that of Albania and Nicaragua (World

Bank World Development Indicators 2005 (http://devdata.worldbank.org/wdi2005).

[276] See Hughes (1999: 105; 2003: 131). Opposition forces maintained some ties to the West, particularly the United States (Hughes 2003: 119–25; Un 2005: 211), but the "peripheral" nature of U.S.–Cambodian relations (Neher 2002: 261) limited the utility of these ties (Hughes 2003).

[277] Neher and Marlay (1995: 185); see also Peou (2000: 95–8).

[278] Hourn (1998: 187).

[279] Hughes (2003: 22); see also Gottesman (2003: 50).

[280] Hughes (2003: 13, 25).

[281] Peou (2000: 210); Gottesman (2003: 226–7).

[282] The Communist Party had only a thousand members in 1984. See Peou (2000: 99), Gottesman (2003: 48–9), and Hughes (2003: 59).

[283] Gottesman (2003: 212).

Over time, however, the Hun Sen government built both a functioning state and a strong party. State capacity appears to have reached medium levels of scope and cohesion by the early 1990s.[284] As Gottesman has shown, the CPP government built a "formidable state administration," with a demonstrated capacity to control society.[285] The army expanded to 100,000 troops, which – combined with a 45-thousand–strong police force – constituted a massive security apparatus in a country of 10 million people.[286] Although the security forces were not very professionalized,[287] they were capable of monitoring and repressing opposition across the territory.[288] Cohesion also increased to medium. The defeat of the Khmer Rouge and organized corruption helped "cement the allegiances of state officials" and, by the mid-1990s, Cambodia had acquired a "cohesive and loyal state apparatus."[289]

The ruling party – which became the CPP in 1991 – also strengthened over time. In the early 1990s, the CPP launched a massive membership drive, drafting tens of thousands of public employees into the party.[290] The party "swiftly became a mass organization,"[291] with as many as three million members and "formidable grassroots networks."[292] Party networks operated "throughout the country, down to the village level."[293] By the mid-1990s, the CPP could mobilize 500,000 activists and place 10-member cells in villages across the country.[294] Thus, party scope was high. We score party cohesion as medium. Although the CPP was not held together by a salient ideology or a history of revolutionary struggle, it developed into an institutionalized patronage-based machine, and its leadership remained intact even during the severe crisis triggered by Vietnam's 1989 withdrawal.[295]

Origins and Evolution of the Regime

Cambodia's regime trajectory may be divided into two periods. Between 1989 and 1993, when Western leverage was highest and state and party structures were still consolidating, UN intervention imposed a competitive regime and the CPP

---

[284] See Peou (2000), Gottesman (2003), and Hughes (2003).

[285] Gottesman (2003: 50–3). For example, military conscription improved considerably, and state officials successfully drafted 150,000 people to build an earthen wall on the Thai border (Gottesman 2003: 226–33).

[286] Um (1994: 76); Hay (1998: 179). The security apparatus also included secret-police units ("A Teams"), military security agencies (S-91, Special Intelligence Battalion), and a "vast network of local militias" (Gottesman 2003: 331–2). See also Ashley (1996: 174–8) and Peou (2000: 198–9).

[287] Shawcross (1994: 24, 72–3).

[288] Hughes (2003).

[289] Hughes (2003: 62). See also Gottesman (2003: 299–335). According to Gottesman (2003: 299–300), patronage and corruption created "networks of happy officials whose loyalty the regime could count on."

[290] Freison (1996a: 188–90); Hughes (2003: 68).

[291] Hughes (2003: 59).

[292] McCargo (2005: 99).

[293] Frieson (1996b: 235); see also Hughes (2003: 60–5).

[294] Frieson (1996a: 188); Hughes (2003: 67–9, 123).

[295] Gottesman (2003). On party cohesion during the 1989 crisis, see Gottesman (2003: 329).

nearly lost power. After 1993, Western attention faded and organizational power increased, which allowed the CPP to reconsolidate power.

The Transition to Competitive Authoritarianism (1989–1993)

Cambodia's transition to multiparty rule was internationally imposed.[296] The withdrawal of Vietnamese troops and Soviet assistance in 1989 left the communist government bankrupt, isolated, and vulnerable to military defeat by the Khmer Rouge.[297] The ruling party was "disintegrating from below," and the police were too weak to block illicit political meetings.[298] Indeed, many observers did not believe the regime would survive Vietnam's departure.[299] With "few allies and no money,"[300] the government entered internationally sponsored peace talks, which culminated in the 1991 Paris Accord.[301] The Paris Accord called for an internationally orchestrated transition, in which CPP would effectively cede power to UN forces.[302] Backed by 16,000 international troops, the UN Transition Authority in Cambodia (UNTAC) established a "mini trusteeship" over the state.[303] UNTAC would oversee the creation of a new army, design an electoral system, and administer elections in 1993.[304]

The UN intervention had a "dehegemonizing" effect on the regime.[305] Opposition forces were very weak in the early 1990s. Civil society was "virtually nonexistent,"[306] and the private sector was "small and underdeveloped."[307] Even the largest opposition party, the royalist National United Front for an Independent, Neutral, Peaceful, and Cooperative Cambodia (FUNCINPEC), lacked a strong organization or a significant rural presence.[308] Yet UNTAC "dramatically altered the balance of... forces,"[309] creating an environment of "internationally sanctioned pluralism."[310] Under UNTAC's protective umbrella, the NGO sector "expanded rapidly" and opposition parties opened hundreds of offices.[311] Independent media outlets proliferated and UNTAC-run television and radio stations "systematically provided air time" for all parties.[312]

External intervention failed to democratize Cambodia, however. UNTAC's control over the state was in many respects "cosmetic"; in several areas, including public finance, local government, and security forces, it failed to dislodge the

---

[296] Hughes (2003: 6).

[297] See Brown and Zasloff (1998: 53–6) and Gottesman (2003: 308–17).

[298] Gottesman (2003: 329, 304–9).

[299] See Doyle (1995: 23) and Heder and Ledgerwood (1996: 9).

[300] Heder and Ledgerwood (1996: 9).

[301] Peou 2000 (2008: 211).

[302] See Doyle (1995), Ojendal (1996), Brown and Timberman (1998), and Brown and Zasloff (1998).

[303] Roberts (2001: 2).

[304] Doyle (1995); Brown and Zasloff (1998).

[305] Peou (2000: 10).

[306] Heder and Ledgerwood (1996: 17).

[307] Hughes (2003: 141).

[308] Curtis (1998: 25–6, 45); Hughes (2002: 170–81; 2003: 116–17). According to Jeldres (1993: 114), FUNCINPEC functioned "more as a royal court than as a political party."

[309] Hughes (2003: 2).

[310] Gottesman (2003: 349).

[311] Brown (1998: 107). Opposition parties opened nearly 1,000 party offices and held more than 1,500 public meetings in 1993 (Jennar 1998: 481; Brown 1998: 93).

[312] Marston (1996: 219); see also Shawcross (1994: 65–7). Indeed, Cambodia was said to have the "freest press in Southeast Asia" in 1992–1993 (Doyle 1995: 45).

CPP from the state.[313] As a result, preexisting power structures – particularly in the security arena – remained "more or less intact."[314] The CPP used its ties to the state to rebuild.[315] Anticipating elections, it mobilized the civil service and security forces in a membership drive that inducted more than two million Cambodians into the party.[316] By early 1993, the CPP had reestablished itself as the strongest organization in the country.[317]

The 1993 elections, held under UN supervision, were unfair. The CPP mobilized public employees en masse, and its control over local government structures provided a huge advantage in reaching rural voters.[318] Moreover, opposition parties suffered "hundreds of attacks" (including assassinations) by paramilitary forces and several opposition candidates were forced into hiding.[319] Nevertheless, UNTAC ensured that the registration, voting, and vote-counting processes were clean, and UNTAC-run radio and television gave opposition parties equal access to the airwaves.[320] These conditions allowed FUNCINPEC – founded by the popular King Norodom Sihanouk and led by his son, Prince Norodom Ranariddh – to score a "stunning victory," capturing 45 percent of the vote compared to 38 percent for the CPP.[321]

The CPP clung to power by "strong-arming" – via threats and attacks – FUNCINPEC into a coalition government, in which FUNCINPEC leader Norodom Ranariddh would be First Prime Minister and CPP leader Hun Sen would be Second Prime Minister.[322] Ministries were to be shared by "co-ministers" from each party, creating a "two-headed" system with parallel hierarchies in each state agency.[323] In fact, FUNCINPEC's control over the state was "never more than illusory," because the CPP retained control of the security forces and local state structures.[324] U.S. opposition notwithstanding,[325] the bulk of the international community accepted this arrangement.[326]

Authoritarian Reconsolidation, 1993–2008

Domestic and international conditions changed considerably after 1993. At home, effective state- and party-building enhanced the capacity of the CPP to

[313] Doyle (1995: 43); see also Doyle (1995: 41–4), Ashley (1998: 54–5), Peou (2000: 213–14), Roberts (2001: 88–91), and Un (2005: 213). Thus, CPP officials "administered around UNTAC" by shifting resources and activities to other parts of the state (Doyle 1995: 44; Brown and Zasloff 1998: 103–6).

[314] Peou (2000: 278).

[315] Frieson (1996a); Hughes (2003: 59–68).

[316] Frieson (1996a: 187–9).

[317] Brown and Zasloff (1998: 213, 223).

[318] See Brown (1998: 92), Doyle (1998: 82), Roberts (2001: 75–6, 89), and Hughes (2003: 65–6).

[319] Frieson (1996a: 196); see also Carney (1993: 4–5), Choo (1993: 21–2), Jeldres (1993: 109),

Heder (1995: 427), Brown and Zasloff 1998: 111–16), and Hughes (2003: 66, 76). According to international observers, the government was responsible for at least 15 deaths during the campaign (Findlay 1995: 81; Doyle 1995: 81).

[320] Carney (1993); Shawcross (1994); Doyle (1995).

[321] Heder (1995: 427).

[322] Jeldres (1996: 149); see also Shawcross (1994: 25–9).

[323] Curtis (1998: 13–24); Roberts (2001: 117–29).

[324] Curtis (1998: 56, 24); see also Shawcross (1994: 41).

[325] Roberts (2001: 114–15).

[326] See Jeldres (1993: 113); Peou (2000: 264–5).

fend off challenges, both on the streets and at the ballot box. At the same time, international scrutiny "declined precipitously."[327] The UN left Cambodia after the election, and Western powers quickly lost interest.[328] Although the United States continued to oppose the government, its influence was limited; Japan, France, and other donors provided Cambodia with more than $500 million a year in aid without conditionality.[329]

Within this more permissive international environment, the CPP reasserted control. It quickly became clear that the post-1993 government was a "paper coalition that rendered FUNCINPEC powerless."[330] Hun Sen remained the dominant force, relegating "First Prime Minister" Ranariddh to junior-partner status.[331] Moreover, the National Assembly was "a rubber stamp for the CPP,"[332] the CPP controlled the courts,[333] and all television stations and nearly all radio stations were operated by individuals with ties to the CPP.[334] The government cracked down on opponents, most notably Sam Rainsy, a popular former Finance Minister who created the Khmer National Party (KNP) after leaving the government.[335] The KNP was denied legal recognition, its headquarters were ransacked by police, and its rural organizing efforts met systematic harassment.[336] The government also arrested newspaper editors, suspended or confiscated newspapers, and occasionally orchestrated attacks on journalists and newspaper offices.[337] By 1996, the independent media was "virtually silenced."[338]

In 1997, FUNCINPEC attempted to assert itself, triggering a regime crisis. Early that year, FUNCINPEC joined the KNP in the opposition National United Front (NUF).[339] The NUF constituted a potential parliamentary majority, and surveys suggested it could win the 1998 election.[340] At the same time, FUNCINPEC began to compete with the CPP for the loyalty of defecting Khmer Rouge units.[341] Viewing Khmer Rouge forces as a potential source of organizational and military muscle, Ranariddh negotiated an accord with Khmer Rouge leader Khieu Samphan and quietly began to import arms.[342] Hun Sen responded

---

[327] Brown and Timberman (1998: 28); see also Hughes (2003: 104).

[328] Brown and Timberman (1998: 13, 21).

[329] Findley (1995: 162–5); Peou (2000: 267, 375–8); Hughes (2003: 99–103). Leverage was further reduced by Cambodia's rapprochement with China, which provided the country with increased military and economic assistance in the late 1990s (Osborne 2000: 107, 90; Peou 2000: 277, 396).

[330] Doyle (1998: 82).

[331] Ashley (1998: 60–1).

[332] Brown (1998: 99–102).

[333] Thus, the courts "never seemed to side with the opposition" (Peou 2000: 309).

[334] See Marston (1996: 237) and Un (2005: 215). Newspapers were more independent but they reached only a small urban elite (Un 2005: 215).

[335] Peou (2000: 191–2).

[336] Peou (2000: 199, 305–8). Rainsy suffered repeated death threats; in 1997, a grenade attack on a KNP rally killed 19 people and nearly killed Rainsy (Brown 1998: 102; Peou 2000: 306–7).

[337] See Jeldres (1996: 154), Lizée (1996: 84), Marston (1996: 239), and Peou (2000: 196–7).

[338] Ojendal (1996: 206).

[339] Peou (2000: 295–6).

[340] Ashley (1998: 63–4); Peou (2000: 343). The CPP preserved its legislative majority by using bribes to engineer a schism in FUNCINPEC (Curtis 1998: 45–6; Peou 2000: 343–4).

[341] Ashley (1998: 60–9); Curtis (1998: 41).

[342] Curtis (1998: 42–51); Hughes (2003: 121–2).

with violence. On July 5, 1997, government troops attacked FUNCINPEC head-quarters and military bases, forcing Ranariddh and much of the party leadership into exile.[343] Opposition offices and most independent media were closed down, hundreds of opposition politicians were arrested, and several dozen were killed.[344] Opposition activists who remained in Cambodia were forced underground.[345]

Regime closure proved costly. The coup "led to a renewed bout of interna-tional scrutiny and intervention."[346] The United States suspended nonhumani-tarian aid and orchestrated the suspension of World Bank and IMF loans, as well as Cambodia's Association of Southeast Asian Nations (ASEAN) membership application.[347] The withdrawal of international assistance "hit hard," as both for-eign investment and tourism declined.[348] In addition, the UN left Cambodia's seat vacant at the opening of the General Assembly.[349]

International pressure induced the CPP to restore a competitive regime. In early 1998, Japan brokered an accord that permitted the return of exiled oppo-sition leaders, the reopening of FUNCINPEC radio and television stations, and international observation of the 1998 election.[350] Indeed, because donor assis-tance, ASEAN membership, and a UN seat hinged on internationally acceptable elections, the CPP was compelled to "hold an election that was freer and fairer than expected."[351] The 1998 race was marked by at least some uncertainty.[352] Opposition parties "campaigned as if they had a chance to win," and as the elec-tion approached, "it began to appear ... that the outcome was not a foregone conclusion."[353]

Yet conditions in 1998 differed markedly from those in 1993. The return to electoral rule masked a major shift in the balance of power.[354] After the 1997 coup, the CPP had purged FUNCINPEC from the state and eliminated its remaining military capacity; repression had destroyed the party's rural patron-age networks and forced its activists into hiding.[355] FUNCINPEC's organi-zation "disintegrated," eventually splitting into eight factions.[356] At the same time, the level of international scrutiny was "severely diminished."[357] Free of

---

343 Brown (1998: 101); Peou (2000: 298, 308).

344 Brown and Zasloff (1998: 263); Doyle (1998: 83); Hay (1998: 172); Peou (2000: 304–8). Even King Sihanouk went into medical "semi-exile" in China (Brown and Zasloff 1998: 265).

345 Hughes (2003: 123).

346 Hughes (2003: 183).

347 Brown and Timberman (1998: 23); Peou (2000: 386–91).

348 Peou (1999: 24); also Curtis (1998: 58).

349 Peou (2000: 386).

350 Curtis (1998: 57); Hay (1998: 171–2).

351 Peou (2000: 399); see also Than (1998: 17–18).

352 Preelection polls showed the CPP running third, and CPP leaders did not expect to win a legislative majority (Peou 2000: 324–5).

353 Brown and Zasloff (1998: 309, 306).

354 Peou (2000); Hughes (2003).

355 Hay (1998: 172); Peou (1998: 72; 2000: 308); Hughes (2003: 122–3). As one FUNCIN-PEC leader observed, "the human struc-ture ... of the party was destroyed.... Many farmers – we can't reach them.... We had 100,000 members. We don't know where they are now." Quoted in Hughes (2003: 122–3).

356 Peou (2000: 345–6); see also Roberts (2001: 175–6). According to one FUNCINPEC member, the party was "chopped up into lit-tle pieces." Quoted in Roberts (2001: 176).

357 Brown and Timberman (1998: 24). Only 800 international observers were present, com-pared to 25,000 UNTAC personnel in 1993 (Peou 2000: 399; Vander Weyden 2000: 619).

UNTAC supervision, the CPP packed the electoral commission,[358] restricted opposition access to the media,[359] abused state resources,[360] violently harassed opposition campaigns,[361] and engaged in "strong-arm electioneering."[362] In a massive "thumbprint campaign" aimed at voter surveillance and intimidation, CPP activists collected millions of rural voters' thumbprints and organized voters into neighborhood "groups," affiliating them with the party, monitoring their activity, and running mock elections to teach them how to vote for the CPP.[363]

The CPP finished first in the election with 41 percent of the vote, which – due to a late change in the seat-allocation system – translated into a parliamentary majority.[364] Opposition forces rejected the results, and in August 1998, 10 thousand protesters began a three week sit-in at a park – dubbed Democracy Square – in front of the National Assembly.[365] FUNCINPEC and the new Sam Rainsy Party (SRP) refused to join a CPP-led government unless Hun Sen resigned – thereby threatening to deprive the government of the two-thirds majority required by the constitution.[366] Following an attack on Hun Sen's residence, the government turned to repression: Police broke up the tent city, triggering a week of violence in which as many as 26 people were killed.[367] Opposition leaders worked hard to mobilize Western support.[368] Nevertheless, all major donors except the United States accepted the election results and the post-election violence triggered little external response.[369] FUNCINPEC eventually rejoined the government and Ranariddh was elected President of the National Assembly.[370]

The CPP reconsolidated power after 1998. Western attention faded and the government's international standing improved.[371] Cambodia secured its UN seat and was admitted to ASEAN, and bilateral assistance – mainly from Japan and

---

[358] The commission was appointed by the National Assembly while the opposition was still in exile, and several of those selected to fill seats reserved for opposition parties and NGOs were actually CPP allies (Roberts 2001: 180–1).

[359] All major television networks were in pro-CPP hands, and radio licenses "proved difficult to get" for the opposition (Lizée 1999: 81; Peou 2000: 325).

[360] Brown and Timberman (1998: 24); Brown and Zasloff (1998: 303–4); Hughes (2001: 115).

[361] Hughes (2002: 170). UN officials reported 16 political killings (Peou 2000: 328).

[362] Hughes (2002: 170).

[363] Hughes (1999: 96–102; 2003: 70); Roberts (2001: 187–8).

[364] FUNCINPEC finished second with 32 percent of the vote. The CPP won 64 of 122 seats. Under the Balinsky/Young formula used in 1993, the CPP would have won between 56 and 59 seats, which would have given the opposition a majority (Brown and

Zasloff 1998: 213; Vander Weyden 2000: 618).

[365] Hughes (2003: 196–7).

[366] Peou (1999: 21–2; 2000: 318–19).

[367] Peou (2000: 319–20).

[368] According to Hughes (2003: 132–3), demonstrations were "oriented toward an international audience." Although opposition leaders knew the protests were unlikely to have a significant domestic impact, they viewed them "as a means of communicating with...donors in a bid to reverse international recognition of the electoral results."

[369] Brown and Zasloff (1998: 213); Peou (2000: 321–2, 400–401); Hughes (2003: 132, 202). Thus, Hun Sen bet that donors were "interested only in the façade of democracy...and were willing to turn a blind eye to almost any abuse of the principles of democracy and human rights in the name of stability. And to a large extent, he [was] proved right" (Ashley 1998: 71).

[370] Roberts (2001: 195–7).

[371] Peou (1999: 20–6); Hughes (2003: 132–4).

France – was restored.[372] On the domestic front, FUNCINPEC "all but ceased to challenge Hun Sen,"[373] which earned it a reputation as a "lap dog."[374] The CPP also consolidated control over the media: By the early 2000s, all six private television stations and all but three radio stations were owned by individuals or firms with ties to the CPP.[375] Finally, resource asymmetries deepened. Vast public resources were channeled into CPP coffers via organized corruption networks, and entrepreneurs with ties to the state lavished money on the CPP.[376] At the same time, the SRP was "starved for funds by a business community told by [the government] that financing SRP was committing economic suicide."[377]

The 2003 election was characterized by less uncertainty than previous elections. With tight control over the media, the finance, and the countryside, the CPP captured a solid parliamentary majority.[378] Despite Rainsy's persistent lobbying in the West, the international community accepted the election.[379] FUNCINPEC eventually returned to the governing coalition and was "paid handsomely" with patronage.[380]

The regime grew more hegemonic after 2003.[381] The SRP, which had emerged as the primary opposition, was repressed. In 2005, several SRP leaders and human-rights activists were imprisoned for libel or defamation, and Rainsy was forced into exile to avoid arrest (he returned in 2006).[382] In 2006, Ranariddh fled Cambodia to avoid adultery charges; FUNCINPEC subsequently divided, bringing the party to the brink of collapse.[383] As the 2008 parliamentary election approached, numerous opposition politicians defected to the CPP.[384] The CPP won overwhelmingly, capturing nearly three quarters of the seats in parliament.[385]

In summary, authoritarian stability in Cambodia was rooted in two developments. First, the Hun Sen government engaged in relatively successful state- and party-building during the 1990s, which enhanced its capacity to monitor,

---

[372] Osborne (2003: 89); McCargo (2005: 101–3).

[373] Roberts (2001: 198).

[374] Marston (2002: 98).

[375] Committee to Protect Journalists (2004: 1); Un (2005: 215). Violence against the media was replaced by a "more vigorous legalistic approach" based on libel suits and denial of licenses (Peou 2000: 197).

[376] Un (2005).

[377] Heder (2005: 118).

[378] Albritton (2004: 102) and Un (2005). See also Committee to Protect Journalists, "Attacks on the Press 2003: Documented Cases from Asia for 2003: Cambodia" (www.cpj.org/attacks03/asia03/cambodia.html). The CPP won 73 of 123 seats.

[379] Un (2005: 208, 211).

[380] McCargo (2005: 108). Ranariddh became President of the National Assembly, and the number of senior government posts was doubled to accommodate the party's patronage needs (Beresford 2005: 135).

[381] According to McCargo (2005: 100), elections came to be viewed as "an exercise in political theater." See also Un (2005).

[382] Freedom House, "Freedom in the World 2008: Cambodia" (http://www.freedomhouse.org).

[383] *The Economist*, November 5, 2005, pp. 46–7 and *The New York Times*, January 9, 2006, p. A3. See also Freedom House, "Freedom in the World 2006: Cambodia" (http://www.freedomhouse.org). FUNCINPEC won only two seats in the 2008 parliamentary election.

[384] Un (2008).

[385] Un (2008).

TABLE 7.1. *Predicted and Actual Competitive Authoritarian Regime Outcomes in Asia*

Case	Linkage	Leverage	Organizational Power	Predicted Outcome	Actual Outcome
Cambodia	Low	High	Medium High	Stable Authoritarianism	Stable Authoritarianism
Malaysia	Medium	Medium	High	Stable Authoritarianism	Stable Authoritarianism
Taiwan	High	Low	High	Democracy	Democracy

co-opt, and – when necessary – repress opposition. In an overwhelmingly rural society, CPP dominance in the countryside proved critical to regime stability. Second, in the absence of linkage, Western democratizing pressure was limited. International pressure faded in the aftermath of the 1993 UN intervention. Particularly after 1997, Sam Rainsy's efforts to lobby Western governments for punitive responses to regime abuses failed repeatedly. Given Cambodia's weak ties to the West, then, it appears that Rainsy's "faith in international action was misplaced."[386]

CONCLUSION

Table 7.1 summarizes the three Asian cases. The Malaysian and Taiwanese cases were similar in several ways. Both regimes possessed high organizational power and both faced a significant domestic push for democratization (although Taiwan's was stronger). Regime outcomes were shaped by the degree to which governing parties were willing to use force to thwart opposition challenges. In Taiwan, where linkage was high, the KMT government refrained from coercion, allowing opposition forces to gather strength. Eventually, the KMT lost control of the political game and, by 2000, the external cost of reasserting control was prohibitive. In Malaysia, where linkage and leverage were medium, the Mahathir government used force to weaken civic and opposition challenges in 1987–1990 and again in 1998–2000. These measures were successful, at least through 2009. In Cambodia, by contrast, lower organizational power and high leverage led to regime vulnerability in the early 1990s, and the CPP nearly lost power. However, effective state- and party-building – in a context of low linkage – helped stabilize the regime after 1997.

Established theories of democratization cannot fully account for these outcomes. For example, economic crisis had little discernible impact. Taiwan democratized despite steady economic growth, whereas the Malaysian regime survived a severe economic crisis in 1997–1998. The outcomes are largely in line with modernization theory. Taiwan was the wealthiest case examined in this book, and there is little question that the social changes generated by industrialization provided an impetus for democratization and facilitated its survival. Likewise,

---

[386] Hughes (2003: 132).

Cambodia's extreme underdevelopment helps explain its persistent authoritarianism. As the case analyses make clear, however, linkage and organizational power were critical to regime outcomes. Although socioeconomic development gave rise to a potent middle-class opposition movement in the 1970s and 1980s, it was high linkage – along with far-reaching geopolitical change – that induced the KMT to underutilize its coercive power during the 1980s and 1990s. By contrast, the Malaysian case shows that when linkage-based pressure is weak, strong party and state structures may be used to thwart even relatively strong opposition movements.

8

Conclusion

Competitive authoritarianism emerged as a distinct, widespread, and often stable regime type during the post–Cold War period. This book explains the diverging fates of these regimes, asking why some of them democratized while others either remained stable and authoritarian or experienced turnover without democratization. We argue that regime outcomes hinged on three main factors. First, where linkage to the West was extensive, competitive authoritarian regimes democratized. By heightening the international salience of abuse (and the likelihood of Western response), increasing the number of domestic actors with a stake in avoiding isolation, and shifting the balance of resources and prestige in favor of oppositions, linkage raised the cost of building and sustaining authoritarian rule. In this context, authoritarian rulers faced strong incentives to cede power rather than crack down in the face of opposition challenges. Linkage also increased the likelihood that successors would rule democratically.

Where linkage was low, external democratizing pressure was weaker. Government abuse was less likely to gain international attention or trigger costly external responses, leaving autocrats with greater room for maneuver. Consequently, regime outcomes were driven primarily by domestic factors, particularly incumbents' organizational power. Where state and/or governing-party organizations were extensive and cohesive, incumbents were better equipped to manage elite conflict and thwart opposition challenges, and competitive authoritarian regimes usually survived. Where state and governing-party structures were weak, regimes were less stable. Because incumbents lacked the organizational and coercive tools to prevent elite defection, steal elections, or crack down on protest, they were vulnerable to even relatively weak opposition challenges. Consequently, outcomes were more contingent than in other cases.

In this context, Western leverage was often decisive. Where leverage was low, authoritarian incumbents generally survived. Where leverage was high, incumbents were more likely to fall. Although turnover in such cases created an opportunity for democratization, the absence of either a strong domestic push for democracy or close ties to the West meant that transitions were more likely to result in the persistence of competitive authoritarianism.

EVALUATING THE THEORY'S PERFORMANCE

The test of our theory lies in the comparative case studies in Chapters 3 through 7; it is only through case analyses that we can demonstrate the causal relationships among linkage, organizational power, and regime outcomes. Nevertheless, Table 8.1 summarizes the theory's performance. As the table shows, our theory correctly predicts regime outcomes in 28 of 35 cases. Among the seven nonmatches, six are "near misses," in that our theory accounts for key aspects of regime evolution and outcomes are close to those predicted by our theory. Only one case – Ghana – falls entirely outside our theoretical framework.

In three near-miss cases (Benin, Mali, and Ukraine), democratization occurred in a context of low linkage, high leverage, and low organizational power, where we predict unstable competitive authoritarianism. Authoritarian incumbents fell, as predicted, but turnover produced democratic governments.[1] In all three cases, however, regime trajectories largely followed the lines of our theory. All three regimes were unstable and competitive authoritarian for most of the period under study,[2] and as the case chapters show, this instability was rooted in state and/or party weakness. Moreover, as we argue in Chapter 2, the combination of low linkage, high leverage, and low organizational power often generates fluid – and highly contingent – regime outcomes. The weakness of both incumbent and opposition forces produces an open environment in which short-term regime outcomes may be shaped by a variety of factors, which creates an opportunity for democratization. Further, because high leverage and low organizational power limit the prospects for authoritarian consolidation, the potential for turnover is high, which may generate multiple opportunities for democratization. Leadership can be decisive in such a context. Where successors underutilize their power, democracy may emerge, as occurred in Benin, Mali, and Ukraine.[3] These regimes were weakly institutionalized, however, and of our democratization cases, they were almost certainly among the most prone to authoritarian regression.[4]

---

[1] Elections in Ukraine (2006 and 2007), Benin (2006), and Mali (2007) were widely considered clean; through 2008, we found little evidence of significant abuse under the Yushchenko, Boni, and Touré governments.

[2] Benin was competitive authoritarian under Soglo (1991–1996) and Kérékou (2001–2006); Ukraine was competitive authoritarian under Kravchuk (1992–1994) and Kuchma (1994–2004); and Mali was competitive authoritarian under Konare (1992–2002).

[3] Similar developments could occur in other cases that combine high leverage and relatively low organizational power, such as Georgia, Madagascar, and Zambia. Although these regimes were competitive authoritarian in 2008, they were less consolidated – and, in most cases, less authoritarian – than other nondemocratizers.

[4] Indeed, there was some evidence of movement in a competitive authoritarian direction in Mali and Ukraine in the late 2000s.

TABLE 8.1. *Predicted and Actual Regime Outcomes*[5]

Case	Linkage	Organizational Power	Leverage	Predicted Outcome	Actual Outcome
Albania	High	Low	High	Democracy	**Unstable Authoritarianism**
Armenia	Medium	High	High	Stable Authoritarianism	Stable Authoritarianism
Belarus	Low	Low	Medium	Stable Authoritarianism	**Unstable Authoritarianism**
Benin	Low	Low	High	Unstable Authoritarianism	**Democracy**
Botswana	Low	High	High	Stable Authoritarianism	Stable Authoritarianism
Cambodia	Low	Medium High	High	Stable Authoritarianism	Stable Authoritarianism
Cameroon	Low	Medium	Medium	Stable Authoritarianism	Stable Authoritarianism
Croatia	High	Medium High	High	Democracy	Democracy
Dominican Republic	High	Medium	High	Democracy	Democracy
Gabon	Medium	High	Medium	Stable Authoritarianism	Stable Authoritarianism
Georgia	Low	Low	High	Unstable Authoritarianism	Unstable Authoritarianism
Ghana	Low	Medium	High	Unstable Authoritarianism	**Democracy**
Guyana	High	High	High	Democracy	Democracy
Haiti	Medium	Low	High	Unstable Authoritarianism	Unstable Authoritarianism
Kenya	Low	Medium	High	Unstable Authoritarianism	Unstable Authoritarianism
Macedonia	High	Low	High	Democracy	Democracy
Madagascar	Low	Low	High	Unstable Authoritarianism	Unstable Authoritarianism
Malawi	Low	Low	High	Unstable Authoritarianism	Unstable Authoritarianism
Malaysia	Medium	High	Medium	Stable Authoritarianism	Stable Authoritarianism
Mali	Low	Low	High	Unstable Authoritarianism	**Democracy**
Mexico	High	High	Low	Democracy	Democracy
Moldova	Medium	Low	High	Unstable Authoritarianism	Unstable Authoritarianism

(continued)

---

[5] Scores on the independent variables are based on the initial competitive authoritarian government (1990–1995). Scores on the dependent variable are from 2008.

TABLE 8.1 *(continued)*

Case	Linkage	Organizational Power	Leverage	Predicted Outcome	Actual Outcome
Mozambique	Low	Medium High	High	Stable Authoritarianism	Stable Authoritarianism
Nicaragua	High	High	High	Democracy	Democracy
Peru	Medium	Low	High	Unstable Authoritarianism	**Democracy**
Romania	High	Medium	High	Democracy	Democracy
Russia	Low	Low	Low	Stable Authoritarianism	Stable Authoritarianism
Senegal	Low	Medium	High	Unstable Authoritarianism	Unstable Authoritarianism
Serbia	High	High	High	Democracy	Democracy
Slovakia	High	Medium High	High	Democracy	Democracy
Taiwan	High	High	Low	Democracy	Democracy
Tanzania	Low	Medium High	High	Stable Authoritarianism	Stable Authoritarianism
Ukraine	Low	Low	High	Unstable Authoritarianism	**Democracy**
Zambia	Low	Medium Low	High	Unstable Authoritarianism	Unstable Authoritarianism
Zimbabwe	Low	High	High	Stable Authoritarianism	Stable Authoritarianism

Note: Outcomes that do not match predictions are in bold.

In a fourth case, Belarus, we expect Russian black knight support to result in authoritarian stability despite low organizational power in the early 1990s. Viacheslau Kebich's defeat in 1994 violates this expectation. In line with our theory, however, Alyaksandr Lukashenka subsequently established a more stable regime, remaining in power – without serious challenge – through 2008.

In Peru, medium linkage and low organizational power yields a prediction of unstable competitive authoritarianism. Although turnover occurred as predicted in 2000, the regime subsequently democratized. Given that Peru's linkage score is close to the threshold for high, this outcome is not surprising; indeed, linkage effects were quite evident in Peru. Opposition leader Alejandro Toledo was a U.S.-educated technocrat with extensive ties to the United States, IOs, and Western NGOs – on winning the presidency, he filled his government with U.S.-oriented technocrats.[6] These ties explain – at least, in part – why turnover resulted in democratization.

Albania – the only high-linkage case that did not democratize – is also a near-miss. Given the structural obstacles to democratization in that country (e.g., underdevelopment, legacies of Stalinist rule, and state collapse in the mid-1990s), a nondemocratic outcome is not particularly surprising. Nevertheless, linkage had a clear and powerful impact on Albania's regime trajectory. Incumbents fell

---

[6] McClintock and Vallas (2003: 161, 167).

three times and, in the face of large-scale Western intervention, governments behaved in an increasingly democratic manner. By the late 2000s, elections were far cleaner and civil-liberties violations far less common than they had been in the 1990s. In fact, although we score Albania as competitive authoritarian in 2008, it was widely viewed as a democracy.

In Ghana, linkage, leverage, and organizational power do not shape regime development in ways predicted by our theory. Ghana is a case of democratization despite low linkage and (at least) medium organizational power. Two factors that lie outside our framework appear to explain this outcome. The first is leadership. In effect, the Rawlings government behaved as if Ghana were a high-linkage case. Heavily invested in its status as a model economic reformer, the government was highly sensitive to its international standing. Like the PRI in Mexico, it strengthened electoral institutions and underutilized its coercive power and, in 1992 and 1996, Rawlings retained power in credible elections. However, the growth of a strong opposition – the second factor – eventually led to his party's defeat. The ability of the NPP opposition to penetrate the countryside enabled it to take advantage of relatively effective electoral institutions and capture the presidency in 2000.

Finally, it is worth noting that our theory appears to perform well even if we expand the sample to include less competitive regimes. As noted in Chapter 1, we excluded from this analysis several "electoral authoritarian" regimes on the grounds that they were hegemonic, rather than competitive.[7] Most of these cases also seem to conform to our theory. For example, in Ethiopia and Uganda, stable authoritarian regimes emerged out of violent struggle; in Azerbaijan and Kazakhstan, regimes benefited from vast state discretionary control over the economy; in Egypt, linkage and leverage were both low. In Kyrgyzstan, authoritarian breakdown in 2005 was clearly driven by state weakness, and in the absence of linkage, turnover did not bring democratization.[8] One case that does not fit our theory is Singapore, which remained authoritarian despite relatively high linkage.

Comparison over Time and across Regions

The key components of our argument may be highlighted through two types of comparison: over time and across region. First, in three cases, scores on our independent variables changed over time in theoretically important ways, which should lead to changes in expected regime outcomes. In Belarus, Cambodia, and Russia, organizational power increased over time, and in all three cases, regimes became more stable. In Belarus, Lukashenka's reassertion of state authority, combined with his decision to preserve state economic control, led to a substantial increase in organizational power after 1994, which – combined with continued

---

[7] These include Azerbaijan, Burkina Faso, Cote d'Ivoire, Egypt, Ethiopia, Kazakhstan, Kyrgyzstan, Singapore, and Uganda.

[8] Way (2008a: 59). Authoritarian breakdown occurred again in 2010 after a few thousand lightly armed protestors overwhelmed police and took over government buildings in the capital. See *The Economist*, April 10, 2010, p. 43.

black knight support from Russia – could be expected to result in greater regime stability. Indeed, the regime stabilized (and grew increasingly closed) between 1995 and 2008. Thus, although our theory cannot explain the 1994 transition, it helps us to understand the 15 years of regime stability that followed.

Cambodia followed a similar pattern. Due to the weakness of the Cambodian state in the early 1990s, organizational power was relatively low just prior to the 1992–1993 transition. Indeed, the CPP barely survived the UN-administered transition and nearly lost power in the 1993 election. Over time, however, state- and party-building enhanced organizational power, which resulted in an increasingly stable – and hegemonic – regime.

Finally, in Russia, organizational power was quite low in the first half of the 1990s, when the state was in disarray and Yeltsin governed without a party. Although the regime survived (due in large part to low leverage), the government faced repeated crises and nearly fell in 1993, 1996, and 1999. After 1999, effective state- and party-building under Putin resulted in increased organizational power, which leads us to expect greater regime stability. Indeed, no serious regime crises emerged in the 2000s, and by decade's end, virtually all serious opposition had disappeared. Putin was easily reelected in 2004 and imposed a successor in 2008.

The utility of our theoretical framework also may be highlighted through selected cross-regional comparisons. For example, the centrality of linkage is seen in a comparison of three post–Cold War international settlement cases: Cambodia, Mozambique, and Nicaragua. All three are cases of poor countries with weak civil societies and no democratic tradition. In the 1980s, all three countries experienced civil wars in which Soviet-backed leftist governments confronted U.S.-backed insurgencies, and each country experienced an externally sponsored settlement that culminated in internationally administered or supervised elections. In each case, Western leverage was very high at the time of founding elections and, in each case, incumbents possessed relatively strong and cohesive parties. Yet regime outcomes diverged considerably, and these differences can be attributed to distinct international environments. In Nicaragua, where linkage was high, the FSLN was compelled to hold a clean election, which the U.S.-backed opposition won. Nicaragua democratized, despite the fact that organizational power was somewhat higher than in either Cambodia or Mozambique. In Cambodia and Mozambique, where linkage was low, governing parties narrowly survived internationally supervised elections in the first half of the 1990s. However, limited international attention after founding elections created a permissive environment in the second half of the decade, which allowed both parties to reconsolidate power.

The role of linkage also is seen in comparing Malaysia and Mexico. Both Malaysia and Mexico possessed relatively favorable conditions for democratization. They were among the most developed countries in the sample and – although both had experienced decades of stable electoral authoritarian rule – years of steady economic growth had produced relatively large, educated middle classes and burgeoning civil societies. Moreover, both countries faced severe economic crises in the 1990s (Mexico in 1994–1995 and Malaysia in 1997–1998) that led to unprecedented electoral challenges (Malaysia in 1999 and Mexico in 2000). Although both the PRI and UMNO enjoyed high organizational power and faced divided oppositions, Mexico democratized whereas the Malaysian regime remained stable. Variation in linkage explains these diverging regime paths. The PRI's technocratic leadership consistently underutilized its coercive capacity during the 1990s, allowing opposition forces to grow to the point where they could compete seriously for power. The Mahathir government, which was less sensitive to Western criticism, engaged in periodic crackdowns that kept opposition forces in check.

A cross-regional comparison also may be used to highlight the role of state coercive capacity. Take Armenia, Georgia, and Madagascar. All three cases were characterized by high leverage, low or medium linkage, and relatively weak civil societies. In each country, incumbents faced major crises (Armenia in 1996, Georgia in 2003, and Madagascar in 2002) when stolen elections triggered protest. Yet, whereas the coercive apparatuses in Madagascar and Georgia were low in both scope and cohesion, Armenia's coercive apparatus was strengthened by a victorious war in Nagorno–Karabakh. In Madagascar, the security forces disintegrated in the face of mass protest, allowing opposition forces to overrun the capital and eventually forcing President Didier Ratsiraka to flee. In Georgia, the police stepped aside in the face of modest-sized demonstrations as opposition activists seized parliament and forced the resignation of President Eduard Shevardnadze. By contrast, in Armenia, war veterans provided the bases for a cohesive and skilled security force that was able to seal off the capital and put down mass demonstrations.

Finally, the role of party strength can be seen in a comparison of five cases: Kenya (2002), Nicaragua (1989–1990), Ukraine (2004), Zambia (1990–1991), and Zimbabwe (2000–2002). In all five cases, unpopular incumbents faced the prospect of imminent defeat, creating incentives for government officials to strategically defect to the opposition. In Kenya, Ukraine, and Zambia, where governing parties lacked any source of cohesion beyond patronage, that is exactly what occurred. Large-scale elite defection weakened incumbents and provided oppositions with the resources they needed to remove them from power. In Nicaragua and Zimbabwe, governing parties – both of which were characterized by high cohesion rooted in military struggle – remained intact. Notwithstanding economic crisis, international isolation, and electoral defeat (Nicaragua) or near-defeat (Zimbabwe), virtually no top-level FSLN or ZANU leaders defected.[9] In Zimbabwe, elite cohesion enabled the government to crack down and – through 2009 – remain in power. In Nicaragua, the FSLN ceded power, but this outcome was rooted in linkage, not low cohesion.

Alternative Explanations

Our theory of linkage and organizational power provides a more compelling explanation of competitive regime outcomes than major alternatives. As discussed

---

[9] ZANU suffered some defection (behind the candidacy of ex–Finance Minister Simba Makoni) in 2008; however, given the depth of the economic and political crises, the level of defection was strikingly low.

in Chapter 2, the modernization variable is of limited utility in this study. All but a few of our cases are low- or lower-middle–income countries – a level of development at which few scholars would predict democratization. Regime outcomes varied considerably among these cases, and as this study demonstrates, much of this variation appears to be rooted in linkage. Indeed, democratization occurred in 9 of 10 lower- and middle-income countries in which linkage was high.[10] By contrast, democratization occurred in only 5 of the 24 low- and middle-income countries in which linkage was medium or low.[11]

Constitutional design also had no notable impact on regime outcomes. Competitive authoritarian regimes with parliamentary systems were no more likely to democratize (and, in fact, were *less* likely to democratize) than those with presidential or semi-presidential systems.[12] Whereas only 1 of 6 parliamentary regimes (Slovakia) democratized, 13 of 29 presidential or semi-presidential cases democratized. Among high-linkage cases, *all* nine presidential or semi-presidential regimes democratized.

Another set of alternative hypotheses centers on the role of exogenous shocks, particularly economic crises.[13] Economic downturn clearly contributed to authoritarian failure in several of our cases.[14] Yet the impact of economic crisis hinged, to a considerable degree, on organizational power. Incumbents with strong state and party organizations – for example, those that emerged from war, revolution, or liberation struggle – were generally able to prevent elite defection, put down protest, and win or steal elections even in a context of declining resources and/or public support. Table 8.2 illustrates the mediating effect of organizational power. We examined the fate of competitive authoritarian incumbents in 65 instances of economic crisis between 1989 and 2008. In cases of low organizational power, turnover occurred in 9 of 35 economic crises. By contrast, where organizational power was medium or high, turnover occurred in only 2 of 30 instances of economic crisis (Nicaragua and Serbia, two high linkage cases). Although hardly definitive, this evidence suggests that the destabilizing impact of economic crisis is far greater where organizational power is already low.

A similar argument may be made regarding a second type of exogenous shock: the death or retirement of authoritarian rulers. Succession challenges have long

---

[10] These were Croatia, the Dominican Republic, Guyana, Mexico, Macedonia, Nicaragua, Romania, Serbia, and Slovakia. (Based on 1991 World Bank classifications; see Table 2.2 in Chapter 2.)

[11] Low- and middle-income democratizers were Benin, Ghana, Mali, Peru, and Ukraine. Nondemocratizers were Armenia, Botswana, Belarus, Cameroon, Cambodia, Gabon, Georgia, Haiti, Kenya, Madagascar, Malawi, Malaysia, Moldova, Mozambique, Russia, Senegal, Tanzania, Zambia, and Zimbabwe.

[12] Parliamentary systems included Albania, Belarus (1992–1994), Botswana, Cambodia,

Malaysia, and Slovakia. We code as parliamentary any case in which the executive is chosen by the legislature rather than by popular vote. Albania and Botswana may be considered mixed presidential–parliamentary because the executive (chosen by the legislature) is elected for a fixed term.

[13] Haggard and Kaufman (1995); Przeworski and Limongi (1997).

[14] This was the case, for example, in Belarus, Malawi, Moldova, Nicaragua, Ukraine, and Zambia in the early 1990s.

TABLE 8.2. *Economic Crisis, Organizational Power, and Turnover, 1989–2008*[15]

Organizational Power	Incumbent Turnover	Incumbent Survival
High	Nicaragua 1989–1990 (turnover 1990)	Armenia 1991, 1992, 1993, 1994
	Serbia 1999 (turnover 2000)	Croatia 1991, 1992, 1993
		Gabon 1999
		Guyana 1989
		Malaysia 1998
		Mexico 1995
		Mozambique 1992
		Serbia 1991, 1992, 1993
		Slovakia 1992
		Zimbabwe 1992, 2000, 2003, 2005, 2006, 2007, 2008
Medium		Cameroon 1990
		Dominican Republic 1990
		Romania 1990, 1991, 1992
Low	Belarus 1993–1994 (turnover 1994)	Albania 1990
	Albania 1991–1992 (turnover 1992), 1997	Belarus 1992, 1995
	Georgia 1991–1992 (turnover 1992)	Georgia 1993, 1994
	Macedonia 2001 (turnover 2002)	Haiti 1994
	Madagascar 1991 (turnover 1992–93)	Macedonia 1991, 1992, 1993
	Malawi 1994	Malawi 1992, 2001
	Moldova 1996	Moldova 1991, 1992, 1994, 1998
	Ukraine 1993–1994 (turnover 1994)	Ukraine 1991, 1992, 1995, 1996
		Russia 1991, 1992, 1993, 1994, 1998
		Zambia 1994

been linked to authoritarian regime instability, and recent studies have pointed to the death or retirement of an autocratic leader as a source of instability in hybrid regimes.[16] When long-standing authoritarian leaders retire, struggles over

---

[15] Sample includes all country years in which GDP declined by at least 5 percent or inflation surpassed 500 percent (World Bank World Development Indicators (online: www.worldbank.org/data)). Cases are scored as turnover if the incumbent lost power during the year of the crisis or the subsequent year. We do not count as instances of turnover those cases in which there is evidence that the incumbent fell prior to the crisis or that the transition contributed to the crisis (e.g., Madagascar in 2002). Cases in which crisis occurs both in the year prior to turnover and the year of turnover are counted as a single crisis.

[16] Hale (2005b); Howard and Roessler (2006).

succession and uncertainty over patronage distribution often trigger elite conflict and defection, which can undermine regime stability. Like economic crises, however, the impact of succession is mediated by organizational power. Where governing parties were weak (e.g., Malawi, Mali, Peru, Russia, and Ukraine), succession issues frequently destabilized competitive authoritarian regimes. Where governing parties were strong and cohesive, however, regimes generally survived one or more successions without serious crisis. In Guyana (1985), Taiwan (1988), Malaysia (2003), and Mozambique (2004), for example, regimes survived the death or retirement of long-standing leaders because cohesive governing parties managed the succession process without falling into crisis. Hence, although succession posed a challenge for competitive authoritarian regimes, it only appears to have undermined regimes where organizational power was already relatively low.

Finally, our focus on incumbent power runs counter to recent studies that highlight the role of opposition protest in bringing down authoritarian regimes.[17] This focus has been especially pronounced in recent work on the post-communist "color revolutions."[18] Opposition mobilization contributed directly to the fall of authoritarian governments in several cases, including Benin (1989–1991), Zambia (1990–1991), Georgia (2003), Madagascar (1991–1993 and 2002), Serbia (2000), and Ukraine (2004). Again, however, the success of opposition mobilization hinged on the organizational power of incumbents. Opposition protest – in some cases, more extensive protest – failed to reverse flawed or stolen elections in the Dominican Republic (1990), Gabon (1993), Armenia (1996, 2003, 2004, and 2008), Cambodia (1998), Peru (2000), Zimbabwe (2002–2003), Belarus (2006), and Kenya (2007); massive strikes and protest failed to dislodge autocrats in Gabon (1990) and Cameroon (1991); and emerging prodemocracy movements were beaten down by repression in Malaysia (1998–1999), Zimbabwe (2000–2005), and Belarus (2006).

Table 8.3 examines the fate of major anti-regime protests between 1990 and 2008. Where organizational power was low, a striking 9 of 14 anti-regime mobilizations succeeded in bringing down governments (either directly or by triggering elections that incumbents lost). Where organizational power was medium or high, only 1 of 24 anti-regime mobilizations succeeded – despite the fact that many of these mobilizations were massive (e.g., Cameroon in 1991, Serbia in the early 1990s, and Armenia in 1996).

To take this point a step further, it appears that opposition mobilization is often endogenous to organizational capacity. Where governing parties were weak, opposition strength was often rooted in elite defection, as politicians who had recently abandoned the government provided critical resources, leadership, and organization to opposition movements. In Ukraine, for example, virtually the entire leadership of the Orange Revolution had defected from the government

---

[17] See Bratton and van de Walle (1997), Thompson and Kuntz (2004, 2005), Bunce and Wolchik (2006b), Beissinger (2007), and Tucker (2007).

[18] See, for example, Bunce and Wolchik (2006a, 2006b), Kuzio (2006a, 2006b), Beissinger (2007), and Tucker (2007). For a critique of this literature, see Way (2008a, 2009a).

TABLE 8.3. *Outcomes of Significant Anti-Regime Protest, 1990–2008*[19]

Organizational Power	Turnover	Incumbent Survival
High	Serbia 2000	Armenia 1993, 1996, 2003, 2004, 2008
		Belarus 2006
		Cambodia 1998
		Gabon 1990, 1993–1994
		Malaysia 1998, 2007
		Mexico 1994
		Serbia 1990, 1991, 1992, 1996–1997
		Taiwan 1990
		Zimbabwe 2003
Medium		Cameroon 1991, 2008
		Dominican Republic 1990
		Kenya 1997, 2007–2008
Low	Albania 1991 (turnover in 1992), 1997	Georgia 1994, 2007
	Benin 1989 (turnover in 1990–1991)	Haiti 2003
	Georgia 2003	Peru 2000
	Madagascar 1991 (turnover in 1992–1993), 2002	Russia 1993
	Ukraine 1993 (turnover in 1994), 2004	
	Zambia 1990 (turnover in 1991)	

just a few years (and in some cases, several months) earlier. Likewise, in Kenya, much of the organizational muscle behind the victorious NARC coalition was provided by politicians who defected from the KANU government only months before the 2002 election. By contrast, where state and governing-party organizations were strong, effective repression frequently preempted opposition protest (e.g., Malaysia and Zimbabwe) or prevented it from emerging in the first place (e.g., Russia under Putin).

A similar pattern is evident in the case of stolen elections. Several scholars have linked authoritarian breakdown to stolen elections.[20] For example, Mark Thompson and Philipp Kuntz argue that stolen elections "create conditions favorable for the outbreak of democratic revolutions" by raising and then dashing popular expectations, providing a focal point for opposition, serving as a trigger for mass

---

[19] Data are drawn from the authors' case analyses. We include all protests of 10,000 people or more, as well as general strikes with at least moderate levels of participation, which were aimed at reversing flawed national election results and/or removing the national-level incumbent.

[20] Thompson and Kuntz (2004, 2005) Tucker (2007).

TABLE 8.4. *Organizational Power and Stolen Elections, 1990–2008*

Organizational Power	Turnover	Incumbent Survival
High	Serbia 2000	Armenia 1996 Belarus 2004 (referendum) Gabon 1990 (parliamentary), 1993 Serbia 1997 Zimbabwe 2002, 2008
Medium	Dominican Republic 1994	Cameroon 1992 Kenya 1997 (parliamentary), 2007
Low	Georgia 2003 (parliamentary) Madagascar 2001–2002 Ukraine 2004	Haiti 2000 (parliamentary) Russia 1993 (referendum) Zambia 2001

Note: Elections are for president unless otherwise indicated.

protest, and generating splits within the governing elite.[21] Thus, where incumbents steal elections, regimes should be "vulnerable to democratic revolution."[22] Among our cases, however, regimes were vulnerable to stolen elections only when organizational power was low. Table 8.4 lists all of the competitive authoritarian elections between 1990 and 2008 that can be credibly claimed to have been stolen.[23] As shown in the table, where organizational power was low, stolen elections triggered regime breakdown in three of six cases. However, where organizational power was medium or high, incumbents almost invariably survived stolen elections (10 of 12 cases). The only exceptions were the Dominican Republic and Serbia, two high-linkage cases that were subject to substantial Western pressure.

A final point merits attention: Even when stolen elections trigger the collapse of authoritarian regimes, they should not necessarily be viewed as an independent cause of that collapse. In many cases, stolen elections are a *product* rather than a cause of regime crisis. Where authoritarian regimes are well entrenched (e.g., Egypt, Singapore, Malaysia, and pre-1988 Mexico), incumbents' control over the electoral process – and the opposition – is often so extensive that they can win elections without having to resort to large-scale fraud.[24] Elections are "won" in the weeks and months prior to the actual vote, as opposition forces are debilitated by repression, denial of resources, co-optation, and a variety of other legal and

---

[21] Thompson and Kuntz (2004: 160–3).

[22] Thompson and Kuntz (2004: 171).

[23] A presidential, parliamentary, or constitutional referendum election is considered stolen if manipulation of the voting or vote-counting process is deemed – by credible scholars and/or international observers – to have likely altered the outcome of the election. This includes cases in which there is credible evidence that fraud enabled the governing party to win a parliamentary major-

ity, as well as cases in which fraud enabled incumbent presidential candidates to avoid a second-round runoff. We exclude cases of large-scale fraud in which few observers believed that the outcome would have been different in the absence of fraud (e.g., Albania in 1996 and Belarus in 2006).

[24] See Magaloni (2006) and Greene (2007).

illegal machinations. In other words, events on election day are the final link in a longer chain of processes. Whether or not incumbents are forced to engage in high risk fraud on election day is mainly a product of how capable they were of dealing with opposition challenges prior to the election. In general, only regimes that are weak or vulnerable from the outset must turn – often in desperation – to stealing elections.

Regime outcomes have myriad causes. No single theory can explain them all. Nevertheless, a theoretical framework that centers on linkage, leverage, and organizational power takes us a long way toward explaining competitive authoritarian regime trajectories after the Cold War. Indeed, it provides a more compelling explanation than variables such as economic development, constitutional design, economic crisis, and opposition protest.

Two caveats are in order when assessing our theory's performance beyond 2008. First, like most mid-range theories, our theory does not claim to predict outcomes indefinitely. Various factors are likely to influence longer-term regime outcomes. For example, although low linkage reduces external democratizing pressure, it does not preclude domestically driven transitions. Because most of our cases were characterized by weak civil societies and opposition parties, the absence of strong and persistent international pressure generally led to nondemocratic outcomes. However, civic and opposition forces may strengthen over time, thereby increasing the likelihood of endogenous democratization. Such change contributed to democratization in Mexico, Taiwan, and Ghana in the 1990s, and it may well contribute to democratization in other cases – for example, Malaysia – in the future. Levels of organizational power also may change, often due to exogenous shocks such as war or economic crisis. For example, the 1999 NATO war weakened Serbia's coercive apparatus, thereby undermining the organizational bases of authoritarian stability. Likewise, Zimbabwe's extraordinary economic collapse – in a context of international isolation and growing personalization of power – clearly eroded state capacity in the 2000s, thereby throwing the regime's future into question.

Second, although high linkage generates powerful constraints on autocratic rule, it cannot preclude the emergence of leaders who (from ideological commitment, miscalculation, or sheer audacity) are willing – at least temporarily – to buck regional pressures. This was the case with Vladimir Mečiar (Slovakia) and Slobodan Milošević (Serbia) in the 1990s, and Daniel Ortega (Nicaragua) and Hugo Chavez (Venezuela) in the 2000s. Nevertheless, our theory predicts that any return to authoritarianism will be accompanied by intense linkage-based pressure that empowers oppositions and imposes heavy costs on incumbents.

THEORETICAL EXTENSIONS

This study raises several theoretical issues that are of broader interest to students of regime change. We focus on four sets of issues: (1) the relationship among linkage, leverage, and democratization; (2) sources of party cohesion and authoritarian durability; (3) the relationship between organizational power and democratic transitions; and (4) the impact of weak political institutions.

Linkage, Leverage, and Democratization

Our research offers new insights into the international dimension of regime change. In particular, we found that linkage was critical to the success of democratic conditionality. In high-linkage cases, because even minor abuses reverberated in the West, authoritarian behavior was more likely to trigger a boomerang effect. Because so many domestic actors held a stake in their country's international status, the specter of external punitive action often generated considerable domestic opposition, which magnified the boomerang effect. For example, after the 1994 fraud in the Dominican Republic, mere rumors of U.S. sanctions or visa restrictions led business leaders to abandon Balaguer and seek a democratic settlement.[25] Likewise, in Slovakia, Prime Minister Mečiar's relatively minor abuses triggered "exaggerated reactions" from the international community and threatened the European integration process.[26] The Prime Minister became so politically radioactive that he could not find partners to form a coalition government, despite winning a plurality in the 1998 parliamentary election. In Nicaragua, when the Sandinista and Liberal parties threatened to unconstitutionally remove President Bolaños in 2005, U.S. officials threatened to restrict visas to Liberal leaders and their families. Because many Liberal politicians lived in exile in the United States in the 1980s and maintained close ties there (e.g., their families shopped in Miami and many had children in U.S. schools), the threat was effective.[27] By contrast, serious abuse in Armenia (fraud), Malawi (arrest of opposition leaders), Madagascar (arrest and exclusion of opposition candidates), and Zambia (fraud and exclusion of opposition candidates) triggered little response from Western powers. And even strong U.S. pressure (including sanctions) had relatively little impact on domestic elites in Belarus, Cambodia, and Zimbabwe.

The dimension of linkage thus helps explain the mixed and often contradictory findings of studies of the impact of political conditionality. Whereas conditionality has been found to have a democratizing impact in Europe and the Americas,[28] it has limited or mixed results elsewhere in the world.[29] Europe and the Americas, of course, are the two regions where linkage to the West is highest.

These findings have clear policy implications. In the late 2000s, most of the world's authoritarian regimes existed in countries with relatively low linkage, in which economic and/or diplomatic disengagement is least likely to be effective. Where low linkage is combined with low leverage (e.g., China and Russia), authoritarian governments are often in a position to simply ignore such pressure. Even where leverage is higher (e.g., Burma and Tajikistan), such measures will not affect a sufficiently broad stratum of the elite to generate domestic resistance to authoritarian behavior. Instead, such policies are likely to discredit and isolate those forces seeking liberalization and engagement with the West. Moreover,

---

[25] Peña (1996: 312) and Lozano (2002a: 122–3).

[26] Skolkay (1997: 201).

[27] *El Nuevo Diario*, October 5, 2005, p. 1; *La Prensa*, October 5, 2005, p. 1.

[28] Pevehouse (2005); Vachudova (2005b).

[29] See Nelson and Eglinton (1992), Stokke (1995a), Bratton and van de Walle (1997), and Crawford (2001).

in poor countries with weak civil societies, reduced engagement may render a greater share of the population dependent on the government for survival, which limits the opposition's capacity for mass mobilization. By reducing the degree to which the elite and citizens have a stake in their country's international standing, then, policies of long-term isolation are likely to erode Western influence.

Although linkage is mainly rooted in long-term structural factors, Western policy choices do matter, particularly over time. As discussed in Chapter 3, Western powers played a major role in building linkage in Eastern Europe. Western states and IOs invested heavily in the region after 1989, creating a vast network of political, economic, technocratic, intergovernmental, and civil-society ties. Combined with the prospect of EU membership, these policies vastly increased the number of stakeholders in European integration. Politicians, businesses, technocrats, NGOs, and even voters who believed they had something to gain from Europe – and much to lose if the integration process were derailed – became constituents for international norm-abiding behavior, which raised the political cost of authoritarian abuse. Consequently, regimes democratized despite obstacles created by weak civil societies, ethnic tension, and/or legacies of sultanistic rule. A similar process unfolded in Mexico. As discussed in Chapter 4, NAFTA expanded and deepened U.S.–Mexican ties on numerous fronts. These ties grew so extensive that even in the absence of conditionality, Mexican governments became so sensitive to their international standing that they restrained from abuse.

The European and Mexican cases thus suggest that Western linkage-building efforts can have a significant medium-term democratizing effect. Although its immediate impact may be limited, engagement at multiple levels (for example, trade and investment, open borders, and educational exchange) over time will magnify the impact of Western pressure. Conversely, policies of sustained isolation – as in the case of U.S. policy toward Burma, Cuba, and Iran – may undermine the prospects for democratization by reducing linkage.

Political Parties, Elite Cohesion, and Authoritarian Durability

The book also contributes to the literature on political parties and authoritarian durability. In particular, it highlights the importance of nonmaterial sources of partisan cohesion in ensuring authoritarian stability. Much of the recent literature assumes that authoritarian ruling parties are organized around patronage.[30] Parties are said to provide institutional mechanisms for resource distribution that lengthen time horizons and encourage elite cooperation over defection. Our study confirms the claim that party-based patronage distribution enhances authoritarian stability, but it also finds that patronage alone is often insufficient. As our case studies demonstrate, even institutionalized patronage-based parties are vulnerable to crises in the form of either economic shocks (e.g., Senegal and Zambia) or leadership succession (e.g., Kenya and Malawi).

---

[30] Geddes (1999); Brownlee (2007a); Magaloni
(2008); Reuter and Remington (2009).

By contrast, parties that also are based on nonmaterial sources of cohesion – such as ethnicity (e.g., UMNO in Malaysia) or a shared history of violent revolution or liberation struggle (e.g., ruling parties in Mozambique, Nicaragua, and Zimbabwe) – have a greater capacity to survive even extreme crises. Such nonmaterial bonds strengthen intra-elite trust and increase the likelihood that party cadres will remain united and disciplined during periods of uncertainty. Revolutionary or liberation struggles also tend to produce a generation of leaders – such as the "elders" in China in 1989 or the *antigos combatentes* in Mozambique – that is unusually cohesive and possesses the necessary legitimacy to impose discipline during crisis.

Indeed, the book's case analyses point to a striking empirical pattern. On the one hand, the record of patronage-based parties was decidedly mixed during the post–Cold War period. Many of them suffered large-scale defection and, in several cases (e.g., Georgia, Malawi, Senegal, Kenya, and Zambia), authoritarian regimes broke down. On the other hand, ruling parties that emerged from violent struggle suffered few defections, even in the face of deep economic crisis and serious opposition threat. With the exception of high-linkage cases (e.g., Guyana and Nicaragua), the regimes governed by such parties survived. These findings suggest a need to pay greater attention to variation in ruling-party strength as well as a need for greater research into the historical roots of this variation.[31]

Organizational Power, Regime Transitions, and Democracy: Two Paradoxes

Our research also highlights two paradoxes in the relationship between organizational power and democracy. The first paradox is related to organizational power and regime transitions. Where organizational power is low, transitions are easy but democratization is difficult. Where state and/or governing-party organizations are weak, regimes may be toppled with relative ease. These are what might be called "rotten-door" transitions, in which protesters essentially knock down a door that has already rotted from within. In some cases, even a small opposition push is sufficient to trigger regime collapse. Indeed, in several of our cases (Georgia, Haiti, and Madagascar), presidents fell because security forces would not or could not carry out orders to repress relatively small protests; thus, they were left defenseless as opponents overran the state. In Haiti, Aristide was toppled by a "rag-tag army of as few as 200 rebels"[32]; in Georgia, police surrounding parliament dissolved so quickly that Shevardnadze was forced to flee mid-speech – leaving his tea on the speaker's rostrum for Saakashvili to gulp down after storming the building.

Rotten-door transitions are often easy in the sense that they require little opposition mobilization. In some cases (e.g., Madagascar, Malawi, and Georgia in 1992), they occurred despite the near-absence of a preexisting democracy movement. Such transitions are often rapid and spectacular-looking. In fact, images of

---

[31] See, for example, Smith (2005).   [32] *The Economist*, March 6, 2004, p. 39.

protesters overrunning parliament, with security forces standing aside or joining them, have led some of these transitions to be labeled "revolutions."

Yet rotten-door transitions frequently do not lead to democracy, for several reasons. First, they often take place in a context of extreme state weakness, in which state agencies cannot enforce the rule of law across the national territory. Although such conditions may aid protesters seeking to storm the capital, they are hardly favorable to stable democratization.[33]

Second, rotten-door transitions often result in power distributions that are unfavorable to democracy. Because rotten-door transitions do not require a strong opposition push, they often take place in countries with weak civil societies, in which few "counterweights to state power" exist after the transition.[34] Opposition weakness is often exacerbated by the disintegration of old governing parties. In Georgia, Malawi, Madagascar, Mali, Moldova, Senegal, and Zambia, ex-ruling parties were decimated by defection to successor governments, leaving the opposition fragmented and weak. Weak oppositions do not favor democratization.

Third, rotten-door transitions often generate little elite turnover. Because transitions are often driven by large-scale (and last-minute) defections from the old regime rather than sustained opposition or prodemocracy movements, many of the most influential transition figures tend to be drawn from the old regime elite.[35] Consequently, post-transition governments often are led by politicians without a clear commitment to democracy – and with considerable experience in authoritarian politics.[36]

Fourth, rotten-door transitions often bring little institutional change. The rapid and chaotic nature of transitions by collapse often means that few real institutional reforms are undertaken. As a result, much of the institutional architecture of competitive authoritarianism is left intact – including weak and corrupt electoral and judicial authorities, state monopolies on the electronic media, politicized bureaucracies and security agencies, and repressive libel and/or internal security laws. Successor governments thus inherit many of the tools of coercion and abuse that characterized the previous regime. In other words, the players change but the playing field remains uneven.

In summary, rotten-door transitions generally occur in a context of state, party, and civil-society weakness. New governments often are filled with elites from the old regime, and they inherit many of the politicized and authoritarian institutions that had characterized the previous regime. Thus, there exist few societal

---

[33] For example, although the disintegration of the Georgian state in 1991 helped bring down an autocrat (i.e., Gamsakhurdia), it led not to democracy but to three years of civil war.

[34] van de Walle (1993: 388).

[35] Thus, the new governing party in post-1994 Malawi was so dominated by former high-level Banda government officials that it was described as a "party of recycles" (Lwanda

1996: 95, 147). In Kenya, most leading officials in the post-2002 Kibaki government were ex-KANU leaders (Throup 2003a: 7), leading observers to claim that "the new tenants are no different from the old" (Ajulu 2003: 7).

[36] On the impact of elite rotation on transition outcomes, see McFaul (2002).

or institutional checks on government abuse. In such a context, a democratic outcome requires extraordinary leadership; successor governments must actively dismantle or underutilize the institutional advantages that are available to them. Such behavior is rare, and as a result, rotten-door transitions frequently lead to another round of competitive authoritarianism.

Where organizational power is high, by contrast, transitions tend to be more difficult. Incumbents with strong party and state organizations often exhibit considerable staying power. They can win elections (e.g., Mexico and Taiwan) and withstand large and sustained opposition protest (e.g., Armenia and Serbia). Consequently, even relatively strong opposition movements may either fail (e.g., Armenia, Malaysia, and Zimbabwe) or take many years (e.g., Mexico, Serbia, and Taiwan) to succeed. When oppositions succeed, however, transitions are more likely to bring democratization. First, post-transition power distributions are more likely to favor democracy. "Hard-door" transitions usually require a strong societal push that is often rooted in a robust civil society. In Mexico and Taiwan, for example, strong civil societies raised the cost of government abuse both before and after transitions. At the same time, strong ruling parties are less likely to collapse after defeat, which should strengthen post-transition oppositions. Thus, in Croatia, Ghana, Mexico, Nicaragua, and Taiwan, ex–ruling parties served as the core of strong oppositions in the post-transition period.

Second, hard-door transitions are generally characterized by more extensive elite turnover. Where ruling parties are strong (e.g., Ghana, Mexico, and Taiwan), transitions rarely trigger large-scale defection and opposition forces are more likely to be led by regime outsiders. Consequently, existing patronage and corruption networks tend to be disrupted, and new governments are more likely to be filled with elites who are less experienced with or socialized into past authoritarian practices. Third, whereas rotten-door transitions generally occur in a context of weak states, hard-door transitions often take place where states are more effective – a condition that favors stable democratization.[37]

Finally, hard-door transitions are more likely to be accompanied by robust institutional change. Because strong ruling parties are often well positioned to win fair elections and because they can expect to remain politically viable even if they lose, they may have less to lose from reforms that level the playing field. Indeed, given the benefits – in terms of domestic and international legitimacy – of winning elections that are widely seen as free and fair, strong governing parties may have incentive to invest in credible and robust electoral institutions. In Ghana and Mexico, for example, incumbents with confidence in their ability to win elections infused newly designed judicial and electoral institutions with resources and high-quality personnel. These investments enhanced the prestige and technical capacity of those institutions and created reformist constituencies within the state that reinforced the stability of those institutions.

---

[37] Not all strong states are the same, of course. Highly militarized states, in which powerful coercive structures are oriented toward internal security, may create obstacles to democratization after hard-door transitions. This was arguably the case in Zimbabwe after 1979–1980, for example (Weitzer 1990).

These findings suggest – *contra* earlier work on modes of transition[38] – that under some conditions, top-down or "imposed" transitions may be more likely to yield stable democratic outcomes. In top-down transitions in Ghana, Mexico, and Taiwan, the organizational strength of incumbents – together with strong oppositions – encouraged the creation of strong democratic institutions. Powerful incumbents, confident in their ability to win elections, undertook institutional reform from above and invested in credible electoral institutions. Over time, both incumbents and oppositions gained a stake in the new institutional arrangements, and the institutions grew in prestige and independence. Eventually, incumbents were trapped. By 2000, incumbents in Ghana, Mexico, and Taiwan faced both strong oppositions and strong democratic institutions that would have been very costly to dismantle.

A second paradox centers on issues of state-building and democracy. Numerous scholars have pointed to state weakness as a major obstacle to achieving stable and effective democracy.[39] Indeed, there is broad consensus that a minimally effective state is a necessary condition for stable democracy. Without an effective state, neither the rule of law nor basic citizenship rights can be systematically enforced, resulting – at best – in "low-intensity" democracy.[40] Indeed, given the extent of state weakness in countries such as Albania, Georgia, Madagascar, and Haiti during the 1990s, it is difficult to imagine the construction of effective democracy under *any* kind of leadership or constitutional design. In such cases, state-building is a virtual precondition for stable democracy. Similar observations have led some scholars to suggest – in line with earlier arguments about "sequencing" and democratization – that state-building must come *prior to* democratization.[41]

There is a paradox here, however. Where state-building occurs in a transitional or nondemocratic context, it can facilitate the consolidation of authoritarian rule.[42] Just as more effective states enhance democratic governments' capacity to protect citizenship rights and enforce the rule of law, more effective states enhance authoritarian governments' capacity to monitor and crack down on opponents. As Way has argued, the pluralism and competition that existed in Belarus, Georgia, Moldova, Russia, and Ukraine in the early and mid-1990s were rooted primarily in state weakness and disorganization.[43] Independent media flourished and opposition candidates won elections not because incumbents were democratic but rather because they lacked the capacity to crack down on them. Similarly, the emergence of civil society and opposition challenges in Benin, Cambodia,

---

[38] See, for example, Karl (1990) and Karl and Schmitter (1991).

[39] See O'Donnell (1993, 1999), Linz and Stepan (1996), Holmes (1997), Mengisteab and Daddieh (1999), Herbst (2001), Carothers (2002), van de Walle (2002), Joseph (2003), Fukuyama (2004), King and Gonzales (2004), Bratton (2005), Yashar (2005), and Bratton and Chang (2006).

[40] O'Donnell (1993, 1999).

[41] See, for example, Zakaria (2003), Fukuyama (2004), and Mansfield and Snyder (2007).

[42] For an insightful analysis of the relationship between state-building and authoritarian consolidation, see Slater (2010).

[43] See Way (2002a, 2004, 2005a).

Madagascar, and Malawi during the late 1980s and early 1990s was rooted in extreme state weakness.

State- and/or party-building allow incumbents to eliminate pluralism by default.[44] State-building generally brings a stronger coercive apparatus and thus a greater capacity to monitor, harass, and repress critics.[45] Moreover, state-building – particularly when rooted in military conflict – fosters elite cohesion, which enhances governments' ability to engage in the type of high-intensity coercion that is often needed to consolidate authoritarian rule.

The relationship between state-building and authoritarian stability is seen in the cases of Armenia, Cambodia, and Russia. Armenia emerged from its war with Azerbaijan in the mid-1990s with a large, cohesive coercive apparatus that – together with paramilitary forces made up of ex-combatants – played a central role in fending off opposition protest in 1996 and thereafter. In Cambodia, where extreme state weakness had led to civil war, UN intervention, and the near-defeat of the CPP in 1993, state-rebuilding allowed the Hun Sen government to reestablish CPP domination of the countryside, dismantle opposition networks, and check the growth of independent media and civil society, thereby resulting in greater regime stability after 1997.[46] In Russia, Putin used his ties to internal-security networks to consolidate effective control over the country's vast coercive and bureaucratic apparatus, which he then used to effectively eliminate opposition and independent media.

In summary, state-building is critical to stable democratization, but it may also provide the bases for stable authoritarianism. This observation has important implications for recent debates about sequencing and democratization.[47] Advocates of sequencing – in which state-building occurs prior to (and thus facilitates) democratization – assume that sequencing postpones rather than precludes democratization. Democracy is simply pushed back to a subsequent stage. However, effective state-building in a transitional or weak authoritarian regime may not be (except in the very long term) an initial step in a sequence that ends in democracy. Rather, it may push regimes down an entirely different path – that of authoritarian consolidation. In other words, instead of postponing democratization, state-building may effectively preclude it.

Institutional Weakness

Finally, our study raises important questions about the role of formal institutions in shaping post–Cold War regime outcomes. As discussed in Chapter 2, recent literature on political regimes has paid considerable attention to constitutional design. These analyses rest on the assumption that formal institutions

---

[44] Way (2005a, 2009b).

[45] In Peru, for example, successful "state-rebuilding" under Fujimori included a massive increase in the size and capabilities of the intelligence apparatus, which gave the government unprecedented capacity to monitor and control civil society (Mauceri 1997, 2004; Rospigliosi 2000; Burt 2004).

[46] Gottesman (2003); Hughes (2003).

[47] See Zakaria (2003), Fukuyama (2004), and the articles in the July 2007 *Journal of Democracy*.

are regularly enforced and minimally stable – that the rules written into parchment actually constrain actors in practice. Although these assumptions hold up relatively well in the advanced industrialized democracies, they travel less well to other parts of the world.[48] In much of the developing world, formal rules of the game – including core state, regime, and market institutions – are unstable and weakly enforced. Constitutional rules and procedures are routinely circumvented, violated, or dismantled.

Institutional weakness is a central characteristic of most competitive authoritarian regimes. Nearly all of the regimes examined in this study were *formally* democratic in that their constitutions met procedural minimum criteria for democracy. They were nondemocracies because constitutional rules were routinely subverted. Supreme Courts or constitutional courts were circumvented or trampled upon in Belarus, Malaysia, Peru, Russia, and Zimbabwe; nominally independent electoral commissions were packed or emasculated in Cambodia, Croatia, the Dominican Republic, Gabon, Georgia, Guyana, Haiti, Madagascar, Malawi, Peru, and Ukraine; and term limits were violated or dismantled in Belarus, Cameroon, the Dominican Republic, Gabon, and Peru.

In such a context, institutional outcomes are often rooted less in parchment rules than in the organizational and power resources available to incumbents. For example, Russia's constitution did not change between 1993 and 2008. However, Putin's access to a more cohesive ruling party and effective state hierarchy allowed him to emasculate parliament and reduce political competition to a degree that Yeltsin – operating within the same super-presidential constitutional framework – could not. Likewise, Moldova's 2000 constitutional reform to strengthen parliament was accompanied by greater authoritarianism rather than democracy. This outcome was due in large part to the rise to power of a relatively well-organized and cohesive Communist Party, which was able to control the state and limit elite defection in a way that its predecessors could not.[49]

Where weak formal institutions *do* exert independent influence in competitive authoritarian regimes, it is often by default. In Malawi and Zambia, for example, constitutional term limits were respected in the early 2000s because Presidents Muluzi and Chiluba lacked the disciplined party structures necessary to overturn them. In both cases, executive-led constitutional-amendment projects were derailed, in large part, by opposition from within. Likewise, in Benin, the constitutional court acted as the "neutral arbiter it was designed to be"[50] only because no party was strong enough to control it. In such cases, the independence of formal institutions is often short-lived. Thus, Moldova's constitutional court was independent during the 1990s, when governing parties were weak; however, this independence eroded after the Communist Party's rise to power.[51] In Gabon, Omar Bongo agreed to create presidential term limits and a nominally independent electoral authority during the early 1990s but eliminated them after reconsolidating power.

---

[48] Levitsky and Murillo (2009).
[49] Way (2002a).
[50] Magnusson (2001: 225–6).
[51] Way (2002a).

Institutional weakness has important implications for causal analysis.[52] Where constitutional rules do not effectively constrain actors, their influence over regime outcomes will be limited. Indeed, in a context of institutional weakness, constitutional arrangements are often endogenous to regime outcomes. Take presidentialism. Presidential (or super-presidential) constitutions have been widely associated with authoritarian outcomes.[53] Yet in several of our cases – including Cameroon, Gabon, Kenya, Malawi, Senegal, Tanzania, and Zambia in the 1960s; Guyana and Zimbabwe in the 1980s; and Belarus, Peru, and Russia in the 1990s – presidential or super-presidential constitutions were imposed *after* autocrats had repressed opponents and consolidated power.

Formal institutions are not uniformly weak in competitive authoritarian regimes. In some cases (e.g., Malaysia and Taiwan), formal institutions were historically strong. In other cases (e.g., Ghana and Mexico), strong democratic institutions emerged during the 1990s where they had previously been weak. In these cases, formal institutions did constrain political actors and exert independent influence over regime outcomes. However, such instances of institutional strength cannot be taken for granted; rather, they must be explained. Indeed, the question of *why* strong institutions emerge – why effective constitutional courts emerged in Benin and Tanzania but not in Gabon, Peru, or Russia, or why independent electoral authorities emerged in Ghana and Mexico but not in Madagascar or Mozambique – is critical (and underexamined) in comparative politics.

CONCLUSION: UNDERSTANDING AUTHORITARIAN PERSISTENCE

This study focuses on competitive authoritarian regimes during one historical period: the post–Cold War era. We do not seek to develop a general theory of regimes. Nevertheless, our theoretical framework has implications for broader questions of authoritarian stability elsewhere in the world.[54] For example, dimensions of linkage and leverage provide insight to the stability of other post–Cold War authoritarian regimes. With strikingly few exceptions, authoritarianism persisted where linkage and leverage were low. In the 2000s, the vast majority of the world's closed regimes existed in countries with weak ties to the West. In 2008, Larry Diamond classified 49 regimes as closed or hegemonic authoritarian.[55] Of these, 48 were located in sub-Saharan Africa (16), Asia/Pacific Islands (13), Middle East/North Africa (12), and the former Soviet Union (7). None was located in Eastern Europe and only one (Cuba) was located in the Americas. Ties to the United States and Western Europe are weaker in the former regions than in the latter ones. Thus, most of the world's remaining authoritarian regimes

---

[52] Levitsky and Murillo (2009).
[53] Linz (1990); Stepan and Skach (1993); Fish (2005, 2006).
[54] Questions of authoritarian stability received considerable (if belated) attention during the 2000s. See Bellin (2004), Smith (2005, 2006),

Schedler (2006a), Way (2005a, 2009b), Magaloni (2006), Brownlee (2007a), Gandhi and Przeworski (2007), Greene (2007), Lust-Okar (2007), Blaydes (forthcoming), and Slater (2010).
[55] See Diamond (2008: Appendix, Table 5).

do not face the kind of linkage-based democratizing pressures described in this book. Moreover, many of the world's remaining authoritarian regimes exist in cases where Western leverage is low. China and Russia are nuclear powers. In much of the Middle East and North Africa, energy resources and/or security issues trump democracy promotion on Western foreign-policy agendas, thereby limiting autocrats' vulnerability to external pressure. Autocrats in Saudi Arabia, Egypt, and Kazakhstan can plausibly argue that political liberalization would put at risk either U.S. security interests or Western access to oil.

Cuba stands out as an exception to these patterns. Although the 1959 revolution and subsequent U.S. trade embargo eroded Cuba's historical ties to the United States, many forms of linkage – particularly immigration ties – remain extensive.[56] Moreover, following the collapse of the Soviet Union, Western leverage was high. Hence, it seems reasonable to suggest that if and when Cuba's communist regime collapses, the likelihood of democratization is greater than in countries such as North Korea or Vietnam.

The dimension of organizational power also is useful in understanding the domestic sources of authoritarian stability elsewhere in the world. For example, it is noteworthy that many of the most surprising cases of authoritarian stability in the 1990s and 2000s are regimes that emerged from violent conflict. We argue that violent origins (whether successful war, revolution, or anticolonial liberation movements) enhance organizational power – and, consequently, regime stability – in several ways. Violent conflict tends to foster the construction of a large and effective coercive apparatus. It also tends to give rise to a generation of cadres with the ideological commitment and "stomach" for the type of large-scale violence that is often necessary to maintain authoritarian rule. Moreover, the generation of cadres that emerges out of a violent struggle – particularly a revolutionary or liberation struggle – is often characterized by a high level of cohesion and legitimacy, which can be critical to ensuring discipline during periods of crisis. Finally, violent struggle often engenders a shared ideology that can bolster regime support even in the face of material hardship.

It is probably not a coincidence that all of the communist regimes that survived into the post–Cold War period – China, Cuba, Laos, North Korea, and Vietnam – emerged from armed conflict and/or indigenous revolution. Regime survival was particularly striking in Cuba and North Korea, which confronted severe economic crises in the wake of the USSR's demise, and China, which faced a serious opposition challenge in 1989. In each case, armed insurgency and violent conflict had resulted in the construction of a powerful coercive apparatus and a cohesive Leninist party. These state and party structures provided governments with powerful tools for facing down the severe challenges that emerged at the end of the Cold War.

Cuba and North Korea were peripheral states that had been subsidized and protected by the Soviet Union. When Soviet aid dried up, Cuba's

---

[56] Eckstein (2004, 2009).

communist regime suffered severe economic contraction and was widely expected to collapse.[57] Nevertheless, the regime survived not only the Soviet collapse but also the physical incapacitation of Fidel Castro and the transfer of power to his brother Raul. Although regime survival in Cuba is rooted in various factors,[58] one of them is clearly its revolutionary origins. The Cuban Revolution gave rise to a vast repressive apparatus with the capacity to infiltrate and preempt opposition challenges. At the same time, the persistence of the revolutionary generation in both the Revolutionary Armed Forces and the Communist Party helped the regime to remain cohesive and survive well into the post–Cold War era.

Similarly, North Korea faced an economic collapse – as well as a famine that left hundreds of thousands dead – following the collapse of the Soviet Union. Moreover, North Korea's efforts to build a nuclear bomb triggered more than a decade of diplomatic isolation. Yet, despite numerous predictions to the contrary,[59] the regime survived the end of the Cold War and the 1994 death of its founding leader, Kim Il Sung.[60] Authoritarian resilience may be explained in part by the regime's violent origins. Although Kim Il Sung seized power in 1945 with the help of Soviet troops rather than via an indigenous revolution, the regime – which was led by veterans of the anticolonial struggle with Japan – survived a massive war against the U.S.-backed forces in the early 1950s.[61] Military conflict – and decades of subsequent military threat – gave rise to an enormous security apparatus, including one of the largest armies in the world.[62] Veterans of the struggles against Japan and the United States retained key leadership positions into the 1990s – a fact that arguably reinforced elite cohesion in the face of enormous external pressure.[63]

The impact of violent struggle is also evident in China. Unlike Cuba or North Korea, China's vast economic and military power meant that it faced limited external pressure to democratize. Moreover, the communist government benefited from robust economic growth throughout the post–Cold War period. Nevertheless, the regime faced a serious challenge in May and June of 1989 when hundreds of thousands of students protested in Beijing in favor of democracy. Available accounts suggest that the Communist Party leadership split over how to respond to the protests. Mark Thompson and Andrew Nathan argue that the survival of the original revolutionary generation in the Party leadership was critical to the decision to crack down.[64] A group of party "elders" drawn from the revolutionary period acted as a cohesive and self-confident "final court of appeals."[65] The elders possessed the legitimacy to impose unity upon a divided elite and

[57] See, for example, Montaner (1990) and Purcell (1992). Cuba's GDP contracted by 30 percent in the early 1990s (Dominguez 1993; Muja-Leon and Busby 2001: 10).

[58] See Domínguez (1993).

[59] On earlier predictions of the demise of the North Korean regime, see Cumings (2007).

[60] Kwon (2003: 294).

[61] The war resulted in the death of as much as a quarter of North Korea's population (Kwon 2003; Martin 2006: 87). Hence, military conflict was "core to regime identity" (Kwon 2003: 287).

[62] Cumings (2007: 4).

[63] Cumings (2007: 20). In 2007, the average age of the regime's top 20 leaders was 76.

[64] Thompson (2001); Nathan (2001).

[65] Nathan (2001: xvi).

provided the party leadership with the cohesion and self-confidence needed to risk the high-intensity coercion of June 1989.

These brief accounts suggest that the regime-strengthening effects of origins in large-scale violence or revolution may have a "best-before" date. Violent struggles most effectively generate cohesion while the revolutionary generation is alive. Subsequent generations are likely to lack sufficient legitimacy to impose unity in crisis, and they often have less experience with high-intensity coercion. For example, the rapid collapse of the Soviet Union beginning in the late 1980s may be attributed partly to the fact that the revolutionary generation had long since died off. Indeed, the regime had largely abandoned high-intensity coercion by the 1960s.[66] As a result, the generation of leaders in power in the 1980s generally lacked the "stomach" to engage in the high-intensity coercion that would have been necessary to put down opposition after 1988.[67] Moreover, the absence of a revolutionary generation equivalent to the Chinese elders arguably made it more difficult for the government to impose unity once the system began to disintegrate. This suggests that other communist regimes may have difficulty surviving crises once the revolutionary generation leaves the stage. Thus, although the Chinese regime may continue to benefit from low leverage and robust economic growth in the 2000s, it is unclear whether it has the capacity to engage in another round of large-scale repression.

The survival of communist regimes in China, Cuba, and North Korea highlights the importance of nonmaterial sources of cohesion in sustaining authoritarian rule. Further research into nonmaterial sources of intra-elite trust and cohesion – almost entirely ignored in studies of democratization – are therefore essential to understanding the strength and character of contemporary nondemocracies.

This book focuses on regime dynamics in the particular international environment that prevailed after the end of the Cold War. The 1990s were characterized by a unipolar geopolitical environment in which liberal Western states emerged as militarily, economically, and ideologically dominant. In that context, peripheral states were particularly dependent on the West, and Western powers were especially likely to promote democracy. That world historical moment may now be coming to an end. By the late 2000s, the global balance of power had shifted considerably, and although the transformation was far from complete, the rise of China and other powers clearly marked the dawn of a more multipolar world. In this new context, external pressure for democracy may weaken in many parts of the world. Greater availability of assistance from China and other states may expand autocratic governments' room to maneuver vis-à-vis Western

---

[66] The Alexeyeva and Chalidze (1985) survey of mass unrest in the USSR between 1953 and 1983 showed that after 1964, the regime largely stopped using large-scale violence to suppress unrest. Between 1953 and 1964, shootings occurred in 6 of 12 cases of unrest.

By contrast, officers fired on demonstrators in just 1 of 21 major instances of unrest between 1965 and 1983 (Alexeyeva and Chalidze 1985: 352).

[67] Beissinger (2002); Way (2009b).

powers. And in the face of new geopolitical rivalries, Western powers may prioritize strategic issues (e.g., security cooperation and geopolitical alliances) over democracy, much as it did during the Cold War. In short, competitive authoritarianism proliferated in the 1990s because the international environment was highly favorable to democracy. Even many hardened autocrats were forced to subject their rule to competitive elections and, in some cases, to accept defeat. The end of the post–Cold War era may loosen these external constraints, creating new possibilities for authoritarian rule – competitive or not.

Appendix I: Measuring Competitive Authoritarianism and Authoritarian Stability

I. FULL AUTHORITARIANISM

Cases are scored as *fully authoritarian* if:

1. National-level multiparty elections for the executive do not exist.
   Or
2. At least *one* of the following indicators is present:
   (a) Major opposition parties and/or candidates are routinely excluded – either formally or effectively – from competing in elections for the national executive.[1]
   (b) Large-scale falsification of electoral results makes voting effectively meaningless.
   (c) Repression is so severe that major civic and opposition groups cannot operate in the public arena; thus, much of the opposition is underground, in prison, or in exile.

II. COMPETITIVE AUTHORITARIANISM

Cases are scored as *competitive authoritarian* if:

1. The criteria for full authoritarianism are not met.
2. There exists broad adult suffrage.
3. The authority of elected governments is not seriously restricted by unelected "tutelary" powers.
4. *At least one* of the following criteria is met:

---

[1] Effective exclusion occurs when physical repression is so severe or the legal, administrative, and financial obstacles are so onerous that most viable candidates are effectively deterred from running.

(1) Unfair Elections

Evidence of *any one* of the following indicators is sufficient to score an election as unfair:

1. At least one major candidate is barred for political reasons.
2. Centrally coordinated or tolerated electoral abuse is asserted by credible independent sources (i.e., known scholars or credible international or nonpartisan domestic observers). Indicators include:
   (a) Serious partisan manipulation of voter rolls
   (b) Large-scale voter intimidation or disruption of voting
   (c) Ballot-box stuffing, multiple voting, or other forms of ballot tampering
   (d) Falsification of results
3. Significant formal or informal impediments – coordinated or tolerated by the national government – prevent the opposition from campaigning nationally on reasonably equal footing. Indicators include:
   (a) Violence against opposition party activists, candidates, or infrastructure
   (b) Use or abuse of laws regulating public meetings limits the opposition's ability to campaign
4. Uneven electoral playing field. Indicators include:
   (a) Electoral authorities systematically biased in favor of incumbent
   (b) Highly uneven access to media (see Appendix I, 3.2 below)
   (c) Highly uneven access to resources (see Appendix I, 3.3 below)

(2) Violation of Civil Liberties[2]

Evidence of *any one* of the following indicators is sufficient for civil liberties to be violated:

1. Frequent harassment of independent media for political reasons. Indicators include:
   (a) Censorship or restrictions on broadcasting
   (b) Legal harassment (e.g., use of libel, defamation, or tax laws; manipulation of debt) by central government (not individual ministers)
   (c) Discretionary use of licenses, concessions, or subsidies to reward/punish private media

---

[2] In measuring civil liberties violations, we examine only government acts against political opposition within the national territory. Thus, primarily ethnic or anti-secessionist repression in enclaves (e.g., Chechnya in Russia and Kosovo in Serbia) or external territories (e.g., Bosnia) is excluded. We also exclude abuse that occurs in areas that are not under the effective control of the national government, such as breakaway regions in Croatia, Georgia, and Moldova.

    (d) Threats and physical attacks on persons and property

    (e) Government pressure to fire journalists/cancel programs

    (f) Restriction/denial, destruction, or confiscation of essential materials (e.g., newsprint, electricity, office space, transmitters, printing presses)

2. Any serious political attack on the media within a one-year period that can reasonably be expected to have a "chilling effect" on independent media activity. Indicators include:

    (a) Closure, suspension, eviction, or physical incapacitation of a major media outlet

    (b) Imprisonment,[3] attempted assassination, killing, or exile of journalist/editor of a major media outlet

    (c) "Legal" actions (e.g., large fines) that have a crippling effect on a major media outlet

3. The government *at least occasionally* engages in (or tolerates and rarely investigates) actions that restrict freedom of political association or speech. Indicators include at least occasional incidents of any of the following:

    (a) Police raids on opposition and civic-association offices

    (b) Enforcement of repressive laws that inhibit speech and association (e.g., sedition laws, libel or defamation laws, preventive detention laws, laws requiring registration of civic groups)

    (c) Political detentions or arrests

    (d) Frequent use of legal or tax system to harass critics

    (e) Physical attacks on government critics, including:

        (1) Threats or physical attacks on individuals

        (2) Attacks on offices, infrastructure

        (3) State or paramilitary repression of protests or public meetings

4. Any serious attack on opposition figures or other government critics within a one-year period that can reasonably be expected to have a "chilling effect" on civic and opposition activity. Indicators include:

    (a) Imprisonment,[4] attempted assassination, killing, or exile of a major politician or civic leader

    (b) Effective delegalization or crippling (via politicized legal or tax action) of a mainstream (i.e., nonextremist) political organization

    (c) Suspensions of basic civil and political rights (e.g., states of emergency) that target or seriously affect opposition activity

    (d) Large-scale physical repression of civic or opposition groups (e.g., repression of protest that causes widespread injury or death)

---

[3] Instances of brief (e.g., overnight) detention are not treated as cases of imprisonment.

[4] Instances of brief (e.g., overnight) detention are not treated as cases of imprisonment.

(3) Uneven Playing Field

Evidence of *any one* of the following indicators is sufficient to score the playing field as uneven:

1. State institutions are widely politicized and deployed frequently by the incumbent in ways that limit the opposition's ability to compete on reasonably equal footing
2. Uneven media access
   (a) State-owned media is the primary source of news for much of the population and is biased in favor of incumbent; or
   (b) A significant share of private media is "packed" by incumbent, via:
      (1) Ownership by proxies linked to incumbent; or
      (2) Manipulation of taxes, debts, state advertising, subsidies, or other resources to bully private media into self-censorship; or
      (3) Systematic bribery by government to slant coverage
3. Uneven access to resources, including:
   (a) Incumbent makes widespread use of public finance, employees, or infrastructure in a way that limits the opposition's ability to compete on reasonably equal footing; or
   (b) Incumbent uses public-policy instruments in a discretionary way to skew access to private-sector finance – either by securing illicit finance for the incumbent party or by systematically denying finance to opposition parties – in a way that limits the opposition's ability to compete on reasonably equal footing

III. DEMOCRACY

Cases are scored as *democratic* if:

1. The criteria for full authoritarianism are not met.
2. The criteria for competitive authoritarianism are not met.
3. There exists near-universal adult suffrage.
4. Basic civil liberties (speech, press, association) are systematically protected.
5. The authority of elected governments is not seriously restricted by unelected "tutelary" powers or major nonstate actors.

CODING REGIME OUTCOMES

Democratization

Cases are scored as *democratic* if they experience three consecutive terms of democracy or were democratic as of December 31, 2008.

Stable Authoritarianism

Cases are scored as *stable authoritarian* if incumbent governments or their chosen successors remain in power for at least three presidential or parliamentary terms following the establishment of competitive authoritarian rule, or in which incumbents remain in power for at least two terms but three full terms had not yet been completed as of December 31, 2008.

Unstable Authoritarianism

Cases are scored as *unstable authoritarian* if a regime experiences one or more instances of turnover, in which both the autocratic incumbent and the ruling party are removed, but the regime does not democratize (i.e., successor governments are not democratic).

Note: Cases are scored anew following each turnover in power.

REGIME SCORES

In the following tables, each "X" indicates the occurrence of abuse in that particular dimension of competitive authoritarianism (i.e., elections, civil liberties, and playing field). The numbers in parentheses refer to the subcategories of violations within each dimension. An "XX" indicates that the case crossed the threshold for full authoritarianism.[5]

CA: Competitive Authoritarianism
Full AR: Fully Authoritarian Regime

1990–1995

Case	Elections	Civil Liberties	Playing Field	Regime Type
Albania	X (1, 2, 3, 4)	X (1, 3, 4)	X (1, 2, 3)	CA
Armenia	X (1, 2, 3, 4)	X (1, 2, 3, 4)	X (1, 2, 3)	CA
Belarus	X (2, 4)	X (1)	X (1, 2, 3)	CA
Benin	X (4)	X (1, 3)	X (2)	CA
Botswana	X (4)		X (2, 3)	CA
Cambodia	X (3)	X (1, 2, 3)	X (1, 2, 3, 4)	CA
Cameroon	X (2, 3, 4)	X (1, 2, 3, 4)	X (1, 2, 3)	CA
Croatia	X (2, 4)	X (1, 3)	X (1, 2, 3)	CA
Dominican Republic	X (2, 4)	X (3)		CA
Gabon	X (2, 4)	X (1, 2, 3)	X (1, 2, 3)	CA
Georgia	X (2, 3, 4)	X (1, , 3)	X (1, 2, 3)	CA
Ghana	X (2, 4)	X (1)	X (1, 2, 3)	CA
Guyana		X (1)	X (1, 2)	CA

(continued)

---

5 It merits emphasis that the scores in this table do not capture variation in the severity of violations. They merely indicate whether the minimum criteria for a particular violation have been met.

Case	Elections	Civil Liberties	Playing Field	Regime Type
Haiti	X (2, 3, 4)	X (1, 2, 3, 4)		CA
Kenya	X (2, 3, 4)	X (1, 3, 4)	X (1, 2, 3)	CA
Macedonia	X (2, 4)	X (1, 3)	X (1, 2, 3)	CA
Madagascar		X (3, 4)	X (2)	CA
Malawi	X (3, 4)	X (1, 3)	X (1, 2, 3)	CA
Malaysia	X (3, 4)	X (1, 3)	X (1, 2, 3)	CA
Mali		X (1)		CA
Mexico	X (2, 4)	X (1, 3)	X (1, 2, 3)	CA
Moldova	X (1, 4)		X (1, 2, 3)	CA
Mozambique	X (4)	X (1)	X (1, 2, 3)	CA
Nicaragua	X (4)	X (3)	X (1, 2, 3)	CA
Peru	X (2, 4)	X (1, 3)	X (1, 3)	CA
Romania	X (2, 3, 4)	X (1, 3, 4)	X (1, 2, 3)	CA
Russia	X (2, 4)	X (1, 3, 4)	X (1, 2, 3)	CA
Senegal	X (2, 4)	X (3, 4)	X (1, 2, 3)	CA
Serbia	X (2, 3, 4)	X (1, 3)	X (1, 2, 3)	CA
Slovakia	X (4)	X (1)	X (1, 2, 3)	CA
Taiwan	X (4)	X (1)	X (1, 2, 3)	CA
Tanzania	X (2, 3, 4)	X (1, 3)	X (1, 2, 3)	CA
Ukraine	X (4)	X (1, 2)	X (1, 2)	CA
Zambia	X (3, 4)	X (1, 3, 4)	X (1, 2, 3)	CA
Zimbabwe	X (3, 4)	X (1, 3, 4)	X (1, 2, 3)	CA

2008

Case	Elections	Civil Liberties	Playing Field	Regime Type
Albania		X (1)		CA
Armenia	X (2, 3, 4)	X (1, 2, 3, 4)	X (1, 2, 3)	CA
Belarus	XX	XX	X (1, 2, 3)	Full AR
Benin				Democracy
Botswana	X (4)		X (2, 3)	CA
Cambodia	X (3, 4)	X (1, 2, 3, 4)	X (1, 2, 3)	CA
Cameroon	X (1, 2, 3, 4)	X (1, 2, 3, 4)	X (1, 2, 3)	CA
Croatia				Democracy
Dominican Republic				Democracy
Gabon	X (2, 4)	X (1, 3)	X (1, 2, 3)	CA
Georgia	X (2, 3, 4)	X (1, 2, 3)	X (1, 2, 3)	CA
Ghana				Democracy
Guyana				Democracy
Haiti		X (1)		CA
Kenya	X (2, 4)	X (1, 3)	X (1, 2)	CA
Macedonia				Democracy
Madagascar	X (1, 3, 4)	X (1, 2, 3, 4)	X (1, 2, 3)	CA
Malawi	X (2, 3, 4)	X (1, 2, 3, 4)	X (1, 2, 3)	CA

Case	Elections	Civil Liberties	Playing Field	Regime Type
Malaysia	X (3, 4)	X (1, 3, 4)	X (1, 2, 3)	CA
Mali				Democracy
Mexico				Democracy
Moldova	X (3, 4)	X (1, 3)	X (1, 2, 3)	CA
Mozambique	X (2, 3 4)	X (1)	X (1, 2, 3)	CA
Nicaragua		X (1, 3)		CA (*)
Peru				Democracy
Romania				Democracy
Russia	XX	X (1, 2, 3, 4)	X (1, 2, 3)	Full AR
Senegal	X (2, 4)	X (1, 2, 3)	X (1, 2, 3)	CA
Serbia				Democracy
Slovakia				Democracy
Taiwan				Democracy
Tanzania	X (2, 3, 4)	X (1)	X (1, 2, 3)	CA
Ukraine				Democracy
Zambia	X (4)	X (1)	X (1, 2, 3)	CA
Zimbabwe	X (2, 3, 4)	X (1, 2, 3, 4)	X (1, 2, 3)	CA

(*) *Note:* Nicaragua is scored as a case of democratization because it was democratic for three presidential terms (1990–2006). It became competitive authoritarian again after 2006.

Appendix II: Measuring Leverage

Low Leverage: Cases that meet at least one of the following criteria:

1. Large Economy: Total GDP more than $100 billion (1995, current US$) (*Source*: World Bank World Development Indicators (online: www.worldbank.org/data))[1]
2. Major Oil Producer: Annual production of more than one million barrels of crude oil per day average (1995) (*Source*: U.S. Energy Information Administration, "International Energy Annual" (online: http://www.eia.doe.gov/emeu/iea/))
3. Possession of/capacity to use nuclear weapons (1990–1995)

Medium Leverage: Cases that meet none of the criteria for low leverage but meet at least one of the following criteria:

1. Medium-Sized Economy: Total GDP between $50 billion and $100 billion (1995, current US$). *Source*: World Bank World Development Indicators (online: www.worldbank.org/data)[2]
2. Secondary Oil Producer: Annual production of 200,000 to one million barrels of crude oil per day average (1995) (*Source*: U.S. Energy Information Administration, "International Energy Annual" (online: http://www.eia.doe.gov/emeu/iea/))
3. Competing Security Issues: Country where there exists a major security-related foreign-policy issue for the United States and/or the EU.
4. Beneficiary of Black Knight Assistance: Country that receives significant bilateral aid (at least 1 percent of GDP), the overwhelming dominant share of which comes from a major power that is not the EU or the United States (1990–1995). A major power is defined as a high-income country (per capita GDP of $10,000 or higher) or a major military power (annual

---

[1] Taiwan GDP data from CIA Factbook 1996 "Taiwan" (online: www.cia.gov).

[2] Taiwan GDP data from CIA Factbook 1996 "Taiwan" (online: www.cia.gov).

military spending in excess of $10 billion, 1990–1995) (*Source*: "Correlates of War," available at www.cow2.la.psu.edu). China, France, Japan, and Russia are considered potential Black Knights.

High Leverage: Cases that meet none of the criteria for low or medium leverage.

Leverage Scores (1990–1995)

Case	Major Economy	Nuclear Power	Major Oil Producer	Medium Economy	Medium Oil Producer	Competing Security Issues	Black Knight Support	Leverage Score
Albania								High
Armenia								High
Belarus							X	Medium
Benin								High
Botswana								High
Cambodia								High
Cameroon							X	Medium
Croatia								High
Dominican Republic								High
Gabon					X		X	Medium
Georgia								High
Ghana								High
Guyana								High
Haiti								High
Kenya								High
Macedonia								High
Madagascar								High
Malawi								High
Malaysia				X	X			Medium
Mali								High
Mexico	X		X					Low
Moldova								High
Mozambique								High
Nicaragua								High
Peru								High
Romania								High
Russia	X	X	X			X		Low
Senegal								High
Serbia								High
Slovakia								High
Taiwan	X					X		Low
Tanzania								High
Ukraine								High
Zambia								High
Zimbabwe								High

Appendix III: Measuring Linkage[1]

Linkage is measured by the following four components:

1. *Economic Ties*: Measured by the extent of trade with the United States and 15 EU member countries[2] (exports and imports over GDP) (log)[3] (1990–2000), excluding years when a country is democratic.[4]
2. *Social Ties*: Measured by the average annual number of a country's citizens traveling to or living in the U.S. and EU (1990–2000) as a share of total country population (log)[5], excluding years when a country is democratic.[6]
3. *Communication Ties*: Measured by per capita average annual international voice traffic 1993–2000 (log) and per capita average annual

---

[1] Two points should be noted regarding our measure of linkage. First, because a significant number of cases gained independence only at the end of the Cold War, we cannot use data from the pre-1990 period. Second, to avoid potential problems of endogeneity associated with an increase in linkage resulting from democratization, we include data only from years when each country was *not* democratic.

[2] All references in this appendix are to the pre-2004 EU member states.

[3] *Source*: International Monetary Fund Direction of Trade Statistics (CD-ROM).

[4] Bilateral trade data were unavailable for Botswana. Botswana's linkage score is calculated as the sum of the three other dimensions divided by the highest possible score for those dimensions. Given its score on the other dimensions, even the highest possible score on

trade would not make Botswana high linkage. In post-communist cases, data are excluded for years prior to a state's independence.

[5] *Sources*: U.S. Department of Homeland Security *2003 Statistical Yearbook*, Tables: "Non-immigrants admitted by selected class of admission and region and selected country of last residence, selected fiscal years 1981–2003" and "Immigrants admitted by region and country of birth, fiscal years 1990–2000" (www.dhs.gov) and Eurostat NewCronos database "Immigration, Population Stocks by Citizenship (MPOPCTZ Table)" (CD-ROM).

[6] EU data include Austria, Denmark, Finland, Germany, Greece, Italy, the Netherlands, Portugal, Spain, Sweden, and the United Kingdom. Data were unavailable for Belgium, France, Ireland, and Luxembourg.

Internet access (1995–2000) (log)[7], excluding years when a country is democratic.[8]

4. *Intergovernmental Ties*: Measured by membership in the Organization of American States (OAS) or potential membership in the EU.[9]

For each of the four dimensions, each country is given a score (1–5) based on its ranking relative to all non-Western countries in the world (5 = highest quintile; 1 = lowest quintile).[10] The scores on the four dimensions are summed into a total score, which was recalculated so that scores range from 0 to 1.

Linkage Scores

High Linkage

Guyana	0.97	Russia	0.31
Croatia	0.94	Senegal	0.31
Slovakia	0.91	Ukraine	0.31
Mexico	0.88	Botswana	0.29
Macedonia	0.84	Belarus	0.28
Serbia	0.78	Ghana	0.28
Nicaragua	0.75	Cameroon	0.25
Albania	0.72	Georgia	0.22
Dominican Republic	0.72	Zimbabwe	0.19
Romania	0.69	Kenya	0.16
Taiwan	0.69	Malawi	0.13
Medium/Low Linkage		Mozambique	0.13
Haiti	0.63	Benin	0.09
Malaysia	0.59	Madagascar	0.09
Peru	0.59	Mali	0.09
Armenia	0.41	Zambia	0.09
Gabon	0.38	Cambodia	0.06
Moldova	0.34	Tanzania	0

---

[7] *Source*: World Bank World Development Indicators (www.worldbank.org/data). Taiwan Internet data are from the 2004 *ITU Yearbook of Statistics*. Geneva, CH: International Telecommunication Union, p. 157.

[8] Years were chosen based on the amount of available data for all countries in the world. Voice traffic data are missing for Haiti and Taiwan. For country years in which there is either no data or in which the country is a democracy, we fill in the missing data in the following way: We multiply the figure from that country's most recent nondemocratic year by the annual rate of change for all competitive authoritarian countries. Due to a lack of data in competitive authoritarian years for Nicaragua (1990) and Guyana (1990–1992), existing data for telephone traffic (1993–2000) and Internet (1995–2000) are used.

[9] Here we include countries that the EU had officially declared eligible for membership as of 2000.

[10] For "communications ties," the country rankings for Internet and voice traffic are averaged together to make a single score for the dimension.

Appendix IV: Measuring Organizational Power

Scope

High: Large, well-trained, and well-equipped internal security apparatus with an effective presence across the national territory. Existence of specialized intelligence or internal security agencies with demonstrated capacity to penetrate civil society and monitor and repress opposition activities at the village and/or neighborhood level across the country.

Medium: Criteria for high scope are not met, but security forces maintain a minimally effective presence across virtually the entire national territory. No evidence of severe deficits of funding, equipment, and training.

Low: Unusually small/underdeveloped security apparatus. Evidence of a lack of minimally effective state presence in significant parts of the national territory or severe deficits of funding, equipment, and training.

Cohesion

High: Evidence of non-material sources of cohesion. This may include:

Recent history of military conflict (leading security officials must be drawn from the generation that participated in the conflict), including:

1. Large-scale external war (without defeat); or
2. Intense and enduring military competition or threat; or
3. Successful revolutionary or anticolonial struggle

or

Pervasive ethnic ties between incumbent party and security forces, in a society that is deeply divided along those ethnic lines or

Shared ideology in a context in which this ideological cleavage is dominant

or

Evidence of consistent ability to use high-intensity coercion in recent past (pre-1990).

Medium: No evidence of non-material sources of cohesion

and

No evidence of previous insubordination (pre-1990), recent defeat in military conflict, or significant wage arrears to security officials

Low: No evidence of non-material sources of cohesion

and

Evidence from the decade prior to the period under analysis of significant insubordination by state security officials, including attempted coups, open rebellion, large-scale desertion, and refusal to carry out major executive orders

or

Recent decisive defeat in a major military conflict

or

Persistent and substantial wage arrears to security officials

PARTY STRENGTH

Scope

High: Mass organization that penetrates virtually all population centers down to village and neighborhood level and/or civil society and/or workplace. Evidence of significant grassroots activity – during and between elections – across the national territory.

Medium: Party does not meet criteria for high scope but possesses a national organization that penetrates most population centers and is capable of carrying out election campaigns and fielding candidates across the national territory.

Low: No party

or

Little or no party organization outside of the capital/major urban centers

Cohesion

High: Single governing party that achieved power via violent conflict, including revolution or national liberation struggle in which much of the current leadership participated or

Established single party (has participated in at least two national multiparty elections) with evidence of non-material source of cohesion, including:

1. Shared ideology in a context in which this ideological cleavage is dominant
2. Shared ethnicity in a context in which this ethnic cleavage is dominant

Medium: Established single party (has participated in at least two national elections) that does not meet the criteria for high cohesion.

or

New party (has participated in fewer than two national elections) with evidence of shared ideology or ethnicity in a context in which that ideological or ethnic cleavage is predominant

Low: Incumbent rules with no party

or

Incumbent rules without a single party but is supported by multiple and competing parties

or

New party (has participated in fewer than two national multiparty elections) and for which there is no evidence of nonmaterial sources of cohesion.

DISCRETIONARY STATE CONTROL OF THE ECONOMY

1. State-controlled mineral sector accounts for more than 50 percent of export revenue
   or
2. Centrally planned economy that does not undergo large-scale privatization

Scoring Organizational Power

Scores for party scope and cohesion and state scope and cohesion (low = 0; medium = 1; high = 2) are summed into a single composite score (0–8).

6–8: High

5: Medium High

4: Medium

3: Medium Low

0–2: Low

Presence of state discretionary control increases the score by one full level – i.e., from low to medium or medium to high.

Organizational Power Scores[1]

Case	Party Scope	Party Cohesion	State Scope	State Cohesion	State Economic Control	Total	Category
Albania	1	1	0	0	0	2	Low
Armenia	1	1	2	2	0	6	High
Belarus 1992–1994	0	0	2	0	0	2	Low
Belarus 1995–2005	0	0	2	1	2	5	Medium High
Benin	0	0	0	0	0	0	Low
Botswana	1	1	1	1	2	6	High
Cambodia	2	1	1	1	0	5	Medium High
Cameroon	1	1	1	1	0	4	Medium
Croatia	1	1	1	2	0	5	Medium High
Dominican Republic	1	1	1	1	0	4	Medium
Gabon	1	1	1	1	2	6	High
Georgia	0	0	0	0	0	0	Low
Ghana	1	1	1	1	0	4	Medium
Guyana	1	2	2	2	0	7	High
Haiti	1	0	0	0	0	1	Low
Kenya	1	1	1	1	0	4	Medium
Macedonia	1	1	0	0	0	2	Low
Madagascar	1	1	0	0	0	2	Low
Malawi	1	1	0	0	0	2	Low
Malaysia	2	2	2	2	0	8	High
Mali	1	0	0	0	0	1	Low
Mexico	2	1	2	2	0	7	High
Moldova	0	0	0	0	0	0	Low
Mozambique	1	2	0	2	0	5	Medium-High
Nicaragua	2	2	2	2	0	8	High
Peru	0	0	1	1	0	2	Low
Romania	1	0	2	1	0	4	Medium
Russia 1992–1999	0	0	2	0	0	2	Low
Russia 2000–2003	1	0	2	1	2	6	Medium-High
Senegal	1	1	1	1	0	4	Medium
Serbia	2	2	2	2	0	8	High
Slovakia	1	1	2	1	0	5	Medium High
Taiwan	2	1	2	2	0	7	High

[1] Scores are for the first government in the 1990s unless otherwise noted. Because Armenia and Croatia were in the middle of wars in the early 1990s, we score state coercive capacity in 1995. We score multiple periods in a single country if organizational power changed significantly.

Case	Party Scope	Party Cohesion	State Scope	State Cohesion	State Economic Control	Total	Category
Tanzania	2	1	1	1	0	5	Medium High
Ukraine	0	0	2	0	0	2	Low
Zambia	1	1	1	0	0	3	Medium Low
Zimbabwe	2	2	2	2	0	8	High

References

Abbott, Jason. 2001b. "Democracy@internet.asia? The Challenges to the Emancipatory Potential of the Net: Lessons from China and Malaysia." *Third World Quarterly* 22, No. 1: 99–114.

Abbott, Jason P. 2004. "The Internet, Reformasi and Democratization in Malaysia." In Edmund Terence Gomez, ed. *The State of Malaysia: Ethnicity, Equity and Reform*. New York: RoutledgeCurzon.

Abdulai, David. 1992. "Rawlings 'Wins' Ghana's Presidential Elections: Establishing a New Constitutional Order." *Africa Today* 39, No. 4: 66–71.

Abrahams, Fred. 1996. "Albania: A Tenuous Separation of Powers." *Transition* 2, No. 3.

Abrahamyan, Gayane. 2008. "Leader of Karabakh War Veterans Struggles with Hobson's Choice." *Eurasia Insight*, June 16.

Acemoglu, Darin, and James A. Robinson. 2005. *Economic Origins of Democracy and Dictatorship*. New York: Cambridge University Press.

Ackermann, Alice. 1999. "Managing Conflicts Non-Violently Through Preventive Action: The Case of the Former Yugoslav Republic of Macedonia." *Journal of Conflict Studies* 19, No. 1: 5-2.

Ackermann, Alice. 2003. "International Intervention in Macedonia: From Preventative Engagement to Peace Implementation." In Peter Siani-Davies, ed. *International Intervention in the Balkans since 1995*. London: Routledge.

Ackroyd, William S. 1991. "Military Professionalism, Education, and Political Behavior in Mexico." *Armed Forces and Society* 18, No. 1: 81–96.

Adar, Korwa G. 2000. "Assessing Democratization in Kenya: A Post-Mortem of the Moi Regime." *Journal of Commonwealth and Comparative Politics* 38, No. 3 (November): 103–30.

Adcock, Robert, and David Collier. 2001. "Measurement Validity: A Shared Standard for Qualitative and Quantitative Research." *American Political Science Review* 95, No. 3 (September): 529–46.

Agh, Attila. 1998. *Emerging Democracies in Central Europe and the Balkans*. Cheltenham, UK: Edward Elgar Publishing.

Aguayo Quezada, Sergio. 1993. "The Inevitability of Democracy in Mexico." In Riordan Roett, ed. *Political and Economic Liberalization in Mexico: At a Critical Juncture?* Boulder, CO: Lynne Rienner Publishers.

Aguayo Quezada, Sergio. 1995a. "A Mexican Milestone." *Journal of Democracy* 6, No. 2 (April): 157–67.

Aguayo Quezada, Sergio. 1995b. "Auge y perspectiva de los derechos humanos en México." In Luis Rubio and Arturo Fernández, eds. *México a la hora del cambio*. Mexico City: Cal y Arena.

Ajulu, Rok. 1998. "Kenya's Democratic Experiment: The 1997 Elections." *Review of African Political Economy* No. 76: 275–88.

Ajulu, Rok. 2001. "Kenya: One Step Forward, Three Steps Back: The Succession Dilemma." *Review of African Political Economy* No. 88: 197–212.

Ajulu, Rok. 2003. "Kenya: A Reflection on the 2002 Elections: Third Time Lucky or More of the Same?" Institute for Global Dialogue, Occasional Paper No. 39. Braamfontein, South Africa: Institute for Global Dialogue.

Akivaga, S. Kichamu. 2002. "Towards a National Movement for Democratic Change in Kenya." In Lawrence Murungu Mute, Wanza Kioko, and Kichamu Akivaga, eds. *Building an Open Society: The Politics of Transition in Kenya*. Nairobi, Kenya: Claripress.

Alagappa, Muthiah. 2001. "Introduction: Presidential Election, Democratization, and Cross-Strait Relations." In Muthiah Alagappa, ed. *Taiwan's Presidential Politics: Democratization and Cross-Strait Relations in the Twenty-First Century*. Armonk, NY: M. E. Sharpe.

Alao, Abiodun. 1995. "The Metamorphasis of the 'Unorthodox': The Integration and Early Development of the Zimbabwean National Army." In Ngwabi Bhebe and Terence Ranger, eds. *Soldiers in Zimbabwe's Liberation War*. London: James Currey, Ltd.

Albats, Evgeniia. 1994. *The State Within a State: The KGB and its Hold on Russia*. New York: Farrar Straus Giroux.

Albritton, Robert B. 2004. "Cambodia in 2003: On the Road to Democratic Consolidation." *Asian Survey* 44, No. 1 (January–February): 102–109.

Alcocer, Jorge V. 1995. "Recent Electoral Reforms in Mexico: Prospects for a Real Multiparty Democracy." In Riordan Roett, ed. *The Challenge of Institutional Reform in Mexico*. Boulder, CO: Lynne Rienner Publishers.

Alden, Christopher. 2000. "From Neglect to 'Virtual Engagement': The United States and its New Paradigm for Africa." *African Affairs* 99, No. 396: 355–71.

Alden, Chris. 2001. *Mozambique and the Construction of the New African State: From Negotiations to Nation Building*. London: Palgrave.

Alden, Chris, and Mark Simpson. 1993. "Mozambique: A Delicate Peace." *Journal of Modern African Studies* 31, No. 1: 109–30.

Alexander, Jocelyn. 1997. "The Local State in Post-War Mozambique: Political Practice and Ideas about Authority." *Africa* 67, No. 1: 1–26.

Alexander, Jocelyn, and Joann McGregor. 1999. "Representing Violence in Matabeland, Zimbabwe: Press and Internet Debates." In Tim Allen and Jean Seaton, eds. *The Media of Conflict: War Reporting and Representations of Ethnic Violence*. London: Zed Books.

Alexander, Peter. 2000. "Zimbabwean Workers, the MDC, and the 2000 Election." *Review of African Political Economy* 27, No. 85: 385–406.

Alexeyeva, Liudmilla, and Valery Chalidze. 1985. "Mass Unrest in the USSR." Report No. 19, Office of Net Assessment of the Department of Defense (August).

Aligica, Paul Dragos. 2001. "Romania's Economic Policy: Before and After the Elections." *East European Constitutional Review* 10, No. 1 (Winter).

Allen, Chris. 1992a. "Restructuring an Authoritarian State: Democratic Renewal in Benin." *Review of African Political Economy* 19, No. 54: 42–58.

Allen, Chris. 1992b. "'Goodbye to All That': The Short and Sad Story of Socialism in Benin." *Journal of Communist Studies* 8: 63–81.

Allen, Philip M. 1995. *Madagascar: Conflicts of Authority in the Great Island.* Boulder, CO: Westview Press.

Allina-Pisano, Jessica. 2005. "Informal Institutional Challenges to Democracy: Administrative Resource in Kuchma's Ukraine." Prepared for presentation at the Danyliw Research Seminar in Contemporary Ukrainian Studies, Chair of Ukrainian Studies; University of Ottawa, 29 September–1 October.

Almond, Gabriel, and Sidney Verba. 1963. *The Civic Culture: Political Attitudes and Democracy in Five Nations.* Princeton, NJ: Princeton University Press.

Alvarez, Michael, Jose Antonio Chiebub, Fernando Limongi, and Adam Przeworski. 1996. "Classifying Political Regimes." *Studies in Comparative International Development* 31, No. 3: 3–36.

Amariei, Razvan. 2005. "Romania: Ghosts from the Past." *Transitions Online*, 20 June.

Amariei, Razvan. 2006. "Romania: A Black Sea Berlusconi?" *Transitions Online*, 8 June.

Amchuk, Leonyd. 2005. Interview with Mykola Martynenko. *Ukrainska Pravda*, 20 April.

Americas Watch. 1985. *Political Freedom in Guyana.* New York: Americas Watch.

Ames, Rolando, Enrique Bernales, Sinesio López, and Rafael Roncagliolo. 2001. *Situación de la Democracia en el Perú.* Lima: Universidad Católica del Peru.

Amin, Julius. 2004. "Paul Biya's Foreign Policy: The Promise and Performance." In John M. Mbaku and Joseph Takougang, eds. *The Leadership Challenge in Africa: Cameroon under Paul Biya.* Trenton, NJ: Africa World Press.

Amnesty International. 2001. "Amnesty International Report 2001: Kenya." New York: Amnesty International.

Amnesty International. 2002a. "Madagascar: Selective Justice." Amnesty International Report, 10 December.

Amnesty International. 2002b. "Amnesty International Report 2002: Kenya." New York: Amnesty International.

Amnesty International. 2003. "Madagascar: Former Prime Minister's Trial Must Respect International Standards of Fairness." Amnesty International Public Statement, 17 December 2003.

Amuwo, 'Kunle. 2003. "The State and the Politics of Democratic Consolidation in Benin, 1990–1999." In Julius Omozuanvbo Ihonvbere and John Mukum Mbaku, eds. *Political Liberalization and Democratization in Africa.* Westport, CT: Praeger.

Anderson, David M. 2003. "Briefing: Kenya's Elections 2002 – The Dawning of a New Era?" *African Affairs* 102: 331–42.

Anderson, Leslie E. 2006. "The Authoritarian Executive? Horizontal and Vertical Accountability in Nicaragua." *Latin American Politics and Society* 48, No. 2 (Summer): 141–69.

Anderson, Leslie, and Lawrence C. Dodd. 2002. "Nicaragua Votes: The Elections of 2001." *Journal of Democracy* 13, No. 3 (July): 80–94.

Anderson, Leslie, and Lawrence C. Dodd. 2005. *Learning Democracy: Citizen Engagement and Electoral Choice in Nicaragua, 1990–2001.* Chicago: University of Chicago Press.

Andrejevich, Milan. 1990a. "Milosevic and the Socialist Party of Serbia." *Report on Eastern Europe.* 3 August: 41–5.

Andrejevich, Milan. 1990b. "Milosevic and the Serbian Opposition." *Report on Eastern Europe.* 19 October: 38–46.

Andrejevich, Milan. 1990c. "The Election Scorecard for Serbia, Montenegro, and Macedonia." *Report on Eastern Europe.* 21 December: 37–9.

Andrejevich, Milan. 1991a. "Macedonia's New Political Leadership." *Report on Eastern Europe.* 17 May: 22–5.

Andrejevich, Milan. 1991b. "Resurgent Nationalism in Macedonia: A Challenge to Pluralism." *Report on Eastern Europe.* 17 May: 26–9.

Andrejevich, Milan. 1991c. "Unrest in Belgrade: A Symptom of Serbia's Crisis." *Report on Eastern Europe.* 29 March: 12–18.

Andrejevich, Milan, and Gordon N. Bardos. 1992. "Media in Regions of Conflict: Serbia and Montenegro." *RFE/RL Research Report.* Vol. 1, No. 39 (2 October): 86–91.

Andrews, Josephine T. 2002. *When Majorities Fail: The Russian Parliament, 1990–1993.* Cambridge: Cambridge University Press.

Anebo, Felix K. G. 1997. "Voting Patterns and Electoral Alliances in Ghana's 1996 Elections." *African Journal of Political Science* 2, No. 2 (December): 38–52.

Angjeli, Anastas. 1995. "Problems of Albanian Democracy." *Mediterranean Quarterly* 6, No. 4: 35–47.

Anjaparidze, Zaal. 2002. "Preparing for the Post-Shevardnadze Era." *Prism* 8, No. 5. Available at http://www.jamestown.org/.

Anokwa, Kwadwo. 1997. "Press Performance under Civilian and Military Regimes in Ghana: A Reassessment of Past and Present Knowledge." In Festus Eribo and William Jong-Ebot, eds. *Press Freedom and Communication in Africa.* Trenton, NJ: Africa World Press, Inc.

Antonic, Slobodan. 2002. "A Captive Nation: Serbia under Slobodan Milosevic." (English summary of *Zarobljena zemlja: Srbija za vlade Slobodana Miloševiãa.*) Beograd: Otkrovenje. Pp. 505–16. Available at www.dekart.f.bg.ac.yu/sociologija/o1%20Osoblje/Antonic_en.htm.

Antonic, Slobodan. 2003. "Serbia after Djindjic." *East European Constitutional Review* 12, No. 2–3: 113–118.

Anuar, Mustafa K. 2002. "Defining Democratic Discourses: The Mainstream Press." In Francis Loh Kik Wah and Khoo Boo Teik, eds. *Democracy in Malaysia: Discourses and Practices.* Richmond, Surrey, UK: Curzon.

ARD, Inc. 2003. "Democracy and Governance Assessment of Tanzania: Transitions from the Single Party State." Report submitted to the U.S. Agency for International Development. Washington, DC: USAID.

Arceneaux, Craig, and David Pion-Berlin. 2005. *Transforming Latin America: The International and Domestic Sources of Change.* Pittsburgh, PA: University of Pittsburgh Press.

Arias Quincot, César. 2001. "La Infama Década del Fujimorato." In Carlos Milla Batres, ed. *Como Fujimori Jodió al Perú.* Lima: Editorial Mill Batres.

Armony, Ariel, and Hector Schamis. 2005. "Babel in Democratization Studies." *Journal of Democracy* 16, No. 4: 113–28.

Aron, Leon. 2000. *Yeltsin: A Revolutionary Life.* New York: St. Martin's Press.

Arrigo, Linda Gail. 1994. "From Democratic Movement to Bourgeois Democracy: The Internal Politics of the Taiwan Democratic Progressive Party in 1991." In Murray A. Rubinstein, ed. *The Other Taiwan: 1945 to the Present.* Armonk, NY: M. E. Sharpe.

Ashley, David W. 1996. "The Nature and Causes of Human Rights Violations in Battambang Province." In Steve Heder and Judy Ledgerwood, eds. *Propaganda, Politics, and Violence in Cambodia: Democratic Transition Under United Nations Peacekeeping.* Armonk, NY: M. E. Sharpe.

Ashley, David W. 1998. "The Failure of Conflict Resolution in Cambodia: Causes and Lessons." In Frederick Z. Brown and David G. Timberman, eds. *Cambodia and the International Community: The Quest for Peace.*

Aslund, Anders. 2002. "Is the Belarusian Economic Model Viable?" In Ann Lewis, ed. *The EU and Belarus: Between Moscow and Brussels.* London: Federal Trust.

Astourian, Stephan. 2000–2001. *From Ter-Petrosian to Kocharian: Leadership Change in Armenia*. Berkeley Program in Soviet and Post-Soviet Studies Working Paper Series (Winter).

Asuagbor, Greg O. 1998. *Democratization and Modernization in a Multilingual Cameroon*. Lewiston, NY: The Edwin Mellen Press.

Atkins, G. Pope. 1981. *Arms and Politics in the Dominican Republic*. Boulder, CO: Westview Press.

Atkins, G. Pope, and Larman C. Wilson. 1998. *The Dominican Republic and the United States: From Imperialism to Transnationalism*. Athens: University of Georgia Press.

Aubynn, Anthony Kwesi. 2002. "Behind the Transparent Ballot Box: The Significance of the 1990s Elections in Ghana." In Michael Cowen and Liisa Laakso, eds. *Multi-Party Elections in Africa*. Oxford, UK: James Currey, Ltd.

Austin, Kathi. 1994. *Invisible Crimes: US Private Intervention and the War in Mozambique*. Washington, DC: APIC.

Austin, Robert. 1993. "What Albania Adds to the Balkan Stew." *Orbis* 37, No. 2 (March): 259–79.

Austin, Robert. 2009. "Less Is More: Towards a Sustainable and Reliable Media in Albania." In Marta Dyczok and Oxana Gaman-Golutvina, eds. *Media, Democracy and Freedom: The Post-Communist Experience*. Bern, Switzerland: Peter Lang.

Avendaño, Jorge. 2001. "La Perpetuidad en el Poder a Través del Congreso (La Corrupción del Poder Judicial y del Sistema Electoral)." In Carlos Milla Batres, ed. *Como Fujimori Jodió al Perú*. Lima, Peru: Editorial Mill Batres.

Aves, Jonathan. 1992. "The Rise and Fall of the Georgian Nationalist Movement, 1987–1991." In Geoffrey A. Hosking, Jonathan Aves, and Peter J. S. Duncan, eds. *The Road to Post-Communism: Independent Political Movements in the Soviet Union 1985–1991*. London: Pinter Publishers.

Aves, Jonathan. 1995. "National Security and Military Issues in the Transcaucasus." In Bruce Parrott, ed. *State-Building and Military Power in Russia and the New States of Eurasia*. Armonk, NY: M. E. Sharpe.

Aves, Jonathan. 1996. "Politics, Parties and Presidents in Transcaucasia." *Caucasian Regional Studies* 1: 5–23. Available at www.poli.vub.ac.be/publi/crs/eng/0101-02.htm.

Avirovic, Pajo. 1995. "Macedonian Postcommunism." *Uncaptive Minds*. Spring: 67–74.

Ayee, Joseph R. A. 1997a. "Ghana's 1996 General Elections: A Post-Mortem." African Association of Political Science Occasional Papers Series, Vol. 1, No. 1. Harare, Zimbabwe: African Association of Political Science.

Ayee, Joseph R. A. 1998b. "Election Management and Democratic Consolidation: The Case of the Electoral Commission of Ghana." In Joseph R. A. Ayee, ed. *The 1996 General Elections and Democratic Consolidation in Ghana*. Accra: University of Ghana, Department of Political Science.

Ayee, Joseph R. A. 1998c. "Elite Consensus and Democratic Consolidation in Ghana: The Inter-Party Advisory Committee (IPAC)." In Joseph R. A. Ayee, ed. *The 1996 General Elections and Democratic Consolidation in Ghana*. Accra: University of Ghana, Department of Political Science.

Ayee, Joseph R. A. 2001. "The 2000 General Elections and Presidential Run-off in Ghana: An Overview." In Joseph R. A. Ayee, ed. *Deepening Democracy in Ghana: Politics of the 2000 Elections (Vol. 1)*. Accra: Freedom Publications.

Ayee, Joseph R. A. 2002. "The 2000 General Elections and Presidential Run-off in Ghana: An Overview." *Democratization* 9, No. 2 (Summer): 148–74.

Ayisi, Ruth Ansah. 1991. "Mozambique: The Problems of Peace." *Africa Report* March–April: 23–5.

Ayissa, Anatole, and Nouhoum Sangaré. 2006. "Mali." In Wuyi Omitoogun and Eboe Hutchful, eds. *Budgeting for the Military Sector in Africa: The Process and Mechanisms of Control*. Oxford, UK: Oxford University Press.

Aywa, Francis Ang'ila, and Francois Grignon. 2001. "As Biased as Ever? The Electoral Commission's Performance Prior to Polling Day." In Marcel Rutten, Alamin Mazrui, and Francois Grignon, eds. *Out for the Count: The 1997 General Elections and Prospects for Democracy in Kenya*. Kampala, Uganda: Fountain Publishers.

Azevedo, Mario. 1995. "Ethnicity and Democratization: Cameroon and Gabon." In Harvey Glickman, ed. *Ethnic Conflict and Democratization in Africa*. Atlanta, GA: African Studies Association Press.

Aziz Nassif, Alberto, and Jorge Alonso Sánchez. 2003. "Votos, Reglas y Partidos." In Alberto Aziz Nassif, ed. *México al inicio del siglo XXI: Democracia, ciudadanía y desarrollo*. Mexico City: CIESAS.

Babb, Sarah. 2001. *Managing Mexico: Economists from Nationalism to Neoliberalism*. Princeton, NJ: Princeton University Press.

Bacinic, Ivan. 1993. "The Croatian Economy: Achievements and Prospects." *RFE/RL Research Report*. 25 June: 33–9.

Bacinic, Ivo, and Iva Dominis. 1992. "Tudjman Remains Dominant after Croatian Elections." *RFE/RL Research Report*. 18 September: 20–6.

Bacinic, Ivo and Iva Dominis. 1993. "The Multi Party Elections in Croatia: Round Two." *RFE/RL Reports*. 7: 17–21.

Baer, Josette. 2001. "Boxing and Politics in Slovakia: 'Mečiarism' Roots, Theory, Practice." *Democratizaion* 8, No. 2 (Summer): 97–116.

Bagley, Bruce M., and Juan G. Tokatlian. 1992. "Dope and Dogma: Explaining the Failure of U.S.–Latin American Drug Policies." In Jonathan Hartlyn, Lars Schoultz, and Augusto Varas, eds. *The United States and Latin America in the 1990s: Beyond the Cold War*. Chapel Hill: The University of North Carolina Press.

Bakalian, Anny P. 1992. *Armenian-Americans: From Being to Feeling Armenian*. New Brunswick, NJ: Transaction.

Baker, Bruce. 2002. "Overstaying One's Welcome: The Presidential Third Term Debate in Africa." *Contemporary Politics* 8, No. 4: 301–85.

Baker, Bruce. 2003. "Policing and the Rule of Law in Mozambique." *Policing and Society* 13, No. 2: 139–58.

Baker, Peter, and Susan Glasser. 2005. *Kremlin Rising: Vladimir Putin's Russia and the End of the Revolution*. New York: Scribner.

Bala, Alban. 2001. "Albania: Ruling Socialist Party Faces Conflicts." *RFE/RL Reports*. 10 December.

Bala, Alban. 2002. "Albania: Development Goals For Next 15 Years Set With UN." *RFE/RL Reports*. 15 July.

Balbi, Carmen Rosa, and David Scott Palmer. 2001. "'Reinventing' Democracy in Peru." *Current History* 100, No. 643 (February): 65–72.

Baldwin, Kate. 2009. "Keeping the Party Going in Zambia." In Larry Diamond and Marc Plattner, eds. *Democratization in Africa*. Baltimore, MD: The Johns Hopkins University Press.

Ballard, John R. 1998. *Upholding Democracy: The United States Military Campaign in Haiti, 1994–97*. Westport, CT: Praeger.

Balzer, Harley. 2003. "Managed Pluralism: Vladimir Putin's Emerging Regime." *Post Soviet Affairs* 19, No. 3 (July): 189–227.

Bardos, Gordon. 2001. "Yugoslavia." In *Nations in Transit 2001*. Washington, DC: Freedom House.

Barkan, Joel D. 1992. "The Rise and Fall of a Governance Realm in Kenya." In Goran Hyden and Michael Bratton, eds. *Governance and Politics in Africa*. Boulder: Lynne Rienner.

Barkan, Joel D. 1993. "Kenya: Lessons from a Flawed Transition." *Journal of Democracy* 4, No. 3 (July): 85–99.

Barkan, Joel D. 1994. "Divergence and Convergence in Kenya and Tanzania: Pressures for Reform." In Joel D. Barkan, ed. *Beyond Capitalism versus Socialism in Kenya and Tanzania*. Boulder, CO: Lynne Rienner Publishers.

Barkan, Joel D. 1998. "Toward a New Constitutional Framework in Kenya." *Africa Today* 45, No. 2 (April–June): 213–26.

Barkan, Joel D. 2003. "New Forces Shaping Kenyan Politics." *CSIS Africa Notes* 18 (May).

Barkan, Joel D. 2004. "Kenya After Moi." *Foreign Affairs* 83, No. 1 (January/February): 87–100.

Barkan, Joel D. 2008. "Breaking the Stalemate in Kenya." Washington, DC: Center for Strategic and International Studies (January 8).

Barkan, Joel, and Njuguna Ng'ethe. 1999. "Kenya Tries Again." In Larry Diamond and Marc Plattner, eds. *Democratization in Africa*. Baltimore, MD: The Johns Hopkins University Press.

Barnes, James F. 1992. *Gabon: Beyond the Colonial Legacy*. Boulder, CO: Westview Press.

Barr, Robert R., and Henry Dietz. 2006. "Fujimori and the Mayors of Lima, 1990–2001: The Impact and Legacy of Neopopulist Rule." In Julio Carrión, ed. *The Fujimori Legacy: The Rise of Electoral Authoritarianism in Peru*. University Park: Pennsylvania State University Press.

Barraclough, Simon. 1985. "The Dynamics of Coercion in the Malaysian Political Process." *Modern Asian Studies* 19, No. 4: 797–822.

Bartlett, David. 2000. "Civil Society and Democracy: a Zambian Case Study." *Journal of Southern African Studies*, 26, No. 3: 429–446.

Basom, Kenneth E. 1995. "Prospects for Democracy in Serbia and Croatia." *East European Quarterly* 29, No. 4: 509–34.

Basombrío, Carlos. 2000. "Civil Society Aid in Peru: Reflections from Experience." In Marina Ottaway and Thomas Carothers, eds. *Funding Virtue: Civil Society Aid and Democracy Promotion*. Washington, DC: Carnegie Endowment for International Peace.

Baturin, Yu, A. Il'in, V. Kalatskii, V. Kostikov, M. Krasnov, A. Livshchits, K. Nikiforov, L. Pikhoia, and G. Satarov. 2001. *Epokha El'tsina: Ocherki politicheskoi istorii*. Moscow: Vagrius.

Baudais, Virginie, and Grégory Chauzal. 2006. "Les partis politiques et l' 'indépendance partisane' d'Amadou Toumani Touré." *Politique Africaine* 104: 61–80.

Baudaisa, Virginie, and Enrico Sborgib. 2008. "The Presidential and Parliamentary Elections in Mali, April and July 2007." *Electoral Studies* 27, No. 4 (December): 769–73.

Bauer, Gretchen, and Scott D. Taylor. 2005. *Politics in Southern Africa: State and Society in Transition*. Boulder, CO: Lynne Rienner Publishers.

Baum, Julian. 1994. "The Money Machine." *Far Eastern Economic Review*. 11 August: 62–6.

Baun, Michael. 2000. *A Wider Europe: The Process and Politics of European Union Enlargement*. Lanham, MD: Rowman and Littlefield.

Bawumia, Mahamudu. 1998. "Understanding the Rural–Urban Voting Patterns in the 1992 Ghanaian Presidential Election: A Closer Look at the Distributional Impact of Ghana's Structural Adjustment Program." *Journal of Modern African Studies* 36, No. 1: 47–70.

Baylies, C., and M. Szeftel. 1992. "The Fall and Rise of Multi-Party Politics in Zambia." *Review of African Political Economy* 19, No. 54: 75–91.

Becarra, Ricardo, Pedro Salazar, and José Woldenberg. 2000. *La mecánica del cambio político en México: Elecciones, partidos y reformas.* Mexico City: Cal y Arena.

Beck, Linda J. 1997. "Senegal's 'Patrimonial Democrats': Incremental Reform and the Obstacles to the Consolidation of Democracy." *Canadian Journal of African Studies* 31, No. 1: 1–31.

Beck, Linda J. 1999. "Senegal's Enlarged Presidential Majority: Deepening Democracy or Detour?" In Richard Joseph, ed. *State, Conflict, and Democracy in Africa.* Boulder, CO: Lynne Rienner Publishers.

Beck, Linda J. 2001. "Reining in the Marabouts? Democratization and Local Governance in Senegal." *African Affairs* 100: 601–21.

Beck, Linda J. 2008. *Brokering Democracy in Africa: The Rise of Clientelist Democracy in Senegal.* New York: Palgrave-Macmillan.

Bedevian, Asghik. 2006. "Ruling Parties Pledge Continued Cooperation." *RFE/RL Armenia Report,* 6 February.

Bedlington, Stanley S. 1978. *Malaysia and Singapore: The Building of New States.* Ithaca, NY: Cornell University Press.

Behrman, Lucy C. 1970. *Muslim Brotherhoods and Politics in Senegal.* Cambridge, MA: Harvard University Press.

Beinin, Henry. 1978. *Armies and Parties in Africa.* New York: Holmes and Meier.

Beissinger, Mark R. 2002. *Nationalist Mobilization and the Collapse of the Soviet State.* New York: Cambridge University Press.

Beissinger, Mark R. 2007. "Structure and Example in Modular Political Phenomena: The Diffusion of Bulldozer/Rose/Orange/Tulip Revolutions." *Perspectives on Politics* 5 (June): 259–76.

Belarusian Institute for Strategic Studies (BISS). 2008. "New Russian President and Belarus: Sluggish Political Emancipation, Active Economic Expansion?" Vilnius, Lithuania, unpublished manuscript.

Belin, Laura, Ralph S. Clem, Peter R. Craumer, and Robert W. Orttung. 1997. *The Russian Parliamentary Elections of 1995: The Battle for the Duma.* Armonk, NY: M. E. Sharpe.

Bellamy, Alex. 2001. "Croatia after Tudjman: The 2000 Parliamentary and Presidential Elections." *Problems of Post-Communism* 48, No. 5 (September–October): 18–31.

Bellamy, Alex J. 2003. *The Formation of Croatian National Identity: A Centuries Old Dream?* Manchester, UK: Manchester University Press.

Bellin, Eva. 2000. "Contingent Democrats: Industrialists, Labor, and the State in Late-Developing Countries." *World Politics* 52, No. 2: 175–205.

Bellin, Eva. 2004. "The Robustness of Authoritarianism in the Middle East: Exceptionalism in Comparative Perspective." *Comparative Politics* 36, No. 2: 139–57.

Belloni, Roberto, and Roberto Morozzo della Rocca. 2008. "Italy and the Balkans: The Rise of a Reluctant Middle Power." *Modern Italy* 13, No. 3: 169–85.

Bendaña, Alejandro. 1992. "Afterward: Elections, Intervention, and Revolution: A Sandinista Perspective." In William Robinson, *A Faustian Bargain: U.S. Intervention in the Nicaraguan Elections and American Foreign Policy in the Post–Cold War Era.* Boulder, CO: Westview Press.

Beresford, Melanie. 2005. "Cambodia: An Artificial Democratization Process." *Asian Survey* 45, No. 1 (January–February): 134–52.

Berg-Schlosser, Dirk, and Rainer Siegler. 1990. *Political Stability and Development: A Comparative Analysis of Kenya, Tanzania, and Uganda.* Boulder, CO: Lynne Rienner Publishers.

Bergamaschi, Isaline. 2008. "Mali: Patterns and Limits of Donor-Driven Ownership." In Lindsay Whitfield, ed. *The Politics of Aid: African Strategies for Dealing with Donors.* Oxford: Oxford University Press.

Berman, Daniel K. 1992. *Words Like Colored Glass: The Role of the Press in Taiwan's Democratization Process.* Boulder, CO: Westview Press.

Bermeo, Nancy. 1990. "Rethinking Regime Change." *Comparative Politics* 22, No. 3 (April): 359–77.

Biberaj, Elez. 1993. "Albania's Road to Democracy." *Current History* 92, No. 577: 381–85.

Biberaj, Elez. 1998. *Albania in Transition: The Rocky Road to Democracy.* Boulder, CO: Westview Press.

Bieber, Florian. 2003. "The Serbian Opposition and Civil Society: Roots of the Delayed Transition in Serbia." *International Journal of Politics, Culture, and Society* 17, No. 1 (Fall): 73–90.

Bieber, Florian. 2006. "Serbia and Montenegro." *Nations in Transit 2006.* New York: Freedom House.

Bienen, Henry. 1967. *Tanzania: Party Transformation and Economic Development.* Princeton, NJ: Princeton University Press.

Bierschenk, Thomas, and Jean-Pierre Olivier de Sardan. 2003. "Powers in the Village: Rural Benin between Democratization and Decentralization." *Africa* 73, No. 2: 145–73.

Bierschenk, Thomas, Elizabeth Thioléron, and Nassirou Bako-Arifari. 2003. "Benin." *Development Policy Review* 21, No. 2: 161–78.

Bing, Rasmus, and B. Szajkowski. 1994. "Romania." In B. Szajkowski, ed. *Political Parties of Eastern Europe, Russia, and the Successor States.* Stockton, UK: Essex.

Birch, Sarah. 2002. "The Presidential Election in Ukraine, October 1999." *Electoral Studies* 21, No. 2 (June): 339–63.

Birch, Sarah. 2003. "The Parliamentary Elections in Ukraine, March 2002." *Electoral Studies* 22, No. 3 (September): 524–31.

Bjelakovic, Nebojsa, and Sava Tatic. 1998. "1997: Another Year of Bleak Continuity." In Gale Stokes and Peter Rutland, eds. *The Challenge of Integration: East West Institute Annual Survey of Eastern Europe and the Former Soviet Union.* New York: EastWest Institute.

Black, Jan Knippers. 1986. *The Dominican Republic: Politics and Development in an Unsovereign State.* Boston: Allen and Unwin.

Blair, David. 2002. *Degrees in Violence: Robert Mugabe and the Struggle for Power in Zimbabwe.* London: Continuum.

Blair, David. 2003. *Degrees in Violence: Robert Mugabe and the Struggle for Power in Zimbabwe* (Revised Edition). London: Continuum.

Blaydes, Lisa. Forthcoming. *Elections and Distributive Politics in Mubarak's Egypt.* New York: Cambridge University Press.

Bluff, Margot. 2008. "Belarus: Authorities Free Another Political Prisoner." *RFE/RL Reports.* February 22.

Bluwey, Gilbert. 1998. "State Organizations and the Transition to Constitutional Democracy." In Kwame A. Ninsin, ed. *Ghana: Transition to Democracy.* Dakar, Senegal: CODESRIA.

Boafo-Arthur, Kwame. 1998a. "Party Organization, Finance and the Democratic Process: The Case of the Opposition Parties." In Joseph R. A. Ayee, ed. *The 1996 General Elections and Democratic Consolidation in Ghana.* Accra: University of Ghana, Department of Political Science.

Boafo-Arthur, Kwame. 1998b. "The International Community and Ghana's Transition to Democracy." In Kwame A. Ninsin, ed. *Ghana: Transition to Democracy.* Dakar, Senegal: CODESRIA.

Boafo-Arthur, Kwame. 1999. "Ghana: Structural Adjustment, Democratization, and the Politics of Continuity." *African Studies Review* 42, No. 2 (September): 41–72.

Boafo-Arthur, Kwame. 2001. "Election Monitoring and Observation in Ghana: Problems and Prospects." In Joseph R. A. Ayee, ed. *Deepening Democracy in Ghana: Politics of the 2000 Elections (Vol. 1)*. Accra: Freedom Publications.

Boafo-Arthur, Kwame. 2003. "Political Parties and Democratic Sustainability in Ghana, 1992–2000." In M. A. Mohamed Salih, ed. *African Political Parties: Evolution, Institutionalization and Governance*. London: Pluto Press.

Boas, Taylor C. 2005. "Television and Neopopulism in Latin America: Media Effects in Brazil and Peru." *Latin American Research Review* 40, No. 2: 27–4.

Bobea, Lilian. 2002. "Recomposición de las Fuerzas de Seguridad en el Caribe y su Impacto en las Relaciones Cívico-Militares." In Lilian Bobea, ed. *Soldados y Ciudadanos en el Caribe*. Santo Domingo: FLACSO.

Boduszynski, Mieczyslaw P., and Kristina Balalovska. 2004. "Between a Rock and a Hard Place: Croatia, Macedonia, and the Battle over Article 98." *Problems of Post-Communism* 51, No. 1 (January–February): 18–30.

Boichenko, O. V. 2004. "Incidence of Wage Arrears in Ukraine." *Magisterium* (National University of Kyiv Mohyla Academy) 14: 22–5.

Boix, Carles. 2003. *Democracy and Redistribution*. New York: Cambridge University Press.

Boix, Carles, and Susan C. Stokes. 2003. "Endogenous Democratization." *World Politics* 55, No. 4 (July): 517–49.

Bojcun, Marko. 2001. "Russia, Ukraine, and European Integration." *EUI Working Paper*, HEC No. 2001/4. Florence, Italy: European University Institute.

Bokeria, Giga, Givi Targamadze, and Levan Ramishvili. 1997. "Georgian Media in the 90s: A Step to Liberty." Discussion Paper Series. Tbilisi: UN Development Programme – Georgia.

Boone, Catherine. 1990. "State Power and Economic Crisis in Senegal." *Comparative Politics* 22, No. 3 (April): 341–57.

Boone, Catherine. 1992. *Merchant Capital and the Roots of State Power in Senegal, 1930–1985*. New York: Cambridge University Press.

Booth, John A. 1985. *The End and the Beginning: The Nicaraguan Revolution, Second Edition*. Boulder, CO: Westview Press.

Booth, John A. 1998. "Electoral Observation and Democratic Transition in Nicaragua." In Kevin Middlebrook, ed. *Electoral Observation and Democratic Transitions in Latin America*. La Jolla, CA: Center for U.S.–Mexican Studies.

Borisov, Vadim, and Simon Clarke. 1994. "Reform and Revolution in the Communist National Park." *Capital & Class*. No. 53 (Summer): 9–13.

Borjas Benavente, Adriana. 2003. *Partido de la Revolución Democrática: Estructura, Organización Interna y Desempeño Público: 1989–2003 (Vol. 2)*. Mexico City: Gernika.

Bosco, Joseph. 1994. "Faction versus Ideology: Mobilization Strategies in Taiwan's Elections." *The China Quarterly* 137 (March): 28–62.

Bossom, Kenneth. 1996. "Prospects for Democracy in Serbia and Croatia." *East European Quarterly* 29, No. 4 (January): 509–28.

Bostrom, Mikael. 1994. "Contagion of Democracy in Latin America: The Case of Paraguay." In Stuart S. Nagel, ed. *Latin American Development and Public Policy*. New York: St. Martin's Press.

Bouman, Marlies. 1987. "A Note on Chiefly and National Policing in Botswana." *Journal of Legal Pluralism* 25 & 26: 275–300.

Bowen, Merle. 1992. "Beyond Reform: Adjustment and Political Power in Contemporary Mozambique." *Journal of Modern African Studies* 30, No. 2 (June): 255–80.

Bowen, Sally, and Jane Holligan. 2003. *El Espía Imperfecto: La Telaraña Siniestra de Vladimiro Montesinos*. Lima, Peru: Peisa.

Bowman, Larry. 1973. *Politics in Rhodesia: White Power in an African State*. Cambridge, MA: Harvard University Press.

Boyer, Allison. 1992. "An exemplary transition." *Africa Report* 37 No. 4: 40–3.

Bratton, Michael. 1992. "Zambia Starts Over." *Journal of Democracy* 3, No. 2 (April): 81–93.

Bratton, Michael. 1994. "Economic Crisis and Political Realignment in Zambia." In Jennifer A. Widner, ed. *Economic Change and Political Liberalization in Sub-Saharan Africa*. Baltimore, MD: The Johns Hopkins University Press.

Bratton, Michael. 2005. "Building Democracy in Africa's Weak States." *Democracy at Large* 1, No. 3: 12–15.

Bratton, Michael, and Eric C. C. Chang. 2006. "State-Building and Democratization in Sub-Saharan Africa: Forwards, Backwards, or Together." *Comparative Political Studies* 39, No. 9: 1059–83.

Bratton, Michael, and Eldred Masunungure. 2006. "Popular Reactions to State Repression: Operation Murambatsvina in Zimbabwe." *African Affairs* 106, No. 422: 21–45.

Bratton, Michael, and Daniel Posner. 1999. "A First Look at Second Elections in Africa, with Illustrations from Zambia." In Richard Joseph, ed. *State, Conflict, and Democracy in Africa*. Boulder, CO: Lynne Rienner Publishers.

Bratton, Michael, and Nicolas van de Walle. 1997. *Democratic Experiments in Africa: Regime Transitions in Comparative Perspective*. New York: Cambridge University Press.

Braun, Janice. 1992. "Is Macedonia Next? Chaos Moves South." *Commonweal* (14 August): 7–8.

Breitinger, Eckhard. 1993. "Lamentations Patriotiques: Writers, Censors and Politics in Cameroon." *African Affairs* 92, No. 369 (October): 557–576.

Bremmer, Ian, and Cory Welt. 1997. "Armenia's New Autocrats." *Journal of Democracy* 8, No. 3: 77–91.

Bresani, Augusto. 2003. *Osaso y Persecución*. Lima, Peru: Bresani Ediciones.

Bricke, Dieter, Zdenek Lukas, and Sona Szomolányi. 1995. "Slovakia." In Werner Weidenfield, ed. *Central and Eastern Europe on the Way into the European Union: Problems and Prospects of Integration*. Guttersloh, Germany: Bertelsmann Foundation Publishers.

Brinegar, Adam, Scott Morgenstern, and Daniel Nielson. 2006. "The PRI's Choice: Balancing Democratic Reform and its Own Salvation." *Party Politics* 12, No. 1: 77–97.

Brinks, Daniel, and Michael Coppedge. 2006. "Diffusion Is No Illusion: Neighbor Emulation in the Third Wave of Democracy." *Comparative Political Studies* 39, No. 4: 463–89.

Brkic, Misa. 1996–1997. "Elections in Serbia: An Unstable Coalition." *Uncaptive Minds* Winter–Spring: 85–9.

Brown, Archie. 2005. "Comparative Politics: A View from Britain." *APSA-CP Newsletter* 16, No. 1: 1–4.

Brown, Frederick Z. 1998. "Cambodia's Rocky Venture in Democracy." In Krishna Kumar, ed. *Postconflict Elections, Democratization, and International Assistance*. Boulder, CO: Lynne Rienner Publishers.

Brown, Frederick Z., and David G. Timberman. 1998. "Introduction: Peace Development, and Democracy in Cambodia – Shattered Hopes." In Frederick Z. Brown and David G. Timberman, eds. *Cambodia and the International Community: The Quest for Peace, Development, and Democracy*. New York: The Asia Society.

Brown, Graham. 2008. "Federal and State Elections in Malaysia, March 2008." *Electoral Studies* 27, 4: 740–73.

Brown, Karen. 2001. "In the Realm of the Double-Headed Eagle: Parapolitics in Macedonia, 1994–1999." In J. Cowan, ed. *Macedonia: The Politics of Identity and Difference*. London: Pluto Press.

Brown, MacAlister, and Joseph J. Zasloff. 1998. *Cambodia Confounds the Peacemakers: 1979–1998*. Ithaca, NY: Cornell University Press.

Brown, Stephen. 2001. "Authoritarian Leaders and Multiparty Elections in Africa: How Foreign Donors Help to Keep Kenya's Daniel arap Moi in Power." *Third World Quarterly* 22, No. 5: 725–739.

Brown, Stephen. 2003. "Quiet Diplomacy and Recurring 'Ethnic Clashes' in Kenya." In Chandra Lekha Sriram and Karin Wermester, eds. *From Promise to Practice: Strengthening UN Capacities for the Prevention of Violent Conflict*. Boulder, CO: Lynne Rienner Publishers.

Brown, Stephen. 2004. "Theorizing Kenya's Protracted Transition to Democracy." *Journal of Contemporary African Studies* 22, No. 3: 325–42.

Brownlee, Jason. 2002. "... And Yet They Persist: Explaining Survival and Transition in Neopatrimonial Regimes." *Studies in Comparative International Development* 37, No. 3: 35–63.

Brownlee, Jason. 2007a. *Durable Authoritarianism in an Age of Democratization*. New York: Cambridge University Press.

Brownlee, Jason. 2007b. "Hereditary Succession in Modern Autocracies." *World Politics* 59, No. 4 (July): 595–628.

Bruhn, Kathleen. 1997. *Taking on Goliath: The Emergence of a New Left Party and the Struggle for Democracy in Mexico*. University Park: Pennsylvania State University Press.

Bryan, Shari, and Denise Baer, eds. 2005. *Money in Politics: A Study of Party Financing Practices in 22 Countries*. Washington, DC: National Democratic Institute.

Bubnova, Nina, and Lucan Way. 1998. *Trends in Financing Regional Expenditures in Transition Economies: The Case of Ukraine*. World Bank Discussion Paper. Washington, DC.

Buechsenschuetz, Ulrich. 2001a. "New Rift in Macedonian Leadership?" *Transitions Online*, 10 August.

Buechsenschuetz, Ulrich. 2001b. "Are Bulgarian-Macedonian Relations Improving?" *Transitions Online*, 27 August.

Bujosevic, Dragan, and Ivan Radovanovic. 2003. *The Fall of Milosevic: The October 5 Revolution*. New York: Palgrave Macmillan.

Bunce, Valerie. 2003. "Rethinking Recent Democratization: Lessons from the Post-Communist Experience." *World Politics* 55, No. 2: 167–92.

Bunce, Valerie, and Sharon Wolchik. 2006a. "Defining and Domesticating the Electoral Model: A Comparison of Slovakia and Serbia." Prepared for the conference, "Waves and Troughs of Post-Communist Transitions: What Role for Domestic vs. External Variables?" Center on Democracy, Development, and the Rule of Law; Stanford, CA, Stanford University. 28–29 April.

Bunce, Valerie, and Sharon Wolchick. 2006b. "Favorable Conditions and Electoral Revolutions." *Journal of Democracy* 17, No. 4: 5–18.

Bureau of European and Eurasian Affairs. 2009. "Foreign Operations Appropriated Assistance." Washington, DC: U.S. Department of State.

Burger, Ethan S., and Viktar Minchuk. 2006. "Alyaksandr Lukashenka's Consolidation of Power." In Joerg Forbrig, David R. Marples, and Pavol Demes, eds. *Prospects for Democracy in Belarus*. Washington, DC: German Marshall Fund of the United States.

Burke, Justin. 2001. "Significant Benefits await Armenia If Road and Rail Blockade Lifted." *Armenia Daily Digest*. 11 June.

Burnell, Peter, ed. 2000a. *Democracy Assistance: International Cooperation for Democratization*. London: Frank Cass.

Burnell, Peter. 2000b. "Democracy Assistance: The State of the Discourse." In Peter Burnell, ed. *Democracy Assistance: International Cooperation for Democratization*. London: Frank Cass.

Burnell, Peter. 2001a. "The Party System and Party Politics in Zambia: Continuities Past, Present and Future." *African Affairs* 100, No. 399: 239–63.

Burnell, Peter. 2001b. "Does Economic Reform Promote Democratization? Evidence from Zambia's Third Republic." *New Political Economy* 6, No. 2: 191–212.

Burnell, Peter. 2003. "The Tripartite Elections in Zambia, December 2001." *Electoral Studies* 22: 388–95.

Burt, Jo-Marie. 1997. "Political Violence and the Grassroots in Lima, Peru." In Douglas A. Chambers, Carlos M. Vilas, Katherine Hite, Scott B. Martin, Kerianne Piester, and Monique Segarra, eds. *The New Politics of Inequality in Latin America: Rethinking Participation and Representation*. New York: Oxford University Press.

Burt, Jo-Marie. 1998. "Unsettled Accounts: Militarization and Memory in Postwar Peru." *NACLA Report on the Americas* 32, No. 2: 35–41.

Burt, Jo-Marie. 2004. "State-Making Against Democracy: The Case of Fujimori's Peru." In Jo-Marie Burt and Philip Mauceri, eds. *Politics in the Andes: Identity, Conflict, Reform*. Pittsburgh, PA: University of Pittsburgh Press.

Bush, Jason. 2005. "How Putin May Hang on to Power." *Business Week*. 6 June.

Butora, Martin, Zora Butorova, and Grigorij Meseznikov. 2003. "Slovakia's Democratic Awakening." In Jacques Rupnik and Jan Zielnka, eds. *The Road to the European Union: The Czech and Slovak Republics*. New York: Manchester University Press.

Buturova, Zora, and Martin Butora. 1995. "Political Parties, Value Orientations and Slovakia's Road to Independence." In G. Wightman, ed. *Party Formation in East Central Europe*. Aldershot, UK: Edward Elgar Publishing.

Cajina, Roberto J. 1997. *Transición política y reconversión militar en Nicaragua, 1990–1995*. Managua, Nicaragua: CRIES.

Calder, Bruce J. 1984. *The Impact of Intervention: The Dominican Republic during the U.S. Occupation of 1916–1924*. Austin: University of Texas Press.

Calderón, Alzati, and Daniel Cazés. 1996. *Las Elecciones Presidenciales de 1994*. Mexico City: La Jornada Ediciones.

Calinescu, Matei, and Vladimir Tismaneanu. 1992. "The 1989 Revolution and Romania's Future." In Daniel Nelson, ed. *Romania after Tyranny*. Boulder, CO: Westview Press.

Callaghy, Thomas M. 1991. "Africa and the World Economy: Caught Between a Rock and a Hard Place." In John W. Harbeson and Donald Rothchild, eds. *Africa in World Politics*. Boulder, CO: Westview Press.

Callaghy, Thomas M. 1993. *Hemmed In: Responses to Africa's Economic Decline*. New York: Columbia University Press.

Cameron, David. 2007. "Post-Communist Democracy: The Impact of the European Union." *Post-Soviet Affairs* 23, No 3: 185–217.

Cameron, Maxwell A. 1994. *Democracy and Authoritarianism in Peru: Political Coalitions and Social Change*. New York: St. Martin's Press.

Cameron, Maxwell A. 1997. "Political and Economic Origins of Regime Change in Peru: The Eighteenth Brumaire of Alberto Fujimori." In Maxwell Cameron and Philip Mauceri, eds. *The Peruvian Labyrinth*. University Park: Pennsylvania State University Press.

Cameron, Maxwell A. 2000. "Elections in a Hybrid Regime: Civil–Military Relations and Caesarism in Peru." Paper prepared for delivery at the 2000 meeting of the Latin American Studies Association; Miami, FL. 16–18 March.

Cameron, Maxwell A. 2006. "Endogenous Regime Breakdown: The Vladivideo and the Fall of Peru's Fujimori." In Julio Carrión, ed. *The Fujimori Legacy*. University Park: Pennsylvania State University Press.

Camp, Roderic A. 1985. *Intellectuals and the State in Twentieth-Century Mexico*. Austin: University of Texas Press.

Camp, Roderic A. 1992. *Generals in the Palacio: The Military in Modern Mexico*. New York: Oxford University Press.

Camp, Roderic A. 1995. "Striving for Mexican Democracy: The PRI and the Opposition." In Donald E. Schulz and Edward J. Williams, eds. *Mexico Faces the 21st Century*. Westport, CT: Greenwood Press.

Camp, Roderic A. 1999. *Politics in Mexico: The Decline of Authoritarianism*. New York: Oxford University Press.

Camp, Roderic A. 2002. *Mexico's Mandarins: Crafting a Power Elite for the Twenty-First Century*. Berkeley: University of California Press.

Camp, Roderic A. 2005. *Mexico's Military on the Democratic Stage*. Washington, DC: Center for Strategic and International Studies and Praeger Publishers.

Canak, Branislav. 1993. "The Power and Powerless: The Media in Serbia." *Uncaptive Minds* (Summer): 81–7.

Caplan, Richard. 1998. "International Diplomacy and the Crisis in Kosovo." *International Affairs* 74, No. 4: 745–62.

Carbone, Giovanni M. 2003. "Emerging Pluralist Politics in Mozambique: The Frelimo–Renamo Party System." Crisis States Programme Working Paper No. 23. London: London School of Economics Development Research Center.

Carbone, Giovanni M. 2005. "Continuidade na Renovação? Ten Years of Multiparty Politics in Mozambique: Roots, Evolution and Stabilisation of the Frelimo–Renamo Party System." *The Journal of Modern African Studies* 43: 417–42.

Carbonell, José. 2002. *El Fin de las Certezas Autoritarias: Hacia la Construcción de un Nuevo Sistema Político y Constitucional para México*. Mexico City: Universidad Nacional Autónoma de México.

Carey, Henry F. 1995. "Irregularities or Rigging: The 1992 Romanian Parliamentary Elections." *East European Quarterly* 29: 43–67.

Carey, Henry F. 1998. "Electoral Observation and Democratization in Haiti." In Kevin Middlebrook, ed. *Electoral Observation and Democratic Transitions in Latin America*. La Jolla, CA: Center for U.S.–Mexican Studies.

Carey, Henry F. 2004. "Conclusion: Ambiguous Democratization?" In H. Carey, ed. *Romania Since 1989: Politics, Economics, and Society*. Boulder, CO: Lexington Books.

Carletto, Calogero, Benjamin Davis, Marco Stampini, and Alberto Zezza. 2006. "A Country on the Move: International Migration in Post-Communist Albania." *International Migration Review* 40, No. 4: 767–85.

Carney, Timothy. 1993. "Compromise and Confrontation: The Cambodian Future." In Timothy Carney and Tan Lian Choo, eds. *Wither Cambodia: Beyond the Election*. Singapore: Institute of Southeast Asian Studies.

Carothers, Thomas. 1991. *In the Name of Democracy: US Policy Toward Latin America in the Reagan Years*. Berkeley: University of California Press.

Carothers, Thomas. 1996. *Assessing Democracy Assistance: The Case of Romania*. Washington D.C.: The Carnegie Endowment for International Peace.

Carothers, Thomas. 1997a. "Democracy without Illusions." *Foreign Affairs* 76 (January–February): 85–99.

Carothers, Thomas. 1997b. "The Observers Observed." *Journal of Democracy* 8, No. 3: 17–31.

Carothers, Thomas. 1997c. "Romania: The Political Background." *Democracy in Romania: Assessment Mission.* Stockholm: IDEA.

Carothers, Thomas. 1999. *Aiding Democracy Abroad: The Learning Curve.* Washington, DC: Carnegie Endowment for International Peace.

Carothers, Thomas. 2000a. "Struggling with Semi-Authoritarians." In Peter Burnell, ed. *Democracy Assistance: International Cooperation for Democratization.* London: Frank Cass.

Carothers, Thomas. 2000b. "Taking Stock of US Democracy Assistance." In Michael Cox, G. John Ikenberry, and Takashi Inoguchi, eds. *American Democracy Promotion: Impulses, Strategies, and Impacts.* Oxford: Oxford University Press.

Carothers, Thomas. 2001. "Ousting Foreign Strongmen: Lessons from Serbia." *Carnegie Endowment for International Peace Policy Brief* 1, No. 5.

Carothers, Thomas. 2002. "The End of the Transition Paradigm." *Journal of Democracy* 13, No. 1: 5–21.

Carothers, Thomas, Ray S. James, Jonathan Soros, and Dorin Tudoran. 1994. *The Moldovan Parliamentary Elections: February 27, 1994.* Washington, DC: International Foundation for Electoral Systems.

Carpenter, Michael. 1997. " Slovakia and the Triumph of Nationalist Populism." *Communist and Post-Communist Studies* 30, No. 2: 205–19.

Carpenter, Ted. 2002. "Kosovo and Macedonia: The West Enhances the Threat." *Mediterranean Quarterly* (Winter): 21–37.

Carrión, Julio F. 2006. "Public Opinion, Market Reforms, and Democracy in Fujimori's Peru." In Julio Carrión, ed. *The Fujimori Legacy: The Rise of Electoral Authoritarianism in Peru.* University Park: Pennsylvania State University Press.

The Carter Center. 2002. "Observing the 2002 Mali Presidential Elections." Atlanta, GA: The Carter Center.

The Carter Center. 2005. "Observing the 2004 Mozambique Elections." Atlanta, GA: The Carter Center.

Carver, Richard. 1994. "The Army Factor." *Africa Report* 39, No. 1: 56–8.

Case, William. 1994. "The UMNO Party Election in Malaysia: One for the Money." *Asian Survey* 34, No. 10: 916–30.

Case, William. 1995. "Comparing Regime Continuity and Change: Indonesia, Thailand and Malaysia." Regime Change and Regime Maintenance in Asia and the Pacific Discussion Paper No. 15, Department of Political and Social Change, Research School of Pacific and Asian Studies, Australian National University.

Case, William. 1996. *Elites and Regimes in Malaysia: Revisiting a Consociational Democracy.* Clayton, Australia: Monash Institute.

Case, William. 1997. "The 1996 UMNO Party Elections: 'Two for the Show.'" *Pacific Affairs* 70, No. 3: 393–411.

Case, William. 2001a. "Malaysia's Resilient Pseudodemocracy." *Journal of Democracy* 12, No. 1: 42–57.

Case, William. 2001b. "Malaysia's General Elections in 1999: A Consolidated and High-Quality Semi-Democracy." *Asian Studies Review* 25, No. 1: 35–55.

Case, William. 2004a. "New Uncertainties for an Old Pseudo-Democracy: The Case of Malaysia." *Comparative Politics* 37, No. 1: 83–104.

Case, William. 2004b. "Testing Malaysia's Pseudodemocracy." In Edmund Terence Gomez, ed. *The State of Malaysia: Ethnicity, Equity and Reform.* New York: Routledge-Curzon.

Case, William. 2008. "Legitimacy Deficits and Stunning Elections: The Malaysian Experience." Paper presented at the Annual Meeting of the American Political Science Association: Boston, MA. 28 August.

Cassá, Roberto. 1995. "Recent Popular Movements in the Dominican Republic." *Latin American Perspectives* 22, No. 3 (Summer): 80–93.

Castañeda, Jorge G. 1994. "Latin America and the End of the Cold War: An Essay in Frustration." In Abraham F. Lowenthal and Gregory F. Trevorton, eds. *Latin America in a New World*. Boulder, CO: Westview Press.

Castañeda, Jorge G. 1995. *The Mexican Shock: Its Meaning for the United States*. New York: The New Press.

Castells, Manuel. 1997. *The Power of Identity in the Information Age: Economy, Society and Culture, Vol. 2*. Oxford, UK: Basil Blackwell Publishers.

Catanese, Anthony V. 1999. *Haitians: Migration and Diaspora*. Boulder, CO: Westview Press.

Cedeño, Víctor Livio. 1999. *Los Partidos Políticos en la Republica Dominicana*. Santo Domingo: Editorial Diálogo.

Centeno, Miguel Ángel. 1994. *Democracy within Reason: Technocratic Revolution in Mexico*. University Park: Pennsylvania State University Press.

Center for Political Education. 2006. *The Fading Pillars of Power in Belarus: 100 days of Milinkevich*. Bratislava: Pontis Foundation's Institute for Civic Diplomacy.

Center for Strategic and International Studies. 2002. "Preview of Kenya's December 27 National Elections." *CSIS Africa Notes* 12 (December).

Chachiua, Martinho. 2000. "Internal Security in Mozambique: Concerns Versus Policies." *African Security Review* 9, No. 1. Available at http://www.iss.co.za/PUBS/ASR/9NO1/%20SecurityMozambique.html

Chan, Stephen. 2003. *Robert Mugabe: A Life of Power and Violence*. London: I. B. Tauris.

Chand, Vikram K. 1997. "Democratization from the Outside In: NGO and International Efforts to Promote Open Elections." *Third World Quarterly* 18, No. 3: 543–61.

Chand, Vikram. 2001. *Mexico's Political Awakening*. Notre Dame, IN: University of Notre Dame Press.

Chanda, Alfred. 2003. *National Integrity Systems Country Study Report: Zambia 2003*. Lusaka: Royal Norwegian Embassy.

Chandler, Andrea. 1998. *Institutions of Isolation: Border Controls in the Soviet Union and Its Successor States, 1917–1993*. Montreal: McGill-Queen's University Press.

Chandler, David P. 1998. "The Burden of Cambodia's Past." In Frederick Z. Brown and David G. Timberman, eds. *Cambodia and the International Community: The Quest for Peace, Development, and Democracy*. New York: The Asia Society.

Chao, Linda, and Ramon H. Myers. 1994. "The First Chinese Democracy: Political Development of the Republic of China on Taiwan, 1986–1994." *Asian Survey* 34, No. 3: 213–30.

Chao, Linda, and Ramon H. Myers. 1997. *Democracy's New Leaders in the Republic of China on Taiwan*. Stanford, CA: Hoover Institution Press.

Chao, Linda, and Ramon H. Myers. 1998. *The First Chinese Democracy: Political Life in the Republic of China on Taiwan*. Baltimore, MD: The Johns Hopkins University Press.

Charlton, Roger. 1993. "The Politics of Elections in Botswana." *Africa* 63, No. 3: 330–70.

Chazan, Naomi. 1983. *An Anatomy of Ghanaian Politics*. Boulder, CO: Westview Press.

Chazan, Naomi. 1991. "The Political Transformation of Ghana under the PNDC." In Donald Rothchild, ed. *Ghana: The Political Economy of Recovery*. Boulder, CO: Lynne Rienner Publishers.

Chazan, Naomi, Peter Lewis, Robert A. Mortimer, Donald Rothchild, and Stephen John Stedman. 1999. *Politics and Society in Contemporary Africa, Third Edition*. Boulder, CO: Lynne Rienner Publishers.

Cheater, Angela. 2001. *Human Rights and Zimbabwe's June 2000 Election*. Harare: Zimbabwe Human Rights NGO Forum Human Rights Special Unit, Special Report 1 (January).

Chebankova, Elena. 2008. "Adaptive Federalism and Federation in Putin's Russia." *Europe–Asia Studies* 60, No. 6 (August): 989–1009.

Chege, Michael. 1994. "The Return of Multi-Party Politics." In Joel Barkan, ed. *Beyond Capitalism vs. Socialism in Kenya and Tanzania*. Boulder, CO: Lynne Rienner Publishers.

Chege, Michael. 1996. "Between Africa's Extremes." In Larry Diamond and Marc F. Plattner, eds. *The Global Resurgence of Democracy*. Baltimore, MD: The Johns Hopkins University Press.

Chege, Michael. 2005. "Democratic Governance in Africa at the Start of the Twenty-First Century: Lessons of Experience." In Leonardo A. Villalón and Peter VonDoepp, eds. *The Fate of Africa's Democratic Experiments: Elites and Institutions*. Bloomington: Indiana University Press.

Chen, Yun Chen. 1998. "State, Media and Democracy in Taiwan." *Media, Culture and Society* 20: 11–29.

Cheng, Li, and Lynn White. 1990. "Elite Transformation and Modern Change in Mainland China and Taiwan: Empirical Data and the Theory of Technocracy." *The China Quarterly* 121 (March): 1–35.

Cheng, Tun-jen. 1989. "Democratizing the Quasi-Leninist Regime in Taiwan." *World Politics* 41, No. 4: 471–99.

Cheng, Tun-jen, and Stephan Haggard. 1992. "Regime Transformation in Taiwan: Theoretical and Comparative Perspectives." In Tun-Jen Cheng and Stephan Haggard, eds. *Political Change in Taiwan*. Boulder, CO: Lynne Rienner Publishers.

Cheng, Tun-jen. 1997. "Taiwan in 1996: From Euphoria to Melodrama." *Asian Survey* 37, No. 1 (January): 43–51.

Cheterian, Vicken. 2000. "The Struggle to Fill the Power Vacuum in Armenia." *Eurasia Insight*. 3 April.

Chikuhwa, Jacob. 2004. *A Crisis of Governance: Zimbabwe*. New York: Algora Publishing.

Chimanikire, Donald P. 2003. "Foreign and Security Policy of Zimbabwe: From Independence to the DRC." In Staffan Darnolf and Liisa Laakso, eds. *Twenty Years of Independence in Zimbabwe: From Liberation to Authoritarianism*. Houndmills, UK: Palgrave Macmillan.

Chin, James. 1997. "Malaysia in 1996: Mahathir-Anwar Bouts, UMNO Election, and Sarawak Surprise." *Asian Survey* 37, No. 2: 181–7.

Chin, James. 1998. "Malaysia in 1997: Mahathir's Annus Horribilis." *Asian Survey* 38, No. 2: 183–9.

Chipanyula, Eunice Nihero. 2003. *Political Reporting Trends in Malawi: 1980s and 1990s*. Makwasa, Malawi: Malamulo Publishing House.

Chipeta, Mapopa. 1992. "Political Process, Civil Society and The State." In Guy C. Z. Mhone, ed. *Malawi at the Crossroads: The Post-Colonial Political Economy*. Harare: SAPES Books.

Chirwa, Wiseman C. 2000. "Civil Society in Malawi's Democratic Transition." In Martin Ott, Kings M. Phiri, and Nandini Patel, eds. *Malawi's Second Democratic Elections: Process, Problems and Prospects*. Blantyre, Malawi: Christian Literature Association in Malawi.

Chitiyo, Knox, and Martin Rupiya. 2005. "Tracking Zimbabwe's Political History: The Zimbabwe Defense Force from 1980–2005." In Martin Rupiya, ed. *Evolutions and Revolutions: A Contemporary History of Revolutions in Southern Africa*. Pretoria, South Africa: Institute for Security Studies.

Choo, Lan Tian. 1993. "The Cambodian Elections: Wither the Future?" In Timothy Carney and Tan Lian Choo, eds. *Wither Cambodia: Beyond the Election*. Singapore: Institute of Southeast Asian Studies.

Christian, Shirley. 1985. *Nicaragua: Revolution in the Family*. New York: Random House.

Chu, J. J. 1993. "Political Liberalization and the Rise of Taiwanese Labor Radicalism." *Journal of Contemporary Asia* 23, No. 2: 173–88.

Chu, Yun-han. 1992. *Crafting Democracy in Taiwan*. Taipei, Taiwan: Institute for National Policy Research.

Chu, Yun-han. 1994a. "Social Protest and Political Democratization in Taiwan." In Murray A. Rubinstein, ed. *The Other Taiwan: 1945 to the Present*. Armonk, NY: M. E. Sharpe.

Chu, Yun-han. 1994b. "The Realignment of Business–Government Relations and Regime Transition in Taiwan." In Andrew MacIntyre, ed. *Business and Government in Industrializing Asia*. Ithaca, NY: Cornell University Press.

Chu, Yun-han. 1998. "Taiwan's Unique Challenges." In Larry Diamond and Marc F. Plattner, eds. *Democracy in East Asia*. Baltimore, MD: The Johns Hopkins University Press.

Chu, Yun-han. 1999. "The Challenges of Democratic Consolidation." In Steve Tsang and Hung-mao Tien, eds. *Democratization in Taiwan: Implications for China*. London: Macmillan.

Chu, Yun-han. 2005. "Taiwan's Year of Stress." *Journal of Democracy* 16, No. 2: 43–57.

Chu, Yun-han, and Larry Diamond. 1999. "Taiwan's 1998 Elections: Implications for Democratic Consolidation." *Asian Survey* 39, No. 5: 808–22.

Chu, Yun-han, Fu Hu, and Chung-in Moon. 1997. "South Korea and Taiwan: The International Context." In Larry Diamond, Marc F. Plattner, Yun-han Chu, and Hung-mao Tien, eds. *Consolidating the Third Wave Democracies: Regional Challenges*. Baltimore, MD: The Johns Hopkins University Press.

Ciobanu, Monica. 2007. "Romania's Travails with Democracy and Accession to the European Union." *Europe–Asia Studies* 59, No. 8 (December): 1429–50.

Clapham, Christopher. 1996. *Africa and the International System: The Politics of State Survival*. Cambridge: Cambridge University Press.

Clark, Andrew F. 2000. "From Military Dictatorship to Democracy: The Democratization Process in Mali." In R. Bingem, D. Robinson, and J. Staatz, eds. *Democracy and Development in Mali*. East Lansing: Michigan State University Press.

Clark, William A. 2006. "Communist Devolution: The Electoral Decline of the KPRF." *Problems of Post-Communism* 53, No. 1 (January–February): 15–25.

Clauson, Thomas. 1998. "Minding the Gap? State–Civil Society Relations in Ghana's Fourth Republic." In Joseph R. A. Ayee, ed. *The 1996 General Elections and Democratic Consolidation in Ghana*. Accra: University of Ghana, Department of Political Science.

Clinkenbeard, Steven E. 2004. "Donors versus Dictators – The Impact of Multilateral Aid Conditionality on Democratization: Kenya and Malawi in Comparative Context, 1990–2004." Ph.D. Diss., Department of Political Science, Massachusetts Institute of Technology.

Close, David. 1988. *Nicaragua: Politics, Economics and Society*. London: Pinter Publishers.

Close, David. 1999. *Nicaragua: The Chamorro Years*. Boulder, CO: Lynne Rienner Publishers.

Close, David. 2004a. "Undoing Democracy in Nicaragua." In David Close and Kalowatie Deonandan, eds. *Undoing Democracy: The Politics of Electoral Caudillismo*. Lanham, MD: Lexington Books.

Close, David. 2004b. "President Bolaños Runs a Reverse, or How Arnoldo Alemán Wound up in Prison." In David Close and Kalowatie Deonandan, eds. *Undoing Democracy: The Politics of Electoral Caudillismo*. Lanham, MD: Lexington Books.

Clough, Ralph N. 1998. "The Enduring Influence of the Republic of China on Taiwan Today." In David Shambaugh, ed. *Contemporary Taiwan*. Oxford, UK: Clarendon Press.

Coatsworth, John H. 1999. "The United States and Democracy in Mexico." In Victor Bulmer-Thomas and James Dunkerley, eds. *The United States and Latin America: The New Agenda*. London: Institute of Latin American Studies.

Cohen, Lenard J. 1997. "Embattled Croatia: Postcommunist Croatia in Transition." In Bruce Parrott and Karen Dawisha, eds. *Politics, Power, and the Struggle for Democracy in South East Europe*. Cambridge: Cambridge University Press.

Cohen, Lenard J. 2001a. *Serpent in the Bosom: The Rise and Fall of Slobodan Milosevic*. Boulder, CO: Westview Press.

Cohen, Lenard J. 2001b. "Post-Milosevic Serbia." *Current History* 100, No. 644: 99–108.

Cohen, Yousef, Brian R. Brown, and A. F. K. Organski. 1981. "The Paradoxical Nature of State-Making: The Violent Creation of Order." *American Political Science Review* 75, No. 4: 901–10.

Cohn, Betsy, and Patricia Hynds. 1987. "The Manipulation of the Religious Issue." In Thomas W. Walker, ed. *Reagan versus the Sandinistas: The Undeclared War on Nicaragua*. Boulder, CO: Westview Press.

Cokorinos, Lee. 1984. "The Political Economy of State and Party Formation in Zimbabwe." In Michael G. Schatzberg, ed. *The Political Economy of Zimbabwe*. New York: Praeger.

Collier, David, Henry E. Brady, and Jason Seawright. 2004a. "Critiques, Responses, and Trade-Offs: Drawing Together the Debate." In Henry E. Brady and David Collier, eds. *Rethinking Social Inquiry: Diverse Tools, Shared Standards*. Lanham, MD: Rowman and Littlefield.

Collier, David, Henry E. Brady, and Jason Seawright. 2004b. "Sources of Leverage in Causal Inference: Toward an Alternative View of Methodology." In Henry E. Brady and David Collier, eds. *Rethinking Social Inquiry: Diverse Tools, Shared Standards*. Lanham, MD: Rowman and Littlefield.

Collier, David, and Steven Levitsky. 1997. "Democracy with Adjectives: Conceptual Innovation in Comparative Research." *World Politics* 49, No. 3: 430–51.

Collier, Ruth Berins. 1992. *The Contradictory Alliance: State-Labor Relations and Regime Change in Mexico*. Berkeley, CA: International and Area Studies.

Collier, Ruth Berins. 1999a. *Pathways toward Democracy: The Working Class and Elites in Western Europe and Latin America*. New York: Cambridge University Press.

Collier, Ruth Berins. 1999b. "The Transformation of Labor-Based One-Partyism at the End of the Twentieth Century: The Case of Mexico." In Hermann Giliomee and Charles Simkins, eds. *The Awkward Embrace: One-Party Domination and Democracy*. Cape Town, South Africa: Tafelberg.

Collier, Ruth Berins, and David Collier. 1991. *Shaping the Political Arena*. Princeton, NJ: Princeton University Press.

Collier, Stephen, and Lucan Way. 2004. "Beyond the Deficit Model: Social Welfare in Post-Soviet Georgia." *Post-Soviet Affairs* 20, No. 3: 258–84.

Collina, Tom Z., and Jon B. Wolfsthal. 2002. "Nuclear Terrorism and Warhead Control in Russia." *Arms Control Today* 32, No. 3: 15–20.

Collins, Kathleen. 2002. "Clans, Pacts and Politics in Central Asia." *Journal of Democracy* 13, No. 3: 137–52.

Collins, Kathleen. 2003. "The Political Role of Clans in Central Asia." *Comparative Politics* 35, No. 2: 171–90.

Collins, Susan M., and Dani Rodrick. 1991. *Eastern Europe and the Soviet Union in the World Economy*. Washington, DC: Institute for International Economics.

Colovic, Ivan. 1996. "Football, Hooligans and War." In N. Popov, ed. *The Road to War in Serbia*. Budapest: Central European University Press.

Colton, Timothy J. 1996. "From the Parliamentary to the Presidential Election: Russians Get Real about Politics." *Democratizatsiya* IV, No. 3 (Summer): 371–79.

Colton, Timothy J. 2008. *Yeltsin: A Life*. New York: Basic Books.

Colton, Timothy J., and Jerry F. Hough. 1998. *Growing Pains: Russian Democracy and the Election of 1993*. Washington, DC: The Brookings Institution Press.

Colton, Timothy J., and Michael McFaul. 2003. *Popular Choice and Managed Democracy: The Russian Elections of 1999 and 2000*. Washington, DC: The Brookings Institution Press.

Colton, Timothy, and Cindy Skach. 2005. "The Russian Predicament." *Journal of Democracy* 16, No. 3: 113–26.

Comisión Andina de Juristas. 2001. *Las Tareas de la Transición Democrática*. Lima, Peru: In Comisión Andina de Juristas.

Commonwealth Observer Group. 2000. "The Parliamentary Elections in Zimbabwe: 24-25 June 2000." London: Commonwealth Secretariat.

Commonwealth Observer Group. 2007. "Kenya General Election." London: Commonwealth Secretariat (December).

Conaghan, Catherine M. 1998. "Stars of the Crisis: The Ascent of Economists in Peruvian Public Life." In Miguel A. Centeno and Patricio Silva, eds. *The Politics of Expertise in Latin America*. London: Macmillan Press.

Conaghan, Catherine M. 2001. "Making and Unmaking Authoritarian Peru: Re-Election, Resistance, and Regime Transition." North–South Agenda Paper No. 47. Miami, FL: University of Miami, North–South Center.

Conaghan, Catherine M. 2005. *Fujimori's Peru: Deception in the Public Sphere*. Pittsburgh, PA: University of Pittsburgh Press.

Conaghan, Catherine M. 2008. "Ecuador: Correa's Plebiscitary Presidency." *Journal of Democracy* 19, No. 2 (April): 46–60.

Conaghan, Catherine M. and Rosario Espinal. 1990. "Unlikely Transitions to Uncertain Regimes? Democracy without Compromise in the Dominican Republic and Ecuador." *Journal of Latin American Studies* 22, No. 3: 553–74.

Conroy, Michael E. 1987. "Patterns of Changing External Trade in Revolutionary Nicaragua: Voluntary and Involuntary Trade Diversification." In Rose J. Spalding, ed. *The Political Economy of Revolutionary Nicaragua*. Boston: Allen and Unwin.

Conroy, Michael E. 1990. "La Política Económica en las Elecciones Nicaraguenses de 1990." *Anuario de Estudios Centroamericanos* 16, No. 2: 47–69.

Copani, Adem, and Constantine Danopoulos. 1995. "The Role of the Military in the Democratization of Marxist–Leninist Regimes: Albania as a Case Study." *Mediterranean Quarterly* 6, No. 2: 117–34.

Copper, John F. 1989. "The Evolution of Political Parties in Taiwan." *Asian Affairs* 16, No. 1: 3–21.

Copper, John F. 1995. "Taiwan's 1994 Gubernatorial and Mayoral Elections." *Asian Affairs* 22, No. 2: 97–118.

Copper, John F. 1997. *The Taiwan Political Miracle: Essays on Political Development, Elections, and Foreign Relations*. Lanham, MD: University Press of America.

Copper, John F. 1998. *Taiwan's Mid-1990s Elections: Taking the Final Step to Democracy.* Westport, CT: Praeger.

Coppieters, Bruno, and Robert Legvold, eds. 2005. *Statehood and Security: Georgia after the Rose Revolution.* Cambridge, MA: The MIT Press.

Corke, Bettina, ed. 1984. *Quien es Quien en la Política y los Gobiernos de America Latina.* New York: Decade Media Books.

Cornelius, Wayne A. 1994. "Mexico's Delayed Democratization." *Foreign Policy* 95, (Summer): 53–71.

Cornelius, Wayne A. 1996. *Mexican Politics in Transition: The Breakdown of a One-Party Dominant Regime.* San Diego, CA: Center for U.S.–Mexican Studies.

Cornelius, Wayne A. 2004. "Mobilized Voting in the 2000 Elections: The Changing Efficacy of Vote Buying and Coercion in Mexican Electoral Politics." In Jorge I. Domínguez and Chappell Lawson, eds. *Mexico's Pivotal Democratic Election: Candidates, Voters, and the Presidential Campaign of 2000.* Stanford, CA: Stanford University Press.

Cornelius, Wayne A., Judith Gentleman, and Peter H. Smith. 1989. "Overview: The Dynamics of Political Change in Mexico." In Wayne A. Cornelius, Judith Gentleman, and Peter H. Smith, eds. *Mexico's Alternative Political Futures.* La Jolla, CA: Center for U.S–Mexico Studies.

Cornell, Svante E. 1999. "International Reactions to Massive Human Rights Violations: The Case of Chechnya," *Europe-Asia Studies* 51, No. 1: 85–100.

Cornell, Svante E. 2001. *Small Nations and Great Powers: A Study of Ethnopolitical Conflict in the Caucasus.* New York: Routledge.

Cornwell, Richard. 2003. "Madagascar: First Test for the African Union." *African Security Review* 12, No. 1: 41–52.

Corrales, Javier, and Michael Penfold. 2007. "Venezuela: Crowding out the Opposition," *Journal of Democracy* 18, No. 2 (April): 99–113.

Corso, Molly. 2004. "Civil Society: Georgian President Saakashvili's Campaign Against Corruption." *Eurasianet.* 22 December.

Corso, Molly. 2006a. "Georgia: Pressure to Report." *Transitions Online.* 27 February.

Corso, Molly. 2006b. "Georgia: Free Enough?" *Transitions Online.* 5 April.

Corten, André. 1993. *El Estado Débil.* Santo Domingo, Dominican Republic: Editora Taller.

Cotler, Julio. 1994. *Política y Sociedad en el Perú.* Lima, Peru: Instituto de Estudios Peruanos.

Cotler, Julio. 2000. "La Gobernabilidad en el Perú: Entre el Autoritarismo y la Democracia." In Julio Cotler and Romeo Grompone, eds. *El Fujimorismo: ascenso y caída de un régimen autoritario.* Lima, Peru: Instituto de Estudios Peruanos.

Cotler, Julio. 2001. "Navegar Contra el Viento: Las Elecciones y la Democracia en el Perú." In Carlos Milla Batres, ed. *Como Fujimori Jodió al Perú.* Lima, Peru: Editorial Mill Batres.

Coulon, Christian. 1988. "Senegal: The Development and Fragility of a Semidemocracy." In Larry Diamond, Juan J. Linz, and Seymour Martin Lipset, eds. *Democracy in Developing Countries: Africa.* Boulder, CO: Lynne Rienner Publishers.

Coulon, Christian, and Donal B. Cruise O'Brien. 1989. "Senegal." In Donal B. Cruise O'Brien, John Dunn, and Richard Rathbone, eds. *Contemporary West African States.* Cambridge: Cambridge University Press.

Coulson, Andrew. 1982. *Tanzania: A Political Economy.* Oxford, UK: Clarendon Press.

Council of Freely Elected Heads of Government/National Democratic Institute for International Affairs. 1990a. *The 1990 Elections in the Dominican Republic: Report of an Observer Delegation.* Atlanta, GA: The Carter Center of Emory University.

Council of Freely Elected Heads of Government. 1990b. *Observing Nicaragua's Elections, 1989–1990*. Atlanta, GA: The Carter Center of Emory University.

Council of Freely Elected Heads of Government. 1993. *Observing Guyana's Electoral Process, 1990–1992*. The Carter Center Special Report #3. Atlanta, GA: The Carter Center of Emory University.

Covell, Maureen. 1987. *Madagascar: Politics, Economics and Society*. London: Frances Pinter.

Cowen, Michael, and Karuti Kanyinga. 2002. "The 1997 Elections in Kenya: The Politics of Communality and Locality." In Michael Cowen and Liisa Laakso, eds. *Multi-Party Elections in Africa*. Oxford, UK: James Currey Ltd.

Cox, Michael G., John Ikenberry, and Takashi Inoguchi, eds. 2000. *American Democracy Promotion: Impulses, Strategies, and Impacts*. Oxford, UK: Oxford University Press.

Crawford, Gordon. 1997. "Foreign Aid and Political Conditionality: Issues of Effectiveness and Consistency." *Democratization* 4, No. 3: 69–108.

Crawford, Gordon. 2001. *Foreign Aid and Political Reform: A Comparative Analysis of Democracy Assistance and Political Conditionality*. New York: Palgrave.

Creevey, Lucy, Paul Ngomo and Richard Vengroff. 2005. "Party Politics and Different Paths to Democratic Transitions: A Comparison of Benin and Senegal." *Party Politics* 11, No. 4: 471–493.

Crespo, José Antonio. 1995. *Urnas de Pandora: Partidos Políticos y Elecciones en el Gobierno de Salinas*. Mexico City: Espasa Calpe.

Crespo, José Antonio. 1999. *Fronteras Democráticas en México: Retos, Peculariaridades y Comparaciones*. Mexico City: Oceano.

Croissant, Aurel, and Wolfgang Merkel. 2004. "Introduction: Democratization in the Early Twenty-First Century." *Democratization* 11, No. 5 (December): 1–9.

Crook, Richard C. 1999. "'No Party' Politics and Local Democracy in Africa: Rawlings' Ghana in the 1990s and 'Ugandan Model.'" *Democratization* 6, No. 4 (Winter): 114–38.

Crouch, Harold. 1992. "Authoritarian Trends, the UMNO Split and the Limits to State Power." In Joel S. Kahn and Francis Loh Kok Wah, eds. *Fragmented Vision: Culture and Politics in Contemporary Malaysia*. North Sydney, Australia: Allen and Unwin.

Crouch, Harold. 1993. "Malaysia: Neither Authoritarian nor Democratic." In Kevin Hewison, Richard Robison, and Gerry Rodan, eds. *Southeast Asia in the 1990s: Authoritarianism, Democracy, and Capitalism*. St. Leonards, Australia: Allen and Unwin.

Crouch, Harold. 1996a. *Government and Society in Malaysia*. Ithaca, NY: Cornell University Press.

Crouch, Harold. 1996b. "Malaysia: Do Elections Make a Difference?" In R. H. Taylor, ed. *The Politics of Elections in Southeast Asia*. Washington, DC: Woodrow Wilson Center Press.

Crowther, William. 1996. "The Moldovan Ethno-National Movement." In Donald L. Dyer, ed. *Studies in Moldovan: The History, Culture, Language and Contemporary Politics of the People of Moldova*. Boulder, CO: East European Monographs.

Crowther, William. 1997. "The Politics of Democratization in Postcommunist Moldova." In Karen Dawisha and Bruce Parrott, eds. *Democratic Changes and Authoritarian Reactions in Russia, Ukraine, Belarus, and Moldova*. New York: Cambridge University Press.

Crowther, William. 2003. "The European Union and Romania: The Politics of Constrained Transition." In Paul Kubicek, ed. *The European Union and Democratization*. London: Routledge.

Crowther, William. 2007. "Moldova, Transnistria and the PCRM's Turn to the West." *East European Quarterly* 61, No. 3: 273–304.

Cruise O'Brien, Donal B. 1971. *The Mourides of Senegal: The Political and Economic Organization of an Islamic Brotherhood*. Oxford, UK: Clarendon Press.

Cruise O'Brien, Donal B. 1975. *Saints and Politicians: Essays in the Organization of a Sene-galese Peasant Society*. Cambridge: Cambridge University Press.

Cruise O'Brien, Donal B. 1978. "Senegal." In John Dunn, ed. *West African States: Failure and Promise*. Cambridge: Cambridge University Press.

Cruz, Arturo J. 1989. *Memoirs of a Counterrevolutionary: Life with the Contras, the Sandinistas, and the CIA*. New York: Doubleday.

Cular, Goran. 2000. "Political Development in Croatia 1990–2000: Fast Transition – Postponed Consolidation." *Politička Misao* 37, No. 5: 30–46.

Cullen, Trevor. 1994. *Malawi: A Turning Point*. Edinburgh, Scotland: The Pentland Press.

Cumings, Bruce. 2007. "Why Didn't North Korea Collapse, and Why Did So Many Influential Americans Think It Would?" Paper prepared for the conference, "Why Didn't Communism Collapse?" Hanover, NH: Dartmouth College. 25–26 May.

Curtis, Grant. 1998. *Cambodia Reborn? The Transition to Democracy and Development*. Washington, DC: The Brookings Institution Press.

Daalder, Ivo H., and Michael E. O'Hanlon. 2000. *Winning Ugly: NATO's War to Save Kosovo*. Washington, DC: The Brookings Institution Press.

Daci, Halic. 1998. *Albanian Military and Regime Changes*. The Netherlands: Centre for European Studies, Harmonie Papers.

Dahl, Robert. 1971. *Polyarchy: Participation and Opposition*. New Haven, CT: Yale University Press.

Dale, Richard. 1978. "The Challenges and Restraints of White Power for a Small African State: Botswana and Its Neighbours."*Africa Today*, 25, no. 3, 7–23.

Dammert, Manuel. 2001. *Fujimori–Montesinos: El Estado Mafioso*. Lima, Peru: El Virrey.

Danielian, Mikael. 1996–1997. "Elections in Armenia: A Funeral for Democracy." *Uncaptive Minds* 9, No. 1–2: 125–31.

Danielyan, Emil. 1998. "Ter-Petrossian Rigged 1996 Election, Fell into 'Depression,' Says Top Ally." *RFE/RL Armenia Report*. 30 December.

Danielyan, Emil. 2004a. "Armenian Ruling Coalition Beset by Renewed Infighting." *Transitions Online*. 10–16 February.

Danielyan, Emil. 2004b. "Armenia: A Dictator in the Making." *Transitions Online*. 24 June.

Danielyan, Emil. 2004c. "The State of Democracy in Armenia." *Transitions Online*. 7 July.

Danielyan, Emil. 2005. "Controversial Arrests Shed Light on Armenia's Murky Security Service." *Eurasia Daily Monitor* 2, No. 199 (October 25).

Danielyan, Emil. 2007a. "Armenian Security Services Suspected of Spying on Opposition Leader." *Eurasia Daily Monitor* 4, No. 85 (May 1).

Danielyan, Emil. 2007b. "West Gives Armenian Leaders a Boost after Disputed Election Win." *Eurasianet*. May 15.

Danielyan, Emil. 2008. "Armenia in Turmoil after Presidential Election Praised by West." *Eurasia Daily Monitor* 5, No. 36.

Danilochkin, Sergei. 2003. "Ukraine: Kuchma Cleared to Run for Third Term." *RFE/RL Reports*. December 30.

Danns, George K. 1982. *Domination and Power in Guyana: A Study of the Police in a Third World Context*. New Brunswick, NJ: Transaction Books.

Danns, George K. 1983. "Decolonization and Militarization in the Caribbean: The Case of Guyana." In Paget Henry and Carl Stone, eds. *The New Caribbean: Decolonization, Democracy, and Development*. Philadelphia, PA: Institute for the Study of Human Issues.

Darden, Keith. 2001. "Graft and Governance: Corruption as an Informal Mechanism of State Control." Paper prepared for the Conference on Informal Institutions and Politics in the Developing World, Weatherhead Center for International Affairs, Cambridge, MA: Harvard University. April 5–6.

Darden, Keith. 2008. "The Integrity of Corrupt States: Graft as an Informal State Institution." *Politics and Society* 36, No. 1: 35–59.

Davidow, Jeffrey. 2004. *The U.S. and Mexico: The Bear and the Porcupine*. Princeton, NJ: Markus Wiener.

Debrah, E. 2001. "Mechanisms for Ensuring Free and Fair 2000 General Elections in Ghana." In Joseph R. A. Ayee, ed. *Deepening Democracy in Ghana: Politics of the 2000 Elections (Vol. 1)*. Accra: Freedom Publications.

De Brito, Luis. 2007. "Rebuilding Frelimo's Hegemony in Mozambique: The Politics of a Presidential Succession." Paper presented at the conference, "The Politics of Nations and Nationalism in Lusophone Africa." Oxford, UK: University of Oxford. December 6.

Decalo, Samuel. 1990. *Coups and Army Rule in Africa: Motivations and Constraints*. New Haven: Yale University Press.

Decalo, Samuel. 1997. "Benin: The First of the New Democracies." In John F. Clark and David E. Gardinier, eds. *Political Reform in Francophone Africa*. Boulder, CO: Westview Press.

Decalo, Samuel. 1998. *The Stable Minority: Civilian Rule in Africa*. Gainesville, FL: Academic Press.

Degregori, Carlos Iván. 2000. *La Década de la Antipolítica: Auge y Huida de Alberto Fujimori y Vladimiro Montesinos*. Lima, Peru: Instituto de Estudios Peruanos.

de Krnjevic-Miskovic, Damjan. 2001. "Serbia's Prudent Revolution." *Journal of Democracy* 12, No. 3: 96–110.

DeLancey, Mark W. 1986. "Cameroon's Foreign Relations." In Michael G. Schatzberg and I. William Zartman, eds. *The Political Economy of Cameroon*. New York: Praeger.

DeLancey, Mark W. 1989. *Cameroon: Dependence and Independence*. Boulder, CO: Westview Press.

Deletant, Dennis. 1995. "The Securitate Legacy in Romania: Who Is in Charge?" *Problems of Post-Communism* 42, No. 6: 23–8.

Deletant, Dennis. 2001a. "The Securitate Legacy in Romania." In Kieran Williams and Dennis Deletant, *Security and Intelligence Services in New Democracies: The Czech Republic, Slovakia, and Romania*. New York: Palgrave. Pp. 159–210.

Deletant, Dennis. 2001b. "The Successors of the Securitate: Old Habits Die Hard." In Kieran Williams and Dennis Deletant, *Security and Intelligence Services in New Democracies: The Czech Republic, Slovakia, and Romania*. New York: Palgrave. Pp. 211–262.

Deletant, Dennis. 2004. "The Security Services Since 1989: Turning over a New Leaf." In Henry Carey, ed. *Romania Since 1989: Politics, Economics, and Society*. Boulder, CO: Lexington Books. Pp. 503–21.

Deletant, Dennis, and Peter Siani-Davies. 1998. "The Romanian Elections of November 1996." *Representation* 35, Nos. 2–3 (Summer): 155–67.

Demetropoulou, Leeda. 2002. "Europe and the Balkans: Membership Aspiration, EU Involvement and Europeanization Capacity in Southeastern Europe." *Southeast European Politics* 3, No. 2–3 (November): 87–106.

Democratic Elections in Ukraine. 1994. *Report on the 1994 Presidential Elections*. Kiev, Ukraine.

Denkabe, Aloysius. 1996. "An Overview of the Non-Governmental Sector in Ghana." In F. K. Drah and Mike Oquaye, eds. *Civil Society in Ghana*. Accra: Friedrich Ebert Stiftung.

Dereta, Miljenko. 1994. "Why Milosevic Won." *Uncaptive Minds* Winter–Spring: 19–26.

Derichs, Claudia. 2004. "Mahathir's Mind Block: Think Tanks and Intellectuals." In Bridget Welsh, ed. *Reflections: The Mahathir Years*. Washington, DC: The Paul H. Nitze School of Advanced International Studies.

Derrick, Jonathan. 1992. "Cameroon: One Party, Many Parties and the State." *Africa Insight* 22, No. 3: 165–78.

De Swaan, Mony, Paola Martorelli, and Juan Molinar Horcasitas. 1998. "Public Financing of Political Parties and Electoral Expenditures in Mexico." In Mónica Serrano, ed. *Governing Mexico: Political Parties and Elections*. London: Institute of Latin American Studies.

Devdariani, Jaba. 2001. "Georgia: CUG Hopelessly Divided: The Dismissal of the Georgian Government Last Week Highlights the Growing Rift between Conservatives and Reformers." *CRS* 104 (6 November).

Devdariani, Jaba. 2002. "Georgia: Stormy Year Breeds Uncertainty." *Transitions Online*. 24 January.

Devdariani, Jaba. 2003. "Georgia: Security at Stake." *Transitions Online*. 9 April.

Devdariani, Jaba. 2004a. "Georgia: The Year of Revolution." *Transitions Online*. 15 April.

Devdariani, Jaba. 2004b. "Georgia's Rose Revolution Grapples with Dilemma: Do Ends Justify Means." *Eurasia Insight*. 26 October.

de Waal, Thomas. 2003. *Black Garden: Armenia and Azerbaijan Through Peace and War*. New York: NYU Press.

de Waal, Thomas. 2005. "Georgia and Its Distant Neighbors." In Bruno Coppieters and Robert Legvold, eds. *Statehood and Security: Georgia after the Rose Revolution*. Cambridge, MA: The MIT Press. Pp. 307–38.

Diamond, Larry. 1992. "Promoting Democracy." *Foreign Policy* 87 (Summer): 25–47.

Diamond, Larry. 1993. "The Globalization of Democracy." In Robert O. Slater, Barry M. Schutz, and Steven R. Dorr, eds. *Global Transformation and the Third World*. Boulder, CO: Lynne Rienner Publishers.

Diamond, Larry. 1995. *Promoting Democracy in the 1990s: Actors and Instruments, Issues and Imperatives*. New York: Carnegie Corporation of New York.

Diamond, Larry. 1999. *Developing Democracy: Toward Consolidation*. Baltimore, MD: The Johns Hopkins University Press.

Diamond, Larry J. 2002. "Thinking about Hybrid Regimes." *Journal of Democracy* 13, No. 2: 21–35.

Diamond, Larry. 2008. *The Spirit of Democracy: The Struggle to Build Free Societies Throughout the World*. New York: Times Books.

Diaw, Aminata, and Mamadou Diouf. 1998. "The Senegalese Opposition and its Quest for Power." In Adebayo O. Olukoshi, ed. *The Politics of Opposition in Contemporary Africa*. Uppsala, Sweden: Nordiska Afrikainstitutet.

Díaz Santana, Juan Bolívar. 1996. *Trauma Electoral*. Santo Domingo, Dominican Republic: MOGRAF.

Dicklitch, Susan. 2002. "Failed Democratic Transition in Cameroon: A Human Rights Explanation." *Human Rights Quarterly* 24: 152–76.

Dickson, Bruce. 1993. "The Lessons of Defeat: The Reorganization of the Kuomintang on Taiwan, 1950–52." *The China Quarterly* 133 (March): 56–84.

Dickson, Bruce. 1996. "The Kuomintang before Democratization: Organizational Change and the Role of Elections." In Hung-mao Tien, ed. *Taiwan's Electoral Politics and Democratic Transition: Riding the Third Wave*. Armonk, NY: M. E. Sharpe.

Dickson, Bruce. 1997. *Democratization in China and Taiwan: The Adaptability of Leninist Parties*. Oxford, UK: Clarendon Press.

Dion, Richard Read. 1997. "Macedonia: Coming in from the Cold." *World Affairs* 160, No. 2: 96–103.

Di Palma, Guiseppe. 1990. *To Craft Democracies*. Berkeley: University of California Press.

Djukic, Slavoljub. 2001. *Milosevic and Markovic: A Lust for Power*. Montreal and Kingston: McGill-Queen's University Press.

Doder, Dusko, and Louis Branson. 1999. *Milosevic: Portrait of a Tyrant*. New York: The Free Press.

Dolidze, Ana. 2007. "Inside Track: Georgia's Path to Authoritarianism." *National Interest Online*. 24 August.

Domínguez, Jorge I. 1993. "The Secrets of Castro's Staying Power." *Foreign Affairs* 72, (Spring): 98–107.

Domínguez, Jorge I., and Rafael Fernández de Castro. 2001. *The United States and Mexico: Between Partnership and Conflict*. New York: Routledge.

Doyle, Michael W. 1995. *UN Peacekeeping in Cambodia: UNTAC's Civil Mandate*. Boulder, CO: Lynne Rienner.

Doyle, Michael W. 1998. "Peacebuilding in Cambodia: The Continuing Quest for Power and Legitimacy." In Frederick Z. Brown and David G. Timberman, eds. *Cambodia and the International Community: The Quest for Peace, Development, and Democracy*. New York: The Asia Society.

Dragaze, Tamara. 1994. "Georgia." In B. Szajkowski, ed. *Political Parties of Eastern Europe, Russia, and the Successor States*. London: Longman.

Dragomir, Marius 2005. "Public TV: Cutting the 'Red Lines.'" *Transitions Online*. 11 October.

Dragović-Soso, Jasna. 2003a. *Saviours of the Nation: Serbia's Intellectual Opposition and the Revival of Nationalism*. Montreal: McGill–Queen's University Press.

Dragović-Soso, Jasna. 2003b. "The Impact of International Intervention on Domestic Political Outcomes: Western Coercive Policies and the Milošević Regime." In Peter Siani-Davies, ed. *International Intervention in the Balkans since 1995*. London: Routledge.

Drake, Paul W. 1998. "The International Causes of Democratization, 1974–1990." In Paul W. Drake and Mathew D. McCubbins, eds. *The Origins of Liberty: Political and Economic Liberalization in the Modern World*. Princeton, NJ: Princeton University Press.

Dresser, Denise. 1996a. "Mexico: The Decline of Dominant-Party Rule." In Jorge I. Domínguez and Abraham F. Lowenthal, eds. *Constructing Democratic Governance: Mexico, Central America, and the Caribbean in the 1990s*. Baltimore, MD: The Johns Hopkins University Press.

Dresser, Denise. 1996b. "Treading Lightly and without a Stick: International Actors and the Promotion of Democracy in Mexico." In Tom Farer, ed. *Beyond Sovereignty: Collectively Defending Democracy in the Americas*. Baltimore, MD: The Johns Hopkins University Press.

Dresser, Denise. 1998. "Post-NAFTA Politics in Mexico: Uneasy, Uncertain, Unpredictable." In Carol Wise, ed. *The Post-NAFTA Political Economy: Mexico and the Western Hemisphere*. University Park: Pennsylvania State University Press.

Dudley, Steven. 2004. "Chronicle of a Coup." *The Progressive* 68, No. 5: 23–8.

Dudwick, Nora. 1997. "Political Transformations in Armenia: Images and Realities." In Karen Dawisha and Bruce Parrott, eds. *Conflict Cleavage and Change in Central Asia and the Caucasus*. Cambridge: Cambridge University Press.

Duffy, Terence. 1995. "Albania: Jumping from the Stalinist Epoch." In Bogdan Goralczyk et al., eds. *In Pursuit of Europe: Transformations of Post-Communist States, 1989–1994*. Warsaw, Poland: Instytut Studiów Politycznych PAN. Pp. 13–25.

Dunlop, John. 1995. *The Rise of Russia and the Fall of the Soviet Empire*. Princeton, NJ: Princeton University Press.

Dunlop, John. 1999. "Sifting through the Rubble of the Yeltsin Years." Washington, DC: Jamestown Foundation Policy Papers.

Dupuy, Alex. 1997. *Haiti in the New World Order: The Limits of the Democratic Revolution*. Boulder, CO: Westview Press.

Dupuy, Alex. 2003. "Who Is Afraid of Democracy in Haiti? A Critical Reflection." *Trinity College Haiti Papers* 7 (June).

Dupuy, Alex. 2007. *The Prophet and Power: Jean Bertrand Aristide, the International Community, and Haiti*. Lanham, MD: Rowman and Littlefield.

Dura, George. 2007. "Moldova." In Adrian Karatnycky, ed. *Nations in Transit*. New York: Freedom House.

Durand, Francisco. 2003. *Riqueza Económica y Pobreza Política: Reflexiones Sobre las Elites del Poder en un País Inestable*. Lima, Peru: Universidad Católica.

Du Toit, Pierre. 1995. *State-Building and Democracy in Southern Africa: Botswana, Zimbabwe, and South Africa*. Washington, DC: U.S. Institute of Peace Press.

Dyczok, Marta. 2000. *Ukraine: Movement Without Change, Change Without Movement*. New York: Routledge.

Dyczok, Marta. 2006. "Was Kuchma's Censorship Effective? Mass Media in Ukraine before 2004." *Europe–Asia Studies* 58, No. 2 (March): 215–38.

Eades, J. S., and Chris Allen. 1996. *Benin*. Oxford, UK: Clio Press.

Easter, Gerald. 1997. "Preference for Presidentialism: Postcommunist Regime Change in Russia and the NIS." *World Politics* 49, No. 2: 184–211.

East European Constitutional Review. 1998. "Constitution Watch: Croatia," 7, No. 2 (Spring). Available at http://www1.law.nyu.edu/eecr/.

East European Constitutional Review. 2002. "Constitution Watch: Yugoslavia," 11, No. 1/2 (Winter/Spring). Available at http://www1.law.nyu.edu/eecr/.

Eckstein, Susan. 2004. "Dollarization and Its Discontents: Remittances and the Remaking of Cuba in the Post-Soviet Era." *Comparative Politics* 36, No. 3 (April): 313–330.

Eckstein, Susan. 2009. *The Immigrant Divide: How Cuban Americans Changed the U.S. and their Homeland*. New York: Routledge.

Edmunds, Timothy. 2007. *Security Sector Reform in Transforming Societies: Croatia, Serbia and Montenegro*. Manchester, UK: Manchester University Press.

Eisenstadt, Todd A. 1999. "Off the Streets and into the Courtrooms: Resolving Postelectoral Conflicts in Mexico." In Andreas Schedler, Larry Diamond, and Marc F. Plattner, eds. *The Self-Restraining State: Power and Accountability in New Democracies*. Boulder, CO: Lynne Rienner Publishers.

Eisenstadt, Todd A. 2003. "Thinking Outside the (Ballot) Box: Informal Electoral Institutions and Mexico's Political Opening." *Latin American Politics and Society* 45: 25–54.

Eisenstadt, Todd A. 2004. *Courting Democracy in Mexico: Party Strategies and Electoral Institutions*. New York: Cambridge University Press.

Ekedahl, Carolyn McGiffert, and Melvin Allan Goodman. 1997. *The Wars of Eduard Shevardnadze*. College Park, PA: Pennsylvania State University Press.

Elbasani, Arolda. 2004. "Albania in Transition: Manipulation or Appropriation of International Norms?" *Southeast European Politics* 5, No. 1: 24–44.

Elbasani, Arolda. 2007. "Exploring the Impact of EU Conditionality upon Democratisation: Cases of Electoral Competition and Civil Service Reforms in Post-Communist Albania." Ph.D. diss., European University Institute, Florence, Italy.

Electoral Institute of Southern Africa (EISA). 2006. "EISA Election Observer Mission Report: Tanzania Presidential National Assembly and Local Government Elections, 14 December 2005." EISA Election Observer Mission Report No. 20. Johannesburg: EISA.

Elizondo, Carlos. 2003. "After the Second of July: Challenges and Opportunities for the Fox Administration." In Joseph S. Tulchin and Andrew D. Selee, eds. *Mexico's Politics and Society in Transition*. Boulder, CO: Lynne Rienner Publishers.

Elklit, Jorgen. 1999. "Electoral Institutional Change and Democratization: You Can Lead a Horse to Water, But You Can't Make It Drink." *Democratization* 6, No. 4: 28–51.

Elklit, Jurgen, and Andrew Reynolds. 2002. "The Impact of Election Administration on the Legitimacy of Emerging Democracies." *Journal of Commonwealth and Comparative Politics* 57: 86–119.

Elklit, Jorgen, and Palle Svensson. 1997. "What Makes Elections Free and Fair?" *Journal of Democracy* 8, No. 3: 32–46.

Ellert, Henrick. 1995. "The Rhodesian Security and Intelligence Community, 1960–1980." In Ngwabi Bhebe and Terence Ranger, eds. *Soldiers in Zimbabwe's Liberation War*. London: James Currey, Ltd.

Ellman, Michael. 2000. "The Russian Economy under El'tsin." *Europe–Asia Studies* 52, No. 8 (December): 1417–32.

Englebert, Pierre. 1996. "Benin: Recent History." In *Africa South of the Sahara 1996*. London: Europa Publications.

Englund, Harri. 2002a. "Introduction: The Culture of Chameleon Politics." In Harri Englund, ed. *A Democracy of Chameleons: Politics and Culture in the New Malawi*. Stockholm: Nordiska Afrikainstitutet.

Englund, Harri. 2002b. "Winning Elections, Losing Legitimacy: Multi-Partyism and the Neopatrimonial State in Malawi." In Michael Cowen and Liisa Laakso, eds. *Multi-Party Elections in Africa*. Oxford, UK: James Currey Ltd.

Enloe, Cynthia H. 1976. "Civilian Control of the Military: Implications in the Plural Societies of Guyana and Malaysia." In Claude F. Welch, ed. *Civilian Control of the Military: Theory and Cases from Developing Countries*. Albany: State University of New York Press.

Enloe, Cynthia. 1980. *Ethnic Soldiers: State Security in a Divided Society*. Harmondsworth, UK: Pelican Books.

Epstein, Rachel A., and Sedelmeier, Ulrich. 2008. "Beyond Conditionality: International Institutions in Postcommunist Europe after Enlargement." *Journal of European Public Policy* 15, No. 6: 795–805.

Erceg, Tena. 2005. "Croatia: Choosing the President." *Transitions Online*. 20 January.

Erikson, Daniel P. 2004. "The Haiti Dilemma." *Brown Journal of World Affairs* 10, No. 2: 285–97.

Erikson, Daniel P. 2005. "Haiti after Aristide: Still on the Brink." *Current History* 104, No. 679. (February): 83–90.

Erikson, Daniel P., and Adam Minson. 2005a. "Haiti: Preparing for Elections." Inter-American Dialogue Conference Report. Washington, DC: Inter-American Dialogue.

Erikson, Daniel P., and Adam Minson. 2005b. "The Caribbean: Democracy Adrift?" *Journal of Democracy* 16, No. 4: 159–71.

Espinal, Rosario. 1987. *Autoritarismo y Democracia en la Politica Dominicana*. San Jose, Costa Rica: CAPEL.

Espinal, Rosario. 1995. "Economic Restructuring, Social Protest, and Democratization in the Dominican Republic." Special issue, *Latin American Perspectives* 22, No. 3: 63–79.

Espinal, Rosario. 1996. "The Dominican Republic: An Ambiguous Democracy." In Jorge I. Domínguez and Abraham F. Lowenthal, eds. *Constructing Democratic Governance: Mexico, Central America, and the Caribbean in the 1990s*. Baltimore, MD: The Johns Hopkins University Press.

Espinal, Rosario. 1998a. "Electoral Observation and Democratization in the Dominican Republic." In Kevin Middlebrook, ed. *Electoral Observation and Democratic Transitions in Latin America*. La Jolla, CA: Center for U.S.–Mexican Studies.

Espinal, Rosario. 1998b. "Business and Politics in the Dominican Republic." In Francisco Durand and Eduardo Silva, eds. *Organized Business, Economic Change, and Democracy in Latin America*. Miami, FL: North–South Center Press.

Espinal, Rosario. 1999. "Conflictos Electorales, Reformas Políticas y Proceso Democrático en la República Dominicana." In Ramonina, Brea, Rosario Espinal, and Fernando Valerio-Holguín, eds. *La Republica Dominicana en el Umbral del Siglo XXI.* Santo Domingo, Dominican Republic: Universidad Catolica Madre y Maestra.

Espinal, Rosario. 2000. "Observing Elections in the Dominican Republic." In Tommie Sue Montgomery, ed. *Peacemaking and Democratization in the Western Hemisphere.* Miami, FL: University of Miami: North–South Center Press.

Espinal, Rosario, and Jonathan Hartlyn. 1998. "Las relaciones entre Estados Unidos y República Dominicana: El tema de la democracia en la Posguerra Fría." In Wilfredo Lozano, ed. *Cambio Político en el Caribe: Escenarios de la Posguerra Fría: Cuba, Haití, y República Dominicana.* Caracas, Venezuela: Editorial Nueva Sociedad.

Espinal, Rosario, and Jonathan Hartlyn. 1999. "The Dominican Republic: The Long and Difficult Struggle for Democracy." In Larry Diamond, Jonathan Hartlyn, Juan J. Linz, and Seymour Martin Lipset, eds. *Democracy in Developing Countries: Latin America* (Second Edition). Boulder, CO: Lynne Rienner.

Ethier, Diane. 2003. "Is Democracy Promotion Effective? Comparing Conditionality and Incentives." *Democratization* 10, No. 1: 99–120.

European Council. 1993. "European Council in Copenhagen 21–22 June 1993: Conclusions of the Presidency." SN 180/1/93 REV. Available at www.ue.edu.int.

European Institute for the Media. 1994. *The 1994 Parliamentary and Presidential Elections in Ukraine.* Dusseldorf, Germany: European Institute for the Media.

European Institute for the Media. 1996. *Final Report: Media and the Russian Presidential Elections.* Dusseldorf, Germany: European Institute for the Media.

European Union Election Observer Mission. 2008a. "Preliminary Statement." Nairobi, Kenya: European Union Election Observer Mission (1 January).

European Union Electoral Observation Mission. 2008b. "Kenya: Final Report, General Elections, 27 December 2007." Brussels: European Union.

Evans, Michael. 1992. "Making an African Army: The Case of Zimbabwe, 1980–87." In Norman Etherington, ed. *Peace, Politics and Violence in the New South Africa.* London: Hans Zell Publishers.

Eyinga, Abel. 1978. "Government by State of Emergency." In Richard Joseph, ed. *Gaullist Africa: Cameroon under Ahmadu Ahidjo.* Enugu, Nigeria: Fourth Dimension Publishers.

Fairbanks, Charles H., Jr. 1995. "The Postcommunist Wars: Armed Forces and Democracy." *Journal of Democracy* 6, No. 4: 18–34.

Fairbanks, Charles H., Jr. 2004. "Georgia's Rose Revolution." *Journal of Democracy* 15, No. 2: 110–24.

Fan, Liang-Shing, and Frank B. Feigert. 1988. "Independents and Independence: Challenges to One-Party Domination in Taiwan." In Kay Lawson and Peter H. Merkl, eds. *When Parties Fail: Emerging Alternative Organizations.* Princeton, NJ: Princeton University Press.

Fane, Daria. 1993. "Moldova: Breaking Loose from Moscow." In Ian Bremmer and Ray Taras, eds. *Nations & Politics in the Post-Soviet Successor States.* New York: Cambridge University Press.

Farer, Tom J. 1988. "Looking at Looking at Nicaragua: The Problematique of Impartiality in Human Rights Inquiries." *Human Rights Quarterly* 10: 141–56.

Farer, Tom. 1993. "Collectively Defending Democracy in a World of Sovereign States: The Western Hemisphere's Prospect." *Human Rights Quarterly* 15: 716–50.

Farer, Tom, ed. 1996a. *Beyond Sovereignty: Collectively Defending Democracy in the Americas.* Baltimore, MD: The Johns Hopkins University Press.

Farer, Tom. 1996b. "Collectively Defending Democracy in the Western Hemisphere: Introduction and Overview." In Tom Farer, ed. *Beyond Sovereignty: Collectively*

Defending Democracy in the Americas. Baltimore, MD: The Johns Hopkins University Press.

Farhi, Farideh. 1990. *States and Urban-Based Revolutions: Iran and Nicaragua*. Urbana: University of Illinois Press.

Fatton, Robert, Jr. 1987. *The Making of a Liberal Democracy: Senegal's Passive Revolution*. Boulder, CO: Lynne Rienner Publishers.

Fatton, Robert, Jr. 2002. *Haiti's Predatory Republic: The Unending Transition to Democracy*. Boulder, CO: Lynne Rienner Publishers.

Fatton, Robert, Jr. 2004. "For Haiti: 200 Years of Mixed Results." *The New York Times*, 4 January: Section 4, 7.

Fauriol, Georges A. 1993. "Inventing Democracy: The Elections of 1990." In Georges Fauriol, ed. *The Haitian Challenge: US Policy Considerations*. Washington, DC: Center for Strategic and International Studies.

Feduta, Aleksandr. 2005. *Lukashenko: Politicheskaia Biografiia*. Moscow: Referendum.

Felch, Jason. 2004. "Have Peru's Press Heroes Gone Too Far?" *Columbia Journalism Review* (July–August): 43–6.

Felker, Greg. 1999. "Malaysia in 1998: A Cornered Tiger Bares Its Claws." *Asian Survey* 39, No. 1: 43–54.

Felker, Greg. 2000. "Malaysia in 1999: Mahathir's Pyrrhic Deliverance." *Asian Survey* 40, No. 1: 49–60.

Ferdinand, Peter, ed. 2000. *The Internet, Democracy, and Democratization*. London: Frank Cass.

Ferguson, James. 1992. *Dominican Republic: Beyond the Lighthouse*. London: Latin America Bureau.

Ferguson, James. 1994. "Presidential Elections: Loser Take All." *NACLA Report on the Americas* 28 (November–December): 10–14.

Ferrero Costa Eduardo. 1993. "Peru's Presidential Coup." *Journal of Democracy* 4, No. 1: 28–40.

Field, Heather. 2001. "Awkward States: EU Enlargement and Slovakia, Croatia, and Serbia." *Perspectives on European Politics and Society*. 1, No. 1: 123–46.

Fields, Karl J. 2002. "KMT, Inc.: Liberalization, Democratization, and the Future of Business in Politics." In Edmund Terence Gomez, ed. *Political Business in East Asia*. London: Routledge.

Filatov, Sergei. 2001. *Sovershenno Nesekretno*. Moscow: Vagrius.

Findlay, Trevor. 1995. *Cambodia: The Legacy and Lessons of UNTAC*. Oxford, UK: Oxford University Press.

Finnegan, William. 1992. *A Complicated War: The Harrowing of Mozambique*. Berkeley: University of California Press.

Fish, M. Steven. 1995. *Democracy from Scratch: Opposition and Regime in the New Russian Revolution*. Princeton, NJ: Princeton University Press.

Fish, M. Steven. 1998. "Mongolia: Democracy without Prerequisites." *Journal of Democracy* 9, No. 3: 127–41.

Fish, M. Steven. 2001a. "Conclusion." In Z. Barany and R. G. Moser, eds. *Russian Politics: Challenges of Democratization*. New York: Cambridge University Press.

Fish, M. Steven. 2001b. "Authoritarianism Despite Elections: Russia in Light of Democratic Theory and Practice." Paper prepared for the 2001 Annual Meeting of the American Political Science Association, San Francisco, CA: 30 August–2 September.

Fish, M. Steven. 2005. *Democracy Derailed in Russia: The Failure of Open Politics*. New York: Cambridge University Press.

Fish, M. Steven. 2006. "Stronger Legislatures, Stronger Democracies." *Journal of Democracy* 17, No. 1: 5–20.

Fish, M. Steven, and Andrej Krickovic. 2003. "Out of the Brown and into the Blue? The Tentative 'Christian-Democratization' of the Croatian Democratic Union." *East European Constitutional Review* 12, No. 2: 104–12.

Fisher, Sharon. 2000a. "Slovakia: A Year of Dramatic Change." In Peter Rutland, ed. *Annual Survey of Eastern Europe and the Former Soviet Union 1998*. New York: EastWest Institute.

Fisher, Sharon. 2000b. "Croatia's EU Odyssey." *Central Europe Review*. 2, No. 19 (May 15). Available at http://www.ce-review.org/00/19/fisher19.html.

Fisher, Sharon. 2006. *Political Change in Post-Communist Slovakia and Croatia: From Nationalist to Europeanist*. New York: Palgrave.

Fitzgerald, David. 2004. "For 118 Million Mexicans: Emigrants and Chicanos in Mexican Politics." In Kevin J. Middlebrook, ed. *Dilemmas of Political Change in Mexico*. London: Institute of Latin American Studies.

Fitzmaurice, John. 1995. "The Slovak Election of September 1994." *Electoral Studies* 14, No. 2 (June): 203–6.

Florini, Ann M., ed. 2000. *The Third Force: The Rise of Transnational Civil Society*. Washington, DC: Carnegie Endowment for International Peace.

Florini, Ann M., and P. J. Simmons. 2000. "What the World Needs Now?" In Ann M. Florini, ed. *The Third Force: The Rise of Transnational Civil Society*. Washington, DC: Carnegie Endowment for International Peace.

Flower, Ken. 1987. *Serving Secretly: An Intelligence Chief on Record. Rhodesia into Zimbabwe, 1964 to 1981*. London: John Murray.

Foeken, D., and T. Dietz. 2000. "Of Ethnicity, Manipulation and Observation: The 1992 and 1997 Elections in Kenya." In Jon Abbink and Gerti Hesseling, eds. *Electoral Observation and Democratization in Africa*. London: MacMillan Press, Ltd.

Fombad, Charles Manga. 1998. "The New Cameroonian Constitutional Council in a Comparative Perspective: Progress or Retrogression?" *Journal of African Law* 42, No. 2: 172–86.

Fombad, Charles Manga. 2002. "The Protection of Freedom of Expression in the Public Service Media in Southern Africa: A Botswana Perspective." *The Modern Law Review* 65, No. 5: 649–75.

Fombad, Charles Manga. 2003. "The Mass Media and Democratization in Africa: Lessons from Cameroon." In John Mukum Mbaku and Julius Omizuanvbo Ihonvbere, eds. *The Transition to Democratic Governance in Africa: The Continuing Struggle*. Westport, CT: Praeger.

Fombad, Charles Manga. 2004. "The Dynamics of Record-Breaking Endemic Corruption and Political Opportunism in Cameroon." In John M. Mbaku and Joseph Takougang, eds. *The Leadership Challenge in Africa: Cameroon under Paul Biya*. Trenton, NJ: Africa World Press.

Fonchingong, Tangie Nsoh. 1998. "Multipartyism and Democratization in Cameroon." *Journal of Third World Studies* XV, No. 2: 119–37.

Foundation for Democratic Process. 2001. *Zambia's 2001 Tripartite Elections*. Lusaka, Zambia.

Fowks, Jacqueline. 2000. *Suma y Resta de la Realidad: Medios de comunicación y elecciones generales 2000 en el Perú*. Lima, Peru: Friedrich Ebert Stiftung.

Fox, Jonathan. 2004. "Assessing Binational Civil Society Coalitions: Lessons from the Mexico–US Experience." In Kevin J. Middlebrook, ed. *Dilemmas of Political Change in Mexico*. London: Institute of Latin American Studies.

Fraser, John M. 2002. "Macedonia: What's the Problem?" *International Journal* 57, No. 3: 349–64.

Frederick, Howard H. 1987. "Electronic Penetration." In Thomas W. Walker, ed. *Reagan versus the Sandinistas: The Undeclared War on Nicaragua.* Boulder, CO: Westview Press.

Freeland, Chrystia. 2000. *Sale of the Century: Russia's Wild Ride from Communism to Capitalism.* New York: Crown Business.

Freire, Maria Raquel. 2003. *Conflict and Security in the Former Soviet Union: The Role of the OSCE.* Surrey, UK: Ashgate.

Frieson, Kate. 1996a. "The Politics of Getting the Vote in Cambodia." In Steve Heder and Judy Ledgerwood, eds. *Propaganda, Politics, and Violence in Cambodia: Democratic Transition under United Nations Peacekeeping.* Armonk, NY: M. E. Sharpe.

Frieson, Kate. 1996b. "The Cambodian Elections of 1993: A Case of Power to the People?" In R. H. Taylor, ed. *The Politics of Elections in Southeast Asia.* Washington, DC: Woodrow Wilson Center Press.

Fru Awason, Nicodemus. 2004. "Autochthonization Politics and the Invention of the Crisis of Citizenship in Cameroon." In John M. Mbaku and Joseph Takougang, eds. *The Leadership Challenge in Africa: Cameroon under Paul Biya.* Trenton, NJ: Africa World Press.

Fukuyama, Francis. 2004. *State-Building: Governance and World Order in the Twenty-First Century.* Ithaca, NY: Cornell University Press.

Fuller, Liz. 1995. "Media: Independent Press in Armenia and Georgia." *Transition,* 6 October.

Fuller, Liz. 1996a. "Armenia: The Fall from Democratic Grace." *Transition,* 15 November.

Fuller, Liz. 1996b. "Media: Georgia's Remotely Controlled Television." *Transition,* 18 October.

Fuller, Liz. 1998a. "Armenia: Political Power Grows out of the Barrel of a Gun." *RFE/RL Caucasus Report.* 12 May. Vol. 1, No. 11.

Fuller, Liz. 1998b. "Coup Attempt in Georgia." *RFE/RL Caucasus Report.* 20 October. Vol. 1, No. 34.

Fuller, Liz. 1998c. "How Serious Is Georgia's Financial Crisis?" *RFE/RL Caucasus Report.* 30 October, Vol. 1, No. 35.

Fuller, Liz. 1998d. "Armenia: Things Fall Apart ... " *RFE/RL Caucasus Report.* 30 October, Vol. 1, No. 35.

Fuller, Liz. 2001a. "Georgia: Papering over the Cracks." *RFE/RL Endnote.* 25 April.

Fuller, Liz. 2001b. "Georgia: Has Zurab Zhvania Overplayed His Hand?" *RFE/RL Caucasus Report.* Vol. 4, No. 31, 10 September.

Fuller, Liz. 2001c. "Has Georgia Reached a Milestone in War on Corruption?" *RFE/RL Caucasus Report.* Vol. 4, No. 41, 13 December.

Fuller, Liz. 2003a. "Armenian Presidential Campaign Kicks Off." *RFE/RL Caucasus Report.* 27 January.

Fuller, Liz. 2003b. "Thousands Protest Armenian Election Falsification." *RFE/RL Caucasus Report.* 24 February. Vol. 7, No. 35.

Fuller, Liz. 2003c. "Armenia: Cold Feet or Steel Nerves?" *RFE/RL Caucasus Report.* 3 March. Vol. 6, No. 9.

Fuller, Liz. 2003d. "Georgia: When Is a Coup Attempt Not a Coup Attempt?" *RFE/RL Caucasus Report.* 7 April. Vol. 6, No. 14.

Fuller, Liz. 2005. "Some Georgian Journalists Feel Less Equal than Others." *RFE/RL Report.* 3 January. Vol. 5, No. 1.

Funston, John. 1999. "Malaysia: A Fateful September." *Southeast Asian Affairs* 1999: 165–84.

Funston, John. 2000. "Election Fervor: Political Contest in Thailand and Malaysia." Trends in Southeast Asia Working Paper. Singapore: Institute of Southeast Asian Studies (September).

Gadzekpo, Audrey. 1997. "The Media and the 1996 Elections." In Kwasi Afriyie Badu and John Larvie, eds. *Elections 96 in Ghana.* Accra: Friedrich Ebert Stiftung/Electoral Commission of Ghana.

Gagnon, V. P. 1994/1995. "Ethnic Nationalism and International Conflict: The Case of Serbia." *International Security* 19, No. 3: 130–66.

Gaidar, Yegor. 1999. *Days of Defeat and Victory.* Seattle: University of Washington Press.

Gallagher, Thomas. 1995. *Romania after Ceausescu.* Edinburgh, Scotland: Edinburgh University Press.

Gallagher, Thomas. 1996. "Ethno-Nationalism: Nationalism and the Romanian Opposition." *Transitions Online.* 12 January. Available at www.tol.org.

Gallagher, Thomas. 2001. "Building Democracy in Romania: Internal Shortcomings and External Neglect." In Jan Zielonka and Alex Pravda, eds. *Democratic Consolidation in Eastern Europe: Volume 2, International and Transnational Factors.* New York: Oxford University Press.

Gallagher, Thomas. 2005. *Theft of a Nation: Romania Since Communism.* London: C. Hurst & Co.

Galvan, Dennis. 2001. "Political Turnover and Social Change in Senegal." *Journal of Democracy* 12, No. 3: 50–62.

Gandhi, Jennifer. 2008. *Political Institutions under Dictatorship.* New York: Cambridge University Press.

Gandhi, Jennifer, and Adam Przeworski. 2007. "Authoritarian Institutions and the Survival of Autocrats." *Comparative Political Studies* 40, No. 11: 1279–301.

Ganev, Vanelin I. 2001. "Bulgaria: The (Ir)relevance of Post-Communist Constitutionalism." In Jan Zielonka, ed. *Democratic Consolidation in Eastern Europe: Institutional Engineering.* New York: Oxford University Press.

Ganev, Vanelin I. 2006. "Bullets, Bribes and State-Building in Bulgaria." *Journal of Democracy* 17, No. 1: 75–89.

García Calderón, Ernesto. 2001. "Peru's Decade of Living Dangerously." *Journal of Democracy* 12, No. 2: 46–58.

Gardinier, David E. 1994. *Historical Dictionary of Gabon.* Second Edition. Metuchen, NJ: The Scarecrow Press.

Gardinier, David E. 1997. "Gabon: Limited Reform and Regime Survival." In John F. Clark and David E. Gardinier, eds. *Political Reform in Francophone Africa.* Boulder, CO: Westview Press.

Gardinier, David E. 2000. "France and Gabon Since 1993: The Reshaping of a Neo-Colonial Relationship." *Journal of Contemporary African Studies* 18, No. 2: 225–42.

Garrido, Luis Javier. 1989. "The Crisis of Presidencialismo." In Wayne A. Cornelius, Judith Gentleman, and Peter H. Smith, eds. *Mexico's Alternative Political Futures.* La Jolla, CA: Center for U.S.–Mexico Studies.

Gashi, Dardan. 1998. "Myth, Wild Capitalism and Democracy in Albania." *Fletcher Forum of World Affairs* 22, No. 1: 29–38.

Gazibo, Mamadou. 2005. "Foreign Aid and Democratization: Benin and Niger Compared." *African Studies Review* 48, No. 3: 67–87.

Geddes, Barbara. 1999. "What Do We Know About Democratization after Twenty Years?" *Annual Review of Political Science* 2: 115–44.

Geisler, Gisela. 1993. "Fair? What Has Fairness Got to Do with It? Vagaries of Election Observation and Democratic Standards." *Journal of Modern African Studies* 31, No. 4: 613–38.

Gellar, Sheldon. 1982. *Senegal: An African Nation Between Islam and the West*. Boulder, CO: Lynne Rienner Publishers.

Gellar, Sheldon. 1995. *Senegal: An African Nation Between Islam and the West* (Second Edition). Boulder, CO: Westview Press.

Gellar, Sheldon. 2005. *Democracy in Senegal: Tocquevillian Analytics in Africa*. New York: Palgrave MacMillan.

Gelman, Vladimir. 2006. "Vozvrashchenie Leviafona? Politika Retsentralizatsii v sovremennoi Rossii." Unpublished manuscript. European University at St. Petersburg, Faculty of Political Sciences and Sociology.

Gelman, Vladimir. 2007. "Politicheskaia oppozitsiia v Rossii: vymiraiushchi vid?" In V. Gelman, ed. *Tretii elektoral'nyi tsikl v Rossii, 2003–2004 gody*. St. Petersburg: European University in St. Petersburg Press.

Gelman, Vladimir. 2008a. "Party Politics in Russia: From Competition to Hierarchy." *Europe–Asia Studies* 60: 6, 913–30.

Gelman, Vladimir. 2008b. "Dynamika subnatsional'nogo avtoritarizma: Rossiia v sravnitel'noi perspektiva." Working paper, European University, St. Petersburg, M-01/08.

General Accounting Office (GAO). 1996. "Haiti: U.S. Assistance for the Electoral Process." U.S. General Accounting Office Report to the Chairman, Committee on International Relations, House of Representatives. Washington, DC: GAO.

Gentleman, Judith, and Voytek Zubek. 1992. "International Integration and Democratic Development: The Cases of Poland and Mexico." *Journal of Interamerican Studies and World Affairs* 34, No. 1: 59–109.

Georgievski, Petre and Svetomir Skaric. 2000. "The Republic of Macedonia." In Henriette Riegler ed. *Transformation Processes in the Yugoslav Successor States between Marginalization an European Integration*. Baden-Baden: Austrian Institute for International Affairs.

GERDDES-Cameroon. 1995. "Financing Political Parties in a Multi-Party Democracy: The Experience of Cameroon." In Kofi Kumado, ed. *Funding Political Parties in West Africa*. Accra: Electoral Commission of Ghana and the Friedrich Ebert Foundation.

Geroski, Branko. 1995. "Media: Waiting for a Second Chance in Macedonia." *Transition*. 6 October.

Gibbons, Elizabeth D. 1999. *Sanctions in Haiti: Human Rights and Democracy under Assault*. Westport, CT: Praeger.

Gilbert, Dennis. 1988. *Sandinistas*. New York: Basil Blackwell.

Giragosian, Richard. 2003. "Armenia: Two Steps Forward, One Step Back." *Transitions Online*. 9 April.

Giragosian, Richard. 2004. "Armenia 2003: Burdened by the Unresolved." *Transitions Online*. 15 April.

Girault, Christian A. 1991. "Society and Politics in Haiti: The Divorce Between the State and the Nation." In Colin Clarke, ed. *Society and Politics in the Caribbean*. Oxford: MacMillan.

Glaurdic, Josip. 2009. "Inside the Serbian War Machine: The Milošević Telephone Intercepts, 1991–1992." *East European Politics and Societies* 23, No. 1: 86–104.

Gledhill, John. 2005. "States of Contention: State-Led Political Violence in Post-Socialist Romania." *East European Politics & Societies* 19, No. 1: 76–104.

Gleditsch, Kristian Skrede. 2002. *All International Politics Is Local: The Diffusion of Conflict, Integration, and Democratization*. Ann Arbor: University of Michigan Press.

Glenny, Misha. 1995. "The Macedonian Question: Still No Answers." *Social Research* 62, No. 1: 143–60.

Gobel, Christian. 2001. "Towards a Consolidated Democracy? Informal and Formal Institutions in Taiwan's Political Process." Paper prepared for the Annual Meetings of the American Political Science Association. San Francisco, CA: August 30–September 2.

Gold, Thomas B. 1986. *State and Society in the Taiwan Miracle*. Armonk, NY: M. E. Sharpe, Inc.

Gold, Thomas B. 1997. "Taiwan: Still Defying the Odds." In Larry Diamond, Marc F. Plattner, Yun-han Chu, and Hung-mao Tien, eds. *Consolidating the Third Wave Democracies: Regional Challenges*. Baltimore, MD: The Johns Hopkins University Press.

Gold, Thomas B. 2000. "The Waning of the Kuomingtang State on Taiwan." In Kjedle Erik Brodsgaard and Susan Young, eds. *State Capacity in East Asia*. Oxford: Oxford University Press.

Goldenberg, Suzanne. 1994. *Pride of Small Nations: The Caucasus and Post-Soviet Disorder*. London: Zed Books.

Goldgeier, James, and Michael McFaul. 2003. *Power and Purpose: U.S. Policy towards Russia after the Cold War*. Washington, DC: The Brookings Institution Press.

Goldman, Marshall I. 2004. "Putin and the Oligarchs." *Foreign Affairs* 83, No. 6: 33–44.

Goldman, Marshall. 2008. *Petrostate: Putin, Power, and the New Russia*. New York: Oxford University Press.

Goldman, Minton. 1999. *Slovakia Since Independence: A Struggle for Democracy*. Westport, CT: Praeger.

Goldman, Stuart D. 2008. "Russia's 2008 Presidential Succession." CRS Report for Congress RL34392.

Goldworthy, David. 1986. "Armies and Politics in Civilian Regimes." In Simon Baynham, ed. *Military Power and Politics in Black Africa*. London: Croom Helm.

Golob, Stephanie R. 1997. "'Making Possible What Is Necessary': Pedro Aspe, the Salinas Team, and the Next Mexican 'Miracle.'" In Jorge I. Domínguez, ed. *Technopols: Freeing Politics and Markets in Latin America in the 1990s*. University Park: Pennsylvania State University Press.

Gomez, Edmund Terence. 1990. *Business in Politics: UMNO's Corporate Investments*. Kuala Lumpur, Malaysia: Forum.

Gomez, Edmund Terence. 1991. *Money Politics in the Barisan Nasional*. Kuala Lumpur, Malaysia: Forum.

Gomez, Edmund Terence. 1995. "The 1995 Malaysian General Elections: A Report and Commentary." Institute for Southeast Asian Studies Occasional Paper No. 93. Singapore: Institute of Southeast Asian Studies.

Gomez, Edmund Terence. 1996. "Electoral Funding of General, State and Party Elections in Malaysia." *Journal of Contemporary Asia* 26, No. 1: 81–99.

Gomez, Edmund Terence. 1998. "Malaysia." In Wolfgang Sachsenroder and Ulrike E. Frings, eds. *Political Party Systems and Democratic Development in East and Southeast Asia*. Aldershot, UK: Ashgate Publishing.

Gomez, Edmund Terence, ed. 2002a. *Political Business in East Asia*. London: Routledge.

Gomez, Edmund Terence. 2002b. "Introduction: Political Business in East Asia." In Edmund Terence Gomez, ed. *Political Business in East Asia*. London: Routledge.

Gomez, Edmund Terence. 2002c. "Political Business in Malaysia: Party Factionalism, Corporate Development, and Economic Crisis." In Edmund Terence Gomez, ed. *Political Business in East Asia*. London: Routledge.

Gomez, Edmund Terence, and K. S. Jomo. 1999. *Malaysia's Political Economy: Politics, Patronage and Profits*. Cambridge: Cambridge University Press.

Gómez Tagle, Silvia. 1993. "Introducción." In Silvia Gómez Tagle, ed. *Elecciones de 1991: La Recuperación Oficial*. Mexico City: García y Valadés.

Gómez Tagle, Silvia. 1994a. "Electoral Violence and Negotiations, 1988–1991." In Mónica Serrano, ed. *Party Politics in 'An Uncommon Democracy': Political Parties and Elections in Mexico*. London: Institute of Latin American Studies.

Gómez Tagle, Silvia. 1994b. *De la Alquimia al Fraude en las Elecciones Mexicanas*. Mexico City: García y Valadés.

Gómez Tagle, Silvia. 2004. "Public Institutions and Electoral Transparency in Mexico." In Kevin J. Middlebrook, ed. *Dilemmas of Political Change in Mexico*. London: Institute of Latin American Studies.

González, Francisco E., and Desmond King. 2004. "The State and Democratization: The United States in Comparative Perspective." *British Journal of Political Science* 34: 193–210.

González, Guadalupe. 2001. "Foreign Policy Strategies in a Globalized World: The Case of Mexico." In Joseph H. Tulchin and Ralph H. Espach, eds. *Latin America in the New International System*. Boulder, CO: Lynne Rienner Publishers.

Good, Kenneth. 1992. "Interpreting the Exceptionality of Botswana." *Journal of Modern African Studies* 30, No. 1: 69–96.

Good, Kenneth. 1996. "Towards Popular Participation in Botswana." *Journal of Modern African Studies* 34, No. 1: 53–78.

Good, Kenneth. 2005. "Resource Dependency and Its Consequences: The Costs of Botswana's Shining Gems." *Journal of Contemporary African Studies* 23, No. 1: 27–49.

Good, Kenneth. 2008. *Diamonds, Dispossession, and Democracy in Botswana*. Auckland Park, South Africa: James Currey.

Good, Kenneth, and Ian Taylor. 2007. "Mounting Repression in Botswana." *The Round Table* 96, No. 390: 275–8.

Good, Kenneth, and Ian Taylor. 2008. "Botswana: A Minimalist Democracy." *Democratization* 15, No. 4: 750–65.

Gordy, Eric. 1999. *The Culture of Power in Serbia: Nationalism and the Destruction of Alternatives*. University Park: Pennsylvania State University Press.

Gordy, Eric. 2000. "Why Milosevic Still?" *Current History* 99, No. 635: 99–103.

Gosse, Van. 1995. "Active Engagement: The Legacy of Central America Solidarity." *NACLA Report on the Americas* 28, No. 5: 22–7.

Gottesman, Evan. 2003. *Cambodia after the Khmer Rouge: Inside the Politics of Nation Building*. New Haven, CT: Yale University Press.

Gould, Jeremy. 2002. "Contesting Democracy: The 1996 Elections in Zambia." In M. Cowen and L. Laakso eds. *Multi-Party Elections in Africa*. Palgrave.

Gould, John A., and Sona Szomolanyi. 2000. "Slovakia: Elite Disunity and Convergence." In J. Higley and G. Lengyel, eds. *Elites after State Socialism: Theories and Analysis*. Lanham, MD: Rowman and Littlefield. Pp. 47–70.

Grabbe, Heather. 2002. "European Union Conditionality and the Acquis Communautaire." *International Political Science Review* 23, No. 3: 249–68.

Grabbe, Heather. 2003. "Challenges of EU Enlargement." In A. Lieven and D. Trenin, eds. *Ambivalent Neighbors: The EU, NATO, and the Price of Membership*. Washington, DC: Carnegie Endowment for International Peace.

Green, Daniel. 1995. "Ghana's 'Adjusted' Democracy." *Review of African Political Economy* 22, No. 66 (December): 577–85.

Green, Daniel. 1998. "Ghana: Structural Adjustment and State (Re)Formation." In Leonardo A. Villalón and Phillip A. Huxtable, eds. *The African State at a Critical Juncture: Between Disintegration and Reconfiguration*. Boulder, CO: Lynne Rienner Publishers.

Greene, Kenneth. 2007. *Why Dominant Parties Lose: Mexico's Democratization in Comparative Perspective.* New York: Cambridge University Press.

Griffith, Ivelaw Lloyd. 1991a. "The Military and the Politics of Change in Guyana." *Journal of Interamerican Studies and World Affairs* 33, No. 2: 141–73.

Griffith, Ivelaw Lloyd. 1991b. "Guyana: The Military and the Politics of Change." In Ivelaw L. Griffith, ed. *Strategy and Security in the Caribbean.* New York: Praeger.

Griffith, Ivelaw Lloyd. 1993. *The Quest for Security in the Caribbean: Problems and Promises in Subordinate States.* Armonk, NY: M. E. Sharpe.

Griffith, Ivelaw Lloyd. 1997a. "Democracy and Human Rights in Guyana." In Ivelaw L. Griffith and Betty N. Sedoc-Dahlberg, eds. *Democracy and Human Rights in the Caribbean.* Boulder, CO: Westview Press.

Griffith, Ivelaw Lloyd. 1997b. "Political Change, Democracy, and Human Rights in Guyana." *Third World Quarterly* 18, No. 2: 267–85.

Grignon, Francois, Marcel Rutten, and Alamin Mazrui. 2001. "Observing and Analyzing the 1997 General Elections: An Introduction." In Marcel Rutten, Alamin Mazrui, and Francois Grignon, eds. *Out for the Count: The 1997 General Elections and Prospects for Democracy in Kenya.* Kampala, Uganda: Fountain Publishers.

Grigorian, Mark. 1997. "Armenia's 1996 Presidential Election Coverage in the Media." *Caucasian Regional Studies* 2, No. 1. Available at www.poli.vub.ac.be/publi/crs/eng/0201–02.htm.

Grigorian, Mark. 2000a. "Armenian Political Upstart Arrested: An Inglorious Protest Meeting in Yerevan Could Mark the End of Arkady Vardanian's Brief Political Career." *CRS* No. 56: 3 November.

Grigorian, Mark. 2000b. "Under Attack in Yerevan." *CRS*, No. 13: 7 January.

Grigoriev, Leonid, and Marsel Salikhov. 2006. "Ukraine – Growth and Gas." *Russia in Global Affairs* 2: April–June.

Grigoryan, Marianna, and Gayane Abrahamyan. 2008. "Deputy Parliamentary Speaker Resigns, Defections to Ter-Petrosian." *Eurasianet.* 22 February.

Grindle, Merilee S. 1996. *Challenging the State: Crisis and Innovation in Latin America and Africa.* New York: Cambridge University Press.

Gros, Jean-Germain. 1995. "The Hard Lessons of Cameroon." *Journal of Democracy* 6, No. 3: 112–27.

Gros, Jean-Germain. 1997. "Haiti's Flagging Transition." *Journal of Democracy* 8, No. 4: 94–109.

Gros, Jean-Germain. 1998a. "Introduction: Understanding Democratization." In Jean-Germain Gros, ed. *Democratization in Late Twentieth-Century Africa: Coping with Uncertainty.* Westport, CT: Greenwood Press.

Gros, Jean-Germain. 1998b. "Leadership and Democratization: The Case of Tanzania." In J. Gros, ed. *Democratization in Late Twentieth-Century Africa: Coping with Uncertainty.* Westport, CT: Greenwood Press. Pp. 98–111.

Gros, Jean-Germain, and Tatah Mentan. 2003. "Elections and Democratization in Cameroon: Problems and Prospects." In Jean-Germain Gros, ed. *Cameroon: Politics and Society in Critical Perspectives.* Lanham, MD: University Press of America.

Grosfoguel, Ramón. 1998. "Geopolítica y migracion caribeña: de la Guerra Fría a la Posguerra Fría." In Wilfredo Lozano, ed. *Cambio Político en el Caribe: Escenarios de la Posguerra Fría: Cuba, Haití, y República Dominicana.* Caracas, Venezuela: Editorial Nueva Sociedad.

Gross, Irena. 1998. "Albania: When Pyramids Collapse." *East European Constitutional Review* 7, No. 1. Available at http://www1.law.nyu.edu/eecr/vol7num1/special/conversation.html.

Grozdanovska, Ljubica. 2007. "Macedonia: Better Luck Next Year." *Transitions Online.* 12 November.

Grubanovic, Sasha. 2004. "Fourth Time Lucky." *Transitions Online.* 28 June.

Grugel, Jean, ed. 1999a. *Democracy without Borders: Transnationalization and Conditionality in New Democracies.* London: Routledge.

Grugel, Jean. 1999b. "Contextualizing Democratization: The Changing Significance of Transnational Factors and Non-State Actors." In Jean Grugel, ed. *Democracy without Borders: Transnationalization and Conditionality in New Democracies.* London: Routledge.

Guan, Lee Hock. 2002. "Malay Dominance and Opposition Politics in Malaysia." *Southeast Asian Affairs* 2002: 177–95.

Guerin, Henriette, Lorenzo Morris, and Pierre Tessier. 1992. *Planning for the 1993 National Elections in Senegal: An Evaluation.* Washington, DC: International Foundation for Electoral Systems.

Gueye, Babacar. 1995. "Regulations on the Funding of Elections in Senegal." In Kofi Kumado, ed. *Funding Political Parties in West Africa.* Accra: Electoral Commission of Ghana/Friedrich Ebert Foundation.

Guo, Jiann-Jong, Shih-Hsin Huang, and Min-Hsiu Chiang. 1998. "Taiwan." In Wolf-gang Sachsenroder and Ulrike E. Frings, eds. *Political Party Systems and Democratic Development in East and Southeast Asia.* Aldershot, UK: Ashgate Publishing.

Guri, Gert. 2005. "The Failure of a Post-Totalitarian State: The Albanian Crisis of 1997." Trenton, NJ: University of Trenton, School of International Studies. Unpublished manuscript.

Gyimah-Boadi, Emmanuel. 1991a. "Tensions in Ghana's Transition to Constitutional Rule." In Kwame A. Ninsin and Francis K. Drah, eds. *Ghana's Transition to Constitutional Rule.* Accra: Ghana University Press.

Gyimah-Boadi, Emmanuel. 1991b. "Notes on Ghana's Current Transition to Constitutional Rule." *Africa Today* 38, No. 4: 5–17.

Gyimah-Boadi, Emmanuel. 1994a. "Associational Life, Civil Society, and Democratization in Ghana." In John W. Harbeson, Donald Rothchild, and Naomi Chazan, eds. *Civil Society and the State in Africa.* Boulder, CO: Lynne Rienner Publishers.

Gyimah-Boadi, Emmanuel. 1994b. "Ghana's Uncertain Political Opening." *Journal of Democracy* 5, No. 2 (April): 75–86.

Gyimah-Boadi, Emmanuel. 1998a. "Institutionalizing Credible Elections in Ghana." In Andreas Schedler, Larry Diamond, and Marc F. Plattner, eds. *The Self-Restraining State: Power and Accountability in New Democracies.* Boulder, CO: Lynne Rienner Publishers.

Gyimah-Boadi, Emmanuel. 1998b. "Managing Electoral Conflicts: Lessons from Ghana." In Timothy D. Sisk and Andrew Reynolds, eds. *Elections and Conflict Management in Africa.* Washington, DC: U.S. Institute of Peace Press.

Gyimah-Boadi, Emmanuel. 1999. "Ghana's Elections: The Challenges Ahead." In Larry Diamond and Marc F. Plattner, eds. *Democratization in Africa.* Baltimore, MD: The Johns Hopkins University Press.

Gyimah-Boadi, Emmanuel. 2001a. "The December 2000 Elections and Prospects for Democratic Consolidation." In Joseph R. A. Ayee, ed. *Deepening Democracy in Ghana: Politics of the 2000 Elections (Vol. 1).* Accra: Freedom Publications.

Gyimah-Boadi, Emmanuel. 2001b. "A Peaceful Turnover in Ghana." *Journal of Democracy* 12, No. 2: 103–17.

Gyimah-Boadi, Emmanuel. 2004a. "Civil Society and Democratic Development." In E. Gyimah-Boadi, ed. *Democratic Reform in Africa: The Quality of Progress.* Boulder, CO: Lynne Rienner Publishers.

Gyimah-Boadi, Emmanuel. 2004b. "Africa: The Quality of Political Reform." In E. Gyimah-Boadi, ed. *Democratic Reform in Africa: The Quality of Progress.* Boulder, CO: Lynne Rienner Publishers.

Haas, Ernst B. 1980. "Why Collaborate? Issue-Linkages and International Regimes." *World Politics* 32: 357–402.

Habasonda, Lee M. 2002. "The Military, Civil Society and Democracy in Zambia." *African Security Review* 11, No. 2: 7–16.

Haggard, Stephan, and Robert R. Kaufman. 1995. *The Political Economy of Democratic Transitions.* Princeton, NJ: Princeton University Press.

Hahn, Jeffrey W. 1996. "Introduction: Analyzing Parliamentary Development in Russia." In Jeffrey Hahn, ed. *Democratization in Russia: The Development of Legislative Institutions.* New York: M. E. Sharpe.

Hakobyan, Anna. 2004a. "Armenia: Authorities Hit Back as Opposition Campaign Mounts." *Transitions Online,* 13 April.

Hakobyan, Anna. 2004b. "Armenia's Opposition: Playing for Power." *Transitions Online.* 30 April.

Hale, Henry. 2004. "The Origins of United Russia and the Putin Presidency: The Role of Contingency in Party-System Development." *Demokratizatsiya: The Journal of Post-Soviet Democratization* 12, No. 2: 169–94.

Hale, Henry. 2005a. "Why Not Parties? Electoral Markets, Party Substitutes, and Stalled Democratization in Russia." *Comparative Politics* 37, No. 2: 147–66.

Hale, Henry. 2005b. "Regime Cycles: Democracy, Autocracy, and Revolution in Post-Soviet Eurasia." *World Politics* 58, No. 1 (October): 133–65.

Hale, Henry. 2006. *Why Not Parties in Russia? Democracy, Federalism, and the State.* New York: Cambridge University Press.

Halperin, Morton H. 1993. "Guaranteeing Democracy." *Foreign Policy* 91 (Summer): 105–22.

Ham, Melinda. 1993. "Zambia: History Repeats Itself." *Africa Report* (May/June): pp. 13–16.

Ham, Melinda, and Mike Hall. 1994. "Malawi: From Tyranny to Tolenance." *Africa Report* 39, No. 6 (November-December): 56–59.

Hanlon, Joe. 2000. "Violence in Mozambique: In Whose Interests?" *Review of African Political Economy* 27, No. 86: 593–7.

Hanlon, Joe. 2002. "Debate Intensifies over Adjustment & Press Freedom in Mozambique." *Review of African Political Economy* 29, No. 91: 113–16.

Hanmer, Lucia, Gerrishon Ikiara, Walter Eberlei, and Carolyn Abong. 2003. "Kenya." *Development Policy Review* 21, No. 2: 179–96.

Hanson, Stephen. E. 2003. "Instrumental Democracy: The End of Ideology and the Decline of Russian Political Parties." In V. Hesli and W. Reisinger, eds. *The 1999–2000 Elections in Russia: Their Impact and Legacy.* New York: Cambridge University Press.

Harbeson, John W. 1998. "Political Crisis and Renewal in Kenya – Prospects for Democratic Consolidation." *Africa Today* 45, No. 2: 161–83.

Harrigan, Jane. 2001. *From Dictatorship to Democracy: Economic Policy in Malawi 1964–2000.* Aldershot, UK: Ashgate Publishing.

Harrington, Joseph, Edward Karns, and Scott Karns. 1995. "American-Romanian Relations, 1989–1994." *East European Quarterly* 29, No. 2: 207–36.

Harris, Erika. 2004. "Europeanization of Slovakia." *Comparative European Politics* 2, No. 2: 185–211.

Harrison, Graham. 1994. "Mozambique: An Unsustainable Democracy." *Review of African Political Economy* 21, No. 61: 429–40.

Harrison, Graham. 1996. "Democracy in Mozambique: The Significance of Multi-Party Elections." *Review of African Political Economy* 23, No. 67: 19–35.

Hartlyn, Jonathan. 1990. "The Dominican Republic's Disputed Elections." *Journal of Democracy* 1, No. 4: 92–103.

Hartlyn, Jonathan. 1993. "The Dominican Republic: Contemporary Problems and Challenges." In Jorge I. Domínguez, Robert A. Pastor, and R. DeLisle Worrell, eds. *Democracy in the Caribbean: Political, Economic, and Social Perspectives*. Baltimore, MD: The Johns Hopkins University Press.

Hartlyn, Jonathan. 1994. "Crisis-Ridden Elections (Again) in the Dominican Republic: Neopatrimonialism, Presidentialism, and Weak Electoral Oversight." *Journal of Interamerican Studies and World Affairs* 36, No. 4: 91–144.

Hartlyn, Jonathan. 1998. *The Struggle for Democratic Politics in the Dominican Republic*. Chapel Hill: University of North Carolina Press.

Hartlyn, Jonathan. 1999. "Transitions from Authoritarianism in Vulnerable States: A Framework and Dominican Case Studies." In Ramonina Brea, Rosario Espinal, and Fernando Valerio-Holguín, eds. *La Republica Dominicana en el Umbral del Siglo XXI*. Santo Domingo, Dominican Republic: Universidad Catolica Madre y Maestra.

Hartlyn, Jonathan, and Jennifer McCoy. 2006. "Observer Paradoxes: How to Assess Electoral Manipulation." In Andreas Schedler, ed. *Electoral Authoritarianism: The Dynamics of Unfree Competition*. Boulder, CO: Lynne Rienner Publishers.

Hassan, Saliha. 2002. "Political Non-Governmental Organizations: Ideals and Realities." In Francis Loh Kik Wah and Khoo Boo Teik, eds. *Democracy in Malaysia: Discourses and Practices*. Richmond, Surrey, UK: Curzon.

Hatchard, John. 1993. *Individual Freedoms and State Security in the African Context: The Case of Zimbabwe*. Harare: Baobab Books.

Haughton, Tim. 2001. "HZDS: The Ideology, Organisation, and Support Base of Slovakia's Most Successful Party." *Europe–Asia Studies* 53, No. 5: 745–69.

Haughton, Tim. 2002. "Vladimõ´r Mečiar and His Role in the 1994–1998 Slovak Coalition Government." *Europe–Asia Studies* 54, No. 2: 1319–1338.

Haughton, Tim. 2003a. "Facilitator and Impeder: The Institutional Framework of Slovak Politics during the Premiership of Vladimir Mečiar." *Slavonic & East European Review* 81, No. 2: 267–90.

Haughton, Tim. 2003b. "'We'll Finish What We've Started': The 2002 Slovak Parliamentary Elections." *Journal of Communist Studies and Transition Politics* 19, No. 4 (December): 65–90.

Haughton, Tim. 2005. *Constraints and Opportunities of Leadership in Post-Communist Europe*. Aldershot, UK: Ashgate Publishing.

Haughton, Tim. 2007. "When Does the EU Make a Difference? Conditionality and the Accession Process in Central and Eastern Europe." *Political Studies Review* 5, No 2: 233–46.

Haughton, Timothy, and Sharon Fisher. 2008. "From the Politics of State-Building to Programmatic Politics: The Post-Federal Experience and the Development of Centre–Right Party Politics in Croatia and Slovakia." *Party Politics* 14, No. 4: 435–54.

Haughton, Tim, and Marek Rybár. 2008. "A Change of Direction: The 2006 Parliamentary Elections and Party Politics in Slovakia." *Journal of Communist Studies and Transition Politics* 24, No. 2: 232–55.

Hay, Lao Mong. 1998. "Building Democracy in Cambodia: Problems and Prospects." In Frederick Z. Brown and David G. Timberman, eds. *Cambodia and the International Community: The Quest for Peace, Development, and Democracy*. New York: The Asia Society.

Haynes, Jeff. 1993. "Sustainable Democracy in Ghana: Problems and Prospects." *Third World Quarterly* 14, No. 3: 451–67.

Haynes, Jeff. 1995. "Ghana: From Personalist to Democratic Rule." In John A. Wiseman, ed. *Democracy and Political Change in Sub-Saharan Africa*. London: Routledge.

Haynes, Jeff. 1999. "The Possibility of Democratic Consolidation in Ghana." *Democratization* 6, No. 1: 105–22.

Healey, Derek T. 1991. "Taiwan's Economic Future: Some Thoughts from a 1990 Vantage Point." In Gary Klintworth, ed. *Modern Taiwan in the 1990s*. Canberra, Australia: Strategic Defense Studies Center.

Heder, Steve. 1995. "Cambodia's Democratic Transition to Neoauthoritarianism." *Current History* 94, No. 596: 425–9.

Heder, Steve. 2005. "Cambodia: Hun Sen's Consolidation: Death or Beginning of Reform?" *Southeast Asian Affairs* 2005: 113–30.

Heder, Steve, and Judy Ledgerwood. 1996. "Politics of Violence: An Introduction." In Steve Heder and Judy Ledgerwood, eds. *Propaganda, Politics, and Violence in Cambodia: Democratic Transition Under United Nations Peacekeeping*. Armonk, NY: M. E. Sharpe.

Heilbrunn, John R. 1993. "Social Origins of National Conferences in Benin and Togo." *Journal of Modern African Studies* 31, No. 2: 277–99.

Heilbrunn, John R. 1997. "Commerce, Politics, and Business Associations in Benin and Togo." *Comparative Politics* 29, No. 4 (July): 473–92.

Heinemann-Gruder, Andreas. 2001. "Germany's Anti-Hitler Coalition in Kosovo." *Mediterranean Quarterly* 12, No. 3: 31–46.

Helly, Damien, and Giorgi Gogia. 2005. "Georgian Security and the Role of the West." In Bruno Coppieters and Robert Legvold, eds. *Statehood and Security: Georgia after the Rose Revolution*. Cambridge, MA: The MIT Press. Pp. 271–306.

Helmke, Gretchen, and Steven Levitsky. 2004. "Informal Institutions and Comparative Politics: A Research Agenda." *Perspectives on Politics* 2, No. 4: 725–40.

Helmke, Gretchen, and Steven Levitsky. 2006. *Informal Institutions and Democracy: Lessons from Latin America*. Baltimore, MD: The Johns Hopkins University Press.

Helsinki Watch. 1993. *Human Rights in Moldova: The Turbulent Dniestr*. New York: Human Rights Watch.

Henderson, Karen. 1999. "Slovakia and the Democratic Criteria for EU Accession." In Karen Henderson, *Back to Europe: Central and Eastern Europe and the European Union*. London: UCL Press.

Henderson, Karen. 2001. "The Path to Democratic Consoidation in the Czech Republic and Slovakia: Divergence or Convergence?" In Geoffrey Pridham and Attila Agh, eds. *Prospects for Democratic Consolidation in East-Central Europe*. Manchester and New York: Manchester University Press.

Henderson, Karen. 2004. "The Slovak Republic: Explaining Defects in Democracy." *Democratization* 11, No. 5 (December): 133–55.

Henderson, Sara. 2002. "Selling Civil Society." *Comparative Political Studies* 35, No. 2: 139–67.

Henderson, Sara L. 2003. *Building Democracy in Contemporary Russia: Western Support for Grassroots Organizations*. Ithaca, NY: Cornell University Press.

Henriksen, Thomas H. 1978. "Marxism and Mozambique." *African Affairs* 77, No. 309 (October): 441–62.

Herbst, Jeffrey. 1990. *State Politics in Zimbabwe*. Berkeley: University of California Press.

Herbst, Jeffrey. 1991a. "The United States and Africa: Issues for the Future." In John W. Harbeson and Donald Rothchild, eds. *Africa in World Politics*. Boulder, CO: Westview Press.

Herbst, Jeffrey. 1991b. "Labor in Ghana under Structural Adjustment: The Politics of Acquiescence." In Donald Rothchild, ed. *Ghana: The Political Economy of Recovery.* Boulder, CO: Lynne Rienner Publishers.

Herbst, Jeffrey. 1993. *The Politics of Reform in Ghana, 1982–1991.* Berkeley: University of California Press.

Herbst, Jeffrey. 1994. "The Dilemmas of Explaining Political Upheaval: Ghana in Comparative Perspective." In Jennifer A. Widner, ed. *Economic Change and Political Liberalization in Sub-Saharan Africa.* Baltimore, MD: The Johns Hopkins University Press.

Herbst, Jeffrey. 2000. *States and Power in Africa: Comparative Lessons in Authority and Control.* Princeton, NJ: Princeton University Press.

Herbst, Jeffrey. 2001. "Political Liberalization in Africa after Ten Years." *Comparative Politics* 33, No. 3: 357–75.

Herbst, Jeffrey. 2007. "Why Were We Wrong about Zimbabwe?" Presentation delivered at the Department of Political Science, University of Toronto. 2 February.

Herrera Zúniga, René. 1994. *Nicaragua, el Derrumbe Negociado.* Mexico City: El Colegio de Mexico.

Hickman, John, and Jonathan Trapp. 1998. "Reporting Romania: A Content Analysis of *The New York Times* Coverage, 1985–1997." *East European Quarterly* 32, No. 3: 395–409.

Higley, John, and Richard Gunther, eds. 1992. *Elites and Democratic Consolidation in Latin America and Southern Europe.* Cambridge: Cambridge University Press.

Higley, John, Tong-yi Huang, and Tse-min Lin. 2001. "Elite Settlement and Democratic Consolidation in Taiwan." Working Papers in Taiwan Series, No. 27. American Political Science Association Conference Group on Taiwan Studies.

Hill, Geoff. 2003. *The Battle for Zimbabwe: The Final Countdown.* Cape Town, South Africa: Zebra Press.

Hill, Ronald J. 2001. "Moldova Votes Backwards: The 2001 Parliamentary Election." *Journal of Communist Studies and Transition Politics* 17, No. 4: 130–9.

Hilley, John. 2001. *Malaysia: Mahathirism, Hegemony and the New Opposition.* London: Zed Books.

Hillion, Christophe. 2005. "The Evolving System of European Union External Relations as Evidenced in the EU Partnership with Russia and Ukraine." Ph.D. diss. Leiden, The Netherlands: Leiden University.

Himbara, David. 1994. *Kenyan Capitalists, the State, and Development.* Boulder, CO: Lynne Rienner Publishers.

Hing, Lo Shiu. 1997. "Liberalization and Democratization in Taiwan: A Class and Functional Perspective." In Anek Loathamatas, ed. *Democratization in Southeast and East Asia.* Singapore: Institute of Southeast Asian Studies.

Hintzen, Percy C. 1989. *The Costs of Regime Survival: Racial Mobilization, Elite Domination and Control of the State in Guyana and Trinidad.* Cambridge: Cambridge University Press.

Hislope, Robert. 1996. "Intra-Ethnic Conflict in Croatia and Serbia: Flanking and the Consequences for Democracy." *East European Quarterly* 30, No. 4: 474–91.

Hislope, Robert. 2004. "Crime and Honor in a Weak State: Paramilitary Forces and Violence in Macedonia." *Problems of Post-Communism* 51, No. 3: 18–26.

Hoel, Jostein L. 2003. "Armenia: Presidential Elections 2003 Report." *Nordem* (September). Available at www.unpan1.un.org/intradoc/groups/public/documents/untc/unpan 014969.mht.

Hoffman, Barak, and Lindsay Robinson. 2009. "Tanzania's Missing Opposition." *Journal of Democracy* 20, No. 4: 123–36.

Hoffman, David. 2003. *The Oligarchs: Wealth and Power in the New Russia*. New York: Public Affairs.

Holbrooke, Richard. 1999. *To End a War*. New York: The Modern Library.

Holm, John D. 1987. "Botswana: A Paternalistic Democracy." *World Affairs* 150, No. 1: 21–30.

Holm, John D. 1993. "Political Culture and Democracy: A Study of Mass Participation in Botswana." In Stephen Stedman, ed. *Botswana: The Political Economy of Democratic Development*. Boulder, CO: Lynne Reiner.

Holm, John D., and Staffan Darnolf. 2000. "Democratizing the Administrative State in Botswana." In Bradshaw York and Stephen N. Ndegwa, eds. *The Uncertain Promise of Southern Africa*. Bloomington: Indiana University Press.

Holm, John D., and Patrick Molutsi, eds. 1990. *Democracy in Botswana*. Athens: Ohio University Press.

Holm, John D., Patrick Molutsi, and Gloria Somolekae. 1996. "The Development of Civil Society in a Democratic State: The Botswana Model." *African Studies Review* 39, No. 2, 43–69.

Holmes, Stephen. 1997. "What Russia Teaches Us Now: How Weak States Threaten Freedom." *American Prospect* 8 (July 1–August 1): 30–39.

Holmes, Stephen. 2002. "Simulations of Power in Putin's Russia." In A. Kuchins, ed. *Russia After the Fall*. Washington, DC: Carnegie Endowment for International Peace.

Holmquest, Frank. 2003. "Kenya's Postelection Euphoria—and Reality." *Current History* 102, No. 664 (May): 200–205.

Holmquist, Frank, and Michael Ford. 1994. "Kenya: State and Civil Society the First Year after the Election." *Africa Today* 41, No. 4: 5–25.

Holmquist, Frank W., Frederick S. Weaver, and Michael D. Ford. 1994. "The Structural Development of Kenya's Political Economy." *African Studies Review* 37, No. 4 (April): 69–105.

Holmquist, Frank, and Michael Ford. 1998. "Kenyan Politics: Toward a Second Transition?" *Africa Today* 45, No. 2 (April–June): 227–58.

Hong, Junhao. 2000. "Democratization in Taiwan and the Liberalization of Taiwan's Media: A Study of Interaction between Media and Politics, their Implications and Problems." Paper presented at the Sixth Annual Conference of the North American Taiwan Studies Association. Cambridge, MA: Harvard University. June 16–19.

Hood, Steven J. 1997. *The Kuomingtang and the Democratization of Taiwan*. Boulder, CO: Westview Press.

Hornsby, Charles. 2001. "Election Day and the Results." In Marcel Rutten, Alamin Mazrui, and Francois Grignon, eds. *Out for the Count: The 1997 General Elections and Prospects for Democracy in Kenya*. Kampala, Uganda: Fountain Publishers.

Horowitz, Donald L. 2006. "Constitutional Courts: A Primer for Decision Makers." *Journal of Democracy* 17, No. 4: 125–37.

Horowitz, Shale. 2005. *From Ethnic Conflict to Stillborn Reform: The Former Soviet Union and Yugoslavia*. College Station: Texas A&M University Press.

Houngnikpo, Mathurin C. 2002. *Determinants of Democratization in Africa: A Comparative Study of Benin and Togo*. Lanham, MD: University Press of America.

Hourn, Kao Kim. 1998. "Cambodia and the International Community: The Road Ahead." In Frederick Z. Brown and David G. Timberman, eds. *Cambodia and the International Community: The Quest for Peace, Development, and Democracy*. New York: The Asia Society.

House-Midamba, Bessie. 1996. "Gender, Democratization, and Associational Life in Kenya." *Africa Today* 32, No. 3 (July–September): 289–305.

Howard, Marc Morje. 2003. *The Weakness of Civil Society in Post-Communist Europe*. New York: Cambridge University Press.

Howard, Marc Morje, and Philip G. Roessler. 2006. "Liberalizing Electoral Outcomes in Competitive Authoritarian Regimes." *American Journal of Political Science* 50, No. 2: 207–25.

Howard, Marc Morje, and Philip G. Roessler. 2009. "Post–Cold War Political Regimes: When Do Elections Matters?" In Staffan I. Lindberg, ed. *Democratization by Elections: A New Mode of Transition*. Baltimore, MD: The Johns Hopkins University Press.

Hoyt, Katherine. 2004. "Parties and Pacts in Contemporary Nicaragua." In David Close and Kalowatie Deonandan, eds. *Undoing Democracy: The Politics of Electoral Caudillismo*. Lanham, MD: Lexington Books.

Huang, Teh-fu. 1996. "Elections and the Evolution of the Kuomintang." In Hung-mao Tien, ed. *Taiwan's Electoral Politics and Democratic Transition: Riding the Third Wave*. Armonk, NY: M. E. Sharpe.

Huber, Evelyne. 1993. "The Future of Democracy in the Caribbean." In Jorge I. Domínguez, Robert A. Pastor, and R. DeLisle Worrell, eds. *Democracy in the Caribbean: Political, Economic, and Social Perspectives*. Baltimore, MD: The Johns Hopkins University Press.

Hufbauer, Gary Clyde, Jeffrey J. Schott, and Kimberly Ann Elliott. 1990. *Economic Sanctions Reconsidered: History and Current Policy*. Washington, DC: Institute for International Economics.

Hughes, Caroline. 1999. "Surveillance and Resistance in the Cambodian Elections: The Prisoners' Dilemma?" *Southeast Asian Affairs* 1999: 92–108.

Hughes, Caroline. 2001. "Cambodia: Democracy or Dictatorship?" *Southeast Asian Affairs* 2001: 113–128.

Hughes, Caroline. 2002. "Parties, Protest and Pluralism in Cambodia." *Democratization* 9, No. 3: 165–86.

Hughes, Caroline. 2003. *The Political Economy of Cambodia's Transition, 1991–2001*. London: RoutledgeCurzon.

Hulterstrom, Karolina. 2004. "In Pursuit of Ethnic Politics: Voters, Parties and Policies in Kenya and Zambia." Ph.D. Diss. Uppsala, Sweden: Department of Political Science, Uppsala University.

Human Rights Watch. 1994. *Restrictions on Freedom of the Press in Romania* 6, No. 10.

Human Rights Watch. 1995. "Haiti: Human Rights after President Aristide's Return." Human Rights Watch Report. Vol. 7, No. 11 (October).

Human Rights Watch. 1997. "Institutional Development of the Haitian National Police." Available at www.hrw.org/reports/1997/haiti/Haiti-03.htm.

Human Rights Watch. 1998. "Zambia: No Model for Democracy: Human Rights Violations," 1 May, A1002, available at: http://www.unhcr.org/refworld/docid/3ae6a7f22 .html.

Human Rights Watch. 1999. "Croatia's Democracy Deficit." Available at www.hrw.org/ legacy/reports/1999/croatia2/Electweb-03.htm.

Human Rights Watch. 2002a. *The Cost of Speech: Violations of Media Freedom in Albania*. Vol. 14, No. 5(D): June.

Human Rights Watch. 2002b. *Playing with Fire: Weapons Proliferation, Political Violence, and Human Rights in Kenya*. New York: Human Rights Watch.

Human Rights Watch. 2003a. "Under a Shadow: Civil and Political Rights in Zimbabwe." Human Rights Watch Briefing Paper (June).

Human Rights Watch. 2003b. "An Imitation of Law: The Use of Administrative Detention in the 2003 Presidential Election in Armenia." Human Rights Watch Briefing Paper, 23 May.

Human Rights Watch. 2003c. *Negotiating the News: Informal Censorship of Ukrainian Television*. New York: Human Rights Watch.

Human Rights Watch. 2004a. "Haiti: Recycled Soldiers and Paramilitaries on the March." Available at www.hrw.org/english/docs/2004/02/27/haiti7677_txt.htm.

Human Rights Watch. 2004b. "Cycle of Repression: Human Rights Violations in Armenia." 4 May.

Human Rights Watch. 2008a. "All Over Again." New York: Human Rights Watch. 18 March.

Human Rights Watch. 2008b. "Bullets for Each of You." New York: Human Rights Watch. 19 June.

Huntington, Samuel P. 1968. *Political Order in Changing Societies*. New Haven, CT: Yale University Press.

Huntington, Samuel. 1970. "Social and Institutional Dynamics of One-Party Systems." In Samuel Huntington and Clement Moore, eds. *Authoritarian Politics in Modern Society: The Dynamics of Established One-Party Systems*. New York: Basic Books.

Huntington, Samuel P. 1989. "The Modest Meaning of Democracy." In Robert Pastor, ed. *Democracy in the Americas: Stopping the Pendulum*. New York: Holmes and Meier.

Huntington, Samuel P. 1991. *The Third Wave*. Norman: University of Oklahoma Press.

Huntington, Samuel, and C. Moore, eds. 1970. *Authoritarian Politics in Modern Society: The Dynamics of Established One-Party Systems*. New York: Basic Books.

Huskey, Eugene. 1999. *Presidential Power in Russia*. Armonk, NY: M. E. Sharpe.

Huskey, Eugene. 2001. "Putin Leadership and the Center-Periphery Struggle: Putin's Administrative Reforms." In Archie Brown and Lilia Shevtsova, eds. *Gorbachev, Yeltsin, and Putin: Political Leadership in Russia's Transition*. Washington, DC: Carnegie Endowment for International Peace. Pp. 113–42.

Hutchful, Eboe. 1997. "Military Policy and Reform in Ghana." *Journal of Modern African Studies* 35, No. 2: 251–78.

Hutchful, Eboe. 2002. "The Fall and Rise of the State in Ghana." In Abdi Ismail Samatar and Ahmed I. Samatar, eds. *The African State: Reconsiderations*. Portsmouth, NH: Heinemann.

Hwang, In-Won. 2003. *Personalized Politics: The Malaysian State Under Mahathir*. Singapore: Institute of Southeast Asian Studies.

Hyde, Susan D., and Nikolay Marinov. 2009. "National Elections across Democracy and Autocracy: Putting the 'Competitive' into Competitive Authoritarianism." Yale University. Unpublished manuscript.

Hyden, Goran. 1999. "Top-Down Democratization in Tanzania." *Journal of Democracy* 10, No. 4 (October): 142–55.

Ichino, Nahomi. 2007. "Thugs and Voters." Harvard University, unpublished manuscript.

Ihonvbere, Julius O. 1996. *Economic Crisis, Civil Society, and Democratization: The Case of Zambia*. Trenton, NJ: Africa World Press.

Ihonvbere, Julius O. 1997. "From Despotism to Democracy: The Rise of Multiparty Politics in Malawi." *Third World Quarterly* 18, No. 2: 225–47.

Ihonvbere, Julius O. 2003a. "A Balance Sheet of Africa's Transition to Democratic Governance." In John Mukum Mbaku and Julius Omozuanvbo Ihonvbere, eds. *The Transition to Democratic Governance in Africa: The Continuing Struggle*. Westport, CT: Praeger.

Ihonvbere, Julius O. 2003b. "Dismantling a Discredited One-Party Regime: Populism and Political Liberalization in Zambia." In Julius O. Ihonvbere and John Mukum Mbaku, eds. *Political Liberalization and Democratization in Africa*. Westport, CT: Praeger.

Ihonvbere, Julius O., John Mukum Mbaku, and Joseph Takougang. 2003. "The Opportunities and Limitations of Opposition Politics in Africa: The SDF and Opposition

Alliances." In John Mukum Mbaku and Julius Omizuanvbo Ihonvbere, eds. *The Transition to Democratic Governance in Africa: The Continuing Struggle*. Westport, CT: Praeger.

Iliffe, John. 1979. *A Modern History of Tanganyika*. Cambridge: Cambridge University Press.

Imholz, Kathleen. 1995. "Can Albania Break the Chain? The 1993–1994 Trials of Former High Communist Officials." *East European Constitutional Review* 4, No. 3: 54–60.

Imholz, Kathleen. 2000. "Albania's Evolving Socialist Party: Some Comments on Post-Communist Party Development and Pluralism." *East European Constitutional Review* 9, No. 3: 82–7.

Imperato, James. 1989. *Mali: A Search for Direction*. Boulder, CO: Westview Press.

Ingle, Clyde R. 1972. "The Ten-House Cell System in Tanzania: A Consideration of an Emerging Village Institution." *Journal of Developing Areas* 6 (January): 211–25.

Inoguchi, Takashi. 2000. "Three Frameworks in Search of a Policy: US Democracy Promotion in Asia-Pacific." In Michael Cox, G. John Ikenberry, and Takashi Inoguchi, eds. *American Democracy Promotion: Impulses, Strategies, and Impacts*. Oxford, UK: Oxford University Press.

International Crisis Group. 2000. "Zimbabwe at the Crossroads." ICG Africa Report No. 22. Harare, Zimbabwe: International Crisis Group.

International Crisis Group. 2005. "Post-Election Zimbabwe: What Next?" ICG Africa Report No. 93 (June 2005). Harare, Zimbabwe: International Crisis Group.

International Foundation for Electoral Systems (IFES). 1994. *Republic of Moldova Parliamentary Elections, February 27, 1994*. Washington, DC: IFES.

Ionescu, Dan. 1990. "The National Salvation Front Starts To Implement Its Program." *Report on Eastern Europe* (2 February): 26–29.

Ionescu, Dan. 1992a. "Romania's Ruling Party Splits." *RFE/RL Research Report* 1, No. 16 (17 April): 8–12.

Ionescu, Dan. 1992b. "Romania Reluctantly Joins Embargo against the Former Republic of Yugoslavia." *RFE/RL Research Report* (26 June): 34–37.

Ionescu, Dan. 1992c. "Another Front for National Salvation." *RFE/RL Research Report* 1, No. 33 (21 August): 17–23.

Ionescu, Dan. 1993. "Romania Signs Association Accord with the EC." *RFE/RL Research Report* 2, No. 10 (5 March): 33–37.

Isaacs, Dan. 1993. "Mozambique: Watching and Waiting." *Africa Report* (July/August): 40–43.

Isaacs, Dan. 1995. "Mozambique: Fulfilling a Dream." *Africa Report* (January/February): 13–21.

Ivanov, Vitali. 2008. *Partiia Putina "Istoriia 'edinoi rossii.'"* Moscow: Olma.

Jackman, Robert W. 1993. *Power without Force: The Political Capacity of Nation-States*. Ann Arbor: The University of Michigan Press.

Jackson, Robert W., and Carl G. Rosberg. 1982. "Why Africa's Weak States Persist: The Empirical and the Juridical in Statehood." *World Politics* 35: 1–24.

Jacoby, Wade. 2004. *The Enlargement of the European Union and NATO: Ordering from the Menu in Central Europe*. New York: Cambridge University Press.

Janos, Andrew. 2000. *East Central Europe in the Modern World: The Politics of the Borderlands from Pre- to Post-Communism*. Stanford, CA: Stanford University Press.

Jarábik, Balázs. 2006. "International Democracy Assistance to Belarus: An Effective Tool?" In Joerg Forbrig, David R. Marples, and Pavol Demes, eds. *Prospects for Democracy in Belarus*. Washington, DC: German Marshall Fund of the United States.

Jasic, Suzana. 2000. "Monitoring the Vote in Croatia." *Journal of Democracy* 11, No. 4: 159–68.

Jean Pierre, Jean. 1994. "The Tenth Department." In James Ridgeway, ed. *The Haiti Files: Decoding the Crisis*. Washington, DC: Essential Books.

Jebuni, Charles D., and Abena D. Oduro. 1998. "Structural Adjustment Program and the Transition to Democracy." In Kwame A. Ninsin, ed. *Ghana: Transition to Democracy*. Dakar, Senegal: CODESRIA.

Jeffrey, Henry B., and Colin Baber. 1986. *Guyana: Politics, Economics and Society: Beyond the Burnham Era*. London: Frances Pinter.

Jeffries, Richard. 1989. "Ghana: The Political Economy of Personal Rule." In Donal B. Cruise O'Brien, John Dunn, and Richard Rathbone, eds. *Contemporary West African States*. Cambridge: Cambridge University Press.

Jeffries, Richard. 1998. "The Ghanaian Elections of 1996: Towards the Consolidation of Democracy?" *African Affairs* 97: 189–208.

Jeldres, Julio A. 1993. "The UN and the Cambodian Transition." *Journal of Democracy* 4, No. 3: 104–16.

Jeldres, Julio A. 1996. "Cambodia's Fading Hopes." *Journal of Democracy* 7, No. 1: 148–57.

Jennar, Raoul M. 1995. *The Cambodian Constitutions (1953–1993)*. Bangkok: White Lotus.

Jennar, Raoul M. 1998. "The 1993 UNTAC Election in the Prospect of the 1998 Cambodian Election." In Kao Kim Hourn and Norbert von Hoffman, eds. *National Elections: Cambodia's Experiences and Expectations*. Phnom Penh: Cambodian Institute for Cooperation and Peace.

Jeshuran, Chandran. 2004. "Malaysian Defense Policy under Mahathir: What Has Changed?" In Bridget Welsh, ed. *Reflections: The Mahathir Years*. Washington, DC: The Paul H. Nitze School of Advanced International Studies.

Jesudason, James V. 1989. *Ethnicity and the Economy: State, Chinese Business and Multinationals in Malaysia*. Singapore: Oxford University Press.

Jesudason, James V. 1995. "Statist Democracy and the Limits to Civil Society in Malaysia." *Journal of Commonwealth and Comparative Politics* 33, No. 3 (November): 335–356.

Jesudason, James V. 1996. "The Syncretic State and the Structuring of Oppositional Politics in Malaysia." In Garry Rodan, ed. *Political Oppositions in Industrializing Asia*. London: Routledge.

Jesudason, James V. 1999. "The Resilience of One-Party Dominance in Malaysia and Singapore." In Hermann Giliomee and Charles Simkins, eds. *The Awkward Embrace: One-Party Domination and Democracy*. Cape Town, South Africa: Tafelberg.

Jiménez, Jacqueline Polanco. 1999. *Los Partidos Políticos en la República Dominicana: Actividad Electoral y Desarrollo Organizativo*. Santo Domingo, Dominican Republic: FLACSO.

Johnson, Alisha M. 2001. "Albania's Relations with the EU: On the Road to Europe?" *Journal of Southern Europe and the Balkans* 3, No. 2: 171–92.

Jomo, Kwame Sundaram. 1996. "Elections' Janus Face: Limitations and Potential in Malaysia." In R. H. Taylor, ed. *The Politics of Elections in Southeast Asia*. Washington, DC: Woodrow Wilson Center Press.

Jomo, Kwame Sundaram, and Ahmad Shabery Cheek. 1992. "Malaysia's Islamic Movements." In Joel S. Kahn and Francis Loh Kok Wah, eds. *Fragmented Vision: Culture and Politics in Contemporary Malaysia*. North Sydney, Australia: Allen and Unwin.

Jones, Stephen F. 1996. "Adventurers or Commanders? Civil Military Relations in Georgia Since Independence." In Constantine Danopoulos and Daniel Zirker, eds. *Civil–Military Relations in the Soviet and Yugoslav Successor States*. Boulder, CO: Westview Press.

Jones, Stephen F. 1997. "Georgia: The Trauma of Statehood." In Ian Bremmer and Ray Taras, eds. *New States, New Politics: Building the Post-Soviet Nations*. Cambridge: Cambridge University Press.

Jones, Stephen F. 1998. "Georgia: Progress amid Privation." *Transitions Online*. 8 January.

Jones, Stephen F. 1999. "Georgia: A Difficult Year." *Transitions Online*. 9 January.

Jones, Stephen F. 2000. "Democracy from Below? Interest Groups in Georgian Society." *Slavic Review* 59, No. 1: 42–73.

Jonyo, Fred. 2002. "Ethnicity in Multiparty Politics." In Ludeki Chweya, ed. *Electoral Politics in Kenya*. Nairobi, Kenya: Claripress.

Joseph, Richard A. 1978a. "Introduction and General Framework." In Richard A. Joseph, ed. *Gaullist Africa: Cameroon under Ahmadu Ahidjo*. Enugu, Nigeria: Fourth Dimension Publishers.

Joseph, Richard A. 1978b. "Epilogue and Conclusion." In Richard A. Joseph, ed. *Gaullist Africa: Cameroon under Ahmadu Ahidjo*. Enugu, Nigeria: Fourth Dimension Publishers.

Joseph, Richard A. 1992. "Zambia: A Model for Democratic Change." *Current History* 91, No. 565: 199–201.

Joseph, Richard A. 1997. "Democratization in Africa after 1989: Comparative and Theoretical Perspectives." *Comparative Politics* 29, No. 3: 363–82.

Joseph, Richard A. 1999a. "The Reconfiguration of Power in Late Twentieth-Century Africa." In Richard Joseph, ed. *State, Conflict, and Democracy in Africa*. Boulder, CO: Lynne Rienner Publishers.

Joseph, Richard A. 1999b. "Africa, 1990–1997: From Abertura to Closure." In Larry Diamond and Marc F. Plattner, eds. *Democratization in Africa*. Baltimore, MD: The Johns Hopkins University Press.

Joseph, Richard A. 2003. "Africa: States in Crisis." *Journal of Democracy* 14, No. 3: 159–70.

Jovanovic, Igor. 2005. "Serbia and the EU: Reforms for Serbia's Own Benefit." *Transitions Online*. 5 December.

Jovanovic, Igor. 2006. "Serbia: A Game Plan for Europe?" *Transitions Online*. 19 July.

Jovanovic, Igor. 2008. "Serbia: Socialists Redux." *Transitions Online*. 7 July.

Jowitt, Ken. 1992. *New World Disorder: The Leninist Extinction*. Berkeley: University of California Press.

Jua, Nantang. 2003. "Problematizing a Transition: The Power Elite, the State, and Transition Politics in Cameroon." In Julius O. Ihonvbere and John K. Mbaku, eds. *Political Liberalization and Democratization in Africa: Lessons from Country Experiences*. Westport, CT: Praeger.

Judah, Tim. 2002. *Kosovo: War and Revenge*. New Haven, CT: Yale University Press.

Justo Duarte, Amaury. 2004. *Partidos Políticos en la Sociedad Dominicana (1844–2004)*. Santo Domingo, Dominican Republic: Editorial Búho.

Kadzamira, Zimani D. 2000. "Management of the Electoral Process during the Second Multi-Party Elections." In Martin Ott, Kings M. Phiri and Nandini Patel, eds. *Malawi's Second Democratic Elections: Process, Problems and Prospects*. Blantyre: Christian Literature Association in Malawi.

Kagan, Robert. 1996. *A Twilight Struggle: American Power and Nicaragua, 1997–1990*. New York: Free Press.

Kagwanja, Peter Mwangi. 2001. "Politics of Marionettes: Extra-legal Violence and the 1997 Elections in Kenya." In Marcel Rutten, Alamin Mazrui, and Francois Grignon, eds. *Out for the Count: The 1997 General Elections and Prospects for Democracy in Kenya*. Kampala, Uganda: Fountain Publishers.

Kahn, Jeffrey. 2002. *Federalism, Democratization, and the Rule of Law in Russia*. New York: Cambridge University Press.

Kaiser, Paul J. 1996. "Structural Adjustment and the Fragile Nation: The Demise of Social Unity in Tanzania." *Journal of Modern African Studies* 34, No. 2 (June): 227–38.

Kalathil, Shanti, and Taylor C. Boas. 2003. *Open Networks, Closed Regimes: The Impact of the Internet on Authoritarian Rule.* Washington, DC: Carnegie Endowment for International Peace.

Kalnyczky, Adele. 1992. "Slovak Television: Back to State Control?" *RFE/RL Research Report* Report 1, No. 45 (13 November): 64–8.

Kanyinga, Karuti. 2003. "Limits of Political Liberalization: Parties and Electoral Politics in Kenya, 1992–2002." In Walter O. Oyugi, Peter Wanyande, and C. Odhiambo Mbai, eds. *The Politics of Transition in Kenya: From KANU to NARC.* Nairobi, Kenya: Heinrich Boll Foundation.

Karapetian, Rita. 2004. "Armenian President Cracks Down: Dozens Are Hurt or Arrested in the Centre of Yerevan as the Armenian Opposition Calls for the Resignation of President Kocharian." *CRS* No. 227, 15 April.

Karatnycky, Adrian. 2001. "Meltdown in Ukaine." *Foreign Affairs* 80, No. 3 (May–June): 73–86.

Karatnycky, Adrian. 2005. "Ukraine's Orange Revolution." *Foreign Affairs* 84, No. 2 (March–April): 35–52.

Karikari, Kwame. 1998. "The Press and the Transition to Multi-Party Democracy in Ghana." In Kwame A. Ninsin, ed. *Ghana: Transition to Democracy.* Dakar, Senegal: CODESRIA.

Karl, Terry Lynn. 1986. "Imposing Consent: Electoralism versus Democratization in El Salvador." In Paul Drake and Eduardo Silva, eds. *Elections and Democratization in Latin America, 1980–85.* La Jolla, CA: Center for Iberian and Latin American Studies.

Karl, Terry Lynn. 1990. "Dilemmas of Democratization in Latin America." *Comparative Politics* 23, No. 1: 1–21.

Karl, Terry Lynn. 1995. "The Hybrid Regimes of Central America." *Journal of Democracy* 6, No. 3: 72–87.

Karl, Terry Lynn, and Philippe C. Schmitter. 1991. "Modes of Transition in Latin America, Southern and Eastern Europe." *International Social Science Journal* (May): 269–84.

Karol, Siarhej. 2006. "The Belarusian Economic Model: A 21st-Century Socialism?" *RFE/RL Reports.* 13 March.

Karume, Shumbana. 2005. "Preelection Political and Constitutional Setting." *Election Update 2005 Tanzania*, No. 1. Available at www.eisa.org.

Karumidze, Zurab, and James V. Wertsch (eds.). 2005. *Enough! The Rose Revolution in the Republic of Georgia 200.* New York: Nova Science Publishers.

Kaskiv, Vladyslav, Iryna Chupryna, and Yevhen Zolotariov. 2007. "It's Time! Pora and the Orange Revolution in Ukraine." In Joerg Forbig and Pavol Demes, eds. *Reclaiming Democracy.* Washington, DC: German Marshall Fund of the United States.

Kaspin, Deborah. 1995. "The Politics of Ethnicity in Malawi's Democratic Transition." *Journal of Modern African Studies* 33, No. 4: 595–620.

Katzikas, Stefanos. 2004. "An Overview of Albania's Foreign Policy-Making in the 1980s." *Slovo* 16, No. 2: 91–106.

Kau, Michael Ying-mao. 1996. "The Power Structure in Taiwan's Political Economy." *Asian Survey* 36, No. 3: 287–305.

Kaufman, Robert R. 1999. "Dominant Party and Opposition Parties in Mexico: From Crisis to Reform to Crisis." In Hermann Giliomee and Charles Simkins, eds. *The Awkward Embrace: One-Party Domination and Democracy.* Cape Town, South Africa: Tafelberg.

Kearns, Ian. 1998. "Croatia: Authoritarianism or Democracy?" *Contemporary Politics* 4, No. 3: 247–58.

Kearns, Ian. 1999. "Western Intervention and the Promotion of Democracy in Serbia." *Political Quarterly* 70, No. 1: 23–31.

Keck, Margaret E., and Kathryn Sikkink. 1998. *Activists Beyond Borders: Advocacy Networks in International Politics*. Ithaca, NY: Cornell University Press.

Kelley, Judith. 2004. "International Actors on the Domestic Scene: Membership Conditionality and Socialization by International Institutions." *International Organization* 58, No. 3: 425–57.

Kennedy, Ryan. 2007. "Moldova: Broadcast Privatization – Reform or Censorship?" *RFE/RL*. 21 February.

Kenney, Charles D. 2003. *Fujimori's Coup and the Breakdown of Democracy in Latin America*. Notre Dame, IN: University of Notre Dame Press.

Keohane, Robert O., and Joseph S. Nye, Jr. 1989. *Power and Interdependence*. Glenview, IL: Scott, Foresman and Company.

Khachatrian, Ruzanna. 2005. "Dashnaks Not Responsible for Referendum Fraud." *RFE/RL Armenia Report*. 22 December.

Khachatrian, Ruzanna. 2006a. "Parliament Fails to Elect New Human Rights Defender." *RFE/RL Armenia Report*. 8 February.

Khachatrian, Ruzanna. 2006b. "Parliament Leaders Condemn 'Illegal' Police Actions Against MP." *RFE/RL Armenia Report*. 2 March.

Khalid, Khadijar. 2004. "Malaysia–Japan Relations under Mahathir: Turning Japanese?" In Bridget Welsh, ed. *Reflections: The Mahathir Years*. Washington, DC: The Paul H. Nitze School of Advanced International Studies.

Kharitonov, Mikhail A. 2003. *Zvezdy I terny Vladimira Egrova*. Minsk: [No Publisher Shown].

Khoo, Boo Teik. 2000. "Black April and Beyond: Reflections on the Future of Barisan Alternatif." *Aliran Monthly* 20, No. 3: 2–6.

Khoo, Kay Jin. 1992. "The Grand Vision: Mahathir and Modernization." In Joel S. Kahn and Francis Loh Kok Wah, eds. *Fragmented Vision: Culture and Politics in Contemporary Malaysia*. North Sydney, Australia: Allen and Unwin.

Khutsidze, Nino. 2004. "Georgia: A Jarring Relationship No More." *Transitions Online*. 21 June.

Kiai, Maina. 1998. "Commentary: A Last Chance for Peaceful Change in Kenya?" *Africa Today* 45, No. 2: 185–92.

Kiat, Liak Teng. 1996. "Malaysia: Mahathir's Last Hurrah?" *Southeast Asian Affairs* 1996: 217–37.

Kibwana, Kivutha. 2002. "Constitution-Making and the Potential for a Democratic Transition in Kenya." In Lawrence Murungu Mute, Wanza Kioko, and Kichamu Akivaga, eds. *Building an Open Society: The Politics of Transition in Kenya*. Nairobi, Kenya: Claripress.

King, Charles. 1994. "Moldova." In B. Szajkowski, ed. *Political Parties of Eastern Europe, Russia, and the Successor States*. London: Longman.

King, Charles. 2000. *The Moldovans: Romania, Russia, and the Politics of Culture*. Palo Alto, CA: Hoover Institution Press.

King, Charles. 2001. "Potemkin Democracy: Four Myths about Post-Soviet Georgia." *National Interest* 64 (Summer): 93–104.

Kinzer, Stephen. 1991. *Blood of Brothers: Life and War in Nicaragua*. New York: Putnam.

Kioko, Wanza. 2002. "The Place of Transitional Justice in Kenya's Impending Political Transition." In Lawrence Murungu Mute, Wanza Kioko, and Kichamu Akivaga, eds. *Building an Open Society: The Politics of Transition in Kenya*. Nairobi, Kenya: Claripress.

Kipiani, Vakhtang. 2005. *Vlada T'my i Temnykiv*. Kiev, Ukraine: Prosvita.

Kirschke, Linda. 2000. "Informal Repression, Zero-Sum Politics and Late Third-Wave Transitions." *Journal of Modern African Studies* 38, No. 3: 383–405.

Klesner, Joseph L. 1994. "Realignment or Dealignment? Consequences of Economic Crisis and Restructuring for the Mexican Party System." In Maria Lorena Cook, Kevin J. Middlebrook, and Juan Molinar Horcasitas, eds. *The Politics of Economic Restructuring: State–Society Relations and Regime Change in Mexico.* San Diego, CA: Center for U.S.–Mexican Studies

Klesner, Joseph L. 2004. "The Structure of the Mexican Electorate: Social, Attitudinal, and Partisan Bases of Vicente Fox's Victory." In Jorge I. Domínguez and Chappell Lawson, eds. *Mexico's Pivotal Democratic Election: Candidates, Voters, and the Presidential Campaign of 2000.* Stanford, CA: Stanford University Press.

Klopp, Jacqueline M. 2001. "'Ethnic Clashes' and Winning Elections: The Case of Kenya's Electoral Despotism." *Canadian Journal of African Studies* 35, No. 3: 473–517.

Knaus, Gerald, and Marcus Cox. 2005. "The Helsinki Moment in Southeastern Europe." *Journal of Democracy* 16, No. 1: 39–53.

Kneen, Peter. 1984. *Soviet Scientists and the State: An Examination of the Social and Political Aspects of Science in the USSR.* Albany, NY: SUNY Press.

Knight, Alan. 1992. "Mexico's Elite Settlement: Conjuncture and Consequences." In John Higley and Richard Gunther, eds. *Elites and Democratic Consolidation in Latin America and Southern Europe.* Cambridge: Cambridge University Press.

Knight, Alan. 1997. "Dealing with the American Political System: An Historical Review 1910–1995." In Rodolfo O. de la Garza and Jesús Velasco, eds. *Bridging the Border: Transforming Mexico–U.S. Relations.* Lanham, MD: Rowman and Littlefield.

Knight, Amy. 1993. "Russian Security Services under Yeltsin." *Post Soviet Affairs* 9, No. 1: 40–65.

Knight, Amy. 1996. *Spies without Cloaks: The KGB's Successors.* Princeton, NJ: Princeton University Press.

Knight, Amy. 2000. "The Enduring Legacy of the KGB in Russian Politics." *Problems of Post-Communism* 47, No. 4: 3–16.

Kofele-Kale, Ndiva. 1986. "Ethnicity, Regionalism, and Political Power: A Post-Mortem of Ahidjo's Cameroon." In Michael G. Schatzberg and I. William Zartman, eds. *The Political Economy of Cameroon.* New York: Praeger.

Komlenovic, Uros. 1997. "Crime and Corruption after Communism: State and Mafia in Yugoslavia." *East European Constitutional Review* 6, No. 4.

Konings, Piet. 2002. "University Students' Revolt, Ethnic Militia, and Violence during Political Liberalization in Cameroon." *African Studies Review* 45, No. 2 (September): 179–204.

Konings, Piet, and Francis B. Nyamnjoh. 1997. "The Anglophone Problem in Cameroon." *Journal of Modern African Studies* 35, No. 2 (June): 207–30.

Konings, Piet, and Francis B. Nyamnjoh. 2003. *Negotiating an Anglophone Identity: A Study of the Politics of Recognition and Representation in Cameroon.* Leiden, The Netherlands: E. J. Brill.

Kopstein, Jeffrey S. 2006. "The Transatlantic Divide over Democracy Promotion." *Washington Quarterly* 29, No. 2: 85–98.

Kopstein, Jeffrey S., and David A. Reilly. 2000. "Geographic Diffusion and the Transformation of the Postcommunist World." *World Politics* 53, No. 1: 1–37.

Korosteleva, Elena. 2006. "The Quality of Democracy in Belarus and Ukraine." In Derek Hutcheson and Elena A. Korosteleva, eds. *The Quality of Democracy in Post-Communist Europe.* London: Routledge.

Korzhakov, Aleksandr. 1997. *Boris El'tsin: Ot rassveta do zakata.* Moscow: Interbuk.

Kostikov, Viacheslav. 1997. *Roman s prezidentom*. Moscow: Vagrius.

Kramer, Jane. 2005. "Painting the Town: How Edi Rama Reinvented Albanian Politics." *The New Yorker*, 27 June.

Kramer, Mark. 1992. "The Armies of the Post-Soviet States." *Current History* 91, No. 567 (October): 327–33.

Krause, Kevin Deegan. 2000. "Accountability and Party Competition in Slovakia and the Czech Republic." Ph.D. Diss. Notre Dame, IL: University of Notre Dame, Department of Government.

Krause, Kevin Deegan. 2003a. "Slovakia's Second Transition." *Journal of Democracy* 14, No. 2: 65–79.

Krause, Kevin Deegan. 2003b. "The Ambivalent Influence of the European Union on Democratization in Slovakia." In Paul Kubicek, ed. *The European Union and Democratization*. London: Routledge.

Krause, Kevin Deegan. 2006. *Elected Affinities: Democracy and Party Competition in Slovakia and the Czech Republic*. Stanford: Stanford University Press.

Krause, Stefan. 1996. "Police: Loyal to the Leaders." *Transition*. 19 April.

Krause, Stefan. 2000. "Macedonia: Surviving a Year of Crisis." *Transitions Online*. 12 January.

Krause, Stefan. 2001. "Macedonia: Another Balancing Act." *Transitions Online*. 8 January.

Krause, Stefan. 2002. "Macedonia: Into the Quagmire." *Transitions Online*. 27 January.

Krause, Stefan. 2003. "Macedonia: Inching Towards Normalization." *Transitions Online*. 4 April.

Krause, Stefan. 2004. "Macedonia: Recovering Lost Ground, Slowly." *Transitions Online*. 15 April.

Kravchuk, Leonid. 2002. *Maemo te, shcho maemo: Spohady i rozdumy*. Kiev, Ukraine: Stolittia.

Krickus, Richard. 1997. *Showdown: The Lithuanian Rebellion and the Breakup of the Soviet Empire*. Washington, DC: Brassey's Publishers.

Krieger, Milton. 1994. "Cameroon's Democratic Crossroads, 1990–4." *Journal of Modern African Studies* 32, No. 4: 605–28.

Kriger, Norma J. 1991. *Zimbabwe's Guerrilla War: Peasant Voices*. Cambridge: Cambridge University Press.

Kriger, Norma. 2000. "Zimbabwe Today: Hope Against Grim Realities." *Review of African Political Economy* 27, No. 85: 443–50.

Kriger, Norma J. 2003a. "Robert Mugabe, Another Too-Long-Serving African Ruler: A Review Essay." *Political Science Quarterly* 118, No. 2: 307–13.

Kriger, Norma. 2003b. "Zimbabwe's War Veterans and the Ruling Party: Continuities in Political Dynamics." In Staffan Darnolf and Liisa Laakso, eds. *Twenty Years of Independence in Zimbabwe: From Liberation to Authoritarianism*. Houndmills, UK: Palgrave Macmillan.

Kriger, Norma J. 2003c. *Guerrilla Veterans in Post-War Zimbabwe: Symbolic and Violent Politics, 1980–1987*. New York: Cambridge University Press.

Krikorian, Robert. 2000. "Armenia 1999: Armenia under Fire." *Transitions Online*. 26 January.

Krushelnycky, Askold. 2002. "Ukraine: Exploring Kuchma's Motives for Moving Toward Parliamentary Democracy." *RFE/RL Report*. 29 August.

Kryshtanovskaia, Olga. 2005. *Anatomiia rossiiskoi elity*. Moscow: Zakharov.

Kryshtanovskaia, Olga. 2008. "The Sovietization of Putin's Russia." Russian Academy of Sciences. Unpublished Manuscript.

Kryshtanovskaya, Olga, and Stephen White. 2003. "Putin's Militocracy." *Post-Soviet Affairs* 19, No. 4: 289–306.

Kryzanek, Michael J., and Howard Wiarda. 1988. *The Politics of External Influence in the Dominican Republic.* New York: Praeger.

Kubicek, Paul. 2000. *Unbroken Ties: The State, Interest Associations, and Corporatism in Post-Soviet Ukraine.* Ann Arbor: University of Michigan Press.

Kudelia, Serhiy. 2008. "Intangible Asset: Society, Elites and the Politics of Constitutional Reform in Ukraine." Ph.D. Diss., Baltimore, MD: Johns Hopkins University, The Paul H. Nitze School of Advanced International Studies (SAIS).

Kudrytski, Alyaksandr. 2005. "Belarus: Alyaksandr vs. Alyaksandr." *Transitions Online.* 10 October.

Kuhn, William S., III, Louis Massicotte, and Bernard Owen. 1992. *Madagascar: A Pre-Election Assessment Report.* Washington, DC: International Foundation for Electoral Systems.

Kulikov, Anatolii. 2002. *Tiazhelie Zvezdy.* Moscow: Voina i Mir.

Kumar, Chetan. 2000. "Transnational Networks and Campaigns for Democracy." In Ann M. Florini, ed. *The Third Force: The Rise of Transnational Civil Society.* Washington, DC: Carnegie Endowment for International Peace.

Kupchinsky, Roman. 2006. "Analysis: Is Ukraine's Richest Man Also Its Future Prime Minister?" *RFE/RL Reports.* March 01.

Kuzio, Taras. 1993. "Coup Talk in Ukraine." *Foreign Report (The Economist).* 9 December.

Kuzio, Taras. 1996. "Kravchuk to Kuchma: The Ukrainian Presidential Elections of 1994." *Journal of Communist Studies and Transition Politics* 12 (June): 117–44.

Kuzio, Taras. 2000. "The Non-Military Security Forces of Ukraine." *The Journal of Slavic Military Studies* 13, No. 4: 29–56

Kuzio, Taras. 2004. "Russians Run Censorship of Ukrainian Media." *Eurasia Daily Monitor* 1, No. 35 (June 20).

Kuzio, Taras. 2005. "Ukraine's Orange Revolution: The Opposition's Road to Success." *Journal of Democracy* 16, No. 2: 117–30.

Kuzio, Taras. 2005c. "Regime Type and Politics in Ukraine under Kuchma." *Communist and Post-Communist Studies* 38, No. 2 (June 2005): 167–90.

Kuzio, Taras. 2006a. "Ukraine Is Not Russia: Comparing Youth Political Activism." *SAIS Review* 26, No. 2: 67–83.

Kuzio, Taras. 2006b. *"Directed Chaos and Non-Violence in Ukraine's Orange Revolution."* Stockholm: Swedish Military Academy.

Kuzio, Taras. 2007. "Time for Yushchenko to Let his Head Rule his Heart." *Business Ukraine.* October 15. Available at www.businessukraine.com.ua.

Kwon, Soyoung. 2003. "State-Building in North Korea: From a 'Self-Reliant' to a 'Military-First' State." *Asian Affairs* 34, No. 3 (November): 286–96.

Laakso, Liisa. 2002a. "When Elections Are Just a Formality: Rural–Urban Dynamics in the Dominant-Party Systems of Zimbabwe." In Michael Cowen and Liisa Laakso, eds. *Multi-Party Elections in Africa.* Oxford, UK: James Currey Ltd.

Laakso, Liisa. 2002b. "The Politics of International Electoral Observation: The Case of Zimbabwe in 2000." *Journal of Modern African Studies* 40, No. 3: 437–64.

Lacayo Oyanguren, Antonio. 2005. *La Difícil Transición Nicaraguense: En el Gobierno con Doña Violeta.* Managua, Nicaragua: Fundación UNO.

Laguerre, Michel S. 1993. *The Military and Society in Haiti.* London: Macmillan.

Laguerre, Michel S. 1997. "The Role of the Diaspora in Haitian Politics." In Robert I. Rotberg, ed. *Haiti Renewed: Political and Economic Prospects.* Washington, DC: The Brookings Institution Press.

Laguerre, Michel S. 1999. "State, Diaspora, and Transnational Politics: Haiti Reconceptualized." *Millennium* 28, No. 3: 633–652.

Lala, Anicia, and Andrea Ostheimer. 2004. "How to Remove the Stains on Mozambique's Democratic Track Record: Challenges for the Democratization Process between 1990 and 2003." *Konrad-Adenauer-Stiftung Occasional Papers.*

Langran, Irene. 2001. "Cambodia in 2000: New Hopes Are Challenged." *Asian Survey* 41, No. 1: 156–63.

Langston, Joy. 2001. "Why Rules Matter: Changes in Candidate Selection in Mexico's PRI, 1988–2000." *Journal of Latin American Studies* 33: 485–511.

Langston, Joy. 2006. "The Birth and Transformation of the Dedazo in Mexico." In Gretchen Helmke and Steven Levitsky, eds. *Informal Institutions and Democracy: Lessons from Latin America*. Baltimore, MD: The Johns Hopkins University Press.

Larmer, Miles, and Alastair Fraser. 2007. "Of Cabbages and King Cobra: Populist Politics and Zambia's 2006 Election." *African Affairs* 106, No. 425: 611–37.

Latin America Bureau. 1984. *Guyana: Fraudulent Revolution*. London: Latin America Bureau.

Latin American Studies Association (LASA). 1984. *The Electoral Process in Nicaragua: Domestic and International Influences: The Report of the LASA Delegation to Observe the Nicaraguan General Election of November 4, 1984*. Pittsburgh, PA: Latin American Studies Association.

Latin American Studies Association (LASA). 1990. *Electoral Democracy under International Pressure: The Report of the LASA Commission to Observe the 1990 Nicaraguan Elections*. Pittsburgh, PA: Latin American Studies Association.

Latin American Studies Association (LASA). 1995. *The 1995 Electoral Process in Peru: A Delegation Report of the Latin American Studies Association*. Miami, FL: University of Miami, North–South Center

Lauth, Hans-Joachim. 2000. "Informal Institutions and Democracy." *Democratization* 7, No. 4: 21–50.

Lawson, Chappell. 2002. *Building the Fourth Estate: Democratization and the Rise of a Free Press in Mexico*. Berkeley: University of California Press.

Lawson, Chappell. 2004a. "Introduction." In Jorge I. Domínguez and Chappell Lawson, eds. *Mexico's Pivotal Democratic Election: Candidates, Voters, and the Presidential Campaign of 2000*. Stanford, CA: Stanford University Press.

Lawson, Chappell. 2004b. "Television Coverage, Vote Choice, and the 2000 Campaign." In Jorge I. Domínguez and Chappell Lawson, eds. *Mexico's Pivotal Democratic Election: Candidates, Voters, and the Presidential Campaign of 2000*. Stanford, CA: Stanford University Press.

Lawson, Chappell. 2004c. "Building the Fourth Estate: Media Opening and Democratization in Mexico." In Kevin J. Middlebrook, ed. *Dilemmas of Political Change in Mexico*. London: Institute of Latin American Studies.

Lawson, Letitia. 1999. "External Democracy Promotion in Africa: Another False Start?" *Commonwealth and Comparative Politics* 37, No. 1: 1–30.

Leao, Ana. 2004. "Weapons in Mozambique: Reducing Availability and Demand." *Institute for Security Studies Monograph*, No. 94 (January). Pretoria, South Africa: Institute for Security Studies.

LeBas, Adrienne. 2006. "Polarization as Craft: Party Formation and State Violence in Zimbabwe." *Comparative Politics* 38, No. 4 (July): 419–38.

LeBor, Adam. 2004. *Milosevic: A Biography*. New Haven, CT: Yale University Press.

Ledgerwood, Judy. 1996. "Patterns of CPP Political Repression and Violence During the UNTAC Period." In Steve Heder and Judy Ledgerwood, eds. *Propaganda, Politics, and Violence in Cambodia: Democratic Transition under United Nations Peace-keeping.* Armonk, NY: M. E. Sharpe.

Lee, Hoong Phun. 1995. *Constitutional Conflict in Contemporary Malaysia.* Singapore: Oxford University Press.

Leff, Carol Skalnik. 1996. "Dysfunctional Democratization? Institutional Conflict in Post-Communist Slovakia." *Problems of Post-Communism* 43, No. 5: 36–50.

Leff, Carol Skalnik. 1997. *The Czech and Slovak Republics: Nation Versus State.* Boulder, CO: Westview Press.

Lehoucq, Fabrice. 2008. "Bolivia's Constitutional Breakdown." *Journal of Democracy* 19, No. 4 (October): 110–24.

Leiken, Robert S. 1990. "Old and New Politics in Managua." *Journal of Democracy* 1, No. 3: 26–38.

Leiken, Robert S. 2003. *Why Nicaragua Vanished: A Story of Reporters and Revolutionaries.* Lanham, MD: Rowman and Littlefield.

Leith, J. Clark. 2005. *Why Botswana Prospered.* Montreal–Kingston: McGill-Queen's University Press.

Leogrande, William M. 1992. "Political Parties and Postrevolutionary Politics in Nicaragua." In Louis W. Goodman, William M. Leogrande, and Johanna Mendelson Forman, eds. *Political Parties and Democracy in Central America.* Boulder, CO: Westview Press.

Le Vine, Victor T. 1986. "Leadership and Regime Changes in Perspective." In Michael G. Schatzberg and I. William Zartman, eds. *The Political Economy of Cameroon.* New York: Praeger.

Le Vine, Victor T. 2004. *Politics in Francophone Africa.* Boulder, CO: Lynne Rienner Publishers.

Levitsky, Steven, and Maxwell Cameron. 2003. "Democracy without Parties? Political Parties and Regime Change in Fujimori's Peru." *Latin American Politics and Society* 45, No. 3: 1–33.

Levitsky, Steven, and María Victoria Murillo. 2009. "Variation in Institutional Strength." *Annual Review of Political Science* 12: 115–33.

Levitsky, Steven, and Lucan A. Way. 2002. "The Rise of Competitive Authoritarianism." *Journal of Democracy* 13, No. 2 (April): 51–65.

Levitsky, Steven, and Lucan A. Way. 2005. "International Linkage and Democratization." *Journal of Democracy* 16, No. 3 (July): 20–34.

Levitsky, Steven, and Lucan A. Way. 2006. "Leverage versus Linkage: Rethinking the International Dimension of Regime Change." *Comparative Politics* 38, No. 4 (July): 379–400.

Levitsky, Steven, and Lucan A. Way. 2010. "Why Democracy Needs a Level Playing Field." *Journal of Democracy* 21, No. 1 (January): 57–68.

Levitz, Philip, and Grigore Pop-Eleches. Forthcoming. "Why No Backsliding? The EU's Impact on Democracy and Governance Before and After Accession." *Comparative Political Studies.*

Levy, Patricia. 1998. *Belarus.* Singapore: Marshall Cavendish.

Li, Chien Pin. 1993. "The Effectiveness of Sanction Linkages: Issues and Actors." *International Studies Quarterly* 37, No. 3: 349–70.

Li, He. 2004. *From Revolution to Reform: A Comparative Study of China and Mexico.* Lanham, MD: University Press of America.

Libaridian, Gerard J. 1999. *The Challenge of Statehood: Armenian Political Thinking Since Independence*. Watertown, MA: Blue Crane Books.

Lim, Honh Hai. 2002. "Public Administration: The Effects of Executive Dominance." In Francis Loh Kik Wah and Khoo Boo Teik, eds. *Democracy in Malaysia: Discourses and Practices*. Richmond, Surrey, UK: Curzon.

Lindberg, Staffan I. 2006a. "The Surprising Significance of African Elections." *Journal of Democracy* 17, No. 1: 139–51.

Lindberg, Staffan I. 2006b. *Democracy and Elections in Africa*. Baltimore, MD: The Johns Hopkins University Press.

Lindberg, Staffan I. 2006c. "Tragic Protest: When Do Opposition Parties Boycott Elections?" In Andreas Schedler, ed. *Electoral Authoritarianism: The Dynamics of Unfree Competition*. Boulder, CO: Lynne Rienner Publishers.

Lindberg, Staffan I., ed. 2009a. "Introduction: Democratization by Elections: A New Mode of Democratic Transition?" In Staffan I. Lindberg, ed. *Democratization by Elections: A New Mode of Transition*. Baltimore, MD: The Johns Hopkins University Press.

Lindberg, Staffan I., ed. 2009b. "The Power of Elections in Africa Revisited." In Staffan I. Lindberg, ed. *Democratization by Elections: A New Mode of Transition*. Baltimore, MD: The Johns Hopkins University Press.

Linden, Ronald H. 1992. "After the Revolution: A Foreign Policy of Bounded Change." In Daniel Nelson, ed. *Romania After Tyranny*. Boulder, CO: Westview Press.

Linden, Ronald H. 2002. *Norms and Nannies: The Impact of Organizations on the Central and East European States*. Lanham, MD: Rowman and Littlefield.

Linden, Ronald. 2008. "EU Accession and the Role of International Actors." In Sharon Wolchik and Jane Curry, eds. *Central and East European Politics: From Communism to Democracy*. Lanham, MD: Rowman and Littlefield.

Linden, Ronald H., and Lisa M. Pohlman. 2003. "Now You See It, Now You Don't: Anti-EU Politics in Central and Southeast Europe." *European Integration* 54, No. 4: 311–34.

Linfield, Michael. 1991. "Human Rights." In Thomas Walker, ed. *Revolution and Counterrevolution in Nicaragua*. Boulder, CO: Westview Press.

Linz, Juan J. 1990. "The Perils of Presidentialism." *Journal of Democracy* 1, No. 1: 51–69.

Linz, Juan J. 2000. *Totalitarian and Authoritarian Regimes*. Boulder, CO: Lynne Rienner Publishers.

Linz, Juan J., and Alfred Stepan. 1996. *Problems of Democratic Transition and Consolidation: Southern Europe, South America, and Post-Communist Europe*. Baltimore, MD: The Johns Hopkins University Press.

Linz, Juan J., and Arturo Valenzuela, eds. 1994. *The Failure of Presidential Democracy*. Baltimore, MD: The Johns Hopkins University Press.

Liotta, P. H., and Cindy Jeb. 2002. "Macedonia: The Beginning of the End or End of the Beginning?" *Parameters* (Spring): 96–111.

Liow, Joseph. 1999. "Crisis, Choice and Change: Malaysian Electoral Politics at the End of the 20th Century." *Asian Journal of Political Science* 7, No. 2: 45–73.

Lipman, Masha, and Michael McFaul. 2001. "'Managed Democracy' in Russia: Putin and the Press." *The Harvard International Journal of Press/Politics* 6, No. 3: 116–27.

Lippman, Hal, and Richard Blue. 1999. "Democracy and Governance and Cross-Sectoral Linkages: Madagascar." US AID Center for Development Information and Evaluation Working Paper (October). Washington, DC:, Center for Development Information and Evaluation: U.S. Agency for International Development.

Lipset, Seymour Martin. 1959/1981. *Political Man: The Social Bases of Politics*. Baltimore, MD: The Johns Hopkins University Press.

Liu, I-chou. 1999. "The Development of the Opposition." In Steve Tsang and Hung-mao Tien, eds. *Democratization in Taiwan: Implications for China*. London: Macmillan.

Lizée, Pierre P. 1996. "Cambodia in 1995: From Hope to Despair?" *Asian Survey* 36, No. 1 (January): 83–88.

Lizée, Pierre P. 1999. "Testing the Limits of Change: Cambodia's Politics after the July Elections." *Southeast Asian Affairs* 1999: 79–91.

Lloyd, Robert. 1995. "Mozambique: The Terror of War, The Tensions of Peace." *Current History*. April: 152–55.

Loaeza, Soledad. 1994. "Political Liberalization and Uncertainty in Mexico." In Maria Lorena Cook, Kevin J. Middlebrook, and Juan Molinar Horcasitas, eds. *The Politics of Economic Restructuring: State–Society Relations and Regime Change in Mexico*. San Diego, CA: Center for U.S.–Mexican Studies.

Loaeza, Soledad. 1999. *El Partido Acción Nacional: La Larga Marcha, 1939–1994: Oposición Leal y Partido de Protesta*. Mexico City: Fondo de Cultura Económica.

Loaeza, Soledad. 2000. "Uncertainty in Mexico's Protracted Transition: The National Action Party and Its Aversion to Risk." *Democratization* 7, No. 3: 93–116.

Loayza Galván, Francisco. 1998. *Montesinos: El Rostro Oscuro del Poder en el Perú* (Expanded Edition) Lima, Peru: Francisco Loayza.

Lobjakas, Ahto. 2009. "The EU's Invisible 'Schengen Wall.'" *RFE/RL Report*, 13 April.

Lodge, Tom. 1998. "The Southern African Post-Colonial State." *Journal of Commonwealth and Comparative Politics* 36, No. 1: 20–47.

Lodge, Tom, Denis Kadima, and David Pottie. 2002. "Mozambique." In Tom Lodge, Denis Kadima, and David Pottie, eds. *Compendium of Elections in Southern Africa*. Johannesburg: Electoral Institute of Southern Africa.

Lohmann, Henning. 1997. "NGOs in the Transition Towards Democracy." In Manfred Glagow, Henning Lohmann, Sibylle Nickolmann, Kirsten Paul, and Sabine Paul, eds. *Non-Governmental Organizations in Malawi: Their Contribution to Development and Democratization*. New Brunswick, NJ: Transaction Publishers.

Longo, Matthew. 2006. "The HDZ's Embattled Mandate: Divergent Leadership, Divided Electorate, 2003–2006." *Problems of Post-Communism* 53, No. 3: 36–43.

López, Sinesio. 2001. "Perú 2000–01: La transición democrática y el gobierno de transición." In *Las Tareas de la Transición Democrática*. Lima, Peru: Comisión Andina de Juristas.

López-Pintor, Rafael. 1998. "Nicaragua's Measured Move to Democracy." In Krishna Kumar, ed. *Postconflict Elections, Democratization, and International Assistance*. Boulder, CO: Lynne Rienner Publishers.

Lowenthal, Abraham F. 1972. *The Dominican Intervention*. Cambridge, MA: Harvard University Press.

Lowenthal, Abraham F. 1990. *Partners in Conflict: The United States and Latin America in the 1990s*. Baltimore, MD: The Johns Hopkins University Press.

Lowenthal, Abraham F., ed. 1991. *Exporting Democracy: The United States and Latin America: Themes and Issues*. Baltimore, MD: The Johns Hopkins University Press.

Lowenthal, Abraham F. 1999. "United States–Latin American Relations at the Century's Turn: Managing the 'Intermestic' Agenda." In Albert Fishlow and James Jones, eds. *The United States and the Americas: A Twenty-First Century View*. New York: W.W. Norton and Company.

Lowenthal, Abraham F., and Gregory F. Trevorton, eds. 1994. *Latin America in a New World*. Boulder, CO: Westview Press.

Loza, Tihomir. 2008. "Serbia: Back in the Saddle, Uneasily." *Transitions Online*, 5 February. Available at www.tol.org.

Lozano, Wilfredo. 1998a. "Transiciones pos-autoritarias, cambio social y sistema politico en República Dominicana: 1961–1996." In Wilfredo Lozano, ed. *Cambio Político en el Caribe: Escenarios de la Posguerra Fría: Cuba, Haití, y República Dominicana.* Caracas, Venezuela: Editorial Nueva Sociedad.

Lozano, Wilfredo. 1998b. "Balance crítico: Seguridad, autoritarismo y democracia en al Caribe de la Posguerra Fría (apuntes para una conclusion futura)." In Wilfredo Lozano, ed. *Cambio Político en el Caribe: Escenarios de la Posguerra Fría: Cuba, Haití, y República Dominicana.* Caracas, Venezuela: Editorial Nueva Sociedad.

Lozano, Wilfredo. 2002a. *Después de los Caudillos: Ensayos Sobre Política y Sociedad en la República Dominicana Contemporánea.* Santo Domingo, Dominican Republic: Ediciones Librería La Trinitaria.

Lozano, Wilfredo. 2002b. "Los Militares y la Política en República Dominicana: De la Muerte de Trujillo al fin del Siglo XX." In Lilian Bobea, ed. *Soldados y Ciudadanos en el Caribe.* Santo Domingo, Dominican Republic: FLACSO.

Luckham, Robin. 1996a. "Faustian Bargains: Democratic Control over Military and Security Establishments." In Robin Luckham and Gordon White, eds. *Democratization in the South: The Jagged Wave.* Manchester, UK: Manchester University Press.

Luckham, Robin. 1996b. "Democracy and the Military: An Epitaph for Frankenstein's Monster?" *Democratization* 3, No. 2: 1–16.

Luckham, Robin. 1996c. "Crafting Democratic Control over the Military: A Comparative Analysis of South Korea, Chile, and Ghana." *Democratization* 3, No. 3 (Autumn): 215–45.

Luckham, Robin. 1998. "Transition to Democracy and Control Over Ghana's Military and Security Establishments." In Kwame A. Ninsin, ed. *Ghana: Transition to Democracy.* Dakar: CODESRIA

Luebbert, Gregory. 1991. *Liberalism, Fascism, or Social Democracy.* New York: Oxford University Press.

Lujambio, Alonso. 2001. "Democratization through Federalism? The National Action Party Strategy, 1939–2000." In Kevin Middlebrook, ed. *Party Politics and the Struggle for Democracy in Mexico: National and State-Level Analyses of the Partido Acción Nacional.* La Jolla, CA: Center for U.S.–Mexican Studies.

Lukashuk, Alexander. 1998. "Yesterday as Tomorrow: Why It Works in Belarus." *East European Constitutional Review* 7, No. 3.

Lust-Okar, Ellen. 2007. *Structuring Conflict in the Arab World: Incumbents, Opponents, and Institutions.* New York: Cambridge University Press.

Lwanda, John Lloyd. 1993. *Kamuzu Banda of Malawi: A Study in Promise, Power and Paralysis.* Glasgow, Scotland: Dudu Nsomba Publications.

Lwanda, John Lloyd. 1996. *Promises, Power, Politics and Poverty: Democratic Transition in Malawi.* Glasgow, Scotland: Dudu Nsomba Publications.

Lynch, Dov. 2006. "A European Strategy Towards Belarus: Becoming 'Real.'" In Joerg Forbrig, David R. Marples, and Pavol Demes, eds. *Prospects for Democracy in Belarus.* Washington, DC: German Marshall Fund of the United States.

Lyon, James. 1996. "Yugoslavia's Hyperinflation, 1993–1994: A Social History." *East European Politics and Societies* 10, no. 2: 293–327.

Lyons, Terrence. 1999. "Ghana's Elections: A Major Step Forward." In Larry Diamond and Marc F. Plattner. *Democratization in Africa.* Baltimore, MD: The Johns Hopkins University Press.

MacBruce, James. 1992. "Domestic and Regional Security." In Simon Baynham, ed. *Zimbabwe in Transition.* Stockholm: Almquist and Wiskell International.

Macgregor, Douglas A. 2001. "The Balkan Limits to Power and Principle." *Orbis* 45, No. 1: 93–101.

MacMillan, John, and Pablo Zoido. 2004. "How to Subvert Democracy: Montesinos in Peru." *CESIFO Working Paper, Category 1: Public Finance*. No. 1173 (April).

Magaloni, Beatriz. 2005. "The Demise of Mexico's One-Party Dominant Regime: Elite Choices and the Masses in the Establishment of Democracy." In Frances Hagopian and Scott P. Mainwaring, eds. *The Third Wave of Democratization in Latin America: Advances and Setbacks*. New York: Cambridge University Press.

Magaloni, Beatriz. 2006. *Voting for Autocracy: Hegemonic Party Survival and its Demise in Mexico*. New York: Cambridge University Press.

Magaloni, Beatriz. 2008. "Credible Power Sharing and the Longevity of Authoritarian Rule." *Comparative Political Studies* 41, Nos. 4–5: 715–41.

Magaloni, Beatriz, and Alejandro Poiré. 2004. "The Issues, the Vote, and the Mandate for Change." In Jorge I. Domínguez and Chappell Lawson, eds. *Mexico's Pivotal Democratic Election: Candidates, Voters, and the Presidential Campaign of 2000*. Stanford, CA: Stanford University Press.

Magnusson, Bruce A. 1999. "Testing Democracy in Benin: Experiments in Institutional Reform." In Richard Joseph, ed. *State, Conflict, and Democracy in Africa*. Boulder, CO: Lynne Rienner Publishers.

Magnusson, Bruce A. 2001. "Democratization and Domestic Insecurity: Navigating the Transition in Benin." *Comparative Politics* 33, No. 2 (January): 211–30.

Magnusson, Bruce A. 2005. "Democratic Legitimacy in Benin: Institutions and Identity in a Regional Context." In Leonardo A. Villalón and Peter VonDoepp, eds. *The Fate of Africa's Democratic Experiments: Elites and Institutions*. Bloomington: Indiana University Press.

Magnusson, Bruce A. and John F. Clark. "Understanding Democratic Survival and Democratic Failure in Africa: Insights from Divergent Democratic Experiments in Benin and Congo (Brazzaville)." *Comparative Studies in Society and History* 47, No. 3 (July): 552–582.

Maguire, Robert. 2002. "Haiti's Political Gridlock." *Journal of Haitian Studies* 8, No. 2: 30–42.

Maguire, Robert E. 2003. "US Policy Toward Haiti: Engagement or Estrangement?" Washington, DC: Trinity College Haiti Papers No. 8 (November).

Maguire, Robert. 2004. "Statement before the Subcommittee on the Western Hemisphere." Hearing on Haiti, Committee on Foreign Relations, U.S. Senate. 10 March.

Maingot, Anthony P. 1992. "Haiti and Aristide: The Legacy of History." *Current History* 91, No. 562: 65–9.

Maingot, Anthony P. 1994. "Grasping the Nettle: A 'National Liberation' Option for Haiti." *North–South Agenda Paper #6* (March). Miami, FL: University of Miami, North–South Center.

Maingot, Anthony P. 1996. "Haiti: Four Old and Two New Hypotheses." In Jorge I. Domínguez and Abraham F. Lowenthal, eds. *Constructing Democratic Governance: Mexico, Central America, and the Caribbean in the 1990s*. Baltimore, MD: The Johns Hopkins University Press.

Maingot, Anthony P., and Wilfredo Lozano. 2005. *The United States and the Caribbean: Transforming Hegemony and Sovereignty*. New York: Routledge.

Mainwaring, Scott. 2003. "Party Objectives in Authoritarian Regimes with Elections or Fragile Democracies: A Dual Game." In Scott Mainwaring and Timothy R. Scully, eds. *Christian Democracy in Latin America: Electoral Competition and Regime Conflicts.* Stanford, CA: Stanford University Press.

Mainwaring, Scott, Daniel Brinks, and Aníbal Pérez-Liñan. 2001. "Classifying Political Regimes in Latin America, 1945–1999." *Studies in Comparative International Development* 36, No. 1: 37–65.

Mainwaring, Scott, and Aníbal, Pérez-Liñan. 2003. "Level of Development and Democracy: Latin American Exceptionalism." *Comparative Political Studies* 36, No. 9: 1031–67.

Mainwaring, Scott, and Aníbal, Pérez-Liñan. 2005. "Latin American Democratization Since 1978: Transitions, Breakdowns, and Erosions." In Frances Hagopian and Scott P. Mainwaring, eds. *The Third Wave of Democratization in Latin America: Advances and Setbacks.* New York: Cambridge University Press.

Makgala, Christian. 2003. "'So Far So Good'? An Appraisal of Dr. Ng'ombe's 1998 Prophecy on the Fate of the BNF." *Pula: Botswana Journal of African Studies* 17, No. 1: 51–66.

Makgala, Christian. 2005. "The Relationship Between Kenneth Koma and the Botswana Democratic Party." *African Affairs* 104, No. 415: 303–23.

Maksymiuk, Jan. 2004. "EU Warns Against Unfair Presidential Referendum – But to What Avail?" *RFE/RL Belarus Ukraine Report.* 15 September.

Makumbe, John. 1991. "The 1990 Elections: Implications for Democracy." In Ibbo Mandaza and Lloyd Sachikonye, eds. *The One-Party State and Democracy.* Harare, Zimbabwe: Southern African Political Economy Trust.

Makumbe, John. 1995. "Proposed Bill to Fund Political Parties: Implications for Democracy in Zimbabwe." In Kufi Kumado, ed. *Funding Political Parties in West Africa.* Accra: Electoral Commission of Ghana.

Makumbe, John. 2002. "Zimbabwe's Hijacked Election." *Journal of Democracy* 13, No. 4: 87–101.

Makumbe, John, and Daniel Compagnon. 2000. *Behind the Smokescreen: The Politics of Zimbabwe's 1995 General Elections.* Harare: University of Zimbabwe Publications.

Malache, Adriano, Paulino Macaringue, and Joao-Paolo Borges Coelho. 2005. "Profound Transformations and Regional Conflagrations: The History of Mozambique's Armed Forces, 1975–2005." In Martin Rupiya, ed. *Evolutions and Revolutions: A Contemporary History of Revolutions in Southern Africa.* Pretoria, South Africa: Institute for Security Studies.

Malila, Ikanyeng S. 1997. "Starting first and finishing last: Democracy and its discontents in Botswana." *Society in Transition* 28, No. 1: 20–26.

Maliyamkono, T. L. 1995. *The Race for the Presidency: The First Multi-Party Democracy in Tanzania.* Dar Es Salaam: Tema Publishers.

Malkasian, Mark. 1996. *"Gha-ra-bagh!" The Emergence of the National Democratic Movement in Armenia.* Detroit, MI: Wayne State Press.

Malone, David. 1998. *Decision-Making in the UN Security Council: The Case of Haiti, 1990–1997.* Oxford, UK: Clarendon Press.

Malova, Darina. 1997. "The Development of Interest Representation in Slovakia after 1989: From Transmisssion Belts to Party-State Corporatism?" In Sona Szomolamyi and John A. Gould, eds. *Slovakia: Problems of Democratic Consolidation and the Struggle for the Rules of the Game.* Bratislava: Slovak Political Science Association.

Malova, Darina. 2001. "From the Ambiguous Constitution to the Dominance of Informal Rules." In Jan Zielonka, ed. *Democratic Consolidation in Eastern Europe: Institutional Engineering.* New York: Oxford University Press.

Malova, Darina, and Marek Rybar. 2003. "The European Union's Policies Towards Slovakia: Carrots and Sticks of Political Conditionality." In Jacques Rupnik and Jan

Zielonka, eds. *The Road to the European Union: The Czech and Slovak Republics.* Manchester and New York: Manchester University Press.

Mambo, Andrew, and Julian Schofield. 2007. "Military Diversion in the 1978 Uganda–Tanzania War." *Journal of Political and Military Sociology* 18, No. 2: 231–66.

Man, Liviu. 1993. "The Independent Press in Romania." *Uncaptive Minds* (Summer): 89–96.

Mann, Michael. 1984. "The Autonomous Power of the State: Its Origins, Mechanisms, and Results." *European Archive of Sociology* 25: 185–212.

Manning, Carrie L. 2001a. "Competition and Accommodation in Post-Conflict Democracy: The Case of Mozambique." *Democratization* 8, No. 2 (Summer): 140–68.

Manning, Carrie L. 2001b. "From Armed Conflict to Civil Opposition: Post-Conflict Party Development in Mozambique, Bosnia, and Kosovo." Paper presented at the African Studies Association. Houston, TX: 15–18 November.

Manning, Carrie L. 2002a. "Elite Habituation to Democracy in Mozambique: The View from Parliament, 1994–2000." *Commonwealth & Comparative Politics* 40, No. 1: 61–80.

Manning, Carrie L. 2002b. *The Politics of Peace in Mozambique: Post-Conflict Democratization, 1992–2000.* Westport, CT: Praeger.

Manning, Carrie L. 2002c. "Conflict Management and Elite Habituation in Postwar Democracy: The Case of Mozambique." *Comparative Politics* 35, No. 1 (October): 63–84.

Manning, Carrie L. 2005. "Assessing Adaptation to Democratic Politics in Mozambique: The Case of Frelimo." In Leonardo A. Villalón and Peter VonDoepp, eds. *The Fate of Africa's Democratic Experiments: Elites and Institutions.* Bloomington: Indiana University Press.

Mansfield, Edward D., and Jack Snyder. 2007. "The Sequencing 'Fallacy.'" *Journal of Democracy* 18, No. 3 (July): 5–10.

Mansoor, Ali, and Bryce Quillin. 2006. *Migration and Remittances: Eastern Europe and the Former Soviet Union.* Washington, DC: The World Bank.

March, Luke. 2002. *The Communist Party in Post-Soviet Russia.* Manchester, UK: Manchester University Press.

March, Luke. 2004. "Socialism with Unclear Characteristics: The Moldovan Communists in Government." *Demokratizatsiya* 12, no. 1: 507–524.

March, Luke. 2005. "The Moldovan Communists: From Leninism to Democracy?" *Journal of Foreign Policy of Moldova* (September): 1–25.

March, Luke, and Graeme P. Herd. 2006. "Moldova Between Europe and Russia: Inoculating Against the Colored Contagion?" *Post-Soviet Affairs* 22, 4: 349–79.

Marcus, Richard R. 2001. "Madagascar: Legitimizing Autocracy." *Current History* 100, No. 646 (May): 226–31.

Marcus, Richard. 2004. "Political Change in Madagascar: Populist Democracy or Neopatrimonialism by Another Name?" *Institute for Security Studies Occasional Paper* #89 (August). Johannesburg, South Africa: Institute for Security Studies.

Marcus, Richard R. 2005. "The Fate of Madagascar's Democracy: Following the Rules while Eroding the Substance." In Leonardo A. Villalón and Peter VonDoepp, eds. *The Fate of Africa's Democratic Experiments: Elites and Institutions.* Bloomington: Indiana University Press.

Marcus, Richard R., and Paul Razafindrakoto. 2003a. "Madagascar: A New Democracy?" *Current History* 102, No. 664 (May): 215–21.

Marcus, Richard R., and Paul Razafindrakoto. 2003b. "Participation and the Poverty of Electoral Democracy in Madagascar." *Afrika Spectrum* 38, No. 1: 27–48.

Marcus, Richard R., and Paul Razafindrakoto. 2005. "Political Parties in Madagascar: Neopatrimonial Tools or Democratic Institutions?" *Party Politics* 11, No. 4: 495–512.

Mariñez, Pablo A. 1988. "Las fuerzas armadas en la República Dominicana: Profesionalización y politicización." In Augusto Varas, ed. *La Autonomía Militar en América Latina*. Caracas, Venezuela: Editorial Nueva Sociedad.

Markotich, Stan. 1993. "Serbia Prepares for Elections." *RFE/RL Research Report* 2, No. 49 (10 December): 15–20.

Markotich, Stan. 1994. "Government's Control over Serbia's Media." *RFE/RL Research Report* 3, 5 (4 February): 35–39.

Markotich, Stan. 1998. "Yugoslavia: Slow to Change." *Transitions Online*. 17 January.

Markov, Ihor. 1993. "The Role of the President in the Ukrainian Political System." *RFE/RL Research Report* (3 December): 31–5.

Markovich, Stephen C. 1998. "Democracy in Croatia: Views from the Opposition." *East European Quarterly* 32, No. 1: 83–93.

Marples, David. 2006. "The Presidential Election Campaign: An Analysis." In Joerg Forbrig, David R. Marples, and Pavol Demes, eds. *Prospects for Democracy in Belarus*. Washington, DC: German Marshall Fund of the United States.

Marston, John. 1996. "Cambodian News Media in the UNTAC Period and After." In Steve Heder and Judy Ledgerwood, eds. *Propaganda, Politics, and Violence in Cambodia: Democratic Transition under United Nations Peacekeeping*. Armonk, NY: M. E. Sharpe.

Marston, John. 2002. "Cambodia: Transnational Pressures and Local Agendas." *Southeast Asian Affairs*: 95–108.

Martin, Bradley. 2006. *Under the Loving Care of the Fatherly Leader: North Korea and the Kim Dynasty*. New York: Thomas Dunne Books.

Martin, Ian. 1999. "Haiti: International Force or National Compromise?" *Journal of Latin American Studies* 31: 711–34.

Martin, Philip, Susan Martin, and Patrick Weil. 2002. "Best Practice Options: Mali." *International Migration* 40, No. 3: 87–101.

Martin, Roderick. 1999. *Transforming Management in Central and Eastern Europe*. New York: Oxford University Press.

Martinez, Patricia. 2001. "Malaysia in 2000: A Year of Contradictions." *Asian Survey* 41, No. 1: 189–200.

Martinez, Patricia. 2002. "Malaysia in 2001: An Interlude of Consolidation." *Asian Survey* 42, No. 1: 133–40.

Masih, Joseph R., and Robert Krikorian. 1999. *Armenia at the Crossroads*. Amsterdam: Harwood Academic Publishers.

Matsheka, Thapelo C., and Mukganedi Z. Botlhomilwe. 2000. "Economic Conditions and Election Outcomes in Botswana: Is the Relationship Spurious?" *Pula: Botswana Journal of African Studies* 14, No. 1: 36–46.

Matviiuk, Maria. 1994. "Evgenii Marchuk – Povyshenie ili Zapadnia." *Zerkalo nedeli* 5 No. 11 (November).

Mauceri, Philip. 1995. "State Reform, Coalitions, and the Neoliberal Autogolpe in Peru." *Latin American Research Review* 30, No. 1: 7–37.

Mauceri, Philip. 1996. *State under Siege: Development and Policy Making in Peru*. Boulder, CO: Westview Press.

Mauceri, Philip. 1997. "State Development and Counter-Insurgency in Peru." In Paul B. Rich and Richard Stubbs, eds. *The Counter-Insurgent State: Guerrilla Warfare and State-Building in the Twentieth Century*. London: Macmillan Press.

Mauceri, Philip. 2004. "State, Elites, and the Response to Insurgency: Some Preliminary Comparisons Between Colombia and Peru." In Jo-Marie Burt and Philip Mauceri, eds. *Politics in the Andes: Identity, Conflict, Reform.* Pittsburgh, PA: University of Pittsburgh Press.

Mauzy, Diane K. 1983. *Barisan Nasional: Coalition Government in Malaysia.* Kuala Lumpur, Malaysia: Marican and Sons.

Mauzy, Diane K. 1992. "Malaysia: Shared Civilian–Military Interests." In Constantine P. Danopolous, ed. *Civilian Rule in the Developing World: Democracy on the March?* Boulder, CO: Westview Press.

Maynes, Charles William. 2004. "Losing Russia." *The St. Petersburg Times.* 17 February.

Mazza, Jacqueline. 2001. *Don't Disturb the Neighbors: The United States and Democracy in Mexico, 1980–1995.* New York: Routledge.

Mbaku, John Mukum. 2002. "Cameroon's Stalled Transition to Democratic Governance: Lessons for Africa's New Democrats." *African and Asian Studies* 1, No. 3: 125–63.

Mbaku, John Mukum. 2004a. "Decolonization, Reunification and Federation in Cameroon." In John M. Mbaku and Joseph Takougang, eds. *The Leadership Challenge in Africa: Cameroon under Paul Biya.* Trenton, NJ: Africa World Press.

Mbaku, John Mukum. 2004b. "Economic Dependence in Cameroon: SAPs and the Bretton Woods Institutions." In John M. Mbaku and Joseph Takougang, eds. *The Leadership Challenge in Africa: Cameroon under Paul Biya.* Trenton, NJ: Africa World Press.

Mbow, Penda. 2008. "Senegal: The Return of Personalism." *Journal of Democracy* 19, No. 1 (January): 156–69.

Mbuagbo, Oben T., and Robert M. Akoko. 2004. "'Motions of Support' and Ethno-Regional Politics in Cameroon." *Journal of Third World Studies* 21, No. 1: 241–57.

McCargo, Duncan. 2005. "Cambodia: Getting Away with Authoritarianism?" *Journal of Democracy* 16, No. 4: 98–112.

McClintock, Cynthia. 1999. "Peru: Precarious Regimes, Authoritarian and Democratic." In Larry Diamond, Jonathan Hartlyn, Juan J. Linz, and Seymour Martin Lipset, eds. *Democracy in Developing Countries: Latin America.* Boulder, CO: Lynne Rienner Publishers.

McClintock, Cynthia. 2001. "The OAS in Peru: Room for Improvement." *Journal of Democracy* 12, No. 4: 137–40.

McClintock, Cynthia. 2006a. "Electoral Authoritarian Versus Partially Democratic Regimes: The Case of the Fujimori Government and the 2000 Elections." In Julio Carrión, ed. *The Fujimori Legacy: The Rise of Electoral Authoritarianism in Peru.* University Park: Pennsylvania State University Press.

McClintock, Cynthia. 2006b. "An Unlikely Comeback in Peru." *Journal of Democracy* 17, No. 4 (October): 95–109.

McClintock, Cynthia, and Fabián, Vallas. 2003. *The United States and Peru: Cooperation at a Cost.* New York: Routledge.

McCoy, Jennifer. 1997. "Introduction: Dismantling the Predatory State – The Conference Report." In Robert I. Rotberg, ed. *Haiti Renewed: Political and Economic Prospects.* Washington, DC: The Brookings Institution Press.

McCoy, Jennifer. 1998. "Monitoring and Mediating Elections during Latin American Democratization." In Kevin Middlebrook, ed. *Electoral Observation and Democratic Transitions in Latin America.* La Jolla, CA: Center for U.S.–Mexican Studies.

McCoy, Jennifer, Larry Garber, and Robert Pastor. 1991. "Pollwatching and Peacemaking." *Journal of Democracy* 2, No. 4: 102–14.

McFaul, Michael. 1994. "Russian Politics: The Calm Before the Storm?" *Current History* 93, No. 585: 313–19.

McFaul, Michael. 1997. *Russia's 1996 Presidential Election: The End of Polarized Politics.* Stanford, CA: Hoover Institution Press.

McFaul, Michael. 1999. "The Perils of a Protracted Transition." *Journal of Democracy* 10, No. 2: 4–18.

McFaul, Michael. 2001. *Russia's Unfinished Revolution: Political Change from Gorbachev to Putin.* Ithaca, NY: Cornell University Press.

McFaul, Michael. 2002. "The Fourth Wave of Democracy and Dictatorship: Noncooperative Transitions in the Postcommunist World." *World Politics* 54, No. 2: 212–44.

McFaul, Michael. 2005a. "Transitions from Postcommunism." *Journal of Democracy* 16, No. 3: 5–19.

McFaul, Michael. 2005b. "American Efforts at Promoting Regime Change in the Soviet Union and Then Russia: Lessons Learned." Washington, DC: American Political Science Association. 2–4 September.

McFaul, Michael. 2007. "Ukraine Imports Democracy: External Influences on the Orange Revolution." *International Security* 32, No. 2: 45–83.

McFaul, Michael, and Nikolai Petrov. 1998. *Almanakh Rossii.* Moscow: Carnegie Endowment for International Peace.

McFaul, Michael, and Nikolai Petrov. 2004. "What the Elections Tell Us." *Journal of Democracy* 15, No. 3: 20–31.

Mchombo, Sam A. 1998. "Democratization in Malawi: Its Roots and Prospects." In Jean-Germain Gros, ed. *Democratization in Late Twentieth-Century Africa: Coping with Uncertainty.* Westport, CT: Greenwood Press.

McMann, Kelly M. 2006. *Economic Autonomy and Democracy: Hybrid Regimes in Russia and Kyrgyzstan.* New York: Cambridge University Press.

Means, Gordon. 1991. *Malaysian Politics: The Next Generation.* Oxford, UK: Oxford University Press.

Meinhardt, Heiko, and Nandini Patel. 2003. *Malawi's Process of Democratic Transition: An Analysis of Political Developments Between 1990 and 2003.* Lilongwe Malawi: Konrad Adenauer Stiftung.

Meldrum, Andrew. 1993a. "Mozambique: Peace at Last." *Africa Report* (March–April): 47–50.

Meldrum, Andrew. 1993b. "Mozambique: Avoiding Another Angola." *Africa Report* (September–October): 46–9.

Membreño, Idiáguez Marcos. 1997. "Whither U.S. Solidarity with Nicaragua?" *Envio Digital* 189 (April).

Mendelson, Sarah Elizabeth. 2001. "Democracy Assistance and Political Transition in Russia: Between Success and Failure." *International Security* 25, No. 4: 68–106.

Mengisteab, Kidane, and Cyril Daddieh. 1999. "Why State-Building Is Still Relevant in Africa and How It Relates to Democratization." In Kidane Mengisteab and Cyril Daddieh, eds. *State-Building and Democratization in Africa: Faith, Hope, and Realities.* Westport, CT: Praeger.

Mentan, Tatah. 1998. "Cameroon: A Flawed Transition to Democracy." In Jean-Germain Gros, ed. *Democratization in Late Twentieth-Century Africa: Coping with Uncertainty.* Westport, CT: Greenwood Press.

Meredith, Martin. 2002. *Our Votes, Our Guns: Robert Mugabe and the Tragedy of Zimbabwe.* New York: PublicAffairs.

Mershon, Carol A. 1994. "Expectations and Informal Rules in Coalition Formation." *Comparative Political Studies* 27, No. 1: 40–79.

Meseznikov, Grigorij. 1997. "The Open-Ended Formation of Slovakia's Party System." In Sona Szomolamyi and John A. Gould, eds. *Slovakia: Problems of Democratic Consolidation and the Struggle for the Rules of the Game.* Bratislava: Slovak Political Science Association.

Messone, Nelson, and Jean-Germain Gros. 1998. "The Irony of Wealth: Democratization in Gabon." In Jean-Germain Gros, ed. *Democratization in Late Twentieth-Century Africa: Coping with Uncertainty*. Westport, CT: Greenwood Press.

Meyer, Lorenzo. 1991. "Mexico: The Exception and the Rule." In Abraham Lowenthal, ed. *Exporting Democracy: The United States and Latin America*. Baltimore, MD: The Johns Hopkins University Press.

Michaels, Marguerite. 1993. "Retreat from Africa." *Foreign Affairs* 72, No. 1: 93–108.

Mickiewicz, Ellen. 1988. *Split Signals: Television and Politics in the Soviet Union*. New York: Oxford University Press.

Mickiewicz, Ellen. 1999. *Changing Channels: Television and the Struggle for Power in Russia*. Oxford, UK: Oxford University Press.

Middlebrook, Kevin J. 1988. "Dilemmas of Change in Mexican Politics." *World Politics* 41, No. 1: 120–41.

Middlebrook, Kevin J. 1995. *The Paradox of Revolution: Labor, the State, and Authoritarianism in Mexico*. Baltimore, MD: The Johns Hopkins University Press.

Middlebrook, Kevin J., ed. 1998. *Electoral Observation and Democratic Transitions in Latin America*. La Jolla, CA: Center for U.S.–Mexican Studies.

Middlebrook, Kevin J. 2001. "Party Politics and Democratization in Mexico: The Partido Acción Nacional in Comparative Perspective." In Kevin Middlebrook, ed. *Party Politics and the Struggle for Democracy in Mexico: National and State-Level Analyses of the Partido Acción Nacional*. La Jolla, CA: Center for U.S.–Mexican Studies.

Middlebrook, Kevin J. 2004. "Mexico's Democratic Transitions: Dynamics and Prospects." In Kevin J. Middlebrook, ed. *Dilemmas of Political Change in Mexico*. London: Institute of Latin American Studies.

Mihyo, Paschal B. 2003. "Chama Cha Mapinduzi (CCM): A Revolutionary Party in Transition." In M. A. Mohamed Salih, ed. *African Political Parties*. London: Pluto Press.

Miklos, Ivan. 1997. "Economic Transition and the Emergence of Clientelist Structures in Slovakia." In Sona Szomolamyi and John A. Gould, eds. *Slovakia: Problems of Democratic Consolidation and the Struggle for the Rules of the Game*. Bratislava: Slovak Political Science Association.

Military Balance. 2006. London: International Institute for Strategic Studies.

Milivojevic, Marko. 1994. "Croatia's Security Services." *Jane's Intelligence Review*. 1 September.

Miller, Norman, and Rodger Yeager. 1994. *Kenya: The Quest for Prosperity*. Boulder, CO: Westview Press.

Millett, Richard L. 1994. "Beyond Sovereignty: International Efforts to Support Latin American Democracy." *Journal of Interamerican Studies and World Affairs* 36, No. 3: 1–23.

Milne, R. S., and Diane K. Mauzy. 1999. *Malaysian Politics under Mahathir*. London: Routledge.

Minasian, Liana. 1999. "The Role of the Military in Armenia's Politics." *CRS* No. 5 (4 November).

Miranda, Roger, and William Ratliff. 1993. *The Civil War in Nicaragua: Inside the Sandinistas*. New Brunswick, NJ: Transaction Publishers.

MISA. 1998. "State of the Media in Southern Africa 1998: Mozambique." Windhoek: Media Institute of Southern Africa.

MISA. 2008. "MISA–Zambia Statement on the Media Coverage of the Just-Ended Presidential Election." Available at www.ifex.org (accessed 13 November).

Mitchell, Lincoln. 2004. "Georgia's Rose Revolution." *Current History* 103, No. 675: 342–53.

Mitchell, Lincoln. 2008. *Uncertain Democracy: U.S. Foreign Policy and Georgia's Rose Revolution*. Philadelphia, PA: University of Pennsylvania Press.

Mitiaev, V. G. 1998. "Vnutripoliticheskie protsessy v nezavisimoi Armenii." In E. M. Kozhokina, ed. *Armeniia: Problemy Nezavisimogo Razvitiia*. Moscow: RISI. Pp. 73–138.

Mitic, Aleksandar. 2004. "Lost in Transition." *Transitions Online*. 25 March.

Mitic, Aleksandar. 2005. "Serbia & Montenegro: A First Step Towards Accession." *Transitions Online*. 7 October.

Mizrahi, Yemile. 2003. *From Martyrdom to Power: The Partido Acción Nacional in Mexico*. Notre Dame, IN: University of Notre Dame Press.

Mkrtchian, Nerses. 1999. "The Place and the Role of Parliamentary Elections in the Process of Establishment of Democratic Practices in Armenia: The Peculiarities of the 1999 Parliamentary Elections." Available at www.forum.am/groups/pol/mat/17.doc.

Mlechin, Leonid. 2002. *KGB: Predsedateli organov gosbezopasnosti rassekrechenye sud'by*. Moscow: Tsentrpoligraf.

Mmuya, Max, and Amon Chaligha. 1994. *Political Parties and Democracy in Tanzania*. Dar Es Salaam: University Press.

Mobekk, Eiren. 2001. "Enforcement of Democracy in Haiti." *Democratization* 8, No. 3: 173–88.

Moeller, Susanne D. 1984. "Government and Opposition in Kenya, 1966–9." *Journal of Modern African Studies* 22, No. 3 (September): 399–427.

Mohammad, Yusoff B. 2005. "Malaysia Bilateral Trade Relations and Economic Growth." *International Journal of Business and Society* 6, No. 2 (July).

Molchanov, Mikhail. 2004. "Ukraine and the European Union: A Perennial Neighbour?" *European Integration* 26, No. 4: 451–73.

Molinar, Horcasitas Juan. 1991. *El Tiempo de la Legitimidad: Elecciones, Autoritarismo y Democracia en Mexico*. Mexico City: Cal y Arena.

Mollison, Thomas A. 1998. "Television Broadcasting Leads Romania's March Toward an Open, Democratic Society." *Journal of Broadcasting & Electronic Media* 42, No. 1 (Winter): 128–38.

Molomo, Mpho. 2001. "Civil–Military Relations in Botswana's Developmental State." *African Studies Quarterly* 5, No. 2.

Molomo, Mpho, and David Sebudubudu. 2006. "Funding of Political Parties: Leveling the Political Playing Field." In Zibani Maundeni, ed. *40 Years of Democracy in Botswana 1965–2005*. Gaborone Botswana: Mmegi Publishing House.

Molutsi, Patrick, and John D. Holm. 1990. "Developing Democracy When Civil Society Is Weak: The Case of Botswana." *African Affairs* 89, No. 356: 322–40.

Momba, Jotham C. 1992. "The 'Pot-Holed' Road to Multi-Party Politics in Zambia." In Jannie H. Hunter and Christo Lombard, eds. *Multi-Party Democracy, Civil Society and Economic Transformation in Southern Africa*. Windhoek: Southern African Universities Social Science Conference.

Momba, Jotham C. 2003. "Democratic Transition and the Crises of an African Nationalist Party: UNIP, Zambia." In Mohammad Salih, ed. *African Political Parties: Evolution, Institutionalisation and Governance*. London: Pluto Press.

Mondlane, Luis. 2003. "Mozambique: Nurturing Justice from Liberation Zones to a Stable Democracy." In A. A. An-Naim, ed. *Human Rights under African Constitutions: Realizing the Promise to Ourselves*. Philadelphia, PA: University of Pennsylvania Press.

Montaner, Carlos Alberto. 1990. "Castro's Last Stand." *Journal of Democracy* 1, No. 3 (Summer): 71–80.

Monteiro, Oscar. 2000. "Governance and Decentralization." In Bernardo Ferraz and Barry Munslow eds. *Sustainable Development in Mozambique*. Trenton, NJ: Africa World Press.

Monzini, Paola. 2007. "Sea-Border Crossings: The Organization of Irregular Migration to Italy." *Mediterranean Politics* 12, No. 2: 163–84.

Moody, Peter R., Jr. 1991. *Political Change in Taiwan: A Study of Ruling Party Adaptability*. Westport, CT: Praeger.

Moore, Barrington. 1966. *Social Origins of Dictatorship and Democracy: Lord and Peasant in the Making of the Modern World*. Boston: Beacon Press.

Moore, Patrick. 1992a. "Yugoslavia: Ethnic Tension Erupts into Civil War." *RFE/RL Research Report*. 3 January: 68–72.

Moore, Patrick. 1992b. "The Media in Regions of Conflict: Croatia." *RFE/RL Research Report*. 2 October: 82–5.

Moore, Patrick. 1993. "Croatia (Survey of East European Media)" *RFE/RL Research Report* (7 May): 25–26.

Moore, Patrick. 1994. "Changes in the Croatian Landscape" *RFE/RL Research Report* (3 June): 10–15.

Moore, Patrick. 1996. "A Turn Toward Peace." In J. F. Brown, ed. *Building Democracy: OMRI Annual Survey 1995 of Eastern Europe and the Former Soviet Union*. Armonk, NY: M. E. Sharpe.

Moore, Patrick. 1999a. "Perisic: Army Will Not Act Against Opposition." *RFE/RL Balkan Report* 3, No. 38 (12 October).

Moore, Patrick. 1999b. "A Fatal – and Fateful – Accident." *RFE/RL Balkan Report* (12 October).

Moore, Patrick. 1999c. "Croatian Archbishop Warns Against Isolation." *RFE/RL Balkan Report* (12 November).

Moore, Patrick. 2000a. "Croatian Opposition Confronts Challenge of Governing." *RFE/RL Endnote* (4 January).

Moore, Patrick. 2000b. "Croatia's Racan Sets Priorities." *RFE/RL Endnote* (12 January).

Moore, Patrick. 2000c. "Mixed Signals for Croatia." *RFE/RL Endnote* (24 July).

Moore, Patrick. 2000d. "Milošević's Montenegrin Gambit." *RFE/RL Balkan Report* (11 July).

Moore, Patrick. 2002a. "Balkans: Half Empty or Half Full?" *RFE/RL Balkan Report* 6, No. 29 (9 August).

Moore, Patrick. 2002b. "The International Community and Albania." *RFE/RL Balkan Report* (1 November).

Moran, John P. 1999. "Praetorians or Professionals? Democratization and Military Intervention in Communist and Post-Communist Russia." *Journal of Communist Studies and Transition Politics* 15, No. 2: 41–68.

Moravcsik, Andrew, and Milada Anna Vachudova. 2003. "National Interests, State Power, and EU Enlargement." *East European Politics and Societies* 17, No. 1: 42–57.

Mørck, Anna Birgitte. 2006. "The United Republic of Tanzania: Presidential and Parliamentary Elections, December 2005." Norway: Nordem Report.

Moreno, Dario. 1995. "Respectable Intervention: The United States and Central American Elections." In Mitchell A. Seligson and John A. Booth, eds. *Elections and Democracy in Central America, Revisited*. Chapel Hill: University of North Carolina Press.

Moreno Ocampo, Luis. ND. "Power Networks and Institutions in Latin America." Cambridge. Unpublished manuscript.

Morley, Morris. 1994. *Washington, Somoza, and the Sandinistas: State and Regime in U.S. Policy toward Nicaragua, 1969–81*. Cambridge: Cambridge University Press.

Morna, Colleen Lowe. 1990. "Tanzania: Nyerere's Turnabout." *Africa Report* 35, No. 4: 23–5.

Morris, Stephen D. 1995. *Political Reformism in Mexico: An Overview of Contemporary Mexican Politics*. Boulder, CO: Lynne Rienner Publishers.

Morrison, John. 1991. *Boris Yeltsin: From Bolshevik to Democrat*. New York: Penguin.

Morrison, Minion K. C. 2004. "Political Parties in Ghana Through Four Republics: A Path to Democratic Consolidation." *Comparative Politics* 36, No. 4 (July): 421–42.

Moser, Robert. 2001a. "Introduction." In Zoltan Barany and Robert G. Moser, eds. *Russian Politics: Challenges of Democratization*. New York: Cambridge University Press.

Moser, Robert. 2001b. *Unexpected Outcomes: Electoral Systems, Political Parties, and Representation in Russia*. Pittsburgh, PA: University of Pittsburgh Press.

Mosley, Layna, 2003. *Global Capital and National Governments*. New York: Cambridge University Press.

Moss, Todd J. 1995. "US Policy and Democratization in Africa: The Limits of Liberal Universalism." *Journal of Modern African Studies* 33, No. 2: 209–89.

Moss, Todd J. 2007. "Zimbabwe's Meltdown: Anatomy of a Peacetime Economic Collapse." *Fletcher Forum of World Affairs* 31, No. 2 (Summer): 133–48.

Moten, Abdul Mashid, and Tunku Mohar Mokhtar. 2006. "The 2004 General Elections in Malaysia." *Asian Survey* 46, No. 3: 319–40.

Motyl, Alexander J. 1986. *Will the Non-Russians Rebel? State, Ethnicity, and Stability in the USSR*. Ithaca, NY: Cornell University Press.

Moya Pons, Frank. 1986. *El Pasado Dominicano*. Santo Domingo, Dominican Republic: Fundación J. A. Caro Alvarez.

Moya Pons, Frank. 1998. *The Dominican Republic: A National History*. Princeton, NJ: Markus Wiener.

Mozaffar, Shaheen. 2001. "The Dilemma of Building a Multiparty Democracy in Haiti." *Georgetown University Haiti Papers*, No. 4 (July).

Mozaffar, Shaheen, and Andreas Schedler. 2002. "The Comparative Study of Electoral Governance – Introduction." *International Political Science Review* 23, No. 1: 5–27.

Mozaffar, Shaheen, and Richard Vengroff. 2002. "A Whole System Approach to the Choice of Electoral Rules in Democratizing Countries: Senegal in Comparative Perspective." *Electoral Studies* 21, No. 4: 601–16.

Mudde, Cas. 2002. "Slovak Elections: Go West!" *RFE/RL Newsline* 4, No. 21 (16 October).

Mueller, John. 2000. "The Banality of Ethnic War." *International Security* 25, No. 1: 42–70.

Muja-Leon, Eusebio, and Joshua Busby. 2001. "Much Ado about Something: Regime Change in Cuba." *Problems of Post Communism* 48, No. 6 (November–December): 6–18.

Mukhin, A. 2002. *Kto est Mister Putin i kto s nim prishel?* Moscow: Gnom I D.

Mulford, David. 1967. *Zambia: The Politics of Independence 1957–1964*. London: Oxford University Press.

Muluzi, Bakili, Yusuf M. Juwayeyi, Mercy Makhambera, and Desmond D. Phiri. 1999. *Democracy with a Price: The History of Malawi Since 1900*. Blantyre, Malawi: Ghango Heinemann.

Munene, Macharia. 2001. *The Politics of Transition in Kenya: 1995–1998*. Nairobi, Kenya: Quest and Insight Publishers.

Mungiu-Pippidi, Alina. 1999. "Romania: From Procedural Democracy to European Integration." In M. Kaldor and I. Vejvoda, eds. *Democratization in Central and Eastern Europe*. London: Pinte Publishers. Pp. 135–49.

Mungiu-Pippidi, Alina. 2006. "Europeanization without Decommunization: A Case of Elite Conversion." In David Phinnemore, ed. *The EU and Romanis: Accession and Beyond*. London: The Federal Trust.

Munro-Kua, Anne. 1996. *Authoritarian Populism in Malaysia*. London: Macmillan Press.

Munslow, Barry. 1983. *Mozambique: The Revolution and Its Origins*. New York: Longman.

Murawiec, Laurent, and Clifford Gaddy. 2002. "The Higher Police: Vladimir Putin and His Predecessors." *The National Interest* Spring: 29–36.

Mutalib, Hussin. 1990. *Islam and Ethnicity in Malay Politics*. Singapore: Oxford University Press.

Mutalib, Hussin. 2000. "Malaysia's 1999 General Election: Signposts to Future Politics." *Asian Journal of Political Science* 8, No. 1 (June): 65–89.

Mutua, Makua. 2001. "Justice Under Siege: The Rule of Law and Judicial Subservience in Kenya." *Human Rights Quarterly* 23: 96–118.

Mutua, Makua. 2008. *Kenya's Quest for Democracy: Taming Leviathan*. Boulder, CO: Lynne Rienner Publishers.

Mutunga, Willy. 1999. *Constitution-Making from the Middle: Civil Society and Transition Politics in Kenya, 1992–1997*. Nairobi, Kenya: SAREAT.

Mutunga, Willy. 2002. "The Unfolding Political Alliances and their Implications for Kenya's Transition." In Lawrence Murungu Mute, Wanza Kioko, and Kichamu Akivaga, eds. *Building an Open Society: The Politics of Transition in Kenya*. Nairobi, Kenya: Claripress.

Mwagiru, Makumi. 2002. "Elections and the Constitutional and Legal Regime in Kenya." In Ludeki Chweya, ed. *Electoral Politics in Kenya*. Nairobi, Kenya: Claripress.

Mwanakatwe, John M. 1994. *End of the Kaunda Era*. Lusaka, Zambia: A Multimedia Publication.

Mwase, Ngila, and Mary Raphael. 2001. "The 1995 Presidential Elections in Tanzania." *The Round Table* 359: 245–69.

Myagkov, Mikhail, and Peter C. Ordeshook. 2001. "The Trail of Votes in Russia's 1999 Duma and 2000 Presidential Elections." *Communist and Post-Communist Studies* 34: 353–70.

Myagkov, Mikhai, Peter C. Ordeshook, and Dimitri Shakin. 2009. *The Forensics of Election Fraud: Russia and Ukraine*. New York: Cambridge University Press.

Myers, Mary. 1998. "The Promotion of Democracy at the Grassroots: The Example of Radio in Mali." *Democratization* 5, No. 2 (Summer): 200–16.

Nain, Zaharom. 2002. "The Structure of the Media Industry: Implications for Democracy." In Francis Loh Kik Wah and Khoo Boo Teik, eds. *Democracy in Malaysia: Discourses and Practices*. Richmond, VA: Curzon.

Nair, Shanti. 1997. *Islam in Malaysian Foreign Policy*. London: Routledge.

Nathan, Andrew J. 2001. "Introduction: The Documents and Their Significance." In A. Nathan and P. Link, eds. *The Tiananmen Papers*. New York: Public Affairs.

Nathan, K. S. 2002. "Malaysia: 11 September and the Politics of Incumbency." *Southeast Asian Affairs*: 159–76.

National Democratic Institute for International Affairs (NDI). 1991. *An Assessment of the Senegalese Electoral Code*. Washington, DC: NDI.

National Democratic Institute for International Affairs. 1993. *An Assessment of the October 11, 1992 Election in Cameroon*. Washington, DC: NDI.

National Democratic Institute for International Affairs/Council of Freely Elected Heads of Government. 1998. *The 1996 Presidential Election in the Dominican Republic*. Washington, DC: NDI.

National Democratic Institute for International Affairs. 2000. *Zimbabwe Parliamentary Elections 2000: Report of the NDI Pre-Election Delegation*. Washington, DC: NDI.

National Democratic Institute for International Affairs. 2006. "Tanzania." Washington, DC: NDI.

National Republican Institute for International Affairs (NRIIA). 1991. "The 1991 Elections in Albania." Report of the NRIIA Election Observer Delegation. Washington, DC: NRIIA.

Ncube, Welshman. 2001. "The Courts of Law in Rhodesia and Zimbabwe: Guardians of Civilization, Human Rights and Justice or Purveyors of Repression, Injustice and

Repression?" In Ngwabi Bhebe and Terence Ranger, eds. *The Historical Dimensions of Democracy and Human Rights in Zimbabwe. Volume 1: Pre-Colonial and Colonial Legacies.* Harare: University of Zimbabwe Publications.

Ndegwa, Stephen N. 1998. "The Incomplete Transition: The Constitutional and Electoral Context in Kenya." *Africa Today* 45, No. 2 (April–June): 193–212.

Ndegwa, Stephen N. 2003. "Kenya: Third Time Lucky?" *Journal of Democracy* 14, No. 3 (July): 145–58.

Ndlovu-Gatsheni, Sabelo. 2006. "Nationalist–Military Alliance and the Fate of Democracy in Zimbabwe." *African Journal of Conflict Resolution* 6, No. 1: 49–80.

Neher, Clark D. 2002. *Southeast Asia in the New International Era.* Boulder, CO: Westview Press.

Neher, Clark D., and Ross Marlay. 1995. *Democracy and Development in Southeast Asia: The Winds of Change.* Boulder, CO: Westview Press.

Neher, Leonardo, and Jessy D. Bakary. 1993. "Gabon: Competing for the Presidency: A Pre-Election Assessment." Washington, DC: International Foundation for Electoral Systems.

Neild, Rachel. 2002. "La Reforma Policial en Haití: Un Triunfo sobre la Historia." In Lilian Bobea, ed. *Soldados y Ciudadanos en el Caribe.* Santo Domingo, Dominican Republic: FLACSO.

Nelson, Daniel N. 2002. "Armies, Security, and Democracy in Southeastern Europe." *Armed Forces & Society* 28, No. 3 (Spring): 427–54.

Nelson, Daniel N. 2004. "Romanian Security." In H. Carey, ed. *Romania Since 1989: Politics, Economics, and Society.* Boulder, CO: Lexington Books. Pp. 461–83.

Nelson, Joan M., and Stephanie J. Eglinton. 1992. *Encouraging Democracy: What Role for Conditioned Aid?* Washington, DC: Overseas Development Council.

Nesvetailova, Anastasia. 2002. "A Friend in Need...Or a Friend in Need? Russia and the Belarusian Economy." In Ann Lewis, ed. *The EU and Belarus: Between Moscow and Brussels.* London: Federal Trust.

Newell, Jonathan. 1995. "A Moment of Truth? The Church and Political Change in Malawi, 1992." *Journal of Modern African Studies* 33, No. 2: 243–62.

Newell, Jonathan. 1999. "'A Difficult Year for Us in Many Respects': Pressure for Change and Government Reaction in Malawi in 1992." In Jonathan Hyslop, ed. *African Democracy in the Era of Globalization.* Johannesburg, South Africa: Witwatersrand University Press.

Ngaiza, Anthony. 1999. "Tanzania." *Report on State of the Media in Southern Africa 1998.* Windhoek: MISA.

Ng'ethe, Njugona, and M. Katumanga. 2003. "Transition and the Politics of Constitution Making: A Comparative Study of Uganda, South Africa and Kenya." In Walter O. Oyugi, Peter Wanyande, and C. Odhiambo Mbai, eds. *The Politics of Transition in Kenya: From KANU to NARC.* Nairobi, Kenya: Heinrich Boll Foundation.

Ngoh, Victor Julius. 2004. "Biya and the Transition to Democracy." In John M. Mbaku and Joseph Takougang, eds. *The Leadership Challenge in Africa: Cameroon under Paul Biya.* Trenton, NJ: Africa World Press.

Ng'ong'ola, Clement. 1996. "Managing the Transition to Political Pluralism in Malawi: Legal and Constitutional Arrangements." *Journal of Commonwealth and Comparative Politics* 34, No. 2: 85–110.

Ng'ong'ola, Clement. 2002. "Judicial Mediation and Electoral Politics in Malawi." In Harri Englund, ed. *A Democracy of Chameleons: Politics and Culture in the New Malawi.* Stockholm: Nordiska Afrikainstitutet.

Nichols, Jim. 2003. "Coup in Georgia [Republic]: Recent Developments and Implications." Report RS21685. Washington, DC: Congressional Research Service.

Nichols, Thomas. 2001. *The Russian Presidency: Society and Politics in the Second Russian Republic*. New York: Palgrave.

Nicholson, Beryl. 1999. "The Beginning of the End of a Rebellion: Southern Albania, May–June 1997." *East European Politics and Societies* 13, No. 3: 543–565.

Nikitchenko, Andrei. 2000. "Ukraine: Heading to Default and Restructuring." *Eastern & Central Europe Credit Research Global Fixed Income* (7 February). Commerzbank. Available at www.ukrainaemb.se/Econ_section/ukr_econ/Ukr_default_kommertz_bank. doc (accessed March 2005).

Nikolayenko, Olena. 2004. "Press Freedom during the 1994 and 1999 Presidential Elections in Ukraine: A Reverse Wave?" *Europe–Asia Studies* 56, No. 5: 661–86.

Ninsin, Kwame A. 1996. *Ghana's Political Transition 1990–1993*. Accra: Freedom Publications.

Ninsin, Kwame A. 1998a. "Introduction." In Kwame A. Ninsin, ed. *Ghana: Transition to Democracy*. Dakar, Senegal: CODESRIA.

Ninsin, Kwame A. 1998b. "Civil Associations and the Transition to Democracy." In Kwame A. Ninsin, ed. *Ghana: Transition to Democracy*. Dakar, Senegal: CODESRIA.

Nivat, Anne. 1997. "Slovak Media under Government Fire." *Transition* 2, No. 9 (May 6).

Njølstad, Olav. 2004. *The Last Decade of the Cold War: From Conflict Escalation to Conflict Transformation*. New York: Routledge.

Nkiwane, Tandeka C. 1998. "Opposition Politics in Zimbabwe: The Struggle within the Struggle." In Adebayo O. Olukoshi, ed. *The Politics of Opposition in Contemporary Africa*. Uppsala, Sweden: Nordiska Afrikainstititet.

Nodia, Ghia. 2005. "Georgia 2004." In Adrian Karatnycky and Alexander J. Motyl, eds. *Nations in Transit*. New York: Freedom House.

Nordlund, Per. 1996. *Organizing the Political Agora: Domination and Democratization in Zambia and Zimbabwe*. Ph.D. diss. Sweden: Uppsala University.

Nugent, Paul. 1995. *Big Men, Small Boys and Politics in Ghana: Power, Ideology and the Burden of History, 1982–1994*. London: Pinter Publishing.

Nuzzi, O'Shaughnessy, Laura Dodson, and Michael Dodson. 1999. "Political Bargaining and Democratic Transitions: A Comparison of Nicaragua and El Salvador." *Journal of Latin American Studies* 31, No. 1: 99–127.

Nwajiaku, Kathryn. 1994. "The National Conferences in Benin and Togo Revisited." *Journal of Modern African Studies* 32, No. 3 (September): 429–47.

Nyamnjoh, Francis B. 1999. "Cameroon: A Country United by Ethnic Ambition and Difference." *African Affairs* 98, No. 390 (January): 101–18.

Nyamnjoh, Francis B. 2005. *Africa's Media: Democracy and the Politics of Belonging*. London: Zed Books.

Nye, Joseph S., Jr. 1999. "Redefining the National Interest." *Foreign Affairs* 78, No. 4: 22–35.

Nyong'o, Peter. 1992. *Thirty Years of Independence in Africa: The Lost Decades?* Nairobi, Kenya: Academy Science Publishers.

Nzunda, Matembo S., and Kenneth R. Ross. 1995. "Introduction." In Matembo S. Nzunda and K. R. Ross, eds. *Church, Law and Political Transition in Malawi: 1992–94*. Gweru, Zimbabwe: Mambo Press.

Oates, Sarah. 2003. "Television, Voters, and the Development of the 'Broadcast Party.'" In Vicki L. Hesli and William M. Reisinger, eds. *The 1999–2000 Elections in Russia: Their Impact and Legacy*. New York: Cambridge University Press.

Obando, Enrique. 1993. "El Poder de los Militares." In Augusto Alvarez Rodrich, ed. *El Poder en el Peru*. Lima, Peru: Editorial Apoyo.

Obando, Enrique. 1994a. "Fuerzas Armadas: Redefiendo el Rol Militar en un Contexto Democrático." In Carlos Fernández Fontenoy, ed. *Sociedad, Partidos y Estado en el Perú: Estudios sobre la Crisis y el Cambio.* Lima, Peru: Universidad de Lima.

Obando, Enrique. 1994b. "The Power of Peru's Armed Forces." In Joseph S. Tulchin and Gary Bland, eds. *Peru in Crisis: Dictatorship or Democracy?* Boulder, CO: Lynne Rienner Publishers.

O'Barr, Jean F. 1972. "Cell Leaders in Tanzania." *African Studies Review* 15, No. 3, 437–65.

Obrman, Jan. 1992. "Slovak Politician Accused of Secret Police Ties." *RFE/RL Research Report* 1, No. 15: 13–17 (10 April).

Obrman, Jan. 1993. "The Slovak Government versus the Media." *RFE/RL Research Report* 2, No. 6: 26–30 (5 February).

Odhiambo-Mbai, C. 2003. "The Rise and Fall of the Autocratic State in Kenya." In Walter O. Oyugi, Peter Wanyande, and C. Odhiambo Mbai, eds. *The Politics of Transition in Kenya: From KANU to NARC.* Nairobi, Kenya: Heinrich Boll Foundation.

ODIHR. 1996a. *Armenian Presidential Elections, September 24, 1996: Final Report.* Warsaw: OSCE.

ODIHR. 1996b. *Final Report on the Presidential and Parliamentary Elections in Romania, 3 and 17 November 1996.* Warsaw: OSCE.

ODIHR. 1996c. *Observations of the Parliamentary Election in Albania, 26 May and 2 June 1996.* Warsaw: OSCE.

ODIHR. 1997a. *Final Report on the Presidential Election in Moldova, 17 November and 1 December 1996.* Warsaw: OSCE.

ODIHR. 1997b. *Final Report. Romanian Parliamentary and Presidential Elections 3rd and 17th November 1997.* Warsaw: OSCE.

ODIHR. 1997c. *Republic of Serbia Parliamentary Election, September 21, 1997, and Presidential Election, September 21 and October 5, 1997.* Warsaw: OSCE.

ODIHR. 1997d. *Final Report: Parliamentary Elections in Albania, 29 June – 6 July 1997.* Warsaw: OSCE.

ODIHR. 1997e. *Statement on the Presidential Election in the Republic of Croatia, June 15, 1997.* Warsaw: OSCE.

ODIHR. 1998a. *Parliamentary Elections in the Former Yugoslav Republic of Macedonia, 18 October and 1 November 1998.* Warsaw: OSCE.

ODIHR. 1998b. *Republic of Armenia: Presidential Election, March 16 and 30, 1998, Final Report.* Warsaw: OSCE.

ODIHR. 1998c. *Final Report on the Parliamentary Elections in Slovakia, 25–26 September 1998.* Warsaw: OSCE.

ODIHR. 1999a. *The Republic of Albania Referendum on The Constitution, 22 November 1998.* Warsaw: OSCE.

ODIHR. 1999b. *Final Report on the Presidential Election in Slovakia, 15 and 29 May 1999.* Warsaw: OSCE.

ODIHR. 2000a. *Former Yugoslav Republic of Macedonia Presidential Elections, 31 October & 14 November 1999, Final Report.* Warsaw: OSCE.

ODIHR. 2000b. *Ukraine Presidential Elections, 31 October and 14 November 1999, Final Report.* Warsaw: OSCE.

ODIHR. 2000c. *Republic of Georgia Presidential Election, 9 April 2000, Final Report.* Warsaw: OSCE.

ODIHR. 2000d. *Georgia: Parliamentary Elections, 31 October & 14 November 1999, Final Report.* Warsaw: OSCE.

ODIHR. 2000e. *Republic of Albania Local Government Elections, 1 and 15 October 2000.* Warsaw: OSCE.

ODIHR. 2000f. *Republic of Croatia Extraordinary Presidential Elections, 24 January and 7 February 2000. Final Report.* Warsaw: OSCE.

ODIHR. 2000g. *Republic of Croatia Parliamentary Elections, 2 and 3 January 2000. Final Report.* Warsaw: OSCE.

ODIHR. 2000h. *Russian Federation Elections to the State Duma, 19 December 1999: Final Report.* Warsaw: OSCE.

ODIHR. 2000i. *Russian Federation Presidential Election, 25 March 2000: Final Report.* Warsaw: OSCE.

ODIHR. 2001a. *Final Report on the Parliamentary Elections in Moldova, 25 February 2001.* Warsaw: OSCE.

ODIHR. 2001b. *Republic of Albania Parliamentary Elections, 24 June – 19 August 2001.* Warsaw: OSCE.

ODIHR. 2001c. *Final Report on the Presidential Election in Belarus, 9 September 2001.* Warsaw: OSCE.

ODIHR. 2001d. *Romania Presidential and Parliamentary Elections, 26 November and 10 December 2000. Final Report.* Warsaw: OSCE.

ODIHR. 2002. *Former Yugoslav Republic of Macedonia Parliamentary Elections, 15 September 2002, OSCE/ODIHR Election Observation Mission, Final Report 20 November 2002.* Warsaw: OSCE.

ODIHR. 2003a. *Republic of Serbia and Montenegro Presidential Election, 16 November 2003. OSCE/ODIHR Election Observation Mission Report.* Warsaw: OSCE.

ODIHR. 2003b. *Republic of Armenia: Presidential Election, March 16 and 30, 2003, Final Report.* Warsaw: OSCE.

ODIHR. 2003c. *Republic of Armenia: Parliamentary Elections, 25 May 2003, Final Report.* Warsaw: OSCE.

ODIHR. 2004a. *Republic of Albania Local Government Elections, 12 October 2003 – 25 January 2004, OSCE/ODIHR Election Observation Mission Report.* Warsaw: OSCE.

ODIHR. 2004b. *Russian Federation Elections to the State Duma, 7 December 2003, OSCE/ODIHR Election Observation Mission Report.* Warsaw: OSCE.

ODIHR. 2004c. *Republic of Serbia and Montenegro Parliamentary Election, 28 December 2003, OSCE/ODIHR Election Observation Mission Report.* Warsaw: OSCE.

ODIHR. 2004d. *Russian Federation Presidential Election, 14 March 2004, OSCE/ODIHR Election Observation Mission Report.* Warsaw: OSCE.

ODIHR. 2004e. *Final Report on the Presidential Election in the Republic of Serbia (Serbia and Montenegro), 13 and 27 June 2004.* Warsaw: OSCE.

ODIHR. 2004f. *Former Yugoslav Republic of Macedonia: Presidential Election, 14 & 28 April 2004, OSCE/ODIHR Election Observation Mission, Final Report, 13 July 2004.* Warsaw: OSCE.

ODIHR. 2004g. *Georgia: Extraordinary Presidential Election, 4 January 2004, Final Report.* Warsaw: OSCE.

ODIHR. 2004h. *Georgia: Partial Repeat Parliamentary Elections, 28 March 2004, OSCE/ODIHR Election Observer Mission Report, Part II.* Warsaw: OSCE.

ODIHR. 2004i. *Final Report on the Parliamentary Elections in Belarus, 17 October 2004.* Warsaw: OSCE.

ODIHR. 2005a. *Romania Presidential and Parliamentary Elections, 28 November and 12 December 2004, Final Report.* Warsaw: OSCE.

ODIHR. 2005b. *Republic of Albania Parliamentary Elections, 3 July 2005, OSCE/ODIHR Election Observation Mission Report.* Warsaw: OSCE.

ODIHR. 2005c. *Moldova: Parliamentary Elections, 6 March 2005, Election Observation Mission Report.* Warsaw: OSCE.

ODIHR. 2006a. *Final Report on the 19 March 2006 Presidential Election in Belarus*. Warsaw: OSCE.

ODIHR. 2006b. *Final Report on the 26 March 2006 Parliamentary Elections in Ukraine*. Warsaw: OSCE.

ODIHR. 2006c. *5 July 2006 Parliamentary Elections in the Former Yugoslav Republic of Macedonia: Final Report*. Warsaw: OSCE.

ODIHR. 2007a. *Republic of Armenia: Parliamentary Elections, 12 May 2007, Final Report*. Warsaw: OSCE.

ODIHR. 2007b. *Final Report on the 30 September 2007 Pre-Term Parliamentary Elections in Ukraine*. Warsaw: OSCE.

ODIHR. 2008a. *Final Report on the 1 June 2008 Parliamentary Elections in the Former Yugoslav Republic of Macedonia*. Warsaw: OSCE.

ODIHR. 2008b. *Republic of Armenia: Presidential Election, 19 February 2008, Final Report*. Warsaw: OSCE.

ODIHR. 2008c. *Georgia: Extraordinary Presidential Election, 5 January 2008, Final Report*. Warsaw: OSCE.

ODIHR 2009a. *Final Report on the 28 June 2009 Parliamentary Elections in the Republic of Albania*. Warsaw: OSCE.

ODIHR. 2009b. *Statement of Preliminary Findings and Conclusions on the 22 March 2009 Presidential and Municipal Elections (First Round) in the Former Yugoslav Republic of Macedonia*. Warsaw: OSCE.

O'Donnell, Guillermo. 1973. *Modernization and Bureaucratic-Authoritarianism: Studies in South American Politics*. Berkeley: Institute of International Studies, University of California.

O'Donnell, Guillermo. 1993. "On the State, Democratization, and Some Conceptual Problems: A Latin American View with Some Post-Communist Countries." *World Development* 21, No. 8: 1355–69.

O'Donnell, Guillermo. 1996. "Illusions about Consolidation." *Journal of Democracy* 7, No. 2: 34–51.

O'Donnell, Guillermo. 1999. "Polyarchies and the (Un)rule of Law in Latin America: A Partial Conclusion." In Juan Mendez, Guillermo O'Donnell, and Paulo Sergio Pinheiro, eds. *The (Un)rule of Law and the Underprivileged in Latin America*. Notre Dame, IN: University of Notre Dame Press. Pp. 303–38.

O'Donnell, Guillermo, and Philippe C. Schmitter. 1986. *Transitions from Authoritarian Rule: Tentative Conclusions about Uncertain Democracies*. Baltimore, MD: The Johns Hopkins University Press.

O'Donnell, James. 1995. "Albania's *Sigurimi*: The Ultimate Agents of Social Control." *Problems of Post-Communism* 42, No. 6: 18–22.

Ognianova, Nina. 2009. "Georgia and Russia: Conquering Television to Control the Narrative." Committee to Protect Journalists: "Attacks on the Press in 2008."

Ojendal, Joakim. 1996. "Democracy Lost? The Fate of the UN-Implemented Democracy in Cambodia." *Contemporary Southeast Asia* 18, No. 2: 193–218.

Okumu, John J., and Frank Holmquist. 1984. "Party and Party–State Relations." In Joel Barkan, ed. *Politics and Public Policy in Kenya and Tanzania*. New York: Praeger.

Ola-Davies, George. 1991. "Mali: People's Resolve." *Africa Events* 7, No. 4 (April): 7–8.

O'Loughlin, John, Michael D. Ward, Corey L. Lafdahl, Jordan S. Coehn, and David S. Brown. 1998. "The Diffusion of Democracy, 1946–1994." *Annals of the Association of American Geographers* 88, No. 4: 545–74.

Olukoshi, Adebayo O. 1998. "Economic Crisis, Multipartyism, and Opposition Politics in Contemporary Africa." In Adebayo O. Olukoshi, ed. *The Politics of Opposition in Contemporary Africa*. Uppsala, Sweden: Nordiska Afrikainstitutet.

Olvera, Alberto J. 2003a. "Las tendencies generales de desarrollo de la sociedad civil en México." In Alberto J. Olvera, ed. *Sociedad civil, esfera pública y democratización en América Latina.* Xalapa, Mexico: Universidad Veracruzana.

Olvera, Alberto J. 2003b. "Movimientos socials prodemocráticos y esfera pública en México: El caso de Alianza Cívica." In Alberto J. Olvera, ed. *Sociedad civil, esfera pública y democratización en América Latina.* Xalapa, Mexico: Universidad Veracruzana.

Olynyk, Stephen D. 1994. "Emerging Post-Soviet Armies: The Case of the Ukraine." *Military Review* 74, No. 3 (March): 5–18.

Omitoogun, Wuyi, and Kenneth Onigo-Itite. 1996. "The National Conference as a Model for Democratic Consolidation: Benin and Nigeria." *Africa Occasional Paper*, No 6. Ibadan, Nigeria: French Institute for Research (IFRA).

Omukada, A. E. 2002. "The Ruling Party in Competitive Elections: The Dialectics of Incumbency in Kenya." In Ludeki Chweya, ed. *Electoral Politics in Kenya*. Nairobi, Kenya: Claripress.

Ooi, Su-Mei. 2009. "The Transnational Protection Regime and Taiwan's Democratization." *Journal of East Asian Studies* 9: 57–85.

Oppenheimer, Andres. 1992. *Castro's Final Hour: The Secret Story Behind the Coming Downfall of Communist Cuba.* New York: Simon and Schuster.

Oppenheimer, Andres. 1996. *Bordering on Chaos: Guerrillas, Stockbrokers, Politicians, and Mexico's Road to Prosperity.* Boston: Little, Brown and Company.

Oquaye, Mike. 1995. "The Ghanaian Elections of 1992: A Dissenting View." *African Affairs* 94, No. 375 (April): 259–75.

Oquaye, Mike. 1998. "Human Rights and the 1996 Elections." In Joseph R. A. Ayee, ed. *The 1996 General Elections and Democratic Consolidation in Ghana.* Accra: University of Ghana, Department of Political Science.

Oquaye, Mike. 2000. "The Process of Democratization in Contemporary Ghana." *Journal of Commonwealth and Comparative Politics.* 38, No. 3 (November): 53–78.

Oquaye, Mike. 2001. *Government and Politics in Contemporary Ghana (1992–1999): A Study.* Accra: Africa Governance Institute.

Oquist, Paul. 1992. "Sociopolitical Dynamics of the 1990 Nicaraguan Elections." In Vanessa Castro and Gary Prevost, eds. *The 1990 Elections in Nicaragua and Their Aftermath.* Lanham, MD: Rowman and Littlefield.

Orenstein, Catherine. 2001. "Aristide, Again." *The Progressive* Volume 65 (January): 20–23.

Orenstein, Mitchell, and Hans Peter Schmitz. 2006. "The New Transnationalism and Comparative Politics." *Comparative Politics* 38, No. 4: 479–500.

Osei-Hwedie, Bertha. 2001. "The Political Opposition in Botswana: The Politics of Factionalism and Fragmentation." *Transformation* 45: 57–77.

O'Rourke, Breffni. 2003. "EU/Balkans: Is the Bloc Doing Enough to Help the Region?" *RFE/RL Reports* (7 January).

Orozco, Manuel. 2002. *International Norms and Mobilization of Democracy: Nicaragua in the World.* Aldershot, UK: Ashgate Publishing.

Osborne, Milton. 2000. "Cambodia: Hun Sen Consolidates Power." *Southeast Asian Affairs* (2000): 101–11.

Osborne, Milton. 2003. "Cambodia: Hun Sen Firmly in Control." *Southeast Asian Affairs* (2003): 83–94.

O'Shea, Brendan. 2001. "Macedonia on the Brink?" *Peacekeeping and International Relations* 30, No. 4: 1–6.

Ostrow, Joel M., Georgiy Saratov, and Irina Khakamada. 2007. *The Consolidation of Dictatorship in Russia.* Westport, CT: Praeger.

Ottaway, Marina. 2003. *Democracy Challenged: The Rise of Semi-Authoritarianism.* Washington, DC: Carnegie Endowment for International Peace.

Ottaway, Marina, and Thomas Carothers, eds. 2000. *Funding Virtue: Civil Society Aid and Democracy Promotion*. Washington, DC: Carnegie Endowment for International Peace.

Ottaway, Marina, and Theresa Chung. 1999. "Debating Democracy Assistance: Toward a New Paradigm." *Journal of Democracy* 10, No. 4: 99–113.

Ottaway, Marina, and Gideon Maltz. 2001. "Croatia's Second Transition and the International Community." *Current History* 100, No. 649: 375–80.

Oviedo, José, and Rosario Espinal. 1986. *Democracia y Proyecto Socialdemocrata en Republica Dominicana*. Santo Domingo, Dominican Republic: Editor Taller.

Oye, Kenneth A., et al. 1979. *Eagle Entangled: U.S. Foreign Policy in a Complex World*. New York: Longman.

Oyugi, Walter O. 1997. "Ethnicity in the Electoral Process: The 1992 General Elections in Kenya." *African Journal of Political Science* 2, No. 1: 41–69.

Oyugi, Walter O. 2003. "The Politics of Transition in Kenya, 1992–2003: Democratic Consolidation or Deconsolidation?" In Walter O. Oyugi, Peter Wanyande, and C. Odhiambo Mbai, eds. *The Politics of Transition in Kenya: From KANU to NARC*. Nairobi, Kenya: Heinrich Boll Foundation.

Ozuna, Marcelino. 2003. *Leonel: Una Biografia*. Santo Domingo, Dominican Republic: Llantén.

Pacheco, Mendez Guadalupe. 1991. "Los Sectores del PRI en las elecciones de 1988." *Mexican Studies/Estudios Mexicanos* 7, No. 2: 253–82.

Packer, George. 2004. "Ten Years After." *The New Yorker*, 1 March.

Palairet, Michael. 2000. "The Economic Consequences of Slobodan Miloševic." *Europe–Asia Studies* 53, No. 6: 903–19.

Palmer, Allen W. 1997. "Reinvesting the Democratic Press of Benin." In Festus Eribo and William Jong-Ebot, eds. *Press Freedom and Communication in Africa*. Trenton, NJ: Africa World Press.

Palmer, David Scott. 2006. "The Often Surprising Outcomes of Asymmetry in Internacional Affaire: United States–Peru Relations in the 1990s." In Julio Carrión, ed. *The Fujimori Legacy: The Rise of Electoral Authoritarianism in Peru*. University Park: Pennsylvania State University Press.

Panford, Kwamina. 1998. "Elections and Democratic Transition in Ghana: 1991–96." In Jean-Germain Gros, ed. *Democratization in Late Twentieth-Century Africa: Coping with Uncertainty*. Westport, CT: Greenwood Press.

Panter-Brick, Keith. 1994. "Prospects for Democracy in Zambia." *Government and Opposition* 29, No. 2 (Spring): 230–47.

Pao-Min, Chang. 1996. "Taiwan: The 1994 Elections." *Asian Affairs* 22, No. 4: 224–38.

Papadimitriou, Dimitris. 2001. "The EU's Strategy in the Post-Communist Balkans." *Southeast European and Black Sea Studies* 1, No. 3: 69–94.

Papadimitriou, Dimitris, and David Phinnemore. 2008. *Romania and the European Union: From Marginalization to Membership*. London: Routledge.

Pârvulescu, Sorana. 2004. "2004 Romanian Elections: Test Case for a True Romanian Democracy." *The Romanian Journal of Political Sciences* 4, No. 2 (Winter): 7–28.

Pascu, Ioan Mircea. 2004. "Perspectives of a Prospective NATO Member." *Mediterranean Quarterly* 15, No. 1: 8–16.

Pastor, Robert A. 1990. "Nicaragua's Choice: The Making of a Free Election." *Journal of Democracy* 1, No. 3: 13–25.

Pastor, Robert A. 1992. "Afterward: Old Habits, New Opportunities in Nicaragua." In William Robinson, *A Faustian Bargain: U.S. Intervention in the Nicaraguan Elections and American Foreign Policy in the Post–Cold War Era*. Boulder, CO: Westview Press.

Pastor, Robert A. 1993. *Integration with Mexico: Options for U.S. Policy.* New York: Twentieth Century Fund Press.

Pastor, Robert A. 1997. "A Popular Democratic Revolution in a Predemocratic Society: The Case of Haiti." In Robert I. Rotberg, ed. *Haiti Renewed: Political and Economic Prospects.* Washington, DC: The Brookings Institution Press.

Pastor, Robert A. 2001. *Exiting the Whirlpool: U.S. Foreign Policy Toward Latin America and the Caribbean.* Boulder, CO: Westview Press.

Pastor, Robert A., and Jorge G. Castañeda. 1988. *Limits to Friendship: The United States and Mexico.* New York: Alfred A. Knopf.

Patel, Nandini. 2000a. "The 1999 Elections. Challenges and Reforms." In Martin Ott, Kings M. Phiri, and Nandini Patel, eds. *Malawi's Second Democratic Elections: Process, Problems and Prospects.* Blantyre, Malawi: Christian Literature Association in Malawi.

Patel, Nandini, 2000b. "Media in the Democratic and Electoral Process." In Martin Ott, Kings M. Phiri, and Nandini Patel, eds. *Malawi's Second Democratic Elections: Process, Problems and Prospects.* Blantyre, Malawi: Christian Literature Association in Malawi.

Patel, Nandini. 2002. "Malawi." In Tom Lodge, Denis Kadima, and David Pottie, eds. *Compendium of Elections in Southern Africa.* Johannesburg: Electoral Institute of Southern Africa.

Pavlakovic, Vjeran. 2005. "Serbia Transformed? Political Dynamics in the Milošević Era and After." In Sabrina P. Ramet and Vjeran Pavlakovic, eds. *Serbia Since 1989: Politics and Society Under Milošević and After.* Seattle: University of Washington Press.

Pavlovic, Dusan, and Arben Qirezi. 2005. "Serbia and Montenegro." In A. Karatnycky, ed. *Nations in Transit 2005.* New York: Freedom House.

Pazderka, Josef. 2005. "Russia: End of a Messy Affair." *Transitions Online.* 7 June.

Pease, García Henry. 2003. *La Autocracia Fujimorista: Del Estado Intervencionista al Estado Mafioso.* Lima: Fondo Editorial del Pontificia Universidad Católica del Perú.

Peceny, Mark. 1999. *Democracy at the Point of Bayonets.* University Park: Pennsylvania State University Press.

Pehe, Jiri. 1989. "An Annotated Survey of Independent Movements in Eastern Europe." *Radio Free Europe Research, RAD Background Report* No. 100 (13 June): 1–29.

Peña, Angela. 1996. *Campañas y Crisis Electorales: La Experiencia Dominicana.* Santo Domingo, Dominican Republic: Editora Lozano.

Peou, Sorpong. 1998. "Cambodia in 1997: Back to Square One?" *Asian Survey* 38, No. 1: 69–74.

Peou, Sorpong. 1999. "Cambodia in 1998: From Despair to Hope?" *Asian Survey* 39, No. 1: 20–6.

Peou, Sorpong. 2000. *Intervention and Change in Cambodia: Towards Democracy?* Bangkok: Silkworm Books.

Pepinsky, Thomas B. 2007. "Malaysia: Turnover without Change." *Journal of Democracy* 18, No. 1: 113–27.

Pepinsky, Thomas B. 2009a. "The 2008 Malaysian Elections: An End to Ethnic Politics?" *Journal of East Asian Studies* 9: 87–120.

Pepinsky, Thomas B. 2009b. *Economic Crisis and the Breakdown of Authoritarian Regimes: Indonesia and Malaysia in Comparative Perspective.* New York: Cambridge University Press.

Peranic, Barbara. 2004. "Croatia 2003: Back to the Future." *Transitions Online.* 24 March.

Pérez-Armendáriz, Clarisa, and David Crow. 2010. "Do Migrants Remit Democracy? International Migration, Political Beliefs, and Behavior in Mexico." *Comparative Political Studies* 43, No. 1: 119–48.

Perry, Duncan. 1992. "The Republic of Macedonia and the Odds for Survival." *RFE/RL Research Report* 1, No. 46: 12–24.

Perry, Duncan. 1994. "Macedonia: From Independence to Recognition." *RFE/RL Research Report*. 7 January.

Perry, Duncan. 1998. "Destiny on Hold: Macedonia and the Dangers of Ethnic Discord." *Current History* 97, No. 617: 119–26.

Perry, Duncan. 2000. "Macedonia's Quest for Security and Stability." *Current History* 99, No. 635: 129–36.

Perusse, Roland I. 1995. *Haitian Democracy Restored: 1991–1995*. Lanham, MD: University Press of America.

Peters, Ralph-Michael. 2001. "Civil Society and the Election Year 1997 in Kenya." In Marcel Rutten, Alamin Mazrui, and Francois Grignon, eds. *Out for the Count: The 1997 General Elections and Prospects for Democracy in Kenya*. Kampala: Fountain Publishers.

Petkovski, Mihail Goce Petreski, and Trajko Slaveski. 1993. "Stabilization Efforts in the Republic of Macedonia." *RFE/RL Research Report* 2, No. 3: 34–7.

Petrosian, Susanna. 2003a. "Armenian Election Clash Looms: Government and Opposition Are Set on a Collision Course Following the Disputed First Round of Armenia's Presidential Election." *CRS*, No. 168 (27 February).

Petrosian, Susanna. 2003b. "Armenian Media Law Hangs in Balance." *CRS* No. 213 (8 January).

Petrov, Nikolai, and Darrell Slider. 2005. "Putin and the Regions." In Dale Herspring, ed. *Putin's Russia: Past Imperfect, Future Uncertain*. Boulder, CO: Rowman and Littlefield.

Pettman, Jan. 1974. "Zambia's Second Republic: The Establishment of a One-Party State." *The Journal of Modern African Studies* 12, No. 2: 231–44.

Peuch, Jean-Christophe. 2004. "Georgia: Critics Say Police Violence, Media Intimidation on the Rise." *Eurasia Insight*. 20 February.

Pevehouse, Jon C. 2005. *Democracy from Above: Regional Organizations and Democratization*. New York: Cambridge University Press.

Philip, George. 1999. "Democracy and State Bias in Latin America: Some Lessons from Mexico, Peru and Venezuela." *Democratization* 6, No. 4: 74–92.

Phillips, Dión E. 2002. "The Military of Guyana." In Lilian Bobea, ed. *Soldados y Ciudadanos en el Caribe*. Santo Domingo, Dominican Republic: FLACSO.

Phinnemore, David. 1999. *Association: Stepping Stone or Alternative to EU Membership?* Sheffield, UK: Sheffield Academic Press.

Phinnemore, David. 2001. "Stuck in the 'Grey Zone'? Fears and Frustrations in Romania's Quest for EU Membership." *Perspectives on European Politics and Society* 10, No. 1: 95–121.

Phiri, Isaac. 1999. "Media in 'Democratic' Zambia: Problems and Prospects." *Africa Today* 46, No. 2: 53–65.

Picard, Louis. 1987. *The Politics of Development on Botswana: A Model for Success?* Boulder, CO: Lynne Rienner Publishers.

Pickering, Paula M., and Mark Baskin. 2008. "What Is to Be Done? Succession from the League of Communists of Croatia." *Communist and Post-Communist Studies* 41, No. 4: 521–40.

Pikhovshek, V'iacheslav. 1998. *Dynamika Elity*. Kiev, Ukraine: Agentsva Ukrainy.

Pilon, Juliana. 1990. "Romania: A Revolution Hijacked." *Uncaptive Minds* (May–June–July): 36–7.

Piñeyro, José Luis. 1988. "Fuerzas armadas mexicanas y modernización military." In Augusto Varas, ed. *La Autonomía Militar en América Latina*. Caracas, Venezuela: Editorial Nueva Sociedad.

Pinkney, Robert. 1997. *Democracy and Dictatorship in Ghana and Tanzania*. New York: St. Martin's Press.

Planas, Pedro. 2000. *La Democracia Volátil: Movimientos, partidos, líderes políticos y conductas electorales en el Perú contemporáneo*. Lima, Peru: Fundación Friedrich Ebert Stiftung.

Plank, David. N. 1993. "Aid, Debt and the End of Sovereignty: Mozambique and Its Donors." *The Journal of Modern African Studies* 31, No. 3 (September): 407–30.

Polhemus, James. 1983. "Botswana Votes: Parties and Elections in an African Democracy." *Journal of Modern African Studies* 21: 397–430.

Pollier, Karine. 2008. *Ukraine Energy Report*. Paris: Enerdata.

Pond, Elizabeth. 2006. *Endgame in the Balkans: Regime Change European Style*. Washington, DC: The Brookings Institution Press.

Ponomarev, Lev. 1993. "The Democratic Russia Movement: Myths and Realities." *Demokratizatsiya* 1, No. 4: 15–21.

Pop-Eleches, Grigore. 1999. "Separated at Birth or Separated by Birth? The Communist Successor Parties in Romania and Hungary." *East European Politics and Societies* 13, No. 1: 117–47.

Pop-Eleches, Grigore. 2001. "Romania's Politics of Dejection." *Journal of Democracy* 12, No. 3: 156–69.

Posner, Daniel. 1995. "Malawi's New Dawn." *Journal of Democracy* 6, No. 1: 131–45.

Poulton, Hugh. 1993. "The Republic of Macedonia after UN Recognition." *RFE/RL Research Report* 2, No. 23: 22–30.

Powaski, Ronald E. 2000. *Return to Armageddon: The United States and the Nuclear Arms Race, 1981–1999*. New York: Oxford University Press.

Power, Samantha. 1995. "Croatia Postcard: Guns and Pigs." *New Republic* 212, No. 21 (22 May).

Pralong, Sandra. 2004. "NGOs and the Development of Civil Society." In H. Carey, ed. *Romania Since 1989: Politics, Economics, and Society*. Boulder, CO: Lexington Books. Pp. 229–43.

Preeg, Ernest H. 1993. "Introduction: The Haitian Challenge in Perspective." In Georges Fauriol, ed. *The Haitian Challenge: US Policy Considerations*. Washington, DC: Center for Strategic and International Studies.

Preeg, Ernest H. 1996. *The Haitian Dilemma: A Case Study in Demographics, Development, and U.S. Foreign Policy*. Washington, DC: Center for Strategic and International Studies.

Premdas, Ralph R. 1993a. "Guyana: The Critical Elections of 1992 and a Regime Change." *Caribbean Affairs* 6, No. 1: 111–40.

Premdas, Ralph R. 1993b. "Race, Politics and Succession in Trinidad and Guyana." In Anthony Payne and Paul Sutton, eds. *Modern Caribbean Politics*. Baltimore, MD: The Johns Hopkins University Press.

Premdas, Ralph R. 1994. "Guyana: Ethnic Politics and the Erosion of Human Rights and Democratic Governance." In Carlene J. Edie, ed. *Democracy in the Caribbean: Myths and Realities*. Westport, CT: Praeger.

Premdas, Ralph R. 1995. *Ethnic Conflict and Development: The Case of Guyana*. Aldershot, UK: Avebury.

Premo, Daniel. 1997. "The Redirection of the Armed Forces." In Thomas Walker, ed. *Nicaragua without Illusions: Regime Transition and Structural Adjustment in the 1990s*. Wilmington, DE: Scholarly Resources, Inc.

Preston, Julia, and Samuel Dillon. 2004. *Opening Mexico: The Making of a Democracy*. New York: Farrar, Straus, and Giroux.

Prevost, Gary. 1991. "The FSLN as Ruling Party." In Thomas Walker, ed. *Revolution and Counterrevolution in Nicaragua*. Boulder, CO: Westview Press.

Prevost, Gary. 1997. "The FSLN." In Thomas Walker, ed. *Nicaragua without Illusions: Regime Transition and Structural Adjustment in the 1990s*. Wilmington, DE: Scholarly Resources, Inc.

Pribicevic, Ognjen. 1996. "Serbia's Strongman Tightens His Grip on Power." *Transition*. 13 December.

Pribicevic, Ognjen. 2004. "Serbia after Milosevic." *Southeast European and Black Sea Studies* 4, No. 1: 107–18.

Pridham, Geoffrey, ed. 1991a. *Encouraging Democracy: The International Context of Regime Transition in Southern Europe*. Leicester, UK: Leicester University Press.

Pridham, Geoffrey. 1991b. "International Influences and Democratic Transition: Problems of Theory and Practice in Linkage Politics." In Geoffrey Pridham, ed. *Encouraging Democracy: The International Context of Regime Transition in Southern Europe*. Leicester, UL: Leicester University Press.

Pridham, Geoffrey. 1991c. "The Politics of the European Community, Transnational Networks and Democratic Transition in Southern Europe." In Geoffrey Pridham, ed. *Encouraging Democracy: The International Context of Regime Transition in Southern Europe*. Leicester, UK: Leicester University Press.

Pridham, Geoffrey. 1999a. "Complying with the European Union's Democratic Conditionality: Transnational Party Linkages and Regime Change in Slovakia, 1993–1998." *Europe–Asia Studies* 51, No. 7: 1221–44.

Pridham, Geoffrey. 1999b. "The European Union, Democratic Conditionality and Transnational Party Linkages." In Jean Grugel, ed. *Democracy without Borders: Transnationalization and Conditionality in New Democracies*. London: Routledge.

Pridham, Geoffrey. 2001. "Uneasy Democratizations: Pariah Regimes, Political conditionality and Reborn Transitions in Central and Eastern Europe." *Democratization* 8, No. 4: 65–94.

Pridham, Geoffrey. 2002. "The European Union's Democratic Conditionality and Domestic Politics in Slovakia: The Meciar and Dzurinda Governments Compared." *Europe–Asia Studies* 54, No. 2: 203–27.

Pridham, Geoffrey. 2005. *Designing Democracy: EU Enlargement and Regime Change in Post-Communist Europe*. London: Palgrave.

Pridham, Geoffrey. 2007. "Romania and EU Membership in Comparative Perspective: A Post-Accession Compliance Problem? – The Case of Political Conditionality." *Perspectives on European Politics and Society* 8, No. 2: 168–88.

Pridham, Geoffrey. 2008. "Status Quo Bias or Institutionalisation for Reversibility?: The EU's Political Conditionality, Post-Accession Tendencies and Democratic Consolidation in Slovakia." *Europe–Asia Studies* 60, No. 3 (May): 423–54.

Pridham, Geoffrey, Eric Herring, and George Sanford, eds. 1997. *Building Democracy? The International Dimension of Democratization in Eastern Europe*. London: Leicester University Press.

Prifti, Peter. 1978. *Socialist Albania since 1944: Domestic and Foreign Developments*. Cambridge, MA: MIT Press.

Primakov, Evgenii. 2007. *Minnoe pole politiki*. Moscow: Molodaia gvardiia.

Pringle, Robert W. 2001–2002. "Putin: The New Andropov?" *International Journal of Intelligence & Counter Intelligence* 14, No. 4 (Winter): 545–59.

Prizel, Ilya. 1999. "Assessing a Decade: Eastern Europe and the FSU after the Fall of the Berlin Wall." *SAIS Review* 19, No. 2: 1–15.

Prud'homme, Jean-Francois. 1998. "The Instituto Federal Electoral (IFE): Building an Impartial Electoral Authority." In Mónica Serrano, ed. *Governing Mexico: Political Parties and Elections*. London: Institute of Latin American Studies.

Przeworski, Adam. 1986. "Some Problems in the Study of the Transition to Democracy." In Guillermo O'Donnell, Philippe C. Schmitter, and Laurence Whitehead, eds. *Transitions from Authoritarian Rule: Comparative Perspectives*. Baltimore, MD: The Johns Hopkins University Press.

Przeworski, Adam. 1991. *Democracy and the Market*. New York: Cambridge University Press.

Przeworski, Adam, Michael E. Alvarez, José Antonio Cheibub, and Fernando Limongi. 2000. *Democracy and Development: Political Institutions and Well-Being in the World, 1950–1990*. New York: Cambridge University Press.

Przeworski, Adam, and Fernando Limongi. 1997. "Modernization: Theories and Facts." *World Politics* 49, No. 2: 155–83.

Puglisi, Rosario. 2003. "Clashing Agendas? Economic Interests, Elite Coalitions and Prospects for Cooperation between Russia and Ukraine." *Europe–Asia Studies* 55, No. 6: 827–45.

Purcell, Susan Kaufman. 1973. "Decision-Making in an Authoritarian Regime: Theoretical Implications from a Mexican Case Study." *World Politics* 26, No. 1: 28–54.

Purcell, Susan Kaufman. 1992. "Collapsing Cuba." *Foreign Affairs* 71, No. 1: 131–45.

Purcell, Susan Kaufman. 1997. "The Changing Nature of US–Mexican Relations." *Journal of Interamerican Studies and World Affairs* 39, No. 1: 137–52.

Pusic, Vesna. 1998. "Croatia at the Crossroads." *Journal of Democracy* 9, No. 1: 111–24.

Puto, Artan. 2006. "Albania: One Step Closer." *Transitions Online*. 15 June.

Quantin, Patrick. 1992. "The 1990 General Elections in Zimbabwe: Step Towards a One-Party State?" In Simon Baynham, ed. *Zimbabwe in Transition*. Stockholm: Almquist and Wiskell International.

Rabobank. 2006. *Country Report Botswana*. The Netherlands.

Radio Free Europe. 1978. "Travel Regulations in Eastern Europe and the Soviet Union." *RAD Background Report (Eastern Europe)* 109: 5 June.

Radnitz, Scott. 2006. "What Really Happened in Kyrgyzstan?" *Journal of Democracy* 17, No. 2 (April): 132–46.

Radu, Michael. 2000. "Mexico: Slouching toward Normality." *The Washington Quarterly* 23, No. 3: 41–56.

Raftopoulos, Brian. 2000. "The State, NGOs and Democratization." In Sam Moyo, John Makumbe and Brian Raftopoulos, eds. *NGOs, the State and Politics in Zimbabwe*. Harare: SAPES Books.

Raftopoulos, Brian. 2001. "The Labor Movement and the Emergence of Opposition Politics." In Brian Raftopoulos and Lloyd Sachikoyne, eds. *Striking Back: The Labor Movement and the Post-Colonial State in Zimbabwe, 1980–2000*. Harare, Zimbabwe: Weaver Press.

Raftopoulos, Brian. 2002. "Briefing: Zimbabwe's 2002 Presidential Election." *African Affairs* 101: 413–26.

Rahman, Embong, Abdul. 2002. *State-Led Modernization and the New Middle Class in Malaysia*. New York: Palgrave.

Raison-Jourde, Francoise. 1995. "The Madagascan Churches in the Political Arena and their Contribution to the Change of Regime 1990–1993." In Paul Gifford, ed. *The Christian Churches and the Democratization of Africa*. Leiden, The Netherlands: E. J. Brill.

Rakipi, Albert. 2002. "Albania and Weak States in the Balkans." In *Institute for Peace Support Management, The Western Balkans*. Vienna: Austrian National Defense Academy.

Rakner, Lise. 2003. *Political and Economic Liberalization in Zambia 1991–2001*. Stockholm: Nordic Africa Institute.

Rakner, Lise, and Lars Svåsand. 2004. "From Dominant to Competitive Party System: The Zambian Experience 1991–2001." *Party Politics* 10, No. 1: 49–68.

Rakner, Lise, and Lars Svåsand. 2005. "Stuck in Transition: Electoral Processes in Zambia 1991–2001." *Democratization* 12, No. 1: 85–105.

Rakner, Lise, and Nicolas van de Walle. 2009. "Opposition Parties and Incumbent Presidents: The New Dynamics of Electoral Competition in Africa." In Staffan I. Lindberg, ed. *Democratization by Elections: A New Mode of Transition.* Baltimore, MD: The Johns Hopkins University Press.

Ramírez Morillo, Belarminio. 1997. *El Fantasma del Fraude: Estudio de los Procesos Electorales en la República Dominicana.* Santo Domingo, Dominican Republic: Editora Diálogo.

Randrianja, Solofo. 1999. "The Endless Quest of Caliban: or The Movement of 1991 and Democratization in Madagascar." In Jonathan Hyslop, ed. *African Democracy in the Era of Globalization.* Johannesburg: Witwatersbrand University Press.

Randrianja, Solofo. 2003. "'Be Not Afraid, Only Believe': Madagascar 2002." *African Affairs* 102: 309–29.

Rauch, Janine, and Elrena Van DerSpuy. 2006. "Recent Experiments in Police Reform in Post-Conflict Africa: A Review." Report submitted to IDASA and Japanese International Cooperation Aid (JICA).

Rawnsley, Gary D., and Ming-Yeh T. Rawsley. 1998. "Regime Transition and the Media in Taiwan." *Democratization* 5, No. 2: 106–24.

Reding, Andrew. 1991. "The Evolution of Governmental Institutions." In Thomas Walker, ed. *Revolution and Counterrevolution in Nicaragua.* Boulder, CO: Westview Press.

Reed, Michael C. 1987. "Gabon: A Neo-Colonial Enclave of Enduring French Interest." *Journal of Modern African Studies* 25, No. 2: 283–320.

Reichardt, David. 2002. "Democracy Promotion in Slovakia: An Import or an Export Business?" *Perspectives: The Central European Review of International Affairs* 18 (Summer): 5–20.

Remington, Robin Alison. 1996. "The Yugoslav Army: Trauma and Transition." In Constantine Danopoulos and Daniel Zirker, eds. *Civil–Military Relations in the Soviet and Yugoslav Successor States.* Boulder, CO: Westview Press. Pp. 153–73.

Remington, Thomas. 1996. "Menage a Trois: The End of Soviet Parliamentarism." In Jeffrey Hahn, ed. *Democratization in Russia: The Development of Legislative Institutions.* Armonk, NY: M. E. Sharpe. Pp. 106–40.

Remington, Thomas. 2003a. "Majorities without Mandates: The Russian Federation Council since 2000." *Europe–Asia Studies* 55, No. 5: 667–91.

Remington, Thomas. 2003b. "Putin, the Duma, and Political Parties." In Dale R. Herspring, ed. *Putin's Russia: Past Imperfect, Future Uncertain.* Lanham, MD: Rowman and Littlefield.

Remington, Thomas F. 2003c. "Coalition Politics in the New Duma." In Vicki Hesli and William Reisinger, eds. *The 1999–2000 Elections in Russia: Their Impact and Legacy.* New York: Cambridge University Press.

Remington, Thomas. 2008. "Patronage and the Party of Power: President–Parliament Relations under Vladimir Putin." *Europe–Asia Studies* 60, No. 6: 959–87.

Remington, Thomas, Steven S. Smith, D. Roderick Kiewit, and Moshe Haspel. 1994. "Transitional Institutions and Parliamentary Alignments in Russia, 1990–1993." In Thomas Remington, ed. *Parliaments in Transition.* Boulder, CO: Westview Press. Pp. 159–80.

Reuter, Ora John, and Thomas F. Remington. 2009. "Dominant Party Regimes and the Commitment Problem: The Case of United Russia." *Comparative Political Studies* 42, No. 4: 501–26.

Reynolds, Andrew. 1999. *Electoral Systems and Democratization in Southern Africa*. Oxford, UK: Oxford University Press.

Rhodes, Matthew. 2001. "Slovakia after Mečiar: A Midterm Report." *Problems of Post-Communism* (July–August): 3–13.

Richard, Patricia Bayer and John A. Booth. 1995. "Election Observation and Democratization: Reflections on the Nicaraguan Case." In Mitchell A. Seligson and John A. Booth, eds. *Elections and Democracy in Central America, Revisited*. Chapel Hill: University of North Carolina Press.

Richmond, Yale. 2008. "Cultural Exchange." In Ruud van Dijk, ed. *Encyclopedia of the Cold War*. New York: Taylor & Francis.

Rigger, Shelley. 1996. "Mobilizational Authoritarianism and Political Opposition in Taiwan." In Garry Rodan, ed. *Political Oppositions in Industrializing Asia*. London: Routledge.

Rigger, Shelley. 1999. "Grassroots Electoral Organization and Political Reform in the ROC on Taiwan and Mexico." In Hermann Giliomee and Charles Simkins, eds. *The Awkward Embrace: One-Party Domination and Democracy*. Cape Town, South Africa: Tafelberg.

Rigger, Shelley. 2000. "Machine Politics and Protracted Transition in Taiwan." *Democratization* 7, No. 3: 135–52.

Rigger, Shelley. 2001a. "The Democratic Progressive Party in 2000: Obstacles and Opportunities." *The China Quarterly* 168 (December): 944–59.

Rigger, Shelley. 2001b. *From Opposition to Power: Taiwan's Democratic Progressive Party*. Boulder, CO: Lynne Rienner Publishers.

Riker, William H. 1982. *Liberalism against Populism*. Prospect Heights, IL: Waveland.

Risse-Kappen, Thomas. 1995a. "Bringing Transnational Relations Back In: Introduction." In Thomas Risse-Kappen, ed. *Bringing Transnational Relations Back In: Non-State Actors, Domestic Structures, and International Institutions*. New York: Cambridge University Press.

Risse-Kappen, Thomas. 1995b. "Structures of Governance and Transnational Relations: What Have We Learned?" In Thomas Risse-Kappen, ed. *Bringing Transnational Relations Back In: Non-State Actors, Domestic Structures, and International Institutions*. New York: Cambridge University Press.

Risse, Thomas, and Stephen C. Ropp. 1999. "International Human Rights Norms and Domestic Change: Conclusion." In Thomas Risse, Stephen C. Ropp, and Kathryn Sikkink, eds. 1999. *The Power of Human Rights: International Norms and Domestic Change*. New York: Cambridge University Press.

Risse, Thomas, Stephen C. Ropp, and Kathryn Sikkink, eds. 1999. *The Power of Human Rights: International Norms and Domestic Change*. New York: Cambridge University Press.

Risse, Thomas, and Kathryn Sikkink. 1999. "The Socialization of International Human Rights Norms into Domestic Practices: Introduction." In Thomas Risse, Stephen C. Ropp, and Kathryn Sikkink, eds. 1999. *The Power of Human Rights: International Norms and Domestic Change*. New York: Cambridge University Press.

Roberts, David W. 2001. *Political Transition in Cambodia 1991–99: Power, Elitism and Democracy*. Richmond, VA: Curzon.

Roberts, Kenneth M. 1990. "Bullying and Bargaining: The United States, Nicaragua, and Conflict Resolution in Central America." *International Security* 15, No. 2: 67–102.

Roberts, Kenneth M. 1995. "Neoliberalism and the Transformation of Populism in Latin America." *World Politics* 48, 1: 82–116.

Roberts, Kenneth M. 1998. *Deepening Democracy? The Modern Left and Social Movements in Chile and Peru*. Stanford, CA: Stanford University Press.

Roberts, Kenneth M. 2002. "Do Parties Matter? Lessons from the Fujimori Experience." Conference Paper. Dante B. Fascell North–South Center at the University of Miami and the University of Delaware's Department of Political Science and International Relations (sponsors). Washington, DC.

Roberts, Kenneth M. 2006a. "Populism, Political Conflict, and Grass-Roots Organization in Latin America." *Comparative Politics* 38, No. 2: 127–48.

Roberts, Kenneth M. 2006b. "Do Parties Matter? Lessons from the Fujimori Experience." In Julio Carrión, ed. *The Fujimori Legacy: The Rise of Electoral Authoritarianism in Peru.* University Park: Pennsylvania State University Press.

Roberts, Kenneth M., and Mark Peceny. 1997. "Human Rights and United States Policy Toward Peru." In Maxwell Cameron and Philip Mauceri, eds. *The Peruvian Labyrinth.* University Park: Pennsylvania State University Press.

Robinson, Thomas W. 1998. "America in Taiwan's Post–Cold War Foreign Relations." In David Shambaugh, ed. *Contemporary Taiwan.* Oxford, UK: Clarendon Press.

Robinson, William I. 1992. *A Faustian Bargain: U.S. Intervention in the Nicaraguan Elections and American Foreign Policy in the Post–Cold War Era.* Boulder, CO: Westview Press.

Robinson, William I. 1996. *Promoting Polyarchy: Globalization, U.S. Intervention, and Hegemony.* New York: Cambridge University Press.

Rochowanski, Almut. 2004. "EU Extends Cooperation with Georgia, but Expresses Caution on Accession Issue." *Eurasia Insight.* 17 June.

Rodan, Garry. 2004. *Transparency and Authoritarian Rule in Southeast Asia: Singapore and Malaysia.* London: Routledge.

Rodríguez Beruff, Jorge. 1998. "Entre la 'narcodemocracia' y el Leviatán antidrogas: Fuerzas de seguridad, Estado pospopulista y nuevas formas de autoritarismo en el Caribe." In Wilfredo Lozano, ed. *Cambio Político en el Caribe: Escenarios de la Posguerra Fría: Cuba, Haití, y República Dominicana.* Caracas, Venezuela: Editorial Nueva Sociedad.

Roeder, Philip G. 1994. "Varieties of Post-Soviet Authoritarian Regimes." *Post-Soviet Affairs* 10, No. 1: 61–101.

Roessler, Philip G. 2005. "Donor-Induced Democratization and the Privatization of State Violence in Kenya and Rwanda." *Comparative Politics* 37, No. 2: 207–25.

Ronen, Dov. 1987. "People's Republic of Benin: The Military, Marxist Ideology, and the Politics of Ethnicity." In John W. Harbeson, ed. *The Military in African Politics.* New York: Praeger.

Ronfeldt, David F. 1984a. "The Modern Mexican Military: An Overview." In David F. Ronfeldt, ed. *The Modern Mexican Military: A Reassessment.* La Jolla, CA: Center for U.S.–Mexican Studies.

Ronfeldt, David F. 1984b. "The Mexican Army and Political Order Since 1940." In David F. Ronfeldt, ed. *The Modern Mexican Military: A Reassessment.* La Jolla, CA: Center for U.S.–Mexican Studies.

Ronfeldt, David F. 1986. "The Modern Mexican Military." In Abraham F. Lowenthal and J. Samuel Fitch, eds. *Armies and Politics in Latin America, Revised Edition.* New York: Holmes and Meier.

Ronfeldt, David F. 1989. "Prospects for Elite Cohesion." In Wayne A. Cornelius, Judith Gentleman, and Peter H. Smith, eds. *Mexico's Alternative Political Futures.* San Diego, CA: Center for U.S.–Mexican Studies.

Ronning, Helge. 2003. "The Media in Zimbabwe: The Struggle between State and Civil Society." In Staffan Darnolf and Liisa Laakso, eds. *Twenty Years of Independence in Zimbabwe: From Liberation to Authoritarianism.* Houndmills, UK: Palgrave Macmillan.

Roper, Steven D. 1999. "Romania." In Julie Smith and Elizabeth Teague, eds. *Democracy in the New Europe: Politics of Post-Communism*. London: The Greycoat Press.

Rose, Euclid A. 2002. *Dependency and Socialism in the Modern Caribbean: Superpower Intervention in Guyana, Jamaica, and Grenada, 1970–1985*. Lanham, MD: Lexington Books.

Rose, Gideon. 2000. "Democracy Promotion and American Foreign Policy: A Review Essay." *International Security* 25, No. 3: 186–203.

Rose, Richard. 1996. "Boris Yeltsin Faces the Electorate: Findings from Public Opinion Polling Data." *Democratizatsiya* 4, No. 3 (Summer): 381–7.

Rosenau, James N. 1969. "Toward the Study of National–International Linkages." In James N. Rosenau, ed. *Linkage Politics: Essays on the Convergence of National and International Systems*. New York: The Free Press.

Rosenau, James N., and W. Michael Fagen. 1994. "Domestic Elections as International Events." In Carl Kaysen, Robert A. Pastor, and Laura W. Reed, eds. *Collective Responses to Regional Problems: The Case of Latin America and the Caribbean*. Cambridge, MA: American Academy of Arts and Sciences.

Rosenberger, Chandler Ross. 1999. "Big Brother in a Small Country: The Subversion of the Rule of Law in Contemporary Slovakia." *Human Rights Review* 1, No. 1 (September): 34–44.

Rospigliosi, Fernando. 1994. "Democracy's Bleak Prospects." In Joseph S. Tulchin and Gary Bland, eds. *Peru in Crisis: Dictatorship or Democracy?* Boulder, CO: Lynne Rienner Publishers.

Rospigliosi, Fernando. 1995. "La Amenaza de la 'Fujimorizacion': Gobernabilidad y Democracia en Condiciones Adversas: Perú y los Países Andinos." In Carina Perelli, Sonia Picado, and Daniel Zoviatto, eds. *Partidos y Clase Politica en America Latina en los 90*. San Jose, Costa Rica: Instituto Interamericano de Derechos Humanos.

Rospigliosi, Fernando. 2000. *Montesinos y las Fuerzas Armadas: Cómo Controló durante una Década las Instituciones Militares*. Lima, Peru: Instituto de Estudios Peruanos.

Ross, Kenneth R. 1995. "Not Catalyst but Ferment: The Distinctive Contribution of the Churches to Political Reform in Malawi 1992–93." In Paul Gifford, ed. *The Christian Churches and the Democratization of Africa*. Leiden, The Netherlands: E. J. Brill.

Ross, Kenneth R. 2004. "'Worrisome Trends': The Voice of the Churches in Malawi's Third Term Debate." *African Affairs* 103: 91–107.

Ross, Michael. 2001. "Does Oil Hinder Democracy?" *World Politics* 53, No. 3: 325–61.

Rotberg, Robert I. 1997. "Preface: Haiti's Last Best Chance." In Robert I. Rotberg, ed. *Haiti Renewed: Political and Economic Prospects*. Washington, D.C.: Brookings Institution Press.

Rothchild, Donald. 1995. "Rawlings and the Engineering of Legitimacy in Ghana." In I. William Zartman, ed. *Collapsed States: The Disintegration and Restoration of Legitimate Authority*. Boulder, CO: Lynne Rienner Publishers.

Roy, Denny. 2003. *Taiwan: A Political History*. Ithaca, NY: Cornell University Press.

Rueschemeyer, Dietrich, Evelyne Huber Stephens, and John D. Stephens. 1992. *Capitalist Development and Democracy*. Chicago: University of Chicago Press.

Rutland, Peter. 2006. "Oil and Politics in Russia." Paper prepared for the American Political Science Association Annual Convention, Philadelphia, PA. 2 September.

Rutten, Marcel. 2000. "The Kenyan General Elections of 1997: Implementing a New Model for International Election Observation in Africa." In Jon Abbink and Gerti Hesseling, eds. *Electoral Observation and Democratization in Africa*. London: MacMillan Press, Ltd.

Ryan, Selwyn. 1992. "Beyond Ethnic Paramountcy." In Dennis Watson and Christine Craig, eds. *Guyana at the Crossroads*. Miami, FL: University of Miami, North-South Center.

Saaka, Yakubu. 1997. "Legitimizing the Illegitimate: The 1992 Presidential Election as a Prelude to Ghana's Fourth Republic." In George Akeya Agbango, ed. *Issues and Trends in Contemporary African Politics: Stability, Development, and Democratization*. New York: Peter Lang.

Sabar, Galia. 2002. *Church, State and Society in Kenya: From Mediation to Opposition 1963–1993*. London: Frank Cass.

Sachikonye, Lloyd. 1991. "The Context of the Democracy Debate." In Ibbo Mandaza and Lloyd Sachikonye, eds. *The One Party State and Democracy*. Harare: Southern African Political Economy Trust.

Sachikonye, Lloyd. 1995. "State and Social Movements in Zimbabwe." In Lloyd Sachikoyne, ed. *Democracy, Civil Society and the State: Social Movements in Southern Africa*. Harare, Zimbabwe: SAPES Books.

Sachikonye, Lloyd. 2001. "The Institutional Development of Unions in Zimbabwe." In Brian Raftopoulos and Lloyd Sachikoyne, eds. *Striking Back: The Labor Movement and the Post-Colonial State in Zimbabwe, 1980–2000*. Harare, Zimbabwe: Weaver Press.

Sachsenroder, Wolfgang. 1998. "Party Politics and Democratic Development in East and Southeast Asia – A Comparative View." In Wolfgang Sachsenroder and Ulrike E. Frings, eds. *Political Party Systems and Democratic Development in East and Southeast Asia*. Aldershot, UK: Ashgate Publishing.

Saghabalian, Anna. 2005. "Armenian Referendum Was Rigged, Says Government Official." *Liberty Armenia and RFE/RL Report*. 28 December.

Sakwa, Richard. 2004. *Putin: Russia's Choice*. New York: Routledge.

Sakwa, Richard. 2007. *Putin: Russia's Choice (Revised Edition)*. New York: Routledge.

Sakwa, Richard. forthcoming. *The Crisis of Russian Democracy: The Dual State, Factionalism, and the Medvedev Succession*. Cambridge, UK: Cambridge University Press.

Salinas de Gortari, Carlos. 2002. *Mexico: The Policy and Politics of Modernization*. Barcelona, Spain: Plaza Janés.

Salleh, Halim. 1999. "Development and the Politics of Social Stability in Malaysia." *Southeast Asian Affairs* 1999: 185–203.

Samatar, Abdi Ismail. 1999. *An African Miracle: State and Class Leadership and Colonial Legacy in Botswana Development*. Portsmouth, NH: Heinemann.

Sanchez, Peter M. 1992. "The Dominican Case." In John Higley and Richard Gunther, eds. *Elites and Democratic Consolidation in Latin America and Southern Europe*. Cambridge: Cambridge University Press.

Sandbrook, Richard, and Jay Oelbaum. 1997. "Reforming Dysfunctional Institutions through Democratization? Reflections on Ghana." *Journal of Modern African Studies* 35, No. 4 (December): 603–46.

Sandbrook, Richard, and Jay Oelbaum. 1999. "Reforming the Political Kingdom: Governance and Development in Ghana's Fourth Republic." *Critical Perspectives Paper* (June 1999). Accra: Center for Democracy and Development.

Sannikov, Andrei. 2005. "The Accidental Dictatorship of Alexander Lukashenko." *School of Advanced International Studies of Johns Hopkins University Review* (Winter–Spring): 75–88.

Sannikov, Andrei, and Inna Kuley. 2006. "Civil Society and the Struggle for Freedom." In Joerg Forbrig, David R. Marples, and Pavol Demes, eds. *Prospects for Democracy in Belarus*. Washington, DC: German Marshall Fund of the United States.

Santiago, Charles, and M. Nadarajah. 1999. "The Anwar Debacle and the Potential for Democratic Reforms in Malaysia." In Kristina N. Gaerlan, ed. *Transitions to Democracy in East and Southeast Asia*. Quezon City, The Philippines: Institute for Popular Democracy.

Sarafyan, Mark. 1994. "Armenia." In B. Szajkowski, ed. *Political Parties of Eastern Europe, Russia, and the Successor States*. Stockton, UK: Essex.

Saravananamuttu, Jojan. 2004. "Iconoclasim and Foreign Policy – The Mahathir Years." In Bridget Welsh, ed. *Reflections: The Mahathir Years*. Washington, DC: The Paul H. Nitze School of Advanced International Studies.

Sasse, Gwendolyn. 2007. *The Crimea Question: Identity, Transition, and Conflict*. Cambridge, MA: Harvard University Press for the Harvard Ukrainian Research Institute.

Saunders, Richard. 2001. "Striking Ahead: Industrial Action and Labor Movement Development in Zimbabwe." In Brian Raftopoulos and Lloyd Sachikoyne, eds. *Striking Back: The Labor Movement and the Post-Colonial State in Zimbabwe, 1980–2000*. Harare, Zimbabwe: Weaver Press.

Saunders, Richard. 2007. "Trade Union Struggles for Autonomy and Democracy in Zimbabwe." In Jon Kraus, ed. *Trade Unions and the Coming of Democracy in Africa*. New York: Palgrave MacMillan.

Sawyer, Jon. 2006. "Georgia's Dangerous Game." *Foreign Policy Online*. 31 October.

Schaefer, Brett D., and Stephen Groves. 2008. "Kenyan Election Signals Need to Overhaul U.S. Policy Toward Nascent Democracies." *WebMemo* No. 1769. Washington, DC: Heritage Foundation.

Schedler, Andreas. 2000. "Mexico's Victory: The Democratic Revelation." *Journal of Democracy* 11, No. 4: 5–19.

Schedler, Andreas. 2002a. "The Nested Game of Democratization by Elections." *International Political Science Review* 23, No. 1: 103–22.

Schedler, Andreas. 2002b. "The Menu of Manipulation." *Journal of Democracy* 13, No. 2: 36–50.

Schedler, Andreas, ed. 2006a. *Electoral Authoritarianism: The Dynamics of Unfree Competition*. Boulder, CO: Lynne Rienner Publishers.

Schedler, Andreas. 2006b. "The Logic of Electoral Authoritarianism." In Andreas Schedler, ed. *Electoral Authoritarianism: The Dynamics of Unfree Competition*. Boulder, CO: Lynne Rienner Publishers.

Schedler, Andreas. 2007. "The Mobilization of Distrust." *Journal of Democracy* 18, No. 1: 88–105.

Schedler, Andreas. 2009a. "Sources of Competition under Electoral Authoritarianism." In Staffan I. Lindberg, ed. *Democratization by Elections: A New Mode of Transition*. Baltimore, MD: The Johns Hopkins University Press.

Schedler, Andreas. 2009b. "The Contingent Power of Authoritarian Elections." In Staffan I. Lindberg, ed. *Democratization by Elections: A New Mode of Transition*. Baltimore, MD: The Johns Hopkins University Press.

Schimmelfennig, Frank. 2001. "The Community Trap: Liberal Norms, Rhetorical Action, and the Eastern Enlargement of the European Union." *International Organization* 55, No. 1: 47–80.

Schimmelfennig, Frank. 2002. "Introduction: The Impact of International Organizations on the Central and Eastern European States – Conceptual and Theoretical Issues." In Ronald Linden, ed. *Norms and Nannies: The Impact of International Organizations on the Central and East European States*. Lanham, MD: Rowman and Littlefield.

Schimmelfennig, Frank. 2008. "EU Political Accession Conditionality after the 2004 Enlargement: Consistency and Effectiveness." *Journal of European Public Policy* 15, No. 6: 918–37.

Schimmelfennig, Frank, Stefan Engert, and Heiko Knobel. 2003. "Costs, Commitment and Compliance: The Impact of EU Democratic Conditionality on Latvia, Slovakia and Turkey." *Journal of Common Market Studies* 41, No. 3: 495–518.

Schimmelfennig, Frank, Stefan Engert, and Heiko Knobel. 2005. "The Impact of EU Political Conditionality." In Frank Schimmelfennig and Ulrich Sedelmeier, eds. *The Europeanization of Central and Eastern Europe*. Ithaca, NY: Cornell University Press.

Schimmelfennig, Frank, Stefan Engert, and Heiko Knobel. 2006. *International Socialization in Europe: European Organizations, Political Conditionality, and Democratic Change*. New York: Palgrave.

Schimmelfennig, Frank, and Ulrich Sedelmeier, eds. 2005. *The Europeanization of Central and Eastern Europe*. Ithaca, NY: Cornell University Press.

Schmidt, Fabian. 1997a. "Albania's Democrats Consolidate Power." *Transition*: 47–8. 7 February.

Schmidt, Fabian. 1997b. "Albanian Government Makes Personnel Changes." *RFE/RL Endnote*. 27 August.

Schmidt, Fabian. 1998a. "Albania Country Report: From Anarchy to an Uncertain Stability." In Peter Rutland ed. *Annual Survey of Eastern Europe and the Former Soviet Union: The Challenge of Integration*. Armonk, NY: M. E. Sharpe.

Schmidt, Fabian. 1998b. "Enemies Far and Near: Macedonia's Fragile Stability." *Problems of Post-Communism* 45, No. 4: 22–31.

Schmidt, Fabian. 1999a. "Albania's New Environment." *RFE/RL Endnote*. 29 July.

Schmidt, Fabian. 1999b. "Albania." In Julie Smith and Elizabeth Teague, eds. *Democracy in the New Europe: Politics of Post-Communism*. London: The Greycoat Press.

Schmidt, Gregory D. 2000. "Delegative Democracy in Peru? Fujimori's 1995 Landslide and the Prospects for 2000." *Journal of Interamerican Studies and World Affairs* 42, No. 1: 99–132.

Schmitter, Philippe C. 1996. "The Influence of the International Context upon the Choice of National Institutions and Policies in Neo-Democracies." In Laurence Whitehead, ed. *The International Dimensions of Democratization: Europe and the Americas*. Oxford, UK: Oxford University Press.

Schmitter, Philippe C., and Terry Lynn Karl. 1991. "What Democracy Is... And Is Not." *Journal of Democracy* 2, No. 3: 75–89.

Schmitz, Hans Peter. 1999. "Transnational Activism and Political Change in Kenya and Uganda." In Thomas Risse, Stephen C. Ropp, and Kathryn Sikkink, eds. 1999. *The Power of Human Rights: International Norms and Domestic Change*. New York: Cambridge University Press.

Schmitz, Hans Peter, and Katrina Sell. 1999. "International Factors in Processes of Political Democratization: Toward a Theoretical Integration." In Jean Grugel, ed. *Democracy without Borders: Transnationalization and Conditionality in New Democracies*. London: Routledge.

Schoffeleers, Mathew. 1999. *In Search of Truth and Justice: Confrontations between Church and State in Malawi, 1960–1994*. Blantyre, Malawi: Christian Literature Association in Malawi.

Schonwalder, Gerd. 2002. *Linking Civil Society and the State: Urban Popular Movements, the Left, and Local Government in Peru, 1980–1992*. University Park: Pennsylvania State University Press.

Schraeder, Peter J. 1994. *United States Foreign Policy Toward Africa: Incrementalism, Crisis and Change*. Cambridge: Cambridge University Press.

Schraeder, Peter J. 1996. "Removing the Shackles? U.S. Foreign Policy Toward Africa after the End of the Cold War." In Edmond J. Keller and Donald Rothchild, eds.

Africa in the New International Order: Rethinking State Sovereignty and Regional Security. Boulder, CO: Lynne Rienner Publishers.

Schraeder, Peter J. 2001. "'Forget the Rhetoric and Boost the Geopolitics': Emerging Trends in the Bush Administration's Policy Towards Africa, 2001." *African Affairs* 100: 387–404.

Schraeder, Peter J., ed. 2002a. *Exporting Democracy: Rhetoric vs. Reality.* Boulder, CO: Lynne Rienner Publishers.

Schraeder, Peter J. 2002b. "Promoting an International Community of Democracies." In Peter J. Schraeder, ed. *Exporting Democracy: Rhetoric vs. Reality.* Boulder, CO: Lynne Rienner Publishers.

Schraeder, Peter J. 2003. "The State of the Art in International Democracy Promotion: Results of a Joint European–North American Research Network." *Democratization* 10, No. 2: 21–44.

Schulz, Donald E. 1996. "Whither Haiti?" Strategic Studies Institute Monograph (April). Carlisle Barracks, PA: Strategic Studies Institute, U.S. Army War College.

Schulz, Donald E. 1997a. "Political Culture, Political Change, and the Etiology of Violence." In Robert I. Rotberg, ed. *Haiti Renewed: Political and Economic Prospects.* Washington, DC: The Brookings Institution Press.

Schulz, Donald E. 1997b. "Haiti Update." Strategic Studies Institute Monograph (January). Carlisle Barracks, PA: Strategic Studies Institute, U.S. Army War College.

Schulz, Donald E. 1997–1998. "Haiti: Will Things Fall Apart?" *Parameters* 27, No. 4: 73–91.

Schulz, Donald E., and Edward J. Williams. 1995. "Crisis or Transformation? The Struggle for the Soul of Mexico." In Donald E. Schulz and Edward J. Williams, eds. *Mexico Faces the 21st Century.* Westport, CT: Greenwood Press.

Schumpeter, Joseph. 1947. *Capitalism, Socialism, and Democracy.* New York: Harper.

Schwartz, Stephen. 1992. *A Strange Silence: The Emergence of Democracy in Nicaragua.* San Francisco, CA: Institute for Contemporary Studies Press.

Scott, Andrew M. 1982. *The Revolution in Statecraft: Intervention in an Age of Interdependence.* Durham, NC: Duke University Press.

Scott, Ian. 1976. "Party Politics in Zambia: A Study of the Organization of the United National Independence Party." Ph.D. Diss. University of Toronto, School of Graduate Studies.

Searle, Peter. 1999. *The Riddle of Malaysian Capitalism.* St. Leonards, Australia: Allen and Unwin.

Sebudubudu, David, and Bertha Osei-Hwedie. 2005. *Democratic Consolidation in SADC: Botswana's 2004 Elections.* Johannesburg, South Africa: EISA.

Sebudubudu, David, and Bertha Osei-Hwedie, 2006. "The Pitfalls of Parliamentary Democracy in Boswana." *Afrika Spectrum* 41, No. 1: 35–53.

Seeger, Annette. 1996. "Revolutionary Armies of Africa: Mozambique and Zimbabwe." In Simon Baynham, ed. *Military Power and Politics in Black Africa.* London: Croom Helm.

Seely, Jennifer 2007. "The Presidential Election in Benin, March 2006." *Electoral Studies* 26: 196–200.

Sekelj, Laslo. 2000. "Parties and Elections: The Federal Republic of Yugoslavia. Change without Transformation." *Europe–Asia Studies* 52, No. 1: 57–75.

Seleti, Yonah. 2000. "The Public Exorcism of the Police in Mozambique: Challenges of Institutional Democratization." *Journal of Southern African Studies* 26, No. 2 (June) 349–64.

Sell, Louis. 2002. *Slobodan Milosevic and the Destruction of Yugoslavia*. Durham, NC: Duke University Press.

Sellin, Frank. 2004. "Democratization in the Shadows: Post-Communist Patrimonialism." In Henry Carey, ed. *Romania Since 1989: Politics, Economics, and Society*. Boulder, CO: Lexington Books.

Selznick, Philip. 1960. *The Organizational Weapon: A Study of Bolshevik Strategy and Tactics*. Glencoe, IL: The Free Press.

Serra, Luis Hector. 1991. "The Grass-Roots Organizations." In Thomas Walker, ed. *Revolution and Counterrevolution in Nicaragua*. Boulder, CO: Westview Press.

Serrano, Mónica. 1995. "The Armed Branch of the State: Civil–Military Relations in Mexico." *Journal of Latin American Studies* 27, No. 2: 423–48.

Serrano, Mónica. 1997. "Estado y Fuerzas Armadas en México." In Marcelo Cavarozzi, ed. *México en el Desfiladero: Los Años de Salinas*. Mexico City: Juan Pablos Editor.

Shafir, Michael. 1992. "Romania's Elections: Why the Democratic Convention Lost." *RFE/RL Research Report* 1, No. 43: 1–7.

Shafir, Michael. 1995a. "Romania: Agony and Death of an Opposition Alliance." *Transition*. 26 May.

Shafir, Michael. 1995b. "Romania: The 'Centripetfugal' Process of Unifying the Liberals." *Transition*. 25 August.

Shafir, Michael. 1996a. "Romania: Anatomy of a Pre-Election Political Divorce." *Transition*. 26 January.

Shafir, Michael. 1996b. "Romania: Three Legacies." *Transition*. 27 December.

Shambaugh, David. 1998. "Taiwan's Security: Maintaining Deterrence amid Political Accountability." In David Shambaugh, ed. *Contemporary Taiwan*. Oxford: Clarendon Press.

Shamsie, Yasmine. 2004. "Building 'Low-Intensity' Democracy in Haiti: The OAS Contribution." *Third World Quarterly* 25, No. 6: 1097–115.

Sharman, J. C., and Roger E. Kanet. 2000. "International Influences on Democratization in Postcommunist Europe." In James F. Hollifield and Calvin Jillson, eds. *Pathways to Democracy: The Political Economy of Democratic Transitions*. New York: Routledge.

Shawcross, William. 1994. "Cambodia's New Deal." *Contemporary Issues Paper*, No. 1. Washington, DC: Carnegie Endowment for International Peace.

Schafferer, Christian. 2003. *The Power of the Ballot Box: Political Development and Election Campaigning in Taiwan*. Boston: Lexington Books.

Shefter, Martin. 1977. "Party and Patronage: Germany, England and Italy." *Politics and Society* 7, No. 4: 403–51.

Shefter, Martin. 1994. *Political Parties and the State: The American Historical Experience*. Princeton, NJ: Princeton University Press.

Shephard, Robin. 2006. "The United States and Europe's Last Dictatorship." In Joerg Forbrig, David R. Marples, and Pavol Demes, eds. *Prospects for Democracy in Belarus*. Washington, DC: German Marshall Fund of the United States.

Shevtsova, Lilia. 1999. *Yeltsin's Russia: Myths and Realities*. Washington, DC: Carnegie Endowment for International Peace.

Shevtsova, Lilia. 2005. *Putin's Russia*. Washinton, DC: Carnegie Endowment for International Peace.

Shiau, Chyuan-jenq. 1999. "Civil Society and Democratization." In Steve Tsang and Hung-mao Tien, eds. *Democratization in Taiwan: Implications for China*. London: Macmillan.

Shillington, Kevin. 1992. *Ghana and the Rawlings Factor*. London: MacMillan.

Shirk, David A. 2001. "Mexico's Democratization and the Organizational Development of the National Action Party." In Kevin Middlebrook, ed. *Party Politics and the Struggle for Democracy in Mexico: National and State-Level Analyses of the Partido Acción Nacional.* La Jolla, CA: Center for U.S.–Mexican Studies.

Shirk, David A. 2005. *Mexico's New Politics: The PAN and Democratic Change.* Boulder: Lynne Rienner.

Shlapentokh, Vladimir. 2006. "Are Today's Authoritarian Leaders Doomed to Be Indicted When They Leave Office? The Russian and Other Post-Soviet Cases." *Communist and Post-Communist Studies* 39, No. 4: 447–73.

Shushkevich, Stanislav. 2002. *Neo kommunizm, v belorusi: ideologiia, praktika, perspektivy.* Smolensk, Russia: Skif.

Siani-Davies, Peter. 2005. *The Romanian Revolution of December 1989.* Ithaca, NY: Cornell University Press.

Sidaway, James, and David Simon. 1993. "Geopolitical Transition and State Formation: The Changing Political Geographies of Angola, Mozambique and Namibia." *Journal of Southern African* 19, No. 1: 6–28.

Siegle, Joseph. 2004. "Developing Democracy: Democratizers' Surprisingly Bright Development Record." *Harvard International Review* 26, No. 2: 2–25.

Sikkink, Kathryn A. 1993. "Human Rights, Principled Issue-Networks, and Sovereignty in Latin America." *International Organization* 47, No. 3: 411–41.

Silber, Laura, and Allan Little. 1996. *Yugoslavia, Death of a Nation.* New York: Penguin Books.

Silina, Tatiana, Sergei Rakhmanin, and Olga Dmitricheva. 2004. "Anatomiia dushi maidana." *Zerkalo nedeli*, No. 50 (525): 11–17 December.

Silitski, Vitali. 2003a. "The Fall of the Patriarch?" *RFE/RL Belarus Ukraine Report.* 3 May.

Silitski, Vitali. 2003b. "What Are the Consequences of the Russian 'Gas Attack'?" *RFE/RL Belarus Ukraine Report.* 23 September.

Silitski, Vitali. 2004a. "Does Arrest of Former Minister Signal a Major Political Campaign?" *RFE/RL Belarus Ukraine Report.* 11 May.

Silitski, Vitali. 2004b. "Minsk Signs Gas Supply Deal with Gazprom." *RFE/RL Belarus Ukraine Report.* 15 June.

Silitski, Vitali. 2004c. *Post-Communist Authoritarianism in Eastern Europe: Serbia and Belarus Compared.* Unpublished manuscript.

Silitski, Vitali. 2005. "Preempting Democracy: The Case of Belarus." *Journal of Democracy* 16, No. 4: 83–97.

Silitski, Vitali. 2006a. "Contagion Deterred: Preemptive Authoritarianism in the Former Soviet Union (the Case of Belarus)." Presented at the conference, "Waves and Troughs of Post-Communist Transitions: What Role for Domestic vs. External Variables?" Stanford, CA: Stanford University, Center on Democracy, Development, and the Rule of Law. 28–29 April.

Silitski, Vitali. 2006b. "Belarus: Learning from Defeat." *Journal of Democracy* 17, No. 4: 139–51.

Silitski, Vasili. 2006c. "Signs of Hope Rather Than a Color Revolution." In Joerg Forbrig, David R. Marples, and Pavol Demes, eds. *Prospects for Democracy in Belarus.* Washington, DC: German Marshall Fund of the United States.

Silitski, Vitali. 2009. "Welcome to Post-Populism?" *BISS Blitz.* 11 January.

Silva, José Adán. 2008. "Politics-Nicaragua: Hard Times for Ortega." *Inter Press Service News Agency Online.* 3 June.

Simon, David. 2005. "Democracy Unrealized: Zambia's Third Republic under Frederick Chiluba." In Leonardo A. Villalón and Peter VonDoepp, eds. *The Fate of Africa's Democratic Experiments: Elites and Institutions.* Bloomington: Indiana University Press.

Simon, Leslie David, ed. 2002a. *Democracy and the Internet: Allies or Adversaries?* Washington, DC: Woodrow Wilson Center Press.

Simon, Leslie David. 2002b. "Democracy and the Net: A Virtuous Circle?" In Leslie David Simon, ed. *Democracy and the Internet: Allies or Adversaries?* Washington, DC: Woodrow Wilson Center Press.

Simonian, Hovann. 2001. "Armenia: Pessimistic Stability." *Transitions Online.* 15 January.

Simpson, Mark. 1993. "Foreign and Domestic Factors in the Transformation of Frelimo." *Journal of Modern African Studies* 31, No. 2 (June): 309–37.

Sindima, Harry J. 2002. *Malawi's First Republic: An Economic and Political Analysis.* Lanham, MD: University Press of America.

Singh, Chaitram. 1988. *Guyana: Politics in a Plantation Society.* New York: Praeger.

Singh, Hari. 1991. "Political Change in Malaysia: The Role of Semangat 46." *Asian Survey* 31, No. 8: 712–28.

Singh, Hari. 2000. "Democratization or Oligarchic Restructuring? The Politics of Reform in Malaysia." *Government and Opposition* 35, No. 4: 520–46.

Sithole, Masipula. 1993. "Is Zimbabwe Poised on a Liberal Path? The State and Prospects of the Parties." *Issue: A Journal of Opinion* 21, Nos. 1–2: 35–43.

Sithole, Masipula. 1997. "Zimbabwe's Eroding Authoritarianism." *Journal of Democracy* 8, No. 1: 127–41.

Sithole, Masipula. 1998. *Zimbabwe's Public Eye: Political Essays (October 1997–October 1998).* Harare, Zimbabwe: Rujeko Publishers.

Sithole, Masipula. 1999. "Zimbabwe: The Erosion of Authoritarianism and Prospects for Democracy." In York Bradshaw and Stephen N. Ndegwa, eds. *The Uncertain Promise of Southern Africa.* Bloomington: Indiana University Press.

Sjoberg, Orjan, and Michael L. Wyzan. 1991. *Economic Change in the Balkan States: Albania, Bulgaria, Romania and Yugoslavia.* London: Pinter Publishers.

Skillen, Daphne. 1995. "Media Coverage in the Elections." In Peter Lentini, ed. *Elections and Political Order in Russia.* Budapest: Central European University Press.

Skocpol, Theda. 1973. "A Critical Review of Barrington Moore's Social Origins of Dictatorship and Democracy." *Politics and Society* 4 (Fall): 1–34.

Skocpol, Theda. 1979. *States and Social Revolutions.* New York: Cambridge University Press.

Skolkay, Andrej. 1997. "The Role of the Mass Media in the Post-Communist Transition of Slovakia." In Sona Szomolamyi and John A. Gould, eds. *Slovakia: Problems of Democratic Consolidation and the Struggle for the Rules of the Game.* Bratislava: Slovak Political Science Association.

Slater, Dan. 2003. "Iron Cage in an Iron Fist: Authoritarian Institutions and the Personalization of Power in Malaysia." *Comparative Politics* 36, No. 1: 81–101.

Slater, Dan. 2004. "Democracy Takes a Thumping: Islamist and Democratic Opposition in Malaysia's Electoral Authoritarian Regime." *Kyoto Review of Southeast Asia* 5 (March).

Slater, Dan. 2010. *Ordering Power: Contentious Politics, State-Building, and Authoritarian Durability in Southeast Asia.* New York: Cambridge University Press.

Sledz, Serhyi. 2005. "Davyd Zvaniia – Ministr MNS." *Dzerkalo tyzhnia* No. 4 (532): 5–11 (February).

Slider, Darrell. 1997. "Democratization in Georgia." In Karen Dawisha and Bruce Parrott, eds. *Conflict, Cleavage, and Change in Central Asia and the Caucasus.* Cambridge: Cambridge University Press. Pp. 156–98.

Smith, Benjamin. 2005. "Life of the Party: The Origins of Regime Breakdown and Persistence under Single-Party Rule." *World Politics* 57, No. 3: 421–51.

Smith, Benjamin. 2006. "The Wrong Kind of Crisis: Why Oil Booms and Busts Rarely Lead to Authoritarian Breakdown." *Studies in Comparative International Development* 40, No. 4: 55–76.

Smith, Benjamin. 2007. *Hard Times in the Land of Plenty: Oil Politics in Iran and Indonesia.* Ithaca, NY: Cornell University Press.

Smith, Clint E. 2000. *Inevitable Partnership: Understanding Mexico–U.S. Relations.* Boulder, CO: Lynne Rienner Publishers.

Smith, Daniel A. 2002. "Consolidating Democracy? The Structural Underpinnings of Ghana's 2000 Elections." *Journal of Modern African Studies* 40, No. 4: 621–50.

Smith, D. A., and Temin J. 2001. "The Media and Ghana's 2000 Elections." In Joseph R. A. Ayee, ed. *Deepening Democracy in Ghana: Politics of the 2000 Elections (Vol. 1).* Accra: Freedom Publications.

Smith, Jackie, and Dawn Wiest. 2005. "The Uneven Geography of Global Civic Society: National and Global Influences on Transnational Association." *Social Forces* 84, No. 2: 621–52.

Smith, Karen. 2004. *The Making of EU Foreign Policy: The Case of Eastern Europe, Second Edition.* London: Palgrave.

Smith, Peter H. 1996. *Talons of the Eagle. Dynamics of U.S.–Latin American Relations.* New York: Oxford University Press.

Smith, Peter H. 2001. "Strategic Options for Latin America." In Joseph H. Tulchin and Ralph H. Espach, eds. *Latin America in the New International System.* Boulder, CO: Lynne Rienner Publishers.

Smith, Tony. 1994. *America's Mission: The United States and the Worldwide Struggle for Democracy in the Twentieth Century.* Princeton, NJ: Princeton University Press.

Smyth, Regina. 2002. "Building State Capacity from the Inside Out: Parties of Power and the Success of the President's Reform Agenda in Russia." *Politics & Society* 30, No. 4: 555–78.

Smyth, Regina. 2004. "What We Have Here Is a Failure to Consolidate: Explaining Russia's Political Development in Comparative Context." Paper presented at the Annual Meeting of the American Political Science Association; Chicago, IL, 2–6 September.

Smyth, Regina, Brandon Wilkening, and Anna Urasova. 2008. "Engineering Victory: Institutional Reform, Informal Institutions and the Formation of a Dominant Party Regime in the Russian Federation." Bloomington: Indiana University. Unpublished manuscript.

Snoeks, Anna, and John McKendy. 1996. "Tanzania's Multi-Party Elections: From 29 October to 19 November 1995." Amsterdam: African–European Institute.

Snyder, Richard. 1998. "Paths out of Sultanistic Regimes: Combining Structural and Voluntarist Perspectives." In Houchang E. Chehabi and Juan J. Linz, eds. *Sultanistic Regimes.* Baltimore, MD: The Johns Hopkins University Press.

Snyder, Richard. 2006. "Beyond Electoral Authoritarianism: The Spectrum of Nondemocratic Regimes." In Andreas Schedler, ed. *Electoral Authoritarianism: The Dynamics of Unfree Competition.* Boulder, CO: Lynne Rienner Publishers.

Soberg, Marius. 2007. "Croatia Since 1989: The HDZ and the Politics of Transition." In Sabrina Ramet and Davorka Matic, eds. *Democratic Transition in Croatia: Value Transformation, Education, & Media.* College Station: Texas A&M University Press.

Sobianin, A. A., and V. G. Sukhovol'skii. 1995. *Demokratiia Ogranichennaia Fal'sifikatsiiami.* Moscow.

Sobyanin, Alexander. 1994. "Political Cleavages among Russian Deputies." In T. Remington, ed. *Parliaments in Transition*. Boulder, CO: Westview Press. Pp. 181–215.

Socor, Vladimir. 1992. "Moldavia Builds a New State." *RFE/RL Research Report* 1, No. 1 (3 January): 42–5.

Soifer, Hillel. 2006. "Authority over Distance: Explaining Variation in State Infrastructural Power in Latin America." Ph.D. diss. Cambridge, MA: Harvard University.

Solchanyk, Roman. 1994. "The Politics of State-Building: Centre-Periphery Relations in Post-Soviet Ukraine." *Europe-Asia Studies* 46, No. 1: 47–68.

Somolekae, Gloria. 1993. "Bureaucracy and Democracy in Botswana: What Kind of Relationship?" In Stephen Stedman, ed. *Botswana: The Political Economy of Democratic Development*. Boulder, CO: Lynne Reiner.

Sorokin, Vladimir. 2008. "PKRM: V Nachale slavnykh del." *Moldavskie vedemosti* (13 March).

Southall, Roger. 1998. "Moi's Flawed Mandate: The Crisis Continues in Kenya." *Review of African Political Economy* 75: 101–11.

Spalding, Rose J. 1994. *Capitalists and Revolution in Nicaragua: Opposition and Accommodation, 1979–1993*. Chapel Hill: University of North Carolina Press.

Spalding, Rose J. 1997. "The Economic Elite." In Thomas Walker, ed. *Nicaragua without Illusions: Regime Transition and Structural Adjustment in the 1990s*. Wilmington, DE: Scholarly Resources, Inc.

Spalding, Rose J. 1998. "Revolution and the Hyperpoliticized Business Peak Association: Nicaragua and el Consejo Superior de la Empresa Privada." In Francisco Durand and Eduardo Silva, eds. *Organized Business, Economic Change, and Democracy in Latin America*. Miami, FL: University of Miami, North–South Center Press.

Sperling, Valerie, ed. 2000. *Building the Russian State: Institutional Crisis and the Quest for Democratic Governance*. Boulder, CO: Westview Press.

Spinner, Thomas J. 1984. *A Political and Social History of Guyana, 1945–1983*. Boulder, CO: Westview Press.

Staar, Richard F., and Corliss A. Tacosa. 2004. "Russia's Security Services." *Mediterranean Quarterly* 15, No. 1 (Winter): 39–57.

Stainton, Michael. 2000. "Creeping Corruption and the Roads of Desire: The 'Dynamic Stability' of the KMT System in Taiwan's Kleptocracy." Paper presented at the Sixth Annual Conference of the North American Taiwan Studies Association. Cambridge, MA: Harvard University. 16–19 June.

Stallings, Barbara. 1992. "International Influences on Economic Policy: Debt, Stabilization, and Structural Reform." In Stephan Haggard and Robert R. Kaufman, eds. *The Politics of Economic Adjustment: International Constraints, Distributive Conflicts, and the State*. Princeton, NJ: Princeton University Press.

Stamm, Andrea L., Dawn Bastian, and Robert A. Myers. 1998. *Mali*. Oxford, UK: Clio Press.

Stan, Lavinia. 2005. "The Opposition Takes Charge: The Romanian General Elections of 2004." *Problems of Post-Communism* 52, No. 3 (May–June): 3–15.

Stan, Valentin. 2000. "Influencing Regime Change in the Balkans: The Role of External Forces in the Transition." In Geoffrey Pridham and Thomas Gallagher, eds. *Experimenting with Democracy: Regime Change in the Balkans*. New York: Routledge.

Starr, Harvey. 1991. "Democratic Dominoes: Diffusion Approaches to the Spread of Democracy in the International System." *Journal of Conflict Resolution* 35, No. 2: 356–81.

Starr, Harvey, and Christina Lindborg. 2003. "Democratic Dominoes Revisited: The Hazards of Governmental Transitions, 1974–1996." *Journal of Conflict Resolution* 47, No. 4: 490–519.

Starr, Pamela. 1999. "Monetary Mismanagement and Inadvertant Democratization in Technocratic Mexico." *Studies in Comparative International Development* (Winter): 35–65.

Stavrova, Biljana. 2004a. "Macedonia: One Step Closer to the EU." *Transitions Online.* 29 March.

Stavrova, Biljana. 2004b. "Macedonia: Crvenkovski Victory Confirmed." *Transitions Online.* 3 May.

Stavrova, Biljana. 2004c. "Macedonia: The Opposition: In Opposition to Itself." *Transitions Online.* 14 July.

Steeves, Jeffrey S. 1999. "The Political Evolution of Kenya: The 1997 Elections and Succession Politics." *Journal of Commonwealth and Comparative Politics* 37, No. 1 (March): 71–94.

Stefanescu, Crisula. 1991. "The Government and Television in Romania."*Report on Eastern Europe* 37. 1 March.

Stefes, Christoph H. 2005. "Elites, Civil Society, and Foreign Assistance: Georgia's Rose Revolution in Comparative Perspective." Unpublished manuscript. Denver: University of Colorado.

Stein, Arthur. 1980. "The Politics of Linkage." *World Politics* 33: 62–81.

Stepan, Alfred. 2005. "Ukraine: Improbable Democratic 'Nation-State' but Possible Democratic 'State-Nation'?" *Post-Soviet Affairs* 21, No. 4: 279–308.

Stepan, Alfred, and Cindy Skach. 1993. "Constitutional Frameworks and Democratic Consolidation: Parliamentarism versus Presidentialism." *World Politics* 46, No. 1: 1–22.

Stepanian, Ruzanna, and Karine Kalantarian. 2005. "More Activists Detained Ahead of Next Opposition Rally." *Liberty Armenia and RFE/RL Report.* 7 December.

Stiff, Peter. 2000. *Cry Zimbabwe: Independence – Twenty Years On.* Alberton, South Africa: Galago Publishing.

Stojkovic, Dragan, 2002. "Yugoslavia: Have the Elections Started?" *Transitions Online.* 23–29 July.

Stokke, Olav. 1995a. *Aid and Political Conditionality.* London: Frank Cass/EADI.

Stokke, Olav. 1995b. "Aid and Political Conditionality: Core Issues and the State of the Art." In Olav Stokke, ed. *Aid and Political Conditionality.* London: Frank Cass/EADI.

Stone, Carl. 1986. *Power in the Caribbean Basin: A Comparative Study of Political Economy.* Philadelphia, PA: Institute for the Study of Human Issues.

Stoneman, Colin, and Lionel Cliffe. 1989. *Zimbabwe: Politics, Economics, and Society.* London: Pinter Publishers.

Stoner-Weiss, Kathryn. 2006. *Resisting the State: Reform and Retrenchment in Post-Soviet Russia.* New York: Cambridge University Press.

Stoner-Weiss, Kathryn. 2008. "Is It Still Putin's Russia?" *Current History* 107, No. 711 (October): 315–21.

Stotzky, Irwin P. 1997. *Silencing the Guns in Haiti: The Promise of Deliberative Democracy.* Chicago: University of Chicago Press.

Strekal, Oleg. 1995. "Ukraine: The New Secret Service." *Transition* 1, No. 10.

Stubbs, Richard. 1997. "The Malayan Emergency and the Development of the Malaysian State." In Paul B. Rich and Richard Stubbs, eds. *The Counter-Insurgent State: Guerrilla Warfare and State-Building in the Twentieth Century.* London: Macmillan Press.

Suárez-Orozco, Marcelo M. 1999. "Latin American Immigration to the United States." In Victor Bulmer-Thomas and James Dunkerley, eds. *The United States and Latin America: The New Agenda.* London: Institute of Latin American Studies.

Sucic, Daria Sito. 1997. "Croatia 1996 Report: A Groundswell of Dissatisfaction." *Transition.* 7 February.

Sullivan, Stacey. 1997. "Albania: Favorite Son." *New Republic* 216, No. 14 (7 April).

Suny, Ronald G. 1994. *The Making of the Georgian Nation*. Bloomington: Indiana University Press.

Suny, Ronald G. 1995. "Elite Transformation in Transcaucasia." In Timothy Colton and Robert Tucker, eds. *Patterns of Post-Soviet Leadership*. Boulder, CO: Westview Press.

Sushko, Oleksandr, and Olena Prystayko. 2006. "Western Influence." In Anders Aslund and Michael McFaul, eds. *Revolution in Orange: The Origins of Ukraine's Democratic Breakthrough*. Washington, DC: Carnegie Endowment for International Peace.

Suzdaltsev, Andrei. 2007. "Lukashenko: Russia's Ally or Sponge?" *RIA Novosti*, 11 January.

Sylvester, Christine. 1991. *Zimbabwe: The Terrain of Contradictory Development*. Boulder, CO: Westview Press.

Sylvester, Christine. 1995. "Whither Opposition in Zimbabwe?" *Journal of Modern African Studies* 33, No. 3: 403–23.

Synge, Richard. 1997. *Mozambique: UN Peacekeeping in Action, 1992–1994*. Washington, DC: United States Institute of Peace.

Szajkowski, Bogdan. 1992. "The 1992 Albanian Elections." *The Journal of Communist Studies* 8, No. 3: 119–29.

Szomolanyi, Szona. 2001. "Socio-Political Development in Slovakia: 'Scenario 2005' Revised." In Grzeorz Gorzelak, Eva Ehrlich, Lubomir Faltan, and Michal Illner, eds. *Central Europe in Transition: Towards EU Membership*. Warsaw: Scholar Publishing House.

Szomolanyi, Szona. 2004. "The Slovak Path to Democracy: From a Deviant Case to a Standard Democracy." In Grigorij Meseznikov and Olga Gyafasova, eds. *Slovakia: Ten Years of Independence and a Year of Reforms*. Bratislava, Slovakia: Institute for Public Affairs.

Takuogang, Joseph. 1993a. "The Post-Ahidjo Era in Cameroon: Continuity and Change." *Journal of Third World Studies* X, No. 2 (Fall): 268–302.

Takuogang, Joseph. 1993b. "Continuity and Change in Cameroon's Foreign Policy in the Post-Ahidjo Era." *The African Review* 20, Nos. 1–2: 135–53.

Takougang, Joseph. 1997. "Cameroon: Biya and Incremental Reform." In John F. Clark and David E. Gardinier, eds. *Political Reform in Francophone Africa*. Boulder, CO: Westview Press.

Takougang, Joseph. 2003a. "The 2002 Legislative Election in Cameroon: A Retrospective on Cameroon's Stalled Democracy Movement." *Journal of Modern African Studies* 41, No. 3: 421–35.

Takougang, Joseph. 2004a. "The Nature of Politics in Cameroon." In John M. Mbaku and Joseph Takougang, eds. *The Leadership Challenge in Africa: Cameroon under Paul Biya*. Trenton, NJ: Africa World Press.

Takougang, Joseph. 2004b. "The Demise of Paul Biya's New Deal in Cameroon, 1982–1992." In John M. Mbaku and Joseph Takougang, eds. *The Leadership Challenge in Africa: Cameroon under Paul Biya*. Trenton, NJ: Africa World Press.

Takougang, Joseph, and Milton Krieger. 1998. *African State and Society in the 1990s. Cameroon's Political Crossroads*. Boulder, CO: Westview Press.

Talbott, Strobe. 2002. *Russia Hand*. New York: Knopf.

Tamarkin, M. 1978. "The Roots of Political Stability in Kenya." *African Affairs* 77, No. 308 (July): 297–320.

Tanaka, Martin. 1998. *Los Espejismos de la Democracia: El colapso del sistema de partidos en el Perú*. Lima, Peru: Instituto de Estudios Peruanos.

Tanaka, Martin. 2001. "Crónica de una Muerte Anunciada? Determinismo, Voluntarismo, Actores y Poderes Estructurales en el Perú, 1980–2000." In Jane Marcus-Delgado and Martín Tanaka, eds. *Lecciones del Final del Fujimorismo*. Lima, Peru: Instituto de Estudios Peruanos.

Tanaka, Martín. 2005. "Peru 1980–2000: Chronicle of a Death Foretold? Determinism, Political Decisions, and Open Outcomes." In Frances Hagopian and Scott P. Mainwaring, eds. *The Third Wave of Democratization in Latin America: Advances and Setbacks.* New York: Cambridge University Press.

Tangwa, Godfrey B. 1998. *Road Companion to Democracy and Meritocracy (Further Essays from an African Perspective).* Bellingham, WA: Kola Tree Press.

Taylor, Ian. 2003. "As Good as It Gets? Botswana's 'Democratic Development.'" *Journal of Contemporary African Studies* 21, No. 2: 215–31.

Taylor, Ian. 2006. "The Limits of the 'African Miracle': Academic Freedom in Botswana and the Deportation of Kenneth Good." *Journal of Contemporary African Studies* 24, No. 1: 101–22.

Teichman, Judith. 1997. "Neoliberalism and the Transformation of Mexican Authoritarianism." *Mexican Studies/Estudios Mexicanos* 13, No. 1: 121–47.

Temin, Jonathan, and Daniel A. Smith. 2002. "Media Matters: Evaluating the Role of the Media in Ghana's 2000 Elections." *African Affairs* 101: 585–605.

Than, Sina. 1998. "The Importance of the 1998 Elections for Cambodia." In Kao Kim Hourn and Norbert von Hoffman, eds. *National Elections: Cambodia's Experiences and Expectations.* Phnom Penh: Cambodian Institute for Cooperation and Peace.

Thioub, Ibrahima Momar-Coumba Diop, and Catherine Boone. 1998. "Economic Liberalization in Senegal: Shifting Politics of Indigenous Business Interests." *African Studies Review* 41, No. 2 (September): 63–89.

Thirkill-White, Ben. 2006. "Political Islam and Malaysian Democracy." *Democratization* 13, No. 3: 421–41.

Thomas, Daniel C. 2006. "Constitutionalization through Enlargement: The Contested Origins of the EU's Democratic Identity." *Journal of European Public Policy* 13, No. 8: 1190–1210.

Thomas, Erwin K. 1990. "Mass Media in Guyana." In Stuart H. Surlin and Walter C. Soderlund, eds. *Mass Media and the Caribbean.* New York: Gordon and Breach.

Thomas, Robert. 1999. *The Politics of Serbia in the 1990s.* New York: Columbia University Press.

Thompson, Mark R. 1993. "The Limits of Democratization in ASEAN." *Third World Quarterly* 14, No. 3: 469–84.

Thompson, Mark R. 2001. "To Shoot or Not to Shoot: Post-Totalitarianism in China and Eastern Europe." *Comparative Politics* 34, No. 1: 63–83.

Thompson, Mark R., and Philip Kuntz. 2004. "Stolen Elections: The Case of the Serbian October." *Journal of Democracy* 15, No. 4: 159–72.

Thompson, Mark R., and Philip Kuntz. 2005. "More Than Just the Final Straw: Stolen Elections as Revolutionary Triggers." Paper presented at the conference, "Authoritarian Regimes: Conditions for Stability and Change." Swedish Institute, Istanbul, 29–31 May.

Throup, David. 1993. "Elections and Political Legitimacy in Kenya." *Africa* 63, No. 3: 371–96.

Throup, David W. 2001. "Kenya: Revolution, Relapse, or Reform?" *Center for Strategic and International Studies (CSIS) Africa Notes* 3 (November). Washington, DC: CSIS.

Throup, David W. 2003a. "Kibaki's Triumph: The Kenyan General Election of December 2002." *Elections in Africa Series: Briefing Paper*, No. 3 (June). London: Royal Institute of International Affairs.

Throup, David W. 2003b. "The Kenya General Election: December 27, 2002." *Center for Strategic and International Studies (CSIS) Africa Notes* 14 (January). Washington, DC: CSIS.

Throup, David W., and Charles Hornsby. 1998. *Multi-Party Politics in Kenya: The Kenyatta and Moi States and the Triumph of the System in the 1992 Election*. Athens: Ohio University Press.

Tien, Hung-mao. 1989. *The Great Transition: Political and Social Change in the Republic of China*. Stanford, CA: Hoover Institution Press.

Tien, Hung-mao. 1992. "Transformation of an Authoritarian Party-State: Taiwan's Development Experience." In Tun-Jen Cheng and Stephan Haggard, eds. *Political Change in Taiwan*. Boulder, CO: Lynne Rienner Publishers.

Tien, Hung-mao. 1996a. "Elections and Taiwan's Democratic Development." In Hung-mao Tien, ed. *Taiwan's Electoral Politics and Democratic Transition: Riding the Third Wave*. Armonk, NY: M. E. Sharpe.

Tien, Hung-mao. 1996b. "Taiwan in 1995: Electoral Politics and Cross-Strait Relations." *Asian Survey* 36, No. 1: 33–40.

Tien, Hung-mao. 1997. "Taiwan's Transformation." In Larry Diamond, Marc F. Plattner, Yun-han Chu, and Hung-Mao Tien, eds. *Consolidating the Third Wave Democracies: Regional Challenges*. Baltimore, MD: The Johns Hopkins University Press.

Tien, Hung-mao, and Tun-jen Cheng. 1999. "Crafting Democratic Institutions." In Steve Tsang and Hung-mao Tien, eds. *Democratization in Taiwan: Implications for China*. London: Macmillan.

Tien, Hung-mao, and Yun-han Chu. 1998. "Building Democracy in Taiwan." In David Shambaugh, ed. *Contemporary Taiwan*. Oxford, UK: Clarendon Press.

Tilly, Charles, ed. 1975. *The Formation of National States in Western Europe*. Princeton, NJ: Princeton University Press.

Tilly, Charles. 1985. "War Making and State Making as Organized Crime." In Peter Evans, Dietrich Rueschemeyer, and Theda Skocpol, eds. *Bringing the State Back In*. Cambridge: Cambridge University Press.

Tilly, Charles. 1992. *Coercion, Capital, and European States, AD 990–1992*. Cambridge, UK: Blackwell.

Tismaneanu, Vladimir. 1993. "The Quasi-Revolution and Its Discontents: Emerging Political Pluralism in Post-Ceauşescu Romania." *East European Politics and Societies* 7, No. 2 (Spring): 309–48.

Tismaneanu, Vladimir. 1996. "Romania: Tenuous Pluralism in the Post-Ceausescu Era." *Transition*. 27 December.

Tismaneanu, Vladimir. 1997. "Romanian Exceptionalism? Democracy, Ethnocracy and Emerging Pluralism in Post-Ceausescu Romania." In Karen Dawisha and Bruce Parrott, eds. *Politics, Power and the Struggle for Democracy in South-East Europe*. Cambridge: Cambridge University Press.

Tismaneanu, Vladimir. 2003. *Stalinism for All Seasons: A Political History of Romanian Communism*. Berkeley: University of California Press.

Tismaneanu, Vladimir, and Gail Kligman. 2001. "Romania's First Postcommunist Decade: From Iliescu to Iliescu." *East European Constitutional Review* 10, No. 1. (Online: www1.law.nyu.edu/eecr).

Tocci, Nathalie. 2004. "EU Intervention in Ethnopolitical Conflicts: The Cases of Cyprus and Serbia-Montenegro." *European Foreign Affairs Review* 9: 551–73.

Toma, Peter A., and Dusan Kováč. 2001. *Slovakia: From Samo to Dzurinda*. Stanford, CA: Hoover Institution Press.

Tordoff, William. 1988. "Political Parties in Zambia." In Vickey Randall, ed. *Political Parties in the Third World*. London: Sage Publications.

Tordoff, William, and Ralph A. Young. 1999. "The Presidential Election in Gabon." *Review of African Political Economy* 80: 269–77.

Torimiro, Frédéric Belle. 1992. "Personal Rule and the Search for Political Pluralism in Cameroon." In Constantine P. Danopolous, ed. *Civilian Rule in the Developing World: Democracy on the March?* Boulder, CO: Westview Press.

Transitions Online. 2002. "Balkan Reconstruction Report." 12 November. Available at www.tol.org.

Transitions Online. 2006. "Macedonia: Just-in-Time Delivery." 11 July. Available at www.tol.org.

Transitions Online. 2008. "Radical Shakeup" 12 September. Available at www.tol.org.

Treisman, Daniel. 1999. *After the Deluge: Regional Crises and Political Consolidation in Russia.* Ann Arbor: University of Michigan Press.

Trejo Delarbre, Raul. 1999. "Los Medios También Votan: Las Campañas de 1997 en Televisión y Prensa. Un Informe Preliminar." In Luis Salazar, ed. *1997: Elecciones y Transición a la Democracia en México.* Mexico City: Cal y Arena.

Trenin, Dmitri. 2006. "Russia's Policy towards Belarus: A Tale of Two Presidents." In Joerg Forbrig, David R. Marples, and Pavol Demes, eds. *Prospects for Democracy in Belarus.* Washington, D.C.: German Marshall Fund of the United States.

Tripodi, Paolo. 2002. "Operation Alba: A Necessary and Successful Preventative Deployment." *International Peacekeeping* 9, No. 4: 89–104.

Tripp, Aili Mari. 2000. "Political Reform in Tanzania: The Struggle for Associational Autonomy." *Comparative Politics* 32, No. 2 (January): 191–214.

Troxel, Tiffany A. 2003. *Parliamentary Power in Russia, 1994–2001.* New York: Palgrave.

Tsang, Steve. 1999. "Transforming a Party State into a Democracy." In Steve Tsang and Hung-mao Tien, eds. *Democratization in Taiwan: Implications for China.* London: Macmillan.

Tsekov, Georgi. 2005. "Macedonia." *Nations in Transit.* New York: Freedom House.

Tucker, Joshua. 2007. "Enough! Electoral Fraud, Collective Action Problems, and the 2nd Wave of Post-Communist Democratic Revolutions." *Perspectives on Politics* 5, No. 3: 537–53.

Tucker, Nancy Bernkopf. 1994. *Taiwan, Hong Kong, and the United States, 1945–1992: Uncertain Friendships.* New York: Twayne Publishers.

Tulchin, Joseph, and Knut Walter. 1991. "Nicaragua: The Limits of Intervention." In Abraham Lowenthal, ed. *Exporting Democracy: The United States and Latin America.* Baltimore, MD: The Johns Hopkins University Press.

Tull, Stephen M. 2003. "The European Union and Croatia: Negotiating 'Europeanization' amid National, Regional and International Interests." In Paul Kubicek, ed. *The European Union and Democratization.* London: Routledge.

Türkes, Mustafa, and Göksu, Gökgöz. 2006. "The European Union's Strategy towards the Western Balkans: Exclusion or Integration?" *East European Politics and Societies* 16, No. 4: 659–90.

Turner, Michael, Sue Nelson, and Kimberly Mahling-Clark. 1998. "Mozambique's Vote for Democratic Governance." In K. Kumar, ed. *Post-Conflict Elections, Democratization, and International Assistance.* Boulder, CO: Lynn Rienner Publishers.

Ufen, Andreas. 2009. "The Transformation of Political Party Opposition in Malaysia and Its Implications for the Electoral Authoritarian Regime." *Democratization* 16, No. 3: 604–27.

Um, Khatharya. 1994. "Cambodia in 1993: Year Zero Plus One." *Asian Survey* 34, No. 1: 72–81.

Un, Kheang. 2005. "Patronage Politics and Hybrid Democracy: Political Change in Cambodia, 1993–2003." *Asian Perspective* 29, No. 2: 203–30.

Un, Kheang. 2008. "Cambodia's 2008 Election: The End of Opposition?" *Open Democracy.* 5 August.

Uncaptive Minds. 1993a. "Interview with Budisa: Opposition in Wartime." Fall: 71–9.

Uncaptive Minds. 1993b. "Interview with Ljupco Georgievski." Fall: 81–9.

Uncaptive Minds. 1994. "Interview with Stojan Obradovic and Goran Vesic." Fall–Winter: 37–43.

United Nations Educational, Scientific and Cultural Organization (UNESCO). 1972. UNESCO Statistical Yearbook. Paris: United Nations.

United Nations Educational, Scientific and Cultural Organization (UNESCO). 1977. UNESCO Statistical Yearbook. Paris: United Nations.

United Nations Educational, Scientific and Cultural Organization (UNESCO). 1983. UNESCO Statistical Yearbook. Paris: United Nations.

Urban, Michael E. 1992. Boris Yeltsin, Democratic Russia and the Campaign for the Russian Presidency. *Soviet Studies* 44, No. 2: 187–207.

Urban, Michael. 1994. "December 1993 Elections as Replication of Late Soviet Electoral Practices." *Post-Soviet Affairs* 10, No. 2: 127–58.

USAID. 2005. "Armenia Political Parties Assessment: Final Report, May 2005." Washington, DC: U.S. Agency for International Development.

U.S. Department of Homeland Security. 2004. *Yearbook of Immigration Statistics: 2003.* Accessed at http://www.dhs.gov/files/statistics/publications/YrBko3TA.shtm.

U.S. Department of State. 1995a. *Moldova Human Rights Practices, 1994.* Washington, DC: U.S. Department of State.

U.S. Department of State. 1995b. *Mozambique Human Rights Practices, 1994.* Washington, DC: U.S. Department of State.

U.S. Department of State. 1996. *Armenia Human Rights Practices, 1995.* Washington, DC: U.S. Department of State.

U.S. Department of State. 1998a. *Haiti Human Rights Practices, 1997.* Washington, DC: U.S. Department of State.

U.S. Department of State. 1998b. *Georgia Human Rights Practices, 1997.* Washington, DC: U.S. Department of State.

U.S. Department of State. 1998c. *Mozambique Human Rights Practices, 1997.* Washington, DC. U.S. Department of State.

U.S. Department of State. 1999a. *Haiti Human Rights Practices, 1998.* Washington, DC: U.S. Department of State.

U.S. Department of State. 1999b. *Albania Human Rights Practices, 1998.* Washington, DC: U.S. Department of State.

U.S. Department of State. 1999c. *Georgia Human Rights Practices, 1998.* Washington, DC: U.S. Department of State.

U.S. Department of State. 2000a. *Haiti Human Rights Practices, 1999.* Washington, DC: U.S. Department of State.

U.S. Department of State. 2000b. *Cameroon Human Rights Practices, 1999.* Washington, DC: U.S. Department of State.

U.S. Department of State. 2000c. *Madagascar Human Rights Practices, 1999.* Washington, DC: U.S. Department of State.

U.S. Department of State. 2001a. *Background Note: Guyana.* Washington, DC: U.S. Department of State.

U.S. Department of State. 2001b. *Guyana Human Rights Practices, 2000.* Washington, DC: U.S. Department of State.

U.S. Department of State. 2001c. *Haiti Human Rights Practices, 2000.* Washington, DC: U.S. Department of State.

U.S. Department of State. 2001d. *Benin Human Rights Practices, 2000.* Washington, DC: U.S. Department of State.

U.S. Department of State. 2001e. *Croatia Human Rights Practices, 2000.* Washington, DC: U.S. Department of State.

U.S. Department of State. 2002a. *Haiti Human Rights Practices, 2001.* Washington, DC: U.S. Department of State.

U.S. Department of State. 2002b. *Malawi Human Rights Practices, 2001.* Washington, DC: U.S. Department of State.

U.S. Department of State. 2002c. *Cameroon Human Rights Practices, 2001.* Washington, DC: U.S. Department of State.

U.S. Department of State. 2002d. *Madagascar Human Rights Practices, 2001.* Washington, DC: U.S. Department of State.

U.S. Department of State. 2002e. *Kenya Human Rights Practices, 2001.* Washington, DC: U.S. Department of State.

U.S. Department of State. 2002f. *Gabon Human Rights Practices, 2001.* Washington, DC: U.S. Department of State.

U.S. Department of State. 2002g. *Albania Human Rights Practices, 2001.* Washington, DC: U.S. Department of State.

U.S. Department of State. 2003a. *Haiti Human Rights Practices, 2002.* Washington, DC: U.S. Department of State.

U.S. Department of State. 2003b. *Benin Human Rights Practices, 2002.* Washington, DC: U.S. Department of State.

U.S. Department of State. 2003c. *Cameroon Human Rights Practices, 2002.* Washington, DC: U.S. Department of State.

U.S. Department of State. 2003d. *Gabon Human Rights Practices, 2002.* Washington, DC: U.S. Department of State.

U.S. Department of State. 2003e. *Senegal Human Rights Practices, 2002.* Washington, DC: U.S. Department of State.

U.S. Department of State. 2003f. *Armenia Human Rights Practices, 2002.* Washington, DC: U.S. Department of State.

U.S. Department of State. 2003g. *Mali Human Rights Practices, 2002.* Washington, DC: U.S. Department of State.

U.S. Department of State. 2004a. *Malawi Human Rights Practices, 2003.* Washington, DC: U.S. Department of State.

U.S. Department of State. 2004b. *Benin Human Rights Practices, 2003.* Washington, DC: U.S. Department of State.

U.S. Department of State. 2004c. *Cameroon Human Rights Practices, 2003.* Washington, DC: U.S. Department of State.

U.S. Department of State. 2004d. *Madagascar Human Rights Practices, 2003.* Washington, DC: U.S. Department of State.

U.S. Department of State. 2004e. *Kenya Human Rights Practices, 2003.* Washington, DC: U.S. Department of State.

U.S. Department of State. 2004f. *Gabon Human Rights Practices, 2003.* Washington, DC: U.S. Department of State.

U.S. Department of State. 2004g. *Senegal Human Rights Practices, 2003.* Washington, DC: U.S. Department of State.

U.S. Department of State. 2004h. *Mali Human Rights Practices, 2003.* Washington, DC: U.S. Department of State.

U.S. Department of State. 2004i. *Mozambique Human Rights Practices, 2003.* Washington, DC: U.S. Department of State.

U.S. Department of State. 2005a. *Malawi Human Rights Practices, 2004.* Washington, DC: U.S. Department of State.

U.S. Department of State. 2005b. *Benin Human Rights Practices, 2004.* Washington, DC: U.S. Department of State.

U.S. Department of State. 2005c. *Cameroon Human Rights Practices, 2004.* Washington, DC: U.S. Department of State.

U.S. Department of State. 2005d. *Madagascar Human Rights Practices, 2004.* Washington, DC: U.S. Department of State.

U.S. Department of State. 2005e. *Mali Human Rights Practices, 2004.* Washington, DC: U.S. Department of State.

U.S. Department of State. 2005f. *Mozambique Human Rights Practices, 2004.* Washington, DC: U.S. Department of State.

U.S. Department of State. 2006a. *Albania Human Rights Practices, 2005.* Washington, DC: U.S. Department of State.

U.S. Department of State. 2006b. *Botswana Human Rights Practices, 2005.* Washington, DC: U.S. Department of State.

U.S. Department of State. 2006c. *Russia Human Rights Practices, 2005.* Washington, DC: U.S. Department of State.

U.S. Department of State. 2007a. *Malawi Human Rights Practices, 2006.* Washington, DC: U.S. Department of State.

U.S. Department of State. 2007b. *Madagascar Human Rights Practices, 2006.* Washington, DC: U.S. Department of State.

U.S. Department of State. 2007c. *Mali Human Rights Practices, 2006.* Washington, DC: U.S. Department of State.

U.S. Department of State. 2007d. *Kenya Human Rights Practices, 2006.* Washington, DC: U.S. Department of State.

U.S. Department of State. 2008a. *Albania Human Rights Practices, 2007.* Washington, DC: U.S. Department of State.

U.S. Department of State. 2008b. *Georgia Human Rights Practices, 2007.* Washington, DC: U.S. Department of State.

U.S. Department of State. 2008c. *Mali Human Rights Practices, 2007.* Washington, DC: U.S. Department of State.

U.S. Department of State. 2008d. "Background Note, Ukraine." Washington, DC: U.S. Department of State.

U.S. Department of State. 2008e. *Moldova Human Rights Practices, 2008.* Washington, DC: U.S. Department of State.

U.S. Department of State. 2008f. *Cameroon Human Rights Practices, 2008.* Washington, DC: U.S. Department of State.

U.S. Department of State. 2009a. *Albania Human Rights Practices, 2008.* Washington, DC: U.S. Department of State.

U.S. Department of State. 2009b. *Haiti Human Rights Practices, 2008.* Washington, DC: U.S. Department of State.

U.S. Department of State. 2009c. *Macedonia Human Rights Practices, 2008.* Washington, DC: U.S. Department of State.

U.S. Department of State. 2009d. *Malawi Human Rights Practices, 2008.* Washington, DC: U.S. Department of State.

U.S. Department of State. 2009e. *Mali Human Rights Practices, 2008.* Washington, DC: U.S. Department of State.

U.S. Department of State. 2009f. *Nicaragua Human Rights Practices, 2008.* Washington, DC: U.S. Department of State.

U.S. Department of State. 2009g. *Romania Human Rights Practices, 2008.* Washington, DC: U.S. Department of State.

U.S. Department of State. 2009h. *Russia Human Rights Practices, 2008.* Washington, DC: U.S. Department of State.

U.S. Department of State. 2009i. *Botswana Human Rights Practices, 2008.* Washington, DC: U.S. Department of State.

Vachudova, Milada. 2005a. "Promoting Political Change and Economic Revitalization in the Western Balkans: The Role of the European Union." *Slovak Foreign Policy Affairs.* 2: 67–73.

Vachudova, Milada. 2005b. *Europe Undivided: Democracy, Leverage and Integration after Communism.* London: Oxford University Press.

Vachudova, Milada, and Tim Snyder. 1997. "Are Transitions Transitory? Two Types of Political Change in Eastern Europe since 1989." *East European Politics and Societies* 11, No. 1: 1–35.

Valdivia, Angharad N. 1991. "The U.S. Intervention in Nicaraguan and Other Latin American Media." In Thomas Walker, ed. *Revolution and Counterrevolution in Nicaragua.* Boulder, CO: Westview Press.

Valenzuela, Arturo. 1997. "Paraguay: The Coup That Didn't Happen," *Journal of Democracy* 8, No. 1: 43–55.

Vanden, Harry E. 1991. "Foreign Policy." In Thomas Walker, ed. *Revolution and Counterrevolution in Nicaragua.* Boulder, CO: Westview Press.

Vanden, Harry E., and Gary Prevost. 1993. *Democracy and Socialism in Sandinista Nicaragua.* Boulder, CO: Lynne Rienner Publishers.

Vanden Heuvel, Jon, and Everette E. Dennis. 1993. *The Unfolding Lotus: East Asia's Changing Media.* New York: Freedom Forum Media Studies Center.

Vander Weyden, Patrick. 2000. "Parliamentary Elections in Cambodia 1998." *Electoral Studies* 19, No. 4: 615–46.

van de Walle, Nicolas. 1993. "The Politics of Nonreform in Cameroon." In Thomas M. Callaghy and John Ravenhill, eds. *Hemmed In: Responses to Africa's Economic Decline.* New York: Columbia University Press.

van de Walle, Nicolas. 1994. "Neopatrimonialism and Democracy in Africa, with an Illustration from Cameroon." In Jennifer A. Widner, ed. *Economic Change and Political Liberalization in Sub-Saharan Africa.* Baltimore, MD: The Johns Hopkins University Press.

van de Walle, Nicolas. 2002. "Africa's Range of Regimes." *Journal of Democracy* 13, No. 2: 66–80.

van de Walle, Nicolas. 2003. "Presidentialism and Clientelism in Africa's Emerging Party Systems." *Journal of Modern African Studies* 41, No. 2: 297–321.

van de Walle, Nicolas. 2006. "Tipping Games: When Do Opposition Parties Coalesce?" In Andreas Schedler, ed. *Electoral Authoritarianism: The Dynamics of Unfree Competition.* Boulder, CO: Lynne Rienner Publishers.

Van Der Schriek, Daan. 2004. "Saakashvili's First 100 Days: Bloom Still on Reforms, but Critics Voice Concern." *Eurasia Insight.* 10 May.

van Dijk, R. 2000. "Secret Worlds, Democratization, and Election Observation in Malawi." In Jon Abbink and Gerti Hesseling, eds. *Election Observation and Democratization in Africa.* London: Routledge.

Van Donge, Jan Kees. 1995a. "Kamuzu's Legacy: The Democratization of Malawi: Or Searching for the Rules of the Game in African Politics." *African Affairs* 94, No. 375: 227–57.

Van Donge, Jan Kees. 1995b. "Zambia: Kaunda and Chiluba: Enduring Patterns of Political Culture." In John A. Wiseman, ed. *Democracy and Political Change in Sub-Saharan Africa*. London: Routledge.

Van Donge, Jan Kees. 2002. "The Fate of an African 'Chaebol': Malawi's Press Corporation after Democratization." *Journal of Modern African Studies* 40, No. 4: 651–81.

Vasi, Ion Bogdan. 2004. "The Fist of the Working Class: The Social Movements of Jiu Valley Miners in Post-Socialist Romania." *East European Politics and Societies* 18, No. 1: 132–57.

Vasic, Milos. 2001. "The Grimmest Inheritance: Milosevic's Secretive, All-Powerful, and Extremely Dangerous State Security Service Is Largely Still in Place." *Transitions Online*. 29 May.

Vener, Jessica. 2000. "Prompting Democratic Transitions from Abroad: International Donors and Multi-Partyism in Tanzania." *Democratization* 7, No. 4 (Winter): 133–62.

Vengroff, Richard. 1993. "Governance and the Transition to Democracy: Political Parties and the Party System in Mali." *The Journal of Modern African Studies*. Vol. 31, No. 4 (December), pp. 541–562.

Vengroff, Richard, and Lucy Creevey. 1997. "Senegal: The Evolution of a Quasi Democracy." In John F. Clark and David E. Gardinier, eds. *Political Reform in Francophone Africa*. Boulder, CO: Westview Press.

Vengroff, Richard, and Moctar Kone. 1995. "Mali: Democracy and Political Change." In A. Wiseman, ed. *Democracy and Political Change in Sub-Saharan Africa*. London: Routledge.

Vengroff, Richard and Michael Magala. 2001. "Democratic Reform, Transformation and Consolidation: Evidence from Senegal's 2000 Presidential Election." *Journal of Modern African Studies* 39, No. 1 (March): 129–162.

Venter, Denis. 1995. "Malawi: The Transition to Multi-Party Politics." In John A. Wiseman, ed. *Democracy and Political Change in Sub-Saharan Africa*. London: Routledge.

Verheijen, Tony. 1994. "The EU and Romania and Bulgaria: Stuck between Visegrad and Minsk." In J. Redmond, ed. *Prospective Europeans: New Members for the European Union*. New York: Harvester Wheatsheaf.

Verma, Vidhu. 2002. *Malaysia: State and Civil Society in Transition*. Boulder, CO: Lynne Rienner Publishers.

Vickers, Miranda, and James Pettifer. 2000. *Albania: From Anarchy to a Balkan Identity*. New York: NYU Press.

Villalón, Leonardo A. 1994. "Democratizing a (Quasi) Democracy: The Senegalese Elections of 1993." *African Affairs* 93, No. 371: 163–93.

Villalón, Leonardo A. 1995. *Islamic Society and State Power in Senegal: Disciples and Citizens in Fatick*. Cambridge: Cambridge University Press.

Villalón, Leonardo A. 1999. "Generational Change, Political Stagnation, and the Evolving Dynamics of Religion and Politics in Senegal." *Africa Today* 46, No. 3–4 (Summer–Fall): 129–47.

Villalón, Leonardo A., and Abdourahmane Idrissa. 2005. "The Tribulations of a Successful Transition: Institutional Dynamics and Elite Rivalry in Mali." In Leonardo A. Villalón and Peter VonDoepp, eds. *The Fate of Africa's Democratic Experiments: Elites and Institutions*. Bloomington: Indiana University Press.

Villalón, Leonardo A., and Ousmane Kane. 1998. "Senegal: The Crisis of Democracy and the Emergence of an Islamic Opposition." In Leonardo A. Villalón and Phillip A. Huxtable, eds. *The African State at a Critical Juncture: Between Disintegration and Reconfiguration*. Boulder, CO: Lynne Rienner Publishers.

Vladisavljevic, Nebojsa. 2008. *Serbia's Anti-Bureaucratic Revolution: Milošević, the Fall of Communism, and Nationalist Mobilization.* New York: Palgrave.

von Beyme, Klaus. 2001. "Institutional Engineering and the Transition to Democracy." In Jan Zielonka, ed. *Democratic Consolidation in Eastern Europe: Institutional Engineering.* New York: Oxford University Press.

von der Mehden, Fred R. 1991. "Malaysia in 1990: Another Electoral Victory." *Asian Survey* 31, No. 2: 164–71.

VonDoepp, Peter. 2001. "The Survival of Malawi's Enfeebled Democracy." *Current History* 100, No. 646: 232–7.

VonDoepp, Peter. 2002. "Are Malawi's Local Clergy Civil Society Activists? The Limiting Impact of Creed, Context and Class." In Harri Englund, ed. *A Democracy of Chameleons: Politics and Culture in the New Malawi.* Stockholm: Nordiska Afrikainstitutet.

VonDoepp, Peter. 2003. "The Battle for Third Term: Party Politics and Institutional Development in Namibia, Malawi, and Zambia." Paper prepared for the 99th Annual Meeting of the American Political Science Association. Philadelphia, PA: 8–31 August.

VonDoepp, Peter. 2005. "Institutions, Resources, and Elite Strategies: Making Sense of Malawi's Democratic Trajectory." In Leonardo A. Villalón and Peter VonDoepp, eds. *The Fate of Africa's Democratic Experiments: Elites and Institutions.* Bloomington: Indiana University Press.

Von Hippel, Karin. 2000. *Democracy by Force: US Military Intervention in the Post–Cold War World.* Cambridge: Cambridge University Press.

Vronskaya, Gene, and Vladimir Chuguev. 1994. *Kto est Kto v Rossii i byvshem SSSR.* Moscow: Terra.

Vujcic, Zeljka. 2004. "Croatia: Running After Mesic." *Transitions Online.* 17 December.

Wachman, Alan M. 1994. *Taiwan: National Identity and Democratization.* Armonk, NY: M. E. Sharpe.

Wager, Stephen J. 1984. "Basic Characteristics of the Modern Mexican Military." In David F. Ronfeldt, ed. *The Modern Mexican Military: A Reassessment.* La Jolla, CA: Center for U.S.–Mexican Studies.

Wager, Stephen J. 1995. "The Mexican Military Approaches the 21st Century: Coping with a New World Order." In Donald E. Schulz and Edward J. Williams, eds. *Mexico Faces the 21st Century.* Westport, CT: Greenwood Press.

Wager, Stephen J., and Donald E. Schulz. 1995. "The Zapatista Revolt and Its Implications for Civil–Military Relations and the Future of Mexico." In Donald E. Schulz and Edward J. Williams, eds. *Mexico Faces the 21st Century.* Westport, CT: Greenwood Press.

Waldner, David. 2005. "Democracy and Dictatorship in the Post-Colonial World." Paper presented at the Comparative Politics Workshop; Department of Political Science, University of Michigan, 23 September.

Walker, Thomas W. 1991. "The Armed Forces." In Thomas Walker, ed. *Revolution and Counterrevolution in Nicaragua.* Boulder, CO: Westview Press.

Walker, Thomas W. 2003. *Nicaragua: Living in the Shadow of the Eagle.* Boulder, CO: Westview Press.

Waller, J. Michael. 1994. *Secret Empire: The KGB in Russia Today.* Boulder, CO: Westview Press.

Wang, Fang. 1994. "The Political Economy of Authoritarian Clientelism in Taiwan." In Luis Roniger and Ayse Gunes-Ayata, eds. *Democracy, Clientelism, and Civil Society.* Boulder, CO: Lynne Rienner Publishers.

Wanjala, Smoking. 2002. "Elections and the Political Transition in Kenya." In Lawrence Murungu Mute, Wanza Kioko, and Kichamu Akivaga, eds. *Building an Open Society: The Politics of Transition in Kenya*. Nairobi, Kenya: Claripress.

Watson, Dennis, and Christine Craig, eds. 1992. *Guyana at the Crossroads*. Miami, FL: University of Miami, North–South Center.

Way, Lucan. 2002a. "Pluralism by Default in Moldova." *Journal of Democracy* 13, No. 4: 127–41.

Way, Lucan. 2002b. "The Dilemmas of Reform in Weak States: The Case of Post-Soviet Fiscal Reform." *Politics and Society* 30, No. 4: 579–98.

Way, Lucan. 2003. "Weak States and Pluralism: The Case of Moldova." *East European Politics and Societies* 17, No. 3: 454–82.

Way, Lucan. 2004. "The Sources and Dynamics of Competitive Authoritarianism in Ukraine." *Journal of Communist Studies and Transition Politics* 20, No. 1: 143–61.

Way, Lucan. 2005a. "Authoritarian State-Building and the Sources of Regime Competitiveness in the Fourth Wave." *World Politics* 57, No. 2: 231–61.

Way, Lucan. 2005b. "Kuchma's Failed Authoritarianism." *Journal of Democracy* 16, No. 2: 131–45.

Way, Lucan. 2008a. "The Real Causes of the Color Revolutions." *Journal of Democracy* 19, No. 3: 55–69.

Way, Lucan. 2008b. "Deer in Headlights: Authoritarian Skill and Regime Trajectories after the Cold War." Prepared for the Africa–Central Asia Cornell Workshop. Ithaca, NY: 26–27 September.

Way, Lucan. 2009a. "A Reply to My Critics." *Journal of Democracy* 20, No. 1: 90–7.

Way, Lucan. 2009b. "Pluralism by Default: The Sources of Political Competition in the Former Soviet Union." University of Toronto. Unpublished manuscript.

Wayland, Sarah V. 2003. "Immigration and Transnational Political Ties: Croatians and Sri Lankan Tamils in Canada." *Canadian Ethnic Studies* 35, No. 2: 61–87.

Weaver, Eric, and William Barnes. 1991. "Opposition Parties and Coalitions." In Thomas Walker, ed. *Revolution and Counterrevolution in Nicaragua*. Boulder, CO: Westview Press.

Weber, Renate. 2001. "Constitutionalism as a Vehicle for Democratic Consolidation in Romania." In Jan Zielonka, ed. *Democratic Consolidation in Eastern Europe: Institutional Engineering*. New York: Oxford University Press.

Weeks, John. 1987. "The Mixed Economy in Nicaragua: The Economic Battlefield." In Rose J. Spalding, ed. *The Political Economy of Revolutionary Nicaragua*. Boston: Allen and Unwin.

Wehrle, Frederic A. 1999. "Slovakia." In Julie Smith and Elizabeth Teague, eds. *Democracy in the New Europe: Politics of Post-Communism*. London: The Greycoat Press.

Weinstein, Brian, and Aaron Segal. 1992. *Haiti: The Failure of Politics*. New York: Praeger.

Weinstein, Jeremy. 2002. "Mozambique: A Fading UN Success Story." *Journal of Democracy* 13, No. 1: 141–56.

Weiss, Meredith L. 2000. "The 1999 Malaysian General Elections." *Asian Survey* 40, No. 3: 413–35.

Weiss, Meredith L. 2004. "Mahathir's Unintended Legacy: Civil Society." In Bridget Welsh, ed. *Reflections: The Mahathir Years*. Washington, DC: The Paul H. Nitze School of Advanced International Studies.

Weitzer, Ronald. 1984a. "In Search of Regime Security: Zimbabwe Since Independence." *Journal of Modern African Studies* 22, No. 4: 529–57.

Weitzer, Ronald. 1984b. "Continuities in the Politics of State Security in Zimbabwe." In Michael G. Schatzberg, ed. *The Political Economy of Zimbabwe*. New York: Praeger.

Weitzer, Ronald. 1990. *Transforming Settler States: Communal Conflict and Internal Security in Northern Ireland and Zimbabwe*. Berkeley: University of California Press.

Weldon, Jeffrey. 1997. "Political Sources of Presidencialismo in Mexico." In Scott Mainwaring and Matthew Soberg Shugart, eds. *Presidentialism and Democracy in Latin America*. New York: Cambridge University Press.

Weldon, Jeffrey. 2004. "Changing Patterns of Executive–Legislative Relations in Mexico." In Kevin J. Middlebrook, ed. *Dilemmas of Political Change in Mexico*. London: Institute of Latin American Studies.

Welsh, Bridget. 2004. "Mahathir's Legacy: A New Society?" In Bridget Welsh, ed. *Reflections: The Mahathir Years*. Washington, DC: The Paul H. Nitze School of Advanced International Studies.

Welsh, Bridget. 2008. "Malaysia's Democratic Opening." *Open Democracy*. 11 March.

Welt, Cory. 2000. "A Return to Eurasia." *Transitions Online*. 11 January.

Welt, Cory. 2006. "Georgia's Rose Revolution: From Regime Weakness to Regime Collapse." Working Paper. Stanford, CA: Center of Democracy Development, and the Rule of Law.

Weyland, Kurt. 2006. "The Rise and Decline of Fujimori's Neopopulist Leadership." In Julio Carrión, ed. *The Fujimori Legacy: The Rise of Electoral Authoritarianism in Peru*. University Park: Pennsylvania State University Press.

Wheatley, Jonathan. 2003. "The Problems of Post-Soviet Regime Change: Dynamic and Static Elements of the Georgian Regime 1989–2001." Ph.D. diss. Florence: European University Institute.

Wheatley, Jonathan. 2004. "Elections and Democratic Governance in the Former Soviet Union: The Case of Georgia." Free University of Berlin. Available at www.oei.fuberlin. de/cscca/Publications/boi_jw_elections_and_democratic_governance.pdf.

Wheatley, Jonathan. 2005. *Georgia from National Awakening to Rose Revolution: Delayed Transition in the Former Soviet Union*. Aldershot, UK: Ashgate Publishing.

White, Stephen, Sarah Oates, and Ian McAllister. 2005. "Media Effects and Russian Elections, 1999–2000." *British Journal of Political Science* 35, No. 2: 191–208.

White, Stephen, Richard Rose, and Ian McAllister. 1996. *How Russia Votes*. Washington, DC: Congressional Quarterly Press.

Whitehead, Laurence. 1991. "Democracy by Convergence and Southern Europe: A Comparative Politics Perspective." In Geoffrey Pridham, ed. *Encouraging Democracy: The International Context of Regime Transition in Southern Europe*. Leicester, UK: Leicester University Press.

Whitehead, Laurence, ed. 1996a. *The International Dimensions of Democratization: Europe and the Americas*. Oxford, UK: Oxford University Press.

Whitehead, Laurence. 1996b. "Three International Dimensions of Democratization." In Laurence Whitehead, ed. *The International Dimensions of Democratization: Europe and the Americas*. Oxford, UK: Oxford University Press.

Whitehead, Laurence. 1996c. "The Imposition of Democracy: The Caribbean." In Laurence Whitehead, ed. *The International Dimensions of Democratization: Europe and the Americas*. Oxford, UK: Oxford University Press.

Whitehead, Laurence. 1996d. "Democracy by Convergence: Southern Europe." In Laurence Whitehead, ed. *The International Dimensions of Democratization: Europe and the Americas*. Oxford, UK: Oxford University Press.

Whitehead, Laurence. 1996e. "Democratic Regions, Ostracism, and Pariahs." In Laurence Whitehead, ed. *The International Dimensions of Democratization: Europe and the Americas*. Oxford, UK: Oxford University Press.

Whitehead, Laurence. 1996f. "The Enlargement of the European Union: A 'Risky' Form of Democracy Promotion." In Laurence Whitehead, ed. *The International Dimensions of Democratization: Europe and the Americas*. Oxford, UK: Oxford University Press.

Whitehead, Laurence. 1999. "Geography and Democratic Destiny: Eastern Europe a Decade Later." *Journal of Democracy* 10, No. 1: 74–9.

Whitmore, Brian. 2006. "Russia/Belarus: Possible Gas Price Hike Could End Warm Ties." *RFE/RL Reports*, 1 June.

Whitmore, Brian. 2008. "Russia: For Some, Dark Horse Remains in the Shadows." *RFE/RL Reports*, 28 January.

Whitmore, Brian. 2009. "Moldova Vote Controversy Highlights Doubts over Monitoring." *RFE/RL Reports*, 21 April.

Wiarda, Howard J. 1997. *Cracks in the Consensus: Debating the Democracy Agenda in U.S. Foreign Policy*. Westport, CT: Praeger.

Wiarda, Howard J. 2003. "Beyond the Pale: The Bureaucratic Politics of U.S. Policy in Mexico." In Armand B. Peschard-Sverdrup, ed. *Forecasting Mexico's Democratic Transition: Scenarios for Policymakers*. Washington, DC: Center for Strategic and International Studies.

Wiarda, Howard, and Michael J. Kryzanek. 1992. *The Dominican Republic: A Caribbean Crucible*. Boulder, CO: Westview Press.

Wibbels, Erik. 2006. "Dependency Revisited: International Markets, Business Cycles, and Social Spending in the Developing World. *International Organization* 60, No. 2 (April): 433–68.

Widner, Jennifer A. 1992a. *The Rise of a Party-State in Kenya: From 'Harambee!' to 'Nyayo'!* Berkeley: University of California Press.

Widner, Jennifer A. 1992b. "Kenya's Slow Progress Toward Multiparty Politics." *Current History* (May): 214–18.

Widner, Jennifer A. 1994. "Political Reform in Anglophone and Francophone African Countries." In Jennifer A. Widner, ed. *Economic Change and Political Liberalization in Sub-Saharan Africa*. Baltimore: The Johns Hopkins University Press.

Will, W. Marvin. 1997. "NGOs and IGOs as Promoters of Liberal Democracy in the Caribbean: Cases from Nicaragua and Guyana." In Ivelaw L. Griffith and Betty N. Sedoc-Dahlberg, eds. *Democracy and Human Rights in the Caribbean*. Boulder, CO: Westview Press.

Williams, Edward J. 1986. "The Evolution of the Mexican Military and Its Implications for Civil–Military Relations." In Roderic A. Camp, ed. *Mexico's Political Stability: The Next Five Years*. Boulder, CO: Westview Press.

Williams, Kieran. 2001a. "Introduction." In Kieran Williams and Dennis Deletant, eds. *Security Intelligence Services in New Democracies: The Czech Republic, Slovakia, and Romania*. New York: Palgrave. Pp. 1–23.

Williams, Kieran. 2001b. "Slovakia since 1993." In Kieran Williams and Dennis Deletant, eds. *Security and Intelligence Services in New Democracies: The Czech Republic, Slovakia, and Romania*. New York: Palgrave. Pp. 123–58.

Williams, Philip J. 1990. "Elections and Democratization in Nicaragua: The 1990 Elections in Perspective." *Journal of Interamerican Studies and World Affairs* 32, No. 4: 13–34.

Williams, Philip J. 1994. "Dual Transitions from Authoritarian Rule: Popular and Electoral Democracy in Nicaragua." *Comparative Politics* 26, No. 2: 169–86.

Williams, T. David. 1978. *Malawi: The Politics of Despair*. Ithaca, NY: Cornell University Press.

Wilson, Andrew. 1993. "The Growing Challenge to Kiev from the Donbas." *RFE/RL Research Report*. 20 August.

Wilson, Andrew. 2005a. *Virtual Politics: Faking Democracy in the Post-Soviet World*. New Haven, CT: Yale University Press.

Wilson, Andrew. 2005b. *Ukraine's Orange Revolution*. New Haven, CT: Yale University Press.

Wilson, Andrew. 2010. "Dealing with Yanukovych's Ukraine." *Europeam Council on Foreign Relations Policy Memo*. March. Accessed at www.ecfr.eu.

Wing, Susanna. 2008. *Constructing Democracy in Transitioning Societies of Africa: Constitutionalism and Deliberation in Mali*. New York: Palgrave.

Winiecki, Jan. 2002. *Transition Economies and Foreign Trade*. London: Routledge

Winland, Daphne. 2004. "Croatian Diaspora." In Carol R. Ember, Melvin Ember, and Ian A. Skoggard, eds. *Encyclopedia of Diasporas: Immigrant and Refugee Cultures Around the World*. New York: Springer.

Wise, Carol. 2003. *Reinventing the State: Economic Strategy and Institutional Change in Peru*. Ann Arbor: University of Michigan Press.

Wiseman, John A. 1996. *The New Struggle for Democracy*. Aldershot, UK: Avebury.

Wiseman, John A. 1998. "The Slow Evolution of the Party System in Botswana." *Journal of Asian and African Studies* 33, No. 3: 241–64.

Wiseman, John A., and Roger Charlton. 1995. "The October 1994 Elections in Botswana." *Electoral Studies* 14, No. 3: 323–8.

Wolchik, Sharon. 1997. "Democratization and Political Participation in Slovakia." In Karen Dawisha and Bruce Parrott, eds. *The Consolidation of Democracy in East Central Europe*. Cambridge: Cambridge University Press.

Woldenberg, José. 2002. *La Construcción de la Democracia*. Mexico City: Plaza Janés.

Wong, Joseph. 2003. "Deepening Democracy in Taiwan." *Pacific Affairs* 74, No. 2: 235–56.

Wong, Kean. 2000. "Malaysia: In the Grip of Government." In Roland Rich and Louise Williams, eds. *Losing Control: Freedom of the Press in Asia*. Canberra, Australia: Asia Pacific Press.

Wood, Elisabeth Jean. 2000. *Forging Democracy from Below: Insurgent Transitions in South Africa and El Salvador*. New York: Cambridge University Press.

Wood, Geoffrey. 1999. "Democratization in Mozambique: Trends and Practices." *Democratization* 6, No. 2 (Summer): 156–70.

World, Bank. 2003. "The Russian Labor Market: Moving from Crisis to Recovery." Washington, DC: World Bank.

Wright, Teresa. 1999. "Student Mobilization in Taiwan: Civil Society and its Discontents." *Asian Survey* 39, No. 6: 986–1008.

Wu, Jaushieh Joseph. 1995. *Taiwan's Democratization: Forces Behind the New Momentum*. Oxford, UK: Oxford University Press.

Wucker, Michele. 2004. "Haiti: So Many Missteps." *World Policy Journal* (Spring): 41–9.

Wuhs, Steven T. 2001. "Barbarians, Bureaucrats, and Bluebloods: Fractional Change in the National Action Party." In Kevin Middlebrook, ed. *Party Politics and the Struggle for Democracy in Mexico: National and State-Level Analyses of the Partido Acción Nacional*. La Jolla, CA: Center for U.S.–Mexican Studies.

Yang, Ma-Li, and Dennis Engbarth. 2000. "Taiwan: All Politics, No Privacy." In Roland Rich and Louise Williams, eds. *Losing Control: Freedom of the Press in Asia*. Canberra, Australia: Asia Pacific Press.

Yashar, Deborah. 2005. *Contesting Citizenship in Latin America*. New York: Cambridge University Press.

Yates, Douglas A. 1996. *The Rentier State in Africa: Oil Rent Dependency and Neocolonialism in the Republic of Gabon.* Trenton, NJ: Africa World Press.

Yeltsin, Boris. 1994. *Zapiski Prezidenta.* Moscow: Ogonek.

Yeltsin, Boris. 2000. *Prezidentskii Marafan.* Moscow: AST.

Young, Crawford. 1999a. "The Third Wave of Democratization in Africa: Ambiguities and Contradictions." In Richard Joseph, ed. *State, Conflict, and Democracy in Africa.* Boulder, CO: Lynne Rienner Publishers.

Young, Crawford. 1999b. "Africa: An Interim Balance Sheet." In Larry Diamond and Marc F. Plattner, eds. *Democratization in Africa.* Baltimore, MD: The Johns Hopkins University Press.

Young, Crawford, and Babacar Kante. 1992. "Governance, Democracy, and the 1988 Senegalese Elections." In Goran Hyden and Michael Bratton, eds. *Governance and Politics in Africa.* Boulder, CO: Lynne Rienner Publishers.

Young, Eric T. 1996. "The Development of the FADM in Mozambique: Internal and External Dynamics." *African Studies Review* 5, No. 1.

Youngers, Coletta A. 2000. *Deconstructing Democracy: Peru under President Alberto Fujimori.* Washington, DC: Washington Office on Latin America.

Youngs, Richard. 2006. "Ukraine." In *Strategies for Democratic Change: Assessing the Global Response.* Democracy Coalition Project. Pp. 97–121.

Yurchuk, Aleksandr. 1999. "Va-Bank ili nogodnyi zaets." *Zerkalo nedeli* No. 50 (271). 18–24 December.

Zaffiro, James. 2000. "Broadcasting Reform and Democratization in Botswana." *Africa Today* 47, No. 1 (Winter): 87–102.

Zaffiro, James J. 2002. *Media and Democracy in Zimbabwe, 1931–2001.* Colorado Springs, CO: International Academic Publishers, Ltd.

Zahariadis, Nikolaos. 2003. "External Interventions and Domestic Ethnic Conflict in Yugoslav Macedonia." *Political Science Quarterly* 118, No. 2: 259–79.

Zakaria, Fareed. 1997. "The Rise of Illiberal Democracy." *Foreign Affairs* 76, No. 6: 22–41.

Zakaria, Fareed. 2003. *The Future of Freedom: Illiberal Democracy at Home and Abroad.* New York: W.W. Norton and Company.

Zakaria, Haji Ahmad. 1985. "Malaysia." In Zakaria Haji Ahmad and Harold Crouch, eds. *Military–Civilian Relations in South-East Asia.* Singapore: Oxford University Press.

Zakaria, Haji Ahmad. 1987. *Government and Politics of Malaysia.* Singapore: Oxford University Press.

Zakarian, Armen. 2005. "Armenian War Veterans Create New Union" *RFE/RL Caucasus Report.* 11 February.

Zanga, Louis. 1991a. "Albania: A Watershed Year." *Report on Eastern Europe* (8 February): 1–6.

Zanga, Louis. 1991b. "The Albanian Democratic Party." *Report on Eastern Europe* (1 March): 1–6.

Zanga, Louis. 1991c. "*Sigurimi* Dissolved and Replaced." *Report on Eastern Europe* (30 August): 19–21.

Zanga, Louis. 1992a. "Albania: Fall of Government Plunges Country into Chaos." *RFE/RL Research Report* (10 January): 17–19.

Zanga, Louis. 1992b. "Renewed Italian Interest in Albania." *RFE/RL Research Report* 1, No. 19: 22–5.

Zanga, Louis. 1993. "Albania: Democratic Revival and Social Upheaval." *RFE/RL Research Report* 2, No. 1: 75–77.

Zanga, Louis. 1994. "Albania's Socialist Party: A Weak Giant." *RFE/RL Research Report* 3, No. 15 (15 April): 10–12.

Zaprudnik, Jan. 1993. *Belarus: At a Crossroads in History*. Boulder, CO: Westview Press.

Zidaru-Barbalescu, Aurel. 1993. "Romania Seeks Admission to the Council of Europe." *RFE/RL Research Report* 2, No. 2: 11–16 (8 January).

Zielonka, Jan. 2003. "Introduction: Enlargement and the Study of European Integration." In Jacques Rupnik and Jan Zielonka, eds. *The Road to the European Union: The Czech and Slovak Republics*. Manchester and New York: Manchester University Press.

Zielonka, Jan, and Alex Pravda, eds. 2001. *Democratic Consolidation in Eastern Europe: Volume 2: International and Transnational Factors*. New York: Oxford University Press.

Zimmerman, William. 1987. *Open Borders, Nonalignment, and the Political Evolution of Yugoslavia*. Princeton, NJ: Princeton University Press.

Zirker, Daniel. 1992. "The Preservation of Civilian Rule in Tanzania." In Constantine Danopoulos, ed. *Civilian Rule in the Developing World*. Boulder, CO: Westview Press.

Zlotnik, Marc. 2003. "Yeltsin and Gorbachev: The Politics of Confrontation." *Journal of Cold War Studies* 5, No. 1: 128–64.

Zolberg, Aristide R. 1966. *Creating Political Order: The Party-States of West Africa*. Chicago: University of Chicago Press.

Zunec, Ozren. 1996. "Democracy in the 'Fog of War': Civil–Military Relations in Croatia." In Constantine Danopoulos and Daniel Zirker, eds. *Civil–Military Relations in the Soviet and Yugoslav Successor States*. Boulder, CO: Westview Press. Pp. 213–32.

Zürcher, Christoph. 2007. *The Post-Soviet Wars: Rebellion, Ethnic Conflict, and Nationhood in the Caucasus*. New York: New York University Press.

Zuzul, Miomir. 1998. "A Just Settlement." *Harvard International Review* 20, No. 2: 16–21.

Index

31 December Women's Movement (Ghana), 300
Abdullah, Badawi, 327–8
ABIM (Malaysian Islamic Youth Movement), 319, 323
Abkhazia, 221, 222
Access to Information and Protection of Privacy Act (Zimbabwe), 243
Action Front for Renewal and Development (Benin), 295
active leverage, 91
acquis communautaire, 88
ADEMA (Alliance for Democracy in Mali), 297–8, 307
Adil (Movement for Social Justice, Malaysia), 325
ADP (Agrarian Democratic Party of Moldova), 230–1
Afghanistan, 46, 109
AFORD (Alliance for Democracy, Malawi), 284, 285
Africa, 4, 35, 236, 239, 252, 255, 259, 266, 274, 282, 283, 292, 293, 297, 305–6
    civil society in, 25, 46, 236; democracy promotion/conditionality in, 40, 236; economy in, 60, 77, 177; leverage in, 237; linkage in, 23, 25, 45, 237; opposition in, 25, 30, 31, 236, 260; organizational power across, 36, 55, 74, 80, 236–7. *See also* countries by name
Afro-Shirazi Party (Zanzibar), 252
Agrarian Democratic Party of Moldova. *See* ADP
Aguayo, Sergio, 151
Aguilar Zinser, Adolfo, 151

Ahidjo, Ahmadou, 258–9
Akayev, Askar, 55
Akufo-Addo, Nana, 305
Albania, 4, 78, 282, 124, 329, 346, 350
    civil society in, 119; competitive authoritarianism in, 12, 21, 22, 82, 87, 119, 121–24, 341, 342, 369, 370; elections, civil liberties and playing field in, 13, 90, 121–4; EU role in, 122–4; leverage in, 119, 122–4, 373; linkage in, 46, 91, 119–24, 375; opposition in, 121–2, 349; organizational power in, 29, 30, 31, 57, 59, 73, 77, 98, 120–1, 128–9, 357, 379–80; UN peacekeeping force in, 122; U.S. role in, 123
Albright, Madeleine, 168
Alemán, Arnoldo, 144
Alia, Ramiz, 121
Aliyev, Heydar, 34
Alliance for Democracy (Malawi). *See* AFORD
Alliance for Democracy in Mali. *See* ADEMA
Alternative Front (Malaysia). *See* BA
Americas, the, 3, 4, 40, 309
    lack of countervailing power in, 41–2; economy in, 67, 236; leverage in, 53, 130–79, 219, 352; linkage in, 23, 25, 36, 44, 50, 53, 70, 85–6, 130–79, 181, 185, 221, 352; OAS role in, 18
Americas Watch, 156
Amoussou, Bruno, 295
Andrianarivo, Tantely, 281
Angola, 32, 46, 109
ANM (Armenian National Movement), 208–11
antigos combatentes, 248, 354
Anwar, Ibrahim, 9, 12, 55, 324–28

493

CPSIA information can be obtained at www.ICGtesting.com
Printed in the USA
LVOW11s0519160614

390182LV00005B/9/P